TYNESIDE IRISH

This book is dedicated to the memory of all ranks of the Tyneside Irish Brigade 1914–18

Tyneside Irish Brigade Headquarters
103 Light Trench Mortar Battery
103 Machine Gun Company

24th(Service) Battalion Northumberland Fusiliers (1st Tyneside Irish)
25th(Service) Battalion Northumberland Fusiliers (2nd Tyneside Irish)
26th(Service) Battalion Northumberland Fusiliers (3rd Tyneside Irish)
27th(Service) Battalion Northumberland Fusiliers (4th Tyneside Irish)
30th(Reserve) Battalion Northumberland Fusiliers (Tyneside Irish)

THE HARP THAT ONCE THROUGH TARA'S HALLS
THE SOUL OF MUSIC SHED
NOW HANGS AS MUTE ON TARA'S WALLS
AS IF THAT SOUL WERE DEAD

TYNESIDE IRISH

24th, 25th & 26th & 27th (Service)
Battalions of the
Northumberland Fusiliers
A HISTORY OF THE TYNESIDE
IRISH BRIGADE RAISED IN THE
NORTH EAST IN WORLD WAR ONE

John Sheen

Pen & Sword
MILITARY

First published in 1998 by Leo Cooper
an imprint of Pen & Sword Books Ltd
47 Church Street, Barnsley, South Yorkshire, S70 2AS
Reprinted in this format 2010

ISBN 978 1 84884 093 5

A CIP catalogue record for this book is available from the British Library.

Typeset by Phoenix Typesetting, Auldgirth, Dumfriesshire.

Printed and bound in England by CPI UK

Pen & Sword Books Ltd incorporates the imprints of Pen & Sword Aviation,
Pen & Sword Maritime, Pen & Sword Military, Wharncliffe Local History,
Pen & Sword Select, Pen & Sword Military Classics and Leo Cooper.

For a complete list of Pen & Sword titles please contact
PEN & SWORD BOOKS LIMITED
47 Church Street, Barnsley, South Yorkshire, S70 2AS England
E-mail: enquiries@pen-and-sword.co.uk
Website: www.pen-and-sword.co.uk

Contents

Acknowledgements

Thanks are due to the following: my wife Beverley for putting up with my obsession for many years. Jim and Mary Connor for their help in correcting my spelling and punctuation. The staff of the following Libraries: Melksham, Wiltshire where my research started, Durham City Library, Newcastle Central Library, Gateshead Central Library. The staff of the enquiries section of The Commonwealth War Graves Commission, in particular Esther Page for her untiring help. Sue Wood at Northumberland Record Office and The Newcastle Society of Antiquarians for allowing the reproduction of the Tyneside Irish recruiting poster. Department of Printed Books at the Imperial War Museum for permission to use illustrations from *The 34th Divisional Memorial Book*. The Keeper of Public Records at the Public Records Office, Kew.

All who loaned photographs, postcards etc from their collections: Andrew Brookes; J. Bratherton; Mrs D Henderson; Graham Stewart; Jimmy Winter; D. Bilton.

Martin Atwell for help with work on the nominal roll of the officers. Captain P H D Marr of The Fusiliers of Northumberland Museum for his help at the museum. Dr R T Swinburn to whom I owe a great deal of thanks for access to his father's papers. Mr Hugh Arnold for the use of his father's unpublished memoirs. Mr Patrick Arnold for the use of letters from Colonel Richardson and CSM Coleman to his father. Mr Brian Falkous for the use of Captain Robert Falkous's letters and photo album. Jim Lawson of BEAMISH MUSEUM photographic archives. Pamela Armstrong for the interviews with Michael Manley and Lew Shaughnessy. Bob Grundy for help in pinpointing locations of some official photographs. *Battleground* author Michael Stedman for photographs. Also all those who did not have a photograph of their relative but passed on anecdotes and information.

The following relatives who loaned photographs and documents

Mr E Allen	Private E Allen, 24th Battalion.
Mr H Arnold	
Mr P Arnold	Captain J Arnold, 24th & 26th Battalions
Tony Barrow	Sergeant G Barrow MM + Bar, 27th Battalion.
Sue Bright	Corporal P Barrett, 26th Battalion.
Tom Cassidy	Private T Cassidy 24th Battalion.
	Private T Gough 26th Battalion.
Jim Connor	Private P Martin, 26th Battalion.
Mary Connor	Corporal J Cross, 24th Battalion.
	Corporal J Harvey, 25th Battalion.
	Sergeant J B Harvey, 27th Battalion.
	Corporal M M Harvey, 27th Battalion.
Mr Harry Coxon	Private W Lonsdale, 27th Battalion.
Mrs Iris Edmonds	Pipe Major J Wilson, 24th Battalion.
June Fairweather	Private Alexander Fairweather, 1st Northern Cyclists & 25th Battalion.
Mr Brian Falkous	Captain R B Falkous 26th & 27th Battalions
Mrs M Hay	Sergeant R Madden, DCM,MM,MID. 27th Battalion.
Mr N Holmes	Private W Holmes, 27th Battalion.
Mr R Holmes	Private W Smith 25th Battalion.
Rev Les Hood	Sergeant F Hood, 27th Battalion.
Paul Kwiatkowski	Private M Jenkinson, West Yorkshire Regiment & 24/27th Battalion.
Ossie Johnson	Private F Ellison, 26th Battalion.

Mrs Ledbridge	Private W Donaldson, 26th Battalion.
Rob Lenaghan	Lance Corporal M Manley, 26th Battalion.
John Lennon	Private J Wilson, 27th Battalion.
	The McGee Brothers, 27th Battalion.
Alice Levitt	Private F Levitt, 25th Battalion.
Mrs Murial Mates	CSM R J Erett, 24th Battalion & Labour Corps.
Matt Miller	Lance Sergeant C Miller, 24th Battalion.
Mrs J McCartney-Cuomo	
	Private J McCartney, 25th Battalion.
Mr Conn McDerrmott	Private P McCabe, 24th Battalion.
	Private F Early, 27th Battalion.
Mrs Ann McKay	Captain T G Farina, 24th Battalion
Mr Bernard Nolan	Lance Corporal J Nolan 24th Battalion.
Mr George Palmer	Private T Fallon, 26th Battalion & RAMC.
Mrs Audrey Pyle	Private M Pyle, 24th Battalion.
M Richardson	Private W Savage, 25th Battalion.
Brian Scollen	Private J Scollen, 27th Battalion.
Mrs Annie Scott	Private J Connolly, 24th Battalion & Labour Corps
Brian Shield	Lance Corporal M Tyman, 26th Battalion.
Mick Stephenson	Private G Stephenson, 26th Battalion.
Dr R T Swinburn	Captain G Swinburn MC, 24th Battalion & ROD RE.
Mrs A Tate	Corporal W H Lofthouse, 29th & 24th Battalions.
Mr W Thorburn	Private W Thorburn, 30th Reserve Battalion & KOYLI.
David Varvill	Private J Kelly, 25th Battalion.
Fr E.V. Wilkinson	Lieutenant J H Wilkinson, 27th & 24th Battalions.
Maurice Wilkinson	Corporal W K Wheatley DCM MM 25th Battalion & E Yorkshire Regiment
Mrs M Wilson	Private J O'Connor, 24th Battalion.

Also the many releatives who supplied photographs after publication of the First Edition, many of which are included in this edition.

Foreword

In the early 1950s I was visiting my paternal grandmother and together we were looking at the photographs on her sideboard, of my father and his brothers, all in battledress uniform. On the end was a photograph of a man in a different uniform, and I asked, 'Who is this, Gran?'

'That's your Grandfather, he was in the Green Howards. By! Those lads could fight, but not like the Tyneside Irish', she replied. I had heard of the Green Howards but not of the Tyneside Irish, so I asked, 'What's the Tyneside Irish? 'Your great grandfather, my father was in the Tyneside Irish, the best fighting Regiment in the Great War'. With that remark tears came into her eyes and she clouted me across the head and told me to mind my own business. Why had I got a clout because of the Tyneside Irish? From that day I wanted to know more about these men.

It could, and should, be said that many of the men of the Tyneside Irish Brigade, had only one day in a major battle, but, on that one day, they wrote the name of the Tyneside Irish Brigade into the history books of the British Army.

John Sheen

Chapter One

The Irish Come to the North East

'Oh Father dear and I often hear you speak of Erin's Isle, her lofty scenes, her valleys green, her mountains rude and wild, They say it is a lovely land, wherein a prince might dwell, Then why did you abandon it? The reason to me tell.' *Skibereen* TRAD

The story of the Tyneside Irish Brigade really begins in Ireland in 1847. The effects of the 'Potato Famine' drove unfortunate men and women from their homes, and many emigrated to America, Australia and New Zealand. Large numbers came to Great Britain. Those who came to the North East of England landed mainly at Whitehaven and other ports on the North West coast. They made their way across country to where they could find work. In the 1840s the North East, in particular County Durham, became a focal point for the Irish immigrant. The growth in coal, iron, chemical, shipbuilding and engineering industries, and the railways, meant there was work for the unskilled, illiterate and often penniless Irish peasant.

The earliest arrivals frequently lived in makeshift camps alongside the railways or out on the fells. The first to arrive were mainly young single men seeking to establish themselves in secure employment, before sending for their families and relatives. These men were usually offered the most menial and lowest paid jobs. While they tried to scrape together the fare for a sweetheart or a younger brother, they were obliged to live in the dirtiest, cheapest lodging houses they could find.

These foreign immigrants were often treated with suspicion and unkindness by the native Geordie. There was also a great animosity against them, for, in the long strike of 1844, Lord Londonderry had evicted

Sinkers at Ludworth Colliery. Sinking colliery shafts was a job done mainly by the Irish.

the Geordie miners from their homes in Seaham, and brought in 150 Irishmen to man his pits. This small number of Irish blacklegs was exaggerated daily by rumour until many thought there were thousands of Irish scabs in Seaham. The stigma remained for decades in the coalfield. Forty or fifty years later, in some collieries the first to be laid off would be the 'Irish', even though they were second and third generation Irish, born and raised in England, and had worked in a particular colliery longer than some of the English miners.

The bad feeling between the English and Irish communities in the region caused trouble to flare throughout the late 1800s. From the press reports of the time, one would believe that all the immigrant Irish were Fenians, and when there was trouble it would be described as a Fenian Insurrection. With the majority of the immigrants being Roman Catholic, the English found it difficult to separate Irish Fenianism and Irish Catholicism. It is not widely known that Orange Lodges were operating in the North East. Although the exact membership is unknown, some of them must have been immigrant Ulstermen. There was always the chance of conflict between the two communities, and a major riot took place on 12 July 1856, when Newcastle and Gateshead Orangemen decided to march through Felling to visit another Orange Lodge. The route chosen was through an area where many Irishmen were employed at the Felling Chemical Works and the march was bound to provoke a reaction from Catholic workers.

As time passed the Irish became more educated and established in their communities, and many second generation immigrants were able to obtain semi-skilled, and, in some cases, skilled employment. However, for the vast majority, labouring jobs were all that could be obtained. By 1871 there was an increase in the Irish working in the pits. Many moved round the colliery villages as work was available. Bernard Connolly worked as a sinker, sinking shafts for new coal mines. Like other Irish workers he worked in many colliery villages and his subsequent large family, born in various locations, joined other children who were frequently sent out to work at an early age. At the age of 11 boys could be employed in the mine and girls in domestic service or farm work.

William Lonsdale with his children in 1913. Many families would be left fatherless by the war. William was killed on 1 July 1916 aged 29 years. At the time he was serving as a Lance Corporal in the Tyneside Irish. The photograph was taken outside his home at Whitfield Street, Crook

The Irish in England gained an unenviable reputation, They had the stigma of being foreigners, potential job-stealers and they came from a distinct religious and ethnic group. The Irish brogue being very different, it stood out amidst the guttural Geordie dialect. This situation led to the Irish congregating into ghettoes in the particular localities they chose to settle; thus Elvet, and latterly Framwellgate in Durham City came to have strong Irish connections. The same thing happened in many towns and cities, Bottle Bank in Birtley and Wrekenton at Gateshead are good examples.

These Irish had a reputation for disease, dirt and drunkeness, which, in some cases, was probably justified, but many families struggled to make progress. They were handicapped, for they had the lowest paid jobs, were living in the poorest slum dwellings imaginable, and were poorly educated. Even when schooling was available, some children would have been regular truants. Then, at the early age previously mentioned they were sent out to work. The large families were often overcrowded because of extended family loyalties. Any tenuous family link was a reason to provide a roof over the heads of long-lost cousins, as well as brothers and sisters. It is perhaps a sad reflection on the state of things in Ireland that so many left and came to live in England where they would be despised and treated with contempt, and in some areas open

Entertainment was self made, St Mary Magdelene's RC Church brass band. Seated on the priest's right is John Scollen, he would be killed on the first day of the Battle of the Somme, 1 July 1916.

hostility. These problems were some-times increased by the political activities of societies such as the Fenian and Hibernian clubs. It is hardly surprising that when an outbreak of typhus in the Gateshead area started to spread amongst the poor Irish, it soon became known as the Irish disease. Later cholera struck in the same area, and demands were made for the Irish to be driven out.

Many areas where the Irish settled contained housing that was damp, dirty and ill-ventilated, and inside, bedding was often verminous and occupied in relays; as one shift of workers went out, the others came in. What entertainment there was, was self-made, with the singing of songs about Ireland well to the fore, especially when some men became maudlin through drink.

Many buildings were divided up into tenements with as many large families in the building as there were rooms to let. There were no sewers or drains in some places and cleanliness was almost impossible. Violence and disturbances through drink often led to the police being involved. Nevertheless many people struggled to make a decent standard of living for themselves and their families.

The immigration of the Irish into the North East brought far reaching consequences for the development of the area. Many monuments bear witness to the labour provided by the Irish. Railway viaducts at Durham and Chester le Street were built by navvies, and yet the majority of the industries that brought them have disappeared. Even the world-famous Durham coalfield no longer has a working colliery. However, at the turn of the century coal was king. It provided work for one of the highest industrial populations of the country, and provided power for other industries. The Durham and Northumberland coalfields were thriving as output increased, with the demand for more steel to make bigger and better warships, as war loomed nearer. 1913 had been a boom year for the coal industry, and, by the summer of 1914, coal was stockpiled high. There was a lull in production and consequently most collieries were working a two or three day fortnight. Unemployment was at a high level and men were travelling all over the region looking for work, in a desperate attempt to feed their families. This then was the background at the time of the raising of the Tyneside Irish Brigade.

The Call to Arms

With the assassination of the Austrian Archduke Franz Ferdinand in Sarajevo on the 28th of June 1914, the fuse was lit. The countries of Europe rushed to mobilise. On the morning of the 4th of August German

Archduke Franz Ferdinand, heir to the Austria-Hungarian Throne, and his wife Sophie, on 28 June 1914, leaving the town hall at Sarajevo a few minutes prior to their deaths at the hands of assassin Gavrilo Princip.

troops crossed the Belgium border, and Great Britain delivered an ultimatum to the German Government that Germany should respect Belgian neutrality. When the ultimatum expired at 11 p.m. Berlin time, Britain was at war. The British Expeditionary Force of six Infantry divisions and one Cavalry division was quickly deployed to France.

On the 5th of August Field Marshal Earl Kitchener had assumed the duties of Secretary of State for War and immediately he asked Parliament to authorise an additional 500,000 men for the army. Kitchener was of the opinion that the war would not be over by Christmas, that it would last at least three years, and that some seventy divisions would be involved. He had been opposed to the formation of the Territorial Force in 1908, and would not use it as the basis of forming his expansion of the army. Instead he intended to start from scratch and raise a 'NEW ARMY'. Every man would be a volunteer, required to enlist for service anywhere for three years, or for the duration of the war.

On the 11th of August, Kitchener's famous proclamation was released. A poster was published with the words:

Your King and Country Need You
A CALL TO ARMS

The poster called for 100,000 men between the ages of 19 and 30 to enlist for general service.

Many young men of Irish descent rushed to join the colours: after all, they thought that it would be over by Christmas, the pits were idle, so what better time was there to have a holiday at the Government's expense? The early Kitchener battalions of the Northumberland Fusiliers, Durham Light Infantry and Green Howards found recruits flocking to their depots and in particular, The Green Howards attracted many recruits because of its name. If it had been The Orange Howards, many Catholic recruits would have joined another regiment. In Durham, Walter and James Sheen, Paddy Burke and Thomas Killian all went to The Green Howards for this reason, but their older relatives Edward Sheen, Joe Burke and Michael

Killian all waited , and eventually joined the First Battalion of the Tyneside Irish.

However there was a movement to have these men transfer to Irish regiments. A letter in the 'Northern Daily Mail' on 22 September 1914, under the heading 'AN IRISH CALL TO ARMS', stated,

> *'Sir - The idea of forming an Irish fighting force in response to the appeal of Lord Kitchener for recruits, has been publicly endorsed by the Prime Minister on the occasion of his visit to Dublin, and it is anticipated that men of Irish birth or descent, resident in Great Britain, will be able to join. Many have already fallen into line by joining Irish units, but of the 2,000 young Irishmen who have joined the colours in South Durham and North Yorkshire during the past two months, the overwhelming majority are not associated with Irish Regiments. It is understood that the War Office will give favourable consideration to applications for transfers to the new Irish Corps, and for that reason I desire to ask all who have Irish relatives in the recent lists of recruits to forward their names either to Mr John Mulcahy, Mitchell St, Birtley, Co Durham, Mr Farrell Keirman, 285 Burley Rd, Leeds, or to myself. The name of the regiments must also be given. I hope that officials of Irish organisations in Darlington, Stockton, Middlesbrough, The Hartlepools and other large centres of population will co-operate in the preparation of as complete a list as possible. Yours truly*
>
> *Robt McLean 37 Charles Street, Redcar.'*

George Barrow before the war. By 1916 he was a sergeant in the 4th Tyneside Irish and he was twice awarded the Military Medal.

But many of these 2,000 young 'Irishmen' had never been within a hundred miles of Ireland. In some cases their grandparents had arrived as long ago as 1850, but because of their religion and the locality in

Recruits for the Green Howards at Durham Railway Station, 3 September 1914. Many of them were of Irish descent. Ringed is the author's grandfather (behind) Walter Sheen and his mate Paddy Burke.

"DO YOUR DUTY BRAVELY. FEAR GOD. HONOUR THE KING."
(Signed) KITCHENER, Field Marshal

Lord Kitchener's portrait was featured in various ways and places throughout the Country in the summer and autumn of 1914. This is a postcard.

which they lived they were still known as 'Irish'. How many transferred under this scheme is unknown, but from research it would appear that very few did. However at least two are known to have transferred to the Tyneside Irish from other Infantry regiments and one, Private Thomas Keogh having served in France with the South Irish Horse, transferred to the Tyneside Irish, to be with his brother Richard.

Many men just wanted to join the army and would travel quite a distance to do so. Some were not particular which regiment they joined whereas others were to join the Tyneside Irish for the sole reason that they worked with an Irishman who was joining the Tyneside Irish Brigade.

'We didn't plan on joining the Tyneside Irish. In fact we would have preferred the Durhams but me and my brothers Sam and Eddy ended up in Sunderland. We couldn't find the DLI recruiting office so we went to the pub where this bloke told us where to find it. It was for the Tyneside Irish so we thought "Oh well" and took the shilling'.

(Lew Shaughnessy, 27th Battalion).

'I could have joined the Durhams but my father was Irish and there was any amount to pick from. Yet there were more English than Irish in the Battalion as I remember. We thought it would be a good holiday and a chance to see different countries.'

(Michael Manley 26th Battalion).

Chapter Two

Raising the Tynside Irish Brigade

'We're not so old in the Army List
But we're not so new at our trade.'
KIPLING

The first indication of the raising of a battalion from the Irish community on Tyneside appeared in a letter to the Editor of 'The Newcastle Evening Chronicle', of Saturday, 12 September 1914. Under the heading, 'TYNESIDE IRISH Proposal to Form a New Regiment', the following was printed:

'It is evident from the statement of Mr Asquith in the House of Commons last night that every available man in the country must be got to join the New Army if the enemy is to be overcome. That there are thousands of suitable men who have not yet come forward cannot be denied, and all citizens must make a strenuous effort to get these men to join the colours at once.

The idea of regiments of "Pals", which has received the sanction of the War Office, and has proved such a huge success all over the country, is a good one, and in order to give it our full support and do our utmost to assist the country in this terrific struggle, we suggest that an Irish Regiment be formed on Tyneside, which Irishmen of all classes and denominations can join. The number of Irishmen resident in this district is a large one, and although great numbers of our countrymen have already joined, we believe it is possible to get the necessary number of men who, no doubt, would prefer to enlist in such a regiment of a distinctive character in which all would be comrades and friends. A meeting to promote this object will be held in the Collingwood Hall, Irish National Club, Clayton Street, Newcastle, on Sunday 13th of September at 3 o'clock, and every representative Irishman on Tyneside, regardless of politics or religion, should consider it his bounden duty to attend.'

The Mayor of Newcastle 1913-1914, Colonel Johnstone Wallace. His term of office coincided with the raising of the Tyneside Irish.

The letter was signed PETER BRADLEY (Newcastle), ALD O'HANLON (Mayor of Wallsend), JOHN FARNON(Newcastle), FELIX LAVERY (Newcastle), P O'RORKE (Newcastle), COUNCILLOR BENNETT (Felling), JOHN I GORMAN (President, Irish National Club), JOHN MAHONEY (Secretary, Irish National Club), JAMES McLARNEY(Secretary, Ancient Order of Hibernians England), J E SCANLAN J.P.(Newcastle).

It can be seen from this letter that the original idea was for a new regiment cutting across religious and

Members and friends of the the Tyneside Irish Committee: 1. Mr J Farnon; 2. Mr J Fewester; 3. Mr J C Doyle; 4. Mr P Bradley; 5. Mr P Bennett; 6. Lieutenant-Colonel M E Byrne; 7. Major J W Prior; 8. Mr N Grattan Doyle; 9. Major W E Jones; 10. Mr E Conway; 11. Father G McBrearty; 12. Right Rev. Dr Collins; 13. Mr M Holohan; 14. Mr J Mulcahy; 15. Dr D K O'Kelly; 16. Mr P O'Rorke

political divides. The first plan for the Tyneside Irish Battalion was to offer its services to the 16th (Irish) Division that was in the process of being formed in Southern Ireland. However, the Commander of the 16th Division, Lieutenant-General L W Parsons declined the offer, saying that he wanted no 'slum birds' in his division, but rather the clean, fine, strong hurley-playing country fellows found in the Munsters, Connaught Rangers and Royal Irish. [One wonders what the 'slum birds' thought of the General.] Within two days a telegram was received from the War Office, in response to the offer to raise a battalion, saying,

> *'The Army Council expresses its sincere thanks for your patriotic offer which will be submitted to the Secretary of State.'*

However, at a meeting on 19th of September, those interested in raising the battalion were informed that, on the 18th of September, a letter had been received from the War Office to the effect that, owing to the number of local battalions already authorised, the Army Council had decided that no more such battalions be sanctioned.

The Army Council thanked the committee for its patriotic offer, but were unable to accept it. It would appear that this was due to the Tyneside Scottish committee arguing with the War Office about the wearing of the kilt.

Most of the initial recruits now dispersed and many enlisted into other regiments, for example, James Fitzpatrick, from Pomeroy, County Tyrone, enlisted in the First Tyneside Scottish and nothing further in the way of recruiting would be done until October.

On Saturday, 10th of October, Lord Haldane visited Newcastle with a request from Lord Kitchener to Sir Thomas Oliver that a Tyneside Scottish Battalion be raised, which led to hopes that something would be done to renew the efforts to raise the Tyneside Irish Battalion. In fact Lord Haldane did not meet Sir Thomas Oliver, but a meeting with the Lord Mayor, Councillor Johnstone Wallace, did take place which led to the War Office recognising the Mayor as the official raiser of the Tyneside Brigades.

A *Chronicle* reporter interviewed one of the Irish committee, who took the view that if the War Office requested the raising of a battalion the work would be done. After Lord Haldane returned to London, the Lord Mayor of Newcastle then received a telegram sanctioning a Tyneside Brigade comprising three battalions, Scottish, Irish and a second Commercial Battalion, so that steps were taken immediately to enrol members, and the Corn Exchange in Newcastle was opened as a recruiting office. The Scottish recruited briskly, but the Irish were much slower, although at the Irish National Club, as many as forty men presented themselves as would-be recruits.

It is interesting to note that, according to *The Evening Chronicle*, the first two names for enrolment were PATRICK BUTLER of Newcastle and JAMES LEACH of Hebburn. However, in the book, *Irish Heroes in the War*, Joseph Keating gives the first recruit as Henry Doyle, the son of one of the Raising Committee. Among this group of men was one ex-regular of the Connaught Rangers who apparently said, 'Put me in with the boys'. From the very beginning then, the Tyneside Irish had an ex-regular cadre who helped bring the Brigade to a high level of training. Many of these ex-regulars were promoted to senior NCO bringing experience of fighting on the North West Frontier, the Sudan and, of course, in South Africa against the Boers. Among them was Jack Erett, who had served in the 18th, The Royal Irish Regiment, who soon became Company Sergeant Major of C Company, and John Connolly who had served in the 1st Northumberland Fusiliers enlisted on the 9th of November. On the morning of the 10th he was promoted corporal and that afternoon he became a sergeant.[1] [24/585 John Connolly, not to be confused with 24/1151 and 26/1386.]

According to the book Irish Heroes Henry Doyle, the son of one of the Raising Committee, was the first recruit. He served as a sergeant in the 24th Battalion and was commissioned into the 26th Battalion.

Captain Arnold, C Company commander remembered his CSM like this,

'I was blessed with a very good sergeant major, Jack Erett, from whom I learned more than I ever could repay. Erett was a native of Waterford and had served through the South African War with the Royal Irish. He was a man who had educated himself far above the standard of rank and file. After his first Army service he had drifted into mining, but had always kept himself in a class distinct from his fellows. Certainly as things stood in the new armies he made an ideal sergeant major, keen, intelligent even tempered and strictly temperate. I liked him from the beginning and we worked together to make the company as good as it could be.'

Lew Shaughnessy also remarked on the ex-regulars in the ranks of the Tyneside Irish,

'Some of the lads in our platoon had been in before and they knew all the dodges.'

The original recruits were described thus by Captain Jack Arnold,

'When I joined the 24th Battalion, I found a motley throng very reminiscent of the types that used to file along the roads to annual militia musters in Ireland. They had no uniforms, no collars, boots that had toes peeping through them and trousers that were more patch than piece; there were old and young, some born in Ireland, some in England of Irish parentage, some having no connection with Ireland beyond the same church or the fact they worked in

Company Sergeant Major Jack Erett. He had served in India and South Africa with The Royal Irish Regiment.

The first recruit according to the Newcastle Chronicle was Sergeant Patrick Butler (No.21 on photo). He became the bombing Sergeant of D Company and was killed 1st July, 1916, after rescuing his Commanding Officer, Lieutenant-Colonel Meredith Howard, who had been wounded.

> *the same pit with an Irishman. An unusually large number were illiterate, the married ones hardly knew how many children they had got and the single ones were not sure if they were married or not and it was evident they had one characteristic in common, many were no stranger to an empty belly'.*

These early recruits were given a piece of green cloth to wear as an armband, to denote that they had volunteered for the Irish Battalion. In the same way, the Newcastle Commercials wore a red lanyard, and the Tyneside Scottish a Royal Stewart armband.

Joseph Cowen's Gift

At a meeting in the Town Hall, the Lord Mayor explained that the costs of what was termed 'Irregular Corps', had to be borne by the raising committees until they were finally taken over by the War Office. He also added that Mr Joseph Cowen, of Stella Hall, had made a magnificent gift of ten thousand pounds to meet any deficiency which might occur before the battalions were taken over by the War Office. This removed the financial difficulties that the committee had faced, so recruiting could now begin in earnest. Sir Thomas Oliver addressed the meeting, the offer was unanimously accepted, and the thanks of the Committee conveyed to Mr Joseph Cowen.

On 19 October 1914 a representative meeting was held in the Council Chamber of Newcastle Town

Advertisements for recruits appeared regularly in the papers.

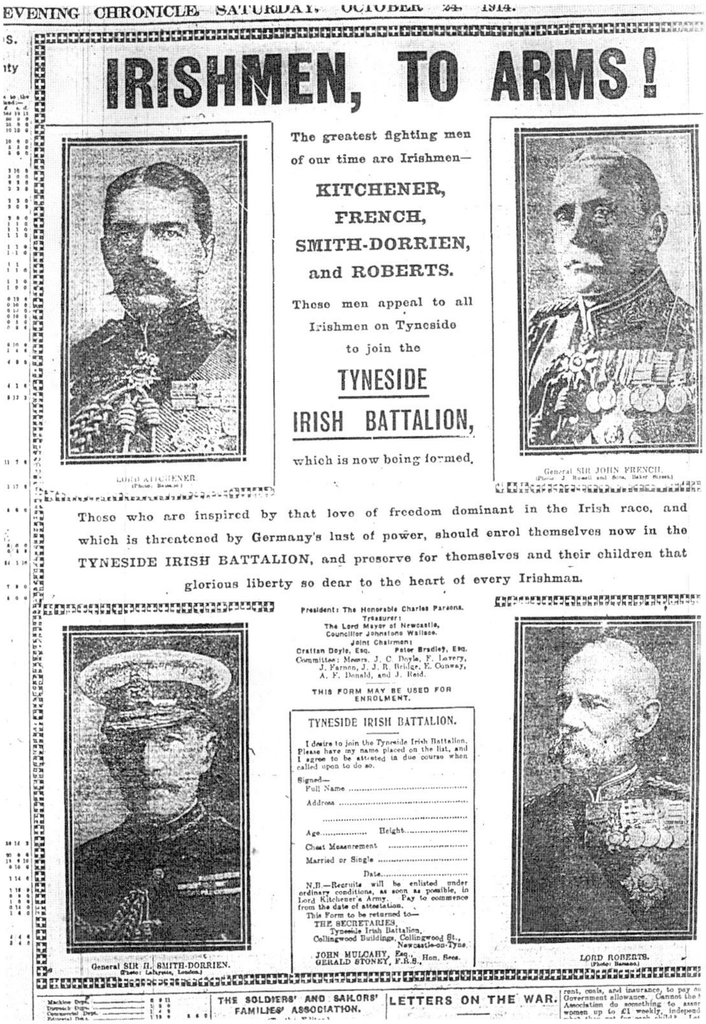

EVENING CHRONICLE, SATURDAY, OCTOBER 24, 1914.

IRISHMEN, TO ARMS!

The greatest fighting men of our time are Irishmen—

KITCHENER, FRENCH, SMITH-DORRIEN, and ROBERTS.

These men appeal to all Irishmen on Tyneside to join the

TYNESIDE IRISH BATTALION,

which is now being formed.

LORD KITCHENER.

General SIR JOHN FRENCH.

Those who are inspired by that love of freedom dominant in the Irish race, and which is threatened by Germany's lust of power, should enrol themselves now in the TYNESIDE IRISH BATTALION, and preserve for themselves and their children that glorious liberty so dear to the heart of every Irishman.

President: The Honorable Charles Parsons.
Treasurer: The Lord Mayor of Newcastle, Councillor Johnstone Wallace.
Joint Chairmen: Grattan Doyle, Esq. Peter Bradley, Esq.
Committee: Messrs. J. C. Doyle, F. Lavery, J. Farnon, J. J. R. Bridge, E. Conway, A. F. Donald, and J. Reid.

THIS FORM MAY BE USED FOR ENROLMENT.

TYNESIDE IRISH BATTALION.

I desire to join the Tyneside Irish Battalion. Please have my name placed on the list, and I agree to be attested in due course when called upon to do so.

Signed—
Full Name ....
Address ....
....
Age .... Height ....
Chest Measurement ....
Married or Single ....
Date ....

N.B.—Recruits will be enlisted under ordinary conditions, as soon as possible, in Lord Kitchener's Army. Pay to commence from the date of attestation.

This Form to be returned to—
THE SECRETARIES,
Tyneside Irish Battalion,
Collingwood Buildings, Collingwood St.,
Newcastle-on-Tyne.
JOHN MULCAHY, Esq., GERALD STONEY, F.R.S., Hon. Secs.

General SIR H. SMITH-DORRIEN.

LORD ROBERTS.

THE SOLDIERS' AND SAILORS' FAMILIES' ASSOCIATION.

LETTERS ON THE WAR.

Hall, when all those who had signed the original letter were present. The Lord Mayor [Councillor Johnstone Wallace who was a Unionist] addressed the meeting and then invited the Mayor of Wallsend (Ald John O'Hanlon) to speak. The Mayor of Wallsend moved the following resolution,

> *'That this meeting, of representative Irishmen on Tyneside, views with grati-tude the proposal to create a Tyneside Irish Battalion for service at the front, and pledges itself, to the utmost of its ability, to carry the proposal to a successful conclusion. The meeting also wishes to place on record its deep appreciation of Mr Joseph Cowen's generous assistance in the matter.'*

Mr Grattan Doyle spoke, as did Father McGill, Dean of St Mary's Roman Catholic Cathedral, and also the Rev C.E. Osborne, representing the Church of England clergy. Officials were elected, and the first meeting of the Executive Committee was set for Wednesday, 21 October 1914, at 8 p.m. A telegram was received from 'The United Irish League' in Westminister by Mr J Mulcahy, one of the secretaries. Mr T P O'Connor MP placed himself at the disposal of the Lord Mayor, and the people of Newcastle, and asked for dates of recruiting meetings at which he could speak.

On Saturday, 24 October 1914, the first recruiting poster appeared in the newspapers, showing the heads of four famous Irish Generals and the headline 'IRISHMEN, TO ARMS!' This poster also had an application form, that a would-be recruit, in an outlying village, could cut out, enter his details, and then forward to the recruiting committee. Also large posters in the Irish colours of green and gold, headed by the words, 'THE CALL TO ARMS! YOUR COUNTRY NEEDS YOU!' were posted in all districts of the North-East.

By 28 October 1914, there was a reported strength of 303. This was the result of postal applications and the work of the recruiting office in the Corn Exchange. Offers of help were also received from Doctors and military and police pensioners who were willing to instruct in drill. Arrangements were said to be well in hand for a great recruiting meeting to be held in the Town Hall on the 31st and on that day, a second recruiting poster appeared in the papers, headed 'IRISHMEN FOR THE BATTLE LINE'.

On 28 of October 1914, it was also stated in 'The Chronicle' that Colonel V.M. Stockley, late Indian Army, had accepted command of The Tyneside Irish Battalion, and that Colonel Ritson had offered two fields behind Jesmond Gardens as a training ground.

The early parades in Eldon Square were a strange sight to the towns-people, when every morning the men gathered for the battalion parade.

> *'Every morning the battalion paraded in Eldon Square at 9 a.m. Major Joe Prior was always in command, he was a man of great physique, over six feet tall and proportionately made. We had a band of fifes and drums. The battalion "shunned," sloped arms (those that had them), formed fours and then to the strains of "The Harp that once through Tara's Hall's", marched off to the Town Moor to begin the day's training.' (Captain Jack Arnold)*

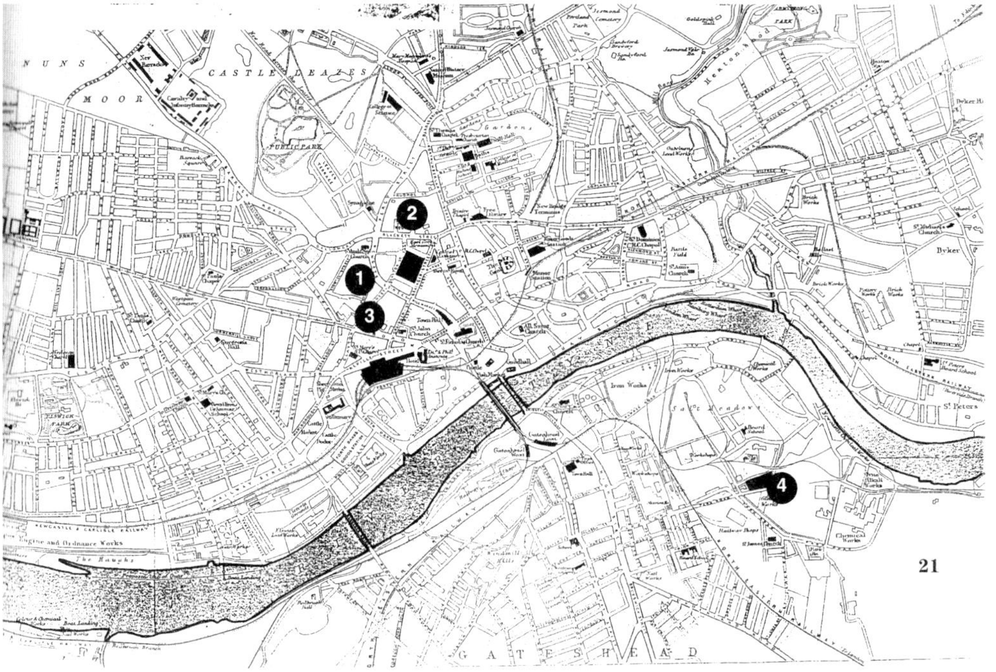

NEWCASTLE AND GATESHEAD 1914

No.1 Dunns Buildings, 24th Battalion billets.
No.2 Eldon Square, 24th Battalion parade ground.
No.3 Westgate Road, Tyneside Irish recruiting office.
No.4 Sunbeam Buildings, 26th Battalion billets.

CHRONICLE, FRIDAY, OCTOBER 30, 1914.

IRISHMEN FOR THE BATTLE LINE.

LORD ROBERTS.
(Photo: J. Russell and Sons, Baker Street.)

The greatest fighting men of our time are Irishmen - KITCHENER, FRENCH, SMITH-DORRIEN, and ROBERTS. These men appeal to all Irishmen on Tyneside to join the

TYNESIDE IRISH BATTALION

which is now being formed.

SIR JOHN FRENCH.
(Photo: Lafayette, London.)

Lord Kitchener makes a direct appeal to every North-Country Irishman. "I feel sure," he writes to the Lord Mayor of Newcastle (Councillor Johnstone Wallace), "that all Irishmen on Tyneside will respond willingly to your Lordship's appeal to defend the Empire." To save your country from the martyrdom of Belgium, you must enlist immediately. Louvain and Malines must be avenged, and this can only be done by your own strong right arm. Fill up the attached Enrolment Form, and return it to the Secretaries (Mr. Gerald Stoney, F.R.S., and Mr. John Mulcahy) immediately.

Lord Kitchener's call is to every man who is fit. For every Irishman the path of duty is clear. If you would preserve your nationality, you must fight for it. Germany, the bully of the nations, must be defeated if free nations are to exist.

Irishmen must take a part in this great struggle. It means risk and sacrifice, but it also means honour, and comradeship, and courage. The cause is worthy and the opportunity great. Will you respond to the call and the hour?

FIELD MARSHAL VISCOUNT KITCHENER.
(Photo: Bassano, 25, Old Bond Street, W.)

Lord Roberts writes:—Dear Lord Mayor,—As an Irishman, I am glad to hear it is proposed to raise a Tyneside Irish Battalion. We are all proud of the way in which English, Scottish, and Irish troops are now fighting on the Continent. They have a hard task before them, and are contending against odds. It should be the pride of every young man of military age to help them, and I have every hope that the ranks of the Tyneside Irish Battalion will soon be filled.

Those who are inspired by that love of freedom dominant in the Irish race, and which is threatened by Germany's lust of power should enrol themselves now in the Tyneside Irish Battalion, and preserve for themselves and their children that glorious liberty so dear to the heart of every Irishman.

SIR H. SMITH-DORRIEN.
(Photo: Lafayette, London.)

Tyneside Irish Battalion.

I desire to join the Tyneside Irish Battalion. Please have my name placed on the list, and I agree to be attested in due course when called upon to do so.

Signed,

Full Name ....

Address ....

....

Age.................. Height.................. Chest Measurement..................

Married or Single.................. Date..................

This Form to be returned to—
THE SECRETARIES,
Tyneside Irish Battalion,
6 and 7, Collingwood Buildings,
Collingwood Street,
Newcastle-on-Tyne.

LORD CHAS. BERESFORD.
(Photo: Record Press.)

THE CALL TO ARMS!
YOUR COUNTRY NEEDS YOU!
JOIN THE
TYNESIDE
IRISH BATTALION

All eligible Irishmen are cordially invited to join at once to fight for the great principles of freedom and the rights of small nations, and against military tyranny and despotism.

Proposal Forms are obtainable in all districts in Northumberland and Durham, or from the
CENTRAL RECRUITING OFFICE,
Corn Exchange, Town Hall,
Newcastle-on-Tyne.

JOHN MULCAHY
GERALD STONEY } Joint Secs.
6 & 7, Collingwood Buildings, Collingwood Street,
Newcastle-on-Tyne.

GOD SAVE OUR KING AND COUNTRY!

North of England Printing Co., Ltd., 40, High Bridge, Newcastle.

Posters printed in green on gold paper were posted throughout the region.

Recruiting Offices for the Tyneside Irish were being opened in all districts of the North-East, as follows:

District	Office	Organiser
Ashington	Catholic Institute	Blaydon
Wood's Cafe	Wesley Place	Mr Patrick Smith
Blyth	Irish National Club	
Consett	Middle Street	Councillor James Daly
Durham City	78 North Road	Mr J M Lynch
Gateshead Labour Exchange	Windmill Hills	
Hebburn	Catholic Institute, Lyon St	Rev E Witty
Jarrow	Grange Road	Mr Patrick Bennett
Newcastle	Town Hall	Mr A M Oliver
Newcastle	Corn Exchange	
Newcastle	57 Westgate Road	Mr McGee
North Shields	Catholic Institute	
South Shields	Irish National Club	
Sunderland	High Street	Councillor Hoey
Wallsend	Catholic Institute	

When the recruits attended the recruiting office, they were issued with a small blue card stating that they had enlisted in the army, and this was signed by the recruiting officer to prove that they had enlisted.

About this time advertisements for retired NCOs appeared in the newspapers, and, somewhat unusually, the Tyneside Irish also invited applications from those wishing to be considered for a commission. No other regiment or unit recruiting in the North-East placed advertisements for Officers and NCOs in this way.

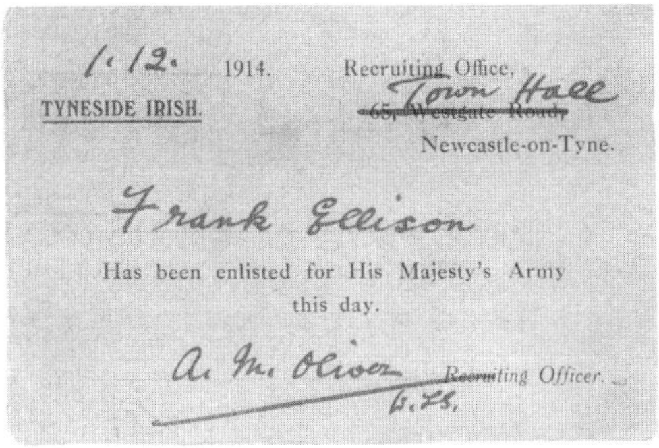

1.12. 1914. Recruiting Office,
TYNESIDE IRISH. Town Hall ~~65, Westgate Road~~
Newcastle-on-Tyne.

Frank Ellison

Has been enlisted for His Majesty's Army this day.

A. M. Oliver Recruiting Officer.

To prove that they had volunteered the recruits were given a small blue card signed by the recruiting officer.

Also, at this time, details of the names and addresses of those enlisting were printed in the newspapers: an idea of Colonel Joseph Reed, who was managing editor of the *Newcastle Chronicle*. The aim was to shame those who had not enlisted into so doing, since arrangements were now well in hand for the 'GREAT RECRUITING MEETING' that was to be held on Saturday, 31 October 1914, which was to be presided over by the Lord Mayor. The chief speakers were to be Mr T P O'Connor M.P. and the Earl of Donoughmore. Also present would be Sir Charles Parsons, the President of the Tyneside Irish Committee and invitations were also sent to Mr Edward Short and Mr Walter Hudson, the Members of Parliament for Newcastle. At the meeting the official announcement was made to the effect that Colonel V.M. Stockley had accepted commmand of the Tyneside Irish Battalion. The Colonel had served from 1874 to 1912, and had fought in Egypt in 1882 and China in 1901, being present at Tel El Kebir and the occupation of Cairo. He only commanded for a very short time before he accepted command of the Second Tyneside Scottish Battalion, and command passed to Colonel Myles Emmet Byrne.

Colonel Joseph Reed managing director of the *Newcastle Chronicle* had the idea of putting the lists of volunteers in the paper.

A great spurt of recruits was expected from this meeting, and on the Saturday morning, it was reported that the Irish Battalion was at half strength, and preparations were being made for attestations to begin on Monday. Now the question of accommodation for the Battalion arose and difficulty was expected as the majority of those enlisting were from outside Newcastle. The Committee asked for suggestions to solve this problem, as most suitable buildings were already occupied by other units. Headquarters of the Battalion was established at 10 Osborne Villas, Osborne Avenue, Jesmond, by the Commanding Officer.

Mr Joseph Cowen now allocated a further £5,000 to the battalion to defray any unforeseen expenses, and Dunn's Buildings, in Low Friar Street, Newcastle, was secured as accommodation for the men. The building was described as being made of concrete, and calculated to be warm and comfortable, with sufficient space to house 800 men. Initially 223 men were quartered in the Town

TYNESIDE IRISH BATTALION.

SPLENDID RESPONSE FROM DURHAM

From this city and neighbourhood there has been a splendid response to the appeal for recruits for the Tyneside Irish Battalion. On Saturday week Mr J. M. Lynch opened a recruiting branch at his premises, 78, North Road, and up to Wednesday 104 applicants had been received. Only a few have been rejected. So long as recruits are required the local branch will remain open from 8.30 a.m. until 8 p.m., and men will be attested at the Assize Courts. The following proposals to join the battalion were sent from the Durham branch:—John Killian, Framwellgate; John Carroll, South Street; Thos. Bowes, Framwellgate; John Bowes, do.; Wm. Atkinson, Millburngate; John Tierney, do.; Jas. Sullivan, Langley Park; Oswald B. Wranghan, Hill Top; Anthony Docherty, Millburngate; Patrick T. Curry, Mowbray Street; Robt. Gaffney, Framwellgate; Alex. Brodie, do.; Michael Glynn, Sacriston; John Bell, Langley Moor; Jas. Nolan, do.; John Tilly, New Brancepeth; Geo. Charlton, do; Harle Mavin, Boyne; Thos. Kelly, Framwellgate; R. Johnson, Crossgate; Jos. Johnson, do.; J. R. Taylor, Langley Moor; A. J. Bennett, do.; Jas. W. Kenworthy, do.; Tweddle Bailey, do.; John Mickle, Crossgate; Andrew C. Taylor, Langley Moor; Dominic McShane, Langley Park; Harry Lockey, Framwellgate; Thos. Johnson, New Elvet; John Bowes, Framwellgate; Wm. C. Bates, New Elvet; Jos. Burke, Framwellgate; Thos. Kelly, Maynard's Row; Allan Lockwood, Gilesgate; Wm. Markham, do.; Patrick McIntyre, Langley Moor; George Humphries, do.; J. Malloy, do.; Jas. Flynn, Millburngate; Chas. Callan, Davy Lamp, Kelloe; Patrick McManus, Framwellgate; Michael Hanley, Millburngate; Patrick Markey, Brandon; J. W. Rourke, Kimblesworth; Hugh Gilroy, Framwellgate; John J. Robinson, Langley Moor; John R. Smith, do.; Geo. Wm. McRoy, Broompark; G. A. Lockey, Langley Moor; Geo. Dagg, Framwellgate; Robt. Ainsley, Langley Moor; Jonathan Malpas, Framwellgate; Ed. Foley, Lawson Terrace; L. Wills, Langley Moor; J. G. Barron, New Brancepeth; Rd. Booth, Langley Moor; Jos. Thornton, do.; J. Ryan, Fowler's Terrace; John Hy. Smith, Court Lane; Abraham Forster, Back Lane; David Keenan, Brandon; Wm. McGrath, Langley Park; John Staff, do.; Jas. Gibson, do.; John Reed, New Brancepeth; Jos. Hanley, Sidegate; Edward Young, Millburngate; John Hanley, Crossgate; John Gavaghan, Sidegate; Rd. Humble, Sunniside, Tow Law; John Miller, Kimblesworth; Jos. S. Turnbull, Gilesgate; George Blagdon, Millburngate; Ed. Sheen, Crossgate Moor; Jas. Brophy, Crossgate Moor; Michael Hook, Lovegreen Street; Jas. Wm. Coleman, New Elvet; Wm. McGair, South Street; Michael Brannen, Anton Stile; John Connolly, Millburngate; Wm. Cummings, Brandon Colliery; Daniel Shanks, Framwellgate; Harry Gibson, do.; John Bowes, Broompark; Thos. Hurst, do.; Hugh Meenan, Millburngate; Martin McNamara, New Brancepeth; John Carroll, New Durham; Frank Scorer, Leamside; Jos. Lowery, Bowburn; J. C. McKewan, do.; James McKeown, do.; Thos. Crosby, Broomside; Benj. Hartley, Framwellgate Moor; Thos. F. Owens, Framwellgate; Geo. Reed, New Brancepeth; Andrew Oughton, Elvet Waterside; Michael Brannen, Crossgate Moor; Jos. Ingledew, Framwellgate Moor.

The first hundred from the Durham City area to volunteer. Among the names are the author's four great uncles and his great grandfather John Connolly. Most of the men on the list served in D Company of the 1st Tyneside Irirsh.

Hall in Newcastle, and the remainder in Dunn's Buildings. Later the Raby Street School became available, and those in the Town Hall were moved there.

Over 100 men were recruited from the meeting on Saturday, 31 October, and by lunch-time on Monday, 2 November 1914, the strength of the Battalion stood at over 900. It was reported that the first attestations were ten ex-NCO's, who could no longer resist the call to arms, as the appeal had been from Irishmen to Irishmen. The Corn Exchange presented a very busy sight as men were enrolled and attested. An appeal was made to the Irish Ladies of Tyneside to attend a meeting to form a Ladies' Committee, in an attempt to provide the men with those things needed to make life more comfortable in billets. Messrs George and Jopling made a motor car available to the main committee to alleviate transport problems.

By the fourth of the month, the Battalion was at full strength with more than enough men to compensate for leakage during attestation. In the book, *Irish Heroes in the War* Joseph Keating writes,

> *'Three days later one thousand and fifty-two splendid young recruits were in the Irish ranks. A Tyneside Irish Battalion had been created in spite of all the difficulties'.*

The average age of these 'young recruits' was in the late thirties; indeed 24/1151 Private John Connolly was 44 and 24/3 Private William Turnbull, 24/63 Private F Finlay and 24/321 Private F Rodgers all aged 42. On the other side of the coin 24/49 Private Athur Walton was 14 and 24/1640 Private Edward Armstrong was 15.

The first Regimental Sergeant Major was soon appointed. RSM P O'Toole was an ex-Drill Sergeant of the Irish Guards. It was under his watchful eye that drill parades were carried out in Eldon Square, although he was not to remain with the battalion, for he was discharged in early 1916 because he was 60 years old. His son, CQMS O'Toole, was killed in action in France in November 1914 with his father's old regiment.

Drill practice was carried out on the Town Moor and the intricacies of ceremonial and company drill were taught and absorbed by the recruits. These were practised for hours and the men patiently trained, although many of the older ones could see little sense in the wheeling and forming and standing immovable for what seemed an age.

Eldon Square as the Tyneside Irish would have known it.

The training was left much in the hands of the company officers, who found there was little that could be achieved in Newcastle. But the one area in which the Tyneside Irish excelled, was the digging of trenches. On the Town Moor therefore an area was set aside and the officers studied the 'Manual of Field Engineering' using terms unfamiliar to the men such as parapet, parados, traverses and communication trench. Before the officers had finished explaining the men would be well on their way underground, as Captain Arnold remarked,

> *'We were probably ahead of most formations, for what the miner of olden days did not know about digging, revetting and drainage was not worth learning.'*

One day not long after the battalion had come together there was to be an inspection by a General, the men were still in 'civvies' and looked like a crowd at a football match.
Captain Arnold also remembered this event.

> *'The populace gaped in curious groups all round the unoccupied parts of the square. No one had the faintest idea of how a General should be received; there could be no proper general salute, no bugle, no presenting of arms. Major Prior was in command, resplendent in well fitting uniform, bright spurs, with a great sword as long as Goliath's stuck in his frog. Amidst the universal panic he alone was confident, calm and collected. After the usual heartrending wait the staff car drove into the square and the old general – he was a dugout of patriarchal age – proceeded to totter towards the battalion. Prior called the battalion to attention in a voice that could be heard across the river, took the regulation number of paces, to meet the inspecting officer and then drawing his Excalibur with a tremendous flourish, which may have included the proper salute, but was delivered with a vigour which suggested the opening of a murderous assault. The tone of the General during the review was now distinctly subdued, and the whole show was carried off with much elan.'*

Major Prior, resplendent in his well tailored uniform, was in command when the visiting General inspected.

The joint secretaries, of the Tyneside Irish Committee Mr Gerald

Stoney and Mr J Mulcahy called a meeting to consider proceeding with the recruiting of a second battalion. In the meantime enrolments continued and on the fourth, a special effort was made to recruit men at Seaham Harbour, when a recruiting meeting was held at which Father Haggerty presided. Seaham, of course, had a large Irish population brought over by Lord Londonderry to work on his estates, and in his mines. Another recruiting meeting was held in the Church Square Schools in West Hartlepool, presided over by the Mayor, Councillor Fryer, with many of the Tyneside Irish committee in attendance. The usual speeches were made but, despite an Irish community amongst the dock workers, not many recruits from the Hartlepool area were obtained.

The Illustrated Chronicle.
LOCAL IRISH FULFIL EXPECTATIONS.
1
3
Those who expected great things from the Irishmen of Tyneside who so readily
sponded to the call to arms, are not likely to be disappointed. Enthusiasm does
t cool nor energy flag. (1), Lieut. T. G. Farina, acting adjutant; (2), Cleaning
the outside of rifles; (3), Fatigue and mess waiters of 1st Battalion.
GS ARE T ALWAYS WHAT THEY SEEM.

The news that the men had enlisted was not always well received by the womenfolk, who would have to stay at home and look after large families. In Framwellgate, for instance, Margaret Connolly had just washed John's pit hoggers, but he deliberately said they were still dirty so as to have an excuse to go out and join up. Margaret threw the trousers at him when he came in with the news. Others, like Matthew Pyle, just sent a post card home with the news.

On the 10th of November a second battalion was officially sanctioned by the War Office, but as recruiting had continued without let, within two days, the battalion was almost full and the Committee had to face the probability of recruiting a third battalion.

The military authorities now called upon the services of 250 men from the First Tyneside Irish, who joined the composite battalion forming for the defence of the coast. Each of the units forming in the district contributed a company, so the battalion consisted of men not only from the Tyneside Irish, but also the First and Second Commercial Battalions and the First Tyneside Scottish Battalion. For three weeks the men were deployed away from the battalion, but after the emergency was over they returned to Dunn's Buildings. An appeal was made for second-hand overcoats and money to buy warm clothing by the Ladies' Committee, with lists of those making donations being placed each evening in the newspaper.

Reverend Father Hartley of Blaydon volunteered to serve as Padre to the Irish Battalion in view of the large number of Roman Catholics among those who were being recruited. The only indication of religion for a whole platoon comes from the company roll book of B Company of the 24th Battalion, kept by Captain George Swinburn. However he only recorded religion for Number 5 Platoon, which had a strength of seventy men, thirty five Roman Catholics, twelve Church of England, three Non-Conformists and twenty unknown. [Looking at the names of these twenty though it is highly probable that the majority were Roman Catholic.]

The third battalion was sanctioned by the War Office on the 23rd of November and received the blessing of the Roman Catholic Bishop of Middlesbrough. At a meeting of the 'Irish Organisation' on Tees-side, it was decided on the 24th of November to support the appeal for recruits for the Tyneside Irish. It was suggested a Tees-side company should be raised by the Bishop of Middlesbrough and one of the most active supporters of this movement was Mr Robert Mclean, afterwards Clerk to Redcar Urban District

Council. In view of the fact that few Middlesbrough men appear in the casualty lists of the Tyneside Irish, and only one or two in the Absentee Voter List give Tyneside Irish regimental numbers, it would seem that this company never reached the Tyneside Irish.

Contracts for clothing and equipment were placed with local companies, and were said to be well in hand. The colour Khaki was said to be the true colour for the Irish and this was a reference to the fact that many of the Kitchener Battalions that were forming were wearing the blue uniforms now known as 'Kitchener Blue'. This was a source of disappointment to many recruits, and the Tyneside Irish Committee hoped that by issuing Khaki uniforms they would attract more men so that as the Khaki uniforms became available, they were issued to the men of the First Battalion and were seen when the Battalion paraded in Eldon Square.

> *'As time went on the men all got into uniform and were fully equipped with rifles, and sidearms. The shuffling and fumbling of the early parades dis-appeared; they sloped arms with wonderful precision, considering that many were over forty and had never handled a rifle before.' (Captain Jack Arnold)*

Colonel Henry M Hatchell, DSO, CO of 2nd Tyneside Irish. Served in the Eygptian, Afghan and Boer Wars with the 18th Royal Irish Regiment.

Recruiting continued throughout December although the lists of names grew shorter towards Christmas. On the 23rd of the month, the First Battalion paraded again in Eldon Square, drawing favourable comment in the newspapers. Christmas dinner, with beer, was provided for those in Dunn's Buildings, and on the 28th, a "Grand Concert" took place in the Town Hall. After Christmas, recruiting picked up again, so much so, that members of the committee went to the War Office in London to obtain permission to recruit a fourth battalion, in order to have a complete Tyneside Irish Brigade.

On 9 January 1915 the First Battalion paraded in Eldon Square completely turned out in khaki, when not a single man was in civilian clothes and some men had full equipment. The parade was led by the band, which played a selection of Irish airs, as the men were inspected by Brigadier-General Colling and General Guisford. Later that afternoon, at 2-15 p.m. the Battalion Rugby Football Fifteen had a resounding success, when they beat the Second Tyneside Scottish 35-0. For some reason the names of the Scottish players were not reported, but the list of the Irish players was as follows:

Pte Carroll Durham
Lt Wilkinson Sunderland
Lt Farina Old Novo's*
Lt Hunt New Brighton
Lt Pringle Old Novo's
Lt Brady Gosforth
Pte Wilson Blaydon*
Pte Dykes Winlaton.

Pte McDonald Durham
Lt A Thompson Gosforth**
Lt Short Cheshire*
Pte Malpas Durham*
Lt Nolan Percy Park*
Sgt Murphy Coldstream
Cpl McMahon Westoe

Those marked * were the scorers in a match which they hoped would become a regular event. The Scottish would even the score later on the soccer field when the battalions were at Alnwick.

The Co-operative store in Birtley was used as a mess hall by men of the 25th Batallion.

Second Tyneside Irish at Birtley

The Second Tyneside Irish Battalion was now ready to be called up, and billets and accommodation were found at Birtley, which was to lead to much controversy as various welcoming committees were formed by different groups in the town. A public meeting was called by the Central Committee of the Tyneside Irish Brigade to make arrangements for the welfare of the men of the Second Battalion, who were to be quartered there. The meeting was attended by Mr Grattan Doyle, joint Chairman, Mr J Mulcahy, joint Secretary, Father Morrell, the Rev W E Farndale, the parish clergy, Mr B Bolam, and a large body of citizens. The chairman, Mr Grattan Doyle, in opening the meeting, said it had been called to see if they could come to some joint arrangement for the benefit of the soldiers to make their lot a pleasant one whilst at Birtley.

Father Morrell, speaking for the Catholic Committee that had been appointed and working for some time, was of the opinion that the committee in Newcastle had gone over their heads and had not

Men of 25/Northumberland Fusiliers in Birtley, kneeling in the centre is 25/324 Private James Keenan of Boldon Lane, South Shields, who would be KiA on 1 July 1916

Second Lieutenant Dunn with some NCOs outside the skating rink at Birtley. The NCOs are (left to right to the rear) Lance Corporals McQuire, Openshaw, Hammil (went absent without leave in England and was court martialled in France for striking a superior officer), Lavell; (either side of the chair) Sergeant A. Black and Corporal Ruddy.

consulted them. Mr Bolam said the question was whether the men would be best served by a joint committee or several sectional committees, but if it were to be done sectionally, he would have nothing further to do with the matter. Mr T Neville replied that, at the invitation of the Central Committee in Newcastle, a Catholic Commmittee had been formed in Birtley, and had worked energetically. He would ask if the General Committee in Newcastle had changed its attitude and if it had now come to the conclusion that a public meeting should be convened to discuss the whole question, and to form one committee. So far as he was concerned, he wished this had taken place six weeks earlier because it would have prevented any ill-feelings that had taken place since then.

Father Morrell then said that the Catholic Committee would do all in its power for the social and moral welfare of the troops. But it was essential that the committee should have time to consider its position. It ought to be able to discuss the position, so that it might decide whether it could join the local joint committee. Father Morrell again spoke saying, that as a Catholic committee had not been dissolved, in mere politeness to them, an intimation should have been sent requesting them, to dissolve. Mr Grattan Doyle replied that he regretted the discussion had taken this turn. He hoped that whatever personal grievances there were, real or imagined, they would allow them to pass, in view of the greater necessity for the common good of the men who were to be amongst them for two months as it was deplorable that these petty local matters should be allowed to interfere or to enter into this great question. The meeting continued in this vein for some time, until the question of the religion of the men arose when Mr Doyle stated that the figures, as to the religion of the men coming to Birtley, were not yet to hand, but with regard to the First Battalion, they knew that 62 out of every 100 were Catholics.

Several more speakers put the point of view of their respective groups, with Father Morrell having the last word, saying that he was not a little bit moved by the pretty rhetoric of the Chairman. It was then agreed the meeting be adjourned until the following Tuesday night.

Men of the 25th Batallion at Birtley, seated at the front is 25/472 Private Jimmy McManus of Crossgate Moor in Durham City.

At the meeting on Tuesday, after considerable discussion, the committees representing the Roman Catholic, Primitive Methodist, Church of England and Wesleyan Churches, all agreed to throw open their halls, and would continue to act independently for the amusement of the men. But for matters concerning the battalion as a whole, a central committee was appointed and it was decided that each of the four churches should have one representative on the committee, whilst 'Ouston, E Pit, Lodge', would have six representatives. The ten gentlemen were elected by the meeting. Mr Doyle was unanimously elected chairman, and agreed to call the first meeting of the Birtley Committee. The members were as follows:

Messrs M Winter, J Hobson, J Adamson, T Mellon, W Willis, T Swinburne, J P Hall, F Knox, B Oliver and H Todd.

The first detachment of the Second Tyneside Irish arrived at Birtley that afternoon and half the battalion, about 550 men, were to be billeted in the skating rink until the end of March, when huts were expected to be ready. The first arrivals, of about 200 men, marched in from Newcastle and presented an exceedingly smart appearance, many of the men being ex-regular soldiers. Excellent arrangements were made for these men whilst they were in the town during which time all meals were taken at the Co-operative Hall, as the society had taken in hand the whole of the catering arrangements and the various religious bodies opened schools and institutions to the men for writing, reading and recreation. This party was under the command of Major Elwy Jones, who was transferred from the King's Liverpool Regiment supported by other officers, notably Messrs Murray, Foley, Bainbridge and Slack.

'I had joined the army on the 16th of November 1914, and was sent home until I was called up for training on the 21st of January 1915. I was in Newcastle for one week, then moved to Birtley.' (Diary of Lance Corporal Ted Colpitts 25th Battalion)

The Second Tyneside Irish settled down in Birtley where Physical Training and Foot Drill was carried out in the streets with Route Marches proceeding through the surrounding villages, and trench digging done on Blackfell, where today the A1(M) motorway passes the Washington Service Area. The first commander of the Second Battalion was Colonel Henry Hatchell DSO who had served in the 18th Royal Irish Regiment during the Egyptian and Afghan wars and had been awarded his DSO for service in the South African war.

In the meantime, in Newcastle, a shooting range for the First Battalion was established at Bath Lane, where early musketry was carried out, and the Officers' Mess was housed in what had been the Variety Artists' Club in Pink Lane. The mess was recalled with great affection by Captain Arnold and he had this to say about it,

'The mess room was in the original bar with a counter at one end and we slept on camp beds in two dormitories up above. The scenes of hilarity that went on there from time to time beggar description. Occasionally some artist, performing at a nearby music hall, would wander in after the show under the misapprehension that the club was still functioning. This would be a heaven sent interlude in the military routine and the fun would wax fast and furious. The life and soul in all these goings on would be Major Joe Prior, the battalion second-in-command.'

The recruiting net spreads wider

The recruiting net was now being spread wider and wider; meetings were arranged for the Cumbrian towns of Workington, Whitehaven, Millom and Cleator Moor, in the hope of raising a Cumbrian Irish Company. In Liverpool, there was a move to form a Liverpool Irish Battalion for Kitchener's Army, but Liverpool already had an Irish Battalion, the 8th (Liverpool Irish) Battalion, a Territorial battalion of the King's Regiment, so the Kitchener Battalion received little support. Those who did enlist were sent to Newcastle to join the Tyneside Irish and arriving in Newcastle on 12 January 1915, were allotted to the First Battalion to be split amongst the companies. The Cumbrians, however, went to the Fourth Battalion, with the majority serving in B Company.

Accommodation was found for the Third Tyneside Irish Battalion at Sunbeam Buildings in Gateshead; this was a large, wooden, three storey building, not ideal for 1,000 men, the home of the Sunbeam Lamp Company a large factory for making oil and electric lamps together with associated products. The men, called up in batches, were kitted out and put into billets and training began. Initially, command of the Third Battalion was given to Lieutenant-Colonel Hussey Walsh who, like the other battalion commanders, brought with him experience of Britain's colonial wars.

Colonel Hussey Walsh commanding the 3rd Tynside Irish.

One of the suggested designs for the Tyneside Irish emblem. The Arms of the City of Newcastle surrounded by a wreath of Shamrock. Taken from a 124 Brigade menu card of 18th February 1915.

Attention was now being given to a special emblem for the Tyneside Irish battalions and it was reported that most favoured a harp surrounded by the letters T.I.N.F. The final choice, however was the Connaught Rangers' Harp with the wording changed to Tyneside Irish, above the battalion number and below the letters N.F. The battalions also learned that they were to be officially numbered in the Northumberland Fusilier sequence, as follows[2]: 24th (Service) Battalion (1st Tyneside Irish), 25th (Service) Battalion (2nd Tyneside Irish), 26th (Service) Battalion (3rd Tyneside Irish) and 27th (Service) Battalion (4th Tyneside Irish). A 30th (Tyneside Irish) Reserve Battalion would be raised in 1915. The Tyneside Irish Brigade was now numbered as the 124 Brigade of the 41st Division, in which the other Brigades were the 122 Brigade comprising the 16th, 18th and 19th Battalions of the Northumberland Fusiliers and the 18th Battalion of the Durham Light Infantry (The Durham Pals), and the 123 Brigade, which consisted of the four Tyneside Scottish battalions.

On the 14th of January, it was reported that the race with the Tyneside Scottish to complete a Brigade was now won, but within days the Tyneside Scottish would also complete their Brigade. It should be pointed out that the Tyneside Scottish had actually raised four battalions first and closed their recruiting offices, but they had not raised depot companies so they had to start all over again.,whereas the Tyneside Irish had been raising men for their depot companies as they went along. The medical condition of many recruits was not up to standard, contrary to the propaganda put out by the raising committee. Particular health problems relating to working in the mines were evident and many men were discharged after only a few weeks with the colours. In one case a one-eyed man, Private T Dodgson of the Second Battalion, managed to serve until June 1915.

The cry now from the Irish Committee was, 'If we were properly backed up by the War Office, we could go for another Brigade. We could get the men; it is the accommodation and officers that are wanted.'

In fact word was received from the War Office that no more Infantry was required at present, but the need for Artillery and Engineers was greater than ever. The Tyneside Irish Committee then agreed to raise

The 3rd Tyneside Irish parade on the streets of Gateshead. Notice the large coke shovels carried by some of the men.

Lieutenants Gilmore, Vernon and Stephenson, 3rd Tyneside Irish, at Sunbeam Buildings, Gateshead February 1915.

these units, but very little is known about them so they may never have been raised and certainly they did not join the Tyneside Irish Infantry Brigade in the field.

The various battalions were now referred to by their number in the Northumberland Fusiliers and will be referred to from now on by those numbers.

Newcastle was now full of battalions of men forming and training and no accommodation could be found to house the 27th Battalion. This lack of accommodation meant that the 27th Battalion could not be called up and men arriving in Newcastle were attested, medically examined, paid, then sent home.

> *'I enlisted on the 26th of December 1914 and was sent back home receiving 27/ 5d a week until actually called up on 29th of March 1915.' (Diary of Sergeant Fred Hood 27th Battalion).*

The fact that the men were at home being paid as soldiers caused a lot of resentment among the other battalions; often soldiers on a weekend pass found recruits in their street or village receiving pay for doing nothing. No accommodation would be available for the 27th Battalion until the 24th moved out of Dunn's Buildings to go to Alnwick.

The 24th Battalion had now been in Newcastle since November and having carried out limited training, was ready for field training. It was decided that, along with the 21st Battalion the Second Tyneside Scottish, the 24th Battalion the First Tyneside Irish should move to the new hutted camp at Alnwick, where the 20th Battalion the First Tyneside Scottish had been for some time.

Attracting large crowds on 12 March 1915, the 24th Battalion paraded in Eldon Square for the last time. Commanded by Colonel Myles Emmett Byrne, it formed up and carried out various drill movements around the square prior to being inspected by the Lord Mayor of Newcastle,

Lieutenants Brown, McAlister and Simons, 3rd Tyneside Irish, at Sunbeam Buildings, Gateshead February 1915.

Alderman John Fitzgerald, whose son Gerald had been commissioned into the 26th Battalion in January. The Lord Mayor was accompanied by the Lady Mayoress (Miss Fitzgerald) and members of the Tyneside Irish Committee; Mr Grattan Doyle, Mr Peter Bradley, Mr J Mulcahy, Mr P O'Rorke, Councillors Donald, Farnon and Messrs Doyle, Middleton, Sheridan, Wedderburn and others. The Lord Mayor congratulated the Battalion on its smart appearance and Colonel Byrne on the rapid progress made over the past months. He also congratulated the men of the Battalion on their exemplary conduct during their stay in the city. They had excited the admiration of the whole community and had acted as soldiers and gentlemen. A long speech followed, ending with the words, 'Their fight would be a gallant one – for freedom, faith and fatherland.' Colonel Byrne thanked the Mayor for his kind words and said that the 24th (Service) Battalion the First Tyneside Irish would do its duty and be a credit to the city. They would endeavour to uphold the great traditions of their regiment, The Northumberland Fusiliers. The Colonel then called for three cheers for the Lord Mayor, the Lady Mayoress, the Honorary Colonel, Councillor Johnstone Wallace and the Tyneside Irish Committee. These were heartily given, and led by the Irish Pipes and Drums, the Fife and Drum Band and the Bugle Band, the Battalion marched by way of Grainger Street to Newcastle Central Station, to depart in two trains for Alnwick.

Brigadier General WA Collings had retired in 1908 but was appointed the first Commander of the Tyneside Irish Brigade

An advance party had left Newcastle a few days before the main party to prepare the camp at Alnwick for the arrival of the main body. The Senior NCO of this party was Sergeant Patrick Butler, who had been the first in line to join the battalion and it was largely due to his energy and foresight that the camp was ready for the main body.

Brigadier-General O'Leary, commanding 124 Brigade.

Command of the Tyneside Irish Brigade was first given to Brigadier-General Collings, who had retired some six years before the outbreak of War after a career that spanned 38 years, including service in Egypt and the Sudan: he was described as robust and breezy, but in his own words his career was that of an ordinary soldier. By May 1915 however, command of the Brigade had passed to Brigadier-General O'Leary, who headed the first parade through Newcastle, and would be in command when His Majesty the King and Lord Kitchener visited Newcastle.

With the departure of the 24th Battalion to Alnwick the 27th Battalion was called up and accommodated in Dunn's Buildings, with command of this battalion being given to Lieutenant-Colonel Grattan Esmonde of the Waterford Royal Field Artillery. This commander of the 27th Battalion had also served in South Africa but like those commanding the other Tyneside Irish battalions he would be in time replaced by a younger man.

The first CO of the 27th Battalion Lieutenant-Colonel Grattan Esmonde.

Recruiting Figures

In the book *Irish Heroes in the War*, by Joseph Keating, we are led to believe that the Brigade was raised by the Irish Nationalist movement on Tyneside. Certainly there can be no doubt that the leaders and committee members did belong to that movement, but as to the actual soldiers, I have my doubts. Many of those born in England of Irish parents did identify with Ireland, and although some did have connections with political causes, some of the figures that are given in the book seem exaggerated.

Enlistments to the Tyneside Irish totalled 7325 other ranks made up as follows:

24th Bn	1737
25th Bn	1547
26th Bn	1487
27th Bn	1560
30th Bn	994

These figures are arrived at by using the highest service number traced in a battalion. Of the total number, 3760 have been traced by home address or village and nearly all those traced were casualties at some time. Many relatives confirmed that their ancestor was in fact second or third generation Irish, whilst others could not understand how or why their English ancestor was serving in the Tyneside Irish. It is interesting to note that nearly all those from a Roman Catholic background, stated that their relative had served in, 'The Tyneside Irish', whereas those from other religous denominations referred to their relatives as having served in, 'The Northumberland Fusiliers'.

Of those traced to a town or village 69.3% came from County Durham and 26.7% from Northumberland; the remaining 4% were from various parts of the U.K and Ireland.

In Northumberland the majority of those recruited were living in Newcastle, 41% of the County total. Many of these men gave their addresses as Rowton House or Tower House in Newcastle, which were lodging houses, and it is a possibility that these men were Irish. The main area for recruiting, after Newcastle, was along the north bank of the Tyne, Walker, Wallsend, Byker, then up around the Blyth and Ashington colliery districts, and a small pocket at Morpeth, which fits in with the settlement of Irish immigrants in Northumberland.

Only four *Absentee Voter Lists* survive for the County of Northumberland, Hexhamshire, Wansbeck, Berwickshire and Newcastle, but none of these was an area of great Irish immigration, except for Newcastle. Within the first three polling districts, fewer than forty Tyneside Irish soldiers registered and by 1918 not many of those living in Newcastle had survived to register for a vote whilst many of those who gave addresses in Newcastle would not be eligible to register. The lack of registers for the rest of the County, in particular the area along the north bank of the Tyne, makes it difficult to give an exact picture of recruiting in the county.

County Durham, on the other hand, was much easier to assess. The existence of the *Absentee Voter Lists*, for much of the County made it possible to trace many more men by home addresses. However, the registers for the County Boroughs of South Shields and Sunderland are missing, and these were two important areas of recruiting for the Tyneside Irish. The main area for recruits was the north and north-west of the County, with strong contingents from Durham City, Sunderland and Seaham districts. This fits in, more or less, with the spread of Irish immigration into the County. A further 1150 volunteers, mainly from County Durham, were identified through news-paper lists, although these names and addresses posed further problems as some were known to have enlisted into other regiments, some did not enlist at all, and of others there was no trace in either the *Absentee Voter Lists* or the *World War 1 Medal Rolls*. This may be owing to the fact that many men were discharged to work on munitions. For example, the 'Section Roll Book', of Corporal Peter Barratt of the 26th Battalion, has three men's names crossed out, and the words 'to munitions' added. If there were an average of three men in each section of each company discharged, then roughly 1,000 men from the Brigade could have been discharged to work on munitions.

Some men, such as Michael Hook and Peter Gaffney,[3] from Durham, are known to have been serving at Alnwick, with the 24th Battalion, although they were both 'killed in action' with the Durham Light Infantry. When the Medal Rolls were checked, to ascertain their Tyneside Irish service numbers, they were found to have entered France with a Durham Light Infantry, Territorial Force service number. This leads to the assumption that a large draft of younger men, were transferred from the Tyneside Irish to the Durham Light Infantry some time in 1915. Also at least five men have been traced in the 1914/15 Star rolls with Tyneside Irish numbers, having entered a theatre of war before the Brigade went overseas in 1916.

Lew Shaughnessy, for example, was at Alnwick with the 24th Battalion, and, although his narrative states he served with the 27th Battalion on the Somme, he has not been traced on the Medal Rolls nor is he in the Absentee Voter List.

Many questions that have arisen from this research will remain unanswered until the release of the surviving soldiers' personal documents to the Public Record Office. Even then the answers will depend on what has actually survived.

Notes

1. With the release of some soldiers documents to the Public Record Office a search was made for members of the Tyneside Irish Brigade. Of those records found, 25% of those volunteering were found to have previous service in the Regular Army or the Volunteer Force, mainly in the Durham Light Infantry.
2. Locally raised battalions were officially numbered in Army Council Instruction 28, dated 3rd of December 1914.
3. Peter Gaffney is recorded on St Godric's and Durham Town Hall War Memorials' as NF.

Chapter Three

Training in England

Now Mary Mahoney she's acting funny
She don't go to Mass on Sunday
she's saving her brass to buy a jackass
to take her to Mass on St Patrick's Day
TRAD

The 24th Battalion had only been in Alnwick for five days when, on 17th March 1915, it held the St Patrick's Day Parade and Holy Mass was celebrated at St Mary's Roman Catholic Church in Bailiffgate, the Reverend Verity Young being the celebrant. At 11 o'clock the Battalion paraded and Miss Johnstone Wallace, the daughter of the Honorary Colonel, presented each man on parade with a sprig of shamrock, the gift of Miss Moira Cavanagh of Castle Creogh in County Cork. The Battalion was due to have sports in the afternoon, but owing to the inclement weather this event was postponed.

The other battalions also had St Patrick's Day parades and the 25th Battalion's parade was held on Blackfell, where Mrs Parsons the wife of the Honorary Colonel, Sir Charles Parsons, did the honours. Sir Charles inspected the parade, took the salute, and afterwards addressed the men.

The 26th Battalion marched into Newcastle, to Eldon Square where,with the band playing a selection of Irish Airs, the Lady Mayoress handed out shamrock to the soldiers. In driving rain she walked the full length of the parade, giving each soldier a sprig of, 'the dear little plant', followed by her sister, who presented each man with a packet of cigarettes. Major O'Grady, commanding the parade in the absence of Colonel Hussey Walsh, thanked the ladies. Three cheers were given for the King, followed by the National Anthem, and then three cheers for the ladies.

After the parade, the officers of the 26th Battalion had a Mess party. Writing to Bob Falkous from the front, a year later, it was recalled by Jack Fleming,

'Last St Patrick's Day, Yes Bob, It was great; I got blind o! that night I gave 5/- to each sentry at Sunbeam, in a glowing mood to keep up the festive time.'

The Depot Company of the 24th Battalion, marched to the home of Colonel Johnstone Wallace, where the men received their shamrock from the hands of Mrs Wallace.

The one company of the 27th Battalion, that had been called up was quartered in Raby St, Schools, and here the Lady who did the honours wished to remain anonymous.

The 24th Battalion sports was held a few days later, and was very popular with the men, with over

Colonel Hussey Walsh delivers a 'punch' to Lieutenant Henry Doyle's chin – high jinks on St Patrick's day, 1915.

The First Tyneside Irish march from Alnwick railway station through the town to the camp

200 entering for the quarter mile race. The whole of the Battalion turned out as spectators, and several ladies, wives and friends of the officers also attended, as did a large number of Alnwick townspeople. The weather was fine, but was described as chilly, and bracing when the preliminary heats were held in the morning. In the afternoon the semi-finals, and finals were decided. An area of great amusement was the boxing match, between two manikin figures, operated by Private Perry, of D Company, from Blaydon. The Battalion Officers were the Judges and Marshalls for the day's proceedings. The Battalion Pipes and Drums and a Fife band played throughout, rendering the popular airs of the day.

At the end of the final races, prizes were presented to the winners by Major Prior. One thing evident from the list of finalists is that there were a number of men present in Alnwick with the 24th Battalion who were subsequently transferred to the other three battalions.

Results were as follows:

Quarter Mile Foot Race
1 Private Blackburn. C Company,
2 Sergeant Kelly. B Company,
3 Private Boyle. C Company,
4 Private M Lowrie. A Company,
5 Private Hethrington. D Company,
6 Private Cooper. D Company.

Tug of War
D Company Pulled twice over C Company.
A Company pulled twice over B Company.
Final D Company pulled twice over A Company and won the competion.

Mounted Mop Fight
1 Privates Mcquire and McNamara. C Company,
2 Privates Redden and Burke. D Company.

Three-Legged Race
1 Privates Burdon and McDonald,
2 Privates Anderson and Cunningham,
3 Privates Mee and McArdle.

High Jump
1 Private J Kelly,

2 Private Blackburn,
3 Private Chisholm all D Company.

Hop, Step and Leap
1 Private Mullarkey, B Company,
2 Private Byrne, C Company,
3 Private Boyle, C Company
4 Private Thirkeld.

100 Yards Sack Race
1 Corporal Lowe, D Company,
2 Private Lockey, Pipes and Drums
3 Private Mullarkey, B Company,
4 Private Hughes, A Company.

All these events took place with the contestants wearing the issue Ammunition boots. An objection was raised if anyone tried to compete in pumps.

The brief stay at Alnwick

The YMCA tent was doing a brisk trade at this time – it had been blown down in the snowstorm early in the month, and had been repaired by the 16th Battalion (Newcastle Commercials) along with the Tyneside Scottish Electrical Staff who assisted in the restoration of the electric light, so that once the tent was operating properly, the staff was handing out over 2,000 sheets of writing paper and envelopes daily. Many officers and men of the Tyneside Irish attended a concert in the tent, given by the Commercials and Mr Llewellyn Stimpson, the manager of the tent, extended a warm welcome to these latest arrivals to Alnwick Camp. Three cheers were given for the Irish Battalion, and the whole audience sang an Irish song in its honour.

A Temperance Roll of Honour was introduced in the YMCA tent, but it is not known how many of the Tyneside Irish signed up as teetotallers. Given the number of men who went AWOL owing to drink, it would not have been a very significant number!

Events at the camp were reported every week in *The Alnwick and County Gazette*, in which on the back page a feature headed 'HUT TOWN NEWS' reported the various activities at the camp.

On the 27th of March all troops in Alnwick paraded in the pasture, near Alnwick Castle, to be inspected by Major-General Lawson, General Officer Commanding Northern Command. Up to 6,000 men were on parade and included the Depot 7th Battalion, 16th (Newcastle Commercials), 20th, 21st (1st & 2nd Tyneside Scottish), 24th (1st Tyneside Irish), and the 2nd Northern Cyclists. The General inspected the battalions in turn and then took the salute, as the men marched past in column of route, each battalion being headed by its band.

Another parade, this time for the Duke of Northumberland, was recalled by Lew Shaughnessy,

> *'One day we paraded for the Duke, no sign of him, we waited longer, down came the rain in buckets. Still no sign. Well we were cursing and swearing, "Come out you old sod!", "Get a move on you old bugger." There we were drenched to the skin, then up he comes, smiling and nodding. If he had heard the names we had been calling him under our breath, he wouldn't have been smiling like that.'*

An order was issued at this time by Garrison Headquarters that all troops should be back in their respective camps by 10-30 pm in an attempt to prevent trouble in the town. It was also reported, that the Tyneside Irish had to enter and leave town by way of the Canongate, and not by the Lion Bridge. This was emphatically denied in the Alnwick and County Gazette but Lew Shaughnessy had this to say,

> *'There was an incident — with some woman — and everyone was barred from going into town as a result. Everyone knew it was the Commercials to blame, but all of us were banned.'*

In fact the Lion Bridge route to town had been put out of bounds to the 20th Battalion as early as January 1915.[1]

Captain Arnold also recalled the ladies of Alnwick,

'How the towns and villages sprang to life in those days, when a battalion decended on them. If the male inhabitants did not respond to the invasion the females certainly enjoyed the time of their lives, and welcomed the troops with open arms.'

The officers' mess was established in the White Swan Hotel which even today retains the atmosphere of an old fashioned English Inn, but the other ranks were in the huts outside the town.

The huts in the Tyneside Irish camp were given names by the occupants and most prominent amongst these was the hut of Sergeant Patrick Butler, who named his hut 'TARA'S HALL', whilst others were named, 'The Handy Hut', 'Shamrock', 'Hibernia' and 'Blaydon Bricks.' Killarney Cottage' The home of RSM O'Toole definitely gave away the occupants home town, whereas others were named after the officer in charge as in 'Wilkinson's Hut' and 'Wedderburn Villa'.

Father George McBrearty. 'Brigadiers, Colonels and Majors may come and go but Father McBrearty went on for ever.'

An announcement, to the effect that the Reverend G McBrearty had been appointed Roman Catholic Chaplain to the Tyneside Irish Brigade was made. This was excellent news for the Brigade and Father George McBrearty came to be regarded as one of the bravest and best loved men to serve in the Tyneside Irish Brigade. Perhaps the best accolade for Father McBrearty comes from a very unexpected source.

'Of Roman Catholic Padres or at least one , I saw a good deal, as we had the same man both at home and at the front right through. Of our own Reverend Father McBrearty, no praise could be too high. He came from a large parish in Newcastle where he already knew many of the men in civil life. As he used to say to me, "I know a lot more about some men in the battalion than you or any other officer is ever likely to find out or even imagine. In due time he became one of the pillars of the Brigade, brigadiers, colonels and majors might come and go, but Father McBrearty was there forever. He has ever seemed to me to be the perfect picture of all that a parish priest and an army chaplain should be.'

This was written by an Elder of the Presbyterian Church, and an Ulster Orangeman, Captain Jack Arnold, whose father was a minister in Dunmurry Belfast.

Sport was frequently played at Alnwick, with inter-unit matches a weekly highlight and Soccer was organised by a committee, in which Private Dan Dunglinson of the 16th Battalion and late of Newcastle United, was a prominent member. Perhaps the best match played by the 24th Battalion was against the 20th Battalion the First Tyneside Scottish, the reporter describing it thus;

'On Saturday a small crowd saw one of the best games of the season.This game was between the First Scottish and the First Irish, The reason there was so few spectators was that the Irish did not turn up until nearly four o'clock having had to wait in camp for their week's pay. The Irish began in great force and against the hill had quite the best of the opening stages. Their centre forward[2]

Officers of the 24th Battalion doing PT at Alnwick. Such was the rigour of the exercises for officers that one didn't even bother to remove his cap or tunic!

(who plays for Wallsend Park Villa) twice beating the custodian of the Scottish goal before the Scottish players could get going. The left wing of the Scottish was very prominent and they worked together almost like a machine, so well did they understand each other. They were ably backed up by the half backs and the full backs, especially the left back who being over six feet was able to use his head to good advantage. They succeeded in reducing the Irish lead with a penalty kick and before the interval managed to score the equalizer; each side having two goals to their credit at half-time. Following the restart a stern fight for the lead began, this was at last obtained by the Scottish who not long after put in a fourth, But this was disallowed by Lt Grieg the referee, who gave the winger off-side. The Irish were not going to take this lying down and a smart attack resulted in the Scottish goalkeeper being given a hot handful. He was pressed a bit at the time and turned round in the goal-mouth with the ball in his hands thereupon the Irish claimed a goal, claiming the ball had crossed the line but the referee decided against them. Thus the game ended with a narrow win for the Scottish. Amongst the Irish the centre forward was perhaps the most prominent and the way he led and fed his wings was worth seeing, The left back too was on form and it was very much due to his ability that another goal or two was not conceded.'

Officers were recruited from various sources, Robert Falkous served as a private with the Newcastle Commercials, prior to gaining a commission in the 3rd Tyneside Irish.

The next game for the Irish was to be against 21st Battalion the Second Scottish who expected, and got, a severe beating at the feet of the First Irish.

Rugby was also played at Alnwick, mainly against the 16th Battalion. *The Growler*, the magazine of the 16th Battalion, described one of these matches as a fine display of 'Falling Plates' on account of the amount of tries scored. The 16th Battalion History records;

2nd. & 3rd. TYNESIDE IRISH BATTALIONS.
NORTHUMBERLAND FUSILIERS.

Headquarters,
10 Osborne Villas,
Osborne Avenue,
Newcastle-on-Tyne.

R. Falkous Esq.
Newcastle Battn. N.F.
Alnwick.

28th. December 1914.

Will you be so good as to come here on Wednesday Morning between the hours of 10 a.m. and 12 noon, to be seen by the Brigadier General Commanding the Tyneside Irish Brigade, pending your being "temporarily" appointed, to the 2nd. & 3rd. Battalions.

H M Hatchell Col. Commdg. 2nd. Tyneside Bn.
Northumberland Fusiliers.

Wm. Kenny Walsh. Lieut. Col. Comm'dg 3rd Tyneside Bn.
Northumberland Fusiliers.

CO

F J Johnston
Major.

The guardroom of the Newcastle Commercials. A similiar scene greeted 'Alnwickite' at A Camp where a 'stalwart son of Erin's Isle' was on guard duty.

'The Tyneside Irish were perhaps our greatest rivals, and although, Lieutenants R.J Lunn, T.G Farina and Arthur Thompson and others had transferred as officers to the Irish Battalion, nevertheless in the several matches played between the battalions the 16th always managed to come home victorious.'

Another member of the 16th, Private Robert Falkous, was summoned to 10 Osborne Villas', on the 28th of December for an interview with Brigadier Colling and was also 'temporarily' appointed to the 26th Battalion. The Tyneside Irish Battalions enrolled officers from many sources, Captain George Swinburn and Lieutenant Thomas Scanlan had originally enlisted in the North East Railway Battalion, Second Lieutenant Thomas Connolly came from the First Birmingham City Battalion, Captain Jack Arnold was an acquaintance of Colonel Byrne and others were senior NCO's from local Territorial units, but only four, whose fathers were on the raising committee could be said to be from a Tyneside Irish background.

During its time at Alnwick the 24th Battalion featured in a moving picture show initiated by a cinema photographer who had taken some footage of the Battalion in Newcastle and further film was shot at Alnwick camp which was shown in the Corn Exchange in Alnwick every night during the second week of April 1915, along with *Little Lord Fauntleroy.*

One day a reporter, who used the name ALNWICKITE had the privilege of being allowed to visit the Irish camp, and gave these impressions of his visit.

'The winter snows had all gone, and sunlight was now flooding the fields. Down the Peth and over the Lion Bridge, and past St Leonard Hospital with a stiffish climb before one reaches the camp. Turning off to the left from the main road a stalwart sentry challenged me, whose brogue proclaimed him to be a son of Erin's Isle, although "St Patrick's Day" was past and gone he was still "wearing the green". When convinced I was not a German spy he allowed me to proceed. I left the guard room on the right, then passing the lower huts reached the dining rooms. Two large rooms 100 feet long and each accommodating 500 men, separated by the cookhouse. It was nearly dinner time and all was hustle and bustle in the kitchen, a long row of ranges with boilers at each end runs down

the centre, and around these the cooks worked like Trojans. As I went out into the fresh air a sigh of relief left me, certainly the heating engineers have done their work well. Facing the dining room stands the dynamo house, small but important for in this shed we have the "Pelaphone" Dynamo which generates electricity for lighting the whole camp. Passing from here I next visited the general stores, which is nothing more than a well—ordered grocers shop. Meat and bread stores are also in the camp so the soldiers lack for nothing. The large avenue between the rows is named "Northumberland Street" and up this street I next directed my steps.

Each hut is appropriately named such as the "Shamrock", "The abode of Love" etc and I noticed here and there a little garden work. A peep in these huts gives the impression of order and discipline. At length I reached the topmost hut over which floats the green flag of old Erin. This I was informed was the hut of Sergeant Butler. The name of this hut is "TARA'S HALL".

Further away to the north I noticed the officers' quarters well on the way to completion. The view from here is grand, in front the castle and behind it the town. In the hollow, soldiers were drilling, their bayonets glinting in the sun. Signallers were posted here and there on the hillocks waving their flags to each other, while further away a company was doing "Swedish drill". Away in the distance stand the Cheviot Hills, here and there covered in patches of snow. Floating up from the valley came the sound of music and I recognised the strains of 'Tipperary' being played on the bagpipes. The bagpipes covered in green with green flags made a pretty picture. After passing the bath house and again the ominous guardroom, I again reached the main road and bid goodbye to the Irish camp'.

RSM O'Toole and his company sergeant-majors. Standing (left to right): CQMS Fletcher, Sergeant Instructor Regan, CSM J McNeill, CSM R J Erett.
Seated: (left) CSM J McKeon, (right) RSM P O'Toole.

Shortly after the arrival of the Irish at Alnwick, the camps were given an identifying letter. Thus, 'A camp' was occupied by the Irish, 'B camp' by the 16th (Newcastle Commercials), 'C camp' by the 20th Battalion, and 'D camp' by the 21st Battalion.

Men were now required for work in munitions and shipbuilding, so those who were skilled were temporarily discharged, to go back to work in these important industries which left some gaps in the ranks, and further recruiting had to be undertaken.

One incident that occurred at Alnwick was on 'Zeppelin' night when the order for 'lights out' was given long before the usual hour in the camps. The result was that soldiers who were up in town had some difficulty in finding their way back since the night was exceedingly dark and there were many collisions as they returned. Some found themselves in the wrong camp, some found it too dark to take their clothes off and were to be found in bed fully clothed and, in at least one case, a soldier was found to be in the wrong bed.

There was not much done in the way of training at Alnwick that had not been done at Newcastle, but at least the whole battalion could now go out and manoeuvre over wide stretches of open country, so that the route marches were extended and the marching power of the troops was tested as never before. It was still early in the year and for part of the time there was a good covering of snow that had fallen heavily in north Northumberland that year.

There was a bad feeling in the 24th Battalion at Easter time when it was realised that there would not

be a general leave granted and many men tried all sorts of dodges to secure a pass. Some of the soldiers' wives very suddenly reached 'death's door' whilst others were unexpectedly in the later stages of confinement as Captain Arnold recalled:

> *'I was just going on parade with the Company on the morning of Easter Saturday when an NCO brought to me a private who presented me with one of those missives and with tears streaming down his face besought me to let him go. I told him to see me again after parade. I told the Sergeant Major to send a telegram of enquiry to the Police Constable where Mrs X, the dying woman, lived. Could he verify whether Mrs X was seriously ill, and if not, what was her condition? After parade Private X was waiting for me, if possible more doleful of countenance than before. I went into my office to see whether an answer had arrived. It read, "Mrs X doing very well and was out doing the shopping when I called". I called Private X in and said to him, " You will be delighted to hear your wife has made a miraculous recovery — it will not be necessary to attend her death bed." I shall never forget the look that came over the face of Private X.*

Notes (1 & 3) Taken from the Battalion Part 1 Orders of the 20th Battalion, preserved in the Imperial War Museum.
(2) Private Peter Mackin who also played for Blyth Spartan's and Willington Athletic, he would be killed in action 9 April 1917.

The Brigade together at Woolsington

Training continued up to battalion level until at last it was felt it was time to bring the Brigade together and the decision was taken to assemble all four battalions at Haltwhistle. However, this provoked an outcry and a new location had to be found so a camping ground was found at Woolsington Hall some three miles outside of Newcastle (the site of Newcastle Airport today) and at the begining of May 1915 the battalions of the Tyneside Irish Brigade began to assemble there.The Brigade was now renumbered 103 Brigade of the 34th Division and command of the Division was given to Major-General E.C. Ingouville-Williams C.B. D.S.O. who had been mentioned in despatches twice already as the Commander

The Camp in the meadow at Woolsington.

of 16 Infantry Brigade with the BEF. The General became known to the men as 'Inky Bill' and was well liked by them, as Captain Arnold recalled,

> *'Inky Bill was a holy terror if ever there was one, but he never spared himself, and the men respected him for it.'*

The other Brigades of the 34th Division were 101 and 102. 102 Brigade was made up of the four Tyneside Scottish Battalions, originally 122 Brigade, but 101 Brigade was a new formation which comprised the following battalions: 15/Royal Scots (1st Edinburgh), 16/Royal Scots (2nd Edinburgh) , 10/Lincolnshire Regiment (Grimsby Chums) and 1/Suffolk Regiment (Cambridge-shire). 101 Brigade was assembled near Ripon close to Divisional Headquarters, and 102 Brigade remained at Alnwick, the other Tyneside Scottish battalions going into the camps vacated by the 16th and 24th Battalions.

Lieutenant Horsburgh, Transport Officer of the 26th Battalion.

At Woolsington the men were housed in tents, in a large pasture close to a lake and on arrival at the camp they were issued with two blankets each, but conditions were so bad, that many who lived close enough went home. When they returned next day, many had had their blankets 'stolen', and others had mysteriously lost them, but many a miner's family was to be glad of those blankets the following winter! A trench system was dug at Ponteland and the men practised trench fighting, living in the trenches, reliefs and all the other things associated with trench warfare. The officers however were lucky enough to have their meals brought out to them in picnic baskets by the mess waiters, who also brought along a bottle of that famous Irish drink, Guinness, for each officer.

On the 20th of May, the Tyneside Irish Brigade, along with many other troops, paraded on the Town Moor in Newcastle to be inspected by His Majesty the King, who was accompanied by Lord Kitchener.

The parade was commanded by Major-General B Burton, GOC Troops in Newcastle area and on parade were the following units: 1/East Riding Yeomanry Scottish Horse Brigade 1, 2 and 3/Scottish

'Waiter, a Guiness please!' Officers of the 26th Battalion behind the trenches at Ponteland. Left to right: Jack Fleming, Archie McCaw; Hugh McConway, Vernon, Falkous, Waiter, Ossy, Dix, A O Foster, Stewart, Billy Murray. In front: Major Chichester, Lying down: Dick Connor.

Horse All of the 2nd Line Northumbrian Division, Artillery, Engineers, Infantry less 2/5 and 2/7 Northumberland Fusiliers, Army Service Corps and Royal Army Medical Corps.

Representing the 'New Army' were Brigadier—General Hunter's Brigade comprising, 16, 18 and 19/Northumberland Fusiliers and 18/Durham Light Infantry, 102 Brigade, the four Tyneside Scottish Battalions and 103 Brigade, the four Tyneside Irish Battalions. The battalions fired their musketry course whilst stationed at Woolsington and each Company in turn went to the ranges on the coast at Whitley Bay. Captain Arnold recalled,

> *'We did our musketry course at Whitley Bay where we spent a delightful week of summer weather and some of us at least managed to hit the target'.*

One frequent occurrence at Woolsington was road traffic accidents, several members of the Brigade were struck by motor vehicles late at night, usually on their way back to camp after having a drink. One man, 24/594 Private William Hunter, was struck in the Ponteland Road on the night of 8 August 1915, and he died shortly afterwards. When his funeral was held in Wheatley Hill, over 100 local soldiers, who were home on leave, attended. The Colliery Brass Band played the Dead March, a Bugler sounded 'Last Post', and a volley was fired over the grave.

One of the main events associated with the Brigade was a recruiting march on August Bank Holiday 1915, when starting from the camp at Woolsington at 09-30 hours, they marched by way of Ponteland Road and Cowgate to Barrack Road thence through Diana Street, Buckingham Street and Westgate Road into Elswick Road; then by way of Ryehill into Scotswood Road. Crossing the Redheugh Bridge, they paraded through the principal streets of Gateshead and reaching Newcastle again by way of the High Level Bridge, the parade followed the main streets of Newcastle, Moseley Street, Grey Street, Market Street and

Colonel Hussey-Walsh with Captains Price, Fagan and Vernon.

Pilgrim Street to the Boer War Memorial, where Major—General Burton CB of Northern Command, accompanied by the Lord Mayor and members of the Tyneside Irish Committee, took the salute. After the salute the Brigade formed up along the North Road and marched back to the camp at Woolsington going via Old Race Course Road, Coxlodge, Kenton Bank Foot and Ponteland Road, arriving back at camp at 4-15 p.m.

Recruiting had continued into the summer of 1915 to replace men discharged for various reasons and one group was recruited from among the coloured dock workers who lived along the banks of the Tyne. Descended from merchant seamen and local girls, these soldiers became known to the Tyneside Irish as 'Smoked Geordies' and racial prejudice did have an effect, as Lew Shaughnessy recalled,

'We had this lad who was a darky from South Shields and we gave him an awful time mucking up his kit before inspection and stupid things like that. There were a few darkies in the Fourth Tyneside Irish as I recall. They weren't much good at soldiering but I expect most of it was because they were darkies'.

Officers of B Company, 26th Battalion at Woolsington.

But then again there was even more prejudice against the middle-class men of the Newcastle Commercials, the 16th Northumberland Fusiliers. Lew Shaughnessy recalled 'The Commercials' like this,

'We were not impressed with the Newcastle Commercials either. They came from rich people. We looked through a window in one of their huts and I'm not kidding either – there was this feather mattress on the bed! They were superior to us of course and could get away with that sort of thing'.

Prize winners at the Brigade sports day, Woolsington 1915. Marked X is Sergeant Patrick Butler who became the bombing Sergeant of D Company.

If they had no respect for the 'darkies' or men of the 16th Battalion, they had for their NCO's, some of whom had a previous reputation. Lew Shaughnessy again,

> *'Most of the sergeants were pit deputies. They were hard lads some of them. I remember How McLaughlin, he had been a well—known bare—knuckle fighter in Seaham. Behind his back we used to call him "Punchy" McLaughlin because he was punch drunk and should never have been made a sergeant. He was a brave man though and never threw his weight around like a bully. In fact he hated bullies and I heard he brayed this bloke, who picked on a lad in his platoon. It was never reported. The lad he thumped knew better, because if he had reported it, we would have all howked him in turn. "How" was a drunk and a little bit crackers but he looked after his lads – even the darky.'*

Lieutenant John H Hedley 26th Battalion transferred to 34th Divisional Cyclist Company.

Another NCO recalled by Lew, was Corporal Jud Wallace. Lew had had trouble with a new pair of boots, rubbing his feet raw. Corporal Jud Wallace an old regular with service on the North West Frontier gave him this advice,

Men of A Company 2nd Tyneside Irish on Salisbury Plain. Standing second from the right is 25/53 Private John Aspinall, from Lintz Colliery. He would survive the war.

'Son, an officer and a gentleman pours whisky in his boots to soften the leather, but, we sons of toil don't have any whisky, so we piss in our boots instead'.

Lew was delighted and said, 'It worked. No more blisters!'

Salisbury Plain

On 27 August 1915, the Tyneside Irish Brigade was taken over by the War Office and ceased to be the responsibility of the Tyneside Irish Committee. At a committee meeting in Newcastle the accounts were presented and a report issued by the joint secretaries and this stated that the Tyneside Irish Brigade was in the last stages of training and would soon take the field. The report also reviewed the experiences during the raising of the Third and Fourth Battalions and expressed thanks to those concerned. The financial statement was read and showed there had been an outlay of £106,844; The money had been expended as follows,

Clothing and equipment	£61,338
Billeting and feeding	£34,878
Recruiting expenses	£ 4,161

A question was asked about the balance of monies, but an answer could not be given as there were still some bills due in for payment.About £103,000 would be payable by the War Office. The question of

Officers of the 26th Battalion entraining at Callerton Station August 1915. Left to right: Lieutenants Andy O'Connor, Billy Russell, Dick Johnson, Foster Stephenson, Percy Cole and Pat Murphy.

Four men of C Company 27th Battalion, standing second from the left is 27/1171 Private Thomas Penman who was KiA in 1917 when serving with 103/Machine Gun Company.

further recruiting was considered, but it was decided to wait until Lord Derby's recruiting scheme had been considered. At the end of August 1915, the 34th Division received orders to assemble on Salisbury Plain and initially the Division was posted to the eastern end of the plain, to Windmill Hill Camp, a tented camp, just north of Tidworth.

The Tyneside Irish Brigade entrained at local railway stations near Woolsington in the last days of August 1915, the 25th Battalion at Ponteland on Saturday the 28th of August,[1] the 26th Battalion from Callerton, where Captain Bob Falkous managed to find time to take a photograph of some of his brother officers on the platform. The 27th Battalion did not leave until 9.40 p.m. on Sunday the 29th of August[2]

Men of the 25th Battalion march through Ludgershall village in Wiltshire on their way to Windmill Hill.

Officers are briefed for manoeuvres, third from the right is a Brigade staff officer. In the background men can be seen resting.

from Ponteland Station. Travelling south, the battalions of the Brigade eventually arrived at Andover in Hampshire where they detrained, stiff and hungry after a journey that took nearly 24 hours and they then marched via the village of Ludgershall to the camp at Windmill Hill. The journey south was recorded by Captain Arnold in these words:

'Somewhere about 5 a.m. on a wet morning near the end of August the whole Brigade entrained and rumbled along south through the long length of a summer day. The dull grey fields and dykes of Northumberland and Durham gave way to the softer tints and flat reaches of the midlands. About

After the attack officers are debriefed.

noon we swung over towards the west and the type of country changed again. We skirted the Quantocks and the Mendips. Instead of the stark mining villages each with its slag heap and cage tower surmounted by two big pit wheels, we came to the old villages of Gloucestershire, some of mellow stone, some with thatched roofs and whitewashed walls — we were in a different world. The men gaped out of the windows in silence, home was left far behind and the war was drawing nearer at last.'

Seated Private George Patterson and friend in Ludgershall.

As the men marched through the village of Ludgershall the local photographer took several pictures as they passed by, and over the next few weeks visited the camp taking more snapshots for the men to send home. Many men when time allowed, visited the village and had more formal posed portraits taken, and the tent in the Ludgershall garden is one of the commonest photographs of men of the Tyneside Irish Brigade. Very little is known about the actual camps occupied by the Tyneside Irish, although a postcard from one man of the 26th Battalion gives his address as Number 6 Camp. The routine at Windmill Hill was very similar to that at Woolsington, musketry, bombing and route marching being the main activities.

Once again Captain Arnold's memoirs give a description of that part of the training of 103 Brigade,

'There were parades from morning till night and sometimes on top of this we had night operations. Cold Kitchen Hill of baleful recollection was a name all the men remembered, and sometimes when they had been through a bad patch at the front they would say it was nearly as bad as a night march over that accursed hill.'

Men of the 25th Battalion in a garden in the village of Ludgershall.

A group of C Company, 25th Battalion at Windmill Hill, standing at the rear in the shirt is 25/1291 Private William Savage of Gilesgate Moor, Durham City.

He recalled one night when the whole brigade was taken out. Each battalion deployed in line, and then with a suitable interval between battalions the whole brigade had to advance for some miles over broken and hilly ground in the inky darkness of an autumn night.

> *'On we went through rough and smooth, the level ground and even the minor hillocks were not so bad, but when it came to plunging down into some defile of which there were many, the bunching and slippping were appalling the curses that rose to heaven from thousands of throats must have been enough to reach the ears of the God of battles. But still we went on, men fell and rolled over into swamps and puddles, caps and accoutrements were lost, straps broke and belts burst. But we pressed on and stormed up Cold Kitchen Hill.'*

The camp at Sutton Veny was, 'a model of their kind'.

Corporal Richard Madden and two other Tyneside Irishmen on leave in October 1915 in the Catholic Institute in Washington.

The Division was only at Windmill Hill for a month. At the end of September the weather broke, and the tents were constantly flooded, so the whole of the 34th Division was moved lock, stock and barrel to the western edge of Salisbury Plain. All along the main road from Salisbury to Warminster, in each village, hutted army camps had sprung up and many villages had five or six camps near them, bringing with them all the problems of a garrison town.

The Division was disposed in the Sutton Veny and Longbridge Deverill area as follows:

101 Brigade Headquarters	No 2 Camp Green Hill Sutton Veny
15/ Royal Scots	No 4 “ “ “ “ “
16/ Royal Scots	No 2 “ “ “ “ “
10/ Lincolnshire	No 5 “ “ “ “ “
11/ Suffolk	No 3 “ “ “ “ “
102 Brigade Headquarters	Sandhill Camp Longbridge Deverill
20/ Northbld Fus 1TS	No 11 Camp Longbridge Deverill
21/ “ “ 2TS	No 12 “ “ “
22/ “ “ 3TS	No 14 “ “ “
23/ “ “ 4TS	No 15 “ “ “
103 Brigade Headquarters	No 9 Camp Sutton Veny
24/ Northb Fus 1TI	No 7 “ “ “
25/ “ “ 2TI	No 10 “ “ “
26/ “ “ 3TI	No 9 “ “ “
27/ “ “ 4TI	No 8 “ “ “
18/ Northbld Fus Pioneers	No 1 Camp Greenhill
HQ Royal Artillery	Elm Lodge
152 Brigade RFA	No 2 Camp Corton
160 “ “	No 3 “ “
175 “ “	No 4 “ “
176 “ “	No 1 “ “

Divisional Mounted Troops
E Squadron North Irish Horse No 13 Camp
34th Divisional Cyclist Coy Cyclist Camp

34th Divisional Signal Coy Royal Engineers Signals Camp
34th Divisional Assistant Provost Marshall Military Police
No 6 Camp
18/ Motor Machine Gun Battery No 6 Camp

Army Service Corps	34th Div Train	)
	229 Coy ASC	) North Camp Warminster
	230 Coy ASC	)
	231 Coy ASC	)
	232 Coy ASC	) No 6 Camp Sutton Veny

Royal Army Medical Corps

102 Field Ambulance	)
103 " "	) No 13 Camp
104 " "	) No 6 Camp
74 Sanitary Sect	)

44 Mobile Veterinary Section Army Veterinary Corps
No 6 Camp.

Unfortunately the camps for the Royal Engineers Field Companies are unknown.

Visit of the Tyneside Irish Committee

Whilst at Sutton Veny the Brigade had a visit from members of the Raising Committee. Mr P O'Rorke put pen to paper and gave these somewhat romantic impressions of his visit.

> *'The first impression one gets, on approaching in the darkness the almost endless rows of huts that afford such excellent accommodation for the troops, is that of a northern mining village in the days when wooden structures were practically the only dwellings of the northern miners; but here the resemblance ends. These temporary billets, scattered in well-ordered regularity over the wide expanse of moorland, leave nothing in wanting in the shape of comfort for the soldiers. Lighted throughout by electricity and fitted up with everything necessary for military purposes they are, even to the eye of a mere civilian, a wonderful improvement on the canvas camp'.*

After an excellent meal, the party was entertained with music and singing and that indispensable modern instrument the gramophone. However, to read the account of the singing of such songs as, 'The West's Awake', 'Clare's Dragoons' and 'The Wearing of the Green', the impression given is that the Brigade was composed entirely of Irishmen fighting for 'The Cause', instead of 70% of the rank and file coming from the colliery villages of County Durham, with many having little or no Irish connection at all. They would of course have joined in the singing.

24th Battalion Helmet Battle Patch belonging to Captain George Swinburn made of good quality red felt.

On Sunday morning Holy Mass was celebrated by Father McBrearty, with some young subalterns acting as altar boys. The Mass was attended by the visitors, and afterwards they were taken on a tour of inspection of the quarters provided for the men. Mr O'Rorke reported that the sleeping, dining and recreation huts were models of

The 27th Battalion shoulder Shamrock.

their kind and the kitchens scrupulously clean. Every part of the camp received a mention, and every part was just right for the soldiers.

A visit was also made to the soldiers of the 24th Battalion. All those not on leave were drawn up on parade and again they were perfect.

'They looked perfect specimens of virile manhood and soldierly courage — keen, steady, alert; a splendid example of military training and discipline, yet full of that dash and daring that so characterises the soldiers of the race from which they come,'

wrote Mr O'Rorke.

Throughout the inspection, the Battalion Pipes and Drums played appropriate Irish Airs and the party then moved on to view field training, including a particularly blood-curdling exhibition of bayonet practice. They then were taken to the Officers' Mess for lunch, prior to a motor car trip to Salisbury in the afternoon.

That evening a farewell tour of the Brigade's various messes was undertaken with more singing of rebel songs, prior to the return to Newcastle. In December 1915 the 34th Divisional Headquarters issued an order for the wearing of battle patches by the infantry battalions of the Division. The scheme adopted within the Division was as follows:

101 Brigade a RECTANGLE
- 15/Royal Scots RED
- 16/Royal Scots BLUE
- 10/Lincolns GREEN
- 11/Suffolks YELLOW

102 Brigade a DIAMOND
- 20/Northbld Fus 1TS RED
- 21/Northbld Fus 2TS YELLOW
- 22/Northbld Fus 2TS BLACK
- 23/Northbld Fus 4TS BLUE

103 Brigade a SHAMROCK, Brigade HQ personnel wore a GREEN SHAMROCK.
- 24/Northbld Fus 1TI RED
- 25/Northbld Fus 2TI BLUE
- 26/Northbld Fus 3TI PURPLE
- 27/Northbld Fus 4TI BLACK

The surviving Battalion Part I Orders for the 20th Battalion repeated from Divisional Orders state:

'that tunics, greatcoats and helmets will have battle patches stitched on, and that Battalion Quartermasters will lay in a suitable amount of the correct coloured cloth to enable this to be carried out'.

It is not clear, however, whether the patches were for steel helmets or for the tropical helmet. In the 24th Battalion the men were given squares of red gingham cloth with instructions to cut out shamrock shapes and sew them on to their tunics,[3] but the officers received good quality patches made of thick red felt.[4] Initially the 34th Division was earmarked for service in the East, firstly Egypt and then East Africa, and for this, tropical kit was issued then withdrawn, and then re-issued and withdrawn again. News of this was quickly relayed to the North East by postcard, for the men's mail was not censored until they went to France.

It would be fair to assume the same orders were issued to all battalions of the Division. Later on the

The rifle range at Sutton Veny.

Tyneside Irish Battalions had a silhouette of the regimental cap badge (The NF Grenade) painted in white on the side of the steel helmet.

Route-marching continued, with the routes getting longer and longer. One route took the Brigade through Warminster, to Westbury turning east, past the famous White Horse, to Lavington, then south across the plain to Codford and back to Sutton Veny. John Jopling, serving in D Company of the 25th Battalion sent a postcard home of the White Horse to his sister, saying he had passed it on three occasions.

One of the big problems throughout the battalions of both the Tyneside Brigades at this time was the number of men who were returning from leave two or three days late, thus holding up the others who were waiting to go home.

An event occurred at Sutton Veny at this time for which the Tyneside Irish were blamed. The proprietress of the local cinema hut was in the habit of charging admission to see the picture and then not showing it, saying that the projector had broken down. This happened to some men from one of the Tyneside Irish Battalions who complained and demanded a refund but the lady refused, saying that the

Sutton Veny village. To the left is 'The Palace', burnt down by some men of the Tyneside Irish.

money was already on its way to the bank. This was not acceptable to the men, who decided that no more soldiers should be treated in this way, and they set fire to the cinema. As it burned, they gathered round and sang, 'Keep the home fires burning'. The piquet from the nearby camp was called out, under the command of a young subaltern who on seeing the crowd of singing men, which far outnumbered his piquet, made enquiries to discover the cause of the trouble, and having some sympathy with the soldiers tactfully withdrew to the guardroom. As the men were embarking for France the following day no action appears to have been taken against them. This event was recalled by the daughter of CSM Erett, six year old Murial, who was living with her mother in a thatched cottage near the camp. Now living in the North East, aged eighty seven she recalled the arrival of the Sutton Veny Fire Brigade,

'an old man very out of breath, with a bucket, a short length of hose and a pump. By the time he got there the Cinema had burnt to the ground.'

In the Sutton Veny and Codford area an army of traders had set up shops of every description, and whilst the majority were honest, there were those who were taking advantage of the soldiers.

One of these appears to have been Mr Vowles, the photographer who was allowed into the camps to take photographs, and doubtless many men stood in line to have their pictures taken. Mr Vowles took payment for the photographs and then ceased to trade, which of course caused a lot of trouble and bad feeling and the Divisional Provost Marshal was involved. The Provost Marshal managed to confiscate those photographs that had been taken and developed, and it was published on Part I Orders throughout the Division, that any soldier who had been photographed, and not received his picture, was to report to the APM Office in Camp 6 to try and identify his snapshot. It is not clear what happened to the soldiers who had paid and were unable to claim their photographs. Did they receive a refund? What happened to Mr Vowles, did he return to business? But at least some of his work has survived in homes in the North East.[5]

At Christmas many towns and villages sent parcels off to their men in uniform, and Sergeant Lewis of the 25th Battalion wrote to the *Chester Le Street Chronicle* to thank the townsfolk.

'Dear Sir, Allow me through the medium of your paper to thank the people of Chester le Street for their kind and very thoughtful present, which I received a few days ago. It makes men like myself feel proud of the town in which he has lived for years, and the manner in which they have answered their countries call, not only in giving up their sons, but in sending such gifts as the one I received. I hope they continue to do their good work until this ghastly and blood thirsty war is finished.'

Sergt R J H Lewis
25th Service Battalion NF
2nd Tyneside Irish
Warminster Wilts.

On Boxing Day 1915 Private William Widdowson of Fencehouses died in hospital at Salisbury and, although he was to be taken home for burial, the battalion decided that he should be given a proper military send off, even if it was only as far as the station. Captain Jack Arnold was given the task of making the necessary arrangements:

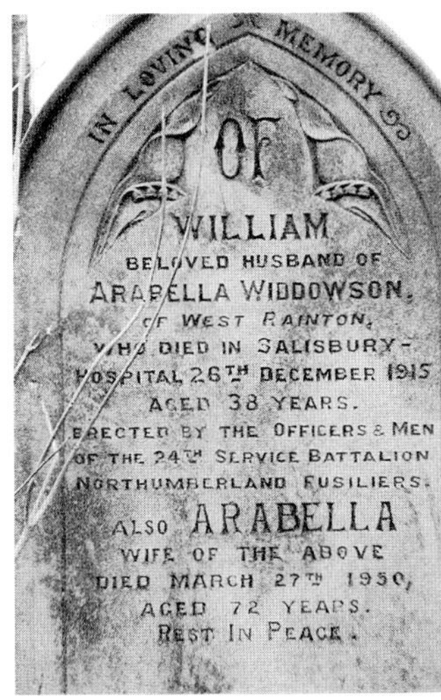

'A lad of the battalion died in hospital and I had my first experience of arranging a funeral, always an important event on home service for the very reason that on active service the prayers said are few and short. The army in those days allowed the quite substantial sum of thirty six shillings for a coffin, but we supplemented that and got something less suggestive of the workhouse ward. We trained the men in the reverse arms and the funeral step, borrowed a Union Jack to enfold the coffin, taught the pipers a lament and muffled the drums in black crepe. Father McBrearty

Tommy Calvert who rolled a training grenade across the floor of the hut.

conducted a short service in the open before we moved off; then the slow measured tread regulated by the throb of the muffled drum, to the sad melody of the lament. We marched behind the gun carriage to the station, where our comrade was to take his last journey home to Tyneside. As the van that carried the remains slowly pulled out of the station, the old Pipe Major (Jack Wilson) played a special lament which is used as the body is committed to the grave, the party presented arms, then we moved into column of route, unfixed bayonets and the band struck up a lively quick step as we marched back to camp.'

The battalion had a collection and an impressive gravestone was purchased and erected over Private Widdowson's grave in West Rainton churchyard County Durham.

One night Private Tommy Calvert arrived back at his hut in Number 8 Camp rather worse for drink. Tommy sat on the end of his bed and began to talk to the hut in general so those who were awake feigned sleep, in the hope he would eventually get into bed and go to sleep. Tommy, aware that some were awake said,

'No one wants to talk to poor Tommy, you're a miserable lot of Buggers, but I bet I can find out who is really asleep.'

He then took a training grenade from his equipment and said out loud,

'I've got a grenade with the pin out and I'm going to blow you all to hell'

He then rolled the training grenade across the wooden floor and in an instant the hut cleared, Tommy picked up his grenade, undressed and got into bed, laughing at his joke, much to the annoyance of his companions.

All surplus personnel were now transferred to the Reserve Battalion in Catterick and some who were medically unfit would be discharged, but others would eventually serve in France with the Tyneside Irish. Some others were posted to different regiments, and would reach the fighting before their comrades who remained with the Brigade. A number of officers were among those transferred, to ensure that the Brigade had a supply of officer reinforcements should casualties be heavy. From the 24th Battalion Captain Jack Arnold said,

'It was a hard wrench to leave the battalion and the company that I had been with so long.'

From the 26th Battalion Captain Bob Falkous was also sent to Catterick, his comments are not recorded but he drew a picture of a fusilier presenting arms and labelled it *NOT ONE OF THE TYNESIDE IRISH.* It was his way of expressing his disgust at being left behind.

Christmas 1915 came and passed. Many of the men had now been training for over a year, and it seemed that the Tyneside Irish would

Not one of the Tyneside Irish

24th Battalion en masse.

never be sent to France. New Year's Day 1916 arrived with still no word, then on 4 January 1916 on the Authority of Headquarters 34th Division Order Number 1329/A.12, the Tyneside Irish Brigade was mobilised for service in France.

Two days before embarkation one soldier had an accident that would keep him out of the fighting. Private Frank McNally of Blyth, serving in D Company of the 24th Battalion, had his leg broken. It happened like this, Frank was standing behind some men, who were sitting on a bench in one of the huts in Number 7 Camp. The men started to lark about and one shoved the bench backwards tipping it over, and knocking Frank to the floor, crushing his leg and breaking the tibia. Frank McNally spent the next fourteen weeks in hospital, where his right leg was found to be shorter than the left. When his leg was better he was sent to join the 30th Battalion, he was then transferred to Army Reserve Class W and was sent home to work in Seaton Delaval Colliery. In April 1918 he was recalled to the colours but on medical examination was classed unfit and returned to the pit.[6]

Those in command of the Tyneside Irish Battalions at the time of embarkation were as follows:

Corporals 26th Northumberland Fusiliers (3rd Tyneside Irish)
1. Cpl M Gates; 2. L/Cpl Calvert; 3. L/Cpl Hutchinson; 4. Cpl Riordan; 5. Cpl J Duffy; 6. Cpl H Lynch; 7. Cpl M Donnelly; 8. L/Cpl J Wynn;
9. Cpl J McCarthy; 10. Cpl I Calvert; 11. Cpl R Dodds; 12. Cpl Trotter MM; 13. Cpl Summers; 14. Cpll Ned Evans; 15. Cpl H Cresswell; 16. L/Cpl R Watson;
17. Cpl Blakey; 18. Cpl G Thompson; 19. RSM D Steele; 20. Captain and Adjutant E C Cobb DSO; 21. L/Cpl Schofield; 22. Cpl P Connelly; 23 Cpl Littlewood

Lt Col Meredith Howard
Comdg 24th Bn.

Lt Col W. E. Richardson DSO
Comdg 26th Bn

Lt Col G. R. V. Steward DSO
Comdg 27th Bn

Brigadier N. G. Cameron
Comdg 103rd Brigade

The 24th Battalion, Lieutenant-Colonel L Meredith Howard, who had seen extensive service in the Boer War with the South African Forces and had joined the 3rd Queen's Royal West Surrey Regiment; in 1914 he become Captain and Adjutant of the 15th Battalion, The West Yorkshire Regiment (1st Leeds) prior to becoming Second-in-Command of the 24th Northumberland Fusiliers.

25th Battalion, Lieutenant-Colonel K Beresford, who was born in Limerick and was commissioned into the Royal Irish Rifles in 1883, serving for twenty eight years, before retiring in 1911.

26th Battalion, Lieutenant-Colonel M.E. Richardson DSO, who joined the 20th Hussars in May 1900 and served during the Boer War. At the outset of the Great War he was serving with The Royal 1st Devon Yeomanry as Adjutant. Rejoining his regiment, he went to France in command of a squadron, serving at Mons, the Marne and the Aisne, being twice Mentioned in Despatches.

27th Battalion, Lieutenant-Colonel G.R.V Steward DSO, who enlisted into the Royal Inniskilling Fusiliers in 1899 and served during the South African War being present at the Relief of Ladysmith. In 1914 he went to France with the 2nd Battalion of his regiment, seeing action at Mons, the Marne, the Aisne and was awarded the DSO at Ypres, before being severely wounded at Festubert on 16 May 1915.

Command of 103 (Tyneside Irish) Brigade had passed to Brigadier-General N.J.G. Cameron, late Cameron Highlanders, who had served with the Nile Expedition in 1898 being Mentioned in Despatches. He served throughout the Boer War and was again Mentioned in Despatches, before going to France in August 1914 where he was wounded at the Aisne on 14 September 1914.

On the Brigade Staff were Captain William Platt DSO of the Northumberland Fusiliers and Major J.H.M. Arden DSO of the Worcestershire Regiment, with Father G.M. McBrearty and Reverend E.F. Duncan as Brigade Chaplains.

When Colonel Howard joined the 24th Battalion for the first time on a route march he heard the men singing *'The Blaydon Races'* as they marched along. He was so impressed with the song he got Captain Swinburn to sing it for him in the mess, and then had it officially recognised as the battalion marching song. Later he tried to get a copy of the words for his wife at Francis and Days in London, but needless to say they had never heard of it and the words had to be obtained from Newcastle.[7]

Notes

1. Diary of Lance Corporal Ted Colpitts 25th Battalion.
2. Diary of Sergeant Fred Hood 27th Battalion.
3. Interview with Mrs Murial Mates daughter of CSM R J Erett.

4+7. Captain George Swinburn's papers.

5. 20th Battalion Part 1 Orders Imperial War Museum.
6. WO/364 World War One Soldiers Documents PRO KEW

Chapter Four

Embarkation and the early days in France

And now the ugly bullets come peckin' through the dust,
And no one wants to face them, but every beggar must.
Kipling

The Brigade was brought up to war strength, and the equipment tables were completed by the 8th of January. All battalion advance parties were warned to be ready to go, and the first to leave was the party of the 26th Battalion on the 9th of January, taking with it all the Battalion baggage and transport. The 26th Battalion's main party was next to go, leaving Warminster Station in two trains at 7 a.m. and 7.30 a.m. on the morning of the 10th of January. This Battalion was to travel via Folkestone to Boulogne arriving at 4 p.m. and spending the night at St Martin's Camp. As they had crossed the channel the boat carrying the 26th Battalion passed a hospital ship. Michael Manley recalled,

We shouted across to them but they called back "You'll soon change your tune", and they were right.'

Next to leave was the 24th Battalion, leaving in three trains at 3.35 a.m., 5.5 a.m. and 6.20 a.m. on the 11th of January. The Battalion travelled to Southampton, arriving at 8.30 a.m. and rested on the docks until embarking on the SS *Mona's Queen* at 2.30.pm. and sailing for Le Havre at 3.30 p.m.

The departure of the 24th Battalion was recorded by Captain George Swinburn in a letter to his fiancee Phoebe,

En Route Southampton

4.50 a.m. Tuesday 11/1/16
My Dear Phoebe
I had a great day but it is over at last. The Major marched at the head of the Unit. I, mounted at the head of B Coy. We entrained at 3.35. The Major and I in a first class compartment together – perfectly happy enjoying a smoke + discussing the future.

The 27th Battalion left at 7.35 a.m., went via Folkestone and arrived in Boulogne by 6.15 p.m. Lew Shaughnessy recalled the voyage of the 27th.

'We went to France on this rotten old ship. I was fascinated by the escort – a fast destroyer, but I couldn't see much of it because it was dark.'

The Isle of Man steam packet SS *Mona's Queen* carried the 24th Battalion from Folkestone to Boulogne on 11th January 1916.

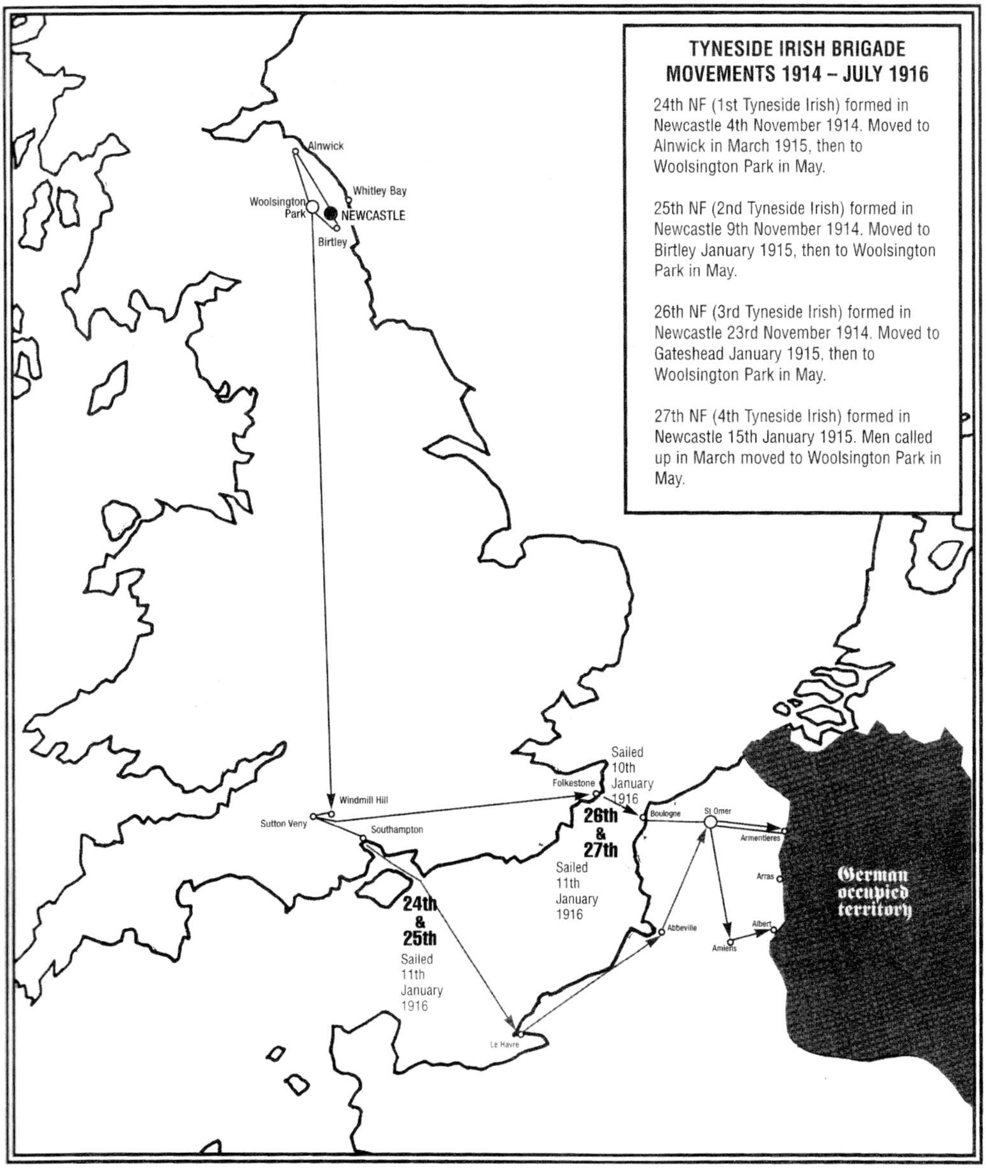
TYNESIDE IRISH BRIGADE
MOVEMENTS 1914 – JULY 1916
24th NF (1st Tyneside Irish) formed in Newcastle 4th November 1914. Moved to Alnwick in March 1915, then to Woolsington Park in May.
25th NF (2nd Tyneside Irish) formed in Newcastle 9th November 1914. Moved to Birtley January 1915, then to Woolsington Park in May.
26th NF (3rd Tyneside Irish) formed in Newcastle 23rd November 1914. Moved to Gateshead January 1915, then to Woolsington Park in May.
27th NF (4th Tyneside Irish) formed in Newcastle 15th January 1915. Men called up in March moved to Woolsington Park in May.
Alnwick
Whitley Bay
Woolsington Park
NEWCASTLE
Birtley
Windmill Hill
Sutton Veny
Southampton
Folkestone
Sailed 10th January 1916
26th & 27th
Sailed 11th January 1916
24th & 25th
Sailed 11th January 1916
Le Havre
Boulogne
St Omer
Armentieres
Arras
Abbeville
Albert
Amiens
German occupied territory

Last but not least, the 25th Battalion were routed via Southampton and starting at 8.40 a.m. they travelled in three trains at hourly intervals. Attached to the 25th were 1 Officer and 22 men of 18/Northumberland Fusiliers; the history of the 18th Battalion records that this was Lieutenant McQuillan with some of his No 5 Platoon but it was not until the 18th of January that this detachment managed to rejoin its own unit. The 25th Battalion embarked on the SS *Caesaria* and the SS *Tudno*, whilst the battalion transport sections of the 24th and 25th Battalions went on the SS *Maidan*. Ted Colpitts recorded in his diary that it was a pleasant voyage.

Left behind in Sutton Veny were the rear parties, made up of men who were being transferred to the 30th (Reserve) Battalion, and who were detailed to clean up and hand over the camp. Sadly, the Brigade had to leave three men in the village churchyard, who had died during the stay in Sutton Veny.

Upon disembarking, battalions went to rest camps near the port,and remained there overnight, but as the 25th was disembarking, a soldier of the Royal Army Medical Corps fell overboard into the dock between the ship and the quay. Lieutenant Hately, who was fully equipped, immediately lowered himself down a rope and tried to fish him out. Whilst doing so a fender was dropped from the ship knocking them both under; in spite of which the Lieutenant managed to rescue the man.

The 26th Battalion, when it disembarked, had to send three sick men to hospital in Boulogne but no other casualties were reported and all officers and other ranks were issued with iron rations and a second gas helmet prior to moving inland.

After the night at the rest camps, the battalions marched at different times to the railhead, where they entrained for St Omer. They travelling in the now famous cattle trucks bearing the sign, *40 men or 8 horses.*

Before the 24th Battalion moved off, Captain George Swinburn got a quick note off to Phoebe, *Wednesday 12/1/16*

> *'My Dear Phoebe I have arrived "Somewhere in France" + I am perfectly happy. All the letters are censored + I am unable to give you any interesting news. It was amusing to hear the remarks as we marched along + the attempts our men made to speak the language. The crossing was alright. I sent you my address so please write with fondest love.*
> *yours George.*

On arrival at St Omer the Tyneside Irish Brigade was given instructions to move to BLENDEQUES where on arrival they detrained and marched to billets in various villages, as follows:

24th to ESQUERDES, 25th A + B to HALLINES C+ D to WIZERNES, 26th to WIZERNES and the 27th to QUIESTEDE.

Training was undertaken: route marches, musketry and inspections of one form or another were the order of the day. Battalion specialists, i.e. signallers, scouts, snipers and bombers, all began intensive training, with men being sent on courses of instruction to the 23rd Divisional School.

On the 17th of January a German aeroplane flew over the 25th Battalion's billets and was fired at by the anti-aircraft artillery. Ted Colpitts recorded in his diary on the 19th that he picked up pieces of a Taube. The other battalions had no such excitement and training carried on until the 20th when the whole of the 34th Division was inspected by Sir Douglas Haig and General Joffre.

The inspection was timed for noon on a very cold and windy day with sleet showers but it was not until three o'clock that the motor vehicles carrying the inspecting officers arrived and drove slowly along the lines of the assembled troops.

The following order was received from Divisional HQ after the inspection.

> *20th January 1916*
> *After Order*
> *Administrative Staff*
> *35 Complimentary*
>
> *General Joffre Commander in Chief of the French Army, has expressed his admiration of the appearance of the 34th Division and was particularly struck by the steady behaviour of all ranks underarms.*
>
> *The Divisional Commander was himself much struck by the steadiness of the battalions and considers the parade reflects much credit on the Division.*
>
> *(Signed) G.H. Nugent.*
> *A.A. & Q.M.G.*
> *34th Division.*

The training continued over the next few days with a party of officers and men testing gas helmets, using actual chlorine gas on the 22nd of January. Another inspection of 103 Brigade took place on the

24th by Lieutenant-General W.P. Poultney KCB DSO commanding III Corps. The Brigade had now moved nearer to the front line preparatory to receiving instruction in trench warfare.

First experiences in the trenches

By the end of the first week of February the battalions were considered ready for the trenches, and were to be attached to other experienced units for instruction. The 24th was to be attached to 24 Brigade. This was a Regular formation that had been transferred to the 23rd Division from the 8th Division. The companies were allotted as follows:

A	Company	24th	attached	to	1/Sherwood Foresters.
B	"	"	"	"	2/East Lancashire Regt.
C	"	"	"	"	2/Northamptonshire Regt.
D	"	"	"	"	1/Worcestershire Regt.

C and D Companies moved off at 9.00 a.m. and marched to Rue Marle where they went into billets. A and B Companies did not move off until 4.30 p.m. and went straight in to the trenches. On the 12th A and B Companies were relieved by C and D Companies. The next day the Battalion had its first casualty when Lieutenant Short of C Company was wounded during a trench-mortar barrage. That night the two companies returned to billets.

On the 14th of the month the Battalion relieved the 2/Northamptonshire Regt, in the line, with A, B, and C Companies in the line and D Company in support in the Bois Grenier line.

The 25th Battalion was attached to 68 Brigade of the 23rd Division, with the companies attached to the various battalions of that Brigade, although the exact allocations are unknown.

During the occupation of the trenches by A and B companies on the12th of January, the enemy heavily shelled the Bois Grenier line, resulting in the death of 25/1102 Private Joseph March of Teresa Street, in

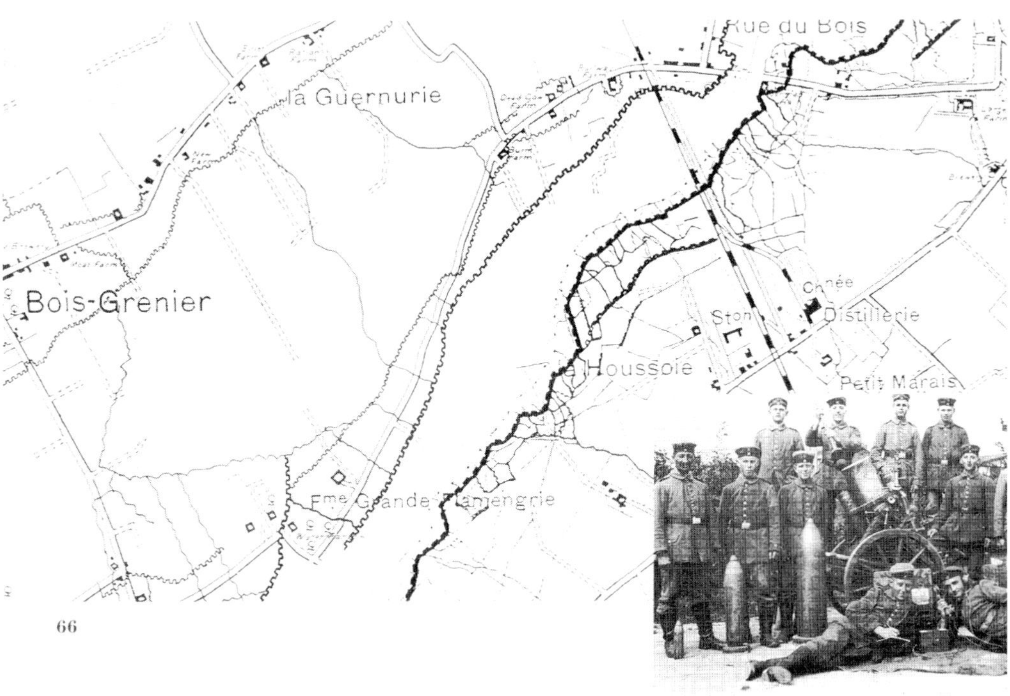

A section of trench map of the Bois Grenier sector of the line where the Tyneside Irish experienced trench warfare for the first time. Inset: A German trench mortar team.

25/637 Private William Smith.

Blaydon, County Durham, and the wounding of four other men. Private William Smith of B Company, a stretcher bearer, from Gateshead, and a member of the Battalion band, put pen to paper and wrote a poem about the incident. Ted Colpitts, being an HQ signaller, did not go in with the companies, but came under attack when German aeroplanes dropped bombs within 50 yards of Battalion HQ. The War Diary records that one of these enemy machines appeared to come down in flames. At 11.a.m. on the 14th of January, the Bombing Officer, the RSM, all CSM's and company signallers of the 25th Battalion began the relief of 1/Worcestershire Regt. At 2.00 p.m. the Company

Commanders went into the line. At 6.00. p.m. the Battalion paraded, and marched off from the billets, reaching the trenches at 7.45.p.m. By 8.40 p.m. the relief was complete, and work started on rebuilding the trenches.

The 26th Battalion received its baptism of trench warfare under the guidance of 2/Rifle Brigade, and 2/Lincolnshire Regt of the 8th Division, with A and B Companies going into the trenches on the 10th of February. Two days later, on the 12th, C and D Companies replaced the other two companies.

It was about now that the 103 Light Trench Mortar Battery was formed, with the personnel found from all four battalions of the Brigade and the War Diary of the 26th Battalion records that Second Lieutenant Brown and 12 other ranks were transferred to the new unit. The CSM came from D Company of the 27th Battalion when Sergeant Richard Madden from Washington was promoted to Company Sergeant Major to fill the vacancy. CSM Madden was to be wounded on 1 July 1916 and subsequently awarded the DCM and the MM with a Mention in Despatches. The Battery was commanded by Captain D H James from the 24th Battalion.

Sergeant Richard Madden Acting CSM 103 Light Trench Mortar Battery.

The Brigade Light Trench Mortar Battery was not very popular with some of those who served in the front line. Captain Jack Fleming described the activities of the Battery to Bob Falkous in a letter:

'My pet aversion, Trench Mortars! Why my pet aversion I'll tell you.The TM Officer here it's the softest job in the Brigade. He stays well behind the firing line and calls up with his satellites occasionally to do a strafe. Locates himself behind a bay and lets fly a dozen or so at the Hun and retires not too gracefully to his lair. Now the Hun with all his faults is some strafer and he always acknowledges receipt. We get the receipt, while the unmentionable TMO is taking his tea in perfect safety somewhere.'

On the 17th of February the 26th took over the line as a battalion for the first time, relieving the 25th Battalion. Patrols were sent out to inspect the wire and work commenced repairing the damaged trenches. One night, during this tour of duty in the trenches, a Zeppelin passed over the Battalion and landed in view behind the enemy lines.

Lieutenant Lance Shackleton described the trench routine in a letter to his fiancée Molly Swinburn at home in Newcastle:

'The parapets which have been blown down have to be repaired. Just at dawn we stand-to again and we go round while rum is issued to everyone. After stand-down the boys are cleaned up & the men get breakfast. Then comes the foot inspection. The men

remove their boots and socks and rub their feet with grease, then their rifles are cleaned and inspected. This goes on for four days and then we wait what seems like an interminable time for the relief to take place'.

Major E A Leather
27th Battalion
KiA 10th February 1916.

(Molly's brother George was serving as a Captain in the 24th Battalion.) On the evening of the 22nd the Battalion was relieved by the 25th and went into rest at Armentières and Erquinghem.

The 27th Battalion received its initial trench training under 70 Brigade, originally with 23rd Division. This Brigade had replaced 24 Brigade in the 8th Division. At 9 am on the 10th of February a party of officers and NCOs of the Battalion proceeded to the trenches for instruction, under 10/Sherwood Foresters and 8/Battalion York and Lancaster Regt.

It was on this day that the Tyneside Irish Brigade had its first fatal battle casualty, Major E.A. Leather O.C. B Company 27th Battalion. Major Leather was not strictly a Tyneside Irishman but had originally joined the 3rd Battalion Northumberland Fusiliers during the Boer War and served with that unit in Malta. On the outbreak of the Great War he had volunteered his services and had been appointed as Second-in-Command of the 10th (Service) Battalion, Northumberland Fusiliers. A bad accident, caused by his horse falling, prevented him from going overseas with the 10th Battalion but on recovery, he was posted to the 15th (Reserve) Battalion. Just before the embarkation of the Tyneside Irish the post of OC B Company of the 27th Battalion fell vacant, and he was appointed to fill the vacancy. Major Leather stood 6ft 3ins, and was the tallest of six brothers who served during both the Boer and Great wars.

In the next three days the Battalion had a fatal casualty every day—on the 11th, 27/1343 Private William Turner, of Silksworth, on the12th, 27/473 Private William McEleavey, of Witton Park, and on the13th, 27/45 Private Joseph Brennan, of Lintz Colliery. Also ten men were wounded and this was soon to become known as daily wastage. Another visit to the Brigade was made by the Raising Committee who stayed a couple of days and were shown round the trenches and the rear areas. On the 22nd of February the 27th Battalion were relieved by the 24th Battalion, now going in for its second tour and the 24th placed D Company on the left, B Company in the centre, and C Company on the right, with A

Above: Lieutenant Wilkinson's platoon, D Company 24th Battalion. Marked X is Lance Sergeant Cuthbert Miller; marked O is Private Connolly.

Company Sergeant Major and Mrs Nicholas Batty, 24th Battalion.

in support. D Company had the 24th Battalion's first soldier killed in action, when 24/1013 Private William Luke, from Thornley, was killed. At the same time the 25th Battalion was relieving the 26th in the same trenches they had held on the previous visit to the line. This then became the pattern for the next few weeks with the battalions holding the line although those supposed to be resting did anything but rest. The War Diaries are full of entries referring to training, route-marching, bomb throwing, fatigues and, of course, the never-ending carrying parties, taking stores and rations to the battalions in the line. For some there were courses of instruction in signalling, transport, bombing and machine guns at Divisional and Army schools.

It was during one of these early tours of duty in the trenches that Sergeant Cuthbert Miller, from Blaydon, of the 24th Battalion, was inspecting the sentries. In one bay he came across Paddy and Geordie in a dugout fast asleep, cuddled up together to keep warm. Lying beside Paddy was his haversack, with a big rat finishing off the contents and at the sight of the sergeant, the rat made off. Moving into the next bay Sergeant Miller was speaking to the sentry when he heard shouting in the bay he had just left. Going back, he found Paddy and Geordie squaring up to each other.

'What's going on?' he asked. 'Sure and hasn't the thievin' son of an Englishman stole me bread!' said Paddy. 'Had away, man. Ah haven't touched yer bread' replied Geordie. Sergeant Miller pointed to the parados where the rat was watching the fight, 'There's the culprit Paddy'

Afterwards the two were the best of friends again. Rat hunting soon became a necessity, as did '*chating*', i.e. hunting for lice, in the seams of the shirt.

Members of Lieutenant Burluraux's Platoon, D Company, 27th Battalion. All but three would become casualties on the opening day of the 'Big Push'. *Left to right back row*: 27/64 G W Broxup (wnd 1/7/16); 27/1175 C Pease MM; 27/1022 R Hill (wnd 1/7/16); 27/17 E Armstrong (wnd 1/7/16); R H Dunn (wnd 1/7/16 k 4/4/18); 27/72 A E Beardsmore (wnd 1/7/16). *Centre row*: 27/585 T Philips (wnd 1/7/16); Lt Burluraux (k 1/7/16); Capt Bibby (DSO 1/7/16) Coy Comd; 27/755 L/Cpl T Ward (wnd 1/7/16); 27/1314 J T Walton (wnd 1/7/16); 27/1204 A Reynolds; 27/1241 C Stephenson (k 1/7/16).

It was reported in *'The Saint George's Gazette'*, that the Adjutant of the 25th resorted to turning his shirt inside out daily, to keep the 'ferocious beasts' on the move.

On the night of the 15—16th of March a German patrol planted a German flag in front of the 27th Battalion and during the day, the battalion snipers shot at the pole, eventually bringing the flag down.

Plans were made to try and recover it during the night when the Company Commander, Captain Davey, had no shortage of volunteers to go out and capture the flag. He therefore chose the best man for the job, Lieutenant C.J. Ervine, together with two men of his platoon but after an hour or so, the party returned without the flag. The enemy were too alert and waiting, and had a patrol covering the flag on one side and a machine gun covering the other. When the three Tyneside Irishmen got to within twenty-five yards of the German flag there was such an outburst of firing that they had to return to the British lines. But in the early hours of St Patrick's Day, Lieutenant Ervine set out again, this time alone and for half-an-hour those in the British trenches waited, until Lieutenant Ervine's Platoon Sergeant went out to the wire to look for him. At quarter-to-three the Germans fired a star shell and those in the trench could see the dark shape of Lieutenant Ervine making his way slowly back to the British lines having managed to recover the prize, but on the way having fallen into a ditch full of muddy water.

While Ervine dried himself, Captain Davey and another officer erected a stout pole with the German ensign nailed to it, and above the ensign the green flag with the golden harp, which had been presented to the Company prior to leaving England. As day broke the Germans started to shoot at the pole in a vain attempt to bring it down, but there it hung throughout St Patrick's Day, attracting admiring visitors to the Tyneside Irish trenches from other parts of the line. Unfortunately, shortly after this episode, Lieutenant Ervine, who hailed from Belfast, was badly wounded and succumbed to his wounds soon afterwards. He was interred in Bailleul communal cemetery. (The German Ensign was presented to the regimental museum by Lieutenant Ervine's brother in 1959.)

The trenches in the Bois Grenier area were known as 'High Command' trenches. This was because water was found a few feet down and consequently the parapet and parados had to be built up with sandbags.

But the fire attracted by the flag, from the German snipers was to have tragic consequences for some of those on duty in the trenches that St Patrick's Day. Early that morning 27/26 Private William Brown and 27/663 Private John Scollen took over sentry duty at a post in the front line. At about 4.15 a.m. the pair were about to be relieved, when a shot from a German soldier hit William Brown in the head, the round ricocheted and then hit John Scollen in the face. As William fell to the floor of the trench, John could see he was badly wounded and needed help urgently. Forgetting his own wounds John Scollen rushed down the trench to the Battalion Aid Post and turned out the stretcher bearers; then he led them back to the front line to where William Brown now lay unconscious, but still alive. The wounded man was placed on a stretcher and evacuated as quickly as possible from the firing line, however although he reached the aid post, he died before the Battalion doctor Lieutenant Cosgrave could reach him.

Mrs Brown was told of her husbands death in a letter from his company commander Captain Davey, who told her of Private Scollen's attempt to save her husband. She also received a letter from his platoon commander, Lieutenant Ernest Blight, who wrote,

Victoria Cross winner Second-Lieutenant Michael O'Leary received an estatic welcome when he visited Newcastle and South Shields on St Patrick's Day, March 1916.

Dear Madam

It is with very great regret that I have to inform you that your husband lost his life on Friday March 17th at about 4.15. in the early morning. He was on sentry in his bay in a trench very close to the Germans, when a bullet struck him. His comrades took him to the dressing station as fast as possible, but the wound proved fatal.

I have not been in charge of this platoon for very long, but during the short time I had your husband under my charge, I was able to see that he was a good soldier and a fearless man. He did his duty thoroughly and died bravely for a worthy cause. I hope that you will be given health and strength to bring up your family and that you will bear up as well as can be expected during this great trial.

I am yours faithfully

E J Blight Lieut.

Mrs Brown had another letter from Lieutenant Ralph Pritchard; although he was now serving in D Company it was less than a fortnight since he had been Private Brown's platoon commander in B Company. Lieutenant Pritchard described William Brown as 'one of the most cheery men in the company'. He went on to say

'No matter how hard the day's work had been your husband always looked upon the bright side and if a laugh was possible Brown always gave it.'

Trying to ease Mrs Brown's loss he went on to write,

'An officer often finds inspiration amongst his men and I am sure your husband's cheerfulness and large heartedness were a source of inspiration to me and helped me very considerably more than once. You will feel his loss keenly I know but I hope that God may give you strength to bear up in this very hard time".

Yours Ralph B Pritchard Lieut.

The Irish soldiers' Flag Day

Meanwhile back in England the Raising Commmitte was still busy collecting, and supplying comforts for the men in France. In March 1916 it was proposed to hold a flag day, in order to raise funds for those serving in the Tyneside Irish, and the other Irish regiments, and for those who were prisoners of war.

The event took place in Newcastle, South Shields and Durham City. In Durham a large committee was formed, with speakers expressing the fact that many men from the city were serving in the Tyneside Irish and that local men of Irish descent were serving in other units. The flag day in Durham was held on Saturday, the 18th of March, as it was felt this would be a better day for collecting money than on the Friday, but in the other locations the flag day was held on the 17th, St Patrick's Day. The principal speaker at Newcastle and South Shields was Second-Lieutenant Micheal O'Leary VC who had won the Victoria Cross while serving as a Corporal in the Irish Guards, and who afterwards was commissioned into 5/Connaught Rangers before transferring to the Tyneside Irish for service with the 30th (Reserve) Battalion. After a civic ceremony of flag purchasing, which took place at the foot of the Cowan Monument in Westgate Road, Second-Lieutenant O'Leary nearly had his arm dislocated by handshaking and so demonstrative did his admirers become, that the police had to form a bodyguard to protect him. Prior to the ceremony the band of the Royal Artillery had played a selection of Irish melodies, at which point the Lord Mayor, Alderman Fitzgerald, addressed an emotionally stirred crowd and explained the purpose of the flag day. Moving on to South Shields, Second-Lieutenant O'Leary was greeted by the Mayor of the Borough, Councillor John Taylor, who delivered an eulogy on the world-famous deed carried out by their guest of honour. Again, scenes of excitement and interest followed the officer, and he was heartily cheered wherever he went. A considerable sum was collected in the three towns, and the proceeds put to good use for the benefit of those serving at the front and those who were held in prison camps in Germany.

In France on the 17th of March, St Patrick's Day, most of the men managed to obtain a piece of shamrock to wear and those lucky enough to have it sent out from home, shared with a friend. Ted Colpitts managed to get some from a chum, whilst the 27th Battalion received its shamrock through the kindness of Mr John Redmond MP, who sent enough for the whole Battalion.

Sniping and patrolling were activities that had to be undertaken and the snipers of the 24th Battalion claimed two Germans on the 19th of March, and those of the 25th Battalion one German cyclist on the same day.

Awards for gallant conduct in the trenches started to be made and the first Military Medal to the Brigade was awarded to 26/474 Lance Corporal Thomas McKenna, from Cornsay Colliery, of D Company of the 26th Battalion, for good patrol work between the 20th of February and the 5th of March. Lamentably Lance Corporal McKenna was killed at 4.20 a.m. on the 8th of April, the day the award was announced. The news of his death was conveyed to Captain Falkous, serving with the Reserve Battalion, by Jack Fleming, in a letter written on the 21st of April,

> *'Did you know Mckenna of D company, a fine big—hearted chap. He was one of the best men and did some excellent patrol work — so excellent that he received the Military Medal the first man in the Army to gain the distinction. The news came too late as poor McKenna got caught by a sniper's bullet while sitting in a fire bay, a most extraordinary thing. How the hell it got him I don't know, but it did.'*

The first Military Cross awarded to the Tyneside Irish Brigade, was given to the bombing officer of the 27th Battalion, Lieutenant J.W. Marshall of South Shields who at great personal risk, crossed

26/474 Lance Corporal Thomas McKenna from Cornsay Colliery was the first man of the Brigade to win the Military Medal.

Major J H Arden took over command of the 25th Battalion.

No—Mans—Land, to where 27/53 Sergeant James Burke, of West Hartlepool, was trapped, badly wounded on the German wire. Lieutenant Marshall carried the wounded NCO back to the British lines under very hot and heavy hostile firing but sad to say, this brave act was in vain, for Sergeant Burke died shortly afterwards at the Battalion aid post.

On the 3rd of April, Lieutenant-Colonel Beresford, who left the 25th Battalion to go on leave, went sick, and did not rejoin. Command of the Battalion passed to Major J.H.M. Arden DSO, of the Worcestershire Regt, who was on the Staff of HQ 103 Brigade.

Captain R R Pirrie RAMC attached 26th Battalion, wounded at Jock's Joy, Bois Grenier, 8th April 1916.

The Battalion Medical Officer of the 26th was wounded the same day that Lance Corporal Mckenna died and Jack Fleming informed Bob Falkous how it happened,

'That day Doc Pirrie called up. He was not supposed to come to the fire trenches but like the dear old chap he was he did. So I went round with him, we passed an "Unknown" near "Jock's Joy" and Doc stopped and said, "It was about here my boy was killed". We strolled along the duck-

A platoon of the 27th Battalion, April 1916. Now they are looking like old soldiers having served in the front line and experienced enemy shell fire.

A group of A Company 27th Battalion, marked X is 27/360 Private Robert Horsman of Grange Villa, by 1918 he was a Sergeant serving in the 8th Battalion where he won the DCM.

boards chatting amiably when the Hun sent a few over. I was leading and half turned to Doc and said, "These devils are starting again", when poor Doc gave a grunt and fell with a chunk of shrapnel as big as an orange near his kidney. I helped the poor fellow all I knew and went with him on the stretcher to the Field Ambulance from where he was taken away.'

Holy Mass, celebrated by Father McBrearty, was a frequent occurrence for those of the Catholic faith and where possible the local French church was used, but often a makeshift altar was set up in a barn. Ted Colpitts recorded going to Mass and many other incidents in his small diary where one of the most poignant entries was for the 6th of April,

'I helped carry Peter Docherty out — Hit in the Head — he died in the DS later. God rest his soul.'

Lance Corporal Peter Docherty of Wallsend was buried the following day in Brewery Orchard Cemetery, along with Private Robert Mundy of D Company of the same battalion.

Three Germans approached the front of the 24th Battalion in the line on the 7th of April. Two of these escaped, but the other, a young Prussian, 21 years old, of the 230th Regiment, was captured by 24/1151 Private John Connolly, of Milburngate in Durham, assisted by other Durham men of D Company. He was the first prisoner taken by the Battalion and the Brigade and word of this must have spread through the Brigade quickly for it is entered in Ted's diary, and the event was also recorded by Captain George Swinburn in his diary.

Another Durham man, 24/398 Private John Carroll serving with A Company, wrote to the 'Durham Advertiser' with news of the Durham City men at the front.

'I write to let you know that my comrades and myself are still in the land of the living, although I have been somewhat poorly. It is very wet and cold out here and we are up to our boot tops in

water. Recently we had a very narrow escape, the Hun sent over a "coalbox" and caught eight out of ten of us, but only one was killed, that was good luck on our part. We could do with a few gamekeepers out here to thin out, not rabbits, but rats. There are millions of rats, some of which we have tamed. We can not get a razor out here as the place has been ruined by shellfire. Every night at "stand to" the Huns shout over to us that the war will be finished in two months. Then the fun starts, it is rat tat tat all night long. I will close now wishing you and all the boys of the city the best of good luck'.

Also writing home that April was 24/1541 Corporal George Kean, serving in B Company. He described a period of German shelling to his mother.

'We were in a farmhouse in the reserve position, just sitting down to tea and toast. We were congratulating ourselves, for we had been told it was impossible to get toast in the line. When all of a sudden "crash" the roof caved in as the Bosche let fly. We all got out, but there was only one casualty, the toast, so we did not get toast in the line after all'.

The Tyneside Irish Brigade was to be withdrawn from the line to begin preparing for the coming summer offensive and, on the 10th of April, the Tyneside Irish began handing over the line to battalions from the 2nd Australian Division arriving in France from Gallipoli via Egypt. Home leave to England had now started and a few lucky officers and men managed to get home for a few days, Lieutenant Shackleton was thinking of marrying Molly and wrote to tell her he would ask for special permission from the CO but before he could do so he was back in the line when during a very heavy bombardment he was badly shellshocked and evacuated home to recover.

Another tragic incident described in a letter to Bob Falkous was the death of Private Jones and Jack Fleming described it thus.

'One of the corporals left one in the breach after stand-to. Another chap's equipment caught on it, and it went off, killing one, "JONES"[1]. Shack (Lieutenant Shackleton) was the Platoon Officer who examined the rifles – He got under close arrest but got off with being put at the bottom of the leave roster – I – well I was acting Company OC that's all. I got strafed and put at the bottom of the leave roster too.'

A later letter in the month described further casualties in the Battalion,

'Russell[2] got a lovely Blighty, he's gone to a hospital at BLANK, Lady Peepee's or some other big shot. The Doc tells me he was almost off his rocker with pain when he dealt with him — Hutchinson[3] the young sergeant with him died, poor young chap.'

Also in the letter was the news that Second Lieutenant Pat Murphy was to face a court martial, for 'Insolence' to a superior officer. The outcome was published in *The Saint George's Gazette* on the 30th of June, when it was reported that Second Lieutenant P J Murphy had lost one year's seniority.

It was around this time that the 34th Divisional Cyclist Company was withdrawn from the Division. Originally formed with men from all the infantry battalions of the Division it was, along with other Divisional Cyclist Companies, used to form III Corps Cyclist Battalion. This left a surplus of men who were then transferred into the 24th Battalion and somewhat unusually, these reinforcements were allocated numbers in the 24th Battalion sequence, 24/1660 being the lowest and 24/1737 the highest located. Original 24th Battalion men were re-allocated their old numbers, so we find men who enlisted for The Tyneside Scottish, The Grimsby Chums, Edinburgh City Battalions, and the Manchester Scottish, who joined the 1st Edinburgh City Battalion, in the casualty lists with Tyneside Irish numbers.

Reinforcements started to come out from the reserve battalions in England and after landing, they went up to the 31st Infantry Base Depot at Etaples, where they received further training prior to joining the battalions up the line. Writing to his mother at Low Fell on the 25th of May, Captain Bob Falkous described the IBD as follows,

'It is a jolly fine place, heaps of good cafes etc.'

and later the same day he wrote,

'In continuation, the night operations turned out to be a gathering of about 600 men and officers under a mob of yellow-backed instructors. We were treated to quite a good lecture and then set off on what sounded like a fearfully exacting stunt. I found myself allocated to a group of New Zealanders. However, the whole business was, as usual, a wash out, and we got back to camp at midnight, feeling not much improved by the experience.'

The IBD was also recalled by Captain Jack Arnold who spent some time there before going up the line.

'The camp itself, which was of enormous proportions, was pitched on base sandhills, in winter or summer the tents were occupied, and the only permanent cover were the mess rooms and stores.'

But unlike Captain Falkous, Captain Arnold spent a period of time with his draft at the 'Bull Ring', a place never to be forgotten and a place to leave as quickly as possible. His memoirs contain a lengthy passage of his experiences there.

'The most abhorred instrument of training was the "Bull Ring" or training area, in which the men were marched out in squads both on Saturdays and Sundays. At the "Bull Ring" they were put through PT, trench assaults and other strenuous exercises under the command of instructors who harried them unmercifully. If you were an officer, you were detailed to take charge of a squad or company and treated in the same way as the men, as far as the instructors dared to.'

He then goes on to describe the various activities that the troops were put through,

'I shall never forget the assault course. It consisted of jumping into trenches with fixed bayonets, climbing over walls, doubling across the open then disembowelling straw filled sandbags, clambering across marshes, bombing imaginary strongpoints and contending with any obstructions that the cruel hearted instructors could devise.'

After a harsh day at the 'Bull Ring' the men were marched back to camp in one long dejected column again mentioned by Captain Arnold.

'But all was not over yet. Usually we had to give the salute to the Camp Commandant who lay in wait at some suitable point on the route, just when everyone was hoping that the day's torture was past. Woe betide the man or officer who was not marching to attention. "Take his name sergeant,—put him down for extra drill." It was not surprising that after a week at the "Bull Ring" every man prayed to be sent up the line.'

From the Infantry Base Depot both Captain Falkous and Captain Arnold were eventually sent up the line to rejoin 103 Brigade, but neither of these officers rejoined their original battalion, Captain Bob Falkous was posted to the 27th Battalion and Captain Jack Arnold went to the 26th Battalion, his journey to the front recalled as follows.

'It was a relief to board the train, once in the train you rumbled along at about ten miles an hour with no indication of direction. I finally decanted at a place called Watten near St Omer, and was told that the division was at rest in billets in the neighborhood. I spent a long day trying to track down the division and it was not until towards evening, that we struck oil. To my great joy I saw

on the roadside a man of my old battalion wearing a shamrock on his shoulder which was the identity mark of the Tyneside Irish Brigade. From then on I was among friends and I soon reported to the CO of the 26th Battalion to whom I had been posted.'

Notes

1. 26/1007 Private Charles Jones.
2. Second Lieutenant John Russell reported wounded 16th March 1916.
3. Lance Sergeant Alfred Hutchinson Died from Wounds 9th of March 1916.

Chapter Five

The Somme Front and Trench Raiding

'The Earth shook and swayed, and the barrage was on
As they leapt o'er the top with a rush, and were gone.'
Anon in 'The Wipers Times'

After handing over to the Australians, the Brigade spent the last days of April and the beginning of May practising the assault on the training area near Moulle. On the 4th of May, the battalions entrained at St Omer and Wizernes for Amiens, detraining at Amiens and marching to St Gratien, where they arrived at 11 p.m. and billeted for the night. This was a long, hot, trying march and several men fell out on the way. Michael Manley recalled the journey,

Lance-Corporal Michael Manley, 26th Battalion.

'We travelled a whole day in this train, shunting about with all these ammunition trains coming up all the time. Eventually we ended up at a place called Amiens. We had to march about 20 miles to get to the front; we were all tired and when we fell out I remember this officer calling over to us, "If you carry on like this you'll miss the Big Push!" Some hope.'

Captain George Swinburn also recorded the march from the station.

'We marched through a large town with the Pipers at the head of the Battalion, under the command of the Major [Prior] because the Colonel is away sick. It is the best reception we just have ever had + the streets + avenues were lined with hundreds of people on both sides. The residents seemed to be greatly impressed by the fitness of the men. We are all sunburnt + look absolutely in the pink. There were shouts of "Vive La France + Vive Angleterre" and the scene was thrilling. I felt quite proud riding at the head of my company. It took us a good hour to march through the town and when we halted in one of the suburbs the people were most kind to the men.'

Captain George Swinburn rode proudly at the head of B Company during the route marches up to the Somme Front.

The journey of the 25th Battalion was noted by Lance Corporal Ted Colpitts, who wrote,

'5 Mile walk - 10 hours ride in train. Arrive Amiens - fine city 12 mile walk an awful march, lots fall out. Arrive tired and footsore, feeling the effect of march now.'

After resting the night in St Gratien, the battalions paraded in Line of March, and continued on the way to the Somme front, the next stopping place being Franvillers. An unamed Padre, writing in the Ushaw College magazine, recorded the arrival of the Tyneside Irish Brigade on the Somme front. A joint Mass for the Padre's Battalion

The Pipes and Drums led the Battalion towards the Somme front.

of London Territorials and the Northumberland Fusiliers had taken place, with Lieutenants E McDool and J Prior acting as altar servers. The same Padre assisted the Tyneside Irish in a cricket match, at the beginning of June, against a York and Lancaster Battalion, in which the Irish were defeated, but in true Irish fashion the Padre recalled that they had finished second.

Captain Bob Falkous, now posted to the 27th Battalion, was to have played in this game, but wrote to his mother saying,

> *'I am going to have a look at a cricket match which I am too late to join due to the shelling. The Boche was having a little target practice as usual today against our place. From below he didn't appear to get so very near judging by the smoke puffs;' shrapnel makes a queer whistling sound,' whilst the 18 pounders, which were banging away within a score of yards, make quite a healthy crash.'*

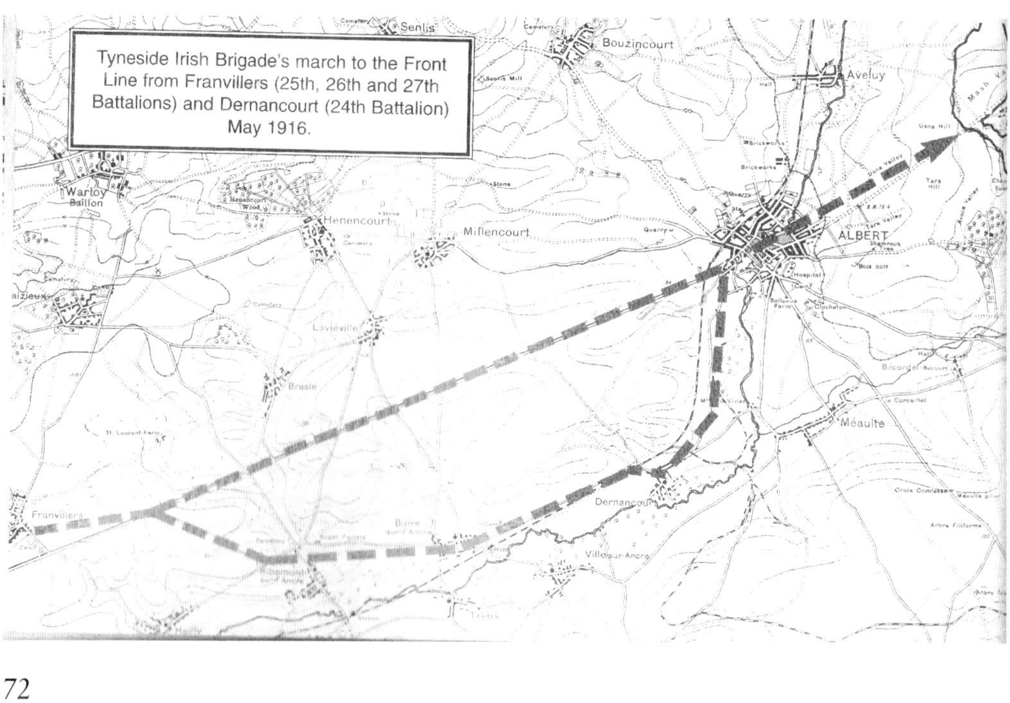

Tyneside Irish Brigade's march to the Front Line from Franvillers (25th, 26th and 27th Battalions) and Dernancourt (24th Battalion) May 1916.

Rubble filled streets in the town of Albert – a sight that greeted the Tyneside Irish battalions en-route to the front line at La Boisselle.

The move from the north was a bit of a tonic for the men. Lew Shaughnessy mentioned this,

'The Somme area was very nice after the Armentieres trenches. It was not nearly so wet and there were plenty of civilians around. Sam had got his stripe by now and went to the signallers, so I felt a little bit lonely without big brother. Albert was in ruins, you went into this cellar and the trench started up the hill.'

The 27th Battalion went into the line first on the 10th of May when there was sporadic shelling and casualties were described as light. The next day the 26th Battalion took over the adjoining section of the front line, and A Company of the 25th Battalion was in support in the soon to be famous Tara and Usna Redoubts astride the Albert–Bapaume road, with the the rest of the battalion in Albert and the 24th Battalion in billets at Dernancourt. On the 15th the 25th Battalion took over from the 26th Battalion in the front line and suffered shelling throughout this tour, with the enemy giving Keats Redoubt, Tummel Street and Athol Street particular attention.

27/1151 Corporal B P Nelson was killed in action 11th May 1916 whilst manning trenches in front of the German fortified village of La Boisselle.

On the night of the 21st of May a German raiding party tried to enter the British trenches on the right, held by D Company of the 25th Battalion. They were forced back after a desperate bombing fight around a post held by six men commanded by Lance Corporal Tom Hilton of Hebburn; after all of his men were either dead or badly wounded, Lance Corporal Hilton kept throwing bombs at the raiders until they were compelled to retire. For this brave action he was awarded the Military Medal.

On the 20th of May, Brigadier Cameron attended a conference at Divisional Headquarters, and was warned to prepare 103 Brigade to carry out a series of trench raids on the enemy in the opposite trenches, near the village of La Boisselle. Accordingly, the battalions were warned to put together and start training raiding parties, in preparation for the forthcoming raids. The parties from the 24th and 26th Battalions were selected to carry out the operation.

On the 22nd of May, the Brigade moved back to Bresle and became the Divisional reserve, supplying working parties for the front line. Meanwhile two groups of raiders started practising; a 'Left Raiding

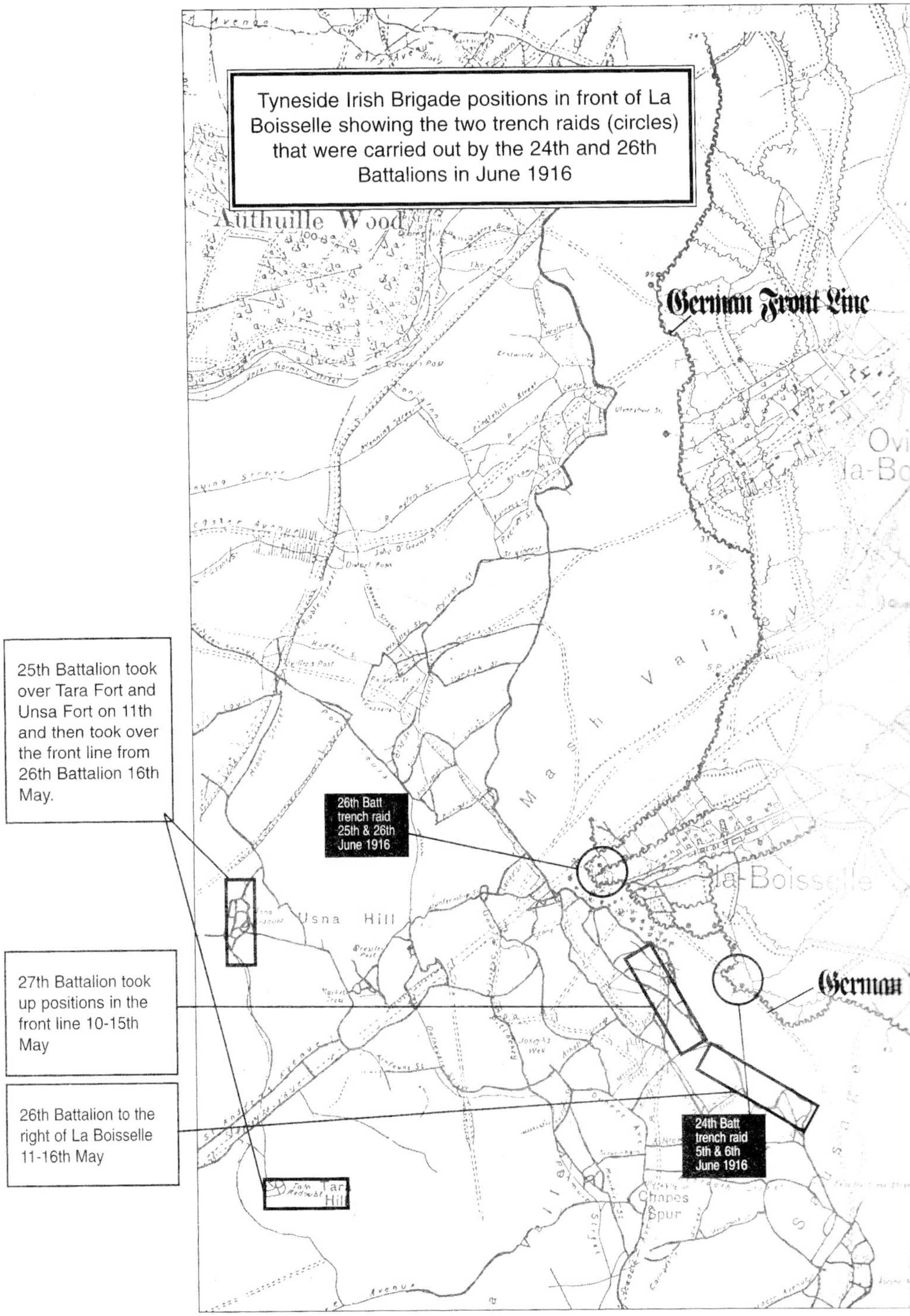
Tyneside Irish Brigade positions in front of La Boisselle showing the two trench raids (circles) that were carried out by the 24th and 26th Battalions in June 1916
Authuille Wood
German Front Line
25th Battalion took over Tara Fort and Unsa Fort on 11th and then took over the front line from 26th Battalion 16th May.
26th Batt trench raid 25th & 26th June 1916
La-Boisselle
Usna Hill
German
27th Battalion took up positions in the front line 10-15th May
26th Battalion to the right of La Boisselle 11-16th May
24th Batt trench raid 5th & 6th June 1916
Tara Hill
Chapes Spur

Party' dug a practice trench and a 'Right Party' found an old trench that resembled their objective. The objectives of the raiders were, Right Raiding Party: The German Salient in X.20.a. Left Raiding Party: The Triangle in the German trenches points X.14.c.01, X.13.b.9.0., X20.a.1/2.2. The Right Raiding Party was found by the 24th Battalion and the Left Raiding Party by the 26th Battalion.

Meanwhile the Officers and NCOs of both parties visited the front line several times to reconnoitre the objective when exact points of departure from the British Line, and point of entry in the German Line, were fixed. Right party would enter at X.20.a.4.5. Left party at X.19.b.9.9. The raid was postponed initially to the 3rd of June and then to the night of the 5th/6th of June. On the 1st and 3rd meetings were held at Divisional Headquarters to ensure that the Artillery programme was fully understood by everyone concerned. Meanwhile the raiders kept practising.

Private Michael Murray 24/877 took part in the raid as a strecher bearer.

Special stores required for the raid by the 24th Battalion were supplied by Division as follows:

140	Mills Grenades
4	Grenade waistcoats
19	Small hand axes
18	Traverser mats
6	Torch rifles
6	Small electric torches
6	Whistles
40	Pairs of wire gloves
300	Yds White tape
3	Sets silent signalling apparatus
4	Wire cutters large
2	Wrist watches

Liaison between 102 Brigade(Tyneside Scottish), who were holding the front line, and 103 Brigade was arranged as follows:

Brigade Commanders to be together in the Advanced Brigade Headquarters in the Tara - Usna Line, close to St Andrews Avenue.

Officer Commanding 24th Battalion to be at A Battalion HQ (Chapes Spur).

Officer Commanding 26th Battalion to be at B Battalion HQ (Maissin).

Right Raid Commander to be in close touch with Left Company Commander A Battalion.

A Captain, detailed by 26th Battalion to be at Advanced Company HQ, Right Company B Battalion.

As the Tyneside Scottish was holding the line, the password was chosen as follows: A soldier of the Scottish, challenging, would say 'SCOTCH', A soldier from the Irish would answer, 'GEORDIE'. A soldier of the Irish, challenging, would say 'IRISH',

A soldier from the Scottish would answer, 'GEORDIE'.

The 24th Battalion raid was to be commanded by Major J P Gallway and would be in two squads, each commanded by a subaltern, comprising:

1	Officer
1	Sergeant
7	Bayonetmen
4	Bombers
3	Carriers
2	Scouts
2	Signallers
2	Stretcher Bearers

27/754 Private James Wooff of Burns Street, Gateshead, died of wounds at the casualty clearing station at Meaulte on 2 June 1916.

No 1 squad would come from D Company and No 2 squad from C Company. In each party there would be at least 1 Corporal and 1 Lance Corporal. Raid HQ would be made up of OC Raid and 2 Telephone Operators.

The plan was for the raiders to leave the British Front Line at the same spot and pass through the British wire. They would then spread out and on reaching the German wire, two bombers and one carrier would throw their traversing mats over the wire and quickly cross, followed by the remainder of the squad, except for one scout, who would return to raid HQ and report that the enemy wire had been crossed.

Two signallers would remain outside the wire and send a signal reporting the wire crossed.

Having crossed the enemy wire, No 1 squad would work to the right and No 2 to the left, and enter the enemy fire trench. Immediately the second scout would return to Raid HQ and report that the trench had been entered and the signallers would also report by sending the prearranged signal.

The bombers and bayonetmen, accompanied by a carrier, would begin working to the flank along the trench protecting the rest of the squad. The remaining bayonetmen, along with the officer and sergeant, would try to capture a prisoner, and if possible, obtain identification. The second party of bombers and bayonetmen would protect the rear of the squad and one stretcher bearer would remain on top of the parapet, whilst the other would enter the enemy trench to assist with the evacuation of any wounded. A late addition to the plan was the inclusion of a Lewis gun team of an officer and two men, who would go out and protect the flank. This was the plan then for the 24th Battalion raid but what actually happened was something quite different.

The raiding party left Franvillers in a motor bus at 6.30 p.m. on the evening of the 5th of June, and were conveyed to Albert, reaching the town at about 8 p.m., so that by 10 p.m. they were assembled in the large dugout at the enemy end of Mercer Street. By the same hour the Brigade and Battalion Commanders were in their respective positions, and communications had been tested and found to be in working order.

Nominal roll of the 24th Battalion Raiding Party 5th/6th June 1916
IN COMMAND
Major J P Gallwey.

No 1 Squad

In Command	Lieut W.A.Brown	348 Sgt P Butler	
Bayonetmen	373 Pte J Reardon	656 Pte H Gilroy	541 Pte J W Creighton
	836 Pte J Brierley	1189 Pte D Cain	1170 Pte H Hughes
	544 Pte H Bowles		
Throwers	1120 Pte R Taylor	1133 Pte J Connolly	1469 Pte O Kehoe
	1518 Pte J Fennelly		
Carriers	220 Cpl A Brodie	1577 L/Cpl Nightingale	
Scouts	701 Lcpl Gray	66 Pte J Donnelly	

Signallers	1375 Pte A T Smith	101 Cpl T Lawler	
Stretcher Bearers	48 Pte T Brown	1027 Pte W McGarr	
Machine Gun Team	204 L/Cpl Nolan	420 Pte Flannigan	1150 Pte Egan
No 2 Squad			
In Command	2nd Lieut J.A.Donnelly	630 Sgt J Leighton	
Bayonetmen	1448 Pte Skelton	1635 Pte Harold	727 Pte Hubbard
	Pte Jones	417 Pte Traynor	70 Pte Wilson
	764 Pte Smith		
Bombers	1015 Pte Cairns	983 Pte Nimmons	1602 Pte Blades
	884 Pte Charters		
Carriers	L/Cpl Stockhill	Pte J Kelly	
Scouts	611 Pte Hughes	448 Cpl Graham	
Signallers	1402 RSM Grailey	1426 Pte Marron	
Stretcher Bearers	234 Pte Welsh	833 Pte Rowell	

There was now almost complete silence over the line, with just an occasional rifle shot heard. At 11 p.m. (Zero Hour) the bombardment started according to the programme and during this bombardment the raiders left the dugout and made their way along the trench to Sap No 6. At the time the barrage was supposed to lift it did not, and with shells landing all around the head of the Sap, Major Gallwey waited for an opportunity to leave the Sap and cross No-Man's-Land, but time ran out. The party had by now had several casualties. Private Joseph Hughes of Spennymoor was killed and Lance Corporals' Stockhill and Blades and Privates Brierley, Cain and Brown, along with Major Gallwey were wounded by British shellfire. Sergeant Patrick Butler and four other soldiers were awarded Divisional Cards of Honour for the part they played in the raid. For Private Brown, who had severe wounds, it was the end of the war and by the time the Battalion was going over the top on the 1st of July, he was well on his way to being discharged, and returning to Usworth.

But what of the 26th Battalion's raiding party? Their raid was planned slightly differently for, although there were two bombing parties, an NCO with nine men would provide a covering force. Things went better for this raid, and, as the barrage moved forward, they crossed No-Man's-Land and entered the enemy front line, where some dugouts were bombed, but no prisoners taken before it was time to withdraw.

More successful than the 24th Battalion raid, it resulted in the award of the Military Cross to Captain Harold Price, the OC Raid. Captain Price was born in Vancouver and had travelled half-way round the world to enlist and receive his commission in the Battalion.

26/389 Lance Corporal Joseph Lee of Craghead was awarded the Military Medal in the same action and promoted to full Corporal. The Germans, too, were active in trench raids, being rather keen to find out as much as possible about the coming offensive and rumours were quick to circulate in the Irish Brigade when some men from the Tyneside Scottish were taken prisoner on the night of the 4th/5th of June. However, it would appear that these men of the Tyneside Scottish followed the Germans back across No-Man's-Land and did not return.

Meanwhile those not involved in the raids were employed on working parties with as many as 600 men a day from each battalion being employed in the Albert, Dernancourt and Franvillers areas. Every sort of stores required for the coming offensive had to be man-handled to dumps in the forward area, rations, ammunition, barbed wire, grenades, sandbags etc, etc. Private John Connolly recalled that,

'the best job was being attached to the tunnellers working on the Y Sap and Lochnagar mines.'

For the Durham miners it was regarded as a home from home since they had already spent the best part of their working lives underground so it was familiar to them, and compared to coalmining, the work was not too heavy.

Captain Jack Arnold had been given the job of Town Major in Dernancourt, a small town a few miles behind Albert on the Somme front and he recalled his time there with these words:

'While I was in the village a large twelve inch gun was brought up by rail and installed almost in the middle of the village. The first time it was loosed off tiles and debris leapt from the roof of almost every house and those that had ceilings very quickly lost them. The mayor came to me in great trepidation to know if the gun could be silenced. I explained to him with some diffidence that as it was the function of guns to fire and as a war happened to be on, it was a tall order to ask that the gun be put out of action. A compromise was reached by which I would convey a warning to the inhabitants what time it was proposed to do a "shoot". The result was the somewhat amusing spectacle of the town crier going round proclaiming the hours at which the performance would begin each day.'

Whilst employed as a Town Major Captain Arnold had a lot of dealings with the local French farmers, but he was not impressed with them and he wrote to the head of his old school in Belfast,

'The fact we were fighting for them never prevented them trying and succeeding in doing us on every possible occasion; each one thought his own particular piece of soil as valuable as, or more valuable than, the whole of France.'

When not employed on working parties, the men were resting or training and the training typically comprised assaulting a position, consolidating and wiring, in preparation for the coming offensive. The working parties were not without danger and on the 18th of June, Privates J Devlin, J Harvey and F Horn of the 25th Battalion were wounded by shellfire.

Captain Falkous described one of these working parties to his mother in a letter written on the 5th of June,

'This morning I set off again with a working party, big motor buses took us right up into the town (Albert). The Boche can see the road in places, it seems as straight as a ruler for 50 miles, and sometimes he drops an iron ration on spec. Fortunately the French habit of lining their roads with trees interferes with his view. When we get to the town we pull up at the church and proceed in single file to the scene of operations. The church is a wonderful sight. The huge gilt Maddonna holding the child aloft is bent over at right angles to the spire, almost as if blessing the troops beneath. Local belief says that when the Madonna falls the war will end. The trenches are being excavated from chalk which is almost painfully white. However the vegetation is so rank that in a short time a line of trench can hardly be seen. They're now at work on St Andrew's Avenue, I hope our friends don't go in for a little retaliation for an hour or two.'

A week later on the 11th of June he wrote again,

'Nothing much of interest has been occurring. Our friends of the T.S. have caught it pretty hot. We have been busy every night on working parties, you see saps, trenches and so on can not be dug in sight of the Hun during the day. It all has to be done at night and very often the earth carried away for a hundred yards or so before it is thrown over the top. Of course the Boche is very well aware of the fact that work is going on and is always having a go at catching the working parties. The job we were on last night we reached by meandering through about 2 miles of trench. This lot of trenches must have been dug by Scotsmen–they are all named after Glasgow and Edinburgh streets. Every-thing was peaceful and quiet last night until we began to come away. Then Fritz started, ours started too, the skyline was a blaze of flashes, Very lights were as common as at a fireworks display. The row was like the thunder of immense waves, so many that individual sounds could not be distinguished. Every now and then the stammering chatter of machine guns would break in. From some miles behind us a battery of monsters was hurling death overhead, it's quite interesting – none of my party was hit.'

During this time, behind the front, many men of the Roman Catholic faith took the opportunity to go to Confession and then to Mass and receive Holy Communion. Captain W Rigby of the 27th Battalion, writing home to Ushaw College, recalled,

'The Padre (Father McBrearty) had a hot time in the confessional that weekend. Long queues of patiently waiting Durham pitmen furiously trying to pray for three hours on end and obviously disappointed with the result.'

Seated is Private Jack Reardon who took part in the trench raid on the night 5/6th June 1916. On 1st July 1916 he was badly wounded and his leg was eventually amputated.

Also in the 27th Battalion, Private Johnny Curran and four friends decided they too would go to Confession, but because of the length of the queue Johnny didn't wait. He was to be the only one to survive out of the group and this would haunt him for the rest of his days.

After the somewhat unsuccessful raids on the night of the 5/6th, Divisional HQ decided that the raiding parties should try again, on the night of 25th/26th of June.

The plan was identical to the previous one with hardly any changes except to the actual personnel involved and even the actual objectives in the German trenches remained the same.

As Major Galwey had been wounded, Major J.M Prior would now command the 24th Battalion's raiding party and, with the majority of the casualties in the previous raid occurring in the D Company squad, A Company was detailed to take part. The majority of the C company squad went again.

The 26th Battalion's raiding party remained under the command of Captain Price and the NCO's were the same.

This time the Germans were well and truly ready for them. On the right, the raiding party under Major Prior reached the enemy parapet but then met with very intense rifle and machine-gun fire and very effective bombing. Forced to retire, they had two men wounded; one managed to walk in under his own power, but the other had a more serious wound, and was carried in by Lieutenant Brady and Private E Hedley of Newcastle. Private Hedley had been constantly absent, while the Battalion was training in England, but he was a good soldier when in the line. He was to be killed in action the following year.

Nominal roll of the 24th Battalion Raiding Party 25th/26th June 1916
IN COMMAND
Major J M Prior

No 1 Squad			
Captain Pringle	264 Sgt T Finneran	1205 Sgt J Jamieson	
Bayonetmen	1503 Pte W Johnson	176 Pte J Docherty	170 Pte J Iley
	79 Pte H Lynn	532 Pte H Forster	156 Pte J Moran
Bombers	99 Pte J Compton	203 L/Cpl P Derrick	249 L/Cpl A Harland
	1348 Pte P Lamb		
Carriers	1514 Pte W Derbyshire	398 Pte P Carroll	9642 Pte Taylor
	154 Pte J Codia		
Scouts	1446 Pte N Fitzpatrick	239 Pte Forster	
Signallers	1537 Pte Hart	49 Pte A O Walton	
Stretcher Bearers	172 Pte Regan	174 Pte J Goundry	1658 Pte J Duffy
Machine Gun Team	204 L/Cpl Nolan	420 Pte Flannigan	842 Pte McKivett
	1150 Pte Egan	1005 Pte T Hedley	

Circled is 24/204 Lance-Corporal James Nolan. He was awarded a Card of Honour for his part in the trench raid 5/6th June 1916. The NCO (square) is Sergeant George Colbey who won the MM in September 1916. He was commissioned to the 25th Battalion and won the MC and Bar in 1918. He became a founder member of the Old Comrades Association after the war.

No 2 Squad

Lieutenant Brady	630 Sgt J Leighton	1625 L/Sgt A Shepardson	
Bayonetmen	930 L/Cpl J Dourish	676 Pte J Staff	727 Pte J Hubbard
	1452 Pte T Trueman	1107 Pte J T Smith	1488 Pte J Skelton
	399 Pte J T May		
Bombers	983 Pte W Nimmons	1015 Pte O Cairns	1633 L/Cpl J Harrold
	884 L/Cpl P A Charters		
Carriers	10046 Pte E Jones	904 Pte R Boyle	
Scouts	611 Pte C Hughes	1649 Pte G Pallon	
Signallers	813 Sgt T M McElhone	1386 Pte J Cummings	
Stretcher Bearers	833 Pte F Rowell	877 Pte M Murray	

Meanwhile, not far to the left, the Germans were playing a more cunning game. As the raiders approached all was quiet and they were allowed to enter the German trenches, but as soon as they were in, they were met with a shower of bombs from each flank and from behind the parados. A hand-to-hand fight ensued in which it was estimated that the enemy suffered more casualties than the raiders. The bombers, moving quickly ,fought their way along the enemy trench and the leading man, 26/73 Private William Bullock, of Blaydon, had a fierce struggle with a German soldier, who had no desire to be taken prisoner. Unable to capture the man, Private Bullock threw him down the steps of a deep dugout, then threw a grenade after him. During the withdrawal, another bomber, 26/850 Private John Clark of Newcastle, assisted those of the raiding party who were wounded. Looking back he spotted two Germans about to open fire, so he threw his last bomb at them, then opened fire with his rifle, before helping the wounded through the German wire. As they crossed

Corporal James Harvey was wounded by shell fire, 18th June 1916. This was the first time he had been wounded – in this photograph he is showing two wound stripes on his left arm.

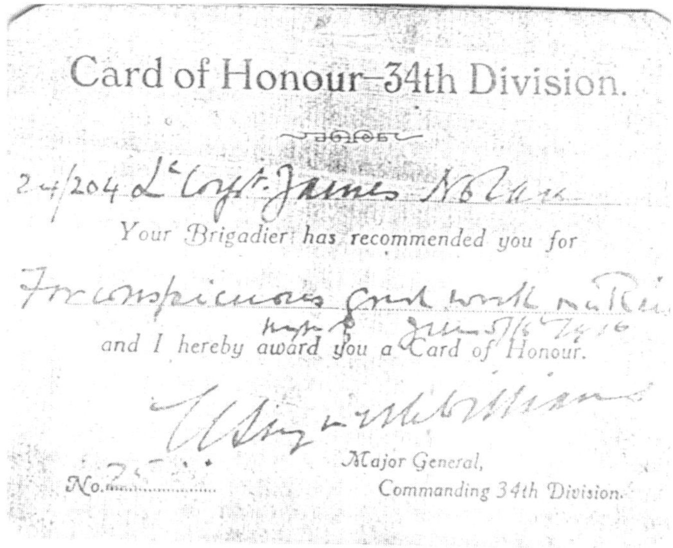

Card of Honour–34th Division.

24/204 Lc Cpl. James Nolan

Your Brigadier has recommended you for

For conspicuous good work in the raid ... June 5/6 1916

and I hereby award you a Card of Honour.

Major General,
Commanding 34th Division.

No. 25

Divisional Card of Honour awarded to 24/204 L/Cpl James Nolan of Langley Moor for his part in the trench raids on the night of 5th/6th June, 1916. He was wounded on 1st July. He was discharged in August 1917.

Captain Brian Desmond Patrick Mullally, wounded and mentioned in despatches for his part in the trench raid 25/26th of June 1916. He was killed on 1st July.

No-Man's-Land, the covering party, under the command of 26/1386 Sergeant John Connolly of Jarrow, headed off a German flank attack, and remained in position until the main party had withdrawn. These members of the 26th Battalion Raiding Party received the Military Medal for their actions during the raid, and Sergeant Connolly was eventually commissioned in the Leinster Regiment. Captain Price was killed as he came back over No-Man's-Land, and other casualties were Captain B.D. Mullally and six other ranks wounded but they remained at duty. Second Lieutenant I Russell and two other ranks were evacuated wounded and one OR was missing 25/1458 Private William Burgess of Blyth. Of the two Royal Engineers who accompanied the raiding party, one was wounded and one was missing so that again the results of the raid were somewhat disappointing.

The raiders did not get much rest, for on the 27th and 28th the battalions began to move forward, in preparation for the opening of the attack. For the previous four days the British artillery had been pounding the German trenches, and every man in the Brigade was aware that the opening of the offensive was very close.

Before they set off for the line men wrote their last letters to their families back home in the north east, 27/663 Private John Scollen who had tried in vain to save his friend the previous March wrote these words to his wife Christina and their seven children in Seaham. It is as if John had forseen his death in the coming battle.

Written this 27th of June 1916 signed John Scollen.

My Dear Wife and children it is with regret I write these last words of farewell to you. We are about to make a charge against these awful Germans. If it is God's Holy will that I should fall I will have done my duty to my King and country and I hope justly in the sight of God. It is hard to part from you but keep a good heart Dear Tina and do not grieve for me for God and His Blessed Mother will watch over you and my bonny little children and I have not the least doubt but that my country will help you. For the sake of one of its soldiers that has done his duty. Well Dear Wife Tina I would ask .....[torn out] I have never had cause because you have been a good wife and mother to look after my canny bairns and I'm sure they will be a credit to both of us.

Dearest wife Christina accept this little souvenir of France, a cross made from a French bullet which I enclose for you.

My Joe, Jack, Tina and Aggie not forgetting my bonny twins Nora and Hugh and my last flower baby whom I have only had the great pleasure of seeing once since he came into the world, God bless them. I will try and get to do my duty whilst on this perilous undertaking and if I fall on the top of a massive bayonet then you will know that I died in God's Holy Grace. Tell all of my friends and yours also that I bid them farewell now. My Dear Wife and children I have not anything more to say only I wish you all God's Holy Grace and Blessing so GOODBYE GOODBYE and think of me in your prayers. I know these are hard words to receive but God's will be done.

From your faithful soldier
Husband and father
John Scollen B Coy 27th SB NF.
Goodbye my loved ones DON'T CRY.
I made the cross myself.

26/1386 Sergeant John Connolly and his wife taken prior to embarkation, he was awarded the Military Medal for his work on the night of 25/26 June 1916. Wounded on 1 July he was eventually commissioned into the Leinster Regiment in August 1917.

However the time for the attack was to be delayed by forty-eight hours, because heavy summer rain had fallen on the 26th and 27th, the High Command had to consider the implications of the battlefield being flooded. On the 28th the decision was taken to postpone the attack and Divisional and Brigade Staff Officers had the job of halting and turning round those battalions on their way towards the front line.

When the offensive was postponed the men of 103 Brigade, who had been sleeping in open fields near Albert, were marched back to the billets where they had started. Back in the billets Captain Falkous snatched a few minutes to write to his mother, describing the events of the past two days.

'I hardly know if my head is on my feet after the last two days. The weather has been rotten which has added greatly to our discomfort. The night before last we set off half an hour after midnight and marched until 4 in the morning when we came to a bivouac, Brrh it was cold, both cold and wet. I got precious little sleep + was called out when my breakfast had only reached the porridge, to accompany a Staff Captain to a blessed dump three-'and-'a-'half miles away to inspect some loads. I ran an officer from 18/NF to earth in a dug out + he gave me a slap up lunch everything just out from home. On returning to camp I was greeted by the cheery news that the Battalion was moving back

26/1095 Private Bernard Morris died of wounds at Rouen on 23 June 1916.

almost immediately. A quick change and then a march back, very little sleep about 21 miles in 24 hours under anything but ideal conditions.'

He then goes on to describe some of his soldiers,

'Murtagh and O'Connell of course are "real" Irish. Several of the other men are "Irish" in the English meaning of the word.'

Describing his men singing, he says,

'The English musical comedy songs weren't sufficiently satisfying, so we had to have several Irish folk songs and lullabies in the original Irish - a most musical if entirely incomprehensible tongue.'

Before the Battalion moved back into the line he managed to get a last letter away to his mother on the morning of the 30th in which he asked,

'You might keep any local cuttings relating to the T.I. will you? They'll be plentiful enough I expect.'

Further on he wrote,

'The new officers are all out on the hill watching matters thro their glasses – quite like a group from one of these imaginative illustrated magazines.'

He ended his last letter home,

'Once again don't worry if you're on short rations in the way of letters for a while, love to all, Your affectionate son Rob.'

Also writing to a loved one back in England was Captain George Swinburn. His letter to his sweetheart Phoebe reflects the mood of many men going into the battle.

Friday 30th June 1916
'My Dear Phoebe
I do not suppose I will have time to write you for a few days. I am fortunately in splendid health and quite look forward to the immediate future because it will be the means to an end. I hope that God will comfort you and bless you – personally I leave my future to him and do so with confidence.
Your own true love. George'

Private Patrick Martin met his brother Frank as he moved up through the artillery lines, but there was only time for a brief handshake.

That afternoon the battalions of 103 Brigade, as in other formations, were paraded in hollow square and messages from the commanding Generals were read out. Captain Swinburn managed to keep a copy of the message from Brigadier-General Cameron the Brigade Commander.

103rd INFANTRY BRIGADE

SPECIAL BRIGADE ORDER

30th JUNE 1916

Officers, Non Commissioned Officers and men of the 103rd Infantry Brigade.
In the past you have won for yourselves a very good name for soldierly conduct in the presence of the enemy and for hard work when necessity arises. Remember this especially tomorrow.
Best wishes to all ranks for good luck and complete success.

Then that evening at 10 p.m. the Brigade began to move forward again making its way into the reserve trenches of the TARA–USNA–BECOURT line. But tragedy was to strike the 24th Battalion before it ever arrived. As the battalion was making its way towards the line it was detailed to collect bombs at a dump but somehow, as a platoon of A company was at the dump, a bomb exploded, wounding eleven men and killing Privates John Pepper and Joseph Armstrong. The sight of dead men before the battle started was thought to be bad for morale, so the bodies were taken with the wounded to the Casualty Clearing Station at Heilly Station, where they were buried.

As the battalions made their way forward, men shook hands and wished each other the best of luck for what lay ahead. The 26th Battalion was marching up through the Artillery positions when 26/1077 Private Patrick Martin, from Willington, saw his brother Frank working on the guns. There was just time for a brief hand shake, and 'All the best' before Patrick moved on towards the communication trenches.

103rd INFANTRY BRIGADE.

SPECIAL BRIGADE ORDER

30th June 1916.

Officers, Non-Commissioned Officers and men of the 103rd Infantry Brigade.

In the past you have won for yourselves a very good name for soldierly conduct in the presence of the enemy and for hard work when necessity arises - Remember this especially to-morrow.

Best wishes to all ranks for good luck and complete success.

[illegible]

Brigadier-General.
Commanding 103rd Infantry Brigade.

Chapter Six

The 1st of July 1916

'The gates of hell were opened and we accepted the invitation to enter'.
26/880 LANCE SERGEANT EDWARD DYKE

The story of the 1st of July 1916, the first day of the Battle of the Somme, has been told many times and I do not intend to go over the whole of the battle. I will concentrate on the part played by the Tyneside Irish Brigade, and touch on the work of the rest of the 34th Division.

General Sir Douglas Haig had given the main part of the Somme Offensive to the Fourth Army commanded by General Sir Henry Rawlinson, and a small diversionary part, to the north, to the Third Army. The Fourth Army comprised, from right to left, XIII, XV, III, X and VII Corps. III Corps was commanded by Lieutenant-General Sir W.P. Pultney, who had under his command the 8th and 34th Divisions holding the line, with the 19th (Western) Division in reserve.

Major-General Ingouville–Williams' plan of attack for the 34th Division was relatively simple. The division would advance in four columns, each three battalions deep. The 34th Division had in the line 101 Brigade on the right and 102 (Tyneside Scottish) Brigade on the left, with 103 (Tyneside Irish) Brigade in reserve along the TARA - USNA line. The first objective of the leading battalions was the German front system consisting of four trenches. The fourth trench, requiring an advance of two thousand yards, was to be reached forty eight minutes after 'zero hour' at 8.18 a.m.

The second objective was the German intermediate line, the 'Kaisergraben', in front of Pozières and Contalmaison villages. This line was to be reached at 8.58 a.m. and when this line was reached, 101 and 102 Brigades would halt and consolidate. 103 Brigade, following close in the rear, would pass through the leading troops, capture Contalmaison village, and having captured the village, would advance to the third and final objective, a line from the eastern edge of Contalmaison to Pozières which would be reached by 10.10 a.m.

103 Brigade was deployed with all four battalions abreast: from right to left, next to Becourt Wood the 27th Battalion, then the 24th, and 26th Battalions while in position on the northern side of the Albert-Bapaume road was the 25th Battalion. The battalions of the Irish Brigade made up the third wave of the divisional attack, with each supporting two battalions of the Brigade in front of them. The plan was very badly flawed, because all the battalions would begin to advance together, which left no room for manoeuvre should anything go wrong, and was to have disastrous consequences for all units of the Division involved in the advance. Another tragic mistake was that the commanding officers and battalion headquarters staff were to advance with the men, leaving no one to take control and to reorganise the battalions later in the day. Each battalion was to advance on a two company front, with each company in a column of platoons. There would be 150 paces between each platoon and the same distance between the following company. The men were heavily equipped in fighting order so that as well as rifles' and bayonets, they were laden down with water bottles, gas helmets, hand grenades and extra bandoliers of rifle ammunition. On their backs they carried a haversack, which had a yellow identity triangle, with 16 inch sides, fastened to it to enable the Artillery Observation Officers to spot the leading troops. Pushed down between the haversack and the back, a soldier would have either a pick or a shovel, ready for the work of digging-in when the objective was reached. Lewis gunners and their number twos carried drums of ammunition and the bombers extra bombs in haversacks. Behind the advancing companies would come signallers, with reels of wire, ready to establish communications between the Battalion and Brigade Headquarters. Also following behind came those detailed as carrying parties, for the Brigade Machine Gun Company, and the Light Trench Mortar Battery. For a lucky few there would be jobs such as waiting on Chapes Spur under cover, as escorts for any prisoners taken.

0730 hrs 1 July 1916 the Tyneside Irish advance. The 103rd Brigade began coming over the hill in beautifully regular lines. Men can be seen advancing with the rifle at the shoulder arms position.

0730 hrs 1 July 1916 the Tyneside Irish advance. One of the best known photographs of the Great War. As the leading wave moves off the next wave can be seen in the trench.

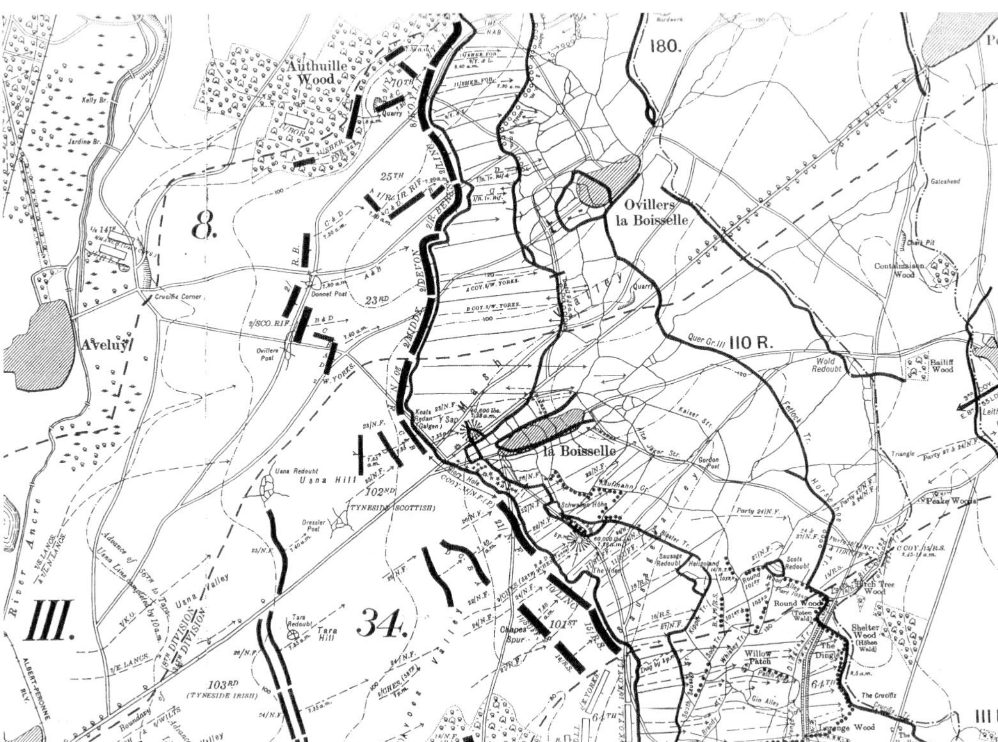

Mr and Mrs McGee and their four soldier sons who served with A Company of the 27th Battalion. *Left to right* 27/468 Sergeant Patsy McGee, 27/1092 Private Peter McGee, 27/1091 Private Michael McGee, 27/1591 Private 27/1092 Tommy McGee.

For many in the Tyneside Irish Brigade, as in other 'Pals' battalions, the first day of the Somme was a family or village affair. In every battalion, brothers, cousins, fathers, sons and workmates would advance together and many would die together. In the 27th Battalion, serving in A Company, were the Caulfield Brothers from Stanley, the McGee's from Usworth and James and Michael Harvey from Stanley, Crook, with their brother-in-law Corporal John Cross in the 24th Battalion. The Norwood brothers, Melville and Thomas went over with C Company and the Shaughnessy brothers Lew, in D Company, and Sam, with the Signal Platoon.

In C Company, of the 24th Battalion, were Peter and Robert Charters. The four Nightingale brothers, Andrew, Matthew, Mark and William went 'over the top', with 7 Platoon of B Company, and the McGill brothers John and James were in A Company, with a third brother Michael in the 25th Battalion. Also going over with the 25th was Robert Stephenson junior. His father, Robert senior, was nearby with the 26th Battalion, where CQMS Gavin Wild and his brother William would both win medals for gallantry before the day was out. Nearly every man named would become a casualty and only a few would survive the war. This is but a small example of the family connections within the Tyneside Irish Brigade.

But what of the men from the villages? Of fifteen men serving in the 26th Battalion from Craghead, only two would survive the war unscathed. Every other man would become a casualty with seven being killed. In many towns and villages the same story applied. Sherburn Hill and Usworth Colliery, both small colliery villages, each had over forty men taking part in the Tyneside Irish advance, whilst from the streets of Framwellgate and Milburngate, in Durham City, there were no less than fifty six men involved, and the larger towns were represented in even greater numbers. After arriving in the assembly trenches time was spent resting, where possible, checking equipment and, in some cases, making a last minute Confession as the padre came round.

'Well I wasn't religious, even though I came from a Catholic family. It was when I saw lads who normally avoided religious things, look serious and go to Mass, that I realised I might not come through.' (Lew Shaugnessy 27th Battalion).

For those lucky enough there was food, and, in some cases, the rum jar found its way to those taking part in the assault. Lew Shaughnessy recalled,

'Eventually our officer turned up with the rum jar and we drank to our success. The officer was just a young lad, and he was as white as a sheet. The rum did the trick and he went quite red in the face, I recall. Well, the officer disappeared around the traverse and we got into place'.

[This was probably 2nd Lt J R C BURLURAUX, who was the only 'young' officer in the company. He would be killed during the day, and is buried in Ovilliers Military Cemetery.]

The waiting to go was stressful and men experienced a range of emotions unknown to those who have not been in battle. Michael Manley said,

'I didn't know what to think. You get all kinds of feelings and you just want to get it over with. You know it's going to be rough, I was scared when the shells came over it didn't half put the wind up you'.

Lew Shaugnessy had this to say,

'Some of the lads took entrenching tools and shoved them into the front of their tunics to protect their bellies when we went over.'

The morning sun was breaking through the mist as the British barrage, pounding the German defences, reached its crescendo, with the German artillery replying. When at 7.28 two minutes before zero, the mines at 'Y sap' and 'Lochnagar' were fired, the ground shook and trembled, and stones and earth rained down on the forward enemy positions. At 'Zero Hour', the British barrage lifted on to the next line of the enemy trenches.

The waiting was almost over; the whistles blew and the Brigade rose from the trenches. Long lines of men, in a formation resembling the fighting at Waterloo, began to advance against well dug-in machine guns.

Many of the accounts by soldiers of the Brigade state that they were facing the Prussian Guard or Prussian Imperial Regiments. However the truth is that the enemy opposite the 34th Division was 56 Reserve Infantry Brigade, with Bavarian Reserve Regiments 110 and 111 under command. These soldiers were well aware that the British attack was coming, for in the last hours before the attack, at 2.45 a.m., one of their listening posts, 'Moritz', in La Boisselle, picked up a message, sent to one of the Tyneside Scottish Battalions, from Headquarters 102 Brigade. This message, passed by a staff officer, confirmed to the waiting enemy that the expected attack would begin the following morning. This information had the German machine gunners alerted and the explosion of the mines confirmed that it was time for the battle to commence.

As the men from Tyneside began to advance an official photographer took photographs of the columns. (These photographs are some of the best known of the Great War, and have been used to illustrate many works.)

'I remember the ladder being placed against the trench wall and the Corporal standing with his foot on the bottom rung. Next thing I remember was being hit by muck and stones from a shell burst as I climbed the ladder.' (Lew Shaughnessy 27th Battalion).

The Y sap mine crater, very few of the 25th Battalion got as far as this. Bodies can be seen lying in No Mans Land.

25/494 Private John McCartney 25th Battalion killed in action 1 July 1916.

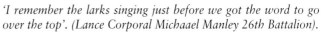

'I remember the larks singing just before we got the word to go over the top'. (Lance Corporal Michaael Manley 26th Battalion).

*'At 7.26 word came along to "**get ready**". Six minutes to go, everything is one buzz of excitement. The word comes to "**mount**" and right well it was responded to.' (Lance Corporal John Higgins 25th Battalion, of Brandon.)*

Out of the trenches there was some confusion as the men sorted themselves into columns of platoons, as laid down in the battle plan. Lew Shaughnessy again,

'On top I looked for the others. There they were, just standing. Just standing, not going forward. They were dressing as they would on parade. I couldn't see our officer, but someone must have given the command and off we went.'

Many accounts tell of the big drum of the Brigade Pipes and Drums being centrally placed, and beating time as the men went forward, although how it was heard, above the noise of the barrage and machine guns remains a mystery. The Pipers also had their part to play, piping the companies over the top. In *Irish Heroes in the War* Joseph Keating says,

'At Albert, an Irish Piper from Tyneside found himself compelled to leap out of the trench at the signal to advance, and play his company over the parapet into action. He marched ahead through a storm of bullets which were wounding or killing his comrades all around him, until he himself fell among the wounded.'

After the war, one piper told his family of how as he went over,

'I played the "Minstrel Boy" because the words seemed the most appropriate that I could think of.' (Private J Brown, Pipes and Drums)

Others reported hearing the strains of 'Tipperary', but the pipers of the Tyneside Scottish and the Royal Scots were also piping their men forward that day.

As the Brigade came over the top of the Tara - Usna ridge, the Pioneers of 18/Northumberland Fusiliers were watching from the edge of Becourt Wood. Their battalion history noted the advance with these words,

'The mines went off and a few minutes later the 103rd Brigade began coming over the hill in beautifully regular lines, dressing and intervals maintained as well as on a ceremonial parade. Everyone felt proud of that lot of Tynesiders.'

27/1020 Corporal Michael Harvey 27th Battalion recited 'Glory be to the Father' at the bottom of a shellhole. Nearby lay the body of his young brother, Sergeant James Harvey.

All accounts of the advance give the same impression of the men going forward in this parade formation, straight through the German counter-barrage. Men were falling, wounded and dying men littered the battlefield and those still standing obeyed orders and filled up the blank files until hit themselves. Lieutenant J A Hately wrote,

'What a glorious sight it was for us to see the men we'd trained going forward as steadily as human beings possibly could and they never kept a better line on manoeuvres than they did that day. I have met officers of the Machine Gun Corps and the REs who said it was simply thrilling to see those "Tyneside Irish chaps", as they were referred to, coming through and past the other troops as-per the programme.'

27/986 Sergeant James Harvey 27th Battalion. Killed in Action 1 July 1916

But the programme did not take account of the German machine gunners or their artillery. Lance Corporal Higgins again,

'We had a lot of open country to traverse before we reached our own front line, but getting there, somewhat reduced in numbers, we reorganised our line. All the while the German machine guns and artillery unmercifully fired away.'

'I was plodding away then I looked to the side and saw men go down as if looking for something – maybe fuse caps or souvenirs. I wanted to find out what they were looking for, it didn't occur to me that they were men in their death agonies kicking and screaming.' (Lew Shaugnessy 27th Battalion).

CSM E G Crawford 27th Battalion, wrote to his wife in Gateshead, after the battle,

'It was glorious to see these men advance under a perfect hail of machine-gun fire and shells. They went on, never faltering, just as if on an ordinary parade, a fitting memorial to the late Lord Kitchener.'

A section of A Company 25th Battalion. Standing second from the right is 25/334 Private James Kelly who had written from Woolsington, 'I hope you and the children will keep strong.' He was killed during the advance.

24/1280 Private James Sedgewick, of C Company, who came from Framwellgate Moor and was employed at Thornley Colliery. He was wounded 1 July 1916 and evacuated to hospital in Kent.

The men kept going forward, disappearing into the morning mist and the smoke and dust from the shellfire. The attack on the left barely reached the British front line, although a few hardy souls did press forward.

'Again we moved forward. Here, for some reason or other, the wire was not cut and many poor men never got through, so fierce was the enemy's fire. Getting tangled therein, they perished. It was a little beyond this point your humble servant was badly fouled, my right leg taken from under me. Of course my part in the operation ended then. From the beginning until I got hit everybody did great.' (Lance Corporal John Higgins 25th Battalion.)

26/934 Private James Gillespie was only 15 when he was wounded on 1 July 1916, when he was runner to the Adjutant of 26/Northumberland Fusiliers, Captain Cobb.

'We tried to find a safe place to cross, but couldn't find one. We had to use the bodies of our mates as a bridge to keep going'. (Lance Corporal Michael Manley 26th Battalion).

A very similar story is told of the advance of the 26th Battalion by Private James Tunney, also from Brandon, although it is a much more romantic account.

'We soon reached the German trenches and when we got about 30 yards from them, we made a rush with fixed bayonets and rifle fire. They asked us to spare them, but we let them see how we could use cold steel. As time went on we got to the second line of German trenches. They came to meet us to fight for their trench back, which we took from them.'

One of the youngest advancing that morning was 26/935 Private, James Gillespie. Born in Kelso in September 1899 his parents had moved to Newcastle before the outbreak of war. In December 1914 he had run away from home and saying he was eighteen he joined the 3rd Tyneside Irish. He told this story of his part that day to his sons after the war.

'I was given the job of Adjutants runner and as such went over the top with Captain Cobb and the RSM. As we advanced down the slope of the ridge and out into No Man's Land, I became fascinated with the sights and sounds of the battlefield and drifted to the left away from the officer. When the Adjutant was wounded the RSM wanted me to look after the Adjutant and blew his whistle to attract my attention. At the sound of the whistle I turned my head to the right, just as a shell exploded in front of me. I was hit in the neck and mouth and knocked unconscious into a shell hole.

Luck was with me the shrapnel in the neck had missed the artery by an eighth of an inch. The chalk in the shell hole helped stop the bleeding and when I woke up I moved and was shot at by a sniper so I lay still until picked up by a sergeant from one of the shire regiments. As I was carried back I passed out again and when I next awoke I was on a stretcher at a railway siding, all my belongings had been stolen, watch, wallet and money.'

In hospital they found out how old I was and I was discharged and sent to work in the pit, but in March 1918 I was called up and sent back to France where after a couple of weeks I was wounded again, this time in the leg.

When he was discharged from hospital the second time he was also discharged from the Army. However he immediately went into a recruiting office and re enlisted in The King's Own Scottish Borderers and served three years in India.

Lying wounded in a shell hole, Corporal Michael Harvey of the 27th Battalion, from Stanley, Crook, thought he was about to die. Nearby lay the body of his brother Sergeant James Harvey. The more he thought about death, the more Michael thought he should say an 'Act of Contrition' and make his peace with God. But he could not remember the words. Eventually he recited the 'Glory be to the Father'. It was the only prayer he could remember.

Further to his left, where the 26th Battalion were advancing, another soldier was taking cover in a shell hole. Private Will Donaldson of Gateshead, who was not a Catholic, found himself sharing the cover with a Roman Catholic. This young lad held his rosary beads and was repeatedly saying the 'Hail Mary'. Before very long, Will was joining in and soon became word perfect.

25/1377 CSM J McAndrews 25th Battalion was badly shellshocked during the advance.

In the same battalion Lance Sergeant Edward Dyke from Gateshead wrote to his brother in Gateshead,

'How anyone got to the German lines I don't know, but we managed it, or rather some of us did. Machine guns mowed us down, shells were bursting all around us and our own artillery pouring shells into the Germans.'

Further on he wrote,

26/918 Private John Gaughan lay for 5 days in a shell hole with 2 dead men. He used their field dressings to dress his own wounds.

26/198 Private Will Donaldson 26th Battalion learned the 'Hail Mary' from a Catholic lad. Wounded in 1917. He had a silver plate put in his head.

Standing right rear is 26/725 CQMS 'Big Billy' Wild DCM and seated is his brother 26/1310 CQMS Gawen Wild MM on the right is their cousin Billy O'Brian.

'Later I got hit with a piece of shell and the earth left me. When I recovered I was blinded by blood. Taking out my field dressing I bandaged my head. The return to safety was as bad as the charge, How I got back is a mystery. My steel helmet, the doctor says, saved my life.'

Others of the same battalion reported that they reached the German second line. Writing with the news of her husband's death, to Mrs Hunter in Clarence Street, Bowburn, CQMS Gawen Wild told this story,

'We got to their second line and the Germans gave us lots of machine-gun fire and I got to within about 20 yards of a German machine gun. A bullet went through my hip and another through my arm. Jackie dragged me about ten yards to a shell hole and just as he pushed me into the safety of the hole, he was shot through the head. A shrapnel shell bursting overhead lodged a piece of shrapnel in me, but I managed to crawl into the hole. I was there about sixteen hours and all the while a lovely sun was burning down. Poor Jackie and I lay all that long burning day together in that shellhole. You can imagine my feelings, lying there with one of my best chums who'd given his life to save mine.'

CQMS Gawen Wild had already done enough to warrant the award of the Military Medal for his work during the day.

Nearby his brother, CQMS William Wild, was carrying out further acts of bravery and since all the officers of his company were casualties, he took command of what was left to lead them on towards the objective. He found the Battalion Adjutant wounded, took over his papers, and keeping in touch with the Battalion, returned to the wounded Adjutant to carry him in under fire. Later having been told that his brother was wounded, he searched for, found, and brought him in under fire. These brave acts resulted in the award of the Distinguished Conduct Medal.

25/222 Corporal J W Grey Killed in Action 1 July 1916.

A third Quartermaster Sergeant of the 26th Battalion was to be awarded a gallantry medal. CQMS Joseph Coleman of Middlesborough also took command of his Company when all the officers became casualties. Having advanced as far as he could, and being down to three men, he went back, gathered together the remnants of the Company, and led them on to capture his objective. (His young brother Peter had joined the 30th Battalion to be with him in the Tyneside Irish. Posted to the 24th Battalion, Peter was killed during the attack.)

In *The Irish on The Somme*, by Michael MacDonagh, Private Knapp of Seaham Harbour serving with A Company of the 27th Battalion told this story of his part in the advance:

'I had just taken the machine gun off my mate to give him a rest, when 'Fritz' opened fire on us from the left with a machine gun,

which played havoc with the Irish. Then I heard my mate shout "Bill, I've been hit," and when I looked round I saw that I was by myself; he, poor chap, had fallen like the rest. Now I had to do the best I could, so I picked up a bag of ammunition for the gun and started off across No-Man's-Land. Once I had to drop into a shell hole to take cover from machine-gun fire. After a short rest I pushed on again and got into the German second line. By this time I was exhausted, for I was carrying a machine gun and 300 rounds of ammunition, besides a rifle and 120 rounds in my pouches, equipment, haversack and waterproof cape, so I had a fair load. I stopped there for a few minutes picking off stray Boches that were kicking about. Then along came a chap, whom I asked to give me a help with the gun, which he did. We had scarcely gone ten yards when a shell burst on top of us. I stood still, I don't think I could have moved had I wanted to. Then I looked around for my chum, but alas! man and gun were missing. Where he went to I don't know, for I have not seen him or my precious weapon since.'

25/1112 Private Thomas Mullen of C Company who came from 32 Milton Street, Jarrow, was transferred to the 12/13th Battalion.

An unnamed Tyneside Irish officer, writing in the *Northern Echo*, stated,

'We left our trenches, the artillery lifted and the Irish were thirsting to get at the foe. The fighting was of the fiercest description, unsurpassed during this or any other campaign. The Irish advance never ceased, in spite of all the unadulterated hell they were going through. The men were fine, no men in the world could have done better. They got it 'in the neck' – enfilade machine-gun fire traversing ankle high, waist high and breast high, over that awful stretch mapped out for us.'

On they went down the open slopes of the Tara–Usna ridge with men falling all the way. Still the survivors kept going. In the 24th Battalion, 24/585 CQMS John Connolly was advancing behind a section and he wrote to his wife in Newcastle,

'It was splendid, and good courage was displayed. Many of the officers and senior NCOs were down early on. It was marvellous. I saw a young Lance Corporal taking a section up as coolly as if they were on parade. He was knocked down just in front of me. I got hit myself a minute afterwards, but I could still see them moving up and falling fast, worse luck.'

The Brigade was now taking tremendous casualties. Brigadier Cameron had been wounded at 7.58. a.m. by a machine-gun bullet and he was carried into an OP, where Captain D H James was watching helpless as the Brigade was being decimated. Brigadier Cameron had a stomach wound but he told Captain James he would be 'alright' and was taken away to the dressing station. Of the four battalion commanders only Lieutenant-Colonel Steward, commanding the 27th Battalion, remained unwounded but when called back to take command of the Brigade, he found virtually no Brigade to command. Officer casualties were very high, as they led the men, and fifteen out of the sixteen company commanders became casualties. In D Company of the 27th Battalion, Captain Falkous was last seen encouraging and helping his men forward when he fell mortally wounded. His batman, Private Greaves, also wounded in the same burst, went to

26/1158 Private John Oliver Killed in Action 1 July 1916.

25/596 Sergeant William Stafford Killed in Action 1 July 1916

27/735 Private Jack Wilson 27th Battalion met his neighbour 'Ginger' Kenny in No Man's Land

his aid, but the Captain refused assistance and implored the private to save himself. Also advancing with D Company was Lew Shaughnessy who had realised that things were not quite as they should be.

> *'We were still going forward but I could see a few groups of men ahead of us. I said to myself, "There's something not right here", but I could see the Corporal over the other side and there seemed to be quite a few men with him. Then I saw them all fling themselves down and instinctively down I went too. I was lying face down in a ditch and there were some plants sticking up above my head. I was gazing at them when all of a sudden the leaves and petals showered down on me. Machine-gun fire meant for me! The Corporal and the others were in the far end of the ditch, so I crept towards them. We were wide eyed – terrified. One lad was crying for his mother and another was swearing and yelling at him to shut up.'*

Nearby Captain Rigby of the same Battalion was advancing with his company and writing from hospital to Ushaw College, he gave a vivid account of the action.

> *'Right and left, stretching away into the haze of battle, were long lines of our men moving slowly and steadily into the white pall which hung over the German line. It was an inspiring moment, no outward enthusiasm, no wild excitement, simply long irregular lines of khaki moving forward slowly but without pause under the hottest fire in the history of the war. Shells and bullets whizzed and banged, men dropped and lay still, but the long lines went always forward, slowly forward without pause. That is all I saw, I was hit in the first five minutes, but not badly. Coming to a convenient trench I collected and reorganised my men, getting two more "scratches" meanwhile. Then came the hell of No-Man's-Land. In that push I only lasted two minutes, for we were hardly through the wire when a bullet in the right knee knocked me out.'*

In C company Jack Wilson from Usworth, and others of his platoon, were taking cover; one man was screaming in absolute terror, and another was shaking uncontrollably. Just as they began to advance again Jack came across 'Ginger' Kenny, a neighbour from the same street, Edith Avenue, who was serving in A Company but they had barely exchanged a word when a shell came and blew 'Ginger' to 'kingdom come'. Jack began to advance again, leaving 'Ginger' for dead, but, he came round and was able to get himself to the Battalion Aid Station, to be evacuated. 'Ginger' Kenny reached 'kingdom come' in October 1918, after he had been transferred to The York and Lancaster Regiment.

The 25th and 26th Battalions advance now ceased and the men who had reached the German front line returned, where possible, to the British front trench. A small pocket of men occupied the Lochnagar crater in the German front line, and a small area in the second line trench, comprising men from a mixture of battalions. The senior officer present was Lieutenant-Colonel Howard, the CO of the 24th Battalion, who was very badly wounded. The 24th was ordered to remain in the German front line, but before the order reached them a party set off towards the next objective. Likewise the men of the 27th Battalion kept on going and some, reaching Round Wood, began to dig in and consolidate. Sergeant Fred Hood in his diary recorded that he got as far as Mametz Wood, but obviously in the heat of battle he had confused his location.

27/324 Private Joe Hall 27th Battalion Killed in Action 1 July 1916.

'I recall the Corporal told me we were in a German trench and the others would be along in a minute. There were some Tyneside Scots[1] there and they didn't seem to have any more idea than we had. They had blocked the trench at the junction with a communication trench and they too were waiting for their officer to come. The Corporal told me to remain with the Scots while he took a look down the trench to find the others. They disappeared round a corner and I never seen any of them again. About quarter of an hour later an officer from another company dropped into the trench with more men, some with horrible wounds. There were plenty of men there but hardly any that I recognised from my platoon. It was then I realised how lucky I had been.' (Lew Shaughnessy 27th Battalion)

Among those from the 27th Battalion, fighting their way through the German communication trenches was Private Wilf Holmes, from Witton Park, serving with D company, as a bomber. They had worked their way forward, bombing several dugouts, with the Germans still inside. Then a German machine-gun post had to be attacked at point blank range and the position was only taken, when, 'our dead were piled up in front of it', Wilf recalled. Shortly after the capture of that position, Wilf received wounds to the head and was blinded, then he was blown into a concrete position and received further injuries from the blast.

In one stretch of captured trench lay a wounded Tyneside Irishman, nearby a German soldier emerged from a dugout and, on seeing the wounded British soldier bayoneted him to death. The German however had failed to notice, that behind him were other men of the Tyneside Irish, who very promptly gave the German the same treatment meted out to their wounded comrade. They then proceeded to bomb the dugout from which he had emerged, not stopping until all the screams of the enemy wounded had stopped. This event caused much anguish and heartache to one of the soldiers involved, and it haunted him for the rest of his life, so much that his family asked that he should not be named.

Witton Park men in the Tyneside Irish. Standing Left to 27/473 Right Private Wm McEleavey Killed in Action 12 February 1916. 27/337 Private Wilf Holmes wounded 1 July 1916. 27/116 Private Tommy Calvert Wounded 1 July 1916. The name of the seated soldier is unknown.

PRIVATE GEORGE PATTERSON,

Northumberland Fusiliers.

KILLED IN ACTION ON JULY 1st, 1916.

Prior to enlisting Private Patterson worked at Ushaw Moor Colliery.

Mrs F. Clark, 50, Crossgate, Durham, has received the following letter:—

"I regret to inform you that your brother, No. 1498, Private George Patterson, was killed in action on 1st July last. It may be consolation to you to know that he helped in a great measure to make the attack the success that it was. Assuring you of the deepest sympathy of all the officers and men of his battalion.—Yours sincerely, [illegible]

27/1498 Private George Patterson resident of Ushaw Moor near Durham City lilled in action 1 July 1916.

Above: Captain Frederick L Vernon 26th Battalion killed in action 1 July 1916.

Meanwhile, Wilf Holmes was lying unconscious in the bottom of the German trench when along came another Witton Park soldier, Private Tommy Calvert, and a few other men from C company, who started to consolidate the trench and taking Wilf for dead they picked him up and threw him over the Parados. Some time later the Germans began shelling the captured trench, and a shell landed in the trench exactly where Wilf had been lying. Shrapnel from the shell wounded Tommy Calvert who was picked up by stretcher bearers, of the 27th Battalion, at the same time as Wilf was rescued. Inadvertently Tommy had saved Wilf's life and years later Tommy said to Wilf, 'Yer bugger we thought you were dead, that's why we threw you out.'

Others of this Battalion reached Birch Tree Wood and linked up with men of the Royal Scots and the Suffolks of 101 Brigade. A few, not enough to make a difference to the battle, got through to the Fricourt-Pozières road whilst another party linked up with the men of the 24th Battalion, pressed on to Acid Drop Copse and reached the outskirts of Contalmaison. A group of men under Second Lieutenant Thompson of the 24th Battalion managed to fight its way back from the village, to the German second line where they took up position, held on, and waited for support. Some of this party fought their way into Contalmaison, were unable to retreat and died there. A small group hid in some dugouts and, when the village was entered by the 1/Worcestershire Regiment on the 7th of July, came back with the survivors of that attack, along with some men of the Tyneside Scottish who had been taken prisoner, and were released by the Worcesters. Although many works make reference to these men who reached the village and hid or were taken prisoner, finding evidence of the facts is difficult. The only account given by a released soldier seems to be in *The North Star* on 19th July 1916. A Press Association report under the heading *'Tales from the Battlefield' 'Brief Captivity'* recorded the following interview. The reporter and the soldier had obviously met before and the reporter described the soldier in the following words,

'The speaker was one of the most war worn in appearance among the last of the wounded to land. He was much graver than the average too. His spirit was alright, I found after talking with him,

but on the surface he showed far less high spirits than most of our wounded show when they get to Blighty and the reason I think was that he had tasted captivity, a brief taste, but it had left its mark on this man.'

The soldier then told the story of how he had been captured and of his subsequent release.

'No, you wouldn't remember me Sir, but I remember you alright. When my Battalion was in training on Salisbury Plain a year ago I ricked my ankle once on a big Divisional do – a three day stunt, it was – over Codford way; and you let your groom take me back to camp on your horse, while you went on with the job on foot. I remember alright and then I saw you again once over the other side. We were passing through one of the villages behind Albert, I misremember the name – never was no good at them French names. I'll wager they don't get many of our boys unwounded, I was past walking when they got me, an' me rifle had been smashed in me hand an' had no stock left. No they don't get our boys putting their hands up asking for it and in that sort of scrapping you don't hardly get unwounded prisoners. There was fourteen of us altogether and I was the only one from my Battalion. It was when the Boches got Contalmaison back an' they got us before we could get away. The chap that found me he looked a likely enough lad. You'd hardly believe he was a Boche until you found the poor chap could speak no other word but his own German. Big open-faced, light haired chap he was, with blue eyes and freckles on his face, like many a farm lad you see in England. A strong chap too for he picked me up and carried me easy, over his shoulder, an I'm no feather-weight, an' what he said sounded friendly enough, My knees were giving out an' I didn't take a lot of notice at the time. Next thing I know I'm in a dug-out, there was eight or nine others all wounded lying there. I was in the front, right in the mouth of the dug-out, where I could see the trench, where a lot of Boche were sitting smoking cigarettes and talking. Bye an' bye a German officer comes along, I knew he was coming by the way they dropped their smokin' an' talkin'. They came to attention pretty smart, I'll say that for them. The officer spoke to the sergeant and we were all dragged out of the dug-out and taken down the trench to another one, down a lot of steps must ha' been twenty five feet down I would say. That was in the afternoon and all that night and the next day and the next day after that we lay there and all that passed our lips was some dirty water in a jar that a tall Boche on sentry in the passage gave us the first morning. You could hear the firing from down there of course, but it was all a bit dull like, so you couldn't tell which side it was coming from, anyway we didn't know our front from our rear. It must have been about the third day, as I reckin it must have been early in the morning, the big gun fire got that heavy one shell seemed to be running into another and all the earth shook and quivered like an earthquake. It went on for a long time like that and at last it eased off a bit, seemed to lift like, and the next thing we know is that bombs were burstin' in the passage just outside. One feller said it was the Boche blowin' us up but I saw we had no sentry an' somehow I reckoned that it must be our boys back in Contalmaison again. I'd have been out of it quick if it hadn't been for my knees. There was a young Lance-corporal next to me, wounded in the shoulder, very sick an' queer he was, I asked him to get along the passage a bit an' shout to tell that we were English in there. He got out

Major Burnett Tabrum Second in Command 26th Battalion wounded during the attack.

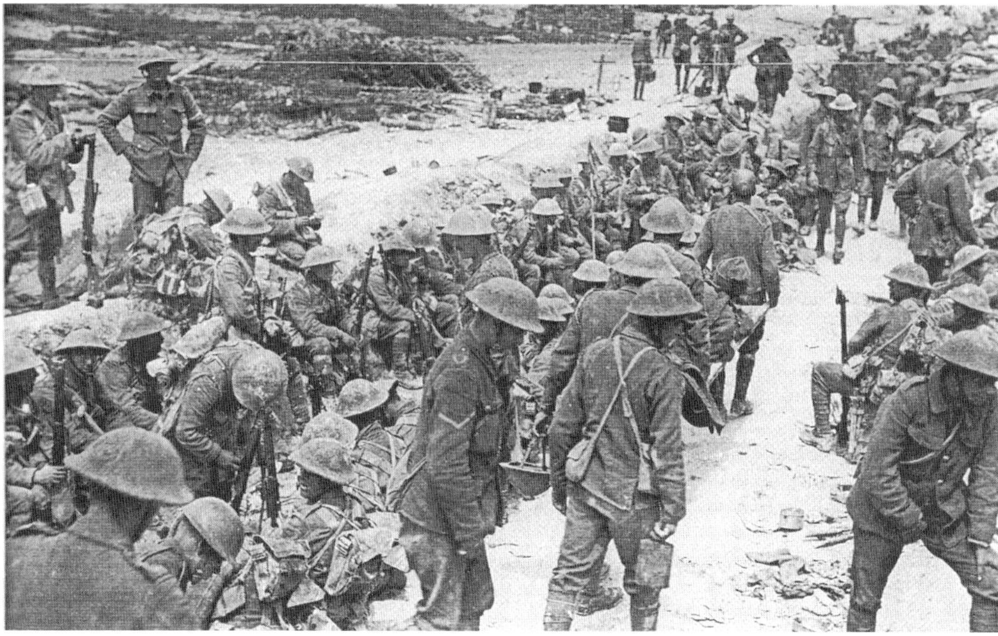

Infantry waiting to move forward into the front line. *(Taylor Library)*

alright, a plucky lad because two more bombs burst after he started. An' then the next thing we knew there was a young English officer down among us, an' half a dozen of our boys after him. My God sir were we glad to see his face! I tried to come to attention and salute him. "Steady Lad" he said to me, "You're not quite fit for parade yet you know, we'll soon have you out and a bit more comfortable." And he did too bless him, that officer gave me a drink of tea with rum in it, out of his own water bottle, an' the stretcher bearers got me soon after that, It was good to know our boys were back in Contalmaison again.'

From this report it is unclear which regiment the soldier came from, the reference to Salisbury Plain leads one to assume he is from 34th Division. However apart from the small parties previously mentioned the vast majority of 103 Brigade and the rest of the Division did not get as far as Contalmaison.

One of those who got into the German fourth line was Private George Lowery of Crook and writing to friends in Willington he said,

'I will never forget the 1st of July, when we got to the first line of German trenches you should have seen the Germans throwing their hands up and shouting, "Mercy Kamerade"! I was hit in the neck about 12.30. It took me about four hours to get back and if I had not had a bomb in my pocket I would not be alive to-day. I got as far as the German fourth line and as I was coming out I met a great big German officer. I had no rifle only this bomb. He fired at me with his revolver and missed me. Just as he was going to fire a second time I threw the bomb, which blew his head off. I managed to get his revolver and flash lamp. I sold the revolver to one of our officers for ten francs but still have the flash lamp which no one will get.'

The men in the Lochnagar crater were from nearly all the regiments of the Division and one officer in the group was Second Lieutenant J H Turnbull of the 10/Lincolns, who writing in *Chequers*, the 34th Divisional OCA magazine, recalled being in the crater,

25/987 Corporal Felix Grugan, C Company 25th Battalion was transferred to the 24th Battalion Royal Fusiliers on 31 August 1918. His brother was killed serving with D company and his cousin was with him in C Company. A third brother was KiA with 6/ Durham LI.

24/981 Private Tommy Cassidy 24th Battalion. He recalled, 'We reached the village and just wandered about, but had to come back because we were out of ammo.'

'A Tyneside Irish officer gave me a drop of whisky, which cheered me up. There were three unhurt officers there. Tried to get a runner back to HQ, sent about four but don't know what happened to them. Later the Tyneside Irish officer went back and got through, but was wounded. For some unknown reason our artillery started shelling us with whizz bangs. Our planes were sailing close overhead and though I shone a mirror up they took no notice. In the end I sent an orderly to Colonel Howard to ask permission to send a red flare up, which he gave. Colonel Howard was badly wounded and has since died.'

Pte Sam Lawrence 26/1028 of Gateshead. Transferred to Royal Scots after being wounded.

When he was wounded Colonel Howard was picked up by two men, the Bombing Sergeant of D Company, Patrick Butler, and Corporal James Bonner. Between them they managed to get their Commanding Officer into a shell hole and from there into the Lochnagar Crater. When the news that Colonel Howard was wounded reached Brigade Headquarters, Captain D H James, the OC of the Trench Mortar Battery, sent forward a stretcher party to bring the Colonel out but he died on the way.[2] (Colonel Howard and Sergeant Butler are buried in Ovillers Military Cemetery, James Bonner is commemorated on the Thiepval Memorial but his rank is given as Private.)

Officers and SNCOs D Company 27th Battalion early 1916.
Standing left to right: Sgt Oswald, Sgt J Thompson (RSM MC), Sgt J Tighe (CSM MiD) CSM J Menham, CQMS T McKenna, Sgt G Wigley (CSM DCM), LSgt J O'Hara.
Officers left to right: Lt R C Burluraux, Capt R B Pritchard (DSO MC), Capt J V Bibby (DSO), 2Lt E J Blight, Lt Simpson, 2Lt D O'Hanlon.
Seated NCO's left to right: Lsgt T Patton, Sgt J Rayne, Sgt R Madden (MSM DCM MM MiD), Sgt T Coates.

By late afternoon it was obvious that the attack had been a disaster, and Major J M Prior with Captain George Swinburn of the 24th Battalion, collected 160 men of the 24th and 27th Battalions, and 75 Royal Engineers from the German front line trench. Taking with them water, food, bombs and ammunition this group then filled the gap between the 34th Division and the 21st Division. In his diary however, Captain Swinburn records that his party actually fought their way into and held Scots Redoubt on the 2nd of July and that they were severely bombarded on a number of occasions.

Captain J V Bibby also took some men of the 27th Battalion and held a gap in the German support line, defending the flank of the 21st Division. Successful bombing raids were carried out against the enemy held positions whilst during the time the party was holding the line the enemy shelled them very heavily, but did not follow up with an infantry assault. Both these parties held their advanced positions until relieved on the morning of the 4th of July by troops of 69 Brigade.

The majority of the wounded had to make their own way out of the trenches, for any stretcher bearers who dared to move in the open were shot down and many of the bandsmen, who were also stretcher bearers, were killed in this way.

> *'Well after being hit, I crawled into a hole and waited about two hours, but the barrage came in conveniently near, so I crawled to our lines and hopped and hobbled to the dressing station. The advance was inspiring, but the sights and sounds of the return journey are not pleasant and are better omitted. That's all, rather an inglorious part in a great enterprise, but my little bit, which I would not have missed for the world.' (Captain Rigby 27th Battalion)*

'Well conscience is a funny thing and I say candidly that I do not wish to see anything like it again.' (Lance Corporal J Higgins 25th Battalion)

> *'It was 10 a.m. when I was blown up in the air by a shell which killed some of our men and wounded a lot. I was knocked sick and was lying in "No-Man's-Land" for about two hours before I knew where I was. Then, hearing the rattle of rifle fire, I crept into a shell hole and lay there for about two hours. It took a bonny long time to creep 400 yards back to our trenches again. I was lost a bit in "No-Man's-Land". I pulled myself together a bit by drinking my water, then found my way out on to the road where the Red Cross vans were taking wounded to safety. I was put in a Red Cross van and taken away down the country.' (Private James Tunney 26th Battalion)*

> *'We had to stagger back over the corpses of our mates, We reached the British trenches and I sat totally stunned. Young lads were all around me, some were sobbing hysterically, they'd seen things no one should have to see.' (Lance Corporal Michael Manley 26th Battalion)*

> *'Afterwards I heard the Battalion rollcall in a small trench. Poor old Tyneside Irish, we made the sacrifice to pave the way for the advance. It has proved a success. The village which was our objective has fallen.' (Lance Sergeant Edward Dyke 26th Battalion)*

But Sergeant Dyke was wrong, for the village of Contalmaison had not fallen and neither had La Boisselle, but this was not for lack of effort on the part of the Tyneside Irish or the other troops of the 34th Division. The blame must be laid squarely on the shoulders of the Corps and Army commanders who ordered the men to advance in such a stupid formation over open ground, in front of an enemy still full of fight, and ready to defend the ground they held.

The lucky ones, and those who were wounded early in the battle, reached the Casualty Clearing Stations quickly and were evacuated on the same day. The surviving records for 3 and 34 Casualty Clearing Stations, held at the Public Record Office, at Kew, show that many slightly wounded, entering on the 1st and 2nd of July, were evacuated on the same day whereas more seriously wounded were stabilised and not evacuated until the 5th. Despite all the accounts of hand to hand fighting and the use of cold steel, only one soldier 24/1550 Private D Howard from Liverpool, is shown as having a bayonet wound but of course the records are far from complete so it may well be that bayonet wounds were taken to other CCS. At least one man, 27/626 Private D Rafferty of Bedlington, lay on the battlefield for nearly

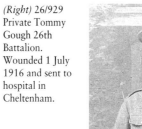

(*Right*) 26/929 Private Tommy Gough 26th Battalion. Wounded 1 July 1916 and sent to hospital in Cheltenham.

24/1524 Private Jeramiah O'Conner 24th Battalion reached the 34th Casualty Clearing Station on the 2nd of July and was evacuated on the 5th.

Miners, discharged soldiers and men on leave in Craghead, 26/206 Pte Frank Ellison kneeling second from left.

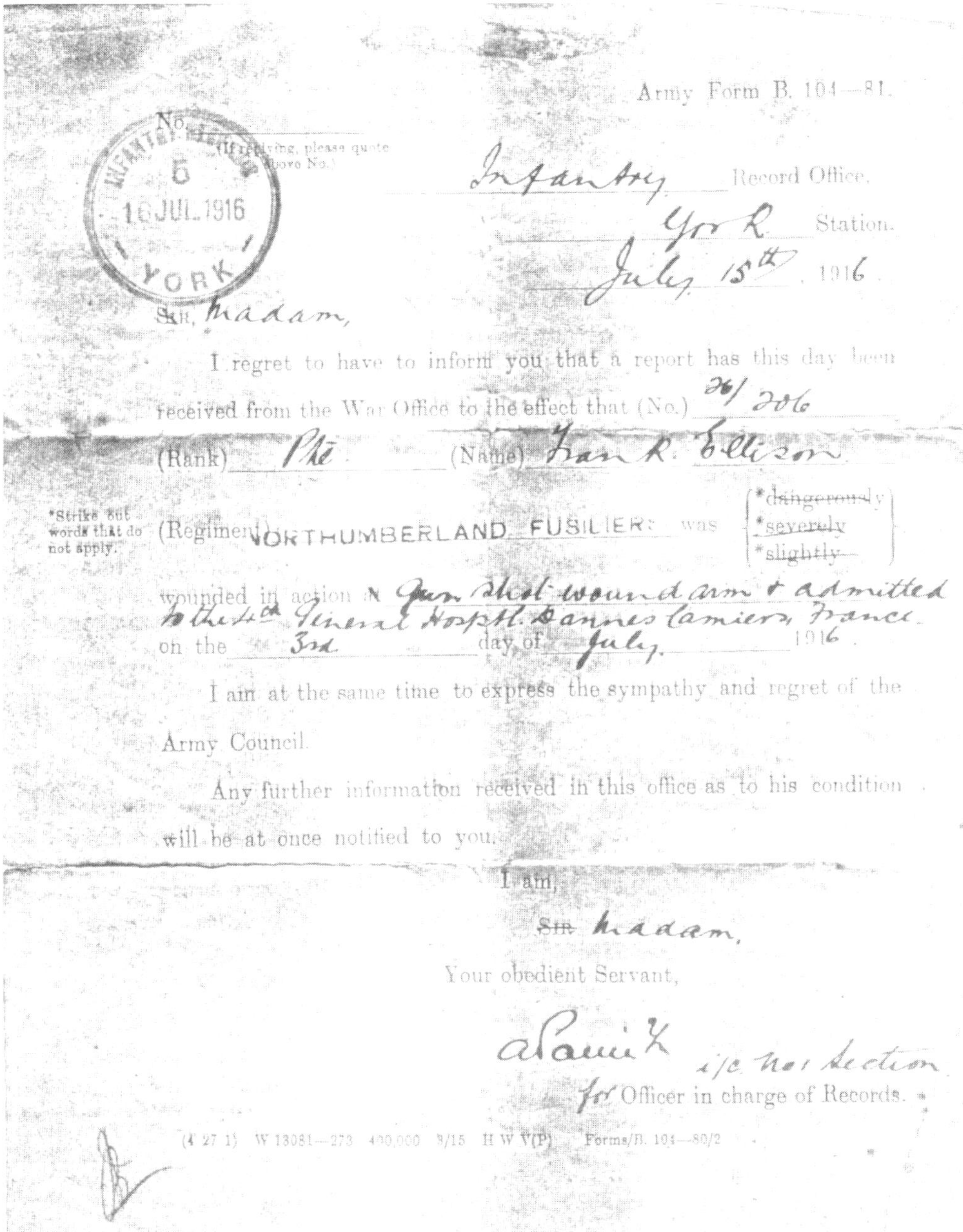

Army Form B. 104—81.

No. ________ (If replying, please quote above No.)

INFANTRY RECORDS 6 16 JUL. 1916 YORK

Infantry Record Office,

York Station.

July 15th 1916.

~~Sir,~~ Madam,

I regret to have to inform you that a report has this day been received from the War Office to the effect that (No.) 26/206

(Rank) Pte (Name) Frank Ellison

*Strike out words that do not apply.

(Regiment) NORTHUMBERLAND FUSILIERS was ~~*dangerously~~ *severely ~~*slightly~~

wounded in action ~~at~~ Gun shot wound arm & admitted to the 4th General Hosptl. Dannes Camiers, France.

on the 3rd day of July 1916.

I am at the same time to express the sympathy and regret of the Army Council.

Any further information received in this office as to his condition will be at once notified to you.

I am,

~~Sir~~ Madam,

Your obedient Servant,

A Lamick i/c No. 1 Section

for Officer in charge of Records.

(4 27 1) W 13081—273 400,000 8/15 H W V(P) Forms/B. 104—80/2

Army Form B 104 sent to Mrs Ellison in Craghead, saying her son Frank was wounded. This was the third one she received. His two brothers were Killed in Action with the Royal Naval Division.

a week and did not reach 34 CCS until the 8th of July. These were the fortunate ones.

The casualties of the Tyneside Irish Brigade, on 1 July 1916 were tremendous but it is sad to relate that the majority of those who died were never identified, and lie in unmarked graves.

The news of the casualties did not take long to reach the North and for the families of well-off middle-class officers there were condolence letters, edged in black, as well as, for many, a card from the Bishop of Durham. But for the hundreds of miners' families, there was just the buff Army Form B 104, notifying that the family breadwinner, or a son, was a casualty.

The news arrived in many ways and in Willington young Rose Cross was waiting for a birthday card from her father, but the only thing the postman brought was the telegram announcing his death. When the telegram arrived, her mother Mary Cross was baking bread. Rose, the capable twelve year old, finished the baking, while her sister Charlotte looked after two year old Frank and the mother meanwhile wrote a letter to her own mother telling her the sad news. She gave the letter to seven year old William who, with a neighbour's son, walked the three miles to Stanley, Crook where both boys expected a nice tea at Grandma Harvey's house, but this was not to be, as this home was also in mourning. Young William found that not only was his father dead, but also his uncle, James Benedict Harvey, and his Uncle Michael had been wounded as also a cousin, another James

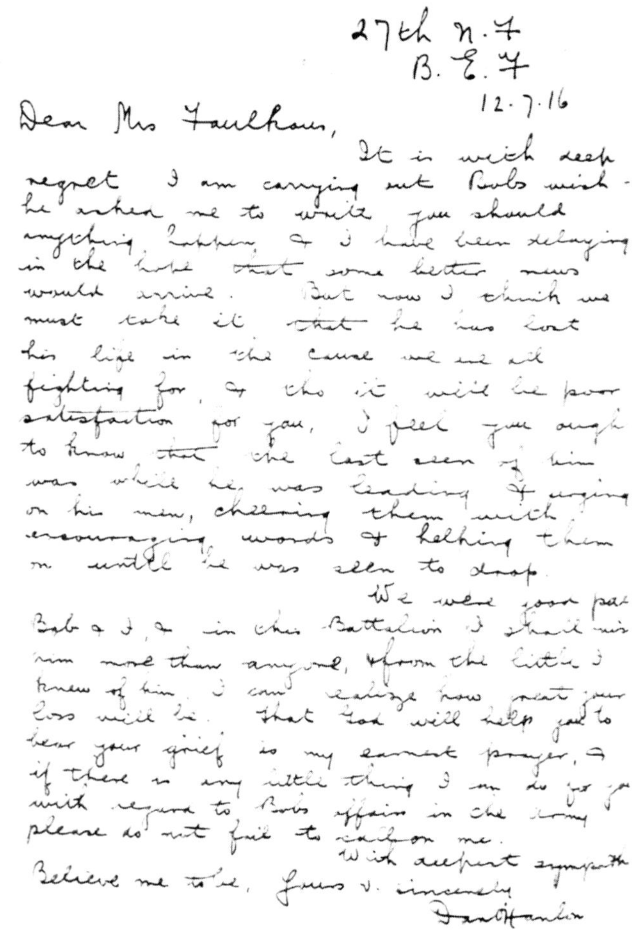

27th N.F
B.E.F
12.7.16

Dear Mrs Faulkous,

It is with deep regret I am carrying out Bobs wish - he asked me to write you should anything happen & I have been delaying in the hope that some better news would arrive. But now I think we must take it that he has lost his life in the cause we are all fighting for, & tho it will be poor satisfaction for you, I feel you ought to know that the last seen of him was while he was leading & urging on his men, cheering them with encouraging words & helping them on until he was seen to drop.

We were good pals Bob & I, & in this Battalion I shall miss him more than anyone, & from the little I knew of him I can't realize how great your loss will be. That God will help you to bear your grief is my earnest prayer, & if there is any little thing I can do for you with regard to Bobs affairs in the Army please do not fail to call on me.

With deepest sympathy

Believe me to be, Yours v. sincerely

Dan O'Hanlon

Captain Robert Falkous 27th Battalion and the letter to his mother from Second Lieutenant Dan O'Hanlon.

Harvey.The following October another cousin, Frank Harvey, would be killed with 12/Durham Light Infantry.

The Quartermaster of the 27th Battalion, Lieutenant & QM Francis Treanor, had the task of going round the dressing-stations trying to locate and list the battalion's wounded. To Michael MacDonagh, for his book *The Irish at The Front*, he wrote,

'The ready jest and witty retort were as abundant as ever, in the dressing-stations afterwards I saw many of them, and there was still the same heroic fortitude and the exchange of comments, many grimly humorous, as the poor fellow who remarked when asked if he had any souvenirs. "Be danged twas no place for picking up jewellery."'

Manning a post just behind the line that weekend was Captain Jack Arnold, who had been left out of battle, a fact he said probably saved his life, but he recalled the wounded coming back.

'On the evening of the 1st of July the walking wounded both men and horses began to trickle back and as luck would have it many men of our brigade passed by my post and I was able to do a little for their comfort. It was not until the following day that we got any inkling of the magnitude of the casualties and the words "dead" were passed from mouth to mouth regarding so many of one's friends.'

In South Shields Mrs Girling having received the official telegram, finally had a letter from her husband's platoon commander, Second Lieutenant Glass, whose letter brought the final confirmation of her husband's death.

B Company
27th NF
B.E.F.
13 July 1916

Dear Madam

It was with the deepest possible regret that I received today the official report of the death of your husband 959 Pte E Girling, who had been reported missing since our attack on the 1st of July.

He was in my own platoon prior to joining the machine gun section and it was a pleasure to be associated with him in any capacity. He deservedly won the esteem and affection of all ranks, who join with me in tendering our heartfelt sympathy to you and all his sorrowing relations and friends.

He fell in one of the bravest attacks ever made by the British soldiers and though the cost in precious lives was considerable the victory was complete.

I am yours very truly
J B Glass 2nd Lt

Not very far away, in Low Fell, a similar letter was delivered and when Mrs Falkous received the news of her son's death, she tried to obtain more information, writing several times to the Army Graves Registration and to the Red Cross. On the 12th of July, Lieutenant Dan O'Hanlon wrote to her,

'Dear Mrs Falkous,

It is with deep regret I am carrying out Bob's wish – he asked me to write you should anything happen + I have been delaying in the hope that some better news would arrive. But now I think we must take it that he has lost his life in the cause we are all fighting for, + tho it will be poor satisfaction to you, I feel you ought to know that the last seen of him was while he was leading + urging on his men, cheering them with encouraging words + helping them on until he was seen to

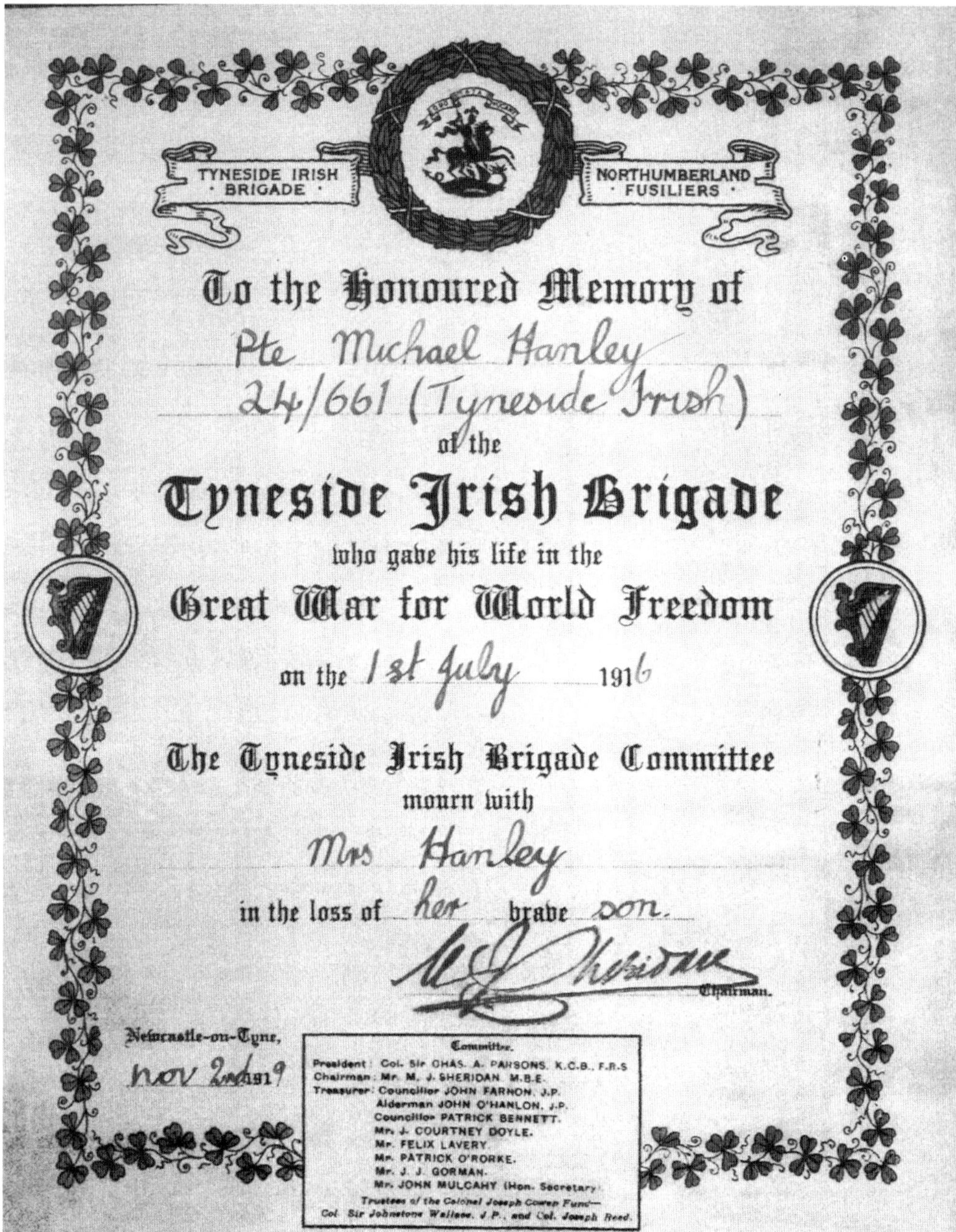

TYNESIDE IRISH · BRIGADE ·

NORTHUMBERLAND · FUSILIERS ·

To the Honoured Memory of

Pte Michael Hanley

24/661 (Tyneside Irish)

of the

Tyneside Irish Brigade

who gave his life in the

Great War for World Freedom

on the 1st July 1916

The Tyneside Irish Brigade Committee

mourn with

Mrs Hanley

in the loss of her brave son.

Chairman.

Newcastle-on-Tyne,

nov 2nd 1919

Committee.

President: Col. Sir CHAS. A. PARSONS, K.C.B., F.R.S

Chairman: Mr. M. J. SHERIDAN M.B.E.

Treasurer: Councillor JOHN FARNON, J.P.

Alderman JOHN O'HANLON, J.P.

Councillor PATRICK BENNETT.

Mr. J. COURTNEY DOYLE.

Mr. FELIX LAVERY.

Mr. PATRICK O'RORKE.

Mr. J. J. GORMAN.

Mr. JOHN MULCAHY (Hon. Secretary)

Trustees of the Colonel Joseph Cowen Fund—

Col. Sir Johnstone Wallace, J.P., and Col. Joseph Reed.

Scroll given to the families of the dead by the Tyneside Irish Committee. The shamrock was in green and St George in black on a gold background.

(Opposite page) Scroll given to the families of the dead. 26/1275 Lance Corporal Michael Tyman Killed in Action 1 July 1916. Buried in Ovillers Military Cemetry.

HE whom this scroll commemorates was numbered among those who, at the call of King and Country, left all that was dear to them, endured hardness, faced danger, and finally passed out of the sight of men by the path of duty and self-sacrifice, giving up their own lives that others might live in freedom.

Let those who come after see to it that his name be not forgotten.

L/Cpl. Michael Tyman
Northumberland Fusiliers

drop. We were good pals Bob + I in this Battalion I shall miss him more than anyone, from the little I knew of him I can realize how great your loss will be. That God will help you to bear your grief is my earnest prayer, + if there is any little thing I can do for you with regards to Bob's affairs in the Army please do not fail to call on me.

With deepest sympathy
Believe me to be Yours v sincerely
Dan O'Hanlon.'

Mrs Falkous also received a short note from the the Captain's batman Private Greaves, stating the circumstances of the Captain's death and his own wounding.

Lieutenant Dan O'Hanlon also wrote to his father Alderman J O'Hanlon the Mayor of Wallsend and again the same story was told,

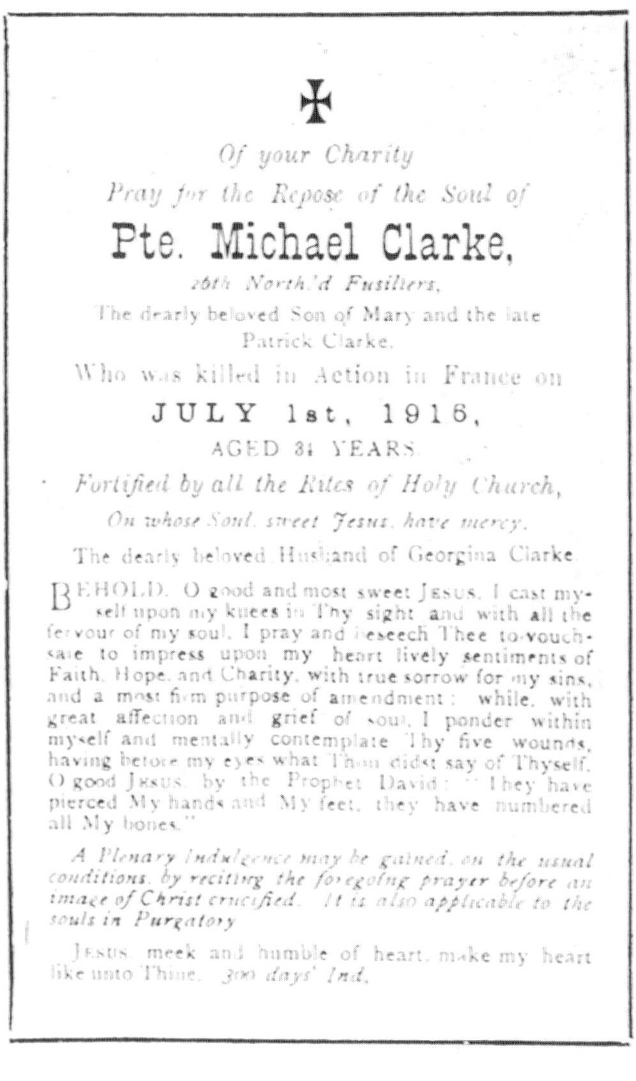
✠

Of your Charity

Pray for the Repose of the Soul of

Pte. Michael Clarke,

26th North'd Fusiliers,

The dearly beloved Son of Mary and the late Patrick Clarke.

Who was killed in Action in France on

JULY 1st, 1916,

AGED 34 YEARS.

Fortified by all the Rites of Holy Church,

On whose Soul, sweet Jesus, have mercy.

The dearly beloved Husband of Georgina Clarke.

BEHOLD, O good and most sweet JESUS, I cast myself upon my knees in Thy sight and with all the fervour of my soul, I pray and beseech Thee to vouchsafe to impress upon my heart lively sentiments of Faith, Hope, and Charity, with true sorrow for my sins, and a most firm purpose of amendment: while, with great affection and grief of soul, I ponder within myself and mentally contemplate Thy five wounds, having before my eyes what Thou didst say of Thyself, O good JESUS, by the Prophet David: "They have pierced My hands and My feet, they have numbered all My bones."

A Plenary Indulgence may be gained, on the usual conditions, by reciting the foregoing prayer before an image of Christ crucified. It is also applicable to the souls in Purgatory.

JESUS, meek and humble of heart, make my heart like unto Thine. *300 days' Ind.*

26/132 Private Michael Clarke 26th Battalion missing in action 1st July 1916, his death was confirmed in February 1917.

'wave after wave going steadily on and on in spite of the fact that all around them their comrades were falling wounded or killed from the hurricane of fire from enemy rifles and machine guns.'

Further on he wrote,

'If individual cases of bravery were always recorded, almost every man of the Brigade would need to be mentioned.'

Many other families applied to the Red Cross for information and the Red Cross produced lists of those missing, about whom they had had requests for information, which were circulated in the hope that someone would be able to pass on news of a loved one. On the 24th July, in Thornley, Mrs Soulsby, unable to bring herself to write, arranged for a letter to be sent to the Casualty Section at the War Office, but it took until the 12th of August to get a reply, which simply stated that her husband 26/643 Private Robert Soulsby had been missing since the 1st of July.

Major-General Ingouville-Williams, commanding the 34th Division wrote to the Chairman of the Tyneside Committees, and referred to his soldiers of 102 and 103 Brigades as,

'MY GALLANT TYNESIDERS'

'To the chairman of the Tyneside Committee, it is with greatest pride and deepest regret that I wish to inform you that the Division which included the Tyneside Irish and Scottish covered itself with glory on 1 July 1916, but its losses were very heavy.

Everyone testifies to the magnificent work they did that day and it is the admiration of all. I, their commander, will never forget their splendid advance through the curtain of German fire. It was simply wonderful and they behaved like veterans. Tyneside can well be proud of them and although they will sorrow for all my brave and faithful comrades, it is some consolation to know they died not in vain and that their gallant attack was of the greatest service to the Army on that day.'

Major General Ingouville Williams (Inky Bill), GOC 34th Division: 'My gallant Tynesiders... they behaved like veterans'.

The NCO's and men who wrote home were concerned with the good name of the Regiment and were keen that it should not be tarnished in any way.

'You know how the old 'Fifth' kept up its traditions. Well the Tyneside Irish lived up to them on Saturday morning, July 1st. The pity is so many were mowed down in upholding the name of the 'Old and Bold'. They were a credit to the old country. The nearest and dearest of those who are no more, when their first sorrow is over, can say with pride, "He was one of the Tyneside Irish".' (CQMS John Connolly 24th Battalion)

'I am sure the traditions of the 'Fighting Fifth' were not disgraced by the display of the Tyneside Irish. They were magnificent and it may be some little consolation to all who have suffered the loss of some dear one, to know that they all died facing their enemy.' (Lance Corporal J Higgins 25th Battalion)

Accurate figures concerning the casualties for 1st July 1916 are not easy to come by, as each battalion presented their figures in a different way. Brigade and Divisional war diaries also give conflicting information. Some men who were missing turned up, whilst some others reported wounded were in fact dead.

The minimum casualties were as follows:-

	Officers		Other ranks	
	Killed	Wounded	**Killed**	Wounded
24th Battalion	5	13	142	474
25th Battalion	4	14	140	351
26th Battalion	8	11	148	322
27th Battalion	5	15	144	375
Totals	**22**	**53**	**574**	**1522**

It is hard to calculate true figures for deaths because some wounded did not die from their wounds until years later. CQMS Connolly died in February 1918 having lost a leg, and 27/311 Private J Harvey, from Crook, of the 27th battalion,[3] was reported in the Durham Advertiser as dying from wounds in 1924. Should they be included with the dead or the wounded?

Trying to calculate the wounded is just as hard. The *Saint George's Gazette*, the regimental journal of the Northumberland Fusiliers, was still reporting 1st of July casualties in the November 1916 issue. Some wounded were not reported in the newspapers at all, so estimated figures are the best available.

24/506 Pte Pat Quin. dow 9 July 1916

24/1168 Private John Wilson of Blackhill was wounded on 1 July 1916 and on his return to the front joined the 25th Battalion.

26/143 Pte Mason Carr. kia 1 July 1916

24/1233 Sergeant Stanley Cox of Easington was wounded on 1 July 1916 and on his return to the front joined the 10th Battalion.

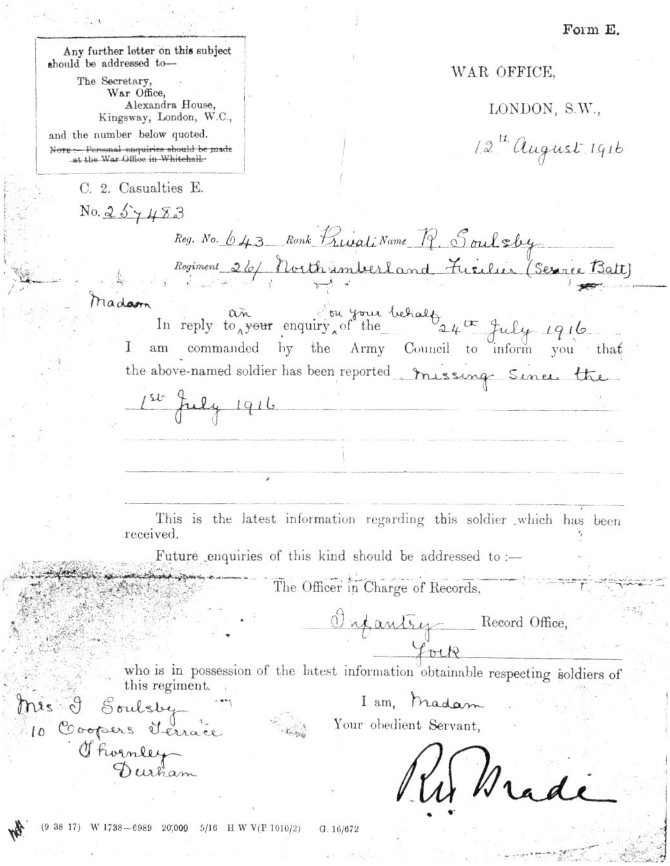
Form E.

Any further letter on this subject should be addressed to—
The Secretary,
War Office,
Alexandra House,
Kingsway, London, W.C.,
and the number below quoted.
~~Note:—Personal enquiries should be made at the War Office in Whitehall.~~

WAR OFFICE,
LONDON, S.W.,
12th August 1916

C. 2. Casualties E.
No. 257483

Reg. No. 643 Rank Private Name R. Soulsby
Regiment 26/ Northumberland Fusiliers (Service Batt)

Madam
In reply to an ~~your~~ enquiry on your behalf of the 24th July 1916 I am commanded by the Army Council to inform you that the above-named soldier has been reported missing since the 1st July 1916

This is the latest information regarding this soldier which has been received.

Future enquiries of this kind should be addressed to :—
The Officer in Charge of Records,
Infantry Record Office,
York
who is in possession of the latest information obtainable respecting soldiers of this regiment.

I am, Madam
Your obedient Servant,
R. W. Brade

Mrs J Soulsby
10 Coopers Terrace
Thornley
Durham

(9 38 17) W 1738—6989 20,000 5/16 H W V(P 1010/2) G. 16/672

26/643 Private and Mrs Soulsby and the letter she received from the War Office.

The Tokens

The Thiepval Memorial to the missing, records the names of 73,412 men who died in 1916 – 1918 and who have no known graves. Of these men the highest number of missing from any one regiment is 2,931 Northumberland Fusiliers. Of this total, 514 are original other ranks of the Tyneside Irish Battalions who died between the 1st and 4th of July 1916. This figure is only exceeded by the Tyneside Scottish Brigade with 590 missing. Therefore the Tyneside Battalions of the 34th Division had between them 37.6% of the whole regimental total of those missing. However, only 63 of those who originally enlisted into the Tyneside Irish Brigade, and who died on 1st July 1916, are buried in marked graves. Why is it that so many of these brave men lie in unknown graves?

The answer is quite simple. The vast majority of the men were coalminers and when working underground, the men filled tubs of coal which had to be sent to the surface. To identify who had filled the tub, the men were given tokens, which were fastened to the men's braces during working hours. When the men enlisted into the army they were issued with the standard British Army identity discs which were roughly the same size as a colliery token, and very quickly became known to the soldier as "me tokens". These also were often fastened to the braces rather than worn round the neck, as they should have been. This was all right until the soldier was killed in action, for when the burial party came along to identify the body, they would open the neck of the tunic to remove the identity disc. Of course, the Tyneside Irish and other Northumberland and Durham miners' identity discs were frequently not around the neck, so the body was placed in an unknown soldier's grave, all because 'the tokens' had been fastened to the man's braces.

Above and below: 24/608 John Cross Pioneer Corporal 24th Battalion whose body was recovererd but his grave destroyed in later fighting.

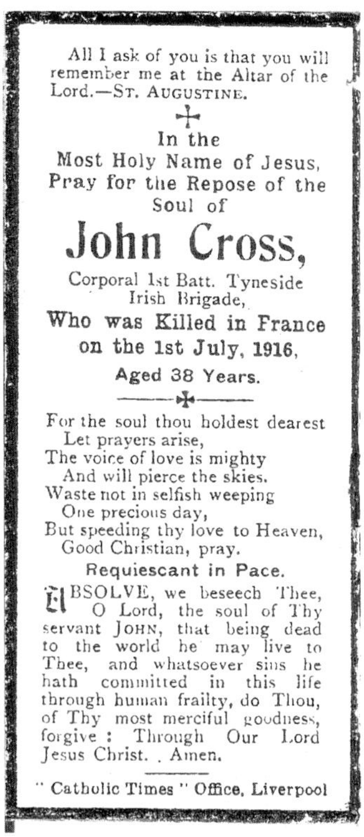

All I ask of you is that you will remember me at the Altar of the Lord.—St. Augustine.

✠

In the
Most Holy Name of Jesus,
Pray for the Repose of the
Soul of

John Cross,

Corporal 1st Batt. Tyneside
Irish Brigade,
**Who was Killed in France
on the 1st July, 1916,
Aged 38 Years.**

✠

For the soul thou holdest dearest
Let prayers arise,
The voice of love is mighty
And will pierce the skies.
Waste not in selfish weeping
One precious day,
But speeding thy love to Heaven,
Good Christian, pray.
Requiescant in Pace.

Absolve, we beseech Thee, O Lord, the soul of Thy servant John, that being dead to the world he may live to Thee, and whatsoever sins he hath committed in this life through human frailty, do Thou, of Thy most merciful goodness, forgive: Through Our Lord Jesus Christ. Amen.

"Catholic Times" Office, Liverpool

Note the figure 514 includes only July 1916 deaths. Other names of Tyneside Irishmen are on the Thiepval Memorial having been killed later in 1916 and in 1917. This fact would therefore increase the size of the Brigade percentage of missing.

On the 11th of July the Pioneers of 19/Northumberland Fusiliers crossed the battlefield. A reconnaissance party from the Battalion saw the results of the attack by the Tyneside Irish and Scottish, and the Battalion history states:

'The battlefield had not been cleared that was an impossibility in the circumstances. Tyneside Scottish and Tyneside Irish dead lay on the blasted field, in shell holes, in bits of trenches but chiefly in the open. Those not in the open seemed to have dragged their mutilated bodies into the partial shelter of the ruined pieces of trench. One man had died with his pay book on his knee, the writing of the first words of his will being his last act on earth. Another lay with his testament open on the ground, his thumb marking the place. Scenes of the battle baffled description.'

Later, in August, the Pioneers of 18/Northumberland Fusiliers were attached to one of the Irish Battalions and their history records,

'In Contalmaison we saw some graves of men of 103 Brigade who had been killed on 1st of July. So some of the brave lads did reach their objective on that dreadful day.'

Many soldiers' bodies were recovered and identified only to be lost in later fighting and Mrs Cross received her husband's personal effects, but yet never knew he had no known grave. Similarly Ted Colpitts' body was found and his diary returned to his next of kin. The last entry made after his death reads,

'1 July 1916, Ted aged 18 years, killed in this big battle - God Bless Him - RIP'

When the burial party recovered the remains of Private Patrick Solan of the 26th Battalion, they removed his home-made identification bracelet, and also one of the Tyneside Irish harps from his shoulder strap and sent them home. The harp had been almost cut in two by a bullet.

Having been presented with information regarding soldiers missing in action but not commemorated on memorials to the missing, on the 13th of March 1996 the Commonwealth War Graves Commission wrote to the author the following:

I write to let you know that the following servicemen have been established as war casualties.

HALL Pte William	25/1014 1 July 1916
ROUELL Cpl Thomas William	27/1186 1 July 1916
THOMPSON Pte William	26/1408 1 July 1916
FAIRHURST Pte Matthew	24/1191 1 July 1916
RAMSHAW L/Cpl James	27/1198 1 July 1916

The names of these casualties will be engraved on the Thiepval Memorial, France, with those of their comrades who died on the same date and have no known grave. These names further increase the Tyneside Irish total.

The work carried out in cross referencing the Tyneside Irish casualties revealed two strange occurrences that had happened during the Great War.

One soldier, Corporal William Henry Lofthouse, of the 24th Battalion, was apparently buried in two different places, Terlincthun Military Cemetery France, and St Nicholas' Cemetery in Durham City. The burial in Durham was noted when the following obituary was read in *The Durham Chronicle* for 14 July 1916.

'SOLDIERS FUNERAL AT DURHAM'

'Amid tokens of general regret, the interment took place at St Nicholas' Cemetery of Corporal William Henry Lofthouse, who died under painfully sad circumstances on Wednesday. Corporal Lofthouse who was a native of Langley Moor, joined the Tyneside Scottish and was afterwards transferred to the Tyneside Irish. He was home on his last leave at Christmas and then married Miss Cryer who resides in Gilesgate. He took part in the great forward movement on the 1st of July and received gunshot wounds in the thigh and back. He was ordered home and whilst on board the hospital ship St George and within sight of England his wounds proved fatal. His remains were brought to Durham on Sunday and interred the same day at St Nicholas Cemetery. Corporal Lofthouse, who was only 24 years of age, was well known in the Langley Moor district, being actively connected with the Independent Order of Good Templars' and was for many years the Superintendent of the Juvenile Tent.

In token of respect for their departed comrade, about fifty 'Good Templars' from Browney, Broompark and Langley Moor, attended in their regalia and headed the procession. Soldiers and buglers were also in attendance, whilst the streets were lined with sympathetic spectators. The coffin which was covered with a Union Jack and the Good Templars' regalia, was carried to

24/1668 Corporal William Henry Lofthouse photographed when he was serving with 34th Divisional Cyclist Company.

Grave of two soldiers on the battlefield. Taken near Ovillers, July 1916.

the hearse by Good Templars and was met at St Nicholas' Church by the Vicar (The Rev W Bothamley). The service in the church was very impressive and included the singing of the hymn "Jesu Lover of my Soul". At the graveside the Good Templars took part in the service and at the conclusion three volleys were fired and the "Last Post" sounded. Many beautiful tributes were received including a globe from his fellow workmen.'

There is nothing unusual about Corporal Lofthouse's obituary which is reproduced above – they appeared in local newspapers in their hundreds throughout the summer and autumn of 1916. However this conflicted with information extracted from the War Graves Register for Terlincthun Military Cemetery in France which showed that the Corporal was buried there.

There was no trace of the grave in St Nicholas' Cemetery, but at the County Record Office in Durham, a check of the burial register gave the following information.

Entry 2155 9th July 1916 William Henry Lofthouse 193 Gilesgate Durham. Age 24. Buried 9/7/16. Died of wounds received during the great advance of the British Forces from Albert, France, July 1916.

William Henry Lofthouse was by trade a coke drawer at Sleetburn Colliery (New Brancepeth) when he enlisted into the 29th (Reserve) Tyneside Scottish Battalion of the Northumberland Fusiliers in the late summer of 1915 and was allotted Regimental Number 29/1688. When the 34th Division assembled on Salisbury Plain he moved south with one of the other battalions of the Tyneside Scottish and on the formation of the 34th Divisional Cyclist Company, men from all the infantry battalions of the division were transferred to the new company. Corporal Lofthouse was among those transferred and as is stated in the obituary, he came home on leave in December and married Mary Cryer, a girl he had been courting for quite a few years. As previously stated, the Divisional Cyclists' were transferred into the 24th Battalion, with whom the unfortunate corporal met his fate.

A letter was sent to the War Graves Commission asking if it could confirm where Corporal Lofthouse was actually buried and while awaiting the reply, an article in the *Northern Echo* led to a meeting with the niece of Corporal Lofthouse, who kindly supplied a copy of a family photograph. Her husband was able to supply the information that, after the war, Mrs Lofthouse was informed that her husband's body had been identified in France. We can only imagine the shock the poor woman must have suffered after having been married for such a short time, and having lost and apparently buried her husband, his remains were now said to be in France.

24/585 CQMS John Connolly 24th Battalion wounded on the 1st of July his leg was amputated at Wharncliffe Hospital Sheffield in September.

After a long search by the Commonwealth War Graves Commission it transpired that the body of the soldier buried in France had been found by a French farmer at the following Grid reference, Sheet 57d X20 a 5. 5. This is just in front of the German front line, not far from the Lochnagar Crater at La Boisselle and this casualty was identified as a soldier from the 24th Battalion because of his shoulder titles and the remains of his Red Shamrock battle patch. There were also the remains of an NCO's rank badge and a British Army boot and for some unexplained reason he was identified as Corporal Lofthouse. Given the information about the burial in Durham, it is now realized that this was incorrect and that it was in fact another man. But who? Six Corporals of the 24th Battalion were killed, missing or died of wounds on 1 July 1916 viz: 24/118 Cpl R Mackie, buried Ovilliers Military Cemetery. 24/608 Cpl J Cross, body recovered and buried but subsequently lost, name on Thiepval Memorial. 24/1668 Cpl W H Lofthouse, buried St Nicholas Cemetery, Durham City. 24/1574 Cpl T Connelly, missing, name on Thiepval Memorial. 24/1703 Cpl A Ramsey, missing, name on Thiepval Memorial. 24/1712 Cpl R Ruse, missing, name on Thiepval Memorial.

The man buried at Terlincthun Military Cemetery must be one of the last three named, given that the casualty was identified as a corporal of the 24th Battalion identified by his badge of rank,

The opening of the Tyneside seat at La Boisselle, the memorial to the Tyneside Irish and Tyneside Scottish Brigades.

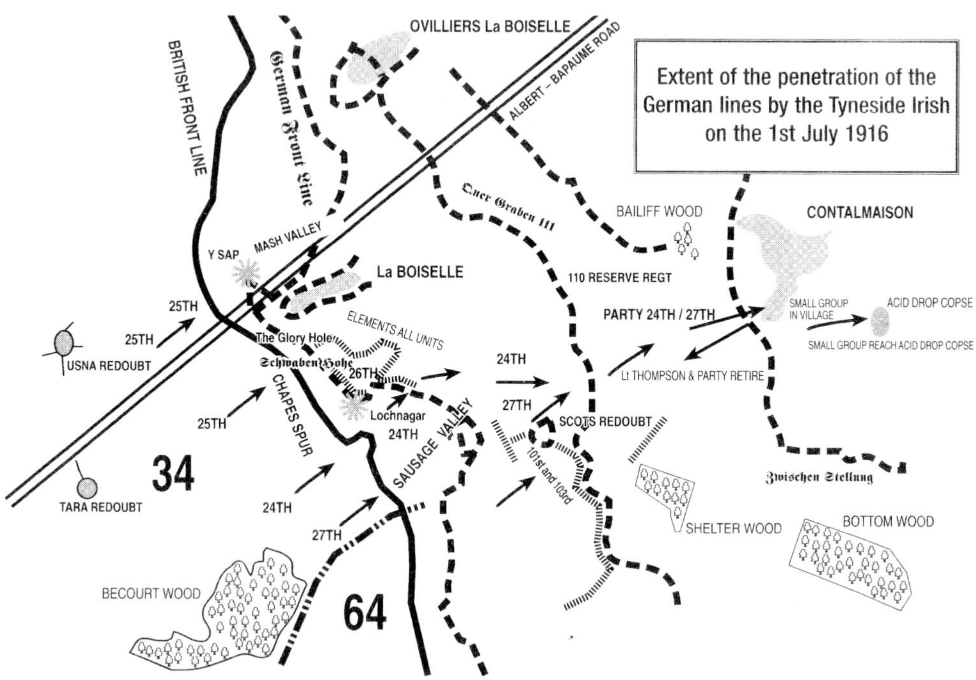

Tyneside Irish shoulder titles and his Red Shamrock battle patch, but who he was perhaps will never be known.

The further and perhaps stranger, facts to turn up are about 24/1543 Private James Clayton.

An Entry on page 102 of Part 10 of *Soldiers Died in the Great War, The Northumberland Fusiliers*, shows that the above named was born in Everton and enlisted in Liverpool, and that he was killed in action on 1st July 1916.

An entry in WO/329 (War and Victory Medal Rolls) in the Public Record Office at Kew, shows that Private Clayton was ineligible for his medals and that they were returned under Para 1743 of King's Regulations.

When trying to locate his place of burial, or the memorial commemorating him, no trace of an entry could be found. Furthermore there was no entry for a Death Certificate at St Catherine's House and when the list of uncommemorated men was submitted to the Commonwealth War Graves Commission, Private Clayton was included in the list. Trying to confirm his service details and his death in action, the CWGC researcher contacted many sources of information on Great War soldiers, Army Records, Department of Social Security etc. In all cases there was no trace of Private Clayton and it is as if he had never existed. Unable to confirm his service details, he is at the moment uncommemorated by the Commonwealth War Graves Commission.

Notes

1. These were probably Royal Scots, the Tyneside Scottish were well to the left of Lew Shaughnessy.
2. Related by Captain D H James in 'Chequers' 1939-40.
3. No relation to Sgt J B and Cpl M Harvey.

Chapter Seven

Re-organisation, replacements, and the rest of 1916

'If machine guns join the muddle–Never mind.
Though you're lying in a puddle–Never mind
MINOR WORRIES FROM THE WIPERS TIMES

The first unit of the Brigade to be withdrawn from action was the 25th Battalion, at 6.00 a.m. on the 2nd of July. Stragglers were collected from all over the battlefield, and the remnants of the shattered Battalion made their way to Belle Vue Farm, where they bivouaced for the night, and stood by in readiness for further fighting, if required. The men stood by all day on the 3rd of July, and at 9.00 a.m. on the following day they moved to Long Valley, near Millencourt, where, in heavy rain, they pitched tents for the remnants of the 34th Division, which was in the process of being withdrawn from the battle. On the 5th of July they struck camp, and moved to Hennencourt Wood, where, with the rest of the Brigade, they were inspected by General Poultney, the Corps Commander.

The 26th Battalion survivors also followed the route via Belle Vue Farm and Long Valley to Hennencourt Wood.

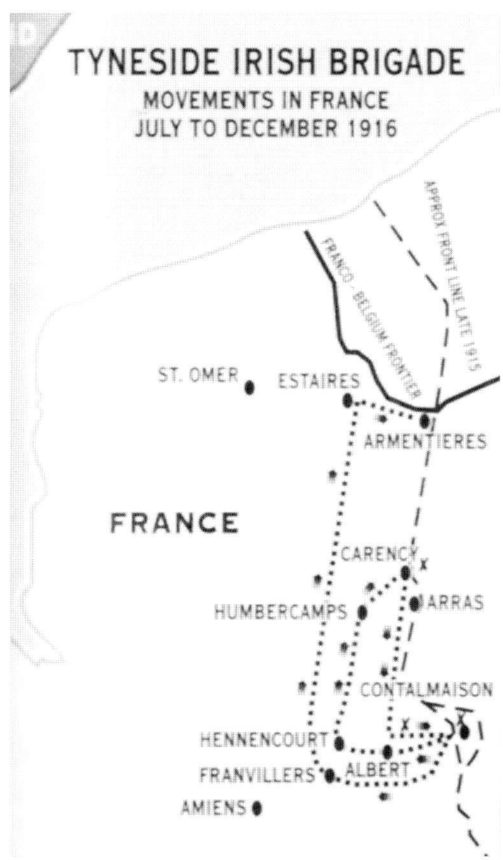

Those of the 24th Battalion were relieved in the line at Scots Redoubt at 4.00 a.m. on the 4th of July by troops of 69 Brigade, and moved to Becourt Wood when, after a short rest they moved to Long Valley and then on to Hennencourt Wood.

The 27th Battalion moved on the 4th of July to Bouzincourt and spent the night there, moving to Hennencourt Wood the following day.

Both of the Tyneside Brigades and 18/Northumberland Fusiliers, were now withdrawn from the 34th Division, and came under command of the 37th Division, which was then holding the line around Monchy au Boi, just north of the Somme sector.

Command of the Battalions now passed as follows:

24th Battalion (1st Tyneside Irish) Major J M Prior; 25th Battalion (2nd Tyneside Irish) Major T D Temple, 27th Battalion; 26th Battalion (3rd Tyneside Irish) Captain J V Bridges Worcester Regiment; 27th Battalion (4th Tyneside Irish) Lieutenant-Colonel E W Hermon, King Edward's Horse.

With Brigadier Cameron wounded, the command of 103 Brigade passed, on the 3rd of July, to Brigadier Herbert Edward Trevor, late King's Own Yorkshire Light Infantry.

Brigadier General H E Trevor C.M.G. DSO assumed command of 103 Brigade on 3 July 1916.

General Ingouville-Williams wrote to the Tyneside Irish Brigade the following message,

'It is with greatest sorrow that I have to part for a time with my gallant 103 Infantry Brigade, but I sincerely trust that so soon as they have refitted they will be returned to my command, as I can command no troops more faithful and brave.'

E C INGOUVILLE-WILLIAMS
Major-Gen
Comdg 34th Division
July 5th 1916

On the 7th of July motor buses arrived and transported the men north to Humbercamps, where time was spent trying to locate those missing, using lists received from the various CCS and Dressing Stations. Refitting and training was commenced, and, within a matter of days, the dreaded working parties began again.

Various inspections and visits by Generals took place, and medals were presented to those who were lucky enough to be still with the Brigade. After a few more moves, the battalions were amalgamated to go back into the line.

The 24th and 27th Battalions joined forces, with the 24th finding Nos 1 and 2 Companies, and the 27th providing Nos 3 and 4. Similarly the 25th and 26th Battalions were combined. Now reinforcements began to arrive, the 24th receiving 122 men from the West Yorkshire Regiment and King's Own Yorkshire Light Infantry, some of whom had only been in the Army for 10 weeks and the 26th Battalion also had a draft of Yorkshiremen from the Duke of Wellington's Regiment. This was the beginning of the end, for although the title Tyneside Irish was retained, the men now joining came from anywhere they could be found, and the Brigade lost much of its original identity. Certainly some drafts did contain

D Company 1/1st Northern Cyclists. This draft was split between the battalions of the Tyneside Irish Brigade.

Lieutenant James Hayes Wilkinson was sent down the line to train the reinforcements

Private Thomas Wilkinson Northern Cyclists on the left was sent out to France and joined the 26th Battalion. He was KiA on 9 April 1917.

Northumberland Fusiliers, but they came from every battalion of the regiment, regulars, territorials, Kitchener men from the early battalions, Tyneside Scottish, Tyneside Pioneers and the North East Railway Battalion. True, some wounded did return to the Brigade, but invariably they were posted to a different battalion. One of the largest drafts to the Brigade came from the Northern Cyclists Battalion whom the Tyneside Irish had last seen at Alnwick, back in March 1915, and among them was Alexander Fairweather, who would eventually be transferred to the 14th Battalion Northumberland Fusiliers.

On the 26th of July, at 12 noon, the combined 24th and 27th Battalions began taking over the line in the Carency sector from 22/London Regiment. The relief was completed by 3 p.m. and a draft, which had arrived only the previous night, went into the line with the rest of the Battalion. Later a draft of 102 other ranks arrived from the Duke of Wellington's Regiment and these men remained at the transport lines until Lieutenant F R Allison and Second Lieutenant J H Wilkinson were sent down from the line, to commence training them. Meanwhile the combined 25th and 26th Battalions, began marching towards the front line again so that at 9.30 p.m. on the night of the 27th of July, the relief of 24/London Regiment began, and was safely completed by 1.30 a.m on the morning of the 28th.

Captain Jack Arnold, commanding one of the companies, had reconnoitred the front line in the dark and was waiting for daylight, so that he could size up the position and make plans accordingly, but as dawn approached he got a shock.

> *'Daylight came and I scrambled about among the sandbags to get a more accurate appreciation of the position we held. On looking over to the enemy trenches I was surprised to see a German officer standing up on his side of the line and calmly viewing the situation as though he were in a field at home. I heaved myself up and bade him the time of day in German, to which he replied with the most cordiality. We proceeded with a conversation and might have had a long talk, when another German officer considerably older - he might have been a Colonel appeared beside him and put up his binoculars, which meant of course that he might identify our unit by the coloured shoulder badges that we wore. I ducked down to avoid this and gave orders that any attempts at fraternisation by the enemy were to be rebuffed.'*

Private Alexander Fairweather, D Company 1/1st Northern Cyclists. Joined the 25th Battalion on 25 July 1916.

The Sappers exploded a mine in front of the 26th Battalion

The weather was very warm now, and the smell of decomposing bodies and the number of flies was very trying for those in the line. This sector had been the scene of fierce fighting in the past, despite the enemy being described in the 25th Battalion War Diary as 'not aggressive'. Further reinforcements arrived for the 26th Battalion, a group of NCOs and men from the Durham Light Infantry. These were a mixture of Regulars and Kitchener men, with a small group from the 'Durham Pals' among them and the next day 134 OR's of the York and Lancaster Regiment joined. The trenches in the Carency sector were dirty and dilapidated, and much energy was spent improving conditions.

Mine warfare was an active occupation in this area, and the miners of the Tyneside Irish, were much in demand by the Tunnelling Companies located nearby. Each battalion sent up to 120 men every night to assist in removing spoil and there was little time for rest during the hours of daylight, because the front line and support trenches were improved by putting in fire bays. Artillery and trench mortar duels were another feature of daily life, but some were lucky enough to get away from the line for a while on specialist courses and amongst these Fred Hood, now a Sergeant, left the trenches on the 3rd of August for ten days at the Divisional Gas School.

CQMS Joseph Coleman DCM.

On the 4th of August, the tunnellers exploded a mine just to the left of Football Crater and a storming party, under Second Lieutenant F H Lampard, of the 26th Battalion, immediately proceeded to consolidate the British front line trench, which had been blown in for a length of about fifty yards. While this was taking place, a party of about fifty Germans left their trench and tried to storm the crater; these were kept at bay by Second Lieutenant Lampard and his party, until assistance arrived, during which Second Lieutenant Lampard was wounded, but remained at his post until the Germans retired.

Writing to his old company commander Captain Arnold in 1917, CQMS Joseph Coleman DCM described the part played by Captain Arnold that night.

'At Vimy when I was serving under your command you saved the situation the night of the explosion. Only by your prompt action

in rallying the men did you divert disaster into success. You left the shelter of a dugout which was your position at the telephone to give a hand with the undertaking, which was more than a younger officer than yourself tried to do.'

On the 7th of August, at 2.13 a.m. it was the Germans' turn to blow a mine, which was quickly followed up by a storming party of about fifty men, some of whom effected an entry into the 25th Battalion line but were driven out by bombs, after a fight of about half-an- hour. On the right, bombers of the 24th Battalion joined in the fight and Lance Corporal Alexander English, of Dipton, throwing over 100 bombs by himself, was immediately recommended for the DCM. Lance Corporal Owen Cairns, of Marley Hill, although wounded in the arm, kept throwing bombs for over half-an-hour, until his arm was so stiff he could throw no more, and he and Private Albert Johnson, who also threw numerous bombs, were both recommended for the MM. All three were responsible for the Germans being driven out, and the consolidation of the lip of the crater.

Only one fatal casualty occurred to the bombers of the 24th, 24/866 Private Edward Allen, of D Company, one of a large group of Lancashire miners, who worked at Wheatley Hill Colliery in County Durham. With no Irish connections among them, they had enlisted at Deaf Hill Recruiting Office into the Tyneside Irish.

Only one fatal casualty was incurred by the bombers of the 24th battlion, 24/866 Private Edward Allen of D Company.

The front fell quiet now, with the enemy daily sending over about fifty HE shells and the British replying in kind. Trench mortars were active on both sides, as were the ever-present snipers.

After the afternoon and evening bombardments there was usually a sort of eerie hush that fell over the scene.

'I went round the line at night, last thing at about midnight, with the company sergeant major and my runner. We would make our way from bay to bay along the front and creep out to the listening posts. Usually I could get up beside the sentry on the parapet, or sit with the man in the listening post for a while. After seeing that the sentry was alert and knew what he was there for, there were few times that I did not have a talk with him about home. We were back away across the channel and up north to Newcastle or in some mining village in Durham, or perhaps in some home far away in Ireland. Most of them had wives and families, they liked to talk about their hopes and fears for them. So on round the line and back to my dugout to get two or three hours sleep before it was time to write my reports. I usually got the reports finished by about five a.m. and then it was time to go up the line for the "rum issue". The rum jar was placed in my dugout each night as it came in. My runner would carry it behind me and I would visit each platoon in turn. Each man would bring his dixie along and amidst a hush a tablespoonful of the sacred liquid would be ladled out to each man.' (Captain Jack Arnold)

Also still alive and serving with the 26th was Michael Manley, who was now employed as a company runner, he recalled sitting in the signals dugout,

'this signaller took a bullet but wasn't dead. One of the lads used the field telephone to send for a doctor, but he didn't come. The signaller was left to die slowly and the lad who made the call got into trouble for using the the telephone. One day me and my mate, another runner, were in the trench talking when Jerry lobbed a shell over and shrapnel got the other lad. When I got to him he was dead, stone cold dead! He had been so happy minutes earlier because he had just had a letter from his wife.'

On the 14th of August the relief of the 24th and 27th Battalions took place by 12/Royal Scots, when the battalions of the Tyneside Irish were pulled out of the line, and sent back for further training. Further reinforcements were arriving, from the 4th and 5th (Territorial) Battalions of the Northumberland

Fusiliers and many of these men were returning to the front, having been wounded at the Second Battle of Ypres, in April and May 1915.

On the 21st of August, the 24th and 25th Battalions each provided a Guard of Honour, at the Chateau de Ranchicourt, on the occasion of medals being presented to men of the French Artillery, who had supported the Corps during recent operations. The inspecting officer General K.C.B. Haking, complimented the Guard on its turn-out, and the men were marched back to their billets. The next day 103 (Tyneside Irish) Brigade came back under command of the 34th Division, which had now returned to the Armentieres area. The battalions at once commenced the journey to rejoin the Division but, on the way, orders were received to proceed south, to the Somme. The Brigade was to be attached to the 15th (Scottish) Division during operations near Contalmaison and on the 26th of August the battalions of 103 Brigade entrained at Merville for Longueau near Amiens, arriving there in the early evening, and going into billets. The next morning the battalions began marching towards the Somme front, with very heavy rain pouring down. The following day saw them arriving back in the Albert area when the 24th Battalion bivouacked at Bois Noir on the Albert - Becourt road, the 25th Battalion in the old front line near Becourt Chateau, the 26th bivouacked South West of Albert, prior to going into Scots Redoubt, and the 27th remained at Albert in Brigade reserve.

In the early hours of the 30th of August, the 24th moved into the support trenches at Contalmaison, relieving 7/Cameron Highlanders. The weather was exceptionally bad and little work was done on the trenches. The enemy shelled the Battalion heavily with Lachyrimatory shells all day but the news was received that the award of the DCM to Lance Corporal English had been confirmed. The 25th also had gone into the front line relieving 8/10/Gordons; they too came under heavy artillery fire, and they lost two men to a sniper whose position they were unable to locate. The Battalion was then replaced in the front line by the 24th Battalion and the 26th Battalion, in the meantime, relieved the 27th Battalion, who moved forward on the 1st of September into support at Contalmaison.

With over half of his platoon dead or wounded 24/287 Sergeant George Hunter (standing on the left) prevented the enemy from entering his section of the front line.

On the 2nd of September the Germans launched a counterattack on Contalmaison, and the front line system came under intense shell- fire. Several men were buried by debris and much damage occurred, with the communication trenches receiving particular attention. At 11 p.m. just as the Battalion was to be relieved, the enemy commenced firing rifle grenades, on the strong points. Whilst the relief was in progress, the Germans came over throwing hand grenades and this attack was supported, by heavy artillery fire on the support line and communication trenches. The Tyneside Irish suffered casualties from this extremely accurate fire, but Lieutenant Thomas Michael Scanlan organised a group of seven men and launched a counterattack which was maintained, until he and five of the men were wounded. CSM George Coleby from Dunston, and Sergeant Stephen O'Neill, of Gateshead, kept the saps clear and supplied bombs to the bombing party, whilst Sergeant George Hunter of Wideopen, with half of his platoon out of action, wounded or dead, kept the enemy from entering his portion of the line. With all but two of Lieutenant Scanlan's party wounded, Private Patrick Connor, of Hebburn, kept throwing bombs, displaying great personal courage until the enemy was forced to retire. The relief was completed by 0800 hours but, owing to enemy shelling, the right flank company, was unable to leave the front line until some time later.

The other battalions were also rotating from reserve to front line and into reserve again, with much digging work coming their way. The 26th Battalion, for instance was digging jumping-off trenches between Cameron Trench and Munster Alley under heavy artillery fire on the night of the 11/12th of September, and then on the 15th of the month levelling a road, from Sanderson Trench to Martinpuich.

The 27th Battalion, however, had the task of assisting the Canadians in an attack to the south of the Bapaume, with the Tyneside Irish Battalion protecting the flank of the Canadians, and then assisting with consolidating the gains. They then dug a communication trench 200 yards long across No-Mans-Land and this work earned the praise of the Canadian Brigade when Colonel Herman, Commanding the Tyneside Irish Battalion, received the following from the neighbouring Canadian Commander.

Men taking a shower in reserve trench.

'Dear Col Herman

Very sorry that I did not see you before we left the trenches. I wish to express to you the sincere thanks of myself, my Officers and men, for the assistance rendered us by your Battalion on the 9th inst.

It was neccesary to have strong support on our right and you certainly gave it to us.

I have much pleasure in bringing to your notice the name of Lieutenant Watts for the excellent work done by him while he was attached to us helping to consolidate our new position. again thanking you.

Believe me
Yours sincerely
A.M.Swift
Lieut Colonel
2nd Battn Canadian 1st Divn.'

Colonel Richardson, now fit, returned from England and resumed command of his old Battalion.

The battalions were withdrawn to the area around Albert and provided working parties for the front line, George Kean now promoted to Sergeant was able to write a few lines to his parents,

'We are once again back for a day or two's rest from this maddening canonade, the guns never cease from morn until night both sides.'

Parties also worked on road improvements in Contalmaison and in one of these working parties, the 24th Battalion had Second Lieutenant V Grossman killed by shellfire. Now the Brigade went back to the area of Franvillers and word was

Lieutenant Thomas Scanlan MC and Paulette Duprey, the little French girl who visited B Company Mess.

received that it would rejoin the 34th Division. The Division was now commanded by Major-General C L Nicholson, for 'Inky Bill' had been killed in action, on July 22nd, whilst the Brigade had been detached from the Division.

The various company messes established themselves in the villages behind the line; the mess of B Company, 24th Battalion commanded by Captain George Swinburn had a regular visitor whom he described to his mother.

> *'At our company HQ there is a darling little girl of seven. Her father was killed in the war. She is a perfect little picture, and we have her in at meals – today I took her for a short walk to a shop and bought her a little smock. She writes her name for you, [The little girl wrote her name on the letter] Paulette Dupre. It is a good French name – really it is sad two little one's left – a fine boy.*
>
> *Well now I must close because I must draw some clothing for the men*
>
> *With fondest love George.'*

The battalions of the Brigade entrained at Longpre for Merville and, after arrival, marched straight to Estaires, arriving at 5 a.m. on the morning of 23 September 1916. After a short rest the Battalion and Company Commanders, along with selected specialists, went forward to reconnoitre the trenches in the L'Epinette sector. 103 Brigade was again detached from 34th Division, and together with 8 Australian Brigade became 'FRANK'S FORCE'. The 26th and 27th Battalions, went straight into the front line system, taking over from Gordon Highlanders of the 51st Division. The 25th Battalion went into the subsidiary line, and the 24th Battalion into reserve at Armentieres, relieving the 7/Black Watch. The 24th Battalion immediately started sending working parties to the front line, likewise the 25th Battalion who also provided smaller parties to assist the 27th Battalion.

After four days the battalions in the line were relieved by those in support, the 27th Battalion returning to the subsidiary line, and the 26th Battalion going back to billets in Armentieres.

Second Lieutenant Albert Murphy 24th Battalion attached 103 Light Trench Mortar Battery, killed in action 3 October 1916.

The beginning of October found the Brigade still holding the L'Epinette sector, with the enemy constantly shelling the rear areas, particularly those known as Japan Dump, and Square Farm, with Minenwerfer and 5.9's. 103 LTMB had bad luck on the 3rd of the month, when Second Lieutenant Albert Murphy, attached from the 24th Battalion, was killed in action, and the Battery Commander Second Lieutenant, Acting Captain, H T White, 26th Battalion, was wounded. Captain White died of his wounds the following day. A period of intense patrol activity began, with the battalions in the line sending out multiple patrols each night.

Lance Corporal Michael Manley recalled one of these patrols in No-Man's-Land,

'There was barbed wire in front of the trenches and every night we would have to replace it as the shelling smashed it up. One night I was picked to be one of the covering party for those doing the work, as we moved across No-Man's-Land we came across a dead German which gave me a hell of a start. The Sergeant said

"take no notice of him yon fella will do you no harm." The Sergeant was a canny fella, but he was soon dead.'

On the 5th of October, 8 Australian Brigade, on the left of the 24th Battalion, discharged gas towards the German trenches, but there was no apparent effect shown by the occupants of the enemy trenches. The nightly patrols reported that the enemy saps were held by bombers near the head of the sap and the 25th Battalion was detailed to raid the area of the Railway Cutting supported by the Divisional Artillery who put down a box-barrage to provide cover for the raiding party. The party was commanded by Lieutenant F S McKellan, with Second Lieutenant Rix as his second-in-command and the raiders entered the German trenches at the point where the Lille–Armentieres railway line crossed the trench lines. On reaching that point, the raiders split into two parties, one going along the enemy trench to the north of the railway cutting, the other to the south. No opposition was encountered, and after about ten minutes the party returned safely to the British front line, but this raid brought artillery retaliation down on the 26th Battalion, who were holding that sector of the front.

On the 12th of the month, the 27th Battalion was ordered to carry out a much stronger raid, involving six officers and one hundred other ranks. Beginning at 7.30. p.m. the artillery, trench mortars and machine guns commenced a bombardment of the enemy front line, in order to provide cover for the raiders to leave the front trenches occupied by the 25th Battalion. The artillery fire had successfully breached the enemy wire on the left, while a Bangalore Torpedo was exploded on the right, making a second breach. Three parties crossed No-Mans-Land and entered the enemy front line at about 7.40. p.m. to discover that the barrage had caused quite considerable damage to the trench and, working along its length, the raiders bombed three dugouts and killed a number of enemy soldiers. A shoulder strap was removed from a dead enemy soldier, to provide identification, before the withdrawal signal was given. The enemy line was described as being fairly well held, and the support line strongly held, so the raiding party had not got off 'scot free', sustaining three officers and eleven other ranks wounded, two other ranks killed and four missing. One of the officers, Second Lieutenant William Harvey later died of his wounds, prompting the CO of the 27th Battalion to write to his parents,

'It is with great regret that I write to tell you of the death of your splendid boy. He had been in France for about four months and engaged in some of the heaviest fighting on the Somme Front. On the evening of the 12th he was one of four officers and a hundred men detailed to make a raid on the enemy trenches. He went off in most splendid spirits, and it was due to his fine example that the party did so well. He was badly wounded just above the knee and his Sergeant, who was also wounded, brought him out to No-Man's-Land and then our Padre went out and fetched him in. He was taken to hospital at Armentieres and the next day to the Australian Hospital at Trois Arbres, Steenwerck. I went over to see him on the 13th but was not able to do so. I regret he died the same night. I saw the poor lad laid to rest alongside many other good fellows who had made the supreme sacrifice for his country. Yours E W Hermon Lt Col.'

The Brigade C of E Padre, Captain the Reverend Ernest Francis Duncan CF on being told that the wounded officer was in No-Man's-Land, had immediately crossed the parapet, to search for him. The Padre was then slightly wounded himself, but brought Second Lieutenant Harvey back to the British front line. For this, and for restoring communication with the raiding party he was awarded the Military Cross.

When the award of the Military Cross to Lieutenant Tom Scanlan was announced for his actions in September, Father Mcbrearty gave a dinner on the evening of 17th of October for the officers of B Company, in honour of the gallant Lieutenant. The food was provided by family and friends at home and named after those who had donated it.

Salmon a la Phoebe.
Soup a la Sally.
Croquettes Donaldo.
Roast Beef a la Wilkie.
Potatoes.

Tranchee Cameron Salad.
Welsh Rabbit a la Tyneside.
Fruit Varie.
Half Blackie.

26/218 Private Thomas Fallon who was unfortunate to be wounded in 19 places at once from the same shell.

The battalions that were out at rest continued to supply the endless working parties to the RE's, and trained when and where possible. With the 25th and 27th Battalions having succesfully carried out raids on the enemy, the staff now decided that the 24th Battalion should be used, so two Officers and thirty-six men began training for a raid on the trenches in the Epinette sector. On the 20th of October the party left the billets at 8.05 p.m. for the front line, and by 10.00.p.m. were ready to go over. They split into two parties, one going north under Lieutenant Donald, the other going south commanded by Second Lieutenant Kerr. The northern party managed to reach the German wire but it was so thick and strong that they could not find a way through. The men under Second Lieutenant Kerr lost touch with one another and only the officer and four men reached the enemy wire. By now the covering barrage had lifted onto the enemy front line, and the raiders were forced to retire back to the British front line trench, doing so without casualties.

Raiding was not limited to the endeavours of the Tyneside Irish however and on the 26th of October, at 5 p.m. the Germans put a heavy barrage down on the front line trench, held by the 25th Battalion. Under the cover of the barrage, a raiding party of unknown strength crossed No-Man's-Land, and despite fierce resistance, they entered the British trenches and captured a Lewis Gun and its team. Casualties sustained by the 25th Battalion, during the raid were given as three OR's killed, thirteen wounded and five missing. Patrolling continued with as many as seven patrols a night going out and one patrol from the 24th Battalion encountered an enemy wiring party out in No-Man's-Land which was dispersed by the Lewis gunners.

On the night of the 30th of October the 24th Battalion War Diary records that the Battalion was supplying the usual working party for the RE's, and that machine-gun and rifle fire were above normal during the night. As one of the working parties was making its way towards the front line, a stray bullet wounded Sergeant George Kean. His Platoon Commander was with him when it happened, and he wrote to the Sergeant's mother, in Liverpool. (Sergeant Kean was well thought of by his Company Commander Captain George Swinburn, for his wounding is recorded in the captain's personal diary, in which only a few OR's are recorded by name.)

24NF B.E.F.
31st October 1916
'Dear Madam,

I am very sorry to inform you that your son Sgt Kean was wounded last night when accompanying a party for rations. I was near him at the time and told him not to worry as I would write to you on his behalf. From what I can judge it seems to have been caused by a stray bullet from the German Front Line half a mile away. It happened about 6 p.m. Your boy was quite cheery and you have every reason to be proud of him. I hardly think that it will turn out to be very serious and hope that you will shortly have good news of him. Please accept my sympathy but at the same time

would ask you to look on the hopeful side of things. I only trust he may reach an English Hospital and soon be able to have a few days with you.
I am madam, sincerely yours,
J L Jones 2nd Lieutenant'

Sergeant Kean was taken to the nearest aid post, and from there he was evacuated to 2 Casualty Clearing Station, which was at that time based in Bailleul. After he was admitted, the Sister in Charge wrote to Mrs Kean to inform her of his admission.

No 2 CCS BEF
31st October 1916
'Dear Mrs Kean
I am exceedingly sorry to have to inform you that your son 1541 Sgt Kean 24/North Fus. was admitted to hospital yesterday 30/10/16 suffering from severe gunshot wound of the abdomen. His condition was such that it necessitated an immediate operation. He is going on as well as can be expected under the circumstances, but he is still very dangerously ill. Rest assured that everything will be done for him that can possibly be done. He has been visited by the Church of England Chaplain [Sgt Kean was an RC] several times. I hope to be able to give you more hopeful accounts of him in a day or two.
With kindest regards Yours very sincerely D McPherson Sister in Charge No 2 Casualty Clearing Station B.E.F. France'

However Sgt Kean did not come through and sadly died of his wounds. Sister McPherson had the unenviable task of informing his mother.

No 2 CCS BEF
1st November 1916
'Dear Mrs Kean
I am exceedingly grieved to have to inform you that your son 1541 Sgt G Kean 24/North Fus. who was admitted to hospital on 30/10/16 suffering from a gunshot wound of the abdomen, passed peacefully away this morning at 2.15.a.m. 1/11/16. Everything was done for him that could possibly be done, but alas of no avail. He was visited frequently by the Chaplain who will also write to you about him. Please accept my most sincere sympathy in this your terrible loss. I am exceedingly sorry but he did not leave any message. I have however, saved you a lock of his hair which I now enclose.
With deepest sympathy

Yours very sincerely
D McPherson
Sister in Charge
No 2 Casualty Clearing Station
B.E.F.
France'

Changes in senior officers took place during the month. Lieutenant-Colonel Prior handed over command of the 24th Battalion, to Lieutenant-Colonel Hermon from the 27th Battalion and reverted to Battalion Second-in-Command.

Lieutenant-Colonel Steward resumed command of the 27th Battalion for a short time, until he was relieved by Lieutenant-Colonel Temple, from the 25th Battalion. Command of that unit passed in quick succession from Captain Beattie-Brown to Major Reay, then, by 2nd of December, Major E.M. Moulton-Barrett D.S.O. assumed command on promotion to Lieutenant-Colonel.

November continued in much the same way as the previous month and on the 1st, the battalions were deployed as follows:- The 25th Battalion were in reserve at Armentieres, supplying working parties for those in the line; the 24th Battalion were in support in the subsidiary line, also supplying the dreaded

Captain and Adjutant Johnny Finlay, 26th Battalion, killed in action 23rd November 1916.

working parties; the 26th and 27th Battalions, were in the front line, coming under trench mortar and 5.9 shellfire. This was destroying the parapet, particularly in the left company of the 26th Battalion, who had eight ORs wounded prior to the Battalion being relieved by the 24th Battalion on the 3rd of the month. At the same time the 25th Battalion relieved the 27th Battalion, who moved into the billets in Armentieres.

Within three hours of the 24th Battalion taking over the front line, they had two patrols out into No-Man's-Land and one of these discovered an enemy wiring party, which was quickly dispersed by fire from a Lewis Gun.

As soon as these patrols returned to the British lines, three other patrols went out and stayed in No-Man's-Land until 04.30 a.m. when they reported the situation as generally quiet. During the day there was shelling on 'Japan' and 'Chicken Farms', but nothing serious occurred and this was the pattern for the rest of the Battalion's tour, with up to seven patrols out nightly. During 'Stand To' on the 5th, two Germans came over and gave themselves up to a sentry, after he had fired at them. The weather was atrocious and the trenches had eighteen inches of water in them, making life unpleasant to say the least. The 25th Battalion also had men out in No-Man's-Land each night and on the 4th of November, Second Lieutenant Collier was severely wounded whilst in charge of a wiring party. Sadly, he died of these wounds the following morning and was buried in TROIS ARBRES Cemetery.

Meanwhile the Battalion had a company of 2/ANZAC Cyclist Battalion attached for training in trench routine and on the 9th of November, the battalions again rotated with the 26th and 27th Battalions again taking over the line. The 26th Battalion reported drafts arriving from 18/Durham LI (The Durham Pals) and from 5/Northumberland Fusiliers. Lieutenant-Colonel Richardson reported sick during the early part of the month, and command of the 26th Battalion passed temporarily to Captain W P Kelly, who was wounded on the 10th, and died of wounds in hospital at Bailleul. Also with the troops in the 26th Battalion was Captain Jack Fleming, who had written of his dislike of the Brigade Trench Mortar Battery. He was detailed to take over command of the said Battery, but unfortunately, his comments have not survived. In the line Lieutenant Lance Shackleton commanding a platoon in D company of the 26th Battalion was looking forward to being relieved. He had married his sweatheart Molly Swinburn when home on convalescent leave at the end of June, and was able to give her news of George,

'I am looking forward to seeing George again, as he will be coming in as we go out.'

> In his diary Captain George Swinburn recorded his meetings with Lance in the line when they would dine together in the company HQ dugout after the hand over. During this time in late 1916 their companies relieved each other several times.

With the trenches waterlogged, much energy was expended trying to drain them. The enemy was quiet, and little hostile shelling was taking place so that the 27th Battalion had only one fatality during this period, when 41954 Private William Stokes, from Catshill, Yorkshire, was accidentally killed.

Out at rest, the 24th Battalion, had once again started training a raiding party and on the night of the 21st at 1 20 a.m. the raiders left the British front line. At the same time, on the right, a party from 2/ANZAC Cyclist Battalion, was to leave the 25th Battalion lines, and also carry out a raid, but for some

Gale and Polden, Ltd.] OFFICERS, 1st Batt. Tyneside Irish Brigade. [24 (S) Batt. N.F.]. [*To face page* 145.

1. Lt. B. C. Brady.
2. 2nd Lt. J. L. Donnelly.
3. Lt. D. M. Dawson.
4. 2nd Lt. J. M. Daizell.
5. ,, J. J. G. Welton.
6. ,, R. Donald.
7. ,, T. W. Thompson.
8. 2nd Lt. H. Wilkinson.
9. ,, H. A. Patterson.
10. ,, J. McLoughlin.
11. Rev. G. McBrearty, C.F.
12. Lt. & Q.M. P. McKenna.
13. 2nd Lt. H. S. Fitzgerald.
14. ,, H. M. Horrox.
15. 2nd Lt. L. F. Byrne.
16. ,, S. A. Jardine.
17. Lt. C. M. Goodall.
18. 2nd Lt. W. A. Short.
19. ,, H. R. C. Sutcliffe.
20. ,, J. R. Wedderburn.
21. ,, R. Loverock.
22. 2nd Lt. F. J. Downey.
23. Lt. A. E. Rogers.
24. Capt. J. H. Pringle.
25. ,, G. Swinburn.
26. ,, K. McKenzie.
27. ,, C. Wallace.
28. Major J. M. Prior.
29. Lt.-Col. L. Meredith Howard, Commanding.
30. 2nd Lt & Adj. W. Waring, Gordon Highlanders.
31. Capt. J. P. Gallwey.
32. ,, E. Pugh.
33. ,, A. Thompson.
34. Lt. T. G. Farina.
35. Lt. C. J. Mate.
36. 2nd Lt. G. Hardy.
37. Capt. W. B. Watson, R.A.M.C.

unknown reason, this party did not leave the front line. The 24th Battalion raiders made their way across No-Man's-Land to the German front line, which was entered, and although the party went for a considerable distance along the trench, in both directions, there was no sign of any recent enemy occupation.

The enemy trenches were found to be damaged by the British artillery fire, and were badly waterlogged but having found nothing, the raiders withdrew without casualties. Two nights later, Second Lieutenant Crichton and fourteen ORs again entered the enemy front line in the same place and this party remained in ambush positions until 5.00. a.m. As no enemy soldiers had appeared by this time, however a concrete dugout was destroyed with gun cotton, and the party retired, without loss, to the British lines.

103 Brigade, was now being relieved by battalions of 9 Australian Infantry Brigade which required that Commanding Officers and specialists remained behind to give instruction to the newcomers. On 30 November 1916, 103 Brigade left 'FRANK's FORCE' and once again came under command of the 34th Division, being placed in Divisional Reserve, in the ERQUINGHEM area. Training was the order of the day with drill, bayonet fighting, musketry and anti-gas drill taking place daily, and there were of course plenty of carrying parties.

On the 11th of December, the Brigade began the relief of their old friends, the Tyneside Scottish, in the RUE DU BOIS and LA CHAPPELLE D'ARMENTIERES sector. Taking over the front line from the 20th Battalion (1st Tyneside Scottish), the 24th Battalion, reported that the enemy artillery was very active, and that the left flank company, C Company, had received a number of 'minnies'. However on the other flank the 25th Battalion, reported that the enemy was inactive. At night the enemy was sweeping No-Man's-Land, and the British parapet with a searchlight, and was bombing his own wire, obviously in the hope of catching a British patrol out in the open.

After six days, the other two battalions took over the line and the 24th and 25th Battalions went into support. The 26th and 27th Battalions had relatively quiet tours, with only one fatal casualty in the 27th Battalion, 41890 Private James Muldowney of Leeds, a reinforcement from the West Yorkshire Regiment. On the 23rd the Brigade was relieved by 102 Brigade and went into Divisional reserve. There were only church parades for the next two days, the men being given a well-earned rest for Christmas 1916. Only the 26th Battalion War Diary gives any additional information for this period, saying that a special 'Christmas Dinner' was held, and that the Battalion was visited by the II (ANZAC) Corps Commander, Lieutenant-General Godley, and the 34th Divisional Commander, Major-General Nicholson.

Captain Jack Arnold recalled with pleasure his mess waiter Private Nelson, who had been a waiter in civilian life.

> *'I have rarely met a finer character than Nelson our mess waiter, the professional touch was always with him. In the trenches when he had established the kitchen and instructed the cook, he carried on the same routine, as if he was in a hotel. The highlight of his catering powers was reached at Christmas 1916. Nelson scoured the countryside for turkey and goose and secured his quarry. The company artist painted menu cards and a French girl in the billet assisted Nelson to write out the cards in faultless French, decorations were run up and lanterns were festooned with ivy. Friends came from near and far and all went like a house on fire. Poor Nelson he was a soldier as well as a waiter and died going over the top at the Battle of Arras.'*

(41406 Lance Corporal John James Nelson from Brampton, Cumberland originally 2nd Barnsley Pals killed in Action 9 April 1917, and buried at Orchard Dump Cemetery.)

For a lucky few there was home leave for Christmas and one of these was Fred Hood of the 27th Battalion, whose trip home to Seaham took two days, but no doubt was well worth it. But home leave was a rare thing at this time and many men resigned themselves to the fact that the only way they would

34th Divisional Christmas card 1916, sent by Captain George Swinburn.

James Bacon and Sons.] OFFICERS, 2nd Batt. Tyneside Irish Brigade. [25 (S) Batt. N.F.]. [*To face page* 161.

1. 2nd Lt. Paul, J.
2. Capt. Bainbridge, J.
3. Lt. Slack, W.R.
4. ,, Hopps, L.
5. 2nd Lt. Broom, P.
6. Lt. Maguire, L.
7. 2nd Lt. Hutchinson, P.
8. 2nd Lt. McLeod, W.
9. ,, Harker, J.
10. Rev. Capt. Duncan.
11. 2nd Lt. Dunn, J.
12. Capt. Pollard, H.
13. Lt. McKellan, C.
14. 2nd Lt. Maitland, A.
15. Capt. Williams, I.
16. 2nd Lt. Robertson, R. R.
17. Lt. Nicholson, R.
18. 2nd Lt. Taylor, J.
19. ,, Kirkup, J.
20. ,, Charlesworth, W.
21. Capt. Rowell, C.
22. Lt. and Q.M. Cooper, R.
23. Lt. Cawson, G.
24. Lt. Hately, J.
25. Lt. de Ridder, S.
26. Capt. Foley, J.
27. ,, Murray, P.
28. Capt. & Adj. Barkworth, C.
29. Lt. Col. Beresford.
30. Maj. Jones, E.
31. ,, Jenkins, H.
32. Capt. Tickler, P.
33. ,, Sheehan, J.
34. Lt. Murphy, J.
35. 2nd Lt. Nichol, W.
36. Lt. Wright, J.
37. 2nd. Lt. Pantin, S.
38. 2nd Lt. Ritchie, R.

get back to England was if they got a 'Blighty' wound. Captain Arnold recalled one soldier who was patiently waiting for his turn on the leave roster.

> *'I remember one old chap called Johnston, who had terrible troubles at home and it was recognised by common consent that he should be placed first in the leave roster. But the leave never seemed to be reached and Johnston had long given up hope of ever seeing home and family again, when one filthy night in the line, permission for one "leave" came through. I told my runner to fetch Johnston from the front line to my dugout but to give no inkling what it was about. In due course Johnston covered in mud and looking as though he was expecting to be shot was brought in. I can see him now in the light of the flickering candle, the misery and mud exuding from him. I looked at him and said, "Well Johnston how would you like a spot of leave to go home to your wife and family? Your turn has come at last." If I ever saw the light of heaven it was in Johnston's face that night. All through the line that night it was whispered that Johnston's leave had come through at last. He had found the pearl of great price. He was marked "unfit" when he reached home and we never saw him again.'*

24/1024 Lance Corporal C Borthwick, 24th Battalion, who became one of the last of the Tyneside Irish casualties of 1916. He was killed on 16 December.

On Boxing Day, the Brigade was back at work, with all battalions supplying working parties to the front line and on the 29th of December, the relief of 101 Brigade in the front line commenced, when the 24th and 25th Battalions took over, with the 26th and 27th Battalions in support. This then was where the Tyneside Irish Brigade welcomed in the New Year and some of the 25th Battalion spent New Year's Eve, putting out wire in No-Man's-Land and the Lewis Gunners fired at gaps in the enemy parapet.

Captain George Swinburn was acting as an Assistant Provost Marshall behind the lines at Bailleul and on New Year's Eve Jack Arnold rode over from Armentieres to spend an evening with him and together with a bottle of gin they rang in 1917.

(Quite separately both men had recorded this event in their papers, much to the author's surprise.)

The last reported fatality for 1916, was from the 25th Battalion, on the 29th of December, when 25/287 A/Corporal David Hood from Gateshead was killed. So ended 1916, a year that began at Sutton Veny, with the Tyneside Irish longing to get to France, and ending with them still in the line.

Chapter Eight

1917 The Battle of Arras

'The Strong point has gone and forward they press
towards their objective in number grown less'
'THE BURNING QUESTION' ANON THE WIPERS' TIMES

The Tyneside Irish entered 1917, with two battalions in the line in the Bois Grenier sector, and two in close support. The 24th Battalion reported that the front was very quiet, but the 25th Battalion fired thirty-six rifle grenades at the German front line, receiving a quantity of artillery fire in return. The next day the battalions rotated, with the 26th and 27th Battalions taking over the front line and on

Eternal rest give unto him O Lord,
And let perpetual light shine upon him.

Of Your Charity
Pray for the Repose of the Soul
OF
John Miller.
2nd West Yorks.
Killed in Action in France,
March 30th. 1917.
Aged 29 Years,
And who was Interred at Nesle,
near St. Quentin.
R. I. P.

PRAYER

Absolve, we beseech Thee O Lord, the soul of Thy servant John, that being dead to this world, he may live to Thee: and whatever sins he hath committed in this life, through human frailty, do Thou, of Thy most merciful goodness, forgive. Through Jesus Christ our Lord.—Amen.

Having recovered from his wounds 24/1101 Private John Miller was transferred to 2/West Yorks with whom he was KiA on 2 March 1917.

Lewis Gun post near Arras.

the night of the 4th/5th January the 26th Battalion sent three patrols out, commanded by Second Lieutenants' Welsh, Lampard and Hunter, each with fifteen men. Their objective was to penetrate the enemy line, and send a smaller patrol further into the enemy rear but none of these patrols was able to find a place to pass through the enemy wire. The Germans, however, were not very alert, and even though it was a bright moonlit night, the patrols were able to walk erect, along the enemy wire and all were able to return safely to the British lines. The routine reliefs continued until the end of the month, when the Brigade was relieved by the Australians and casualties during this period were relatively light, with only six OR's and one officer, Second Lieutenant Wallace of the 27th Battalion, killed. Perhaps one of the more interesting entries in the War Diaries is that on the 10th of January, the 26th Battalion gave a dinner for all those who had come out with the Battalion exactly one year before. Of the original battalion, only seven officers and 180 Other Ranks sat down to the meal, or roughly 17% of those embarking on the 10th of January, 1916. One of those at the meal was 2nd Lieutenant Henry Doyle, one of the first recruits to the Brigade, but within the week he was dead – killed in action on the 17th, and buried behind the lines at Ration Farm.

Drafts were arriving on a regular basis; both the 25th and 26th Battalions gave the numbers of men arriving, but identified no previous units. The Brigade was withdrawn at the beginning of February and began training; the 25th Battalion being employed on the Second Army Rifle Ranges near St Omer where musketry was carried out and some men were used as demonstration troops for senior officers. On the 18th of the month news came that the 34th Division was to be transferred, from the Second Army to the Third Army and this was done by route march. Leaving the training area, the battalions moved south east, each day moving a little closer to the Arras Front, and the forthcoming offensive. By the beginning of March 1917, the Brigade was assembled in the area of ECOIVRES, in a camp known as 'X Hutments', with detachments forward in Arras, providing working parties for the front. The 24th Battalion took over the front line in the Arras sector on the 8th of March for a six-day tour of duty and six men were killed and twelve wounded, during their period in the line. On the 11th of March, the Germans launched a raid on the unit to the right of the 25th Battalion when, after heavy shelling, tragedy struck in the rear. Over 300 shells fell on Arras, close to where the Reverend Captain E. F. Duncan MC CF was taking a service, near the Headquarters of the 27th Battalion and, seeing some men wounded and unable to take cover, the padre ran out to help them, but was caught in the open, and killed by the next shell to fall. He was an Irishman from Fintona, County Tyrone and was buried in Arras shortly afterwards.

The Rev. E.F. Duncan, M.C., 4th Class Chaplains' Dept. Himself wounded, he rescued a wounded officer under heavy fire.

At 5.00 a.m. on the morning of the 15th of March the enemy attempted a raid on the 25th Battalion, but this was forced back by heavy Lewis Gun fire. That night, an officer's patrol, from the 26th Battalion, commanded by Second Lieutenant Hopper, went out with the objective of carrying out a reconnaissance of the enemy trenches. The patrol crossed the German wire, and entered the enemy front line on the south side of a point known as 'POPE'S NOSE'. The front line was found to be empty, so they continued and crossed towards the support line, which was manned by sentries and very deep. This line was also crossed, and a search was made of the area behind the support line from where, after a short while, the patrol recrossed both lines, and left the enemy trenches on the north side of 'POPE'S NOSE'. This patrol resulted in the award of the Military Cross to Second Lieutenant Hopper.

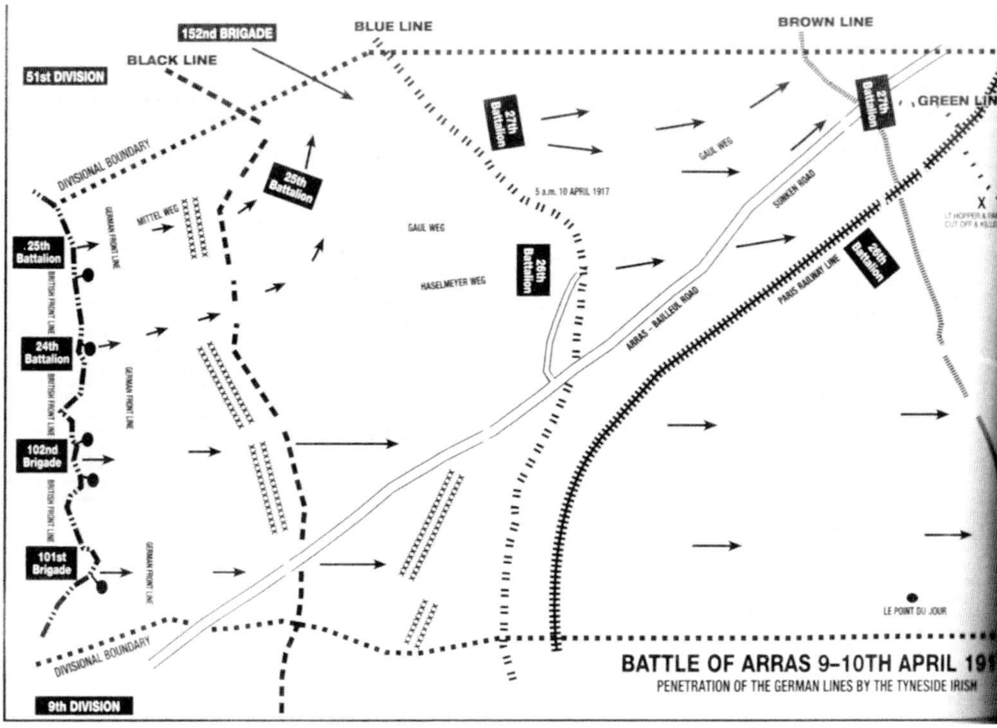

The 25th Battalion was not taking the German raids lying down and, on the night of the 18th of March, they returned the compliment, but did not achieve the success hoped for. Under the command of Captain Maguire, the raiding party managed to enter the enemy trenches, but no prisoners were taken, and the raiders had one officer and four other ranks wounded, together with one NCO missing, 37729 Arthur Crosier of Blyth, who was one of the draft from the Northern Cyclist's Battalion.

The Tyneside Irish Brigade was now withdrawn to billets and training for the coming offensive was carried out in which rifle platoons practised the assault, and the training of the battalion specialists, Lewis Gunners, Signallers, Rifle Grenadiers and Stretcher Bearers was given priority.

The plan for an attack on the Arras Front had been drawn up as far back as June 1916, but had been delayed, owing to the high casualties suffered during the Somme battles of 1916. Once again the Germans knew that an offensive was about to take place since three weeks of 'wire cutting', and a five day bombardment by the British artillery, gave them plenty of notice. However, to be fair to General Allenby, the Third Army

Usworth men in France. *Left to right*, Privates McCartney, Jordan and McGee. They all lived in Edith Avenue Usworth.

Sergeant Fred Hood seated on the left. Fred met his brother as he moved up to the Arras front.

Commander, he had tried to reduce the bombardment to forty eight hours but had been overruled by General Headquarters, who had his artillery adviser, General Holland, promoted and moved to another post. The Third Army had under command for the battle, VII, VI and XVII Corps whilst also involved on the left flank of the Third Army, were the Canadian Corps of First Army, who were detailed to assault and capture Vimy Ridge.

Lieutenant-General Ferguson, who commanded XVII Corps, had four divisions under him for the coming operations, 9th (Scottish), 34th, 51st (Highland) and 4th Divisions. He placed the first three named in the line, with the 4th Division behind, ready to leapfrog through the 9th (Scottish) Division on the right flank whereas on the left flank, the 51st (Highland) Division was to link up with the Canadians. The 34th Division, which he had placed in the centre, had all three brigades in the line each brigade having two battalions in the front line, one in support, and one in reserve.

The Corps plan of attack depended on the 34th Division taking the High Ridge on which stood the farm, Le Point du Jour as all the low ground to the south was commanded from here, and the success of the 9th Division depended upon its capture.

On the 4th of April the Tyneside Irish Brigade, left its billets in the rear area, and the 24th Battalion took over a portion of the front line in the Roclincourt sector. After two days in the line the Battalion was relieved by the 25th, and marched back to billets in Arras. The 25th Battalion carried out a large raid at 9.30 p.m on

A platoon halt on the march up to the front. At such a halt Fred Hood met his brother Ted when, fast asleep, he came down the road astride a donkey.

the night of the 7th of April when four officers and 100 other ranks left the British lines and, finding that the wire was cut, were able to penetrate as far as the enemy second line. The Germans however could not be persuaded to leave their dugouts, so no prisoners were taken. The raid resulted in one officer missing, Second Lieutenant H E Howard, two OR's killed, ten wounded and retaliation in the form of a heavy artillery barrage on the following morning, the 8th of April.

The other battalions were now making their way forward, as the 24th Battalion left Arras to return to the Front Line. The enemy was shelling the town, and 24/731 CQMS Thomas King of Gateshead was killed. The 26th and 27th Battalions also were moving forward into support positions and, after marching for some time, the 27th Battalion stopped for a ten minute rest when Fred Hood's platoon, of C Company, fell out on the roadside. Looking up the road, Fred saw a man on a donkey coming towards them, and as the donkey drew nearer, Fred could see that the man, a soldier of the Army Service Corps, was fast asleep. The command was given for the platoon to fall in and as he stepped onto the road, the donkey drew level with him at which point it was quite a shock to find that sitting asleep on the donkey's back was his younger brother Ted. There was just time for a quick 'hello', and for Fred to be told that the donkey knew its way home, before Fred marched off, and Ted went back to sleep. They would not meet again until 1919.

The Tyneside Irish Brigade had in the front line on the right, the 24th Battalion, and on the left, the 25th Battalion whilst the 26th Battalion was in support positions, in CEMETERY ALLEY south of Roclincourt, with the 27th Battalion held in Divisional reserve in the ROCLINCOURT LINE. The Brigade objectives were three lines of German trenches, Black, Blue and Brown. The 24th and 25th Battalions, were to take the German Front Line, then the Black Line, and after consolidating the Black Line, they were to go on and capture the Brown Line. After the capture of the Brown Line, a further advance was to take place and a new line, The Green Line had to be dug. At 5.30 a.m on the morning of 9 April 1917, Easter Monday, the British barrage fell onto the German front line for four minutes and during this time the leading waves of the 24th and 25th Battalions crept out into No-Man's-Land and got as close to the barrage as they could. The morning was dull and misty, and the two battalions had little trouble clearing the enemy front line trenches. On the 25th Battalion front, A and B companies crossed the enemy front line, and left mopping-up parties in it, then proceeded to the support trench which was taken on time. Two Maxim guns were captured and some prisoners taken, then C and D companies, commanded by Lieutenant McClachlan and Captain Beattie-Brown respectively, came up and passed through the other companies. The barrage lifted precisely on time at Zero hour plus 34 minutes, and the Black Line was taken, but the two companies lost all their officers, killed or wounded before it was time to move on to the Blue Line. In the Black Line no less than nine enemy mortars were captured, many dugouts were cleared, and many prisoners taken.

Lt Col E W Hermon Commander of 24th Northumberland Fusiliers killed crossing No Man's Land, 9 April 1917.

Meanwhile the 24th Battalion had taken the Black Line on time. The Battalion Headquarters of both units was ordered forward, at 6 20. a.m. by Brigade, but as the Commanding Officer of the 24th, Lieutenant-Colonel Hermon, crossed No-Man's-Land he was killed. The companies of both battalions now closed up behind the barrage and re-formed ready to move on to the Blue Line as the barrage lifted. Things began to go wrong for, as the re-formed companies started to advance towards the Blue Line, they came under extremely heavy and accurate machine-gun fire from the left flank. Casualties were heavy, particularly in B company of the 25th Battalion, caused by the delayed arrival

Highlanders bringing in PoWs, 152 Brigade of the 51st Division cut across the front of the Tyneside Irish Brigade.

Lance Corporal Thomas Bryan VC 25th Battalion.

of 152 Brigade of the 51st (Highland) Division. They too came under fire when they arrived and they moved to their right into the path of the 25th Battalion, causing much confusion, with troops of the different battalions being mixed up in the Mittel Weg. This confusion, which was further added to when men of the 26th Battalion began to arrive, was sorted out, and the Highlanders made a further advance, capturing their portion of the Blue Line. While this was going on, A and C companies, protected by a ridge from the machine-gun fire, had managed to reach the Blue Line. Second Lieutenant's Kirkup and Snee, with about eighty men, started to work their way to the left, to try and capture the machine gun, but they were forced back by Highlanders advancing diagonally across the 25th Battalion line of advance. Parties were now sent along Gaul Weg and Zehner Weg, on the left of the 25th Battalion while CSM R E Forster and thirteen men started to fight their way up towards the machine gun. For his leadership and devotion to duty, in rallying and reorganising the company, and for the successful capture of the machine gun, CSM Forster was awarded a bar to the DCM he had previously won.

B Company commander, Lieutenant Huntley, taking with him Lance Corporal Thomas Bryan, of Castleford, Yorkshire, went out to see if he could locate the machine gun, which was well hidden. Trying to locate the gun with his binoculars Lieutenant Huntley was killed and the story of what happened next is told by Lance Corporal Bryan in the St George's Gazette in June 1917.

'On this great day our lads were held up by a machine gun, which was so well hidden we couldn't check its deadly work. I therefore made up my mind to put a stop to its activities, so creeping over the top, I went from shell hole to shell hole. Whilst working my way along, I was spotted by one of the enemy, who, letting drive, caught me in the right arm. Following this bit of hard luck, I decided to try a bit of rapid fire on the place where I thought the machine gun was placed, and on this being carried out, the gun which had been spitting forth its fire of death barked no more.'

Lance Corporal Bryan then went on to say that two of the gun team tried to escape and that he shot them, but those who saw him, testified that they saw his bayonet flashing as he completed the destruction of the gun crew. These actions of Lance Corporal

Bryan brought him the award of The VICTORIA CROSS, the first awarded to a Northumberland Fusilier in the Great War.

With the machine gun out of action the way was now clear to recommence the attack on the Blue Line so that 103 Brigade Headquarters ordered the 27th Battalion forward, from reserve, and they, together with the 26th Battalion, and the Highlanders carried the unoccupied portion of the Blue Line.

Lance Corporal Michael Manley recalled the 26th Battalions advance,

> *'Our officer said "you're going over the top and a lot of you are going to get killed." He came straight out with it, then he said "even more of you will be wounded but I don't want you calling out for stretcher bearers, they've got plenty to do, so just carry on."*
>
> *Later as we advanced I saw this same officer lying in a pool of his own blood. He'd had the cheeks of his arse shot off and was lying there shouting for the stretcher bearers. We told him to stop shouting as they had enough to do. Then we left him, you should have heard him shout.'*

48237 Private Henry Gee from Sunderland served with the DLI in England before being posted to the 24th Battalion. He was Missing in Action at Arras on 9 April 1917 and has no known grave and is commemmorated on the Arras Memorial to the Missing.

Meanwhile the 24th Battalion had also managed to move forward and take their portion of the Blue Line. Command of this battalion had passed to Major R R Brewin, and many acts of courage were being displayed as typified by 24/904 Private Richard Boyle, from Usworth, who was awarded the DCM for handling his machine gun with great courage when although all his team were casualties he went forward and captured an enemy machine gun. In the 26th Battalion, 26/1297 Corporal Matthew Whelan, a member of the band, single handedly captured two enemy officers and thirty-seven men, to gain the same award. An attempt was next made to try and capture the Brown Line.

The 26th and 27th Battalions left the Blue Line, and began advancing towards the enemy held trench when suddenly heavy sustained machine-gun fire from the left flank cut them down. Wounded men were left lying out in the open, and Private Ernest Sykes, from Mossley, despite the heavy fire, went out four times, and each time brought back a wounded man. Private Sykes made a fifth journey, across ground where to move in the open meant almost certain death and he stayed out in the open to bandage all those too seriously wounded to be moved. Private Sykes was also awarded the VICTORIA CROSS.

The machine gun that had caused the damage was firing from a position in the Brown Line on the front of 152 Brigade. The Highlanders were reporting to 51st Division Headquarters that they occupied the Brown Line, but this was a mistake, for they had lost direction and were at right angles to the line of

Infantry waiting to advance, an officer is moving behind the leading wave checking equipment.

Shells explode in the distance as the infantry begin to advance.

advance. It subsequently transpired that the officer who reported he was in the Brown Line, was actually in 'Tommy Trench' and that the enemy still held the Brown Line.[1]

During the night, the 26th Battalion on the right, linked up with the 22nd Battalion of 102 Brigade, who had successfully taken the portion of the Brown Line on their front, and had put out a flank- guard to join up with the Tyneside Irish Battalion. The men spent a very uncomfortable night as the weather deteriorated; the evening rain got heavier, the wind became a howling gale, and later, the rain changed to snow. During the night, orders were given for another attack on the Brown Line, to be carried out by the 21st Battalion of 102 Brigade on the right, the 26th and 27th Battalions on 103 Brigade front, and 5/Gordon Highlanders of 152 Brigade on the left. This attack was planned to start at 5.00 a.m. in order to surprise the enemy, and it was completely successful. The 26th and 27th Battalions met with some organised resistance, with the enemy fire coming from a position known as the Maison de la Cote, but the 27th Battalion carried out a flanking movement along Gaul Weg, on the left, and the sunken road on the right. Once in position, the battalion assaulted the Maison de la Cote and carried the position. Many Germans were seen to be running away down the slope to the east as the tired Tyneside Irishmen entered the Brown Line. The Lewis guns were used to great effect on the retreating enemy, and the men of the battalion cheered as the Germans ran. Over thirty German dead were found in the position and over fifty prisoners were taken in the Maison de la Cote. After some time the 27th and 26th Battalions linked up and secured the Brown Line at last, and then pushed patrols forward to the Green line. During this assault by the 27th Battalion, Sergeant, Acting CSM G T Wigley of Crook, won the DCM for Conspicuous Gallantry, when he took command of his company and reorganised them on the objective.

One of the patrols from the 26th Battalion proceeded along the right of the railway and was cut off by a larger group of the enemy, when Lieutenant Hopper and fifteen men were killed. The remainder of the

The Lewis guns were used to great effect on the retreating enemy.

A stretcher bearer attends to a wounded man. Likely to be a posed picture for the camera man's benefit.

party, all wounded, managed to return to the battalion later that night but at 8 p.m. the enemy launched a counterattack to try to retake Maison de la Cote. This attack was broken up however with a very accurate and heavy barrage from 152 Brigade Royal Field Artillery.

The casualties had been particularly heavy amongst the officers, the 25th Battalion having all its Company Commanders amongst the casualties. Casualties given in the Battalion War Diaries are as follows:-

	Officers		Other Ranks		
	Killed	Wounded	**Killed**	Wounded	**Missing**
24th Bn	4	9		Not Given	
25th Bn	5	8	19	135	63
26th Bn	6	6	22	66	54
27th Bn	3	9		88	49

Many of those missing were of course dead, but the bulk of the casualties were among the reinforcements. Of the original enlistments to the Brigade, there were the following numbers killed in action on the 9th/10th of April 1917:

24th Bn 11, 25th Bn 7, 26th Bn 3, 27th Bn 5.

Of these twenty-six men, only three are recorded on the 'Arras Memorial to the Missing', the difference between a successful battle, and the failure of the 1st of July the previous year. But among those killed in action on the 9th of April was CSM Stephen O'Neill DCM, one of the earliest enlistments to the Tyneside Irish. His company commander, Captain George Swinburn, wrote of him:

> *'I shall never forget Stevie O'Neill a rough diamond, but what a character, he often said to me when we were doing our rounds in all sorts of weather, "I am ready if it should come," NO! I shall never forget O'Neill as long as I live, Heaven is a richer place for his presence.'*

27/1048 Private Richard Keogh, born in Maryborough, Queens County, Ireland. Wounded on the Somme with the 27th Battalion. He was transferred to the 25th Battalion and KiA on 9 April 1917.

After consolidating the position, 103 Brigade handed over a portion of the line captured to the 51st Division, and 101 and 102 Brigades lengthened their fronts to cover what remained of 103 Brigade Front. After the hand over, 103 Brigade Headquarters was withdrawn during the night to the Black Line, where they became the Divisional reserve. The Black Line was occupied by the 26th and 27th Battalions; the 24th and 25th Battalions were forward of them in the Blue Line. At 8 p.m. on the evening of the 10th of April, there was a warning of an imminent attack on the Brown Line, and the battalions in the Blue Line stood to in support of the front line. Fortunately the counterattack failed and the 25th and 26th Battalions were reformed, with each battalion having only two companies. Meanwhile the 27th Battalion was employed carrying stores to the front line and the 25th on salvage work. On the 13th of the month, the 26th Battalion went forward and took over the front line from the 20th Battalion on either side of the GAVRELLER WEG. In the afternoon of the 14th of April the relief of the Brigade commenced, with units of the 63rd (Royal Naval) Division taking over the trenches held by the Tyneside Irish battalions. After marching back to Arras, the battalions travelled by motor bus to the area just east of St Pol, where the battalions were located in separate villages a few kilometres apart as follows:- The 24th and 27th Battlions in Bailleul-Aux-Cornailles, the 25th Battalion in Marquay and the 26th Battalion in Ternas. Here reinforcements were received and the work of rebuilding the Brigade commenced again although once more very few of the men arriving had any front line experience, as many had only been in the army a few months, and some had never fired a rifle.

24/251 CSM Stephen O'neill 'Heaven is the richer for his presence'.

One of these reinforcements was 50300 Private Morris Jenkinson, from Killamarsh, near Sheffield, who joined the 27th Battalion on the 16th of April and one of the first tasks he was given in the trenches was to go and draw water for his section. He related this story to his family,

'The battalion had just occupied this section of trench and was settling in. I was given directions to the well and told to go and fetch some water. When I got to the well, much to my horror and disgust, I found the trench piled high with corpses. I had to move them to get to the water, as I pulled at an arm it came away from the body and I nearly fainted. I then tried to pull at the man's belt and I slipped and landed knees first on the body, which gave a loud belch and let forth a foul stinking gas, at which point I vomited. After this I got the water and got back to the section as fast as I could'.

Lieutenants Simons and Shackleton in 1915. Lance Shackleton's platoon attack on the chemical works at Roeux was described as 'a very gallant attempt.'

Specialists, such as Lewis gunners and Signallers, had to be trained, and there was little time to do this and to weld the men into the efficient fighting force needed to go back into the line. However, back to the line they did go, for after only seven days in the rest billets, a tactical train carried the battalions forward to Y HUTS at Maroeuil, where they arrrived on the evening of the 21st of April. Twenty four hours later, the Brigade left Y Huts and marched back towards the Arras front and the evening of St George's Day saw them in position on the Arras-Lens railway embankment. The Brigade had come under command of the 51st Division, and the 25th and 26th Battalions went forward towards Roeux, and relieved battalions of the Highlanders.

The enemy still held the village of Roeux and had machine guns and snipers in and about the Chemical Works and the Chateau. During the relief, the 25th Battalion had Second Lieutenant Snee and six other ranks killed by machine-gun fire and later on that night, Second Lieutenant Cox and two men patrolled 'Cawdor Trench' in front of the line held, and found it empty, but, under machine-gun fire from the Chemical Works.

Major T Reay D.S.O. severely wounded 9 April 1917. 26th Northumberland Fusiliers.

The 26th Battalion now made an attempt to take the Chemical Works and the Chateau, and Lieutenant Shackleton and his platoon were given the task. The 34th Divisional History describes this as a 'very gallant attempt', but unfortunately, the platoon had many casualties and the platoon commander died from his wounds. On being told that his brother-in-law had died from his wounds Captain George Swinburn asked for permission to go and try to recover his body. On his way forward he met with the Methodist Padre of the 26th Battalion, Captain Stanley Hinchcliffe CF, who accompanied him towards the front line, but the advanced dressing station was under very heavy shellfire and it was some time before they could get forward and bring the body of Lieutenant Shackleton away to be buried. [It was not until June 1917 that George Swinburn was able to erect a cross over Lance Shackleton's grave. Molly Shackleton never remarried and lived with Granny Shackleton until old age, she visited Lance's grave at Crump Trench Cemetery at the time the Arras Memorial was opened in the 1920's.]

The 26th Battalion now found that it was being shot at from the rear, enemy snipers were located in a house on the right-rear flank and had to be disposed of.

The Light Trench Mortar Battery put down a barrage on the house and as the snipers broke cover they were shot down so that of the nine enemy within the house, seven were killed and two were taken prisoner.

Digging and consolidating the trenches was now required and the 26th Battalion dug a line west of Rouex under sniper fire. The 24th and 25th Battalions also were employed in this way and CAM TRENCH was deepened and cleared from the front line to its junction with CAWDOR TRENCH, a distance of some 800 yards. This was done under heavy shellfire, and the 25th Battalion had three killed and six wounded. The battalions were now in the OPPY LINE preparing for the assault on Rouex which was to take place at 4.25 a.m. on the morning of 27 April 1917.

Lt.(Acting Capt.) T. W. Blott 24th Northumberland Fusiliers. Killed in Battle of Arras.

For the attack General Nicholson had placed 101 Brigade on the right and 103 Brigade on the left. 103 Brigade had the 24th Battalion on the right, with its right flank resting on the railway embankment, and on the left the 25th Battalion continued the line as far as CLYDE TRENCH. Attached to each of the leading battalions were two guns of 103 Machine Gun Company with the 26th and 27th Battalions held in support. The barrage missed the enemy front line, falling in the rear, and caused very few casualties amongst the defenders so that, as the attack began, the leading companies came under heavy machine-gun and rifle fire from an unregistered position in front of the 25th Battalion and from the Chemical Works and other buildings in Rouex. The left flank of the 25th Battalion reached the objective and started to dig in, but the enemy fire made this a difficult task. The 24th Battalion were severely held up by machine guns, particularly in the

Captain (Acting Major) F. J. Downey M.C., D.C.M. 24th Northumberland Fusiliers, wounded four times.

buildings north of the railway line and its attack petered out as the men took cover or became casualties.

Some of the 24th Battalion managed to enter the village but were forced out by a counterattack from south of the railway. The 27th Battalion, brought up in support, occupied a trench to the north of the village and several attempts to pass information back by a runner failed, as men fell prey to the German machine guns. A German counter-attack was made against 101 Brigade at 11 a.m. on the 28th of April when over 600 Germans passed across the front of 103 Brigade, but they were halted by machine-gun and artillery fire from the British line to the south.

To the rear of the 25th Battalion a pocket of Germans remained, and their snipers made life unpleasant for the battalion throughout the day. At nightfall the enemy tried to surround the survivors, and the men, with practically all the officers casualties, withdrew to the original front line later that night.

Casualties for the 28th of April are once again difficult to assess. Battalion War Diaries give varying information and the 24th Battalion gives none at all. The 25th gives the following:

Officers 1 killed, 3 wounded, 4 missing, other ranks total 135.

The 26th Battalion divides the casualties up as follows:

		Officers	Other Ranks
9th to 14th of April			
	Killed	6	22
	Wounded	6	160
	Missing	–	54
23rd to 30th of April			
	Killed	3	25
	Wounded	1	110
	Missing	–	11

The 27th Battlion reported as follows:

24/4/17 to 27/4/17 Officers 1 Killed 2 Wounded, 74 OR's Wounded and Missing.

28/4/17 Officers 2 Killed 2 Wounded 2 Missing, OR's 151 Wounded and Missing.

Pte Godfrey Sedgewick killed in action 9 April 1917.

Bertie Edmondson killed in action 21 April 1917 aged 20.

Private Edward Fawcett, of Gargrave. Killed in action 28 April 1917 aged 28.

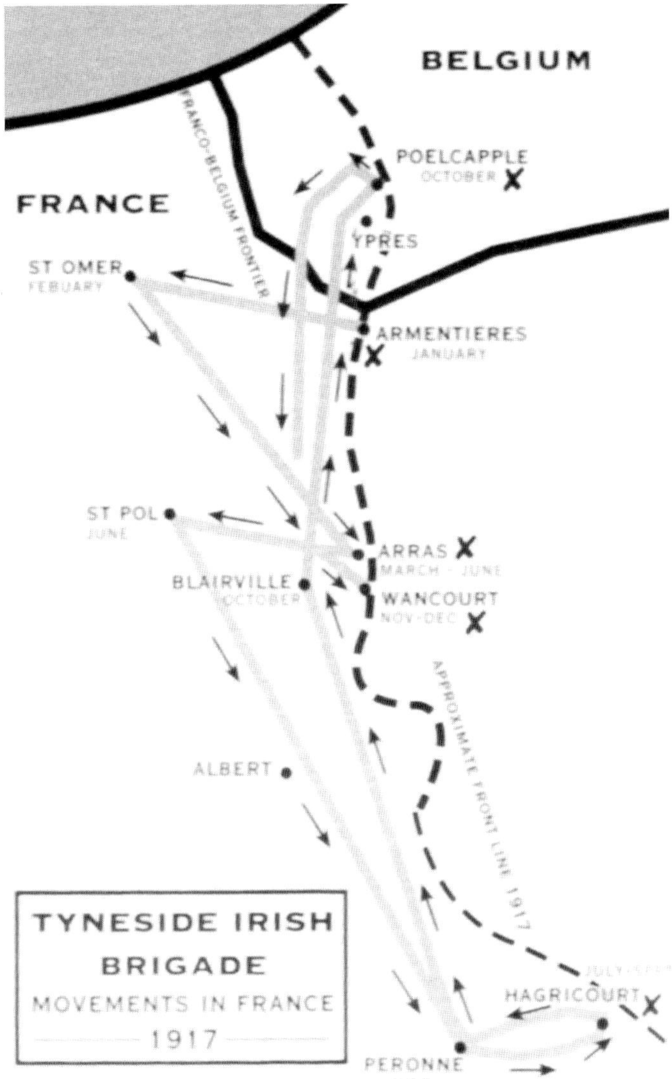

Once again the casualties were high, and the fact that the battle was a qualified success is reflected in the names that are recorded on the 'Arras Memorial to the Missing'. It is a very sad reflection on the casualties, sustained by the Brigade, that there were now very few of the original enlistments left to be recorded on any memorial. The figures for original enlistments killed in action during the Second Battle of the Scarpe, are as follows:

	Killed	Arras Memorial	Known Grave
24th Bn	7	5	2
25th Bn	10	9	1
26th Bn	5	2	3
27th Bn	7	4	3

Further to these names, there were several of the reserve battalion killed during this battle who served with other units. Their names are also recorded on the Arras Memorial.

On the 29th of April, after the battle, the Tyneside Irish Brigade started to hand over the line and withdraw to the OPPY LINE. Once again the casualties were such that the battalions were organised on a two company basis. The Brigade was ordered back to bivouacs in St Nicholas, where the work of rebuilding commenced as gradually new men were absorbed by the shattered remnants, and training programmes were worked out. Every type of infantry training imaginable was carried out, starting with the basic range practices and working up through bayonet fighting, attacking a strong point, and attacking in waves in artillery formation. In the evening the officers gave lectures on anti-aircraft defence by infantry, attack formation in woods, and anti-gas drill. These emphasised the way the fighting was progressing on the Western Front and the idea behind this training was that the 34th Division was trying to return to the rifle as the main infantry weapon, and not rely so much on the hand grenade.

Note

1. 51st Divisional History page 157.

Chapter Nine

1917 Hagricourt and Poelcapelle

'Two blighties a struggle through mud to get back
To the old ADS down a rough duckboard track'
'THE BURNING QUESTION' ANON

All through May 1917, the Tyneside Irish Brigade was located on the training area at Bonneville. Twice on the 23rd and the 26th of May, the men were given a half-day holiday. On the 27th it was time to start heading back towards the line and the transport went by route-march via Candas, Doullens and Moncourt, where the night was spent. The journey continued via Arras and St Nicholas until the Scarpe was crossed and St Nicholas' Camp on the north bank was reached. The remainder of the battalions entrained at Candas station on the 28th and were moved back to Arras by rail, where they arrived in the early afternoon, and then moved on foot to the camp site. The Commanding Officer and one officer from each company and four NCO's from the 24th and 25th Battalions, were met by guides at 8 a.m. on the morning of the 29th of May, and they proceeded to reconnoitre the trenches prior to taking over. That night, the 24th and 25th Battalions took over the front line, the 26th Battalion moved to the railway cutting in support, and the 27th Battalion were placed in reserve.

The transport section of the 24th Battalion was heavily shelled as it brought up the rations to the battalion in the line and casualties were particularly heavy; the Transport Officer, Second Lieutenant Cunningham was wounded and RQMS Wright and CQMS Harnett were killed.

The sector taken over was known as the Gavrelle Line and much work was needed to bring the trenches to a defendable state. Deepening, shoring-up and constructing strong points was commenced, with the wiring parties being hindered at their work by enemy machine guns. For a period the battalions in the front line were relieved by those in support but every battalion had men out in No-Man's-Land digging new trenches and it was during one of these operations that Captain Jack Arnold was severely wounded and some of his men killed.

'The role assigned to my company was to follow the first party over the top and construct a switch line which was to be pegged out for us by the engineers in a move to the flank of a line occupied by the enemy. In due course we went over and came to where the line was pegged out and set to work digging in but I was doubtful about the lay of the line from the start as it appeared to lead more into the enemy's front than to his flank. We were soon under heavy fire and men and officers began to fall, but we stuck to the job although by this time I had only one officer left besides myself, my runner was dead and the whole company sadly thinned. Just as dawn was beginning to appear I went with a supply of bombs to establish a "block" at the furthest point which our line had reached. It was at this point that I was hit. Whatever it was went right through my thigh bone and I knew I could walk no further. I collapsed and crawled into a nearby shellhole. I was quite conscious and sent a note to the only officer left that he was to take over. There was one unwounded man and two or three wounded lying near me.'

Captain Jack Arnold wounded in June 1917 with the 26th Battalion.

They had to lie still all day, not daring to move as this brought rifle fire from the German held trench. Captain Arnold's wound began to bleed and the battalion Doctor, Captain Danahar RAMC, crawled along to him and bandaged the wound and treated the other men also. The day dragged on. Late in the morning the CSM managed to bring a dixie of tea along the trench.

'At last the shadows began to creep down on the longest day in my memory and in due course the stretcher bearers came out to gather in the wounded.'

While he was at 42 Casualty Clearing Station in Aubigny, Captain Arnold received a letter from his CO, Colonel Richardson.

'You had a very nasty job that night and the way you got your men to stick to the work was really splendid. It could never have been done without the personal example of those in charge.'

The colonel went on to congratulate him and then he wrote about the casualties,

'I am dreadfully sorry about poor little Stewart. He is a great loss to the battalion: a more conscientious officer or one more devoted to duty I never knew: well he is one more added to the list of heroes of the 26th.'

Captain Jack Arnold was in hospital and convalescing until June 1918 and never returned to the front.

An unknown Corporal of the 27th Battalion in full Battle Order complete with mud from the trenches. The shoulder badges worn on the collar were adopted in mid 1917. The original picture postcard had the words 'To Maggie love Billie' on the back.

Meanwhile in France with the 27th Battalion, Morris Jenkinson and his pal Bob Quinn, had been on a working party all day, returning to their dugout they were both placed on guard duty but before long due to fatigue they both fell asleep. To teach them a lesson the platoon sergeant had the rest of the section drag a dead German officer into the trench, and prop the corpse up in front of the sleeping men. The sergeant then made a noise loud enough to wake the sentries, who, on seeing the German started screaming, and Maurice shot the dead German again. Of course the 'old hands' thought this hilarious, but the NCO made them realise that they could have been shot for sleeping on duty.

On the 25th Battalion front, a covering party from B Company were in position at 10.30 p.m. and were followed by Royal Engineers who taped the positions to be dug. At 11 p.m. forty eight men of A Company went forward and proceeded to dig the new line, which was to consist of two platoon posts, each with three fire-bays, eighteen feet long, connected by two twelve-feet traverses. During the hours of darkness the men dug as quietly as possible and succeeded in reaching a depth of four feet six inches, then just before daylight the covering party was withdrawn to the old front line, and A Company became the front line garrison. Two Lewis guns were left with them and an officer with his signaller, established himself in the right-hand post. Sufficient tools and sandbags were supplied to enable the men to improve the posts during the hours of daylight, and carrying parties brought up rations, water, bombs and ammunition. This work, carried out within thirty yards of the enemy, was done without any casualties, and was carried on until the 21st Battalion arrived to relieve the 25th Battalion, on the night of the 11th of June. The Brigade now went into reserve, and moved back to the camp at St Nicholas, where the battalions began the process of refitting and training once again.

On 18 June 1917 the 3/4 Royal West Kent Regiment was attached to the Brigade, and the various companies of that Battalion were allotted to the Tyneside Irish Battalions as follows:-

A Company to the 24th Battalion,
HQ & B Company to the 25th Battalion,
C Company to the 26th Battalion and
D Company to the 27th Battalion.

The 24th Battalion took over the line, in front of the Chemical Works at Rouex from 10/Lincolnshire Regiment. The Royal West Kents had their first casualties, three killed and seven wounded, whilst the more experienced Tyneside Irish Battalion had only one fatal casualty, and two wounded. The other battalions had moved forward too, and much work was done by all ranks in improving the Gavrelle line when fire steps were added to the trench, and, where possible, shelters were constructed. On the 22nd of the month 52 Brigade, of the 17th Division, commenced the relief of 103 Brigade, and the Tyneside Irish battalions once again headed for the rear area and the camp at St Nicholas. The 34th Division now went into reserve, and the Brigade was moved to quarters in the Maizieres area near St Pol where training became the order of the day for all battalions until the 5th of July, when they were moved by train to Peronne. On arrival, the billets were found to be in a dreadful state, so the first task was to clean up their own accommodation so for the next three days working parties were allocated to the Town Major in Peronne, and the task of clearing the rubble, caused by enemy shelling, was given to the men of 103 Brigade. By the 9th of July, the 34th Division was relieving the 4th and 5th Cavalry Divisions in the line, but 103 Brigade remained in reserve until the 17th.

In the 26th Battalion Captain Jack Fleming had relinquished command of 103 Light Trench Mortar Battery, and rejoined his old battalion, just in time to take over command of one of the companies as they took over the front line from the Royal Scots of 101 Brigade.

Corporal Peter Barratt (standing) 26th Battalion.

Patrolling No-Man's-Land once again became a priority, and the 26th Battalion had at least three patrols out every night. One patrol waited in Somerville Wood through the daylight hours of the 21st, but no enemy was encountered until that night, at about 10.45 p.m., suspicious sounds were heard on the right flank, to the front of a point known as Lone Tree Post. Five minutes later a whistle blast was heard, and the enemy artillery opened fire on the post but the German gunners had the range wrong, and all the shells fell to the rear. At 10.55 p.m. the Officer Commanding Lone Tree Post had fired an SOS Signal, but there had been no answer from the British Artillery for over five minutes. The enemy infantry then began to fire rifle grenades and throw bombs, and rifle fire was heard from the front. The garrison of the post had stood-to immediately and the enemy fire was returned until 11.15 p.m. when enemy firing ceased. Meanwhile a patrol from the 26th Battalion had been crawling over No-Man's-Land, and had heard a large party of Germans retreating towards their own lines. They opened fire with rifles and Lewis guns, causing great confusion amongst the foe and there was a great deal of noise, particularly from some wounded, who were apparently being carried to safety.

The following morning, at first light, the front line wire was examined, and three gaps were found to have been cut by the raiders, although initially no enemy dead were found, only four caps and three rifles. As daylight grew stronger however two dead German soldiers and a number of caps and rifles were found and the following night another patrol from the same battalion came across an enemy patrol, apparently searching for the bodies of their dead comrades resulting in a sharp fight before both sides withdrew. When the 25th Battalion took over from the 26th Battalion, on the 26th of July, both battalions provided patrols into Somerville Wood, to cover the relief that was taking place. Every night at 10.15 p.m a patrol of one officer and twenty men, of the 25th Battalion left 'Dragoon Post' and stayed out in No-Man's-Land until relieved the following night. It was not until the night of the 31st of July, that two enemy patrols wereencountered when at 10.15 p.m. a small enemy patrol was engaged near Angle Wood by the patrol in Somerville Wood. Fifteen minutes later a second enemy party, with an estimated strength of fifty men, was encountered by a fighting patrol of the 25th Battalion and this enemy patrol, being engaged by Lewis gun fire, were encouraged to retire towards their own lines. The 24th Battalion was also actively carrying out patrol work, but once again they were dogged by bad luck, for on the night of the 30th of July Second-Lieutenant J B Innes was wounded through the neck, and although he was carried in, and reached the Casualty Clearing Station, he died of his wounds a few days later. At midnight on the 31st of July Second Lieutenant C J Pleasance of the same battalion was killed in action.

On the 6th of August the 27th Battalion was to carry out a raid on a copse in No-Man's-Land, known as Little Bill and the story of this raid was told in *Chequers* by an unnamed subaltern of the battalion.

'When we took over the Hagricourt sector the foe had the run of No-Man's-Land. Our job was to prod the Boche out of two copses in No-Man's-Land. Starting from Grand Priel-Ascension Farm posts, one party of a hundred was to comb "Big Bill". Another, of two officers and fifty men from the 27th Battalion had to raid "Little Bill". We got to within fifty yards and lay down, awaiting "Zero" with strained nerves, as "Little Bill" was to be shelled for five minutes, the other "Bill" being a silent raid. When the guns opened the shells screeched uncomfortably near our heads, falling shorter and shorter. So the senior "Sub" wisely decided to withdraw down the slope a little. To this I demurred, foolishly, as I found out a few minutes later; for when we advanced again the ground we had lain on was pitted with our short falling shells. The other officer went round the N.W. edge of the copse with half of the men, to take it in the flank, while I with the other half advanced across the open in a frontal attack.

We got fairly close when a guttural voice challenged us "Wer da"? with that the tension snapped; the chest was relieved of its strangle and the stomach rose to its normal equilibrium; the exitement of battle inherited from thousands of progenitors, rose in me. Caution now useless, action decidely urgent. So I dashed forward yelling "Charge"! At that moment, whether from nerves, accidentally or from sheer elation, someone let off his rifle. As so frequently happens one man can make or mar the efforts of a multitude. A subtle contagion spreads like lightning from man to man and, inexplicably this one became the "Wrong un". To my dismay and upswelling rage, instead of following they started firing, retreating a few steps between each round, and I found myself alone with bullets whistling past my ears and between my legs. I saw "red" to let the show down like this was unthinkable. What would the other two Brigades of the Division think of us? And the honour of the Company, The Battalion, even the Division would be smeared, the "Fighting" prefix of the "Fifth Fusiliers" buried in "Little Bill"copse! What should I do? To advance alone was foolish; to go back was even more so, for then I could never have rallied my men, as they would naturally have looked upon it as "wind up" on my part. If a second before was the time for action then now it was infinitely more so. In that split second I decided to combine both a strategic retreat and a rally as the only possible way of saving the situation and "face". Boiling with anger I started running diagonally across our "front" quite oblivious to the danger of being hit in the dark: once the battle is joined bullets do not exist – 'till one stops one!

Urging them forward and rasping my throat with curses, I dashed sideways to the nearest man. Pushing him I ordered him to remain there. Then to the next one, repeating the process, and so on in a zig zag retreat till I had brought them all up into line, firing away to keep them occupied.'

So the raiders were brought back to the British lines under control but heavily shot at by the now wide awake Germans in Little Bill Copse.

There was now a severe shortage of reinforcements, for there were not enough men to bring the four Tyneside Irish battalions up to strength. The decision was taken to reduce the number of battalions to three, and this was done by the amalgamation of the 24th and 27th Battalions on the 9th of August, to form the 24th/27th Battalion North-umberland Fusiliers. To bring 103 Brigade back up to its establishment of four battalions, 9/North-umberland Fusiliers was transferred from the 17th Division. Corporal Peter Barratt's section roll book, which lists his whole platoon for this period, reveals just how mixed the battalions had become. Of the forty-five men named, five are original enlistments, the others are reinforcements from many different battalions and regiments.

Private Percy Hawkswell, 26th Battalion killed in action 18th November, 1917.

The early part of August 1917 was spent in refitting and training once again and the 25th Battalion actually spent the morning of the 4th of August doing saluting drill and sentry duties, whilst the 26th found the time to run an inter-platoon rifle meeting, with 11 Platoon of C Company the eventual winners. The sergeants and corporals had an inter-company shoot, with the NCOs of B Company winning. The 26th Battalion also received a draft of men from the 24th and 27th Battalions, who were surplus to strength at the time of amalgamation. When the 25th Battalion went back into the line on the 16th of August, B Company became the right hand unit of the British Expeditionary Force. On the south of the River Omnigon the line was held by the French 62nd Regiment, whilst the line on the northern side of the river, held by 103 Brigade, consisted mainly of a series of posts, constructed by and named after the regiments of the Canadian Cavalry Brigade, e.g. Fort Garry, Dragoon, Rifleman and Hussar posts.

On the night of the 16th/17th of August, the men of the 25th Battalion could see the town of St Quentin and the burning spires of the cathedral which had been set on fire by the Germans. Much patrol work was being carried out before the Brigade was relieved by the MHOW Regiment of the Indian Cavalry Brigade. 101 and 102 Brigades were now given the task of taking the German trenches in front of the Hagricourt Sector, where the troops involved fought their way into the enemy lines and were able, after much fighting, to consolidate the position. Two battalions of 103 Brigade, 9/Northumberland Fusiliers and the 24/27th Battalion, were now given the task of taking the high ground to the south of Railway Trench. On the evening of the 26th of August, the weather changed and rain began falling, which made life very miserable for the troops, and movement became very difficult indeed, with men floundering, waist deep in mud and water. In preparation for the coming attack, the Divisional Artillery commenced cutting the enemy wire, and later shelled the objective but the progress of the 24/27th Battalion to the jumping-off point was very slow indeed and by zero-hour the battalion had not arrived at the start line. The CO of 9/Northumberland Fusiliers decided that he would not attack alone, and in consequence 9/Northumberland Fusiliers were withdrawn. When the 24/27th Battalion did arrive, an unsuccessful attempt was made to advance on Railway Trench when

An unidentified soldier of the newly amalgamated battalions. He is wearing the black shamrock of the 27th Battalion superimposed over the red shamrock of the 24th.

Lieutenant Burns and about thirty men of his platoon actually managed to enter Farm Trench. They were unsupported, and began to consolidate and at daybreak were found by the CO of 15/Royal Scots. The rest of the 24/27th Battalion had been withdrawn under the cover of darkness so Lieutenant Burns was relieved and the platoon made its way back to join the rest of the battalion which was moving back into Brigade reserve.

Meanwhile the other battalions were supplying the usual working parties and, when in the line, patrols were out every night. The 25th Battalion War Diary records that nightly large quantities of barbed wire was being placed in front of the trenches and on the night of the 3rd of September the 26th Battalion attacked TRIANGLE TRENCH, losing Second Lieutenant N A Hunter killed, and Second Lieutenant H P Dixon missing, with four other ranks killed, nine wounded and three missing. During the morning of the 4th of September, the German artillery were busy shelling, with the support line receiving over three hundred shells in four hours. The 26th Battalion was relieved by the 24/27th Battalion on the night of the 5th.

Second Lieutenant M Melia 26th Battalion formerly a CQMS in C Company of the 27th Battalion was awarded the MC for his work during the operations at Triangle Trench. The 24/27th Battalion made a very successful attack on Triangle Trench on the morning of the 9th of September, inflicting heavy casualties on the defenders, taking thirty-eight men and a dog prisoner, and suffering only light casualties, one killed and seven wounded, in return. But at dawn the enemy began bombarding the trench it had lost when the shelling, lasting eight minutes, was repeated every half hour until 12.30 a.m. At 2.10 p.m. a very heavy bombardment, lasting for forty minutes, took place, rendering the trench in this area untenable and the men were accordingly withdrawn. As there was no artillery support available the ground taken the previous day was lost.

One evening about this time Morris Jenkinson was sitting in a dugout beside Bob Quinn whilst around

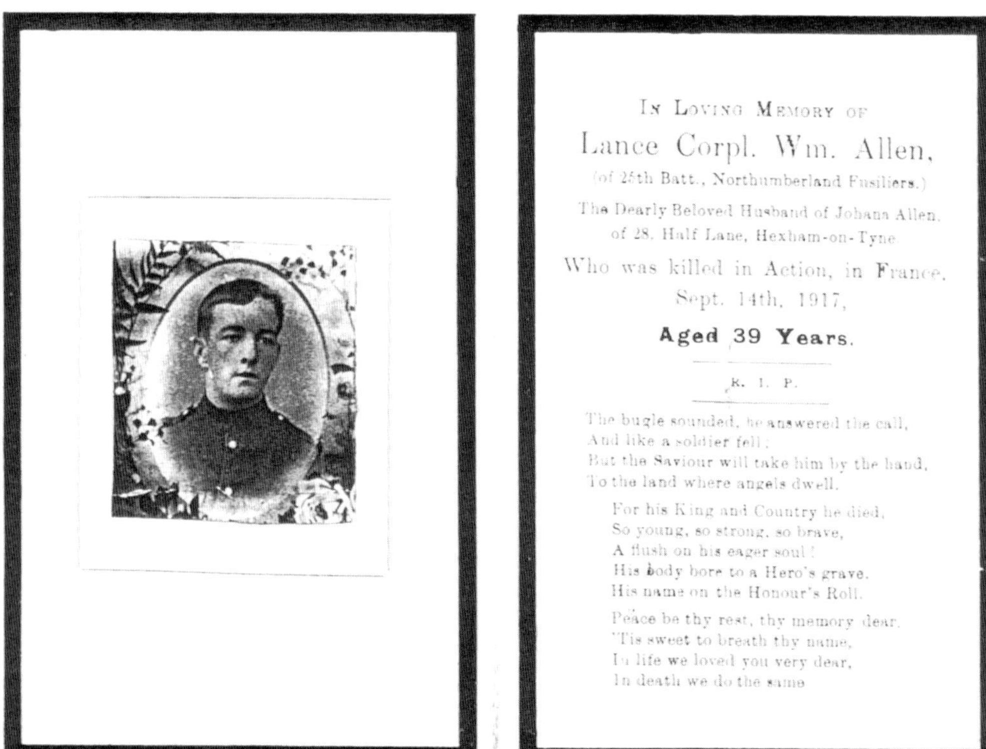

Memorial card for Lance Corporal William Allen, 25th Battalion, killed in action 14th September 1917.

46996 Lance Corporal Arthur Vernon Vallender was one of a a large number of Royal Engineers transferred into the Tyneside Irish. He was KiA in the Ypres Salient on 12 October 1917. He has no known grave and is commemorated on the Tyne Cot Memorial to the Missing.

Private J Early of Seaham, 27th Battalion, discharged sick in 1917.

them men were sitting talking and drinking tea, when Morris noticed that one man was getting edgy saying he could not take the war any longer. Suddenly he ran out of the dugout and before anyone could stop him, he jumped up on the parapet and began to sing 'Roses are blooming in Picardy'. The Germans shot up 'Very lights' which silhouetted the singer, but they did not shoot. The whole section were watching in horror, expecting the Germans to start bombarding their position with trench mortars but, as the soldier finished the last verse, a single shot rang out from the German lines and the singer fell back into the British trench dead!

On another occassion, Morris and his friend Bob were detailed for a patrol in No-Man's-Land when all went well until the Germans heard something, and fired a Very light to light up the ground. The patrol 'froze' and tried to remain perfectly still but all night long flares went up, and there was no chance to get back to the British lines. Daybreak found them still in No-Man's-Land; hoping that the enemy would think they were dead, they lay there throughout the day, until at last as night fell they were able to return to their own trenches.

After spending time in rest, on the 25th of September 103 Brigade took over in the left sub-sector of the Hagricourt section of the line. However, they were only there for four days when the 34th Division was relieved by the 24th Division. The battalions made their way, by various routes, in motor buses to Peronne where they spent the night. On the 30th of September, the Brigade was moved by train to VI Corps rest area, the 24/27th and 26th Battalions going into a hutted camp at Blairville, and the 25th Battalion going to Hendencourt. The 34th Division was now placed in Corps reserve and during the next week new drafts arrived and a lot of training was done. On the 2nd of the month the order came that the Division would move to Fifth Army. The GOC 34th Division, General Nicholson, inspected the battalions

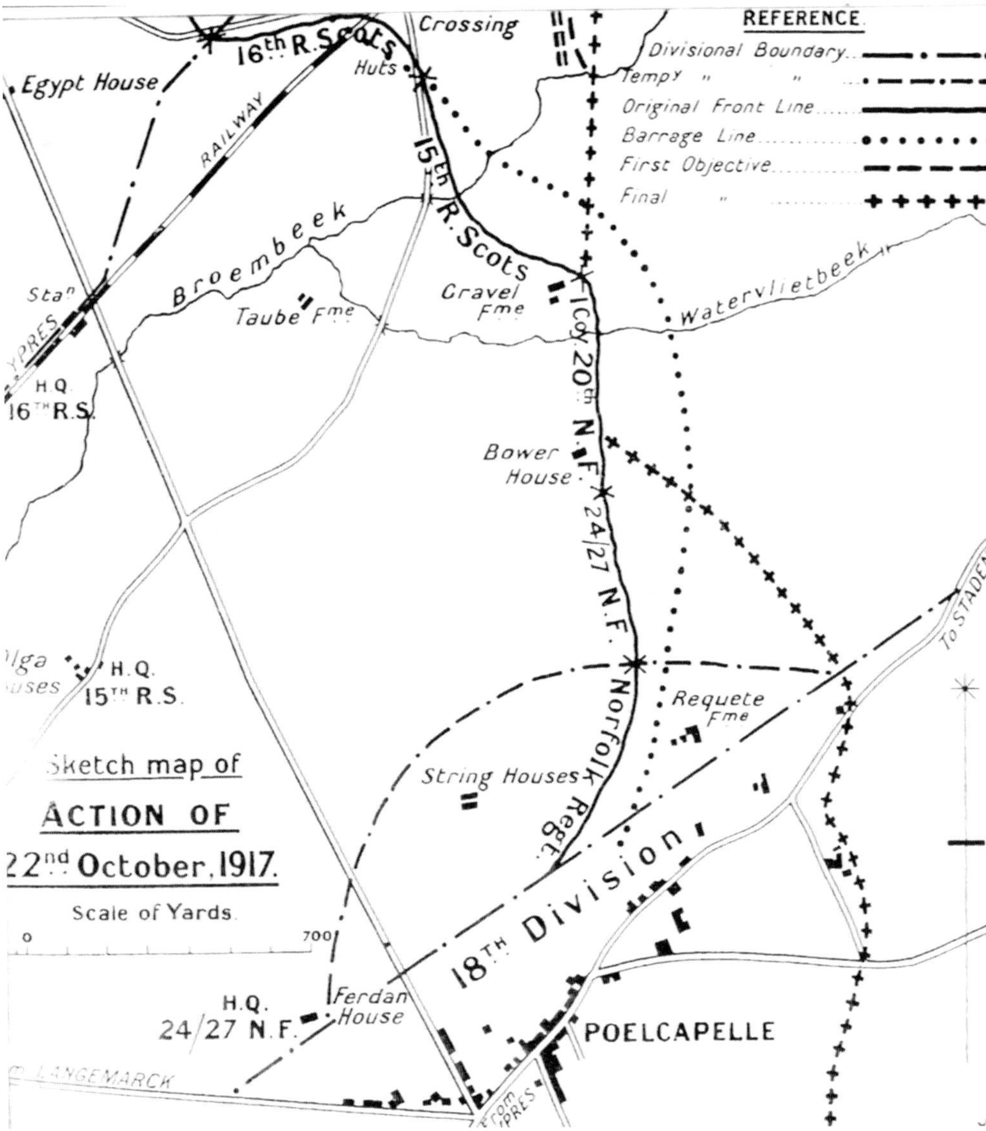

in their respective camps on the 4th of October after which on the 7th of that month the move north to the infamous 'WIPERS' began.

On arrival in Flanders the battalions detrained at or near Proven and marched into camps as follows, 24/27th Battalion to Piccadilly Camp, 25th Battalion to Penton Camp and the 26th Battalion to Paddington Camp. The training of the new drafts commenced at once, for these men had very little service and once again it was found that some had never fired a rifle whereas those who had been in the line before came from an assortment of regiments. The weather was extremely cold and wet when on the 12th of October the battalions entrained at Proven station for Boesinghe.

Left behind were the battalion nucleus, a number of NCO's and specialists, on which to rebuild the battalions should they have high casualties. Also left behind were the bands and transport sections and a number of the new men who were insufficiently trained. On arrival at Boesinghe the battalions detrained and marched to Stray Farm where the 24/27th Battalion came under shellfire and had two officers wounded and twenty-six other ranks killed or wounded. The area of the line to be taken over was described by the 26th Battalion as, 'conditions very bad - country half flooded with water - whole battalion area one sea of mud.' Two battalions of the Brigade, the 25th and 26th were now detailed to commence the relief of the 4th Division N.W. of Poelcapelle, but in the conditions described, it was found almost impossible to move forward and the relief was not complete until the following day. The battalions were not long in the line before being relieved and moved back to Stray Farm Camp but in the twenty-four hour period for the 15th - 16th of October the 24/27th Battalion had over fifty casualties.

Working parties trying to take rations forward lost heavily, and between the 17th and 22nd, the 26th Battalion had over eighty killed and wounded, with a number of missing unaccounted for. In the same period Captain Jack Fleming, attached to the 25th Battalion from the 26th Battalion, was killed in action. In 1901 he had been the amateur middle-weight boxing champion of Ireland, and was a well known racing cyclist.

The 24/27th Battalion was now attached to 102 Brigade to assist in their attack north-west of Poelcapelle and the particular task of the Battalion was to cover the flank of the 18th Division, on their right, and to pivot on the left, where a company of the 20th Battalion would stand fast and provide covering fire. The Battalion formed up and, under the cover of the barrage, began to advance. Things were going well, but the commander of the company on the right, Lieutenant M R Steel, noticed that the Norfolks of the 18th Division had bypassed Requete Farm. Very quickly the company was reorganised, moved to the right, and the defenders of the farm were driven out. Two machine guns and twenty-five prisoners were taken, allowing the advance to be continued towards the objective which was taken and consolidated. Communication was maintained with the Norfolks on the right. The story of the advance was related to his family by 50300 Private Morris Jenkinson

'We stood in the trench waiting for 'zero hour', next to me was Bob Quinn and about four men to my left was the Company Commander. We were watching him for the signal to go over the top, and as the barrage lifted he blew his whistle, and scrambled up over the parapet with C Company following him. He only took a couple of steps before he was cut down.[1] *Bob and I advanced from shellhole to shellhole in short rushes, the last rush was to a shellhole close to a German machine-gun post, and we flung ourselves in to the hole amid a hail of small-arms fire. Seconds later a third soldier, who I did not know, landed in the hole. I was lying on the right and Bob was lying on his back in the middle, we had been there for a couple of minutes when we heard the sound of a whizzbang coming straight for the hole. We knew, just knew, it was going to hit us, and sure enough the shell exploded on the lip of the crater. I had tucked myself as deep as I could into the ground and was struck on the head as earth rained down from the explosion. When everything settled down I went to brush the earth from me and was horrified to see that it was not earth but Bob's leg which had been blown off just below the hip. Bob didn't speak, but looked at me his eyes pleading for help. The other chap was just moaning, he was a mass of torn flesh, blood, dirt and tattered uniform from his back to his thighs. I tried to move over to Bob, but as I did so my left leg gave way when I put my weight on it. Reaching down I felt my leg was wet and when I brought my hand back up it was covered in blood. I got over to Bob, reached into his haversack and took his towel out and dressed the wounded as best I could. Then I took my puttee off and saw my leg was a pulp of flesh and bone, so I pulled my own towel out and used it to dress my own wound. Now I crawled over to the other fellow, the German gunner had another go at me as I moved about in the shellhole but by the time I got to the other side of the hole the man had stopped moaning and had died from his terrible injuries.*

Private Morris Jenkinson, 24/27th Battalion, Badly wounded at Poelcapele 23rd October 1917.

The two of us lay there for some time until I realised I would have to go back, Bob needed medical attention as soon as possible if he was to live. I told Bob where I was going and he acknowl-

Captain Billy Murray 26th Battalion wounded for the second time on 19th October 1917, near Langemarck.

edged with a feeble nod as I set off crawling back. I crawled from shellhole to shellhole until I came upon an officer. I reported the position to him and asked him to help, but he said it was impossible and that I should make my way back to the dressing station. With that he looked over the lip of the shellhole and was shot in the forehead. His body slumped back against me and I had a job to shove him off. As I was sitting there I noticed he had a pearl handled revolver and as I had left my rifle behind I armed myself with this instead.[1]

After some time I managed to crawl back to the old front line where I found two stretcher bearers resting, I told them about Bob and pleaded with them to go for him, I even offered them the revolver if they would, but to no avail. They did say however that they would take me to the aid station, I thought I might get some help for Bob there, so I looked back at the churned up battlefield to try and remember the whereabouts of Bob's location. The stretcher bearers loaded me onto the stretcher and we set off down the duckboard track towards the aid station. After a short distance one of the bearers slipped and went into the mud, after a struggle we got him out and off we went again. We hadn't gone far when in he went again, this time it was even harder to get him out of the devouring morass. Well away we went again and a third time he fell in and this time we all ended up in the quagmire. At this point I decided that I would be better off crawling, to which the stretcher bearers readily agreed. Over two hours later I managed to reach the aid station, in a captured pillbox, and was taken inside and laid on a table. A medical orderly came and cut my webbing off and took my money and the pearl handled revolver for 'safe keeping'. Some time later another orderly came and cut the trouser leg and my puttee away and removed my boot, then he washed the wound as best he could. I was then taken outside and left to wait on a bench, ambulances were coming and going all the time and eventually I was loaded into one and taken to a Casualty Clearing Station. While I was there I heard that Bob had lived for forty-eight hours until the stretcher bearers had reached him, just as they lifted him onto the stretcher he had succumbed to his awful wounds.'

[Private Robert Quinn has no known grave and is not commemorated on the Tyne Cot Memorial, action has been taken to rectify this.]

Casualties were described in the Battalion War Diary as light; there were in fact less than twenty dead, but among them were 24/310 Sergeant Frank Skinnan, a coalminer, originally from Limerick, but living at Deafhill, Co Durham and 24/168 Private Charles Gettings, from Dunston, two of the remaining original members of the Brigade.

At midday on the 24th of October the relief of the Battalion commenced and it made its way back to Boesinghe Station and entrained for Proven, where it remained for three nights until the 28th of October. The welcome news was received that the 34th Division was to move back to VI Corps, and few were sorry to leave Belgium when they entrained at Hopoutre Station on the 28th of October. The conditions in the Ypres Salient were among the worst that the Brigade ever experienced, not only in the state of the ground and the weather, but because of the number of gas shells that the Germans were using. On arrival in the new sector, the 25th and 26th Battalions took over

Captain Jack Fleming 26th Battalion attached 25th. Killed in action in the Ypres Salient 13th October 1917. His letters to Captain Bob Falkous are quoted extensively in Chapter 5.

the front line, with the 24/27th Battalion in Brigade reserve, relieving battalions of the 51st Highland Division.

On the morning of the 8th of November the Headquarters of the 26th Battalion came under fire from German Artillery, and the Headquarters' mess cookhouse was destroyed, the cook, 26/74 Private Fred Bullock killed, and the mess waiter wounded. The sector taken over was relatively quiet, so much so that the war diary of the 24/27th Battalion records on the 27th of November,

> *'As nothing unusual had occurred up to this time normal conditions of trench warfare were resumed.'*

24/27th Battalion wounded in hospital. Standing, Privates Brian and Bell; seated, Lance Corporal Jones and Corporal Porter.

As November drew to a close, the Tyneside Irish Battalions were in and out of the line in the Wancourt sector but information extracted from a German prisoner pointed to a large scale enemy offensive, so, as a precaution, battalions 'stood to' every morning, and afterwards large working parties were provided for work on the defensive lines.

On the night of the 5th of December the 26th Battalion attempted a raid against the enemy north west of Fontaine Les Croisilles where the objective was to take a prisoner and to destroy the enemy dugouts. Four officers and seventy-four men, were to take part and they had been detached from the Battalion at the beginning of the month, in order to train in the rear area. As had happened to the Tyneside Irish previously, the enemy seemed to be expecting them and were well prepared. One small party under Second Lieutenant J Jenkins actually managed to enter a section of the enemy lines, which were found to be empty but the other parties came under heavy and accurate machine-gun and rifle fire. Casualties were two officers, Second Lieutenants' D Kinnaird and G Laughton killed, three other ranks killed and seven wounded. The Battalion diary described this as a very strenuous tour of duty when the artillery of both sides was active and the 25th Battalion reported the shelling of Battalion Headquarters on the 16th of December. Each morning, just before dawn, patrols went forward to observe the enemy to give advance warning of any massing of troops or movement indicating an attack was imminent. Home leave was well under way and officers and men took leave in turn although one of the major problems, owing to the weather, was that large numbers of men were going sick and being admitted to hospital, which caused a shortage of manpower and of course more work for those still with the battalions. On 19th December 1917 the Germans attempted to raid a post of the 24/27th Battalion, creeping forward silently without the cover of a barrage but an alert sentry spotted the enemy, and they were successfully driven off, leaving one dead NCO in the hands of the 24/27th Battalion. By the 22nd of the month, the 25th Battalion had taken over the front line from the 9/Northumberland Fusiliers but nothing unusual was reported; heavy artillery and trench mortar fire and patrols continuing as normal. The 26th Battalion reported that the Corps boxing championship was to take place in Bapaume and Two men from the battalion had fought their way into the championship, Private Herron at Light-Weight and Private Elliott at Bantam-Weight. Private Herron reached the final round, but came up against the reigning Army Champion, losing the bout on points. Unfortunately Private Elliott's performance is not recorded. The 24/27th Battalion managed to celebrate Christmas in reserve and the companies were allowed to come together for the purpose but as the other battalions were in the front line their celebrations had to be delayed until they were relieved. Special greetings from His Majesty The King were relayed to all ranks but 1917 drew to a sorrowful close, when on the 27th of December, the 24/27th Battalion had Lance Corporal Allen Craigen killed and three men wounded. The next day the Battalion was relieved by the 26th Battalion and went into Brigade reserve; the 26th Battalion had A and B companies in the front line, C in support and D in reserve. Likewise the 25th Battalion relieved the 9/Northumberland Fusiliers in the front line placing, in the front line, A Company on the right and B on the left, D Company was in support and C Company in reserve. New Year 1918 was heralded in by the artillery carrying out a shoot on the enemy front line. Patrols were also out in No-Man's-Land and they reported the sounds of hammering from the German trenches. Hard frost and snow hampered work on the positions as the year 1917 finally came to an end.

Note

1. The only two officers killed in action that day were Second Lieutenant's Herbert Middlemis and Harold Lewis. Both commemorated on the Tyne Cot Memorial to the missing.

Chapter Ten

1918 The Disbandments and the German advance

'Now the Hun comes o'er the sandbags, in one long unbroken mass
just in time the welcome message, indent now for helmets gas.'

ANON THE WIPERS TIMES

January 1918 began quietly with the battalions in the line providing working parties for the general maintenance of the line. Daily the Trench Mortar Battery and the Artillery would fire on the enemy positions and nightly patrols would go out into No-Man's-Land trying to find out what the Germans were up to. On the night of the 11th of January a patrol from the 24/27th Battalion captured three Germans and, under interrogation they provided much needed information. The weather began to thaw, the trenches began to crumble and cave in, and much time and effort was expended in trying to remedy the damage. Drafts were still arriving but their numbers were small and the various battalions were under strength. On the evening of the 13th the Commanding Officer of the 26th battalion hosted a dinner for those members of the battalion who had come out with the 34th Division in January 1916 but lamentably the diary does not record how many actually sat down to the meal. Little was happening in the front line, but events in London, and in Whitehall, were to have a profound effect on the Tyneside Irish battalions. A Cabinet Committee, meeting to discuss man power shortages, drew up some plans for the distribution of the available manpower. The BEF would need, in 1918, 615,000 men to keep it up to strength; the Ministry of National Service estimated that there would be only 100,000 men available and suggested two methods of dealing with the shortfall, (A), by reducing the wastage and (B) by making more men available for frontline service.

The Committee made a proposal that the number of Infantry battalions in a division should be reduced

(Left) 17211 Lance Corporal John Callaghan served with 1/NF prior to joining 25th Battalion. Posted to 8/NF in 1918 he was KiA on 28 September 1918.

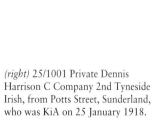

(right) 25/1001 Private Dennis Harrison C Company 2nd Tyneside Irish, from Potts Street, Sunderland, who was KiA on 25 January 1918.

No.11 (The Irish) Platoon, 8th Battalion Northumberland Fusiliers. The photograph was taken 20th June 1918. The 24/27th Battalion sent 10 officers and 200 men to the 8th Battalion in February 1918.

from twelve to nine, the divisional Pioneer battalion would be retained but would be reduced from four companies to three. Various facts and figures were presented to the Committee by the Army Council who protested at the drastic measures involved, and issued a warning to the War Cabinet that the prospects of heavy fighting on the Western Front could leave divisions exhausted and unable to fight on until the Americans arrived. On 10th January 1918 the orders for the reorganisation were issued from the War Office. The orders were not simple, for it was laid down that no Regular, First Line Territorial or Yeomanry battalions were to be disbanded, but the most recently raised Second Line Territorial and Service (Kitcheners New Army) Battalions were to be broken up. The Commander-in-Chief was given a list of 145 Battalions from which to choose and his choice in the 34th Division had drastic effects on the two Tyneside Brigades. In 102 (Tyneside Scottish) Brigade the 20th and 21st Battalions, (1st and 2nd Tyneside Scottish) would be disbanded. In 103 (Tyneside Irish) Brigade the 24/27th and 26th Battalions, (1/4th and 3rd Tyneside Irish) would be disbanded, and the 25th Battalion (2nd Tyneside Irish) would be transferred to 102 Brigade to bring it up to the new three battalion establishment.

Captain Foster Stephenson, 26th Battalion, posted to the 1st Battalion Northumberland Fusliliers when the 26th was disbanded.

The news of the disbandment was received by both battalions of the Tyneside Irish Brigade on 31 January 1918 and the work of winding up the battalions began on the 1st of February. Both battalion war diaries give a list of the disposal of the men of the battalions as follows:

24/27th Battalion

Company	*Officers*	*Other Ranks*	*To*
A Company	10	200	8th Bn Northbd Fus
B Company	7	150	19th Bn Northbd Fus
C Company	7	150	14th Bn Northbd Fus
D Company split up to bring the other companies up to strength			
	4	51	9th Bn Northbd Fus
		14	25th Bn Northbd Fus
	17 Signallers	23rd Bn Northbd Fus	
	38 classified PB to Base Depot Etaples		
	Transport personnel to 103rd Brigade HQ		
Surplus personnel to VI Corps Surplus Personnel Camp at Basseux			

On the 6th at 2.15p.m. the first draft left by rail to join the 14th Battalion, in the 21st Division, and the party to join the 9th Battalion marched to their new camp. At 9.30 a.m. on the 7th, those for transfer to the 8th Battalion, entrained, followed at 2.30. p.m. by the draft to the 19th Battalion. Those who were transferred to battalions serving in the 34th Division left that afternoon also to join their respective new units. Those who remained behind proceeded to No 4 Camp at Blairville, where the final work of clearing up the Battalion's affairs was completed, and on 26 February 1918 the 24/27th Battalion (Tyneside Irish) Northumberland Fusiliers officially ceased to exist. The bulk of those who were left proceeded to the

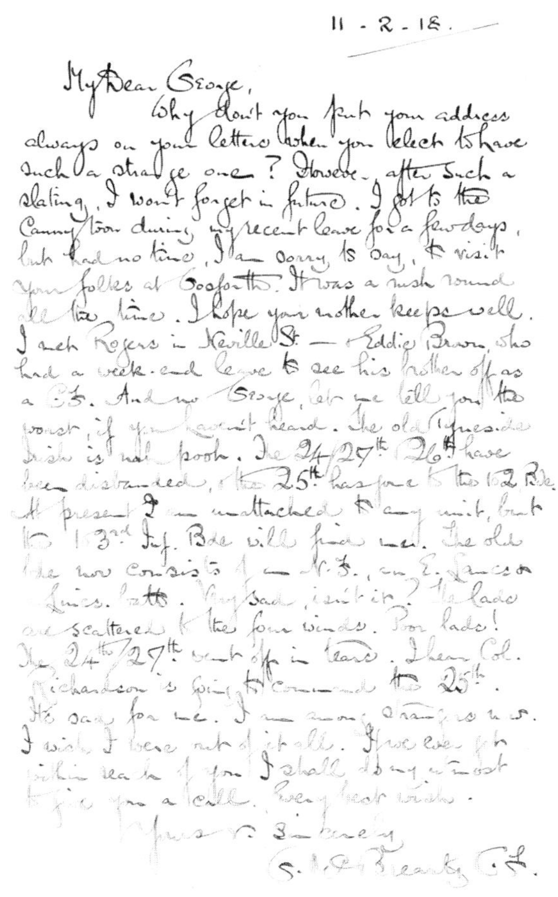

11 - 2 - 18.

My Dear George,
Why don't you put your address always on your letters when you elect to have such a strange one? However, after such a slating, I won't forget in future. I got to the Canny Toon during my recent leave for a few days, but had no time, I am sorry to say, to visit your folks at Gosforth. It was a rush round all the time. I hope your mother keeps well. I met Rogers in Neville St. — Eddie Brown, who had a week-end leave to see his brother off as a C.F. And now George, let me tell you the worst if you haven't heard. The old Tyneside Irish is napooh. The 24/27th & 26th have been disbanded, & the 25th has gone to the 102 Bde. At present I am unattached to any unit, but the 103rd Inf. Bde will find me. The old Bde now consists of [illegible] N.F., [illegible] E. Lancs & Lincs. batts. Very sad, isn't it? The lads are scattered to the four winds. Poor lads! The 24th/27th went off in tears. I hear Col. Richardson is going to command the 25th. It's sad for me. I am among strangers now. I wish I were out of it all. If I'm ever [illegible] within reach of you I shall do my utmost to give you a call. Every best wish.
Yours v. sincerely,
G. McBrearty C.F.

Father George McBrearty's letter to Captain George Swinburn detailing the Tyneside Irish Brigade's disbandment.

25/1015 Private Thomas Henderson was transferred to 19/NF.

17 Signallers were transferred to 23/Northumberland Fusiliers. Here a Corporal signaller of the Tyneside Irish poses with three signallers of the 23rd Battalion.

VI Corps Surplus Personnel Camp whilst Battalion Headquarters and the remainder joined the 34th Battalion Machine Gun Corps.

The disbandment of the 24/27th Battalion was watched with great sadness by, Father George McBrearty CF and on the 11th of February he wrote to Captain George Swinburn, who was now serving with the Railway Operating Division RE, with the news of the disbandment.

'Now George let me tell you the worst, if you havn't heard. The old Tyneside Irish is 'NAH POOH'. The 24/27th + 26th have been disbanded + the 25th has gone to 102 Bde. At present I am unattached to any unit, but the 103 Inf Bde will find me. The old Bde now consists of NF, E Lancs + Lincs Bns. Very sad isn't it? The lads are scattered to the four winds, POOR LADS. The 24/27th went off IN TEARS. I hear Col Richardson is getting command of the 25th. It is sad for me I am going among strangers now. I wish I were out of it all. If we ever get within reach of you I shall do my utmost to give you a call. With every best wish.

Yours Very sincerely G McBrearty CF'

The 26th Battalion meanwhile was engaged on a similar exercise when, on the morning of 1 February 1918 the Commanding Officer Lieutenant-Colonel M E Richardson paraded the Battalion and read out a letter from the Third Army Commander, General Byng. After explaining the shortages and reasons for disbandments, the CO addressed the men, after which the Battalion marched past and the work of breaking up the unit commenced.

The drafts started to leave the 26th Battalion on the 3rd of February as follows:

Second Lieutenant F L Brocklehurst and 70 ORs to 9th Bn Northbd Fus

Second Lieutenant C Robson and 50 ORs to 18th Bn Northbd Fus

Second Lieutenant N C Henry and 50 ORs to 22nd Bn Northbd Fus

Second Lieutenant J C Rodger and 50 ORs to 23rd Bn Northbd Fus

Lieutenant P A Gamble and 50 ORs to 25th Bn Northbd Fus

70 Other Ranks were classified PB by the ADMS and were sent to the Base Depot at Etaples. Then on the 6th of February drafts including all the battalion signallers proceeded to new units as follows:

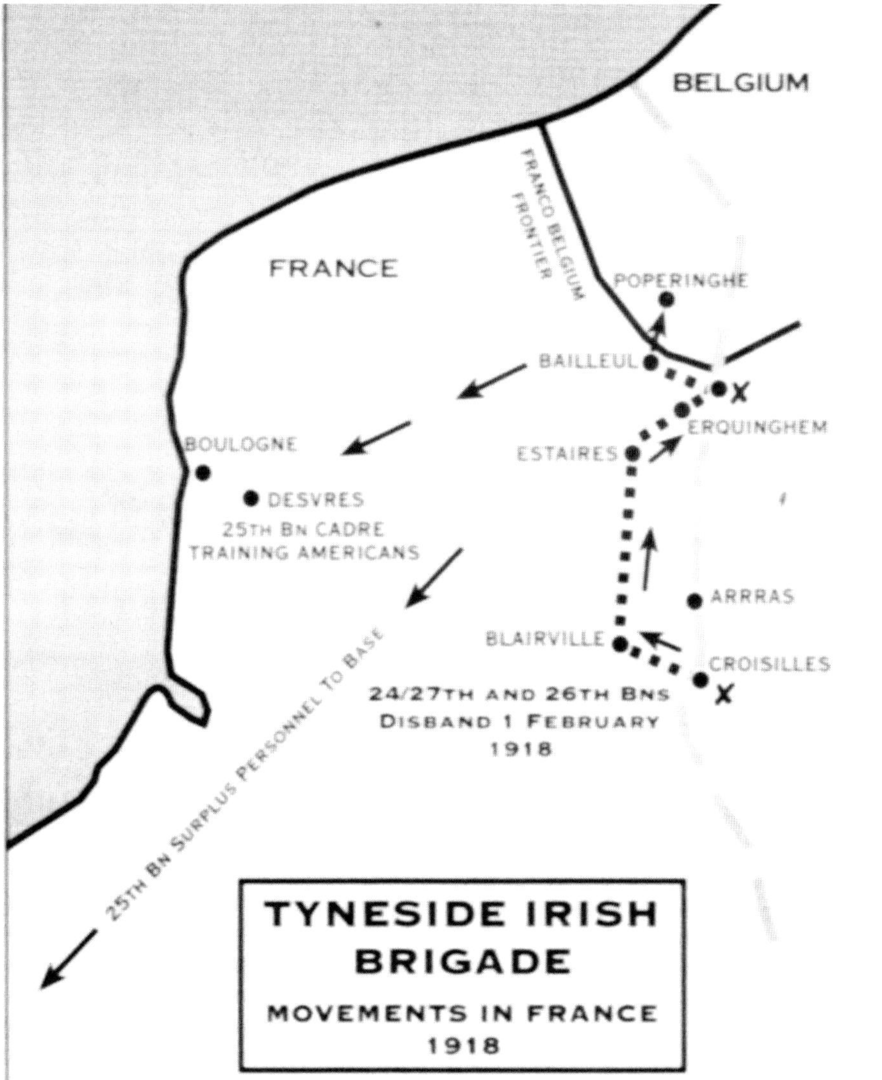

Other ranks	*To*
22	1st Bn Northbd Fus
75	18th Bn Northbd Fus
10	25th Bn Northbd Fus
7	9th Bn Northbd Fus
9	22nd Bn Northbd Fus

34 ORs of the Battalion Transport Section under Captain W Stafford proceeded to join Headquarters 11 Brigade in the 4th Infantry Division and on the following day a draft of 22 men left to join the 12/13th Battalion Northumberland Fus whilst the remainder joined forces with the remnants of the 24/27th Battalion. On the 9th all remaining men of the 26th Battalion except the CO, 2i/c, QM, three batmen and the Orderly Room Clerk were given orders to march to VI Corps Reinforcement Depot at Basseux. Word was received that the majority of these men joined the 9th Entrenching Battalion and were quartered in Arras. Lieutenant-Colonel Richardson was given command of 11/Suffolk Regiment in 101 Brigade and

left what remained of the Battalion on the 16th. Four days later Second Lieutenant A S Hunter left for England and two NCOs 41439 Sergeant G W Boddy and 35594 Corporal F Pearson proceeded to England for commissions. Later the QM and the RQMS and Major H H Neeves dispersed and the work of disbanding the 26th (Service) Battalion Northumberland Fusiliers (3rd Tyneside Irish) was complete.

The men who left these two units upheld the name of the Tyneside Irish, and several were awarded gallantry medals with the units that they joined. The draft that joined the 19/Northumberland Fusiliers was described by the Battalion's historian in the following words,

> *'Later there came a big draft from the disbanded 24/27th Battalion (Tyneside Irish) complete with their officers. That was A DRAFT OF MEN. They proved themselves time and time again in the strenuous and anxious days to come.' (March 1918)*

27/594 CQMS H P Quinn was transferred to 34th Battalion Machine Gun Corps. He served with the 34th Division from its formation until his discharge in March 1919.

Of the draft 24/580 Sergeant C Keegan was awarded the French Croix de Guerre, and Privates 27/667 J Simpson and 24/868 W Timlin each received the Military Medal.

Likewise in the draft to 9/Northumberland Fusiliers CSM R Madden, and Corporals 26/934 W Gilmore and 25/227 W T Granville were awarded the Distinguished Conduct Medal. 27/360 Sergeant R Horsman with the draft to 8/Northumberland Fusiliers received the same decoration and much hard fighting was the lot of the men transferred to the other battalions but right until the end in November 1918 those who were drafted fought on with their new battalions. Many others, having recovered from wounds, were transferred to other regiments, and some men died whilst serving in those regiments. In the last days of the war Corporal William Wheatley of Milburngate in Durham, originally with C Company of the 25th Battalion, but now with the East Yorkshire Regiment, was awarded the Military Medal and the Distinguished Conduct Medal for showing great courage, endurance and initiative in an attack.

Lance Corporal William Timlin, MM, 24th Battalion, won his medal with the 19th Battalion.

But the story of the Tyneside Irish is not yet complete. The 25th Battalion was relieved by 8/Kings Own Royal Lancaster Regiment on the 27th of January and moved to No 4 Camp Blairville, and began cleaning up prior to joining 102 Brigade. On the 28th, 67238 Corporal Stidolph, of the 25th Battalion, met Sergeant Kelly of the 1/Munster Fusiliers in the LightWeight Boxing Championship of the Third Army and the bout went to the Tyneside Irishman on points after a hard fought contest.

Each company provided 10 men daily to work on the building of sandbag protection around the huts as enemy aircraft were frequently bombing the rear areas, making this a necessity. On 3 February 1918 the 25th Battalion officially came under command of 102 Brigade, and moved to Durham Lines in Boisleux au Mont. The now familiar pattern of

Corporal William Wheatley, 25th Battalion, won the DCM and the MM after being transferred to the East Yorkshire Regiment. He was killed by a fall of stone in Bowburn Colliery in 1922.

training began once more, as the Battalion took in the drafts and tried to weld them into a disciplined, cohesive, fighting unit. For the remainder of the month the Battalion remained in Durham Lines training, as the Army High Command were aware of a possible German offensive, but the men spent at least forty-five minutes each day practising ceremonial drill. By the 25th of February the Battalion was 'Falling in on the beat of the drum'. This is a difficult thing to do even for the Brigade of Guards, as no word of command is given, and every movement is ordered by just a single 'tap' on the drum. Every man of the Battalion was shown how to load and fire the Lewis Gun, and anti-gas drill was also carried out by all companies. On the 26th of February, Lieutenant-General Sir J.A.L. Haldane, the GOC VI Corps, inspected the whole of 102 Brigade on the football ground, west of Ambrines. It was a portend that the Brigade would be soon on its way back to the line and the next morning at 8.20 a.m. the 25th Battalion started its march back to the front. The first day's slog took them to Berles au Bois, which they reached at 2 p.m. and the following day they moved to Enniskillen Camp at Ervillers, arriving at 2.30 p.m. When the Battalion started on this journey, seven officers and seven other ranks left by motor bus for Mory, where they began to carry out a

Private Robert Clazie, 30th Battalion, joined the Tyneside Irish in France and was transferred to 103 Machine Gun Company. He was taken prisoner with 206 Machine Gun Company in March 1918. He died in December 1918 attempting to walk home across Germany – he reached the French border before succumbing.

Lt Colonel Leith-Hay-Clarke taken prisoner 21st March 1918

Corporal Coyne escaped from Bunhill Row Trench after it was captured by the Germans 21st March 1918.

reconnaissance of the front line. On the night of the 2nd of March the 25th Battalion took over the front line from the 2/5 Sherwood Foresters, placing the companies as follows:- D Company on the right, B Company on the left, A Company in support and C company in reserve. The War Diary for the remainder of the month was lost in action on the 21st of March, but from what was written up later it appears that the Battalion spent a lot of time on gas training and gas inspections. 102 Brigade was relieved by 103 Brigade on the 7th and went into reserve for some days but on the 19th of March again took over the front line. Prisoners who were taken provided information that a large enemy offensive was imminent, and on the 15th of March the enemy cut gaps in its own barbed wire in preparation for an assault. The 25th Battalion was in Brigade support and rehearsed the counter-attack positions that would be taken up if the enemy did attack. In expectation of being outflanked, the 34th Division prepared flank defences so that, in theory, when the time came everyone knew where to go and what to do. On the night of the 19th heavy rain fell and the afternoon of the 20th was warm and sunny which led to a thick fog on the morning of the 21st of March.

That morning started very quietly but at 2.35 a.m. the front line troops spotted and drove away an enemy patrol, and then at about 4.30. a.m. the front line came under heavy artillery fire. The barrage consisted of a mixture of gas and high explosive and the Germans kept up this bombardment for four hours after which there was a short lull, before the barrage again came down. This time it consisted of nearly all high explosive shells but the men had been wearing gas masks almost since the beginning of the

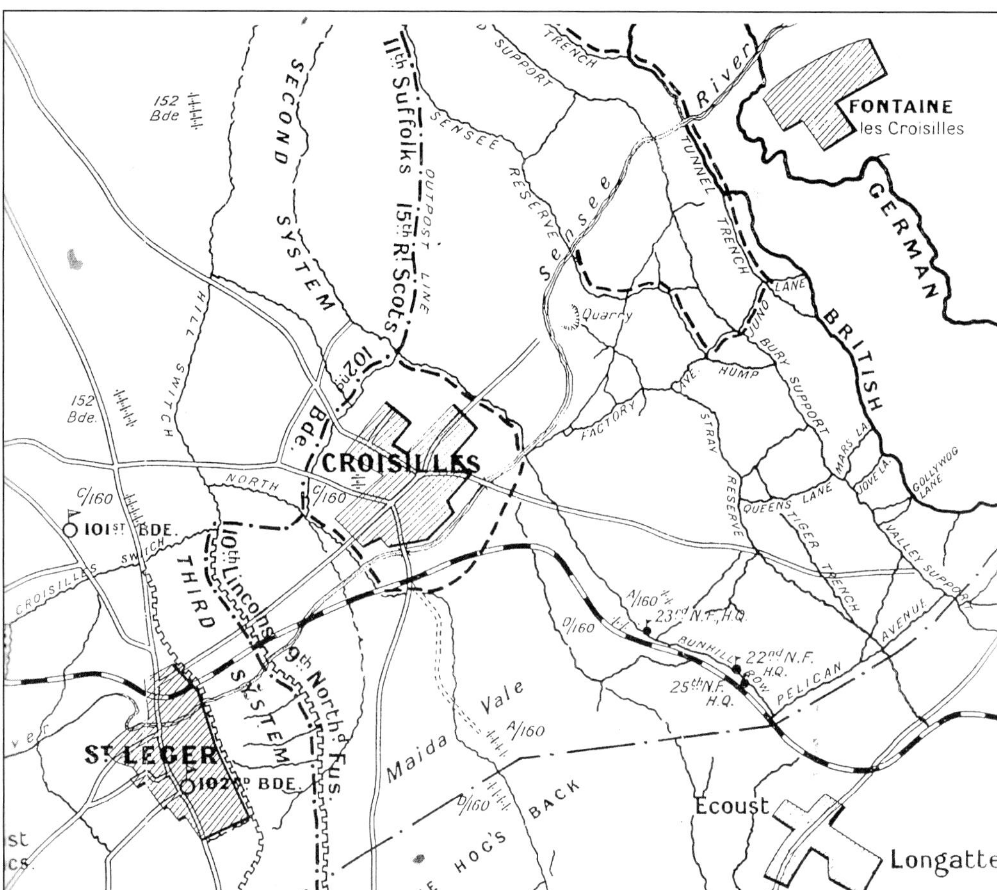

Penetration of 34 Division positions by the Germans, 21 March 1918

barrage, which made movement and communicating difficult, to say the least. 102 Brigade did not come under infantry attack for some time, but the 59th Division on the right flank was pushed back by about 10 a.m. On seeing this, the 22nd Battalion carried out the plan and threw back a flank guard, which was lengthened by the support company along the feature known as The Hogs Back. At 11 a.m. Captain McLachlan MC, commanding C Company of the 25th Battalion, received orders to prepare for a counter-attack on 'Tiger trench'. About an hour later, before the counter-attack took place further orders were received to the effect that a defensive flank was to be formed on the right. Captain McLachlan, in compliance with this order, sent two platoons under Second Lieutenant Bowmer along Bunhill Row towards Leg Lane, and took the other two platoons of the company along the Croisilles - Ecoust road himself. As soon as these two platoons reached the crest of the hill they could see masses of enemy between three and five hundred yards in the right rear of its new position. These Germans were advancing north westerly and very quickly brought rapid rifle and machine-gun fire to bear on the soldiers of the Tyneside Irish Battalion. This fire inflicted many casualties and Captain McLachlan decided to withdraw, at the same time sending out a party to the flank in an effort to prevent the enemy surrounding him. On reaching a trench that ran southwards, he tried to man this and it was here he was joined by A Company under the command of Second Lieutenant Vipond.

Sergeant Faill escaped from Bunhill Row Trench after it was captured by the Germans 21st March 1918.

Meanwhile the Germans had managed to surround the three battalion headquarters of 102 Brigade that were located close together in Bunhill Row. The events at the battalion headquarters are recorded by the battalion HQ cook, Corporal J Coyne, in the Divisional Old Comrades Magazine 'Chequers'.

> *'Dawn 21st March 1918. Artillery fire of a thunderous kind can be heard for miles along the front. Clouds of sickly gas from the enemy lines is affecting us. Severe machine-gun fire from one end of the trench which we occupy forces us to take cover. Colonel Leith-Hay-Clark receives a message from a runner and we are told to prepare to move back. A German aeroplane is dropping bombs on us and the runner, Lance Corporal Jobson[1] and many others are killed outright. Stealthily we move along the 'Hogs Back' towards Courcelles. Scores of officers and men are lying mutilated in holes in the side of this huge trench. We tried to do something for them but are powerless on account of the shell-fire. The Germans are now seen advancing in massed formation and the Colonel and his officers descend into a deep dugout and order us to find shelter. About fifty yards away we found a deep dugout. An officer ordered us to take off our equipment and discard our rifles and he would surrender us. This certainly seemed the wisest procedure, under the circumstances, to save our lives. Some of our artillery gunners joined us, they were carrying the breech blocks from their field guns. Hordes of enemy were near at hand and we were ready to become prisoners. Suddenly a huge gap opened in the ranks of the approaching enemy. One of our heavy guns miles away is in action and made no mistake in finding a target. Here was a chance for me to make a bid to get into our lines further back. After running and crouching along a trench I came across a wounded Tommy shot through the leg. I helped him into a railway cutting and then with one of his arms round my neck we managed to do a three-legged hobble to safety. We reached the village of Courcelles, just in time to catch our battalion transport moving off on the retreat. I reported all that had transpired since dawn to Captain Treanor. He was glad to see me and was anxious to know what had happened to the HQ Staff. Of course, by this time I felt certain they would all be prisoners.'*

Corporal Coyne was correct, the only other man known to escape from the 25th Battalion HQ in Bunhill Row was 27/1413 Sergeant David Faill of Shotton Colliery.

Colonel Leith-Hay-Clark had ordered the burning of all the documents in the Battalion HQ dugout and the Adjutant, Captain McKellen, along with Captain Kirkup, set up an all-round defence. The enemy was

On the left Second Lieutenant Thomas Taylor 25th Battalion in a POW Camp after being taken prisoner during the battles of March and April 1918.

counter-attacked and largely due to the skill and leadership of Captain McKellen, a single Lewis gun with only one magazine was kept in action. The survivors managed to hold out until about 5.30 p.m. when the Germans sent a message, that if the garrison did not surrender they would be blown up. Very reluctantly the Commanding Officer decided, because of his wounded and the fact there was no hope of rescue, that he must surrender. Thus the defence of Bunhill Row ended; the majority of the garrison were either wounded or gassed, but had fought until there was no chance of being relieved.

While all this was taking place Captain McLachlan was still under pressure. Having been joined by A Company, he again extended his flank to the right and placed a strong party on the mound of a windmill. The enemy was, however, moving round him on the right and at 2 p.m. he was again forced to withdraw, to prevent his force from being surrounded. Forming a flank along the railway embankment, Captain McLachlan now found that he had too few men for the task at hand and had to make a further withdrawal. It was now that B Company, under the command of Second Lieutenant Coleby MM, formerly a Company Sergeant Major in the 24th Battalion, arrived in the nick of time.

Runners were sent back to 102 Brigade Headquarters with the position of the survivors of the three companies, asking for assistance on the flanks. This position was prepared for defence and whilst they were doing so they were joined by men who were drifting back in ones and twos, having managed to avoid being captured. At this stage reinforcements arrived in the shape of a platoon from 9/Northumberland Fusiliers and with these men at his disposal, Captain McLachlan now tried again to take the high ground, but every time the men showed themselves they were cut down by accurate machine-gun and rifle fire from the Germans. Information was now received, from an officer of the Royal Scots that Nelly Avenue, on the left, was the new front line, so Captain McLachlan tried to link up in that direction. This attempt had to be abandoned when the Germans again brought pressure on the right flank and there were not enough men for the length of trench to be manned. More men for the defence came at about 5 p.m. when some men of the Brigade Pioneer Company, B Company of the 18/Northumberland Fusiliers, arrived with orders to link up. This allowed Captain Mclachlan to withdraw some men from his right and get in touch with the Royal Scots of 101 Brigade on the left. At about 7 p.m. the survivors of the three companies of the 25th Battalion received orders to retire, and preparations were made. The first group were just about to leave when the Germans made a strong attack and tried to take the Sunken Road but this attack was beaten off with fire from rifle, Lewis gun and rifle grenades. Then at about 8 p.m. the withdrawal to the new position began and this new line was prepared for defence whilst the men rested where possible, until in the early hours of the morning some two hundred and fifty men of the 23rd Battalion arrived to supplement the depleted garrison. Listening patrols were out and a patrol went forward into the village to try and locate the enemy, but everything was quiet and no trace could be found.

The next morning was ideal for the Germans to continue their advance, for a thick mist lay over the battlefield shrouding any movement from British eyes. As dawn broke a large group of enemy massed behind the ridge in front of Captain McLachlan's position which he reported to Brigade HQ and, hoping for some artillery support, he arranged some assistance with an artillery liaison officer, however, no artillery support was forthcoming. The enemy now attacked in small parties, but they were beaten back by rifle and Lewis Gun fire until a large attack began at about 8 a.m. which succeeded in breaking into the 25th Battalion positions. Immediately Captain McLachlan organised a counter-attack under the command of Second Lieutenants Vipond, Coleby and Bowmer. This counter-attack was successful and the enemy was driven back yet again, but, at this moment the Germans managed to force back the Royal Scots of 101 Brigade. This flank had to be protected and there was no choice but to form a defensive flank on the left and withdraw under the cover of it. The enemy now pressed home his attack and Captain McLachlan was obliged to get his men away, but owing to the difficulty of communicating orders, some parties were left behind.

Captain's Francis Treanor and George Coleby MC MM after the fighting of March and April 1918, George Coleby wrote a citation for Francis Treanor to be awarded the MC for his part in bringing supplies up to the Battalion, but he was promoted to Captain instead.

Second Lieutenant Cuthbert Peckston was last seen alive in this position, cut off but still fighting; his body was never recovered, so his name is recorded on the Arras Memorial to the missing. The men who got away with Captain McLachlan were now back at Hill Switch, where they immediately set about preparing a defence. Here they were subject to a heavy barrage from the German gunners, who succeeded in breaking the line of the Royal Scots on the left. Without warning the two battalions retired, leaving the flank of 25th Battalion exposed and once again a flank guard was thrown out, this time under Second Lieutenant Bowmer, whilst the men under Captain McLachlan withdrew to the third trench system. This retirement was just completed, when the enemy broke through in front of St Leger and the order to withdraw was given once again. By now dusk was falling and things settled down for the night, although the Germans were sending up lots of different coloured flares, and no further attacks took place on the 25th Battalion that night. During the night the Germans brought up a trench mortar and a machine gun in preparation for the following day when, as daylight broke, masses of enemy troops were to be seen, crossing the valley in front of the 25th Battalion positions.

Private Thomes Core, 25th Battalion, killed in action 21st March 1918.

Captain McLachlan was now able to get a message through to the artillery, and he brought a heavy barrage down on the advancing Germans and at the same time he opened fire with his Lewis Guns and rifles. A German attack on the Battalion front did not take place, but they did strike further to the left. At 9 a.m. on the 23rd of March the leading platoons of 92 Brigade of the 31st Division began to arrive, to relieve the hard pressed 102 Brigade. The prospect of a German attack interfered with the relief, and it was not until about 3 p.m. that the survivors of the 25th Battalion left the line and marched to Ablainzeville. After

A sergeant of the 25th Battalion. He is wearing cloth NF shoulder titles above his shamrock and lower down cross rifles indicate that he is a marksman.

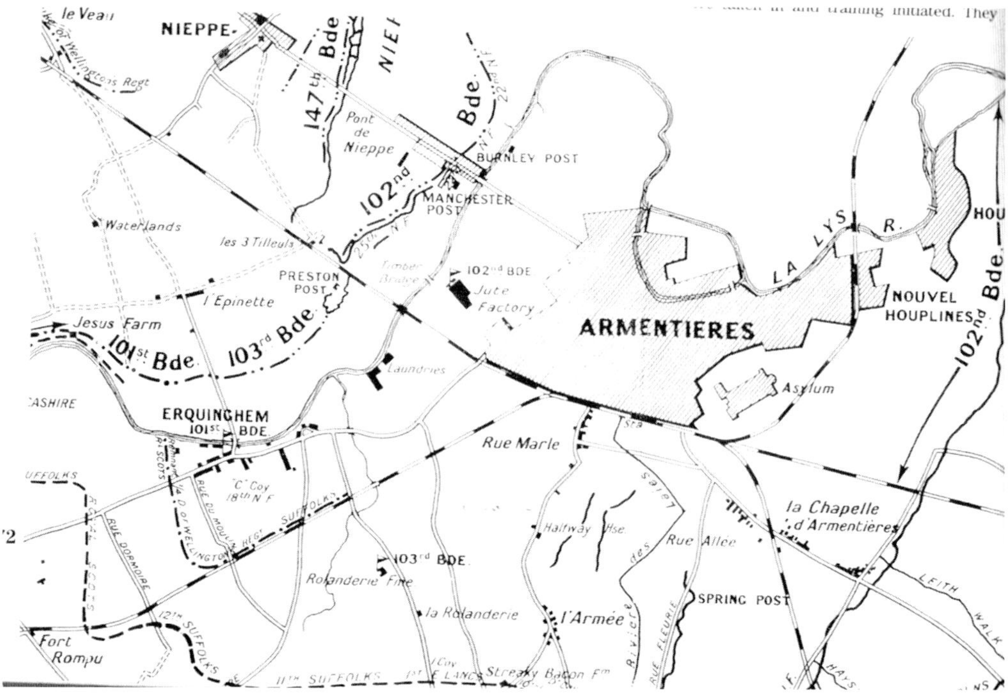

Withdrawal from Armentieres April 1918.

Private Frank Crawford joined with the draft from 8th Border Regiment.

two days of heavy shelling, gas attacks, repeated infantry assault and being continuously outflanked, the 25th Battalion had managed to hold on. With bayonets fixed, a round in the breech and gas masks at the ready, the last seen of many of the men was when they had disappeared into the fog, in order to counter-attack and drive back the enemy. The majority of those killed in action have their names inscribed on the Arras Memorial to the Missing.

After being relieved the Battalion began marching to the rear, until by the 27th of March they reached Frevent, where they entrained for Steenbecque. On arrival in the new area the Battalion was marched to billets in Erquinghem, where once again drafts of men joined the Battalion and training commenced. One large draft was received from 8/Border Regiment, but they were transferred to the 12/13 Northumberland Fusiliers at the end of April. New kit was issued by the quartermaster's department, and the re-organisation of the Battalion back into four companies took place. On the 1st of April all the officers went forward and carried out a reconnaissance of the front line in preparation for the Battalion moving

British troops in battle order await orders to move.

back into the line. At 8 p.m. on the 6th of April, the 25th Battalion began to take over the front line in the Houplines sector from the 15/Royal Scots. B and C Companies went into the front line and A and D Companies were in billets in the Asylum in Armentieres.

The front line companies sent out patrols to try and locate the enemy, and during the night a barrage was put down by the British artillery on the enemy front line. To this shelling the enemy replied with light and medium trench mortars, which shelled the front line. whilst heavier 4.2 and 5.9 artillery began shelling the communication trenches and rear areas. During the 7th of April, German aircraft were very busy over the 34th Division, but there was little else going on. That night at about 8 p.m. the Germans began shelling Armentieres with gas shells and this shelling went on through the night until 9 a.m. the next day. The gas shelling had been carefully planned by the Germans, and affected all the troops in the town which caused the Battalion Headquarters, and the two companies of the 25th Battalion in support, to be put out of action. All these men had to be evacuated, and, on the 8th, the Battalion, now only two companies strong, was reinforced by C Company of 15/Royal Scots, who replaced the gassed companies in support. That night the Royal Engineers exploded a mine in front of the 25th Battalion, and, to prevent the Germans investigating, two fighting patrols were sent out. The next day enemy aircraft were again overhead, and once again the enemy artillery heavily shelled the 25th Battalion area but that night fighting patrols again went out and kept the enemy at bay overnight.

Private Walter Slight of Hull died of wounds 13th April 1918.

The next day the Royal Scots were withdrawn from the now very weak 25th Battalion, and the enemy stepped up the shelling of the British communications trenches and the support line. Enemy aircraft were strafing the Battalion during the day and although these were answered by the Lewis gunners, none were shot down. Then after a heavy barrage the Germans began an assault on the 25th Division on the left of the 34th Division when they managed to penetrate between the two divisions. As had happened the previous month, with the flank gone, the Battalion had to withdraw and orders came that they would

Men of the 25th Battalion behind the lines at Armentières April 1918. Seated second from left is Private F Levitt of Seaham.

This group comprises the veterans of the Brigade, mostly non- commissioned officers specially chosen for training purposes

Officers of Training Cadre, 25th Northumberland Fusiliers (2nd Tyneside Irish). Standing left to right, Captain and QM F Treanor; Lieutenant Ross; Lieutenant Collins; Lieutenant Swindon; Lieutenant Sayers; Captain Blake. Seated, Captain Douglas CF; Captain Bowman; Lieutenant Colonel Catchpole; Captain Rodgers.

withdraw to the North bank of the River Lys. This withdrawal was conducted in an orderly manner until the bridge allotted to the 25th Battalion was reached when it was found that this particular bridge was under German machine-gun fire, and the Battalion could not get across. Owing to the fact the bridge could not be crossed safely, the Battalion moved eastwards along the river bank and half of the Battalion managed to cross by the stone bridge at Nieppe and the remainder over a pontoon bridge erected by the Royal Engineers. The two companies were now given positions to hold near Nieppe and C Company was on the north bank of the River Lys, east of the Armentières railway line, whilst B Company were in support in the Nieppe Switch.

The next morning a fierce assault was launched on C Company which repulsed the enemy several

(left) 25/1152 Company Quarter Master Sergeant McKenna; 26/1484 Sergeant R B Wood; 25/1274 Lance Corporal W Sweeney. CQMS McKenna had been home on leave to Ireland and was drowned when SS *Leinster* was torpedoed as he travelled back to France. Sgt R B Wood served with four of the five battalions (26th, 27th, 24/27th and 25th) of the Tyneside Irish.

During the time spent on the coast the 25th Battalion cadre formed a football team but nothing is recorded about any of its matches.

times, but, as the enemy were round on the flank, a withdrawal once more took place to a line east of the Armentières railway near to Nieppe Station. The remaining men held these positions under continuous machine-gun fire until at 7 p.m. orders for a further withdrawal were received. Moving back, the Battalion took up positions in a prepared line, where the men were fed and everyone had a few hours sleep. Owing to the number of casualties sustained, 102 Brigade was reorganised, as a battalion, with each battalion providing a company. The 25th Battalion Company came under the command of Second Lieutenant Coleby. The enemy again forced back troops on the left flank, but the remnants of the Tyneside Irish hung on until orders were received to withdraw. At 2 a.m. on the 14th of April, a withdrawal was made through lines occupied by fresh troops, and 102 Composite Battalion assembled about one kilometre east of Bailleul. At 3 p.m., after a rest, the 25th Composite Company was reorganised into four platoons, and Second Lieutenant Coleby took the officers forward and sited defensive positions, and then the men were brought up and trenches dug. They remained here throughout the night, but as no attack materialised, they were withdrawn to Hooginacker Camp for a further rest but about 5 p.m. the camp came under heavy shellfire and had to be cleared. Initially positions were taken up in trenches near the camp, but at 7 p.m. a move was made to trenches near the Mount Noir - Baileull road and at 9 a.m. the following morning, these positions became the front line as the troops in front withdrew through the Company positions. The enemy advance now was running out of steam and although during the next three days the 25th was shelled with high explosive and gas, the enemy made no attempt to follow up with infantry. Then at 10 30 p.m. on the night of the 20th of April the relief of the Company by the French commenced and the 25th Battalion was now reorganised on a four-company basis once again when reinforcements were taken in and training initiated. They moved north into Belgium and provided working parties for the Poperinghe Army Line but the Battalion was kept in reserve in case of a hostile attack and would man trenches between the Poperinghe–Ypres road and the Poper-inghe–Reninghelst road. Daily until the end of the month working parties were provided to the engineers, who were constructing the defensive line. Farms and out-buildings were placed in a state of defence and the wiring and concealing of machine-gun posts and strong points undertaken. Through the early days of May the Battalion worked under 208 Field Company Royal Engineers, until they were relieved at 6 p.m. on the 5th of May by the 9/Northumberland Fusiliers. For the next week, the training of specialists was given priority, and once again Lewis Gunners, Signallers and Stretcher Bearers were trained ready to go back into the line. But it was never to be, for the days of the Tyneside Irish as fighting troops were over when on the 15th of May the 25th Battalion was reduced to Training Cadre. On the 17th of May all surplus personnel were paraded and proceeded to Desvres where they entrained for the base, to be transferred to other battalions. The 25th Battalion Training Cadre was now put to work training American troops who were arriving in France in growing numbers. The first unit that the Battalion worked with was 110 US Infantry Regiment, of the 28th American Division. British instructors were allotted to the American companies so that by the 8th of June, 110 Regiment were considered ready for the line, and the Battalion Cadre moved to Le Wast. Here they began training 309 Machine Gun Battalion of the US 78th Division and this training went on throughout the whole of July 1918 until at last the Americans were considered ready and they too moved on up the line. In August the 25th Battalion Cadre was at work preparing a camp for reinforcements who were suffering from malaria; the first batch from the 22nd Division in Salonika came from the Cheshire, East Lancashire and Manchester regiments followed by further drafts from the Royal Dublin, Royal Irish and Inniskilling Fusiliers of the 10th (Irish) Division. All these men were rekitted and processed before being sent up the line. The War ended in this way, with the Cadre still training drafts for the line until in December 1918, with no more drafts required, attention was turned to demobilisation. The 25th Battalion took over No 1 Rest Camp at Le Havre and began demobilising miners from Salonika and Italy, and that is how the year ended. After the hard fighting withdrawals of March and April, the 25th Battalion finished the war in the rear area as a training unit.

Note

1. The author has been unable to trace a L/Cpl Jobson, killed in action 21st March 1918.

Chapter Eleven

The Last Act, Demobilisation 1919

'So sleeps the pride of former day's
So glory's thrill is o'er.'

'THE HARP THAT ONCE' MOORE.

On the morning of 2 May 1919, the 25th Battalion Cadre, now part of 116 Infantry Brigade, fell in alongside the Cadres of 18 and 23/Northumberland Fusiliers. Along with the other Infantry battalions of the 39th Division, they paraded before their Divisional Commander near Le Havre. Major-General Uniacke, commanding the 39th Division, presented each battalion in turn with its Colour, on which were emblazoned all Battle Honours. The task of demobilisation was now carried out, with the miners being the first to go, although there were precious few of the original miners left with the Battalion.

Gradually, over the early months of 1919, the Division slowly disappeared, until at last it came to the 25th Battalion's turn. The Cadre handed in the remaining stores and the few remaining men were dispatched to England. In June the Colour, along with those of 18 and 23/Northumberland Fusiliers were despatched to Newcastle and amid a large crowd, the Colours arrived at Central Station at 4 o'clock, on the 12th of June. After a welcome by a reception committee, the Colours were played out of the station by the Tyneside Scottish Pipers, and were paraded through the streets to the Exchange. Many local dignitaries were present when the Lord Mayor, Councillor A Munro-Sutherland, and The Sheriff, Councillor G J Cole, gave the Colour Parties a civic welcome. The 25th Battalion Colour Party was commanded by Captain Francis Treanor, who had served with the Tyneside Irish from the beginning and also with him, as escort to the Colour, were CQMS C Goodhead, Sergeant Williams and Corporal Dempster.

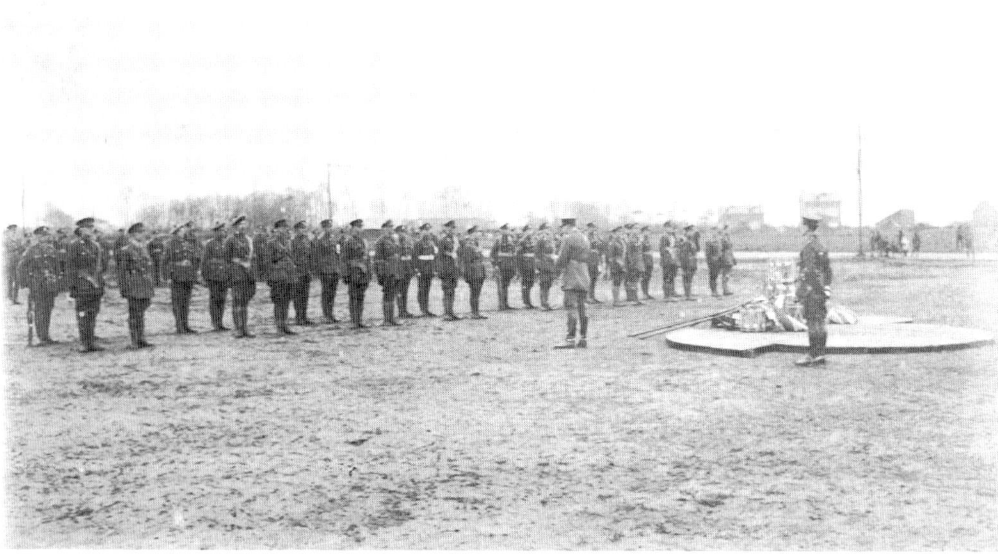

A photographer was present when the King's Colour was presented to the 25th Battalion Cadre and took this series of shots.

The Colours at Newcastle Guildhall 12 June 1919.

Captain Francis Treanor carries the 25th Battalion Colour to St Mary's Cathedral escorted by CQMS Goodhead, Sergeant Williams and Corporal Dempster. Behind march the 25th Battalion cadre.

Speeches of welcome were made by members of the Raising Committees i.e. the Newcastle Chamber of Commerce, the Tyneside Scottish Committee and the Tyneside Irish Committee. After Mr Herbert Shaw and Sir Thomas Oliver spoke for their respective committees, Colonel Johnstone Wallace was the first of the Irish Committee to speak. He said that Captain Treanor wished him to say that they had only done their bit, and that if they had to go through the same again in 1919 as they had from 1914 onwards, they would do it, even if it cost them the supreme sacrifice. After Colonel Wallace spoke, Mr N Grattan Doyle referred to the part he played in the raising of the Tyneside Irish Brigade. He had appealed to men, who needed no appealing to, as they had quickly rallied round the Colours. He then asked what could be done for the men, who had not only saved their country, but had also saved Christianity and Civilisation. These men should be their first charge. Nothing they could do would be equal to the gallantry they had shown and the victory they had won. The Sheriff recognised the work done by the Newcastle battalions, and, on the call of the Lord Mayor, three cheers were given for the Colour Parties. After a reply by the Commanding Officer of the 18th Battalion, Lieutenant-Colonel Methuen, the Lord Mayor was presented with an Iron Cross captured from a German. The Colour Parties then marched to the Mansion House and had tea with the Lord Mayor. Captain Treanor recalled how, when the men had first arrived at Woolsington Park in the rain, all the army blankets had disappeared. The men had gone home, rather than sleep on the wet ground in tents. The officers and men of the Colour Parties were, at the end of the proceedings, presented with a card of welcome by the Lord Mayor.

A few days later, the Colour of the 25th (Service) Battalion (2nd Tyneside Irish) Northumberland Fusiliers was brought from the Officers' Mess on to the parade ground in Fenham Barracks by Captain Treanor and the escort. Assembled on parade were over 100 discharged and demobilised men, and a number of their officers, Captain G Swinburn, Captain T G Farina and Lieutenant G Barker all of the 24th Battalion, and Major T Reay, and Captain J G Kirkup of the 25th Battalion. When the Colour was uncased, the parade was called to attention and the officers saluted.

A large crowd of serving soldiers watched, as those survivors of the Tyneside Irish Brigade formed fours and moved into column of route. Then, headed by the Irish wolf hound, mascot of the Brigade, and the Colour Party, and preceded by the Band of the 9th Durham Light Infantry, the men marched out of the barracks. The route taken was via Barrack Road and Clayton Street to St Mary's Roman Catholic Cathedral, where the Colour was to be laid up. Large crowds of people watched the parade pass by, and

Members of the Tyneside Irish and Tyneside Scottish Committees and serving officers at the laying up of the 25th Battalion Colour.
Third row left to right, Lieutenant G Barker, Unknown, Captain T G Farina. Centre, Sir Thomas Oliver, Captain F Treanor, Sir Charles Parsons, Captain G Swinburn MC, Unknown, Centre of front row, Father George McBrearty CF. Holding dog is the Secretary of the Tyneside Irish Committee Mr J Mulcahy.

The Band of 9/Durham LI and the Irish Wolfhound lead the parade to Eldon Square.

nearer the Cathedral the crowd was described as immense. St Mary's Cathedral was packed with people and some had to be left outside, but preference was given to those who had lost a loved one who had served with the Tyneside Irish Brigade. Amongst the congregation were Colonel Joseph Reed, Lady Parsons and Lady Wallace and also present were the seventeen survivors of the Ushaw College contingent, all that remained of the seventy who had been training for Holy Orders when they had enlisted. At the Presbytery adjoining the Cathedral, the Colour was met by a civic and military procession, headed by the Lord Mayor. Nearly all of the members of the Tyneside Irish Committee and the City Council were in attendance.

The procession passed through the west door of the Cathedral and moved up the aisle. The colour was reverently laid on the altar, and the Corpus Christi Mass was celebrated by Father Newsham, assisted by the Dean of St Cuthbert's Grammar School, Father Wilkinson, as Deacon. At the end of the Mass a Te Deum was rendered by the choir, led by Mr Holloway. At the request of all surviving men of the Brigade who were attending, the sermon was given by Father George McBrearty, who, as Brigade Chaplain, had served throughout the war, until wounded only a week before the Armistice. Father McBrearty delivered a striking address, as follows:

'Four and a half years ago , they had in St Mary's the first church parade of the Tyneside Irish. Few of those who watched the fine men who assembled there that day realised what was before them. None of them dreamt for a moment that, when their grim task was over, only a mere handful would be left to return to their native Tyneside. Certainly there were men among them who had been watching Germany for years previous to the outbreak of war – men who could have told them, they

were up against a very grim task in trying to snatch victory from so powerful, so well prepared an enemy. But even these men, even the men who knew Germany's immense power, little dreamed the war would last so long, or that the belligerents would be able to pay the cost in life and material which it was to demand. In the Tyneside Irish Brigade itself, in camp in England, during the months of preparation, and afterwards in France, before the experience had been learned of those decimating campaigns which began with the Somme fighting in July 1916, both officers and men used to amuse themselves by picturing the victorious return of the Brigade to Newcastle, their triumphant march up Grainger Street, and the ovation from all their friends and admirers gathered to welcome them home. But behold today, all that returned is a small party of one of the four battalions, come to place its Colours before God's altar!'

Father McBrearty went on to say that, they welcomed the representatives of the Second Tyneside Irish there that day, and he assured them that the Colours they came to deposit would be regarded with the deepest reverence. Furthermore, he said,

'When the eyes of the people are turned to those Colours, those eyes will be saddened at the recollection of the men who laid down their lives in France. Many eyes will fill with tears as a mother, wife or sister says a prayer for a dear dead one, whose body lies in a foreign land.'

Father McBrearty then had strong words to say about why only one Colour had been returned to Tyneside,

'Why, must I ask, is there only one standard? Why have we not got four? Were there not four battalions of the Tyneside Irish? Why have we not got the Colours of the other battalions, the 24th, with the Red Shamrock on their sleeves, the 26th and 27th? Is it because they no longer officially exist? Is it because they fought practically to the last man? Because although they no longer officially exist, their memory will never fade on Tyneside. or it will be to the eternal shame of Tyneside if it does.'

Father McBrearty then continued with his sermon, by saying,

'I hope when we teach our children the history of the war, that we shall teach them first and foremost what their own brave north country men did in the war,'

He said he remembered the bitter disappointment they felt, when, in the first days of the Somme offensive, they looked at a London paper and saw a list of the regiments engaged in the fighting. No mention was made of Northumberland Fusiliers or of the Durhams and yet at the moment of the attack, there had been sixteen battalions of Northumberland Fusiliers engaged. The brave Chaplain then went on to recall a sermon he had given to the men on one occasion during the Battle of Arras. He told them he knew of no class of men whose lives so closely resembled the life on earth of our Divine Saviour. He had asked them to examine the resemblance. Our Saviour had left Heaven and had come down to earth to die for us. The soldiers had left their homes, the care of mothers and the affection of wives and the love of children, to go forth to foreign lands, to fight in battle and protect us from an unscrupulous enemy. He then compared Our Lord's life of suffering and his journey, known as 'The Way of the Cross', His Body torn and cut and weighed down by the weight of the cross He carried. How often had the soldiers marched along their own 'Way of the Cross' along bad roads, under the worst conditions, their packs were heavy, and the burden of rifle and ammunition added considerably to the load. Too often the only thing left standing in a ruined French village was the Crucifix, amid the complete encircling devastation. 'But what of ourselves?' he had gone on to ask,

'We had much to learn by the example of fidelity and self-sacrifice of the men who had died in France. They had to learn too that when God's grace was at hand to assist, there was no difficulty too great, no weakness so extreme, that it might not be overcome.'

At the close of the Mass Sir Charles Parsons handed over the Colour to Father Newsham, who thanked the officials for having brought the Colour to St Mary's Cathedral.

The ex-soldiers were then marched through the town to Eldon Square, where the Parade was dismissed. It is fitting that the place that was the first parade ground of the Tyneside Irish was where the survivors 'fell out' after laying-up the Colour. Afterwards the Colours of the other battalions were sent to the North. The 24th Battalion Colour is today hanging in St Nicholas' Cathedral, the 26th Battalion Colour was in Gateshead, and was, it is believed, destroyed when the Church burnt to the ground. The 27th Battalion Colour was in Newcastle Guildhall[1]. On visiting St Mary's to look at the Colour of the 25th the author was informed that it had been stolen many years ago.

Private Patrick McCabe born in Seaham County Durham. His mother spoke of all the 'Irish Lads' who had died for King and Country.

During the Peace Celebrations, flags and bunting were hung out in the streets of the towns and villages across the country. In the 'Irish Catholic' areas of the North East, not only was red, white and blue displayed, but also the green, white and gold colours of the 'Auld Country'. Of course by then, the Home Rule Bill was going through, and the Irish Free State would soon be no longer part of the Union. The hanging out of 'foreign' colours brought some comment in parts of County Durham. Private Patrick McCabe's mother didn't have an Irish flag or any green bunting, so she took a double bed sheet, and dyed it emerald green. As she was hanging it outside her house in a colliery row in Seaham, she was asked what she was doing. In no uncertain terms the questioner was told of all the 'Irish Lads' that had died for King and Country. He then retreated very quickly under the wrath of the bereaved mother.

Lieutenant R J Erett, Secretary and driving force behind the Tyneside Irish OCA.

In the centre of Eldon Square today stands the Newcastle City War Memorial, a statue of St George killing the Dragon. It was here, on St Patrick's Day, for many years that the survivors of the Tyneside Irish Brigade paid annual homage to their dead comrades, until one St Patrick's Day, no one turned up.

Once peace arrived and the survivors had returned to their homes, many expressed a wish to have an Old Comrades Association, but, this met with little support initially. However, Lieutenant R J (Jack) Erett, and Captain George Coleby MC and Bar, MM, both who were Company Sergeant Major's in the 24th Battalion pressed ahead and managed to get things moving. At the first meeting about fifty ex members attended and the following officials were elected:- Mr H Caulfield Chairman, Mr R J Erett Secretary, Mr G Coleby Treasurer, and a committee of six comprising, Messers Blackburn (Consett), Collins (Newcastle), Prudhoe (Winlaton), Wilson (Shiremoor), Doyle (Newcastle) and Duffy (Stanley). The committee wrote to Mr J Mulcahy and requested the use of any remaining funds belonging to the Brigade and things began to happen. 'Re-union smokers' were organised with entertainment provided by the men themselves, prominent among the singers were Messers Donnelly, Blackburn and Reynolds.

Sergeant H Caulfield, Chairman Tyneside Irish OCA. Corporal J Caulfield, committee member for the 27th Battalion.

But of course the 'big' day was St Patrick's Day, Mr Erett obtained shamrock from The Sisters of Charity at Ballaghaderin in County May, for distribution to the men. The men gathered in Castle Garth and were formed up under the command of

Old Comrades march to the war memorial led by Pipe Major Jack Wilson playing, 'The Banks of the Shannon'.

Veterans pay their respects at the War Memorial in Eldon Square standing on the left is 24/49 Private Arthur Walton who 'went over the top' at the age of sixteen.

The Colour of the 27th Battalion was restored and is now in St Mary's Cathedral in Newcastle.

Colonel J M Prior. Led by Pipe Major Wilson, playing 'The Banks of the Shannon' the parade marched to Eldon Square, where after two minutes silence wreaths of Flanders poppies were laid, then the lament, 'After the Battle', was played by the Pipe Major. Speeches were made by the Lord Mayor of Newcastle and Father George McBrearty. This was the pattern throughout the late twenties and the thirties, with many regular attenders, among them Captains Farina, Doyle, Swinburn and Rogers and from the 'other ranks' Arthur Walton of Gateshead, who was numbered /49 in A Company of the First Tyneside Irish, in October 1914 when he enlisted, he was barely fourteen years old, at sixteen he had taken part in the trench raids on the Somme and then been wounded in the legs on the 1st of July. In the evening after the parade there was the re-union smoker. These events gradually faded away but that was not quite the end of the Tyneside Irish, as war clouds loomed in 1939, Colonel J M Prior contacted the War Office and offered to raise a Tyneside Irish Battalion in the event of war breaking out. The offer was declined!

However those who were young enough to enlist did so, and once again took up arms against the foe. Notable amongst these men was Captain G Coleby MC and Bar, MM who served in the Auxiliary Pioneer Corps. Private Will Donaldson crossed the Tyne Bridge once more, and went to the Northumberland Fusiliers Depot in Fenham Barracks. He re-enlisted, ready once more to do his bit, but after a while the Army discovered that he had a silver plate in his head from wounds in the previous conflict. He was honourably discharged very soon afterwards. Those that had survived gradually died. Private John

Connolly died in 1949, and was buried, still with his tokens fastened to his braces. His number /1151 was used as a nom-de-plume on his betting slips, in the days when betting was illegal, because it was his 'LUCKY' number. The other three men with this number 25/1151, 26/1151 and 27/1151 were all killed in action. The last known original to die was 26/1064 Lance Corporal Michael Manley, who died at 11 o'clock on the 11th of November 1994, aged 104, at the very hour that the nation was remembering its war dead.

The regimental motto of the Northumberland Fusiliers is, QUO FATA VOCANT translated into English, this means 'Where the Fates Lead' or translated into Geordie it means 'We gan where we're telt', certainly the men of the Tyneside Irish Brigade, lived up to that motto, and when the whistles blew, at 0730 hours, on the First of July 1916 they 'Went where they were telt'.

Whilst researching photographs for this book the author found that the Regimental Colour of the 27th Battalion had been handed to Beamish Museum. When Councillor Barney Rice of Newcastle City Council learned of this through reading the book, he discussed the matter with Councillor John O'Shea, both felt that the colour should be restored and put on public display.

They convened a meeting of interested parties who felt as they did that; the colour should be rescued from obscurity and put on display. Those present were;

Father Michael Campion, Administrator of St Mary's Cathedral,
Tony Corcoran, Director of the Tyneside Irish Festival,
Joe O'Niell, Chairman of the Tyneside Irish Centre,
Captain Peter Marr, Regimental Secretary of The Royal Regiment Of Fusiliers
John Sheen, the author,
Ned Buick, Arts Director of the Grainger Town Project,
Les Forster, Representing the Chief Executive of Newcastle City Council,
Major Ted Cawthorn, who oversaw the publicity of the project.

Newcastle City Council arranged a long term loan of the colour with Beamish Museum on the understanding that the colour was restored and conserved. The cost of £1200 was met by donations of £500 from the Regimental Association and £500 from the Tyneside Irish Centre with the shortfall made up by Newcastle City Council.

At the authors suggestion the date of Saturday 7 April 2001 was set for the rededication, being the closest date to 9 April the anniversary of the winning of two Victoria Crosses by the Tyneside Irish Brigade.

At Father Campion's suggestion the author was asked to provide the wording for the plaque that would go underneath the colour once it was hung in the Cathedral.

In the mean time the author learned that a set of the original War Pipes was in the possession of Vincent Robinson a road car inspector on the Long Island Railway in New York. The family originally from Willington, County Durham, had been given the pipes by Father McBrearty after the war. The Pipes had been restored and Vincent a piper with an Irish Pipe Band in New York was invited to bring them to Newcastle and play during the service.

On 7 April 2001, as the Northumbrian Band of the Royal Regiment of Fusiliers played a selection of Irish and Geordie airs, St Mary's Cathedral was packed with relatives of members of the Tyneside Irish Brigade, most of whom had supplied photographs for the book. At the door two soldiers of the Royal Regiment of Fusiliers carried the colour in its sealed glass case. The Commanding Officer of 1/Royal Irish Regiment had allowed Pipe Major Wilson to be present to pipe the colour to the altar. Playing the slow march 'Let Erin Remember' the procession made its way to the altar where the colour was handed over to the safe keeping of its spiritual home. Then Vincent Robinson played 'The Minstrel Boy' on the very pipes that had led the Brigade forward on that fateful day in July 1916.

Afterwards the Lord Mayor hosted a reception for the family's which proved a great success.

But that's not the end of the story! At 14:30 hours on Tuesday 16 September 2003 the congregation was back in St Mary's, which was again packed. Outside the skirl of the pipes was heard playing 'The Minstrel Boy' as Vincent Robinson led The President of Ireland Mary McAleese into the Cathedral. In her address the President said, 'I get piped into many functions in my capacity as President but I have never been piped in by pipes with such a history behind them'

At the end of her address the President made her way to the rear of the Cathedral where the Regimental Colour is on display, here she unveiled the brass plaque with the wording done by the author.

The King's Colour
27th (Service) Battalion Northumberland Fusiliers
4th Tyneside Irish
1914–1918

This colour was rededicated on 7th April 2001 and placed here in St Mary's Cathedral

In memory of all ranks who served with
The 103rd (Tyneside Irish) Infantry Brigade
during the Great war
1914–1918

"Their memory will never fade on Tyneside"

"QUO FATA VOCANT"

After unveiling the plaque the President was introduced to several people among them the author to whom she said a few words of praise for the book.

Since then scarcely a month goes by without some letter or email requesting information about a soldier of the brigade many of them from Australia, New Zealand and Canada proving that 'Their memory has never faded'.

Chapter Twelve

The Bands of the Tyneside Irish and The Reserve Battalions

'The Minstrel Boy to the wars has gone.
In the ranks of death you will find him'

TRAD

Music played a part in the Tyneside Irish Brigade from early days. The earliest sounds were provided by Boy Scout buglers attached to the 24th Battalion on war service and Fred Green, now living in Colchester, recalled that in October 1914, at the age of 13, he was sent as a bugler and messenger to the Tyneside Irish. He was billeted on the first floor of Dunn's Buildings and each morning would sound 'Reveille' and later 'Fall In' as the Battalion assembled in Eldon Square. Fred wanted to join up as a junior bandsman but his parents would not agree, and on his 14th birthday, in January 1915, he was taken home to start work. The early parades in Eldon Square were accompanied by a band, but the Irish wanted something special so that Colonel Byrne, at that time the Commanding Officer, suggested that the First Tyneside Irish Battalion should not only have a band but an effort should be made to provide the national instrument, 'The War Pipes of Erin' or the 'Piob Mor' Irish War Pipes. Mr Edward Conway a member of the Executive Committee was asked to take the matter in hand and the Irish War Pipes were provided. However finding a piping instuctor was to prove more difficult as no expert Irish piper was to be found outside Ireland. Eventually Mr Charles Gordon, a teacher at Skerry's College in Newcastle, who was a professional Scottish piper, was recommended. Not only was he an expert piper, but a first class shot also, having won the King's Prize at Bisley. Mr Gordon had served in territorial battalions of the Black Watch and Highland Light Infantry, winning many piping competitions.

The Tyneside Irish were the only band in the army at that time using the Irish War Pipes. Two pipers were borrowed from the Tyneside Scottish, father and son, called Wilson, from Backworth in Northumberland. The father, Jack Wilson, liked the Irish Battalion, and stayed to become Pipe Major of the First Tyneside Irish; the son, John Wilson, returned to the Tyneside Scottish to become Pipe Major of the First Tyneside Scottish, winning the Military Medal piping the Battalion into action on 1 July 1916.

The Pipers of the Tyneside Irish had green cuffs added to their khaki jackets and bandsman's wings on the shoulder, with green cord lanyards as well as green pipe banners and green pipe bags.

'The Pipes came in for some criticism and for a time were dropped in favour of a brass band'. (Captain J B Arnold).

After the Brigade went to France the Pipes and Drums were posted en masse to the 26th Battalion, as Captain Arnold recalled,

Pipe Major Jack Wilson taken on 26th June 1918, when he was serving with the 25th Battalion.

'In the 26th we had a Pipe Major called Scott who was also a member of my Company and a great character. He was one of the trick musicians who probably could not read a note of music but

Band of the 26th Battalion. The young boys are from Felling St Patrick's Catholic Boys Brigade. Ringed is Corporal H Cresswell of Usworth, wounded 1st July 1916, who was transferred to Royal Defence Corps.

could play any instrument that he took up. He only had four marching tunes in his repertoire, "Bonny Dundee", "Father O'Flynn", "Believe me, if all those endearing young charms" – that beautiful melody of Moore's' and "God save Ireland", which is simply the old measure of "Tramp, Tramp, Tramp, the boys are marching" I have foot slogged miles and miles to those tunes and I never hear them now but I am back with the old battalion on the muddy highways of France marching on the right of the road, with the horrible strip of pave in the middle.'

Piper Cunningham with his Irish War Pipes. The two drones can be clearly seen, Scottish pipes have three.

The Second Battalion Tyneside Irish had a Fife and Drum band led by Drum Major L D Edwards and this band played at many recruiting drives around Newcastle. According to the August 1916 issue of the St George's Gazette, this band was started by the regular Adjutant, Captain H R Barkworth, but he did not join the battalion until September 1915, long after the band's activities had been reported in the local papers. Drum Major Edwards was subsequently transferred to the 30th (Reserve) Battalion and did not accompany the Battalion overseas. At least two of this band were to die acting as stretcher bearers in France, Privates Willam Smith on 1 July and Wilf Johnson on 8 July 1916.

The Third Tyneside Irish had by far the most successful band, having recruited en masse the Felling St Patrick's Catholic Boys' Brigade Band. These young boys are very evident in the photograph and this band was very prominent in the recruiting campaign, drawing favourable comment in the local newspapers. One particular member of the band, 26/1297 Bandsman, later Corporal, Matthew Whelan was to win the Distinguished Conduct Medal and the Military Medal in 1917 but was killed in action in September of that year.

The Pipes and Drums of the 24th Battalion.

The Fife and
Drum Band of the
25th Battalion.

Gale and Polden, Ltd.]

BANDSMEN AND PIPERS. Tyneside Irish Brigade.

1. Pte. McGarr.
2. ,, Slaser.
3. ,, Ross.
4. ,, Duffy.
5. ,, Howie.
6. ,, Goundry.
7. Pte. Cassidy.
8. ,, McQinn.
9. ,, Brown.
10. ,, Whitfield.
11. Cpl. Gallagher.
12. Pte. Brown.
13. Pte. Grey.
14. ,, Rodgers.
15. ,, Brown.
16. ,, Kelly.
17. ,, Talbot.
18. ,, Conway.
19. Pte. Rowell.
20. ,, Smith.
21. ,, Welch.
22. ,, McArthur.
23. ,, Grimer.
24. ,, Railton.
25. Pte. Brown.
26. ,, Cunningham.
27. Major Payne Gallwey.
28. Pipe-Major Wilson.
29. Monaghan.
30. Pte. Locky.

27th Battalion Band. Circled is Private John Scollen. Squared is Sergeant Tyrie.

A Bandsman of the Tyneside Irish.

After the 26th Battalion was disbanded in 1918, the big bass drum, which had been presented to the band by Councillor John McCoy, the Lord Mayor of Gateshead, was placed in the care of Felix Lavery. Many years later in 1955 Felix Lavery's home Forth House in Newcastle was sold, and during building work the drum was found and the new owner of Forth House a Newcastle business man, Mr A Barnett, presented the drum to the Royal Northumberland Fusiliers' Museum. This was the first relic of the Tyneside Irish to be handed in, thirty-six years after the Tyneside Irish disbanded.

Very little is known about the band of the Fourth Tyneside Irish, but in April 1915 the band is reported to have purchased from Messrs Boosey and Co, Italian Bersaglieri horns. It was stated that these were a vast improvement on the field bugle, as anything in C, including the regimental march, could be played upon them. The Battalion Band was made up of men from all the companies of the Battalion, a large proportion of whom would be killed in action. The majority of all the bandsmen had been involved in the brass band movement in peacetime and Privates John Scollen and F Early, both from Seaham, had played in Seaham St Mary Magdalene's Roman Catholic brass band. When some of the older bandsmen, and those who were unfit for foreign service were transferred to the

30th Battalion Band. Circled is Private John Armstrong.

30th (Reserve) Battalion, a band was formed for that unit and by this stage the Tyneside Irish Harp had been painted on the big drum. The trombonist 24/796 Private John Romanus Armstrong originally enlisted into the First Tyneside Irish but did not serve overseas with that unit.

The Reserve Battalions

In July 1915, the Depot companies of the Tyneside Irish Battalions based at Woolsington joined together to form the Tyneside Irish (Reserve) Battalion and this Battalion was numbered 30th in the Northumberland Fusiliers. A recruiting campaign started in Newcastle on 27th of August and lists of those volunteering appeared in the papers. However the lists were short indeed compared to those of the previous Winter.

One group of volunteers who enlisted for the 30th Battalion came from Ushaw College, the Roman Catholic college just outside Durham City. With the possibility of conscription looming these young men, who were training to be priests and teachers, decided to enlist, and over eighty of them joined the Tyneside Irish. Very few however served with the Brigade overseas but a large draft of these Ushaw students went out to France and served with the King's Own Yorkshire Light Infantry.

Of these Sergeant Matthew Clancy was shot in the abdomen whilst going over the top at Arras on Easter Monday 1917 and although he lived long enough to receive the Last Sacraments from an Ushaw Chaplain, Father J L Prescott CF, Sergeant Clancy died shortly after-

Lieutenant-Colonel H F Barclay, the Commanding Officer of the 30th Battalion.

James Bacon and Sons.] OFFICERS, Tyneside Irish Brigade. [30th (R) Batt. N.F.]. [*To face page* 227.

1. 2nd Lt. T. M. Scanlan.
2. ,, J. McVey.
3. ,, S. H. Shaw.
4. ,, P. C. Cox.
5. ,, E. G. Pattison.
6. ,, N. S. Lees.
7. ,, A. V. Simpson.
8. ,, W. A. R. Dabell.
9. Lt. L. V. Naughton.
10. Capt. W. A. Goss.
11. 2nd Lt. M. O'Leary, V.C.
12. ,, A. Murphy.
13. ,, F. J. McDonnell.
14. ,, D. McLeod.
15. ,, J. Harker.
16. ,, F. W. Lumley.
17. 2nd Lt. H. S. Hobson.
18. Lieut. J. R. Lunn.
19. 2nd Lt. J. R. Taylor.
20. ,, J. L. Jones.
21. ,, J. M. Dalzell.
22. ,, T. F. Lister.
23. ,, W. Byrne.
24. ,, P. L. H. Brough.
25. 2nd Lt. G. W. Hoggan.
26. ,, L. J. Gavin.
27. ,, H. S. A. Ryley.
28. ,, H. E. Crean.
29. ,, G. T. Sheridan.
30. ,, C. A. Naylor.
31. ,, P. McGuiness.
32. Lt. C. Cameron.
33. Lt. D. McElduff.
34. Capt. T. Doyle.
35. ,, J. Wright.
36. Major A. S. O'Brien.
37. Lt.-Col. H. F. Barclay.
38. Capt. W. J. Rix.
39. Lt. & Q.M. A. P. O'Reilly.
40. Capt. J. C. Arnold.
41. Capt. J. Gay.
42. 2nd Lt. R. Redham.

Private William Thorburn seated on the right, enlisted under the Derby scheme and was posted to the 30th Battalion.

wards. Another of the group, Corporal Bernard McDermott was awarded the Military Medal with 6/KOYLI and among those to survive from this group was Richard Crawford who was wounded in the head on Passchendaele Ridge in October 1917. He was very unfortunate to receive eight other wounds at the same time and he was discharged in March 1918 to be back at Ushaw studying by September of that year.

A few were retained in England as instructors and did not go out to France until the dark days of March 1918 and one of these was Arthur McCormack, who arrived in France at Easter 1918 but ten days later was wounded; his jaw being broken by a bullet. He was in hospital until September 1918 but was able to resume his studies at Ushaw in January 1919.

More than a few of them were commissioned, among these was Francis McNiff who, having been promoted to Sergeant, was sent to a cadet school, and in March 1917, was commissioned in the 24th Battalion. Later he transferred to the Royal Flying Corps where he was killed when his machine was involved in an accident. Another who was commissioned from the ranks of the Ushaw College students, was Austin Tumelty who after reaching the rank of Corporal received a Commission in the Royal Dublin Fusiliers and was killed on a night patrol in No-Man's-Land on 10 November 1917.

Another large batch of recruits for the 30th Battalion came from West Yorkshire, although why they joined the Tyneside Irish is unclear. One theory put forward is that they had been recruited for a Yorkshire Pals unit that did not materialise. A similar number of men from West Yorkshire were serving in the 29th Battalion, the Tyneside Scottish Reserve Battalion and many of these men went out to France to join 13/Northumberland Fusiliers serving in 62 Brigade of the 21st Division.

By November 1915 the Battalion had moved from Woolsington down to Richmond in North Yorkshire, and it was here that they became part of the 20th Reserve Brigade. However, recruiting was not going as well as expected and articles appeared in the newspapers trying to attract recruits. A recruiting office for the battalion was opened at 86 New Bridge Street, Newcastle, and it remained open until 8 p.m. some evenings. These articles in the newspapers also stated that anyone who had attested under Lord Derby's scheme could, if they wished, join the Tyneside Irish, or Scottish, by intimating their wishes to the recruiting officer. In the month of November well over two hundred men joined the 30th Battalion, but how many were Derby men is unknown. On the thirteenth of December, William Thorburn of Frankham High Houses, attested at Hexham, under Lord Derby's scheme. He was called up in January and posted to the 30th Battalion, serving with it until he too was transferred to the King's

26/508 Private John Nowley was posted to 1st Garrison Battalion and served in Malta throughout the war. He arrived home on Christmas Day 1918.

A group of the 85th Training Reserve Battalion wearing the 85 Cloth Badges, the Sergeant wears Harp collar badges of the 25th Battalion.

Lieutenant Thomas Doyle of the 30th Battalion.

A private of the 85th Training Reserve Battalion. Note cloth '85' Cap Badge.

Own Yorkshire Light Infantry. William was another who was wounded at Arras with the KOYLI and was discharged on 15 September 1917.

The 30th Battalion moved to Catterick Garrison in North Yorkshire in December and it was there on 22 January 1916 that one of the ex-regular senior NCOs died, Sergeant Michael Finan of Milburngate in Durham City, who had served for twenty years in 2/Durham Light Infantry, sixteen of them in India and was fifty four years old when he enlisted once again. He had been home on leave and shortly after his return to Catterick a cold he had caught developed into pneumonia. When his funeral cortege passed up North Road in Durham the street was lined with a multitude of spectators, The coffin was carried by four senior NCOs of the Tyneside Irish headed by the band of 8/Durham Light Infantry and following behind came his family and many mourners. The medical facilities where Sergeant Finan passed away were described by Captain Jack Arnold,

> *'Amenities there were none – there was not even a proper hospital and anyone who was sick was dumped into a hut where the male equivalent of nursing orderlies, men who were unfit for the line, could do little for them: they died or somehow got back to the battalion.*

Then came a move to Hornsea in April 1916, where once again the men of the 30th Battalion found themselves under canvas. The tents were pitched in what had in days gone by been a potato field and the CO insisted that the lines of tents should be perfectly straight, which meant that some tents were in hollows, and when it rained the men found that they were lying in little rivers as the water flowed down the field.

In June the 30th Battalion was split into two and a 34th (Reserve) Battalion was formed at Hornsea,

James Bacon and Sons.] OFFICERS, 3rd Batt. Tyneside Irish Brigade. [26 (S) Batt. N.F.]. *[To face page* 185.

1. 2nd Lt. Murray, W.P. 2. ,, Coupon. 3. ,, Scarf. 4. ,, Kendrick. 5. Lt. Shackleton. 6. 2nd Lt. McAlister. 7. 2nd Lt. Ryley. 8. Lt. Horsborough. 9. Rev. Bateman. 10. 2nd Lt. Murray, M.J. 11. ,, Russell. 12. Lt. Young. 13. 2nd Lt. Murphy. 14. Lt. Cole. 15. 2nd Lt. Gavin. 16. Lt McConway. 17. ,, Dr Perric. 18. 2n Lt. Fortune. 19. Lt. McGillicuddy. 20. ,, J. F ndlay. 21. Capt. Gilmore. 22. ,, Falkous. 23. ,, Price, M.C. 24. Major Tabrum. 25. Major Chichester, O.C. 26. Capt. Cobb, Adj., D.S.O. 27. ,, Copley. 28. ,, Stephenson. 29. 2nd Lt. Brown. 30. Lt. Mullally. 31. 2nd Lt. O'Connor. 32. Capt. Hedley. 33. 2nd Lt. Fitzgerald. 34. Lt. Dix.

but only one man has been traced with a 34th Battalion number. 34/4 Private W Poulson killed in action on 27th September 1916.

The plan was that the 30th Battalion would supply drafts to the 24th and 25th Battalions, with the 34th sending men out to the 26th and 27th Battalions. However, before this system could become operational there was further reorganisation of the reserves in the UK and on the 1 September 1916 the 30th (Reserve) Battalion became the 85th Training Reserve Battalion at Hornsea, part of the 20th Reserve Brigade; similarly the 34th (Reserve) Battalion was absorbed by the Training Reserve Battalions of the 20th Reserve Brigade. Many wounded and sick men spent time with the 85th Training Reserve Battalion, and from the information gathered from the Silver War Badge lists, it would seem that a large number of these men were discharged from that unit.

Badges worn by the Reserve Battalions are as follows:

1. Tyneside Irish Harps with 30 numerals and the letters NF.
2 A 20th Brigade numeral on the left arm. The colour scheme of this is uncertain, but it is thought that the Irish had Green numerals. The other colours in the scheme were white*, red and blue.
3. On formation of the 85th Training Reserve Battalion, recruits are seen with a cloth numeral 85 worn as a cap badge. However the officers and senior non-commissioned officers appear to have retained their parent unit insignia.

* Known to be worn by the 29th Bn Tyneside Scottish Reserve Bn.

Chapter Thirteen

Absenteeism, Desertion and Execution

'Its pack drill for me and a fortnights C.B.
For drunk and resisting the guard.'

KIPLING

One of the original ideas of this work was to trace as much about the men of the Tyneside Irish as possible but an area overlooked by many historians is that of absenteeism and desertion, although it may have been accidentally or deliberately overlooked, so as not to blacken the reputation of a particular unit. Some articles appeared in local newspapers about men being arrested and sentenced before being handed over to a military escort. Some of these articles were about members of the Tyneside Irish Brigade, and these snippets of information helped add background to many individuals, and to the story of the Brigade.

Initial research pointed to the fact that some soldiers of the Tyneside Irish Brigade were persistent absentees, but this gave a false picture, since later research showed that the Tyneside Scottish and the Territorials also had their problems with absenteeism and desertion. From the very start, men who had absolutely no intention of soldiering were enlisting for the shilling and then deserting. This was a favourite trick of merchant seamen, who, short of money, with the ship due to sail, would go into Newcastle, enlist in the army under a false name, then sail with the next tide. A number of these appear in the 'Police Gazette' during 1915, yet it appears that they were never apprehended, nor did they give themselves up.

One young man, George Mason aged 16, appeared in court in Durham having enlisted consecutively

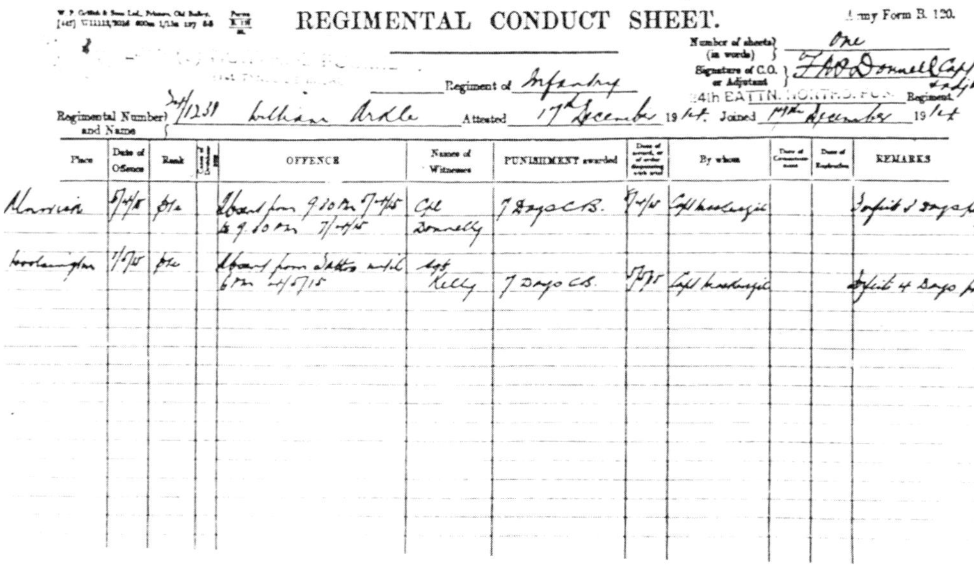

REGIMENTAL CONDUCT SHEET.

Army Form B. 120.

Number of sheets (in words): One

Signature of C.O. or Adjutant: F. O'Donnell Capt Adjt

Regiment of Infantry

24th BATTN. NORTH'D. FUS. Regiment.

Regimental Number and Name: 24/1231 William Arkle

Attested 17th December 1914. Joined 17th December 1914

Place	Date of Offence	Rank		OFFENCE	Names of Witnesses	PUNISHMENT awarded	Date of award	By whom	Date of	Date of	REMARKS
Alnwick	5/4/15	Pte		Absent from 9.30 pm 5-4-15 to 9.30 pm 7-4-15	Cpl Donnelly	7 Days C.B.	9-4-15	Capt Mackenzie			Forfeit 3 Days pay
Woolsington	7/5/15	Pte		Absent from Duties until 6 pm 11/5/15	Sgt Kelly	7 Days C.B.	13/5/15	Capt Mackenzie			Forfeit 4 Days pay

Company Conduct Sheet for Private William Arkle, showing he was AWOL in April and May 1915 prior to being discharged. Of the NCOs involved Corporal Donnelly would be killed in action 1 July 1916 and Sergeant Kelly wounded the same day.

in the Northumberland Fusiliers, Durham Light Infantry, Royal Naval Division and the Tyneside Irish. Charged with obtaining money by false pretences, he was sentenced to one month's hard labour, as was 26/713 Private Patrick Ward who, on 23 April 1915 at 11.5 p.m., was found very drunk in Cemetery Road Blackhill whilst resisting arrest he struck a constable with a whisky bottle. Private Ward served his time and returned to the Battalion, only to go absent without leave in July 1915. In 1917 he was transferred to 783 Labour Company, having survived the Somme, Arras and Passchendaele.

Initially there was little problem with absenteeism, but when the Brigade assembled at Woolsington, Newcastle was easy to reach, and from there it was only a short trip home, in most cases. But once in Newcastle or at home the demon drink took over and men would overstay their time. In some villages, the village policeman would give the men a few days then tell them to be on their way but in Durham the police were constantly on the lookout for deserters and absentees. A particular place the police seemed to wait was on Framwellgate Bridge and it was here that David Summers was arrested. The policeman was granted five shillings by the Judge and Private Summers was remanded to the police cells to await military escort. Captain Arnold, who in civilian life had been called to the Bar, had many recollections of the company orderly room and the soldiers who appeared before him.

'One day I was taking orderly room in my tent on a Tuesday morning: there had been a terrible crop of absentees and late arrivals on the Monday morning as the men were still able to get home easily and a large proportion had weekend or Sunday leave. They had all only one excuse, an attack of diarrhoea and sickness on Monday morning, which retarded their arrival in spite of the most strenuous efforts to make it - "I was on my way to the station when it took me sudden, Sir, and I had to run" - the run always took them home again. There was a big line of men outside and I said in a voice that must have carried, "The next man who has not got a better excuse than diarrhoea and sickness will get a double penalty." In marched the youngest lad of the company, a bugle boy of about sixteen, - "Absent on Monday morning, what have you got to say?" "On Saturday Sir, I got my pay - a halfcrown and a shilling, the rest went as an allotment to my mother, and I started off for the train with the two coins in my pocket. I had a penny in my pocket as well as my pay and I could not resist giving it to a blind man who sits outside the church at the top of Northumberland Road. But when I got home I found that I had given him the halfcrown. I could not afford such a loss and I got up early on Monday morning determined to see him on the way to camp and collect it from him. But, Sir he is one of these men who changes his seat about the town from day to day. I went from place to place looking for him, that is what kept me late." Under a battalion order the bugler had to be remanded for the Colonel, but I told him if he told the same story he would probably get off.'

Private Wilf Holmes stamped himself a leave pass and went AWOL.

The sequel to this story came years later at a reunion when Captain Arnold told the story to the assembled 'Old Comrades', the bugler now reaching middle age was there and was more delighted than if he had been given a fiver.

Another story relating this time to the Battalion Orderly Room was also told by Captain Arnold, but this time it concerned Major Joe Prior.

'In the battalion was an expert lock picker – who could always escape from the guard room with the utmost ease. One day after breaking out he was apprehended and brought before the Major, who sentenced him to a further period of detention and observed "Since you were in the guard-room last we have had the locks strengthened by an expert, and you won't escape this time. But speaking as a sportsman, if you do escape I will give you five shillings when you are recaptured." Sure enough the man escaped again and when he was brought back, Prior solemly handed him the five shillings in the orderly room before locking him up again, but this time there was no offer of another five shillings.'

Two men of the 27th Battalion went AWOL in late 1915, the first being Tommy Calvert who, as an old regular soldier, had seen action during the Boer War, and at some time had been a regimental policeman. During his time with the regimental police, Tommy had learned the *Manual of Military Law* and *King's Regulations*, 'inside out', so whenever he was in trouble he always managed to 'get off' on a lesser charge. Frequently promoted to Lance Corporal, and then reduced for some misdemeanur, he decided to have a few days' at home in Witton Park. Within two days, a couple of regimental policemen arrived at Tommy's house in John Street, to escort him back to Sutton Veny. Meanwhile, due to the number of men going astray, the camp was closed and no one was allowed out without a pass. At guard mount one night Wilf Holmes was appointed 'stick man', that is the best turned out man on parade. He was then relieved from duty and told to wait in the 'Orderly Room', where on the table was a book of passes, and the unit stamp. Quickly Wilf stamped himself a pass and as soon as he came off duty he was on his way to Witton Park. When the train pulled into Witton Park, Wilf quickly made his way up the street towards his home, but there coming down on the other side under escort was Tommy Calvert. 'Get that bugger too, he's a deserter as well', shouted Tommy hoping the police would leave him and chase Wilf. Wilf knowing Tommy's reputation for escaping shouted, 'Don't leave him he'll escape'. This threw the regimental policemen into a quandary, they knew Tommy would run off if they left him, so deciding that their job was to take Tommy back, they let Wilf continue on his way. Wilf had a day or two at home and then returned to Sutton Veny, when on his return he was paraded in front of the Company Commander and questioned as to how he had got out of the camp. The officer cajoled and bribed him with no punishment, but Wilf said nothing.

'if they had known I forged the pass, they would have thrown the book at me,'

he recalled,

'The ten days C.B. was well worth the two in Witton Park'.

Others became almost permanently absent, but when the time came they went out to France, and met their fate with the rest of the Brigade, as did the Lambton brothers, Peter and Robert, from Byker. They were absent in April, May, June and July of 1915, but both were to die of wounds in 1916. Others were so bad, like James Kirton, that they were posted out of the Brigade and the court registers are the only evidence of their service with the Tyneside Irish. From a letter from his grand daughter it would appear that James Kirton was discharged from the Tyneside Irish. He then made his way to Cardiff where he enlisted in the Welsh Regiment. He was posted to 2/Welsh Regiment and was killed in action at Passchendaele on 8 November 1917, he has no known grave and is commemorated on the Tyne Cot Memorial to the Missing. If his service in the Tyneside Irish was below standard he certainly made up for it. Many of these men do not appear in casualty or absentee voter lists, nor do their names appear in WO/329, the First World War Medal Rolls at the Public Record Office. Some men were found hiding under beds, others gave any excuse they could think of, many suddenly became ill, but nearly all were taken to the police station and the next day to Court, where they were remanded for escort. Some, such as Joseph Hammil, were not picked up by the police for a long time and Private Hammil was only arrested because he was 'mad drunk', when the police arrived at The Grapes Inn in Claypath, Durham where Sergeant Haggie recognised Hammil as a deserter and arrested him. He had been on the run for three months, and he was given ten days' hard labour before being handed over to the Army. Another

24/1317 Private Arthur Fenwick was up in court in Durham for fighting after a man in a pub insulted the Red Shamrock on his shoulder.

man, Michael Riley, who was living in a lodging house in Framwellgate, was in trouble before he was called up. On being sentenced to a month's imprisonment, he said to the Judge, 'I am in the Tyneside Irish. How if I am called up?' The reply was 'They will have to wait until you come out.'

This problem with absenteeism in the Tyneside Brigades was frustrating for those in higher command and something had to be done about it. Captain Arnold related how General Ingouville-Williams tried to stamp it out.

'I remember one cold day in November the whole brigade was paraded and marched for miles and miles over some of the bleakest territory in the whole of Salisbury Plain. At last we came to a sort of windswept plateau more bleak, if possible, than anything we had yet been through. Here we halted and "Inky Bill" drew the brigade together into close formation and addressed them in tones that could be heard even by the most distant files. He told off the brigade for frequent absences – a number of men had been given their embarkation leave and had been slow to return. His words flayed the ranks like whips made from scorpions; he could do it well and the whole setting was suitable to the occassion. It was as if a victim had been taken to some lonely spot in order to be done in and we marched back with our tails between our legs, having been made to suffer for those who were still absent.' (The Tyneside Scottish had the same problem.)

But then some men like William Moore of Framwellgate went absent in late 1915 to try and sort out family problems and although the court was sympathetic he was still remanded for escort. Going out to France, William Moore survived all the major battles in which the brigade was involved. In June 1918, on his way back to the front after a spell at the depot, the train carrying him south had to pass through Durham, and hoping to catch a glimpse of his family, he was leaning out of the window as the train approached Crookhall Junction. The door came open, and William fell from the train, and was fatally injured, less than half a mile from his home. He was taken to the VAD Hospital at Brancepeth where he died of his injuries and was buried in Brandon Cemetery.

The problem did not end when the Brigade went overseas. Some of those returning wounded still managed to fall foul of the law and as usual drink was a major part of the problem. Corporal Alex Brodie of Framwellgate, having taken part in the Trench Raid on the night of 5/6th of June 1916, was wounded on the 1st of July. On convalescent leave in August, he fell foul of the police in Durham, but the magistrate took into consideration his service to his country and dismissed the charges, with the hope he would take a warning and, 'leave off the drink.'

The four Stephenson brothers – George is standing at the back. He was wounded in the head 1st July 1916 and deserted rather than return to the front. However, after one of his brothers was killed he went back.

The true scale of absenteeism cannot be gauged accurately because of missing court ledgers and also the Tynemouth Court Clerk gave no unit details, only the fact that the man was a soldier. However, from those records that do survive the following chart gives a good idea of the scale of the problem. Further research carried out in 1996 revealed a further 104 men listed in *The Police Gazette* between January and August 1915. Of these 86 were not known to the author, they could not be traced in the medal rolls, and the majority did not appear in the lists of names of those volunteering for the Tyneside Irish in 1914. The lists in *The Police Gazette* gave a description of each deserter including, in many cases, tattoo marks and scars.

ABSENTEEISM AND DESERTION WHILST
IN UK TRAINING

BATTALION	24	25	26	27	30	
COURT						
DURHAM	8	2	8	2	0	
NEWCASTLE	61	49	54	23	11	
GATESHEAD	20	21	58	16	8	
SOUTH SHIELDS	1	4	4	12	0	
SUNDERLAND	6	6	7	6	0	
HOUGHTON				1	1	
SEAHAM			1			
BEDLINGTON/BLYTH	2	2	1			
MORPETH	1	1	4			
TOTAL	**99**	**85**	**136**	**61**	**20**	
BRIGADE TOTAL						401
POLICE GAZETTE ADDITONAL DESERTERS						84
TOTAL						**485**

Some of those who served in France deserted after being wounded and one of these was 26/1248 Private George Stephenson who wounded in the head on 1st July 1916,was evacuated to hospital in Rouen. After reaching England he decided not to go back to France, quite understandably, and today he would be diagnosed as having Post Traumatic Stress, but in those days there was no such thing. George found work in Easington Colliery, where many members of the village were serving in his battalion, but no one turned him in. Eventually however, he did return to the Army and by 1918 was registered as an absent voter, to be once again serving at the front in France.

DESERTIONS IN FRANCE BY ORIGINAL
MEMBERS OF THE BRIGADE

BATTALION	24	25	26	27	TOTAL
PREVIOUSLY OR SUBSEQUENTLY WOUNDED	14	6	9	8	37
SUBSEQUENTLY KILLED	7	3	7	2	**19**

Those that were casualties 22

As was said earlier Captain Jack Arnold had experience of courts in civilian life and some of the stories in his memoirs relate to Courts Martial in France. In one case he was called to defend a young soldier charged with refusing to obey a lawful order in the front line, something which in those days might very well have been a capital offence and he recalled,

> *'It was a hopeless case in which to secure an acquittal, but there was enough evidence in it to show that the order given, though not unlawful, was one that put an unfair strain on the accused and*

gave him the justifiable impression that he was being given more than his fair crack of the whip. He was found guilty, but the punishment was for those days comparatively light.'

On more than one occassion Captain Arnold was called upon to defend his soldiers of the Tyneside Irish after some misdemeanur, but he recalled that the most interesting case he took part in was as a member of the court and not as a defending officer. This was one of those cases that never ought to have been brought – a charge of drunkenness against a Sergeant of the Tyneside Scottish well behind the lines and on New Year's Eve of all days, the one night of the year when a little licence might be given to members of a northern regiment. Captain Arnold recorded the facts of the case,

'According to the evidence an officer (whose reputation for tactlessness was notorious in the Tyneside Scottish Brigade) found the sergeant lying on the roadside, incapable and smelling of drink. The officer sent a party to bring him in and had him examined by the doctor, who pronounced him drunk and a charge was laid. The men who brought him in could only say he was incapable and smelt of liquor and the doctor, who obviously did not like the job, gave his evidence very fairly. "I asked him what he based his conclusion on that the sergeant was drunk." He said "He breathed stertorously, was incapable of looking after himself and smelt of liquor." I said to him, "Doctor, let us look at these symptoms in isolation. You would not say a man was drunk because he was breathing stertorously? It might be from a fit or an affliction of the nose?" The Doctor cordially agreed. "You would not say he was drunk because he was incapable of movement? that might be due to a fit or some sort of weak turn?" The Doctor was quite willing to take that from me. "Now with regard to the fact that the man smelt of liquor you are not going to say of course that that is proof of drunkeness? Where would we all be if you did?" This hardly required an answer and the Court retired to consider the finding. It is sufficient to say that we found the prisoner not guilty.'

There was a sequel to this story. A week or two afterwards when he was in the front line Captain Arnold received a 'snorting' letter from the Brigadier-General Commanding 102 Brigade [Brigadier-General Trevor Ternan CB CMG DSO]. The letter commented upon what the Brigadier considered to be the absurdity of the finding as being against the weight of evidence and virtually put the members of the court on the carpet for dereliction of duty. Captain Arnold wrote,

'I did not like it at all and though I was commanding in the line and had my hands full I sent out for a copy of "KR's" and the "Manual of Military Law". I had an idea that the Brigadier had exceeded his duty so I looked up the jurisdiction of the "Confirming Authority" which in this case was the Brigade. I found that the authority had the right to comment on a finding of "guilty" or to comment upon the sentence given by the court, but had no right to comment in a case of a finding of "not guilty." That was enough for me and I communicated with the Brigade Major chapter and verse. The answer was what I expected that he knew the position as well as I did, but that he had acted at the Brigadier's dictation. I never knew if my reply reached the Brigadier but I got a sense of satisfaction over that discovery of a point of law at a time when I was far away from libraries and reports.'

Courts Martial' in France appear to have varied from battalion to battalion within the brigade, but between January and September 1916 no less than thirty-six Warrant Officers, NCO's and men of the Tyneside Irish Brigade appeared in front of Field General Courts Martial. The main charge against the soldiers at these courts martial was Section 40 of King's Regulations, closely followed by drunkenness.

However many were charged with more than one offence, mainly absence and drunkenness. In one case a man was found not guilty of self- inflicted wounds, yet his medal roll sheet in WO/329 in the Public Record Office at Kew shows that his medals were forfeited for this offence. The same man's brother, an NCO, serving in the same battalion was also court martialled for sleeping at his post, a capital offence for which some men were executed, however his sentence was to be reduced in rank. In one case an NCO was reduced in rank in April 1916 for being drunk yet by June 1916 he was a Sergeant, would win the Military Medal and was subsequently commissioned. Punishment varied from two soldiers receiving Field

Punishment Number 2, to in two cases the soldiers involved receiving two years' hard labour which was subsequently reduced to ninety-one days Field Punishment Number 1. In the case of Warrant Officers and NCOs the main punishment handed out was reduction in rank. Awards of Field Punishment Number 1 varied from twenty-one days to 168 days although the latter was reduced to eighty-four days and this was for striking a superior. The punishment handed out to the soldiers of the 27th Battalion seems lighter than that of the other battalions, and the question must be asked 'Is this a reflection on the Commanding Officer?' The 27th Battalion was the only one commanded by the same officer throughout the period, a regular infantry officer. The 25th Battalion had had a change of Commanding Officers and after the arrival of Major Arden in April, another regular infantry officer, only two soldiers from the 25th Battalion were tried by FGCM.

It is known however that at least three officers of the Tyneside Irish Brigade were Court Martialled and that two of these were dismissed the service although, at the time of writing, case files or ledgers have not been seen.

FIELD GENERAL COURTS MARTIAL
FRANCE JANUARY TO SEPTEMBER 1916

Charge Battalion	**24**	**25**	**26**	**27**	**Total**
Section 40	4(1)	3(1)	5(1)	2	14
Dunkenness		2	5	1	8
Insubordination	1				1
Absence	4	4	1		9
Striking a Superior	1(1)	1			2
Sleeping at Post		1			1
Disobedience		1			1
Total	10	12	11	3	36
(1)Not Guilty					
Total Not Guilty	2	1	1		4
Convicted by FGCM					32

The executions of Corporal Short and Private Milburn

Two soldiers of the Tyneside Irish Brigade paid with their lives for their personal lack of discipline. Both were executed in the autumn of 1917 and, whatever the rights and wrongs of both cases, military law at

An execution by a British firing squad during the war.

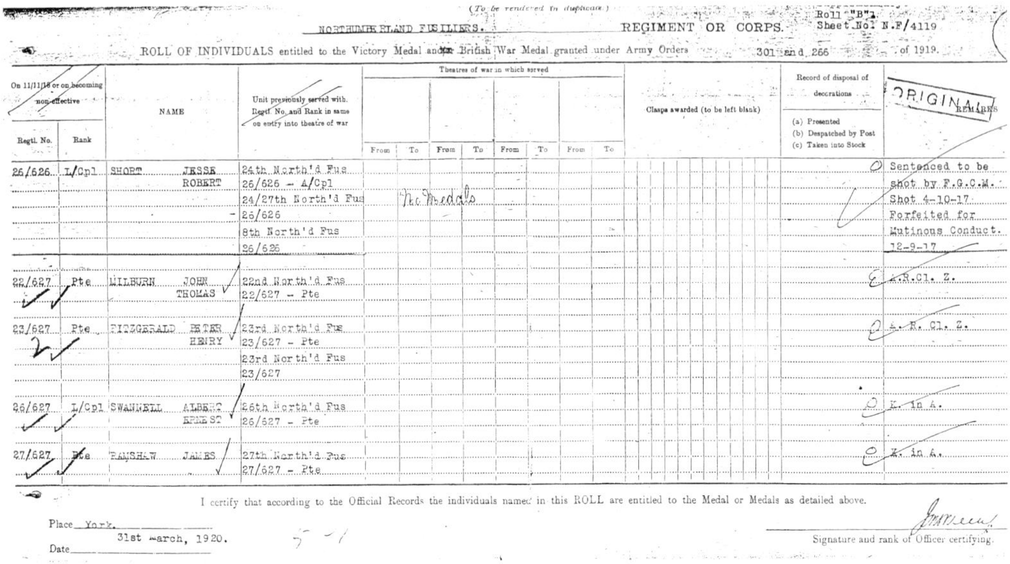
(To be rendered in duplicate.)

NORTHUMBERLAND FUSILIERS. REGIMENT OR CORPS. Roll "B"1. Sheet No. N.F/4119

ROLL OF INDIVIDUALS entitled to the Victory Medal and British War Medal granted under Army Orders 301 and 266 of 1919.

ORIGINAL

Regtl. No.	Rank	NAME	Unit previously served with. Regtl. No. and Rank in same on entry into theatre of war	Theatres of war in which served	Clasps awarded (to be left blank)	Record of disposal of decorations (a) Presented (b) Despatched by Post (c) Taken into Stock	REMARKS
26/626	L/Cpl	SHORT JESSE ROBERT	24th North'd Fus 26/626 – A/Cpl; 24/27th North'd Fus 26/626; 8th North'd Fus 26/626	No Medals		O	Sentenced to be shot by F.G.C.M. Shot 4-10-17. Forfeited for Mutinous Conduct. 12-9-17
22/627	Pte	MILBURN JOHN THOMAS	22nd North'd Fus 22/627 – Pte			E	A.R.Cl. Z.
23/627	Pte	FITZGERALD PETER HENRY	23rd North'd Fus 23/627 – Pte; 23rd North'd Fus 23/627			O	A. R. Cl. Z.
26/627	L/Cpl	SWANNELL ALBERT ERNEST	26th North'd Fus 26/627 – Pte			O	K. in A.
27/627	Pte	RAWSHAW JAMES	27th North'd Fus 27/627 – Pte			E	K. in A.

I certify that according to the Official Records the individuals named in this ROLL are entitled to the Medal or Medals as detailed above.

Place York.

Date 31st March, 1920.

Signature and rank of Officer certifying.

WO/329 sheet 4119, Medal Roll showing that Corporal J R Short forfeited his medals and was executed on the 4th October 1917.

the time allowed the death penalty, and both men would have been aware of this fact. The first to be executed was an original enlistment to the Tyneside Irish Brigade, 26/626 Corporal Jesse Robert Short, who died for the part he played in the mutiny at Etaples in September 1917.

The case of Corporal Short is well covered in, *Shot at Dawn* by Sykes and Putkowski, a book about the execution of British soldiers by their own side, during the First World War. However, at the time of the mutiny there were over two hundred men of the Tyneside Irish in Etaples. The Brigade had been medically inspected and all the older men, and those unfit through wounds and debility, were reclassified, and sent to the base for transfer to the Labour Corps.

It has been fairly easy to ascertain that many Tyneside Irishmen, as well as Tyneside Scots and Tyneside Pioneers of the 34th Division, were in Etaples at the time of the mutiny, because of the Regimental numbers allotted within the Labour Corps. 25/724 Private J Wood was transferred to 287 Labour Company on 26 September 1917.

23/441 Private J Walker originally with the Tyneside Scottish, and transferred to the 26th Battalion, was transferred to 762 Area Employment Company, Labour Corps, on 1 October. When the mutiny was discussed, more than one relative knew that their soldier ancestor had been in Etaples at the time, but invariably the soldier had never spoken, or had said very little, about the mutiny. Furthermore the son of one officer said that his father had refused point blank to command a firing squad, and it appears that the officer had spoken more about the subject than the soldiers.

One of the main causes behind the mutiny was the unjust and inhuman treatment of the front line 'Tommy' by the 'Canaries', the instructors, so called because of their yellow badges. This treatment led to a great deal of discontent and resentment among the men. Given the political situation in Russia and elsewhere, and the fact that men were tired and fed up with the war, it is hardly surprising that the British Army mutinied. What is surprising is that only one man was shot, and it is sad that he was a soldier of the Tyneside Irish.

The other member of the Brigade to face the firing squad was 45688 Private John Milburn, a reinforcement to the 24/27th Battalion. Already under a suspended prison sentence, he again deserted and this time paid with his life. However this was contrary to the wishes of the Divisional Commander, for the Divisional AQMG's War Diary records, at 0600 Hrs on the morning of 8 November, 1917, 'Division are trying to get a stay of execution for Private Milburn'. Then a little later an entry records, 'Word received that, Private Milburn executed at 0620 Hrs this morning'. At the time the 24th/27th Battalion were in Brigade reserve in the Hindenburg Line.

But in at least one case a soldier of the Tyneside Irish was saved from the firing squad, and again the memoirs of Captain Jack Arnold tell the story.

> *'Another case on which I sat as a member of the Court Martial turned on a rather remarkable piece of evidence, which in the circumstances saved the accused from facing the firing squad. The company to which the man belonged was to go over the top at zero hour on a certain day and his name appeared on the nominal roll which was taken shortly before the order to advance was given. After the attack the man was missing and within a day or two he was arrested by the Military Police at Boulogne without a pass and with no explanation of how he got there. It seemed to be an obvious case of deserting one's post in the firing line, for which in those days the penalty was death. But the accused produced a piece of paper which he had carefully preserved, on which was written the words "Private X (Name and number) has permission to stay in a dugout until further orders." Fortunately the handwriting on the paper could be identified; it was that of an officer in the man's company who had been killed during the attack on the day in question. The man said he had been given it by the officer shortly before the attack, but could tender no clear explanation of the purpose for which it was written or handed to him. It was a difficult situation to deal with but we acquitted the prisoner of desertion. The inference was that for some reason, which seemed good to the officer, the man had been thought unfit for duty and in these circumstances it would have been wrong to find him guilty of desertion. If he had lost that piece of paper nothing could have saved him.*

Each reader will have his or her own personal view on the execution of a soldier by his own side, this is a very emotive subject and very controversial, some who were shot were guilty of murder and would have faced the death penalty in a civilian court. The author can only say that a man not pulling his weight, or one who leaves his comrades in the lurch, makes the task of those men in the line that much harder. It seems that those who have never been on active service, or have never been in the forces, make the most noise about military discipline.

Appendix I

GALLANTRY AWARDS TO MEMBERS OF THE TYNESIDE IRISH BRIGADE

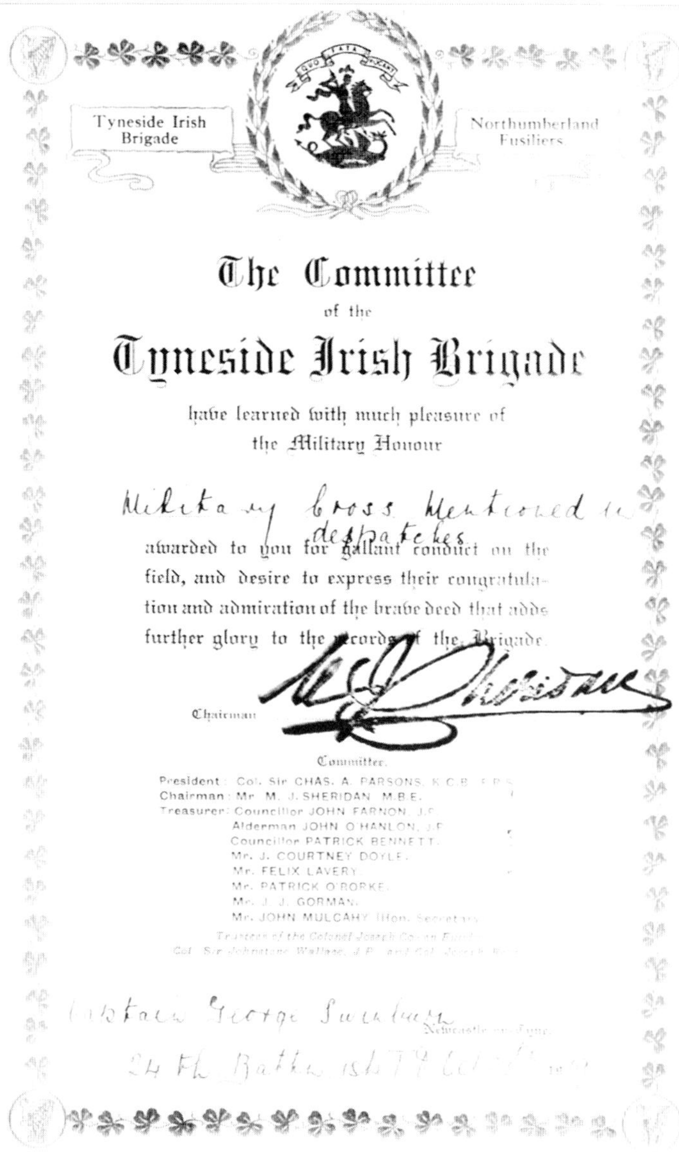
Tyneside Irish Brigade

Northumberland Fusiliers

The Committee

of the

Tyneside Irish Brigade

have learned with much pleasure of the Military Honour

Military Cross Mentioned in despatches

awarded to you for gallant conduct on the field, and desire to express their congratulation and admiration of the brave deed that adds further glory to the records of the Brigade.

Chairman

Committee.

President: Col. Sir CHAS. A. PARSONS, K.C.B., F.R.S.
Chairman: Mr. M. J. SHERIDAN, M.B.E.
Treasurer: Councillor JOHN FARNON, J.P.
Alderman JOHN O'HANLON, J.P.
Councillor PATRICK BENNETT.
Mr. J. COURTNEY DOYLE.
Mr. FELIX LAVERY.
Mr. PATRICK O'RORKE.
Mr. J. J. GORMAN.
Mr. JOHN MULCAHY (Hon. Secretary).

Captain George Swinburne

Newcastle-on-Tyne.

24 Fh Battn

Commemmorative certificate presented to Captain George Swinburne MC by the Tyneside Irish Committee.

The Victoria Cross

22040 Lance Corporal THOMAS BRYAN
25th Battalion

22040 Lance Corporal THOMAS BRYAN
25th Battalion
ARRAS 9 APRIL 1917

For conspicuous bravery during an attack. Although wounded this NCO went forward alone with a view to silencing a machine gun which was inflicting much damage. He worked up most skillfully along a communication trench, approached the gun from behind, disabled it and killed two of the team as they were abandoning the gun. As this machine gun had been a serious obsticale in the the advance to the second objective, the results obtained by Lance Corporal Bryan were very far reaching.

Lance Corporal Thomas Bryan was born in 1882, at Stourbridge in Worcestershire. By 1915 he was employed as a miner at Castleford, Yorkshire, where he lived with his wife and four children. He enlisted into a Reserve Battalion of the Northumberland Fusiliers in April 1915, and was drafted to a Service Battalion in France in December 1915. In April 1916 he fractured an ankle and was sent home, he was then drafted to the 25th (Service) Battalion (2nd Tyneside Irish) in December 1916. After being wounded in the right arm, during the action that brought him the award of the Victoria Cross, he was evacuated to hospital in Alnwick, where he made a good recovery.

On the 17th of June 1917, Lance Corporal Bryan was decorated with the Victoria Cross in front of 40,000 people at St James' Park in Newcastle.

The newspapers carried this report of the occasion:-

'As the first member of the Northumberland Fusiliers to win the Victoria Cross since the days of the Indian Mutiny, Lance Corporal Bryan was easily the most popular war hero and he recieved vociferous applause when he stepped before the King to have the cross pinned to his breast. The gallant non-commissioned officer stood erect facing his sovereign as the brave action which won him such fame was read out. This was the only instance in which the full Gazette announcement of the reasons for the bestowal of the most coveted military honour was read out in full, and their Majesties were all interested with the others on the dias. His Majesty, after pinning the medal on engaged in conversation with Bryan and wished him long life to wear the decoration, cordially shaking him by the hand. Bryan then left the royal presence, wreathed in smiles, to the accompaniment of thunderous appla-use.'

On the 23rd of June Lance Corporal Bryan arrived home in Castleford. Accompanied by his wife and children he was given a civic welcome at the station. Then led by three bands there was a procession through the town, where the streets were thronged with people. Signs were hung from houses, 'Long live Tom Bryan VC', 'Well played Bryan' and 'Good luck to all our boys' are just a few examples. The *Castleford Express* published a commemorative booklet in 1917 in which Mr Mat Evans wrote this poem about Thomas Bryan's exploits.

Lance Corporal T Bryan
The Pitman VC

The Great war has brought many changes
In almost every sphere of life;
We've had plenty of dogs in mangers,
And espionage has been very rife.

We shall not forget in the early stages,
When the Huns raped both mother and lass;
They placed floating mines in our waters,
and used the most poisonous gas.

They murdered women and children,
It filled every true heart with pain;
The shooting down of refugees
And sacking of Louvain.

Then came Kitchener's call to the country,
For more recruits to man the guns,
to defend old England's honour
From the tyranny of the Huns.

There were thousands and thousands responded
most nobly to Kitchener's call;
Some from the labourers cottage,
And some from the rich man's hall

There were lads came out of the workshops,
And some came out of the mine,
To fight the barbarious Prussians,
And chase them back over the Rhine.

This one, who proved such a hero,
This brave chap, Lance-Corporal Bryan,
Has proved by his gallant action
There is still pluck in the old British lion.

It was one day early in April-
How well we remember the time;
The battalion was held up by gun-fire,
When this collier lad, out of the mine,

Said to his officer, "May I sir,
Go out to capture that gun?"
But the officer said, sadly smiling
"Single-handed it cannot be done."

But our hero persists. 'Let me try sir,
For I have worked out a plan,
To capture that gun from the Germans
Without losing a single man.'

Off went Bryan in a moment,
His pals stood with bated breath;
He had gone alone on a journey
Which they thought meant certain death.

He went on his perilous journey
Determined to outwit the Hun;
He worked his way around them,
'Great Scot ! he has captured the gun'.

He had worked his way behind them,
And had shot down two of the team;
The others (brave chaps) they bolted
As if awakened from a terrible dream.

It is such gallant lads as these,
Whether it's Tommy or Jack on the foam,
That make all hearts beat with pride
Which he has left here at home.

And when the war is over,
How happy we all shall be;
We'll give the boys the same welcome home
that we gave to our brave VC.

For 'tis our lads, with great gallant deeds,
That have made Great Britain mighty;
We wish them luck and a safe return
Back home to dear old Blighty.

On the 14th of June, in the House of Commons, Mr McVeagh MP asked whether the War Office had any and, if so, what, objection to it being announced that Lance Corporal Bryan was serving in the Tyneside Irish. For the War Office Mr Macpherson replied: For Military reasons the particular battalion to which an officer or man belongs is never given, the regiment alone being stated.

Lance Corporal Thomas Bryan VC returned to the 25th Battalion in France and was wounded a further twice before the war ended. He died on the 13 October 1945 at Bradley, near Doncaster and was buried with full military honours. A burial party was provided by the Gordon Highlanders who fired three volleys over the grave, then the Last Post was sounded by a bugler of the Royal Artillery. In Castleford Civic Centre a memorial plaque gives details of his bravery and Bryan Close in Castleford is named after him.

40989 Private ERNEST SYKES
27th Battalion
ARRAS 9 APRIL 1917

For most conspicuous bravery and devotion to duty when his battalion in attack was held up about 350 yards in advance of our lines by intense fire from front and flank, and suffered heavy casualties.

Private Sykes, despite this heavy fire went forward and brought back four wounded – he made a fifth journey and remained out under conditions which appeared to be certain death, until he had bandaged all those who were too badly wounded to be moved. These gallant actions, performed under incessant machine gun and rifle fire, showed utter contempt of danger.

40989 Private ERNEST SYKES 27th Battalion

Private Ernest Sykes who was married with two children, was living in Bank Street, Mossley, near Ashton under Lyne and prior to enlisting was a platelayer on the London and North Western Railway. On the outbreak of war he enlisted into The West Riding Regiment (The Duke of Wellington's Regiment) and served at Gallipoli. He was badly wounded in the foot and evacuated, firstly to Egypt and then to England. Initially it was proposed to amputate the foot but Private Sykes would not give permission. He was then ordered to attend a Medical Board and he was passed fit for home service. Yet shortly after leaving hospital he was drafted to the 27th Northumberland Fusiliers in France with whom he won his VC.

After the war Private Sykes returned to his employment on the railways, being employed as a ticket collecter and then a guard, eventually he settled at Lockwood, near Huddersfield. In the Second World War he served in the 25th Battalion (West Riding) Home Guard. The London Midland Scottish Railway Company named a Patriot class locomotive, number 45537, Private E Sykes VC after him. At the age of 64, on the 3rd of August 1949, Private Ernest Sykes VC died at Lockwood, He was buried at Woodfield Cemetery, Lockwood, on the 6th of August. In 1967 the nameplate of the steam engine, Private E Sykes VC, was presented to the Northumberland Fusiliers museum.

The Distinguished Service Order

Lieutenant-Colonel **JOHN HENRY MORRIS ARDEN** 25th Northumberland Fusiliers (2nd Tyneside Irish)

With his former unit 1st Battalion Worcestershire Regiment At Neuve Chapelle March 12th 1915, when the battalion on his right were driven from their trenches, he joined his company under heavy fire, counter attacked the Germans with great determination, thereby enabling the battalion to reoccupy their trenches.

Captain **JAMES VICTOR BIBBY** 27th Northumberland Fusiliers (4th Tyneside Irish) 1st - 3rd July 1916

For conspicuous gallantry when, during operations, he held his own three days and two nights in an exposed position, organising and leading successful bomb attacks and being himself constantly attacked.

Captain J V Bibby DSO.

Major **J V BRIDGES** Worcestershire Regiment attached 25th Northumberland Fusiliers (2nd Tyneside Irish)

Captain and Adjutant **EDWARD CHARLES COBB** Northamptonshire Regiment attached 26th Northumberland Fusiliers (3rd Tyneside Irish) 1st July 1916

Though wounded and unable to move controlled his unit (twenty men) and established a small bombing post in the shellhole where he lay until night.

Major **ERIC C GUINNESS** Royal Irish Regiment attached 27th Northumberland Fusiliers (4th Tyneside Irish)

Major **E M MOULTON BARRATT** 25th Northumberland Fusiliers (2nd Tyneside Irish) D.S.O. Gazetted 23rd June 1915 while serving with previous unit.

Captain acting Major **T McLACHLAN** MC 25th Northumberland Fusiliers (2nd Tyneside Irish) LG 16/9/18

When his commanding officer became a casualty he brought the remnants of the battalion out of action after two and a half days continuous fighting. Through his untiring energy and good leadership, both in counter-attacking and organising successive lines of defence, very heavy losses were inflicted upon the enemy and their advance was materially checked.

Second Lieutenant acting Captain **HORACE HUNTER NEEVES** MC 27th Northumberland Fusiliers (4th Tyneside Irish) LG 18/7/17

For conspicous gallantry and devotion to duty in handling his company during an attack on the enemy position. His skillful leading and determined courage enabled him in spite of enemy flanking and reverse fire, to get his men within a few yards of the enemy's rear position. Owing to many casualties however, he was compelled to withdraw. On his return he gave his Battalion Commander a full and lucid report on the situation - the only accurate one received. It was subsequently found he had been wounded in the lungs early in the attack and had remained with his men under fire twenty three hours after being wounded.

Captain **RALPH BLOOMFIELD PRITCHARD** MC 27th Northumberland Fusiliers (4th Tyneside Irish) attached 14th Battalion LG 16/9/18

When the battalion was ordered to fill a gap in the front line, this officer in charge of the advanced guard, acted with such dash that it was mainly through his fine work that the battalion was able to do so. Later, he again advanced and occupied the old line, getting into touch with the flanks, and capturing three men of an enemy patrol. He held the line for the next four days under heavy fire, and finally was severely wounded when leading his company in a counter-attack as it gained its first objective.

Captain R B Pritchard DSO, MC, Killed in Action 26th April 1918.

Major temporary Lieutenant-Colonel **MORRIS ERNALD RICHARDSON** 26th Northumberland Fusiliers (3rd Tyneside Irish)

For conspicuous gallantry in action. When he had received three wounds in the attack he refused to go back till he had given orders to his successor. He remained two hours in a dangerous spot, and then he walked back to Brigade Headquarters and personally reported the situation.

Major **T REAY** 25th Northumberland Fusiliers (2nd Tyneside Irish)

Lieutenant-Colonel **GODFREY ROBERT VIVEASH STEWARD** 27th Northumberland Fusiliers (4th Tyneside Irish)

Lieutenant-Colonel **RICHARD DURAND TEMPLE** 27th Northumberland Fusiliers (4th Tyneside Irish)

Bar to the Distinguished Service Order

Lieutenant-Colonel **E M MOULTON BARRATT** DSO 25th Northumberland Fusiliers (2nd Tyneside Irish)

Throughout two days fighting his courage and resource were an example to all. On receipt of orders he cleverly withdrew his battalion from close contact with the enemy without a casualty. Some days after he was wounded while holding his headquarters in the support line against heavy hostile attacks, using a rifle himself.

Military Cross

Second Lieutenant **BARTOLD ADAMS** 25th BN LG 23/4/18 For conspicuous gallantry and devotion to duty in re-organising his company, having frequently to go over the top from shell hole to shell hole exposed to the enemy's snipers. He went out and bandaged several wounded who were lying in the open, and remained with his company although wounded.

Second Lieutenant **FRANK ARCHER** MM 25th BN LG 11/1/19 Attached 2nd BN The Lincolnshire Regiment When in in command of a platoon during an advance his company was held up by intense machine-gun fire. He worked his platoon round skillfully to a flank, in spite of heavy casualties, thus materially assisting the advance to be continued. He showed complete disregard of danger, and his example and conspicuous courage imbued his men with confidence which ensured success.

Second Lieutenant **ARTHUR ALEXANDER** MM 25th BN Attached 2/7th BN The King's Liverpool Regiment. For conspicuous gallantry and resource when leading his platoon through a village. So quickly did he follow up the barrage that he reached the enemy machine-guns before they were able to come into action. It was largely due to this officer that the operation was a complete success, his platoon taking 150 prisoners and fifteen machine-guns.

Lieutenant **BOOTH C H** 25th BN

Second Lieutenant **JOHN SIMPSON BOWMER** 25th BN LG 16/9/18 For conspicuous gallantry and devotion to duty. He took up a position in a railway embankment, and under very heavy shell and machine-gun fire held the enemy in check with the men and machine-guns at his disposal. He covered the withdrawl of the forward companies and checked the enemy advance, enabling the left companies to come up and the battalion to reorganise. Next day he took part in a counter attack and was largely responsible for the success of the operation.

Second Lieutenant **BRIAN CHALLONER BRADY** 24th BN

Lieutenant **GUSTAVE CAWSON** 25th BN LG 19/8/16 For conspicuous gallantry when leading his Company through a heavy barrage of artillery fire and through rifle and machine gun fire. He was seriously wounded.

Second Lieutenant **GEORGE COLEBY** 25th BN MM LG 16/9/18 For conspicuous gallantry and devotion to duty while commanding a company. He handled his men admirably, using them to the best advantage and inflicting heavy casualties on the enemy. He did splendid work.

Second Lieutenant **THOMAS DOMINIC CONWAY** 24th BN LG 18/3/18 For conspicuous gallantry and devotion to duty when in charge of an assaulting party after the officer in command was wounded. He held the position gained against practically continuous bombing attacks, although fifty per cent of the assaulting party became casualties.

Lieutenant **CECIL COWLEY** 25th BN LG 14/11/16 For able leading of a raiding party into the enemy's first line. He personally bombed a dug out, showing great coolness, and finally withdrew his party without casualties.

Lieutenant **W A RICHMOND DABELL** 24th BN attached 8th BN. For conspicuous gallantry and leadership whilst in command of a company. On 28th September 1918, after the successful capture of Oisy le Verger, he advanced his posts to within 200 yards of the Canal de la Sensee. On 1st October 1918 he led his company to the successful assault of the railway in M25, near Abancourt, where he consolidated and remained in position, though for some time unprotected, until the battalion was relieved.

Lieutenant **ROBERT DONALD** 24th BN LG 18/7/17 For conspicuous gallantry and devotion to duty. He displayed the greatest energy and initiative when commanding bombing parties of different units, and by means of grenades he and his party succeeded in inflicting severe casualties.

Captain **FREDERICK JOHN DOWNEY** 24th BN

Reverend Captain **ERNEST FRANCIS DUNCAN** CF BRIGADE C of E PADRE On the night, 12th October 1916, during a raid on enemy trenches, went over parapet and brought wounded officer in from No-Man's-Land. Also restored communication with raiding party. Slightly wounded.

Lieutenant and Quartermaster **A ERRINGTON** 26th BN

Second Lieutenant **HAROLD WHITELEY FIRTH** 27th BN LG 18/7/17 For conspicuous gallantry and devotion to duty. He led his company with utmost ability and determination for nine hours after he was wounded. His energy and gallantry were most marked in reducing an obstinate strong point.

Lieutenant **JOHN DALTON FORSYTH** 25th BN LG 15/10/18 For conspicuous gallantry and skilfull leardership in an attack when commanding the two assault platoons. He established three out of his four posts at their objective and then led his party forward under heavy machine gun fire and formed a protective flank. His previous reconnaissance and fine leadership secured the success of his command.

Second Lieutenant **GEORGE ROY FORTUNE** 26th BN

Major **CECIL JAMES FRANCIS** 25th BN with 18th BN.

Second Lieutenant **DOUGLAS RENTON GRANT** 24th BN For conspicuous gallantry and devotion to duty. He went forward with a fighting patrol to search a village and to establish listening posts. He then returned for reinforcements, with which he attempted to drive the enemy out of the village, where they had a good footing. Throughout the attack he displayed great courage and leadership until severely wounded.

Second Lieutenant **GEORGE OSWIN HENZELL** 27th BN LG 18/3/18 For conspicuous gallantry and devotion to duty in leading a night attack on the enemy's trenches. Having gained his objective, he was heavily counter attacked with bombs and rifle grenades. Though wounded in several places and losing several of his men, he held his position, refusing to leave the trench until reinforcements were brought up and he had given full instructions to the NCO in charge. His courage and determination contributed largely to the success of the operation.

Second Lieutenant **JAMES ARTHUR HOPPER** 26th BN For conspicuous gallantry and devotion to duty. Accompanied by an NCO, he penetrated the enemy's line and brought back most valuable information. He previously carried out most valuable patrol work.

Second Lieutenant **ARNOLD FRED JACKSON** 25th BN DCM + BAR LG 7/11/18 For remarkable skill and courage with a reconnaisance of two men, when he rushed a machine-gun post, capturing two guns and seven prisoners and killing two men. He then went back for two extra sections and proceeded to rush another machine-gun, capturing the gun and one prisoner and killing eight of the enemy.

Second Lieutenant **JAMES JENKINS** 26th BN LG 5/7/18 For conspicuous gallantry and devotion to duty. During a raid, owing to heavy machine-gun fire and rifle fire, the majority of the raiding troops found it impossible to enter the enemy trenches, but he, with two men, managed to effect an entry, and in spite of fire, proceeded to his objective in the support line. Having obtained important information regarding the enemy trench system, and when he had given orders for his men to withdraw, he proceeded to search for wounded in No Man's Land, finding two cases and causing them to be brought in. He showed great determination and coolness under heavy fire.

Second Lieutenant **ALFRED GEORGE JENNINGS** 27th BN LG 18/7/17 For conspicuous gallantry and devotion to duty. He led his platoon with great skill against an enemy machine-gun strong point. He succeeded in capturing the position, which was holding up the line, and would have caused heavy casualties.

Captain **JOHN GEORGE KIRKUP** 25th BN LG 18/7/17 For conspicuous gallantry and devotion to duty. He led his company with great dash and initiative, re-formed the men under the barrage and reached his final objective. Throughout he set a splendid example of courage and coolness.

Second Lieutenant **FREDERICK NORMAN STOKEN LAMPARD** 26th BN LG 22/9/16 For conspicuous gallantry. When a mine was sprung by us, he was in charge of the covering party during the consolidation of the crater. The enemy left their trenches and attacked the party with bomb and rifle, but 2Lt Lampard with an R.E. Officer, kept them at bay till reinforcements arrived. Though wounded in the head he stuck to his post till morning. This incident took place on the night of 4/5th of August 1916.

Second Lieutenant **GEORGE Van WYKE LAUGHTON** 26th BN LG 18/7/17 For conspicuous gallantry and devotion to duty. During twenty four hours he was sent on a picquet in front of our lines and conducted

George Laughton a Canadian had enlisted in the CEF prior to being commissioned into the 26th Battalion. He was awarded the MC for gallantry at Arras in 1917.

a daylight patrol to within three hundred yards of the enemy trenches. Throughout he displayed the greatest courage and determination.

Second Lieutenant **ROBERT VICTOR LEES** 24th BN LG 18/7/17 For conspicuous gallantry and devotion to duty. He displayed untiring energy and ability in organising the advance to the second objective. He did splendid work in capturing and consolidating the position. He was mainly responsible for the capturing of the machine-guns which were giving so much trouble.

Temporary Captain later Lieutenant Colonel **PHILIP LIONEL LINCOLN** 25th BN Although severely wounded, he led his company in the attack with great courage and determination.

Second Lieutenant **ARNOLD FRED LOCKWOOD** 25th BN

Second Lieutenant **CHARLES LOVATT** 26th BN attached 4th Bedfordshire Regt. For conspicuous gallantry and devotion to duty. When an enemy machine gun was enfilading his position, he crawled out alone in daylight to within ten yards of the gun, and having located it, returned to the position and directed rifle, grenade and Lewis gun on to the gun, causing casualties to the crew, who hastily withdrew. His promptitude and total disregard of danger undoubtedly saved a large number of casualties.

Major **NORMAN LUNN** 27th BN LG 10/1/17

Second Lieutenant **ROBERT ALDRIDGE MAQUIRE** 25th BN

Lieutenant **JOHN WOODALL MARSHALL** 27th BN LG 10/5/16 For conspicuous gallantry. He went to the assistance of an NCO wounded on patrol and carried him into safety under heavy fire.

Second Lieutenant **MICHAEL MELIA** 26th BN LG 18/3/18 For conspicuous gallantry and devotion to duty when in charge of a special wiring party during a minor operation. He succeeded in wiring 350 yards outside the newly won area under very heavy fire. He had to stop several times to open fire on the enemy in shell holes.

Captain **WILLIAM JOSEPH MORROGH** 27th BN LG 23/4/18 For conspicuous gallantry and devotion to duty as Adjutant of his battalion. He collected reports from wounded and other sources, and guided ration parties to their destination. His efforts throughout were a material factor in the success of the operations.

Lieutenant **MICHAEL JOHN MURRAY** 26th BN LG 18/7/17 For conspicuous gallantry and devotion

Second Lieutenant Michael Melia a Jarrow policeman before the war won his MC on a wiring party.

to duty. During the advance he led his company with great courage and determination. He displayed a total disregard for personal safety, and throughout set a magnificent example to all.

Lieutenant **WILLIAM PATRICK MURRAY** 26th BN

Captain **DANIEL McELDUFF** 25th BN LG 14/11/16 For conspicuous gallantry during operations. He was in charge of the covering force of a large working party close to the enemy's trenches. When the enemy opened heavy shell fire on the working party he kept his men out for twenty minutes with great determination, thus allowing the working party to retire in safety. He set a fine example and displayed great coolness.

Lieutenant **FREDERICK SMITH MOULT McKELLEN** 25th BN

Lieutenant **THOMAS McLACHLAN** 25th BN LG 10/1/17

Captain **M McREA** 25th BN

Second Lieutenant **HORACE HUNTER NEEVES** 27th BN LG 1/1/17 For conspicuous gallantry and devotion to duty. He was in command of one of the leading companies in the advance. Not only did he maintain his own company during a long and difficult advance, but also took command of another company involved in the front line attack. He set a splendid example.

Captain **HAROLD PRICE** 26th BN LG 24/6/16 For the good leadership of a minor enterprise on the night 5/6th of June 1916

Second Lieutenant **STANLEY DIXON PROFFITT** 27th BN LG 18/7/17 For conspicuous gallantry and devotion to duty. He displayed great ability and courage in re-forming his platoon at each successive point in the advance. During the hostile counter attack later his energy was invaluable, especially in patrol work when the counter attack had been driven off.

Second Lieutenant Stanley Proffitt originally served with the University and Public Schools Battalion of the Royal Fusiliers before being commissioned.

Second Lieutenant **LESLIE WILLIAM WHITWORTH QUINN** 27th BN He led a raiding party with great courage and skill, maintaining his position for one and a half hours. He set a splendid example to his men.

Second Lieutenant **THOMAS MICHAEL SCANLAN** 24th BN LG 14/11/16 For conspicuous gallantry in action. When his battalion was being relieved, and under heavy shell fire, he gathered a party of men, and beat back an enemy patrol with great courage and determination. He was wounded.

Captain **JOHN GUY SIMONS** 26th BN LG 18/7/17 For conspicuous gallantry and devotion to duty. He led his company with great energy and resource, displaying a total disregard of danger. Throughout he set a magnificent example of courage and coolness.

Second Lieutenant **JOSEPH SNEE** 25th BN LG 18/7/17 For conspicuous gallantry and devotion to duty. He led his company with great skill and courage. He re-organised under the barrage and got into his final objective, doing great execution with bombs. He displayed great gallantry throughout.

Lieutenant **M R STEEL** 1st BN attached 24th BN LG 23/4/18 For conspicous gallantry and devotion to duty. He led his company in an attack and captured the objective. Then, seeing that the enemy stronghold in front of the division on his right had not been taken, and was likely to hamper their advance, he attacked and captured it with part of his company, taking twenty five prisoners, two machine guns, and two granatenwerfer, and held it throughout the operations.

Captain **GEORGE SWINBURN** 24th BN attached ROD RE LG 6/4/18 For conspicous gallantry and devotion to duty. When the RNAS hangers were set on fire during air raids, he took out a party of his men and assisted to remove aeroplanes and spare parts when bombs were dropping around the aerodrome.

27/ 720 WO1 RSM **JOHN THOMAS THOMPSON** LG 1/1/18 no citation.

27/270 Regimental Sergeant Major John Thomas Thompson MC.

Lieutenant **THOMAS WILFRED THOMPSON** 24th BN On 1st of July 1916 went forward with twelve men after his company were out of action and held a piece of German trench, having bombed the enemy out, for two days.

Second Lieutenant **ERNEST JOHN VIPOND** 25th BN LG 16/9/18 For conspicuous gallantry and devotion to duty. For gallantry and initiative in selecting and holding defensive positions in the face of persistent enemy attacks. Leading a counter attack, he drove the enemy back in disorder, being wounded twice during these operations.

Captain **TREVOR LOTHERINGTON WILLIAMS** 24th BN LG 19/8/16 For conspicuous gallantry when leading the left of his battalion through a heavy barrage of artillery fire and through machine gun and rifle fire.

Lieutenant **JOHN LINDSAY YOUNG** 26th BN LG 16/9/18 For conspicuous gallantry and devotion to duty. During ten days operations this officer, after the battery had fired all its ammunition and the guns had been destroyed, fought with his men as infantry. Owing to severe casualties, he was in command of the battalion when it was attacked, and later took command of a company. He set a fine example throughout, steadying his men and helping them beat off repeated attacks.

Bar to the Military Cross

Second Lieutenant **F ARCHER** MC MM 27th BN attached 2nd BN The Lincolnshire Regiment LG 1/2/19 For conspicuous gallantry and devotion to duty on the 8th of October near Walincourt. When the two leading companies were held up by fire from the right flank he led forward two Lewis gun teams, together with a captured gun and drove the enemy down a road, at the end of which he captured two field guns and forty four prisoners. His deternmination and drive had an inspiring effect on all ranks.

Second Lieutenant **GEORGE COLEBY** MC MM 25th BN LG 16/9/18 For conspicuous gallantry and devotion to duty throughout a fortnights operations. During heavy enemy bombardments this officer; at great personal risk, walked up and down the line amongst the men, keeping up their spirits by his cheerfulness. On one occasion he showed great skill in handling his company, repulsing attacks under most difficult circumstances.

Captain **WILLIAM JOSEPH MORROGH** MC 27th BN During an enemy attack this officer on several occasions displayed the greatest skill and judgement in handling the situation. His company held up the advance of the enemy for several hours, and it was largely due to the admirable way in which he commanded his men and controlled the fire.

Second Lieutenant **HORACE HUNTER NEEVES** DSO MC 27th BN LG 18/7/17 He was in command of one of the leading companies in the advance. Not only did he maintain his own Company during a long and difficult advance but also took command of another Company involved in the front line attack. He set a splendid example throughout.

Lieutenant Acting Captain **THOMAS MICHAEL SCANLAN** MC 24th BN attached 1st BN LG 2/12/18 For conspicuous gallantry in command of a company which formed a defensive flank in close proximity to enemy machine-gun positions. He organised and led an attack on a machine-gun nest, resulting in the capture of three machine-guns, three officers and fifty six other ranks. His cheerfulness, courage and energy inspired all under him.

Lieutenant **M R STEEL** 1st BN attached 24th Bn LG 10/2/19 (serving with another battalion) For marked gallantry and able leadership of a company. On 27th September 1918, he led his company in the successful attack on Oisly Le Verger, and consolidated posts some distance in advance of the objective. Again on 1st October 1918, after three succesful assaults on the railway near Abencourt, where he established posts and sent back information to headquarters. This position was maintained for for four days.

Croix De Geurre (Belgian)
Second Lieutenant **ISACC SPAIN** (with 18th BN)

Croix De Geurre (French)
Lieutenant-Colonel **RICHARD DURAND TEMPLE** 27th BN.

Order of the British Empire
Major **WILLIAM HAMILTON DAVEY** 27th BN.

Mentioned in Despatches

Captain **FREDERICK ROWLAND ALLISON** 25th BN, Captain **HUMPHREY ROBERTSON BARKWORTH** 25th BN, Captain **JAMES VICTOR BIBBY** 27th BN, Lieutenant **PETER H L BROUGH** 27th BN, Captain **EDWARD CHARLES COBB** 26th BN, Captain **BURLEY COPLEY** 26th BN, Lieutenant **G R FORTUNE** 26th BN, Major **JOHN PAYNE GALLWEY** 24th BN, Major Temporary Lieutenant-Colonel **E W HERMON** 27th BN, Captain **F A HOBBS** 25th BN, Captain **ROBERT ALDRIDGE MAQUIRE** 25th BN, Lieutenant **V MESSITER** 25th BN, Captain **C H MONTAGUE** 24th BN, Captain **WILLIAM JOSEPH MORROGH** 27th BN, Major Acting Lieutenant-Colonel **E M MOULTON BARRETT** DSO, 25th BN, Sir Douglas Haig's Despatches 9 Apr 17, 7 Nov 17, 14 Dec 17. Captain **BRIAN DESMOND MULLALLY** 26th BN, Captain **WILLIAM PATRICK MURRAY** 26th BN, Lieutenant Acting Captain **MICHAEL JOHN MURRAY** 26th BN, Captain **JOHN JOSEPH McCORMACK** 27th BN, Captain **H H NEEVES** D.S.O. M.C. + BAR 27th BN, Captain **RALPH BLOOMFIELD PRITCHARD** 27th BN Major **JOSEPH MERRIMAN PRIOR** 24th BN Lieutenant-Colonel **MORRIS ERNOLD RICHARDSON** 26th BN, Major **T REAY** 25th BN, Lieutenant **R R ROBERTSON** 25th BN, Captain **GEORGE SWINBURN** 24th BN, Captain **HERBERT THOMAS WHITE** 26th BN, Captain **R W WRIGHT** 25th BN.

Distiguished Conduct Medal

41297 Private **F BARKER** 26th Bn (with 103rd LTMB) LG 16/8/17 For conspicous gallantry and devotion to duty in picking up a shell that was fusing, and throwing it over the parapet, when it immediately exploded: by his prompt and gallant action he saved the lives of many officers and men who were in the trench.

41297 Private Frank Barker DCM of Sheffield. served with B Company, 26th Battalion attached to 103 Light Trench Mortar Battery. Died of Wounds 22nd August 1917.

25/ 770 Sergeant **J BLYTHE** MM (with 103rd LTMB), LG 14/11/16 For conspicuous gallantry in action. When himself and his machine-gun had been buried, he freed himself and dug out his gun and continued to fire. He has on many occasions done very fine work.

24/ 904 Corporal **R BOYLE**, LG 18/7/17 For conspicous gallantry and devotion to duty. He handled his machine-gun with great courage and daring in taking up most advanced positions. Although most of his team were casualties he went forward and captured an enemy machine-gun.

26/ 828 CQMS **J COLEMAN**, LG 19/8/16 For conspicous gallantry and ability. When all the officers and the CSM had become casualties, he took command of his company and did fine work as long as the battalion was in action. Later he called for volunteers and went back for the wounded.

27/ 852 CSM **J CUNNINGHAM** (with 24/27th BN), LG 4/3/18 For conspicous gallantry and devotion to duty. He continually visited the men of his company under very heavy shell fire, cheering and encouraging them. Later, when enemy snipers were active, he organised a party of men, took up position in front of the line and carried out succesful sniping operations against the enemy, thus preventing many casualties among his men. His personal example and disregard of danger were an inspiration to all his men.

25/ 947 Lance Corporal **A DEVENISH**, LG 17/4/18 For conspicous gallantry and devotion to duty. When an enemy raiding party attempted to enter our lines he took up an advanced position in a sap on his own initiative, and by bombing the enemy materially assisted to break up the attack. He also did excellent work during an advance, and has always set a splendid example of courage and untiring energy.

18757 Lance Sergeant **R DINNINGTON** 24/27th Bn LG 6/2/18 For conspicous gallantry and devotion to duty in leading a bombing attack down a trench: He encountered a strong party of the enemy and personally bayonetted three of them, including an officer. His party captured a position, yielding thirty three prisoners and ten dead, and succeeded in holding it until relieved.

24/9 Private C Bishop DCM, MM of Gateshead, wounded March 1916. Although he is wearing the ribbons of the DCM and the MM the author has been unable to confirm these awards.

25/ 935 Lance Corporal **J DUFFY**, LG 22/9/16 For conspicous gallantry. When the enemy exploded a mine, wrecking part of the defences, and then rushed forward in large numbers to the attack, Lance Corporal Duffy, with a private, posted themselves behind the first defensible traverse and held up the enemy with bombs. After about twenty minutes he led a bombing attack, drove the enemy out and enabled us to occupy the crater.

24/ 764 Lance Corporal **A ENGLISH**, LG 22/9/16 For conspicous gallantry. When the enemy exploded a mine and tried to capture the crater, he fired 103 bombs at the attacking party at great personal risk. He also threw six full boxes of bombs at the enemy after detaching the pin from one of them and replacing it in the box. His gallant action gained the crater for us.

25/ 955 Sergeant Acting CSM **R E FOSTER**, LG 11/5/17 For conspicous gallantry and devotion to duty. He went forward and heard an enemy raiding party assembling, and gave warning, which enabled artillery fire to be brought to bear on the place of assembly. He has previously done fine work.

26/ 934 Corporal **W GILMORE** MM MiD (with 9th Bn), LG 17/4/18 For conspicous gallantry and devotion to duty. He did valuable work in keeping up communications during two engagements and was always ready and eager to carry out any difficult and dangerous task. He has shown the greatest energy and determination in his work.

25/ 227 Acting Corporal **W T GRANVILLE** (with 9th Bn), LG 2/12/19 For conspicous gallantry during the attack on Bermerain on the 24th of October 1918. When his section leader was killed he showed great pluck and initiative, taking command of his section, and seeing that his company was held up by machine-guns on the left, led his section with great dash, capturing the guns and thirteen prisoners. Shortly after, when troops on the left were being checked, he succesfully led his section to the final objective. He set a great example and inspired his men with confidence.

27/ 360 Sergeant **R HORSMAN** (with 8th Bn), LG 10/1/20 On 1st of October 1918, in the attack on the railway near Abancourt, this NCO and one man rushed two machine-guns and a party of twenty men who were holding the embankment, killing ten and capturing the remainder. He displayed marked courage and cheerfullness throughout the operations.

25/1070 Lance Corporal **M LENNARD** MM LG 17/4/18 For conspicous gallantry and devotion to duty. He set a splendid example of courage and determination during an attack and rendered valuable service by taking command and consolidating the captured ground when his officers and senior NCO's became casualties.

27/ 492 Staff Sergeant **R MADDEN** MM MiD (with 9th Bn), LG 3/10/18 For conspicous gallantry and devotion to duty when in charge of half the battery. The half battery was isolated and under heavy fire and S/Sgt Madden with great skill and courage, fought the half battery back and very considerablly assisted in delaying the enemy advance

25/1099 CSM **J MITCHELL** MiD, LG 3/9/18 For conspicous gallantry and devotion to duty. Throughout heavy bombardment and repeated enemy attacks, he rendered invaluable service in organising and leading isolated and mixed parties in the absence of officers. He was responsible for the sufficient supply of ammunition from the forward dump to the firing line. He set a fine example to the men.

24/ 251 Sergeant **S O'NIELL**, LG 13/2/17 For conspicous gallantry in action. He assisted another NCO in keeping a sap clear, thereby enabling the supply of bombs to the bomb post, to be sent by this sap. Later, he assisted in extricating several buried men.

24/1148 Sergeant **H T ROBSON**, LG 9/7/17 For conspicous gallantry and devotion to duty. He has consistently performed good work throughout, and has at all times set a fine example.

40948 Sergeant **E S SCOTT** 27th Bn LG 18/7/17 For conspicous gallantry and devotion to duty: He took command of his platoon and led them with utmost gallantry and initiative. His personal courage and coolness under heavy fire set a fine example to his men.

25/ 702 Corporal **W K WHEATLEY** (with 12th EAST YORKS), LG 21/10/18 For conspicous gallantry and devotion to duty. This NCO has been with the battalion for two and a half years, having previously served with another unit until wounded. He has shown courage and initiative in attacking and in minor enterprises, and both in and out of the line his example of endurance and industry has been a good effect on the men.

26/1297 Corporal **M WHELAN** MM LG 18/7/17 For conspicous gallantry and devotion to duty. During the advance he entered an enemy dug out and captured two officers and thirty seven other ranks. Throughout the operations he rendered most valuable services.

Sergeant, Acting Company Sergeant Major GT Wigley DCM.

27/1318 Sergeant Acting CSM **G T WIGLEY**, LG 18/7/17 For conspicous gallantry and devotion to duty. He showed great courage and ability when acting as CSM. During the advance, he took command of the company and carrying them forward, reorganised them in the new position entirely on his own initiative. He set a fine example throughout.

26/ 725 CQMS **W WILD**, LG 19/8/16 For conspicous gallantry. He took command of three platoons and commanded them ably throughout the action. He went to his adjutant who was lying wounded, took over papers and information from him, and acting for him, kept in touch with the advanced line. Later he carried his adjutant and his own brother, who was wounded to safety under heavy fire.

41393 Sergeant **A WILLIAMS** 26th Bn LG 21/10/18 For conspicous gallantry and devotion to duty as acting CSM while relieving another unit under heavy shell fire, the guide got lost and the company became scattered. He collected what men he could find and got them to their positions; He was of great assistance in organising the line and during relief his constant cheerfulness and courage were a fine example to all ranks.

Bar to Distinguished Conduct Medal

25/ 955 CSM **R E FOSTER**, LG 18/7/17 For conspicous gallantry and devotion to duty. He rallied and reorganised his company under heavy fire, and taking command succeeded in capturing an enemy machine-gun.

Military Medal

Lance Corporal F Parkin, Military Medal.

25/ 6 CSGT **W APPELBY**, 34669 PTE **T APPLEYARD** 24/27th Bn, 41245 PTE **J W ATKINSON** 26th Bn, 46064 CPL **F BAILEY** 25th Bn, 41557 PTE **BARRACLOUGH** 24th Bn, 27/ 50 SGT **G BARROW**, 27/ 85 LCPL **G E BEATTIE** 37938 PTE **E BELL**, 24/ 511 PTE **I BELL**, 27/ 60 PTE **E BEWICK**, 40985 LCPL **J BIRKS** 24/27th Bn, 25/ 770 **SGT J BLYTHE** D.C.M., 26/ 775 PTE **J BOLAM**, 27/ 824 LCPL **G BOND**, 27/ 827 LCPL **M BOND**, 18/ 663 CQMS **V BOWERBANK** 27th Bn, 38909 LCPL **G E BRITTON** 25th Bn, 26/ 73 PTE **W BULLOCK**, 37544 PTE **W BUNTING** 26th Bn, 25/ 873 PTE **J CABLE**, 24/1015 PTE **O CAIRNS**, 9322 ACPL **T CAIRNS** 26th Bn, 27/ 144 PTE **F CASTLING**, 26/ 850 PTE **J CLARK**, 27/ 110

27/902 Private William Richardson served on Malta with the 1st Garrison Battalion Northumberland Fusiliers. Posted to France he joined the 27th Battalion and was awarded the Military Medal in October 1917 when serving with the 24/27th Battalion as a stretcher bearer.

Sergeant A W Peters, Military Medal.

Private J Devanney MM. On 1st July 1916 he carried ammunition forward for his Lewis gun, quite alone through heavy fire over No Man's Land.

LCPL **J S CLARK**, 24/ 987 CSM **G COLEBY**, 6590 PTE **H COLLINS**, 26/ 112 LCPL **P COLLINS**, 26/1386 SGT **J E CONNOLLY**, 24/ 295 PTE **P CONNOR**, 27/ 151 PTE **R CRAIGIE** with 2nd Bn, 26/ 189 PTE **J DAYKIN** with 1/4th Bn, 25/ 903 PTE **J DEVANNEY**, 25/ 192 SGT **G DICKENSON**, 30/ 131 CPL **W DOCK** with 25th Bn, 24/ 35 SGT **J A DUPREY**, 24719 PTE **T EDGAR** 26th Bn, 25/1420 CPL **T H ENGLISH**, 42502 CPL **E D FENWICK** 25th Bn, 24/ 264 SGT **T FINNERAN**, 26/ 905 PTE **H FISHER**, 24/1391 CPL **D FOSTER** with 27th Bn, 41610 SGT **A FYMAN** 24th Bn, 26/ 919 PTE **J GEARY**, 24/ 330 PTE **J W GETTINGS**, 26/ 539 SGT **W H GILBERT**, 26/ 934 SGT **W GILMORE** D.C.M., 235131 PTE **J C GLASS** 25th Bn, 26/ 928 PTE **F J GRAHAM**, 41647 PTE **E GRAY** 24th Bn, 24/ 761 LCPL **J GRAY**, 36066 PTE **E E GREEN** 25th Bn, 25/ 987 PTE **F GROGHAN**, 30/ 137 PTE **A GUTHRIE** with 25th Bn, 26/ 963 SGT **S HALEY**, 26/1467 PTE **M HARDCASTLE**, 24/1398 PTE **W HATTLE**, 25/ 290 CPL **J HILTON**, 702 PTE **J HILL** with 26th Bn, 27/1555 PTE **G HODGSON**, 41012 PTE **A HUGHES** 27th Bn, 26/ 989 LCPL **B HUGHES**, 26/ 959 PTE **O HUGHES**, 24/ 287 SGT **H HUNTER**, 25/ 302 PTE **J JEFFRIES**, 30/ 60 PTE **A W JOHNSTONE** with 24th Bn, 27/1547 PTE **J T KENNEDY**, 24/ 278 PTE **M KIERNAN**, 27/ 396 SGT **J C KIRKUP**, 25/1077 PTE **G LAWSON**, 26/ 389 LCPL **J LEE**, 25/1070 PTE **M LEONARD**, 24/ 630 LSGT **J LEIGHTON**, 41329 PTE **W H LEIGHTON** 26th Bn, 35562 PTE **E J LOURIE** 25th Bn, 25/1056 PTE **R LIDDELL**, 41450 PTE **H LOCKWOOD** 26th Bn, 38957 PTE **H LOUGHRAN** 25th Bn, 27/1064 SGT **J LUGTON**, 25/1365 SGT **R W LUKE**, 27/ 492 SGT **R MADDEN**, 38371 PTE **J MAYBERRY** 24th Bn, 41333 CPL **G B MOODY** 26th Bn, 27/1421 PTE **F MORGAN**, 25/1124 CPL **M MORPETH**, 25/ 435 SGT **W MORRALEE**, 25/1127 PTE **D**

Private J Daykin, Military Medal.

MORRIS, 47066 CPL R J MUNDY 25th Bn, 26/ 487 LSGT J McCAFFERY, 30/ 190 CPL B McDERRMOTT with 6th KOYLI, 26/474 LCPL T McKENNA, 25/1181 PTE P McPARTLIN, 24/1577 PTE A NIGHTINGALE, 45985 PTE A H OVEREND 24/27th Bn, 27/ 587 PTE J PARKER, 27/ 582 LCPL F PARKIN with 1/4th Bn, 25/ 535 A/SGT T PARKIN with 1st Bn, 38876 PTE G H PAYLOR, 27/1175 PTE C PEASE, 47033 PTE A J PERRY 25th Bn, 30/ 253 LSGT A W PETERS with 1/4th Bn, 50307 PTE H PRESTON 25th Bn, 38916 PTE H QUARTON 25th Bn, 26/ 601 LCPL J H RACE, 26/1183 SGT E REARDON with 103LTMB, 27/902 PTE W RICHARDSON, 24/27 BA, 25/1415 PTE G ROBSON, 25/1233 LCPL J ROBSON, 28433 PTE H ROEBUCK 25th Bn, 47048 SGT W P ROGERS 25th Bn, 26/ 625 PTE J H SCOTT, 25/ 625 PTE T R SCOTT, 26/ 650 PTE W H SCOTT, 27/ 667 PTE J SIMPSON with 19th Bn, 27/1232 PTE T STEPHENSON, 27/ 696 PTE T D STONEHOUSE, 41348 PTE F SUMMERFIELD 26th Bn, 26/ 645 SGT C H SYKES, 24/1709 PTE E TAYLOR with 12/13th Bn, 38876 PTE G H TAYLOR 25th Bn, 47641 PTE S TAYLOR 26th Bn, 25/1307 LSGT J TAQUE, 34635 PTE J TELFORD 26th Bn, 24/ 868 PTE W TIMLIN with 19th Bn, 26/ 675 SGT A TROTTER, 25/ 700 PTE A WALSH, 38807 PTE H WATERHOUSE, 24/ 177 CPL M WELSH, 25/ 702 SGT W K WHEATLEY D.C.M. with 6th EAST YORKS, 26/1297 CPL M WHELAN, 26/1445 PTE J W WHITE with 9th Bn, 40904 PTE W WHITEHEAD 27th Bn, 26/1310 CQMS G WILD, 27/1285 LCPL G WILSON, 46998 PTE F WREN 25th Bn.

Bar to the Military Medal

27/ 50 SGT G BARROW, 27/ 827 CSM M BOND with 19th Bn, 36066 PTE E E GREEN 25th Bn, 26/1183 SGT E REARDON with 103rd LTMB.

Croix de Guerre
24/1580 SGT C KEEGAN with 19th Bn, 30/ 9 PTE J FOX.

Medal Millitaire
37563 PTE C FERGUSON 26th Bn.

Russian Crs of St George 3rd class
27/ 827 LCPL M BOND M.M.+BAR

Meritorious Service Medal
27/ 37 LCPL W BLACKBURN, 25/ 242 SGT P GAINES, 25/1418 PTE T MILLER 16/961 RSM J HARNBY with 25th Bn.

Mention in Despatches
24/ 257 CSM N BATTY, 30200 PTE F W BEAUMONT 26th Bn, 24/ 891 SGT J B BIRKETT, 24/ 550 SGT W BURKE, 41436 ACSM COOPER 26th Bn, 26/ 934 SGT W GILMORE, 26/ 323 CSM G HALL, 24/ 287 SGT G H HUNTER 27/ 396, SGT J C KIRKUP, 26/ 400 CSM W LITTLEWOOD, 27/ 492 SGT R MADDEN, 24/ 399 PTE J T MAY, 25/1099 CSM J MITCHELL, 24932 ASGT W J MOSS 26th Bn, 25/1152 CQMS S McKENNA, 27/1367 RSM J F McNIECE, 41566 LSGT J F SAGAR 24th Bn, 27/ 717 CSM J TIGHE.

34th Div Cards of Honour
27/ 824 LCPL G BOND, 24/ 348 SGT P BUTLER, 26/ 833 LCPL J W CAREY, 235305 PTE F CESS-

FORD 26th Bn, TWO AWARDS, 26/ 137 PTE **G CUNNINGHAM**, 34186 CPL **W S DICKSON**, 25/ 917 PTE M **DEIGHAN**, 24/ 35 LSGT **J DUPREY**, 24719 PTE T **EDGAR**, 24/ 264 LSGT **T FINNERAN**, 10515 CPL **J G FULCHER** 26th Bn, 24/ 656 PTE **H GILROY**, 26/ 928 LCPL **F J GRAHAM**, 24/ 442 CPL **J T GRAHAM**, 24/ 761 LCPL **J GRAY**, 24/1070 PTE **J HUGHES**, 25/1365 SGT **R W LUKE**, 26/1064 PTE **M MANLEY**, 41333 CPL **G B MOODY** 26th Bn, 24/1577 LCPL **A NIGHTINGALE** 24/ 204, LCPL **J NOLAN** 26/ 625 LCPL **J H SCOTT**, 26/ 619 PTE **J SMITH**, 41294 PTE **W C TOZER**, 26th Bn 26/1304 PTE **J WILLIAMS**.

Nominal Rolls

Sources used in compiling Battalion Nominal Rolls

When the work of compiling the battalion nominal rolls was started it was as a hobby, to try and locate as many of the soldiers of the Tyneside Irish Brigade as possible. When this work became a book, more and more sources of information were located and used. Battalion nominal rolls in *Irish Heroes in the War* by Joseph Keating, London 1917; *War Grave Registers*, North West Europe, Italy, British Isles, Malta. Published by the Commonwealth War Graves Commission. *Memorials to the Missing* registers for Thiepval, Arras, Tyne Cot, Pozieres, Vis-en-Artois, Nieuport, Soissons, Ploegsteert, Giovera (Italy). Published by the Commonwealth War Graves Commission. *Soldiers Died in the Great War*, HMSO re-published 1989.

Every volume was consulted, in order to identify men who had been killed or died when serving with other regiments. Absentee Voters Lists for Barnard Castle, Bishop Aukland, Blaydon, Chester le Street, Durham City, Houghton Le Spring, Jarrow, Seaham, Sedgefield, Spennymoor, held at Durham County Record Office. Gateshead, Hartlepool, Darlington, Middlesbrough, Newcastle, held in the various city and town libraries. Hexamshire, Berwickshire, Wansbeck, held at Northumberland County Record Office.

Local Newspapers, recruiting articles and casualty lists, *Alnwick and Northumberland Gazette*; *County Chronicle*, *Durham Advertizer*; *Durham Chronicle*; *Darlington Evening Despatch*; *Middlesbrough Evening Gazette*; *Newcastle Illustrated Chronicle*; *Newcastle Daily Chronicle*; *Newcastle Evening Chronicle*; *Newcastle Journal*; *Northern Echo*; *North East Railway Magazine*; *North Mail*, *Northern Daily Mail*; *Sunderland Echo*; *South Shields Gazette*; *St George's Gazette*; the *Regimental Journal of the Northumberland Fusiliers*. Volumes for 1914, 15, 16, 17, 18, 19, 1920.

Medical Health Records MH/106 PRO Kew. Admission registers for the 3rd and 34th Casualty Clearing Stations and the 2nd and 18th General Hospitals.

WO/329 PRO Kew First World War:

1914/18 War & Victory Medal Rolls, 1914/15 Star Rolls, Silver War Badge lists. Volumes for many regiments other than the Northumberland Fusiliers were consulted, this enabled large drafts of men to other regiments to be identified.

Petty Sessions Registers, for courts in Durham, Newcastle, Sunderland, Gateshead, South Shields, Houghton Le Spring, Blyth, Morpeth, this identified many absentees and deserters who are not mentioned in other sources. Held at County Record Offices in Durham, Tyne and Wear and Northumberland.

Rolls of Honour: various battalions, colliery, engineering works, town/village Rolls of Honour.

War Diaries, 34th Division, 103rd Brigade, 24th, 25th, 26th and 27th Battalions. WO/95 PRO Kew.

Police Gazette 1915 lists of deserters. British Library Colindale. Red Cross lists of missing for October 1916 and October 1918. Courts Martial Registers January - September 1916 France WO 213/7 -12 PRO Kew.

Officers Died in the Great War. The *Army List* and *Army List Supplements.* The *London Gazette. St Georges Gazette* extracts from the *London Gazette.*

It is very much regretted that these nominal rolls only contain

information on the original enlistments to the Brigade. After extracting information on over 8,000 reinforcements it was realised that it would be both impossible and impracticable to try and produce an accurate list of all reinforcements to the Tyneside Irish Brigade. I hope therefore that the reader will excuse the inclusion of those reinforcements who won gallantry awards and the few of whom I have been lucky enough to obtain a photograph. To be fair I would have preferred to include every man who served.

Notes on the Nominal Rolls

The first columns are self explanatory, **Name, Initials, Rank, Number, Company, Address** and **Town or Village**.

Enlisted, this date comes from the *Silver War Badge List*, or it is the date that the soldier's name appeared in one of the local newspapers as having enlisted.

Discharged, this date is taken from the *Silver War Badge List*, the Medal Rolls, or in some cases the soldier's discharge certificate.

Cause of Discharge, in this column the date of death or the cause of discharge is given. Once again this information was extracted from the above sources.

Wounded, generally a month is given, this is the month the casualty was recorded in the *Saint George's Gazette*. Casualties recorded between July and November 1916 are nearly all from the 1st of July 1916.

Buried, the cemetery or churchyard of burial, this column also records those commemorated on memorials to the missing.

Transfer, other units that the soldier served with. Mainly extracted from the medal rolls, but some information included from *Absentee Voters Lists* and *Soldiers Died in the Great War*. Where the battalion of a new regiment is known this is recorded behind the regiment thus: Kings Own Yorkshire LI(9th BN). This was done for indexing purposes on the computer. eg 1st, 12th, 16th BNS, this shows that the soldier was transferred to and served with the 1st then the 12th and finally the 16th Battalions of the Northumberland Fusiliers.

Additional information, this column records any extra information noted, especially from Medical Health Records and Petty Sessions Registers.

To include as much information as possible it was found necessary to abbreviate many unit titles, and words thus: 34CCS = the 34th Casualty Clearing Station. 2GENHOSP or 18GHOSP = the 2nd or 18th General Hospitals. 21AMBT = 21st Ambulance Train. WND = Wounded R or L = Right or Left e.g WND R ARM+L BUTTOCK. AWOL = ABSENT WITHOUT LEAVE. ST BEARER = Stretcher Bearer. EVAC = Evacuated. BN = Battalion. CONV DEPOT = Convalescent Depot. LAB COY = Labour Company e.g. 101 LAB COY. No = NUMBER, Where a new regimental number has been allotted e.g. LAB CORPS No 123456. SHIP OR HSHIP = casualty has been transferred to a Hospital

Appendix II

ALPHABETICAL NOMINAL ROLL OF OFFICERS THAT SERVED WITH THE TYNESIDE IRISH BRIGADE

NUMBER ON ROLL **573**

KILLED OR DIED OF WOUNDS **137**

KNOWN WOUNDED, GASSED SICK ETC **158**

TOTAL KNOWN CASUALTIES **295** OR **51.4%**

SURNAME	FIRST_NAMS	BA	RANK	COMMISION	WOUNDED	DIED	BUR_MEM	AWARDS	ADD_INFO	REMARKS
ABBEY	F A	27	2 Lt	4/12/15					FROM 3rd BN	
ADAMS	BARTOLD	25	2 Lt	1/3/17				M.C.	JOINED FOR DUTY 10/5/17. WAR DIARY 13/11/17.	Lt 1/9/18, RELINQUISHED COMMISSION 23/3/19 DUE TO WOUNDS.
ADAMSON	JOHN CONWAY	27	2 Lt	1/7/15		4/10/17	TYNE COT MEM		FROM NF SPECIAL RESERVE KIA ATT 1st LINCS REGT	
AIREY	F	25	2 Lt	28/3/17					JOINED FOR DUTY 10/6/17, TO TRG RES BN 1918	Lt 28/9/18
AITCHISON	G	27	2 Lt	16/7/15					FROM NF SPECIAL RESERVE	
ALLAN	F L	25	CAPT	17/3/16					CAPT 9/6/18	
ALLISON	FREDERICK ROWLAND	25	2 Lt	3/2/15				MiD	FROM GENERAL LIST Lt 1/6/15, TO 30th BN 3/9/15.	CAPT 6/12/16, TRF TO REGULAR BN.
ALLISON	HERBERT	30	2 Lt	8/11/15					BORN JARROW 1886. TO 24th BN 3/8/16, TO 8th BN 1918.	
ANDERSON	C S	27	2 Lt	30/5/17						
ARCHER	F	27	2 Lt	28/11/17				M.C.+ BAR	TO 25th BN, THEN ATT 2nd BN LINCOLNSHIRE REGT.	ACTING CAPT COMMANDING POW CAMP 1/8/19.
ARDEN	JOHN HENRY MORRIS	25	LT COL	17/4/16(LT	1/7/16	22/7/18	ALEXANDRIA	DSO MiD	ASSUMED COMMAND 16/4/16. KiA ATTACHED TO R.A.F.	
ARMSTRONG	NEWMAN BYCROFT	30	2 Lt	6/11/15					BORN KEYWORTH NOTTS 1886, Lt 1/7/17.	TO GEN LIST 10/16, TO SERVICE BN 5/8/19.
ARNOLD	D	24	2 Lt	28/3/17						
ARNOLD	JACK CORRY	24	CAPT	18/11/14	6/6/17				TO 30th 6/11/15,TO 26th BN, REJOINED FROM HOSP 18/9/16	
ARTHUR	ALEXANDER	25	2 Lt	1/8/17		1/10/18	BUCQOUY RD CEM	M.C. M.M.	PTE No 1730, KiA att KINGS LIVERPOOL REGT.	130 HOTSPUR STREET HEATON NEWCASTLE.
AYLING	ARTHUR HENRY	25	2 Lt	25/1/17		28/4/17	ARRAS MEMORIAL		AGE 21 FROM SOUTHWICK SUSSEX.	
BABBITT	M	27	2 Lt	30/5/17					Lt 30/11/18.	
BACCUS	F	24	2 Lt	27/6/17					TO 23rd BN 1918, RELQ COMM 1/6/19 DUE TO ILL HEALTH.	
BAINBRIDGE	JACK	25	CAPT	4/1/15	OCT 16				BORN GATESHEAD 1893,O.C.No 1 COY 25/26 BN 9/7/16. C.O.1/8/16	Lt 1/6/15, CAPT 2/9/15, TO 27th BN DLI 15/12/18 STAFF CAPT.
BAKER	DOUGLAS JAMES	24	2 Lt	7/4/17		28/4/17	BROWNS COPSE		AGE 27, BORN SELBY YORKS, FORMERLY CPL ROYAL FUSILIERS.	
BANKS	S S	27	2 Lt	26/4/17					TO 25th BN 1918, Lt 26/10/18.	
BANKS	W M	25	2 Lt	27/6/17					Lt 27/12/18.	
BARBER	WILLIAM MacKENZIE	34	2 Lt	5/8/16					FROM 34th BN GAZ 20/10/16.	
BARCLAY	HUBERT FREDERICK	30	LT COL	4/3/1888					BORN BIRMINGHAM 1865.SERVED S AFRICA, C.O. 6 BEDFS BEF 1915.	RELINQUISHED COMMISSION 1/9/16.
BARKWORTH	HUMPHREY ROBERTSON	25	CAPT& ADJT	16/11/15	1/7/16	3/7/16	WARLOY BAILLON	MiD	BORN LONDON 1891, SERVED IN FRANCE WITH 2nd NF.	ADJUTANT 16/11/15.
BARNETT	DAVID	26	2 Lt	1/2/15					Lt 1/6/15, CAPT 1/6/15 TO 30th BN 3/9/15.	
BATY	J A	25	2 Lt	19/2/16	5/4/17				TO 1st BN NF 1917, Lt 19/6/18.	
BAYNES	V	24	Lt	21/6/16	1/7/16				CPL LONDON REGT COMMISSIONED 21st BN, TO 84 TR BN 1/9/16.	TO REG BN 10/1/17, TO 27th BN AS Lt 21/12/17, TO 24th BN.
BEASLEY	CECIL CRANBOURNE	24	Lt	1/3/17					Lt 1/9/18, A/CAPT 30/10/17.	
BEATTIE BROWN	WILLIAM	25	CAPT	1/1/16(CAP	GAZ JUNE 17	9/4/17	ARRAS MEMORIAL		2Lt 27/1/15(17th BN) TO 28th BN 3/9/15, C.O. 25th 4/11/16,	SERVED QUEENS EDINBURGH VOLUNTEERS.
BEAVON	JOHN LEONARD	26	2 Lt			1/7/16	THIEPVAL MEM		FROM REGULAR BN.	
BEEMING	A	25	2 Lt	26/4/17						
BELL	G B	25	2 Lt	28/3/17						
BENNETT	B D	24	2 Lt	10/9/16					TO REGULAR BN NOVEMBER 1917.	
BENTLEY	HARRY	25	2 Lt	26/4/17		10/10/18	HOLYBROOK		EMPLOYED MINISTRY OF MUNITIONS, DROWNED.	
BERESFORD	J	26	2 Lt	21/10/15					JOINED 14/5/17,ATT 209 COY RE 30/12/17.TRF MGC 16/1/18	FROM SPECIAL RESERVE BN, COMMISSIONED 12th BN.
BERESFORD	KENNEON	25	Lt Col	20/7/15					28 YEARS IN R IRISH RIFLES, BORN LIMERICK 1862,UK LEAVE 4/16	MAJOR 2i/c 13/1/15, RELINQUISHED LT COL 17/4/16.
BESTFORD	G	25	2 Lt	31/10/17					Lt 1/5/19.	
BIBBY	JAMES VICTOR	27	CAPT	2/7/15				DSO MiD	BORN NEWCASTLE 1887 ENLISTED 6th NF 1908, SGT 1912 CSGT 1914	CAPT 20/8/15, 2i/c 16/8/16, TO REGULAR BN 14/10/17.
BIRKETT	ALAN	25	Lt	6/1/16					FROM 31st BN.	
BLACK	A J	25	2 Lt	28/3/17					JOINED FOR DUTY 18/5/17, Lt 28/9/18.	
BLAIR	B D V	25	2 Lt	28/3/17					JOINED FOR DUTY 9/6/17, RELINQUISHED COMMISSION 31/7/18	DUE TO ILL HEALTH.
BLAKE	A	25	2 Lt	28/11/17					Lt 28/5/19.	
BLIGHT	ERNEST JAMES	27	2 Lt	10/7/15		11/3/17	F.D.A. ARRAS		BORN GUERNSEY 1885, VOLUNTEERED 11/8/14, 6th R IRISH REGT.	
BLOTT	THOMAS WATKIN	24	2 Lt	2/6/16		9/4/17	ROCLINCOURT		FROM INNS OF COURT OTC TO 32nd BN, TO 24th BN 24/8/16.	AGE 34 FROM LONDON.
BODDY	J A	24	2 Lt	19/12/16					EX CADET	
BOGGON	N G	24	2 Lt	1/4/17					EMPLOYED MINISTRY OF MUNITIONS UNTIL NOVEMBER 1917 POSTED	TO REGULAR BN, TRF TO R.A.F. 29/6/18.
BOOTH	C H	25	Lt	16/9/15				M.C.	R.A.M.C. ATTACHED.	
BOTTING	W	26	2 Lt	30/5/17					JOINED FOR DUTY 13/1/18, TO 8th BN 1918.	
BOULTER	W E	26	2 Lt	26/4/17	17/10/17, TO UK 19/10/17				JOINED FOR DUTY 27/6/17, EMPLOYED MINISTRY OF LABOUR 1918.	SERVICE COMPLETED 15/8/19.
BOURNE	WARREN JAMES	25	Lt	13/1/15	1/7/16				TO 30th BN 10/1/16, TO 21st BN 22/6/16.	
BOWDEN	W R	26	2 Lt	28/3/17	6/6/17				FROM 3rd BN, JOINED 26th FOR DUTY 14/5/17.	
BOWMAN	H B	30	2 Lt	7/1/16						
BOWMER	JOHN SIMPSON	25	2 Lt	31/10/17				M.C.	LCPL 16/359 6 PLATOON B COMPANY, EMBARKED 23/11/15.	AT THIEPVAL 1/7/16, 25th WAR DIARY 20/5/18
BRADY	BRIAN CHALLONER	24	Lt	13/11/14				M.C.	IN RANKS 3rd NF, NORTHERN CYCLISTS 2 YEARS.	CARRIED IN WOUNDED 25/6/16, CAPT 2/7/16, ADJ 15/10/18.
BREWIN	B R	24	MAJOR	14/8/14					Lt FROM 6th WEST RIDING REGT,	A/LT COL 25/4/17 TO 27th BN 26/5/17.

SURNAME	FIRST_NAMS	BA RANK	COMMISION	WOUNDED	DIED	BUR_MEM	AWARDS	ADD_INFO	REMARKS
BREWIS	C	26 2 Lt	28/3/17	HOSP 27/8/17				JOINED FOR DUTY 13/7/17, TO UK 7/9/17	RELINQUISHED COMMISSION DUE TO ILL HEALTH 8/6/18.
BRIDGES	JOHN VICTOR	26 CAPT	11/12/07				D.S.O.	FROM WORCESTERSHIRE REGT, CAPT 7/8/16, C.O. 7/7/16.	
BROCKBANK	HERBERT	27 2 Lt	5/9/16		28/4/17	ARRAS MEMORIAL		TO 27th BN 6/12/16, AGE 31.	
BROCKLEHURST	F L	26 2 Lt	26/4/17					FROM 3rd BN, JOINED FOR DUTY 27/6/17, POSTED 9th NF 3/2/18	
BROUGH	PETER HILLARY LLOYD	27 2 Lt	16/6/15				MiD	BORN CHELSEA 1895, TO 30th BN 22/10/15.	TO 24th BN 3/8/16, Lt 1/7/17.
BROWN	EDWARD STANISLAUS	26 2 Lt	11/3/15	JUNE 17				BORN NEWCASTLE 1892,ENLISTED 16th NF 1914,MORTAR CSE 12/2/16	
BROWN	J	25 2 Lt	26/4/17						
BROWN	J A	24 2 Lt	28/3/17					Lt 28/9/18 TO REGULAR BN.	
BROWN	LESLIE EWART	26 2 Lt	24/4/16					FROM INNS OF COURT OTC, TO 32nd BN24/4/16.	TO 26th BN 8/7/16, STRUCK OFF STRENGTH 28/7/17.
BROWN	WILLIAM AELRED	24 2 Lt	18/11/14	1/7/16				EDUCATED USHAW COLLEGE, AGE 25. Lt 1/9/15	
BROWNE	LANGFORD KYFFIN	27 2 Lt	26/5/16		9/4/17	ROCLINCOURT VAL		CHARTERED ACCOUNTANT, S AMERICA, RETURNED TO UK SEPT 1915	ENL ARTIST RIFLES OTC, TO 32nd, 25th BNS, AGE 25 BORN JERSEY
BUCKMAN	FREDERICK WILLIAM STANLEY	27 CAPT & ADJ	3/7/15					BORN BRIGHTON 1871, ENLISTED 1892, 21 YEARS COLDSTREAM GDS.	
BULL	H	25 2 Lt	31/10/17						
BURBRIDGE	D G	24 2 Lt	16/9/17	TO UK SICK 29/8/18				FROM LONDON REGT(TF) TO REGULAR BN.	TO 24th, 24/27th BNS, POSTED TO 19th BN 6/2/18.
BURLEY	P J	25 2 Lt	30/5/17						
BURLURAUX	JOHN RENE CORNELIUS	27 2 Lt	28/5/15		1/7/16	OVILLIERS		BORN NEWCASTLE 1891, ENLISTED 18th NF 1914.	SERVED WITH D COY. AGE 25.
BURN	F D	25 2 Lt						JOINED FOR DUTY 18/5/17.	
BURNS	H N	24 Lt	1/3/17					FROM 1st BN, CAPTURED ENEMY TRENCHES 26/8/17.	
BYRNE	LOUIS FREDERICK SHERIDAN	24 2 Lt	13/11/14		1/7/16	GORDON DUMP		BORN DUBLIN 1894, ENLISTED 1914.	
BYRNE	MYLES EMMETT	24 LT COL	3/11/14					C.O. FROM 3/11/14 UNTIL 28/8/15 RELINQUISHED COMMISSION.	
BYRNE	WILLIAM	27 2 Lt	23/9/15		26/9/16	BAILLEUL		BORN OLDHAM 1895, SERVED 20th UPS BN R FUSILIERS.	TO 30th BN 2/11/15, TO 34th BN 12/7/16, TO 27th BN 24/8/16.
CALDER	E	25 2 Lt	1/8/17					Lt 1/2/19.	
CAMERON	CLAUDE	24 2 Lt	15/2/15					TO 30th BN 3/9/15, Lt 27/9/15, TO REGULAR BN 1/9/16.	RELINQUISHED COMMISSION 13/7/17.
CARSWELL	JAMES	27 2 Lt	1/3/17					EX CADET, TO REGULAR BN NOVEMBER 1917, Lt 1/9/18.	
CASTLING	W R	25 2 Lt	27/6/17					TO COMMAND DEPOT 1918.	
CATCHPOLE	A H	25 MAJOR						A/LT COL & C.O. 3/10/18 FROM 10th BN LINCOLNSHIRE REGT	(SPECIAL RESERVE).
CATNATCH	THOMAS BURNEY	26 2 Lt	26/9/16	9/4/17	19/4/17	ETAPLES		FROM 1st BN, AGE 23, GROSVENOR PLACE NEWCASTLE.	SERVED IN THE RANKS 1914 - 16.
CAWSON	GUSTAVE	25 Lt	1/1/15	1/7/16			M.C.	SERVED 1st V.B. QUEENS WEST SURREY REGT 1903-06. BORN 1885	Lt 1/6/15, CAPT 10/8/16.
CHARLESWORTH	THOMAS STEPHENS	25 2 Lt	4/3/15	1/7/16	10/7/16	GORDON DUMP		BORN MANCHESTER 1895, ENLISTED 13th NF 1914.	TO 30th BN 13/1/16.
CHARLTON	R	25 2 Lt	27/6/17						
CHICHESTER	ARTHUR GEORGE	26 MAJOR	12/3/03					BORN RANDELSTOWN 1865, JOINED CONNAUGHT RANGERS 1885.	RETIRED 4/3/11, JOINED 26th BN JAN 15, TO 34th BN 1/6/16.
CHICK	H T	30 2 Lt	8/11/15						
CHRISTOPHERS	E	34 LT COL	8/7/16				D.S.O.	FROM DCLI, CO 34 RES BN UNTIL 1/9/16, TO 84 TR BN AS 2 i/c.	
CLARK	J C	26 2 Lt	28/3/17	HOSP SICK 17/11/17				JOINED FOR DUTY 25/5/17, TO A COY 20/8/17.	
COATES	DONALD NEWTON	25 2 Lt	31/10/17		21/3/18	ARRAS MEMORIAL		FROM BORDER REGT, AGE 28.	
COBB	EDWARD CHARLES	26 CAPT& ADJT	16/9/15	1/7/16			DSO MiD	BORN FALKLAND ISLANDS 1891. ENLISTED 2nd NORTHANTS REGT 1911	
COCKS	B C	24 2 Lt	28/3/17					TO REGULAR BN JANUARY 1918, Lt 28/9/18.	
COLE	PERCY	26 Lt	11/3/15	1/7/16				BORN NEWCASTLE 1891, ENLISTED 9th BN DLI 1908 SERGEANT.	Lt 15/9/15, CAPT 13/11/16.
COLEBY	GEORGE	25 2 Lt	30/5/17				MC+BAR MM	CSM 24th BN 24/987. WAR DIARIES FOR 24th 9/16+25th 3/18+5/18	A/CAPT 2/4/18, Lt 30/11/18.
COLEMAN	ARTHUR	27 2 Lt	14/6/15	1/7/16				TO 30th BN 27/12/15, REPORTED MISSING 1/7/16.	
COLLIER	BERTRAM	25 2 Lt	3/4/15	4/11/16	5/11/16	TROIS ARBRES		16th TO 28TH 3/9/15, 28th TO 31st TO 34th BNS.	34th BN TO 25th BN 3/8/16, AGE 19 BORN JOHANNESBURG S.A.
COLLIER	W D	25 2 Lt		9/4/17					
CONNELLY	THOMAS PHILIP	27 2 Lt	7/6/15	1/7/16				BORN EDGEBASTON 1891,ENL R WARWICKS 14/244 1st B/HAM CITY BN	TO 30th BN 13/1/16, TO TYNESIDE SCOTTISH REP MISSING 1/7/16
CONNOR	RICHARD JAMES WILFRED	26 2 Lt	21/1/15					BORN WALLSEND 1894, TO 30th BN.	
CONWAY	THOMAS DOMINIC	24 2 Lt	1/3/17				M.C.	1/3/17	
COOK	H	27 2 Lt	24/7/15					FROM NF SEPECIAL RESERVE.	
COOPER	GEORGE THOMAS	25 Lt & ADJT	12/7/15					ENLISTED 6/2/1885 CSGT ROYAL SCOTS FUSILIERS.	TO 34th RESERVE BN AS ADJT 10/6/16, TO 85 TR BN 1/9/16 ADJT
COPLEY	BURLEY	26 CAPT	12/1/15	1/7/16			MiD 2/1/17	BORN MANCHESTER 1890, SERVED CHESHIRE REGT AUG - DEC 1914	CAPT 3/2/15, TO REGULAR BN 27/1/18.
COPPLESTONE	GEORGE BRIGSTOCKE	27 2 Lt	1/3/17						
COSBY	GEORGE SLADE	27 CAPT	2/3/15					BORN MANCHESTER 1875, FROM 8th OX & BUCKS LI 14/6/15.	CAPT 20/8/15 TO 30th BN 28/9/15, TO REGULAR BN 1/9/16.
COSGRAVE	ALEXANDER KIRKPATRICK	27 Lt	30/12/15					BORN DUBLIN 1885, RAMC ATT, 3YRS MALAYA STATES RIFLE VOL.	DEPUTY DIRECTOR OF MEDICAL SERVICES 1917.
COULSON	BASIL JOHN BLENKINSOP	26 LT COL	5/7/1899					K.O.S.B RETIRED 4/12/09, C.O. 20/7/16 TO HOSPITAL 6/8/16.	
COUPON		26 2 Lt						ON BN PHOTO IN IRISH HEROES.	
COVENTRY	A G	24 2 Lt	31/10/17					TO 8th BN.	
COWLEY	CECIL	25 Lt	13/5/16				M.C.	ENLISTED 24th BN, A/CAPT COMDG A COY 6/6/17, CAPT 18/9/17.	RELINQUISHED COMMISSION DUE TO ILL HEALTH 15/9/18.
COWLING	F F	26 2 Lt	28/3/17					JOINED FOR DUTY 26/6/17, TO UK 23/8/17, TO REGULAR BN 1918.	

SURNAME	FIRST_NAMS	BA	RANK	COMMISION	WOUNDED	DIED	BUR_MEM	AWARDS	ADD_INFO	REMARKS
COX	PERCY CYRIL	25	2 Lt	1/6/16		28/4/17	ARRAS MEMORIAL		PATROL'S "CAWDOR TRENCH" 24/4/17. REP MISSING 28/4/17	30th BN TO 25th BN 24/8/16, Lt 18/4/17, AGE 21.
COXON	WILLIAM BASIL	26	2 Lt	19/12/16		11/4/18	TROIS ARBRES		JOINED FOR DUTY 31/3/17	
CRAFT	T M	26	2 Lt	28/3/17	TO UK SICK 3/9/17				JOINED FOR DUTY 26/6/17, Lt 28/9/18, TO REGULAR BN 1918.	
CREAN	HAROLD ETHELWALD	27	2 Lt	22/4/15					BORN NEW BRIGHTON 1892, SERVED 6th BN KINGS REGT	TO 30th BN 13/1/16.
CREASEY	HERBERT HUDSON	24	2 Lt	1/3/17					RELINQUISHED COMMISSION ON COMPLETION OF SERVICE 5/4/19.	
CRITCHEN	THOMAS SMITH	24	Lt	7/5/15					COMMISSIONED 20th BN, TO 29th BN 7/1/16, TO 24th 22/6/16.	
CROWE	G H	25	2 Lt	31/10/17						
CUNNINGHAM	T O	24	Lt		29/5/17				BN TRANSPORT OFFICER.	
DABELL	W A RICHMOND	24	2 Lt	8/11/15	1/7/16, GAZ JUNE 17			M.C.	BORN NOTTINGHAM 1896, MILITARY CROSS WITH 8th BN NF.	30th TO 24th 29/6/16, Lt 1/7/17, CAPT 12/10/18, DIS 20/4/19.
DALZELL	JOHN MURRAY	24	2 Lt	19/7/15	1/7/15				BORN BELFAST 1889,TO 30th BN, Lt 22/3/17 ATT 86th TRG RES BN	
DANAHAR		26	CAPT	15/2/16					R.A.M.C. ATTACHED, TO UK ON LEAVE 1/11/17	
DAVEY	WILLIAM HAMILTON	27	CAPT	19/3/15				O.B.E.	BORN CARRICKFERRGUS 1885, CAPT 20/5/15, A/MJR 23/7/17.	MAJOR TO 24th 14/10/17,ATT REG BN 22/2/18,DIS SICK 29/8/20.
DAVIDSON	NORMAN	24	2 Lt	1/3/17						
DAVIS	JOSEPH LANGLEY	34	2 Lt	5/8/16					FROM 34th BN GAZ 20/10/16.	
DAWSON	DAN McGILL	24	Lt	4/11/14	SEPT 16	8/9/16	ST SEVER ROUEN		BORN 1889, DIED of GAS, TRF 30th BN, A COY 24th BN, AGE 27	
DEAN	R E S	25	2 Lt	27/6/17						
DEW	ALBERT WILLIAM JOHN	26	2 Lt	16/6/16		10/4/17	ARRAS MEM		ENL INNS OF COURT OTC 3/16. COMMISSIONED 7th BN 8/16.	JOINED 26th BN FOR DUTY 10/10/16, AGE 21.
DIX	OSWALD SIDNEY	26	Lt	21/1/15					BORN GLASGOW 1894, ENLISTED 16th NF 1914.	Lt 5/5/15
DIXON	HENRY PHILIP NORMAN	26	2 Lt	26/4/17		4/9/17	THIEPVAL MEM		JOINED FOR DUTY 26/6/17, TO A COY 20/8/17, MISSING 3/9/17.	
DONALD	LESLIE JOHN	27	2 Lt	15/3/15	1/7/15				BORN NEWCASTLE 1892, Lt 1/12/15.	
DONALD	ROBERT	24	Lt	19/11/14		28/4/17	ARRAS MEMORIAL	M.C.	IN RANKS 6th NF 1908-10, AGE 27. Lt 1/7/16.	ON PATROL 20/10/16.
DONNELLY	JOHN LAWLER	24	2 Lt	10/5/15					IN RANKS KING EDWARDS HORSE, AGE 20.	Lt 6/12/16, TO REGULAR BN 22/2/18.
DONNELLY	THOMAS GEOFFERY	24	2 Lt	18/11/14					RELINQUISHED COMMISSION 30/7/15 DUE TO ILL HEALTH	
DOWEND	JOHN MIDDLETON	26	2Lt	24/4/16		24/11/17	ST MARTIN CALV		FROM INNS OF COURT OTC TO 32nd BN, TO 26th BN 8/7/16.	A/CAPT, O.C. A COY 20/8/17.
DOWNEY	FREDERICK JOHN	24	CAPT	8/7/15	JUNE 16, FEB 17, JULY 17			MC DCM	SERVED IN 14th Coy 5th IMP YEOMANRY DCM 1900, CAPT 6/11/15	TO REGULAR BN 14/10/17, RELQ COMM DUE TO WOUNDS 12/6/19.
DOYLE	HENRY	26	2 Lt	21/1/15		17/1/17	RATION FARM CEM		BORN NEWCASTLE 1887,SGT 24/101 1st TYNESIDE IRISH	TRF TO 34th DIV CYC COY - TO 26th BN.
DOYLE	THOMAS	27	Lt	10/7/15					Lt 2/8/15 TO 30th BN 3/9/15, CAPT 23/4/16,TO 34th BN 1/6/16.	TO HOME SERVICE GARRISON BN YORKSHIRE REGT 13/11/16.
DUFF	JOHN	25	Lt & QM	13/2/15					RELINQUISHED COMMISSION DUE TO ILL HEALTH 10/7/15	
DUNCAN	ERNEST FRANCIS	27	CAPT C.F.	5/5/15		11/3/17	F D A ARRAS	M.C.	BRIGADE C of E PADRE, OF FINTONA Co TYRONE, AGE 32,	
DUNN	NORMAN ABLE	24	2 Lt	4/2/15	1/7/16				BORN BLAYDON 1892, SERVED 6th BN NF.	TO 30th BN 10/1/16, TO 85th TRG RES BN 17/10/16.
EDMUND JENKINS	WILLIAM HART	25	MAJOR	1900	1/7/16	3/7/16	ALBERT COM CEM		BORN 1881, SERVED IN SEVERAL REGTS, WAR DIARY 12/2, 28/4/16	MAJOR 4/2/15, TO TRENCHES 12/2/16, AGE 35.
ERRINGTON	A	26	Lt & QM	26/6/17				M.C.	JOINED FOR DUTY 9/7/17	
ERVINE	CHARLES JAMES	27	2 Lt	28/7/15		6/4/16	BAILLEUL COM		BORN BELFAST 1894, AGE 22.	
ESMONDE	GEOFFREY	27	2 Lt	22/3/15		7/10/16	CITE BON JEAN		BORN 1897, TO 30th BN 11/1/16, JOINED 26th FOR DUTY 21/7/16.	IN ST G GAZ 24/8/16.
ESMONDE	J L	27	2 Lt	19/11/14					FROM 6th BN R IRISH RIFLES 22/3/15, CAPT 20/5/15	TO 30th BN 8/11/15.
EVERED	HENRY ROBERT HASTINGS	27	2 Lt	24/8/15		1/7/16	THIEPVAL MEM		BORN KINGSTON UPON THAMES 1895, SERVED TERRITORIALS+OTC.	TO 30th BN 11/1/16, TO 27th BN 29/6/16.
EWART	HERBERT JONES	26	2 Lt	24/4/16					FROM INNS OF COURT OTC, TO 32nd BN, TO 26th BN 8/7/16	Lt 24/10/17, TO 27th BN.
FAGAN	DAVID PATRICK	26	CAPT	20/1/15					CAPT 20/1/15 TO 30th BN 17/9/15, TO 2nd GARRISON BN 7/12/15.	TO GEN LIST 12/5/17, TO SERVICE BN 12/5/19.
FAIRCLOUGH	D F C	24	2 Lt	1/4/17					EMPLOYED MINISTRY OF MUNITIONS TO NOV 17,	TO REGULAR BN 1/10/18, RESIGNED COMMISSION 16/4/19 SVC COMPL
FAIRMAN	A	25	2 Lt	30/5/17						
FALKOUS	ROBERT	26	CAPT	31/12/14		1/7/16	THIEPVAL MEM		BORN WITTON GILBERT 1892,ENL 16th NF 1914, CAPT 3/5/15	TO 30th BN 3/9/15,TO 26th BN 2/10/15, TO 30th BN 8/1/16.
FARINA	THOMAS GARIBALDI	24	Lt	12/11/14	GAZ JUNE 17				SERVED 16th BN NF,SEPT-NOV 14. AGE 21, CAPT 20/11/15	TO 24th FOR DUTY 31/10/16, TO REGULAR BN 14/10/17.
FENWICK	FREDERICK	27	2 Lt	25/1/17					TO REGULAR BN NOV 1917, Lt 25/7/18	RELINQUISHED COMMISSION DUE TO ILL HEALTH 19/11/18.
FIELDS	EDWARD COTMAN	27	2 Lt			22/6/16	CORBIE		AGE 34, COMMISSIONED FROM THE RANKS AFTER ACTIVE SERVICE AT	FESTUBERT & LOOS.
FINLAY	JOHN CUTHBERT	26	CAPT	3/1/15		23/11/16	CITE BON JEAN		BORN NEWCASTLE 1882, O.C. B COMPANY, Lt & QM 8/7/16.	Lt 5/1/15, ADJT WHEN KiA.
FIRTH	HAROLD WHITELY	27	2 Lt	15/1/16	GAZ JUNE 17			M.C.	CADET OTC TO 32nd BN 15/1/16, TO 27th BN 24/8/16, Lt 15/7/17	
FISHER	R E	24	2 Lt	16/9/17					FROM LONDON REGT(TF).	
FITZGERALD	GERALD	26	2 Lt	16/1/15		1/7/16	BAPAUME POST		BORN NEWCASTLE 1899, SON OF THE MAYOR OF NEWCASTLE.	PLATOON COMMANDER C COMPANY.
FITZGERALD	HAROLD SNOWDEN	24	2 Lt	19/11/14					THE DOWER HOUSE RIDING MILL 1918.	
FLEMING	JOHN JOSEPH	26	CAPT	23/2/15		13/10/17	TYNE COT MEM		BORN TRALEE 1883, TO 34th DIV HQ, O.C. 103LTMB, ATT 25th BN.	Lt 1/5/15, CAPT 12/7/15.
FLETCHER	ALBERT EDWARD	27	2 Lt	25/1/17					EX CADET	
FLETCHER	WILLIAM ARTHUR	27	2 Lt	1/3/17					EX CADET Lt 1/9/18.	
FLINT	CHARLES WILLIAM	26	2 Lt	6/1/16		1/7/16	THIEPVAL MEM		CADET ARTIST RIFLES OTC TO 32nd BN. AGE 35.	
FLYNN	JOSEPH MICHEAL	25	2 Lt	31/10/17		11/5/18	MOSTON LANCS			
FOLEY	JOHN	25	CAPT	2/1/15	1/7/16	1/7/16	THIEPVAL MEM		BORN CHARLEVILLE 1886, UK LEAVE 28/4/16.	Lt 1/3/15, CAPT 1/6/16, AGE 29 RESIDENT SUNDERLAND.
FORSTER	ARTHUR OSWIN	26	2 Lt	23/2/15					FROM 13th BN NF, TO 30th BN 3/9/15, RELINQUISHED COMMISSION	12/3/16.

SURNAME	FIRST_NAMS	BA RANK	COMMISION	WOUNDED	DIED	BUR_MEM	AWARDS	ADD_INFO	REMARKS
FORSYTH	JOHN DALTON	25 2 Lt	3/6/16	9/4/17			M.C.	FROM ARTISTS RIFLES OTC. TO 25th BN 24/8/16, Lt 1/5/17.	
FORTUNE	GEORGE ROY	26 2 Lt	2/7/15	TO UK SICK 24/7/17			MiD	BORN GLASGOW 1895,SIGS OFF CSE 3/2/16, PROMOTED Lt 3/7/17	CAPT 14/11/16.
FRANCIS	CECIL JAMES	25 MAJOR	30/8/16				M.C.	JOINED FOR DUTY 29/6/17, M.C. WON WITH 18th BN.	
FRASER	J K	25 Lt	20/7/17					ATTACHED FROM 7th BN.	
FRIEND	LEONARD MICHAEL	24 2 Lt	1/3/17						
FROMANT	HERBERT DUDLEY SANDS	26 2 Lt	1/3/17		29/4/17	AVESNES LE COMT		JOINED FOR DUTY 16/4/17	
FRYERS	ROBERT FURNESS	25 2 Lt	23/2/15					Lt 1/6/15, RELINQUISHED COMMISSION 18/11/15.	
GAILEN	D	25 2 Lt	1/8/17						
GALE	G P	27 2 Lt	29/11/15						
GALLWEY	JOHN PAYNE	24 MAJOR	17/11/14	C 5/6/16 DURING TRENCH RAID			MiD	MAJOR 1/11/15, TO REGULAR BN 3/2/17.	
GAMBLE	PERCY ALEXANDER	26 2 Lt	6/1/16					FROM ARTIST RIFLES TO 32nd BN 6/1/16, JOINED 26th 23/2/17	Lt 6/6/17.UK LEAVE 8/12/17, TO 25th 3/2/18.
GAVIN	LEONARD JOSEPH	26 2 Lt	18/4/15					BORN BRADFORD 1892, TO 30th BN 16/11/15.	
GAY	JOHN	30 CAPT & ADJ	26/10/14		29/5/16	HORNSEA		BORN STAMFORD LINCS 1853,SERVED 2nd ROYAL SCOTS CSM INDIA.	CEASED TO BE ADJT 10/3/16
GIBSON	H	25 2 Lt	31/10/17						
GILLESPIE	F S	26 CAPT	23/9/14					R.A.M.C. ATTACHED FOR DUTY 7/8/16.	
GILMORE	THOMAS EDWARD	26 CAPT	4/1/15					BORN NEWCASTLE 1881, LEFT S AMERICA AUGUST 1914 TO ENLIST.	CAPT 4/2/15, TO 30th BN 22/12/15, TO REGULAR BN 1/9/16.
GLASS	JOHN BIRCH	27 2 Lt	28/7/15	GAZ JUNE 17				BORN BELFAST 1884, Lt 1/7/17, TO REGULAR BN ../11/17.	COMMISSIONED 1st BN.
GLEDSTONE	HERBERT REGINALD	27 2 Lt	5/8/16	14/10/17	25/5/18	POZIERES		COMM 34th BN, POSTED TO 26th BN 11/8/17, UK LEAVE 1/9/17	A/CAPT 1/1/18. ATT 4th BEDFORDSHIRE REGT WHEN KiA.
GODFREY	JOHN AUBREY	27 2 Lt	1/3/17					EX CADET	
GODWARD	GRAHAM	26 2 Lt	16/1/16					FROM ARTISTS RIFLES OTC TO 32nd BN, JOINED FOR DUTY 28/7/16.	
GOODALL	CHARLE MOTAGUE	24 Lt	16/4/15				MiD	IN RANKS H.A.C. 1912-14. AGE 24. Lt 1/9/15	CAPT 2/7/16, ATTACHED REGULAR BN 2/2/18.
GOSS	WILLIAM ARTHUR	27 Lt	14/4/15					BORN SOUTH SHIELDS 1890,SERVED R.G.A., SEPT 14 - DEPOT N.F.	Lt 2/7/15, 30th BN 3/9/15, CAPT 16/4/16, TO 85th TRB 1/9/16.
GOWANS	WILLIAM IRELAND	25 2 Lt	28/3/17		13/10/17	TYNE COT MEM		FROM 1st BN, JOINED FOR DUTY 9/6/17, AGE 25.	
GRACIE	T	30 2 Lt	7/1/16						
GRANT	DOUGLAS ROLSTON	24 2 Lt	31/10/17	31/3/18			M.C.	24/27th BN POSTED TO 19th BN 6/2/18.	
GREEN	H F	27 2 Lt	26/4/17						
GREGERSON	C S	27 2 Lt	1/3/17						
GREGG	A E	26 Lt	13/3/15	17/10/17				WITH BN 8/7/16, TO A COY 20/8/17	
GREVILLE	HERBERT GEORGE E	26 2 Lt	1/3/17	TO UK SICK 29/9/17				JOINED FOR DUTY 24/8/17, UK LEAVE 11/9/17, TO 24th 11/17,	Lt 1/9/18, TO REGULAR BN 1918.
GROOM	THOMAS RICHARD	25 2 Lt	24/3/15					BORN LONGLEN 1895, ENLISTED 1914, TO 30th BN 3/9/15.	
GROSSMAN	VICTOR DAVID	24 2 Lt	2/6/16		15/9/16	BECOURT MIL CEM		FROM INNS OF COURT OTC TO 32nd BN, TO 24th BN 24/8/16,	AGE 18, BORN INDIA.
GUINNESS	ERIC C	27 Lt & ADJT	13/12/15	1/7/16			D.S.O.	FROM ROYAL IRISH REGT, CAPT 23/2/17, ATT REGULAR BN 22/2/18.	
HALL	G H	26 2 Lt	16/4/17	17/12/17				JOINED 16/4/17,ARMY ORDERS 5/7/17,UK LEAVE 8/11/17	ATT REGULAR BN 1918.
HALL	P	26 2 Lt	13/6/16					PRIVATE MACHINE GUN CORPS.	
HALLITT	WILLIAM	26 2 Lt	15/1/16					CADET OTC TO 32nd BN, TO 26th BN 24/8/16.	TRANSFERRED TO ROYAL FLYING CORPS 21/10/16.
HAMER	SAMUEL	26 2Lt	24/4/16	FEB 17	14/4/17	BAILLEUL RD EAS		FROM INNS OF COURT OTC TO 32nd BN, TO 26th BN 8/7/16, A/CAPT	WAR DIARY 11-12/9/16, FROM CHESHIRE AGE 32.
HANSON	WILLIAM EDWARD	26 2 Lt	1/3/17		28/4/17	ARRAS MEMORIAL		CADET OTC JOINED FOR DUTY 16/4/17, AGE 25.	
HARDY	GEORGE	24 2 Lt	7/12/14					TO 30th BN 11/1/16, JOINED 25th BN FOR DUTY 14/5/17.	Lt 1/7/17.
HARKER	JOHN	25 2 Lt	27/8/15					BORN NEWCASTLE 1884, TO 30th BN 13/1/16, TO 24th BN 3/8/16.	
HARRISON	F A	25 2 Lt	31/10/17						
HARRISON	HERBERT HENRY	30 2 Lt	5/8/16					EX CADET	
HARVEY	WILLIAM	27 2 Lt			14/10/16	TROIS ARBRES			
HASELGROVE	V	25 Lt	28/3/17					Lt 28/9/18.	
HATCHELL	HENRY MELVILLE	25 LT COL	28/2/1874				D.S.O.	SERVED S AFRICA ROYAL IRISH REGT, D.S.O.	RETIRED ROYAL GARRISON REGT 26/2/06, LT COLONEL 3TI 10/12/14
HATELY	JAMES ARCHIBOLD	25 Lt	5/1/15	1/7/16				RESCUED SOLDIER FROM THE WATER 12/1/16, BORN 1886.	Lt 1/6/15, TO REGULAR BN 3/2/17.
HEADS	J W	26 2 Lt	28/3/17					JOINED FOR DUTY 26/6/17, TO REGULAR BN 1918.	
HEATH	L C	24 2 Lt	28/11/16					CAPT 5/4/17.	
HEDLEY	JOHN HERBERT	26 CAPT	3/1/15					BORN NORTH SHIELDS 1889, NORTHERN CYCLIST BN 6/1910-2/1/15	26th BN-26/7/15,34 DIV CYC COY-9/11/15,26th-7/12/15,30th BN.
HEIGHAM	WILLIAM THOMPSON	25 2 Lt	11/4/16					Lt 24/5/16, TRANSPORT OFFICER.	RESIGNS COMMISSION DUE TO ILL HEALTH 9/2/17.
HENRY	N C	26 2 Lt	26/4/17					JOINED DUTY 27/6/17,UK LEAVE 20/11/17, POSTED 22nd NF 3/2/18	
HENZELL	GEORGE OSWIN	27 2 Lt	5/9/16	DEC 17			M.C.	ORIGINALLY PTE 26/1428, TO 27th BN 6/12/16, WITH 24/27th BN.	
HERDMAN	F F	26 2 Lt	26/4/17					JOINED FOR DUTY 22/4/17	
HERDMAN	T A	25 2 Lt	26/9/16					FROM 4th BN.	
HERMON	ERNEST WILLIAM	24 LT COL	24/8/16 LT		9/4/17	ROCLINCOURT VAL	DSO MiD	TOOK OVER BN 26/10/16 FROM KING EDWARDS HORSE	SERVED IN SOUTH AFRICA, AGE 38.
HERROD	BERNARD JOHN	30 2 Lt	6/11/15					BORN SHARDLOW 1894, TO 26th 15/4/17 A/ADJT 26th BN 15/6/17.	A/CAPT 1/8-17/8/16,Lt 25/4/17,CAPT 3/8/17,TO REG BN 22/2/18
HIGHAM	W	25 2 Lt	31/10/17					FROM ROYAL LANCASTER REGT.	

SURNAME	FIRST_NAMS	BA	RANK	COMMISION	WOUNDED	DIED	BUR_MEM	AWARDS	ADD_INFO	REMARKS
HILLHOUSE	J P	26	2 Lt	28/3/17	GASSED WITH 18th BN				JOINED FOR DUTY 19/5/17, POSTED TO 18th NF 10/6/17.	Lt 28/9/18.
HINCHCLIFFE	STANLEY	26	CAPT C.F.	10/12/15					BRIGADE METHODIST PADRE.	
HOBBS	FREDERICK ARTHUR	25	2 Lt	27/4/15				MiD	BORN TUNBRIDGE WELLS 1893, Lt 1/12/15, TO 27th BN.	TEMPY CAPT 22/2/17, TO 24th BN 14/10/17, ATT REG BN 22/2/18.
HOBSON	H S	25	Lt	23/10/15					FROM 30th BN GAZ 3/8/16, Lt 10/4/17, CAPT & ADJT 18/5/18.	
HOGGAN	G W	24	2 Lt	17/4/15					BORN INDIA 1894, TO 30th BN 1/11/15.	
HOPKINS	H G	26	2 Lt	28/3/17	HOSP 14/4/17				COMMISSIONED 25th BN, TO 26th BN 1917, ATT 103 LTMB.	ATT REGULAR BN 1918, Lt 28/9/18.
HOPPER	JAMES ARTHUR	26	2 Lt	7/7/16		10/4/17	BAILLEUL RD EAS	M.C.	COMMISSIONED 30th BN, JOINED FOR DUTY 15/10/16.	AGE 33 FROM WHITLEY BAY.
HOPPS	WILLIAM LEONARD	25	2 Lt	3/3/15	20/5/16	22/5/16	LA NEUVILLE		BORN KIMBOLTON 1893, SIGNALS COURSE 5-24/3/16, WND 10 PLACES	AGE 22 FROM EDINBURGH.
HORROX	HENRY M	24	2 Lt	17/4/15	1/7/16	1/7/16	THIEPVAL MEM		BORN EDINBURGH 1897, TO 30th BN 4/11/15, TO 24th BN 3/8/16.	AGE 19.
HORSBURGH	HERBERT ALEXANDER	26	Lt	7/11/14					COMMISSIONED INTO 24th BN TO 26th BN 4/5/15, Lt 4/5/15	TRANSPORT OFFICER TO 30th BN 31/12/15.
HOWARD	HARRY ELSMORE	25	2 Lt	20/1/16	REP WOUNDED 7/16 NOT WND 9/16	8/4/17	ROCLINCOURT VAL		REP MISSING 7/4/17 ORIGINALLY BURIED IN KITE CRATER, AGE 29	COMMISSIONED 30th BN, TO 29th BN, TO 25th BN 20/10/16.
HOWARD	LOUIS MEREDITH	24	LT COL	28/8/15	1/7/16	2/7/16	OVILLIERS		AGE 38 IN 1914, SERVED WITH S.A. FORCES BOER WAR.	MAJOR FROM WEST YORKS
HUNT	RALPH BOWDEN	24	Lt	2/12/14					IN RANKS DUKE OF LANCASTERS YEOMANRY, AGE 24, Lt 1/8/15	
HUNTER	ARTHUR STANLEY	26	2 Lt	5/8/16					FROM INNS OF COURT OTC,COMM 30th BN JOINED FOR DUTY 20/9/16.	Lt 20/2/18 POSTED TO UK 20/2/18.
HUNTER	JOHN KELSO	27	2 Lt	1/3/17						
HUNTER	NORMAN ARCHIBALD	26	2 Lt	26/4/17		3/9/17	HAGRICOURT		JOINED FOR DUTY 27/6/17, TO A COY 20/8/17	FROM WOOLER AGE 22.
HUNTER	W	25	2 Lt	27/6/17						
HUNTLEY	JOHN FENWICK	25	Lt	19/5/16		9/4/17	ROCLINCOURT VAL		TO 25th BN 4/11/16, AGE 30 FROM WHITLEY BAY.	T/CAPT WHILST COMDG COY 4/11/16.
HUNTRODS	R M	27	Lt	19/6/18					2 Lt, ATT REGULAR BN NOVEMBER 17, A/CAPT 21/4/18, TO 25th BN	
HURN	F L	25	2 Lt	10/4/17						
HUSSEY WALSH	W H	26	LT COL	10/12/14					COMMISSIONED 1st CHESHIRE REGT.	
HUTCHINSON	HUGH MAXWELL	26	2 Lt	1/8/17	24/11/17	29/11/17	BUCQOUY RD		FORMERLY L/SGT 12324 REGULAR BN, JOINED FOR DUTY 25/9/17	AGE 23 FROM CHESHIRE.
HUTCHINSON	RALPH de HEPPLE	25	2 Lt	19/2/15					BORN PORTSMOUTH 1897.	
HUTTON	C W C	25	2 Lt	26/12/14					TRF FROM 8tH BN SOUTH LANCS REGT 23/4/15, Lt 24/4/15	
HYMAN	WALTER WILLIAM	26	2 Lt		1/7/16	1/7/16	THIEPVAL			
INNES	JAMES DAVID	24	2 Lt	28/3/17	30/7/17	5/8/17	TINCOURT		FORMERLY 7/8th BN GORDON HIGHLANDERS, BORN BILBAO SPAIN	AGE 20.
IRVINE	R M	25	2 Lt	28/3/17						
JACKSON	A F	25	2 Lt	28/11/17				MC,DCM+BAR		
JAMES	D H	24	Lt	17/4/15					IN RANKS IMPERIAL LIGHT HORSE 1906.AGE 34, Lt 1/11/15	CAPT 11/3/16 TO GEN LIST WHILST COMDG DIV TRENCH MORTAR BTY
JAMES	HENRY JOHN	24	2 Lt	10/1/17		9/4/17	ROCLINCOURT		SGT FROM 13th SERVICE BN NF, AGE 34	
JARDINE	S A	24	2 Lt	17/4/15	1/7/16				IN RANKS RFA 1/2/15-16/4/15, AGE 33.ATT 103 LTMB.	
JARVIS	W C	26	2 Lt	22/1/16					TO 26th BN 8/7/16., Lt 22/7/17, TO MINISTRY OF MUNITIONS.	
JENKINS	JAMES	26	2 Lt	27/6/17				M.C.	COMMISSIONED 30th BN,JOINED FOR DUTY 3/9/17, RAID 5-6/12/17	ATTACHED REGULAR BN 1918.
JENNINGS	ALFRED GEORGE McIVOR	27	2 Lt	25/1/17				M.C.	EX CADET, TO REGULAR BN 1918.	
JETT	R L	26	CAPT						U.S. ARMY MEDICAL CORPS, RELIEVED CAPT SVENSON 1/11/17	
JOHNSON	RICHARD	26	2 Lt	8/12/14					TO 30th BN, PHOTO'S IN CAPT FALKOUS' ALBUM.	FROM 16th BN 27/4/15.
JOHNSTONE	A F	25	2 Lt	10/4/17					JOINED FOR DUTY 18/5/17, RELINQUISHED COMMISSION DUE TO ILL	HEALTH 6/2/18.
JONES	JOHN LLEWLYN	24	2 Lt	6/7/15					BORN SILVERDALE 1884, SERVED NORTHUMBRIAN FLD AMB TF RAMC	TO 30th BN 20/10/15, JOINED 24th FOR DUTY 21/9/16.
JONES	R M	24	2 Lt	21/6/16					Lt 2/12/17.	
JONES	R M	27	2 Lt	2/6/16					FROM 32nd BN TO 27th 24/8/16.	
JONES	WALTER ELWEY	25	MAJOR	1904					SERVED IN SEVERAL REGTS, BORN 1886, MAJOR 10/2/15	REJOINED 25TH BN 11/1/16.
JULIAN	L T	26	2 Lt	28/3/17	6/6/17				JOINED FOR DUTY 19/5/17, OFF STRENGTH 8/1/18	TO 86th TRB, Lt 28/9/18.
KELLY	WILLIAM PETER	27	2 Lt	3/3/1915	10/11/16	12/11/16	BAILLEUL		BORN BIRKENHEAD 1885. ENLISTED 2nd DRAGOON GUARDS 12/10/14	CAPT 1/5/15 TO 30th BN 3/9/15, TO 26th BN 11/1/16.
KENDRICK	E H	27	CAPT	24/11/15					FROM R INNISKILLING FUS 25/11/15.	
KENDRICK	JOHN EVERSLEIGH	26	2 Lt	18/3/15					BORN GOSFORTH 1895, WITH BN 8/7/16.	TO GEN LIST WHILST DRAFT CONDUCTING OFFICER 7/2/17.
KERR	H R	24	2 Lt	17/4/15	GAZ JUNE 17				ON PATROL 20/10/16.	
KIETH	F L	26	Lt		7/8/16				R.A.M.C. ATTACHED FOR DUTY 3/7/16.	
KILFORD	W D	25	2 Lt	25/10/16	9/4/17				Lt 25/4/18.	
KINNAIRD	DAVID	26	2 Lt	30/5/17		5/12/17	ST MARTIN CAL		JOINED FOR DUTY 28/7/17, RAID 5-6/12/17	AGE 22, FROM EAST LOTHIAN.
KIRKSBY-BOWES	R	26	2 Lt	30/5/17					JOINED FOR DUTY 28/7/17,UK LEAVE 29/11/17	TO REGULAR BN 1918.
KIRKUP	JOHN GEORGE	25	2 Lt	5/3/15	1/7/16			M.C.	BORN NEWCASTLE 1894, Lt 4/2/17, O.C. A+B COYS 11/4/17.	CAPT 10/12/17.
KNOX-GORE	ANNESLEY ST GEORGE	25	CAPT	1/7/1881					BORN BALLYNONA Co CORK, SERVED 6th CONNAUGHT RANGERS.	CAPT 23/6/15, TO 30th BN, 86th TRB 1/9/16.
LAMBERT	JOHN HENRY	25	CAPT	6/1/15	7/8/16	9/8/16	BARLIN COM CEM		Lt 1/6/15, ACTING ADJUTANT 8/16, CAPT 2/7/16.	AGE 31 FROM NEWCASTLE.
LAMBERT	PERCY GERALD	25	2 Lt	28/3/17		21/3/18	ARRAS MEMORIAL		FROM CITY OF LONDON YEOMANRY, WAR DIARY 15/3/16.	AGE 33 FROM BAYSWATER LONDON.
LAMPARD	FREDERICK NORMAN STOKEN	26	2 Lt	24/12/15	4/8/16, GAZ JUNE 17			M.C.	COMMISSIONED 15th BN. WITH 26th BN 8/7/16, Lt 15/5/17.	RELINQUISHED COMMISSION ON COMPLETION OF SERVICE 8/10/19.
LAUGHTON	GEOFFREY	26	2 Lt	26/4/17		5/12/17	ST MARTIN CAL		JOINED FOR DUTY 7/3/17, RAID 5-6/12/17	AGE 19 FROM LEEDS.

SURNAME	FIRST_NAMS	BA RANK	COMMISION	WOUNDED	DIED	BUR_MEM	AWARDS	ADD_INFO	REMARKS
LAUGHTON	GEORGE Van WYCK	26 2 Lt	19/12/16				M.C.	JOINED FOR DUTY 27/6/17, RELINQUISHED COMM DUE TO ILL HEALTH	25/4/18.
LAWSON	A O	24 Lt & Adj	/5/14	1/7/16				COMMISSIONED IN 5th NF, SERVED OVERSEAS, TO T.I. JUNE 1915	
LEATHER	ERNEST ARTHUR	27 MAJOR			10/2/16	RUE DAVID		COMMISSIONED 15th BN, CAPT 3rd BN, S.A. 1900-02, ORIGINALLY	10th BN UNTIL INJURED, AGE 48.
LECKENBY	HAROLD	26 2 Lt	29/1/16		9/4/17	ROCLINCOURT		FROM 32nd BN TO 26th BN, WITH BN 8/7/16, C COMPANY AGE 26.	
LEE	D S	26 2 Lt	26/4/17					JOINED FOR DUTY 27/6/17, TO REGULAR BN 1918.	
LEES	NORMAN SAMUEL	30 2 Lt	6/11/15	JULY 17				BORN WEST BRIDGFORD NOTTS 1895, TO 24th BN 3/8/16, Lt 1/7/17	
LEES	ROBERT VICTOR	24 2 Lt	15/11/16	JULY 17			M.C.	CQMS SERVICE BN RIFLE BRIGADE, DUTY ON LIGHT RAILWAY 17/7/16	Lt 15/5/18, A/CAPT 16/3/17 TO REGULAR BN 22/2/18.
LEITHEAD	J G	25 2 Lt	28/3/17					JOINED FOR DUTY 9/6/17	
LENNARD	RICHARD GRAINGER	24 2 Lt	7/4/17		6/5/17	LIEGE		LCPL DRAGOON GUARDS.	
LESLIE	J W	26 2 Lt	31/10/17					TO REGULAR BN JANUARY 1918.	
LEWIS	HAROLD LOCKWOOD	24 2 Lt	28/3/17		23/10/17	TYNE COT MEM			
LINCOLN	P L	25 LT COL	8/5/18				M.C.		
LINFORD	H J	26 2 Lt	31/10/17					JOINED FOR DUTY 13/1/18, TO 23rd BN 3/2/18	
LISTER	THOMAS FREDERICK	27 2 Lt	6/11/15		28/4/17	ARRAS MEMORIAL		BORN MANCHESTER 1893, TO 30th BN, TO 27th BN 3/8/16, AGE 24.	
LOCKWOOD	ARNOLD FRED	25 2 Lt	28/11/17				MC DCM+BAR		
LOVATT	CHARLES	26 2 Lt	1/8/17	23/10/17	12/4/18	AVELEUX WOOD	M.C.	JOINED FOR DUTY 25/9/17, REJOINS FROM HOSP 14/11/17	M.C. ATT 4th BN BEDFORDSHIRE REGT.
LOVERICK	ROBERT	24 2 Lt	6/7/15	1/7/16				AGE 32, Lt 1/7/17, RELINQUISHED COMMISSION ON COMPLETION OF	SERVICE 5/8/19.
LOWE	J E	25 2 Lt	28/3/17					JOINED FOR DUTY 25/5/17	
LOWTHER	GARNER HOLMES	25 2 Lt	16/12/15					31st BN TO 25th BN 3/9/16, FROM TRB TO REG BN ATT HQ 1/12/17	Lt 1/7/17, RELINQUISHED COMMISSION 13/7/19 DUE TO ILL HEALTH
LUMLEY	FREDERICK WILLIAM	24 2 Lt	17/4/15		10/4/17	ARRAS MEMORIAL		TO 30th BN 3/9/15, TO 27th BN 21/7/16.	
LUNN	JOHN RAMSEY	25 Lt	9/2/15					Lt 1/6/15 TO 30th BN 3/9/15,34th BN 12/7/16,85th TRB 1/9/16	TO REGULAR BN. RELINQUISHED COMMISSION DUE TO WOUNDS 15/2/17
LUNN	NORMAN	27 MAJOR	7/10/14	1/7/16			M.C.	BORN GOSFORTH 1888, ENL B COY 9th BN, FROM 16th BN 9/8/15,	Lt 1/7/15, CAPT 20/8/15, MAJOR 9/6/16.
MACKENZIE	KENNETH	24 CAPT	15/1/15	1/7/16	1/7/16	THIEPVAL MEM		SERVED 9th KRRC 1901-06,BRITISH COLUMBIA HORSE 1911-14	LORD STRATHCONA'S HORSE 1914-15 AGE 33.
MAIN	SYDNEY	27 2 Lt	16/8/15					15th BN, TO 84th TRB A/CAPT & ADJT 15/8/15, TO 27th BN.	Lt 1/7/17, RELINQUISHED COMMISSION DUE TO WOUNDS 2/1/19.
MAITLAND	ANDREW	25 2 Lt	6/1/15					BORN LONDON 1882, TO 30th BN 4/1/16, Lt 1/7/17	
MAKEPEACE	IVOR WILLIAM	24 2 Lt	23/4/15	1/7/16				COMM 20th BN TO 29th BN 3/9/15, TO 24th BN 22/6/16,	TO REGULAR BN 22/2/18.
MALCOLM	F R	25 2 Lt	25/10/16	9/4/17				Lt 25/4/18, RELINQUISHED COMM DUE TO ILL HEALTH 17/10/19.	
MALLORY	JOHN CHARLES	26 2 Lt	2/6/16		9/4/17	ROCLINCOURT V		1st BN ATTACHED 26th, AGE 22, FROM HULL.	
MANN	L	25 2 Lt	25/10/16	18/3/17				Lt 25/4/18, EMPLOYED MINISTRY OF MUNITIONS 11/18.	
MANWARING	V W	25 2 Lt	28/11/17						
MAQUIRE	ROBERT ALDRIDGE	25 2 Lt	15/1/15				MiD	ENLISTED 1914, Lt 17/11/15, O.C. RAIDING PARTY 3/3/17.	CAPT 10/2/17, MAJOR 18/9/17.
MARKHAM	R S	25 2 Lt	27/6/17						
MARSHALL	JOHN WOODHALL	27 Lt	3/3/15	1/7/16	1/7/16	GORDON DUMP	M.C.	BORN SOUTH SHIELDS 1892, ENLISTED TERRITORIAL FORCE 1910.	Lt 1/12/15, AGE 24, CARRIED IN SGT BURKE FROM NO-MANS LAND.
MARSLAND	P E	26 2 Lt	29/8/17	HOSP 30/11/17				JOINED FOR DUTY 14/11/17, REJOINED FROM HOSP 3/1/18	
MASSETT		26 2 Lt						REJOINED FROM HOSP 27/12/17	
MATE	C J	24 Lt	25/11/15					ON BN PHOTO.	
MELIA	MICHAEL	26 2 Lt	30/5/17	17/10/17, TO UK 19/10/17			M.C.	FORMERLY CQMS 27/1386.JOINED 26th FOR DUTY 28/7/17.	Lt 30/11/18, TO REGULAR BN JANUARY 1918.
MESSITER	V	25 CAPT & ADJ	30/8/15	9/4/17				COMM 17th BN, TO 28th BN 3/9/15, TO 32nd BN 14/12/15,	Lt 18/5/16, CAPT 1/5/17, FROM 32nd BN TO 25th 1/9/16.
MIDDLEMIS	HERBERT	24 2 Lt	14/9/17		23/10/17	TYNE COT MEM		SERGEANT COLDSTREAM GUARDS.	
MILLS	HORACE ALGERNON WILLIAM	24 2 Lt	22/11/16					EX CADET, TO REGULAR BN NOVEMBER 17.	
MILN	WILLIAM WALLACE	26 Lt	28/3/17		24/5/18	SOISSONS MEM		JOINED FOR DUTY 25/5/17,O.C. D COY 24/11/17.	TO REGULAR BN 1918, ATTACHED 4th BEDFORDS WHEN KiA.
MITCHELL	WILLIAM	25 2 Lt	1/3/17		28/4/17	ARRAS MEMORIAL		REP MISSING 28/4/17, AGE 22 FROM BLYTH.	
MORANT	WILLIAM HEDLEY	24 2 Lt			25/10/16	VERMELLES		1st BN ATTACHED 24th,SENIOR CLASSICAL SCHOLAR AT OXFORD 1908	AGE 27.
MORROGH	WILLIAM JOSEPH	27 CAPT	15/6/15	1/7/16			MC+BAR MiD	BORN CORK 1891, LT 1/12/15, CAPT 13/2/17, ADJ 10/8/17,	TO 24th BN 14/10/17.
MOSELEY	JOE EDWARD	26 2 Lt	15/1/16	31/10/16				CADET OTC TO 32nd BN 15/1/16, JOINED 26th FOR DUTY 28/7/16.	RELINQUISHED COMMISSION DUE TO ILL HEALTH FROM WNDS 25/5/17
MOULTON BARRATT	EDWARD MORRIS	25 MAJOR	18/6/1892				DSO+BARMiD	MAJOR 2nd BN 23/11/09,LT COL 9/12/16,C.O. 25th BN 10/12/16.	RELINQUISHED RANK 29/3/18, LT COLONEL 14/10/18.
MULLALLY	BRIAN DESMOND PATRICK	26 CAPT	1/1/15	25/6/16 AT DUTY	1/7/16	OVILLIERS	MiD 2/1/17	BORN GLASGOW 1896, Lt 2/5/15, CAPT 22/12/15.	
MUNTZ	GEORGE BRIAN	24 Lt	1/3/17					Lt 1/9/18 EMPLOYED WAR OFFICE.	
MURPHY	ALBERT	26 2 Lt	18/5/15		3/10/16	CITE BON JEAN		TO 30th BN 3/9/15, TO 24th BN IN FRANCE 21/7/16.	ATTACHED TO 103rd LIGHT TRENCH MORTAR BATTERY.
MURPHY	JAMES KENNEDY	25 2 Lt	17/4/15	1/7/16,9/4/17				BORN AYR 1886, SERVED 2nd LOWLAND FLD AMB RAMC 1914-15.	Lt 4/2/17 TO 86th TRB 1/11/17.
MURPHY	PATRICK JOSEPH	26 2 Lt	8/4/15	1/7/16				BORN WALLSEND 1892.PATROL NO MANS LAND 27/2/16.	LOSS OF SENIORITY 26/4/16.
MURRAY	MICHAEL JOHN	26 Lt	8/4/15				M.C. MiD	BORN GREENOCK 1892.TPT OFF 8/7/16, TO UK 11/10/17	Lt 11/1/16, CAPT 15/11/16.
MURRAY	PATRICK AUSTIN	25 CAPT	1/1/15		1/7/16	THIEPVAL MEM		BORN NEWCASTLE 1882, SERVED NORTHUMBERLAND YEOMANRY S AFRICA	Lt 1/3/15, CAPT 1/6/15, TO TRENCHES 12/2/16.
MURRAY	T J	26 2 Lt	28/3/17					TO REGULAR BN JANUARY 1918.	
MURRAY	WILLIAM PATRICK	26 2 Lt	8/4/15	1/7/16,19/10/17,TO UK 28/10/17			M.C. MiD	BORN BALLYGOWAN 1890, A/CAPT COMDG D COY 10/6/17.	Lt 2/7/16, CAPT 15/5/17.
MURTAGH	MICHAEL	27 CAPT	7/7/15	1/7/16				BORN DUBLIN 1866, CONNAUGHT RANGERS 23 YRS, CSM T.I.	CAPT 5/8/15,RELINQUISHED COMMISSION DUE TO ILL HEALTH 5/1/19

SURNAME	FIRST_NAMS	BA	RANK	COMMISION	WOUNDED	DIED	BUR_MEM	AWARDS	ADD_INFO	REMARKS
MUSSETT	A	26	2 Lt	1/8/17	HOSP SICK 7/12/17				JOINED FOR DUTY 25/9/17	
MacCOY	NORMAN	26	2 Lt	22/2/15					Lt 4/5/15 TO 30th BN 3/9/15.	
MacGREGOR	W	26	2 Lt	1/8/17	24/11/17				JOINED FOR DUTY 25/9/17, REJOINS 8/1/18, TO REGULAR BN 1918.	
McALISTER	GEORGE MALCOLM STUART	26	2 Lt	8/3/15	S SHOCK 15/5/16,HOSP 6/17,1/18				BORN SHEFFIELD 1894. BOMBING CSE 6/3/16.REJOINED 20/9/16.	ATT MGC 5/16, ATT WEST INDIES REGT 1918, CAPT 14/11/16
McBREARTY	GEORGE	24	CAPT C.F.	23/3/15	/11/18				BRIGADE R.C. PADRE, AGE 35.	
McCALLUM	D	24	Capt & Adj	17/4/15						
McCAW	ARCHIBALD	26	2 Lt	8/4/15					BORN NEWCASTLE 1894, ENLISTED NORTHERN CYCLIST BN TF 1912	TO 30th BN 15/11/15,REL COMM 20/2/16 ILL HEALTH ON ACT SERV
McCLARENCE	STANLEY	27	2 Lt	15/11/16		10/4/17	BAILLEUL RD EAS		PRIVATE LONDON REGIMENT (TF) AGE 27.	
McCONNELL	E	25	2 Lt	27/6/17					TO COMMAND DEPOT.	
McCONWAY	HUGH PERCY	26	Lt	8/4/15	15/5/16, HOSP 23/1/18				BORN HEBBURN 1888, BOMBING CSE 14/3/16 ASST ADJT 8/7/16.	Lt 15/9/15, TO REGULAR BN 22/2/18.
McCORMACK	JOHN JOSEPH	27	CAPT	20/5/15		28/4/17	BROWNS COPSE	MiD	BORN NEWAGH 1889, Lt 2/7/15, CAPT 2/7/16.	
McDONALD	T J	26	2 Lt	5/1/17					JOINED FOR DUTY 3/9/17	
McDONNELL	FRANCIS JOSEPH	24	CAPT &ADJT	6/11/14					CAPT 6/11/14, RELINQUISHED COMMISSION 15/10/15.	
McDONNELL	FRANCIS JOSEPH	27	2 Lt	2/7/15		26/5/18	LIVERPOOL FORD		TO 30th BN 3/9/15, TO 27th BN 24/8/16.	
McDONNELL	THOMAS JOHN	26	2 Lt			1/11/17	ARRAS MEM		ATTACHED FROM 12/13th BN.	
McDOOL	ERNEST	30	2 Lt	22/1/16					TO 24th BN, TO REGULAR BN 22/2/18, TRF ROYAL FLYING CORPS.	STUDENT AT USHAW COLLEGE, ORIGINALLY O.R. 30th BN.
McELDUFF	DANIEL	25	2 Lt	26/3/15				M.C.	TO 30th BN 3/9/15, TO 34th BN 1/6/16, CAPT 26/6/16	BACK TO 30th BN, TO REGULAR BN 1/9/16, RELQ COMM 3/4/18 WNDS
McGILLYCUDDY	JOHN	26	Lt	24/3/15	1/7/16	1/7/16	BAPAUME POST		BORN HIGHGATE 1882, ENLISTED 1900 SERVED S AFRICA, INDIA.	Lt 12/7/15
McGLIP	A R	26	2 Lt	27/6/17	17/10/17				JOINED FOR DUTY 3/9/17, TO REGULAR BN 1918.	CASHIERED BY SENTENCE OF GENERAL COURT MARTIAL 5/9/18.
McGUINESS	PHILIP ALOYSIOS	24	2 Lt	5/2/15					ENLISTED 16th IRISH DIVISION 12/9/14	TO 30th BN 3/9/15.
McINTYRE	J A	26	2 Lt	1/8/17					JOINED FOR DUTY 4/10/17	
McINTYRE	JAMES	27	2 Lt	23/7/15					BORN BISHOP AUKLAND 1893. Lt 2/9/16, TO 24th BN 14/10/17.	
McKELLEN	FREDERICK SMITH MOLT	25	Lt	15/2/15	1/7/16			M.C.	BORN MANCHESTER 1884.ON PATROL 23/2/16, ADJT PoW 21/3/18.	Lt 2/2/16. CAPT & ADJT 10/4/17.
McKENNA	PETER	24	Lt & QM	3/11/14					IN RANKS EAST YORKS + 5th YORKS 1904-1914. AGE 49.	
McLACHLAN	THOMAS	25	Lt	12/2/15	9/4/17			DSO MC	ENLISTED 15th BN. LARGE REPORT ON OPS 21/3/18 IN WAR DIARY.	Lt 2/7/16.
McLEAN	ALFRED KNOWLES	24	2 Lt	1/3/17					EX CADET	
McLEAN	C E	24	2 Lt	1/3/17						
McLEOD	DANIEL	25	2 Lt	17/4/15					BORN GREENOCK 1874. SERVED 5th A&S HLDRS, TO 30th BN.	TO REG BN AS Lt 1/7/17, RELINQUISHED COMM 11/6/19 WOUNDS.
McLOUGHLIN	JAMES	24	2 Lt	16/11/14	1/7/16				SHELLSHOCK, AGE 31.	
McNIFF	FRANCIS JOSEPH	24	2 Lt	28/3/17		13/3/18	CERISSY-GAILY		FROM 30th BN 30/228, ENLISTED ./1/16, ATT ROYAL FLYING CORPS	STUDENT AT USHAW COLLEGE.
McREA	M	25	CAPT	7/3/17				M.C.	R.A.M.C. ATT.	
McVEY	JOHN	27	2 Lt	30/8/15	1/7/16				BORN KINGSHORN 1893,ENLISTED R.E. 26/2/15.TO 30th BN 2/11/15	TO 27th 29/6/16,85 TRB 1/9/16,Lt 26th 14/11/17,TO REG BN9/18
NAUGHTON	LEONARD VINCENT	27	2 Lt	24/6/15					BORN LONDON 1895, ENLISTED AS A PRIVATE, Lt 28/6/15.	TO 30th BN 2/11/15,TO REG BN 17/12/17,RELQ COMM 15/7/19 WNDS
NAYLOR	C A	25	2 Lt	3/11/15	28/4/17				FROM 30th BN 3/8/16, Lt 10/4/17.	
NEEVES	HORACE HUNTER	27	2 Lt	1/1/16	JULY 17 gaz			DSO MC+BAR	COMMISSION 15th BN,MAJOR JOINS 26th 11/9/17, A/C.O. 21/10/17	A/CAPT COMDG A COY 1/8/16. ATT FRENCH ARMY 31/1/18
NEILAN	GERALD ALOYSIOUS	24	2 Lt	17/12/14		24/4/16	DUBLIN CITY		BORN ROSCOMMON 1881,S FORESTERS 1899, WND TRANSVAAL 6/3/02.	TO 30th BN 3/9/15, TO 10th ROYAL DUBLIN FUSILIERS.
NETTLESHIP	THOMAS	24	2 Lt	31/10/17		22/3/18	POZIERES		TO REGULAR BN, ATTACHED 1/5th BN(KiA)	
NEWBOLT	B P	27	MAJOR	27/10/14					FROM BEDFORDSHIRE REGT 13/12/15, SERVED S AFRICA.	
NEWBY	J H	25	2 Lt	27/6/17						
NEWSUM	T M	25	2 Lt	19/12/16	28/4/17					
NICHOL	JAMES	25	2 Lt	17/4/15					BORN DUNDEE 1894.	
NICHOLSON	BERNARD GEORGE MAURICE	27	2 Lt	28/3/17		19/10/18	WESTMINSTER		ATTACHED 13th BN.	
NICHOLSON	G	25	2 Lt	28/3/17					JOINED FOR DUTY 26/10/17.	
NICHOLSON	THOMAS EDWARD	25	Lt	9/2/15		1/7/16	THIEPVAL MEM		BORN AMBLE 1890, ENLISTED 16th NF 9/9/14, Lt 1/9/15	
NOBLE	THOMAS FRASER	25	2 Lt	17/4/15					BORN BELLSHILL 1887, TO 30th BN 11/11/15,TO 26th 15/10/16.	TO UK 9/1/17.DISMISSED SERVICE BY GEN COURT MARTIAL 26/1/17.
NOLAN	WALTER SPEAR	24	2 Lt	9/11/14					TRF GENERAL LIST 19/6/15 AS BRIGADE MACHINE GUN OFFICER	
NUTTALL	THOMAS JOHN	26	2 Lt	1/3/17					FORMERLY 17/1191,JOINED FOR DUTY 22/4/17,CHURCH RD LOW FELL	TO REG BN 1918, Lt 1/9/18, ATT 4th BEDFORD REGT.
O'BRIEN	A S	30	MAJOR	22/10/14 C					BORN 1877 DURHAM, CSM, Lt&QM, CAPT & ADJT 16th NF	2i/c 27th BN,TO 30th BN 8/12/18, RELQ COMM 27/3/19 WNDS.
O'CONNELL	MAURICE	27	Lt	26/3/15	1/7/16				BORN ARDNAGHEHA Co CORK 1888, Lt 5/8/15, CAPT 2/9/16.	
O'CONNER	ANDREW SEBASTIAN	26	2 Lt	8/4/15					BORN NEWCASTLE 1892, REJOINED 20/9/16. OFF STRENGTH 28/9/17	RELINQUISHED COMMISSION 6/10/17 ILL HEALTH FROM ACT SERVICE
O'GRADY	HUGH HAMMOND MASSEY	26	MAJOR	9/9/14					RETIRED R SUSSEX REGT 28/9/03, 2i/c 20/1/15 - JAN 16.	SERVED SOUDAN, S AFRICA.
O'HANLON	DANIEL JOSEPH	27	2 Lt	14/5/15	OCT 16				BORN WALLSEND 1887,A/ADJT AUG-SEP 1915,TO 30th BN 13/1/16	TO D COY 27th BN, 24/27th BN, 19th BN 6/2/18,TO MGC 20/3/18
O'LEARY	MICHAEL	30	2 Lt	23/10/15				V.C.	CPL IRISH GUARDS V.C. COMMISSIONED 5th BN CONNAUGHT RANGERS	TRANSFERRED TO 30th BN NORTHUMBERLAND FUSILIERS.
O'REILLY	ARTHUR PERCY	30	Lt & QM	19/11/15					SERVED YORKSHIRE REGT S AFRICA 1899 - 1901.	
O'SULLIVAN	BRENDAN	27	2 Lt	9/8/15					TO 30th BN 3/9/15, Lt 22/11/15.	
OATES	JOHN	25	2 Lt	1/3/17					EX CADET, Lt 1/9/18.	

SURNAME	FIRST_NAMS	BA RANK	COMMISION	WOUNDED	DIED	BUR_MEM	AWARDS	ADD_INFO	REMARKS
OLIVER	ROBERT DAVISON	27 CAPT	12/4/15					BORN NEWCASTLE 1889, 6th NF 1912, SGT 1914.	CAPT 1/5/15 TO 30th BN 10/1/16.
OWEN	A G	26 2 Lt	29/8/17					JOINED FOR DUTY 14/11/17	
OXTOBY	A H	25 2 Lt	1/3/17					JOINED FOR DUTY 10/5/17. REPORT IN WAR DIARY 21/3/18	Lt 1/9/18.
PANTIN	A	25 Lt	17/4/15	1/7/16				BOMBING COURSE 10/2/16, HOLDING THE LINE 15/2/16.	Lt 2/7/16,CAPT 21/8/17.RELQ COMM ON APPOINTMENT TO R.A.F.
PARK	ANDREW	26 2 Lt	7/9/15		14/7/16	THIEPVAL MEM		EMBARKED 23/11/15 COMMANDER 2 PLATOON A COMPANY 16th BN.	TO 26th BN.
PARKER	JAMES	26 Lt		1/7/16	1/7/16	THIEPVAL MEM		Lt 11/1/16 FROM 32nd BN, FROM THE ISLE OF WIGHT.	
PARKIN	W G	25 2 Lt	1/3/17					JOINED FOR DUTY 10/5/15.	
PATTERSON	HAROLD ALEXANDER	24 2 Lt	12/7/15	1/7/16				AGE 30, Lt 1/7/17, TO REGULAR BN DEC 1917	RELINQUISHED COMMISSION DUE TO WOUNDS 2/2/18.
PATTISON	EDWARD GLADSTONE	30 2 Lt	8/11/15					BORN NEWCASTLE 1897, ENLISTED NORTHUMBRIAN FLD AMB 16/4/14	TO 25th BN 3/8/16, TO REGULAR BN 17/12/17.
PAUL	THOMAS GUTHRIE	25 2 Lt	17/4/15		9/4/17	ROCLINCOURT VAL		BORN COATBRIDGE 1892, REPORTED MISSING 1/7/16.	
PEARSON	S	27 2 Lt	29/1/16					TO 27th BN 3/8/16, A/Lt 3/9/16 TO REGULAR BN 29/1/18.	
PECKSTON	CUTHBERT JOSEPH	25 2 Lt	28/5/17		22/3/18	ARRAS MEMORIAL		30/217 PRIVATE C COMPANY 30th BN.	
PECKSTON	ROBERT HENRY	26 2 Lt	10/6/16		22/10/17	STOCKTON onTEES		JOINED FOR DUTY 10/10/16, FROM 7th BN	
PENDER		26 2 Lt						COMMISSIONED 15th BN, JOINED 26th FOR DUTY 3/4/16.	
PENNEY	HERBERT GILLIES	24 CAPT	5/1/15	1/7/16				BORN WESTOE 1885, SERVED R.F.A.TF 1908-11.	TO 30th BN 3/9/15, TO REGULAR BN 1/9/16.
PETTETT	HERBERT CHARLES	25 2 Lt	1/3/17					EX CADET	
PICKER	CHARLES EDWARD	24 2 Lt	1/3/17					EX CADET, Lt 1/9/18, TO REGULAR BN NOVEMBER 1917.	RELINQUISHED COMMISSION DUE TO WOUNDS 25/4/19.
PIGG	J W	24 Lt	28/3/17					Lt 28/9/18 EMPLOYED MINISTRY OF SHIPPING 1918.	RELINQUISHED COMMISSION DUE TO ILL HEALTH 20/2/19.
PIRRIE	R R	26 CAPT		8/4/16				BORN BELFAST, RAMC ATTACHED T.I. DEC 1914.	
PITHETHLEY	W B	26 2 Lt	31/10/17					JOINED FOR DUTY 13/1/18, TO 23rd BN FEBRUARY 1918.	
PLEASANCE	CHARLES JOSEPH	24 2 Lt	28/3/17	30/7/17	31/7/17	VANDENCOURT		AGE 36 FROM BLACKPOOL.	
POLLARD	GEORGE EMBLETON FOX	25 CAPT	24/4/15					SERVED IN SOUTH AFRICA, BORN CASTLE POLLARD 1872.	TO DIVISION AS AN ANTI GAS INSTRUCTOR.
PORTER	F S	25 2 Lt	28/11/17					RELINQUISHED COMMISSION DUE TO ILL HEALTH 30/3/19.	
POTTER	A E	27 2 Lt	12/3/16						
POTTER	R D	25 2 Lt	1/8/17					Lt 10/9/17.	
PRICE	HAROLD	26 CAPT	31/12/14		26/6/16	ALBERT COM CEM	M.C.	BORN VANCOUVER 1890.BROUGHT IN Lt RUSSELL 16/3/16.	ADJT 31/12/14 - 12/10/15.
PRICE	JOSEPH WILLIAM JAMES	26 2 Lt	19/12/16	GAZ JUNE 17	22/4/17	ETAPLES		JOINED FOR DUTY 7/3/17 FROM 3rd BN, AGE 29 FROM SUSSEX.	
PRINGLE	JOHN HEDLEY	24 Lt	12/11/14	1/7/16				OC SQUAD TRENCH RAID 25/6/16, AGE 30, CAPT 21/1/15	
PRIOR	JOHN PETER	24 2 Lt	10/7/15		9/4/17	BAILLEUL RD EAS		BORN DARLINGTON 1889, ENL 11th YORKS REGT 1914.	TO 30th BN 12/1/16, WITH 24th BN 6/16.
PRIOR	JOSEPH MERRIMAN	24 MAJOR	6/11/14				MiD	2i/c, ACTING CO 9/5/16, 12 YRS NORTHUMBERLAND YEOMANRY.	LT COL 1916.
PRITCHARD	RALPH BLOOMFIELD	27 CAPT	27/5/15	1/7/16	26/4/18	MENDINGHEM	DSO MC MiD	BORN NEWCASTLE 1892,ENL 16th NF 1914 ,KIA 14th BN.	Lt 20/11/15, CAPT 11/2/16, TO 24th BN 14/10/17.
PROBERT	ARTHUR JAMES	1 2 Lt	10/7/15		9/4/17	ROCLINCOURT		BORN SOUTH SHIELDS, ATTACHED 25th BN, AGE 23, A JOURNALIST.	O.R. ARTISTS RIFLES, ENTERED FRANCE 1914.
PROCTOR	L B	26 2 Lt	7/10/14	1/7/16				Lt 2/6/15 TO 86th TRB 17/10/16 FROM 16th BN.	JOINED 26th FOR DUTY 13/2/17.
PROFFITT	STANLEY DIXON	27 2 Lt	5/9/16				M.C.	TO 27th BN 6/12/16, TO 24th BN 1917-18, TO REGULAR BN 5/3/18	
PROSSER	DONALD SYDNEY	27 2 Lt	22/4/16					FROM INNS OF COURT OTC, TO 32nd BN, TO 27th BN 24/8/16.	Lt 22/10/17, TO 24th BN.
PRUDHAM	THOMAS PEARSON	25 2 Lt	1/3/17		28/4/17	ARRAS MEMORIAL		REP MISSSING 28/4/17	
PRYOR	ARTHUR HENRY	27 2 Lt			10/4/17	ARRAS MEMORIAL		AGE 20, SON OF MR & MRS ALFRED PRYOR ROYAL MEWS BUCKINGHAM	PALACE LONDON. ATT REGULAR BN SEPTEMBER 1916.
PUGH	EDWARD RHODES	24 CAPT	26/11/14		2/12/18	EAST AFRICA		TO 30th BN 20/11/15, ADJT 85th TRB 1/9/16.	ATT 1 K AFRICAN RIFLES
PULLEIN	THOMAS HAROLD	25 2 Lt	1/10/17		21/3/18	ARRAS MEMORIAL		AGE 23 FROM LEEDS.	
QUINN	H A	26 2 Lt	1/8/17	17/10/17				JOINED FOR DUTY 4/10/17, TO REGULAR BN 1918.	
QUINN	LESLIE WILLIAM WHITWORTH	27 2 Lt	24/4/16		24/4/17	ARRAS MEMORIAL	M.C.	COMMISSIONED 3rd BN, AGE 23, CAME FROM AMERICA TO ENLIST.	EDUCATED TEMPLE GROVE AND FELSTED, KILLED BY A SNIPER.
RAYNHAM	WILLIAM WRIGHT	26 2 Lt	25/12/15					FROM 26th TO 34th BN 1/6/16, CAPT 25/4/16 TO 85 TR BN 1/7/16	TO REGULAR BN 1918, RAIL TRANSPORT OFFICER 8/1/19.
REAY	T	25 MAJOR	22/10/14	JULY 17			D.S.O. MiD	CAPT & ADJT 18th BN, WAR DIARY BN 2i/c 25/2/17.	
REDDER	SIDNEY de	25 2 Lt	6/1/15	1/7/16				BORN SOUTH SHIELDS 1895,TO 30th BN 4/1/16,TO 21st BN 22/6/16	RELINQUISHED COMMISSION 22/8/17 ILL HEALTH FROM WOUNDS.
REDPATH	F J	26 2 Lt	1/3/17	TO UK SICK 29/6/17,				JOINED FOR DUTY 26/6/17	
REED	JOHN HASTINGS	27 2 Lt	1/6/15					BORN LEEDS 1894, Lt 11/12/16, TO 85th TRB 1/9/16.	
RENSHAW	W A	25 2 Lt	1/8/17					RESIGNED COMMISSION ON TRF TO THE ROYAL AIR FORCE 14/9/18.	
RICHARDSON	JOHN SHERBROOKE	26 2 Lt	19/12/16		9/4/17	ROCLINCOURT		BORN 1877, EDUCATED CHARTERHOUSE AND CAMBRIDGE, MARRIED 1903	ENLISTED DERBY SCHEME MAY 1916, JOINED FOR DUTY 13/2/17.
RICHARDSON	MORRIS ERNOLD	26 LT COL	23/5/1900	1/7/16			DSO MiD	COMM 20th HUSSARS. SERVED IN S AFRICA. Lt 13/12/01,	CAPT 12/10/06, MAJOR 20/5/14, LT COL 8/12/15,SEE WAR DIARY.
RIDING	GEORGE ALBERT	24 2 Lt	22/4/16					FROM INNS OF COURT OTC TO 32nd BN, TO 24th BN, Lt 22/10/17	RELINQUISHED COMMISSION ON COMPLETION OF SERVICE 2/7/19.
RIGBY	H	25 2 Lt	28/11/17						
RIGBY	WILLIAM HENRY	27 CAPT	25/3/15	1/7/16				BORN ST HELEN'S 1890. EDUCATED USHAW COLLEGE.	Lt 5/8/15, CAPT 10/1/16, ATT TRENCH MORTAR BTY 30/5/16
RITCHIE	FRANK A	25 2 Lt	17/4/15					BORN FORFAR 1890. SERVED 2nd BN SCOTS GUARDS B.E.F.1914.	
RIX	HENRY	27 2 Lt	22/9/15					TO 30th BN 2/11/15, JOINED 25th BN IN FRANCE 3/8/16.	WAR DIARY 29/9/16 + 6/10/16,183 SUNDERLAND RD GATESHEAD.
RIX	WILTON JOHN	30 CAPT	25/9/14					BORN BECCLES 1871,1888 2 VB NORFOLK REGT, FROM ARMY CYCLISTS	TO 30th BN 22/1/16,TO 85th TRB 1/9/16,TO REGULAR BN 14/12/17
ROBBINS	E	25 2 Lt	25/1/17	9/4/17				JOINED FOR DUTY 25/5/17, Lt 25/7/18.	EMPLOYED MINISTRY OF LABOUR 1918.

SURNAME	FIRST_NAMS	BA RANK	COMMISION	WOUNDED	DIED	BUR_MEM	AWARDS	ADD_INFO	REMARKS
ROBERTSON	ROGER R	25 2 Lt	17/4/15				MiD	BORN MOUNT VERNON 1894,ABBEVILLE 11/2/16,TO 103 BDE HQ 6/17.	
ROBSON	CHARLES	26 2 Lt	31/10/17	16/4/18	2/12/18	HARTON ST PETER		JOINED FOR DUTY 13/1/18, POSTED 18th NF 3/2/18, AGE 26.	
ROBSON	F	25 2 Lt	28/3/17					Lt 22/4/18, A/CAPT 28/9/18.	
ROBSON	J C	26 2 Lt	31/10/17					JOINED FOR DUTY 13/1/18, TO 23rd BN 3/2/18.	RELINQUISHED COMMISSION DUE TO WOUNDS 11/2/19
RODDIS	F A N	27 2 Lt	26/4/17					Lt 26/10/18 TO 23rd BN.	
RODGER	J C	26 2 Lt	31/10/17					JOINED FOR DUTY 13/1/18, POSTED 23rd NF 3/2/18	
RODHAM	ROBERT	26 2 Lt	17/4/15		17/10/17	TALANA FARM		BORN WILLINGTON QUAY 1892, TO 30th BN 4/11/15, Lt 1/7/16	TO 34th BN 12/7/16, TO 26th BN 24/8/16, KiA WITH 9th BN.
ROGERS	ALBERT EDWARD	24 Lt	18/11/14	1/7/16 REP MISSING				IN RANKS R.E. 1901-04. AGE 29, LT 1/9/15	TO REGULAR BN 14/10/17.
ROGERS	F C	26 2 Lt	31/10/17					JOINED FOR DUTY 13/1/18, TO 23rd BN 3/2/18.	RELINQUISHED COMMISSION 11/2/19 DUE TO WOUNDS.
ROGERSON	JAMES V	26 2 Lt	17/4/15					RELINQUISHED COMMISSION 13/7/15.	
ROLLO	J N	25 2 Lt	28/11/17						
ROWE	A	25 2 Lt	27/6/17	../4/18				TO 18th BN.	
ROWELL	CHARLES	25 CAPT	18/1/15	1/7/16 REP MISSING				BORN TYNEMOUTH 1883,ENLISTED N CYCLISTS BN 1914.Lt 1/6/15	CAPT 3/9/15 TO TRB,TO REGULAR BN 14/12/17,RELQ COMM 22/5/19
RUDDOCK	R B	26 2 Lt						REJOINS FOR DUTY 25/10/17,LEAVE 28/10/17, O.C A COY 24/11/17	A/CAPT 5/11/17, FROM 6th BN NF.
RUSSELL	JOHN	26 2 Lt	17/4/15	16/3/16, 25/6/16, GAZ JUNE 17.				BORN LISCARD 1890, PATROLS WIRE 28/2/16, 29/2/16, 16/3/16.	Lt 2/7/16 TO REGULAR BN 14/12/17.
RUSSELL	WILLIAM FRANCIS	26 2 Lt	18/4/15					BORN HEXAM. TO 30th BN 4/11/15, 85th TRB 1/9/16.	TO REGULAR BN 1918, SERVICE COMPLETED 21/5/19.
RUTHERFORD	WILLIAM CECIL	2 Lt	1/8/17		10/3/19	ST OMER		24/27th BN POSTED TO 19th BN 6/2/18.	
RYLEY	H S A	26 2 Lt	17/4/15					BORN BOLTON 1891, TO 24th BN 1917, Lt 1/7/17.	
SCANLAN	THOMAS MICHAEL	24 2 Lt	11/12/14	9/11/16, FEB 17			M.C.+ BAR	BORN NEWCASTLE 1894, TO 30th BN 23/7/15, 34th BN 1/6/16,	24th BVN 3/8/16, 85th TRB, TO REGULAR BN 1918.
SCARFF	J G R	26 2 Lt	17/4/15	12/5/16,SICK16/6/17,UK 23/6/17				BORN GLASGOW 1894, ASST ADJT 19/12/16, COMDG C COY 15/6/17	Lt 7/8/16.
SCOTT	STEPHEN STUART	27 2 Lt	28/5/15					BORN PORT OF SPAIN 1893, ENLISTED RAMC 1914.	EDUCATED AT USHAW COLLEGE, Lt 2/7/16, TO R.N.V.R 24/2/18.
SHACKLETON	WILLIAM LAUNCELOT COLLIER	26 Lt	21/12/14	SSHOCK 13/5/16, JULY 17	24/4/17	CRUMP TRENCH		BORN NEWCASTLE 1886.PLN CMDR B COMPANY, TO D COY 29/3/16	Lt 21/4/15, MARRIED IN NEWCASTLE 14/6/16. REJOINED 27/10/16
SHAW	J B	27 2 Lt	25/10/16						
SHAW	S H	30 2 Lt	6/11/15						
SHEEHAN	T	25 CAPT	/3/15					RAMC ATTATCHED. BORN MALLOW Co CORK 1885, WAR DIARY 15/3/16.	
SHERIDAN	GERALD THOMAS	27 2 Lt	22/6/15					TO 30th BN 3/9/15, Lt 26/4/16, TO REGULAR BN 1/9/16.	
SHERINGHAM	G	25 2 Lt	28/3/17					A/CAPT 20/3/17.	
SHORT	WILLIAM ANDERSON	24 Lt	1/1/15	13/2/16				IN RANKS 9th KINGS LIVERPOOL REGT, AGE 25, LT 20/11/15	TO REGULAR BN 3/2/17.
SHOWELL	HAROLD GEORGE	27 2 Lt	28/3/17		16/7/17	JEANCOURT		AGE 21, BORN GREENWICH.	
SIGNEY	G S	27 2 Lt	26/4/17					TO REGULAR BN JANUARY 1918, Lt 26/10/18.	T/CAPT & COMNDT POW CAMP UNTIL 27/9/19.
SIM	G S	24 2 Lt	27/6/17					TO 23rd BN 1918	
SIMONS	JOHN GUY	26 CAPT	31/12/14	12/5/16,JUNE 17.HOSP 14/10/17			M.C.	BORN ENISKILLEN 1895, REJOINED 20/9/16.O.C. C COY 28/9/17	Lt 8/5/15, CAPT 7/8/16.
SIMPSON	ARCHIBALD VERE	30 2 Lt	8/11/15					BORN NOTTINGHAM 1889,SERVED 7th SHERWOOD FORESTERS 1905-06.	TO 85th TRB 1/9/16, 24th BN 1917, REGULAR BN DECEMBER 1917.
SIMPSON	THOMAS	27 Lt	31/3/15		1/7/16	THIEPVAL		BORN NEWCASTLE 1888, Lt 25/11/15	
SINCLAIR	W	25 2 Lt	30/5/17						
SKIDMORE	H S	27 2 Lt	28/3/17					FROM LINCOLNSHIRE REGT 7/3/18, Lt 28/9/18.	
SKINNER	WILLIAM JOHN	25 2 Lt	30/5/17					18 ALBION STREET, MURTON, Co DURHAM 1918	
SLACK	WALTER RENTON	25 Lt	5/1/15	1/7/16				BORN DURHAM 1893, ENLISTED 9/9/14, WAR DIARY 27/3/16.	Lt 1/6/15,85th TRB 1/9/16.48 ALBERT ST DURHAM 1918 TO 2nd NF
SLADIN	J H	25 2 Lt	28/11/17					RELINQUISHED COMMISSION DUE TO ILL HEALTH 20/7/18.	
SMAILES	R G F	24 2 Lt	31/10/17					24/27th BN POSTED TO 19th BN 6/2/18, DEMOBILISED 1/2/19.	
SMALES	M E	25 2 Lt	28/3/17	SICK TO UK 22/11/17				COMM 28th BN, JOINED 26th FOR DUTY 10/6/17, TO A COY 20/8/17	Lt 28/9/18, TO REGULAR BN 1918.
SMITH	A C	24 2 Lt	30/5/17						
SMITH	J P G	24 2 Lt	31/10/17	29/3/18			M.M.	24/27th BN POSTED TO 19th BN 6/2/18	
SMITH	T A	24 2 Lt	31/10/17						
SNAILHAM	JOHN JOSEPH	27 2 Lt	23/7/15	1/7/16				BORN GAINFORD 1895. ENLISTED 24th BN 1914.	
SNEE	JOSEPH	25 2 Lt	22/1/16	24/4/17			M.C.	ENLISTED 30th BN, HOLDING STRONG POINT 10/4/17, Lt 19/4/17	EMPLOYED MINISTRY OF MUNITIONS NOV 1918. RELQ COMM 22/6/19.
SNELL	FREDERICK WALTER	25 2 Lt & QM	1/3/17						
SNOWBALL	G N	25 2 Lt	28/3/17					JOINED FOR DUTY 9/6/17, Lt 28/9/18.	
SNOWDON	G C	25 Lt	7/7/16					Lt 7/1/18	
SPAIN	ISAAC	24 2 Lt	16/12/14				CdeGUERRE	TO 30th BN 1/12/15, TO TRB 1/9/16.	TO 18th BN, Lt 1/7/17.
SPELMAN	R W R	24 2 Lt	31/10/17					TO 8th BN, Lt 1/5/19.	
SPILLER	F W	24 2 Lt	31/10/17					TO 18th BN 23/2/17. WOUNDED WITH 18th BN.	
SPRENGER	OLIVER HOWARD	26 2 Lt	28/3/17		5/6/17	ARRAS MEMORIAL		JOINED FOR DUTY 19/5/17, AGE 24 FROM DERBY.	
STAFFORD	WILLIAM	27 2 Lt	7/8/15	SEPT 16				TO 30th BN 2/11/15,Lt 5/11/16,CAPT 3/7/17,TO 2 G BN 24/8/16	TO 26th BN, TO REG BN 22/2/18, GENERAL COURT MARTIAL 27/9/19
STEEL	M R	27 Lt	23/3/16				M.C.+ BAR	FROM 3rd BN TO 24th BN, A/CAPT 14/10/17.	
STEPHENSON	A	26 MAJOR	KOYLI					C.O. 3/7/16. POSTED OUT 7/7/16.	

SURNAME	FIRST_NAMS	BA RANK	COMMISION	WOUNDED	DIED	BUR_MEM	AWARDS	ADD_INFO	REMARKS
STEPHENSON	FOSTER	26 CAPT	25/1/15					BORN BLYTH 1894. WAR DIARY 8/7/16. REP REJOINED BN 26/6/17	CAPT 2/5/15, TO REGULAR BN 27/1/18.
STEVENS	C A	26 2 Lt	26/4/17					Lt 26/10/18.	
STEWARD	GODFREY ROBERT VIVEASH	27 LT COL	20/9/15				D.S.O.	BORN MANCHESTER 1881, COMMISIONED R INNISKILLING FUS 1899.	
STEWART	GEORGE	26 2 Lt	17/4/15	1/7/16	5/6/17	ARRAS MEMORIAL		REJOINS BN 31/3/17, A/CAPT.	
STRONACH	DONALD GRANT	24 2 Lt	15/1/16					FROM 28th BN, TO 19th BN 26/7/16, Lt TO U.K. SICK 30/3/18	Lt 15/7/17.
SUTCLIFFE	HERBERT RICHARD CHARLES	24 2 Lt	2/3/15		1/7/16	OVILLIERS		IN RANKS B Coy 9th NF 9/14-3/15, ATT Z/24 TMB, AGE 24.	
SVENSON	R	26 CAPT	5/10/16					R.A.M.C. ATTACHED, JOINED FOR DUTY 1/11/17 RELIEVED SAME DAY	
SWINBURN	GEORGE	24 CAPT	5/11/14				M.C. MiD	HOLDING FRONT LINE 2/7/16 - 4/7/16, AGE 33, CAPT 21/1/15	
TABRUM	BURNETT	26 MAJOR	13/1/15	REP MISSING 1/7/16				BORN LONDON 1877, TO REGULAR BN 4/2/17.	RELINQUISHED COMMISSION DUE TO WOUNDS 23/4/19.
TATE	ANDREW	2 Lt	31/10/17		20/1/18	WANCOURT		SERVING WITH 24/27th BN, AGE 20 FROM GOSFORTH.	
TAYLOR	J S	26 2 Lt	17/4/15					TO 30th BN 3/9/15.	
TAYLOR	JOHN ROBERT	25 2 Lt	5/3/15					BORN NEWBIGGIN 1870, SERVED NORTHUMBERLAND YEO S AFRICA.	TO 30th BN 13/1/16, TO 27th BN.
TAYLOR	S G	25 2 Lt	28/11/17						
TAYLOR	T H	25 2 Lt	1/8/17						
TEMPLE	RICHARD DURAND	27 Lt Col	11/8/00				DSO CdG	TO 25th BN C.O. 6/7/16, 24th BN C.O. 25/5/17.27th 19/7/17	MAJOR 2 i/c 23/12/14, LT COL 1/8/16, LABOUR COMDT 24/2/18.
THOMPSON	A. A	26 2 Lt	17/4/15					BORN GALASHIELS 1894, ENLISTED 5th WEST YORKS 1914.	
THOMPSON	ARTHUR	24 2 Lt	11/9/15		23/10/17	TYNE COT MEM		KiA ATTACHED LINCOLNSHIRE REGT.	
THOMPSON	ARTHUR	24 CAPT	12/11/14		1/7/16	OVILLIERS		AGE 25, CAPT 21/1/15	
THOMPSON	CHARLES MILBURN	27 2 Lt	26/4/17		26/8/17	HAGRICOURT		3rd BN ATT 24/27th BN, AGE 20 FROM SUNDERLAND.	
THOMPSON	G L	24 MAJOR	8/2/16					WORKING PARTY IN NO-MANS LAND 10/6/17.	
THOMPSON	THOMAS WILFRED	24 Lt	6/7/15				M.C.	IN RANKS 16th NF 10/14-6/15, Lt 3/7/16.	AGE 20. MC FOR WORK ON 1/7/16.
THORNLEY	A	27 2 Lt	28/3/17					TO REGULAR BN NOVEMBER 17, Lt 28/9/18.	
TICKLER	P E	25 CAPT	20/4/15					BORN GRIMSBY 1890, CAPT 1/9/15, SHELLSHOCK 1/7/16.	FROM 8th ROYAL LANCASTER REGT.
TOWNSEND	L	26 2 Lt	28/3/17						
TREANOR	FRANCIS	27 Lt & QM	3/3/15					BORN Co MONOGHAN 1879, ENLISTED R.E.(VOLUNTEERS) 1898.	TO 25th BN, RETURNED AS Oi/c COLOUR PARTY 6/19.
TREVOR	WILLIAM	25 CAPT						BORN SWANSEA 1880.	
TURNER	A B	24 2 Lt	28/3/17					TO 26th BN, TO REGULAR BN JANUARY 18, Lt 28/9/18.	TRANSFERRED TO ROYAL AIR FORCE.
TURNER	FREDERICK MARK	26 2 Lt	5/8/16					COMMISSIONED 34th BN, TO 26th BN 20/10/16.	RELINQUISHED COMMISSION ON COMPLETION OF SERVICE 8/5/19.
URWIN	G	26 2 Lt	1/3/17	TO UK SICK 20/8/17				EX CADET OTC, JOINED FOR DUTY 22/4/17, OFF STRENGTH 8/1/18	
VERNON	FREDERICK LEWIS	26 Lt	25/1/15		1/7/16	OVILLIERS		BORN NEWPORT MONMOUTH 1884, CAPT 25/1/15, AGE 30.	
VICKERS	WALTER EDWIN	25 2 Lt	1/3/17	28/4/17				EX CADET OTC.	
VIPOND	ERNEST JOHN	25 2 Lt	1/3/17				M.C.	COMMISSIONED 24th BN EX CADET, A/CAPT 20/2/18	
WALKER	WILLIAM FRANCIS	26 2 Lt	29/8/17		9/4/18	PLOEGSTEERT MEM		JOINED FOR DUTY 14/11/17,REJOINS 8/1/18, KiA ATTACHED 9th BN	
WALLACE	CHARLES	24 Capt	7/12/14	1/7/16				SERVED 2 YEARS IN VOLUNTEER ARTILLERY, AGE 43	COMMISSIONED FROM TF RESERVE LIST, MAJOR 6/12/16.
WALLACE	CYRIL JOHN GEORGE	24 Lt	1/7/17		9/9/18	ETAPLES		DIED OF GAS POISONING, AGE 22.	
WALLACE	HARRY HERBERT	27 2 Lt	5/9/16		21/1/17	TROIS ARBRES		TO 27th BN 6/12/16, D COMPANY, AGE 20 FROM ESSEX.	NAME HENRY IN CWGC REGISTER.
WALLER	THOMAS JENKINSON	26 2 Lt	28/3/17		28/9/18	BOIS LEUX ST MA		FROM 2nd BN JOINED FOR DUTY 10/6/17, TO UK ON LEAVE 15/11/17	DoW ATTACHED 4th BEDFORDSHIRE REGT.
WALMSLEY	G	30 CAPT	10/4/16					Lt & ADJT FROM KRRC 10/4/16.	
WALTON	HAROLD FOSTER	27 2 Lt	25/1/17		11/4/17	AUBIGNY COM CEM		AGE 23 FROM ALNWICK.	
WARD	ALWYN PERCY	25 2 Lt	15/1/16	2/10/16				WOUNDED ON PATROL IN NO MANS LAND, Lt 15/7/17.	CADET OTC TO 32nd BN 15/1/16, TO 25th BN 3/8/16.
WARDEN	H L	25 LT COL						JOINED FOR DUTY 15/5/17,C.O. 19/7/17, TO 27th BN 24/6/17.	
WARING	WILLIAM	24 Lt & ADJT	10/10/14					FROM GORDON HIGHLANDERS, Lt 15/10/15, ADJT 10/10/14-12/1/16.	
WATSON	W B	24 Capt	10/10/15					RAMC ATT, JOINED BN 10/10/15, AGE 32.	
WATTS	HUBERT	27 2 Lt	19/5/15		8/12/18	ST ANDREWS		FROM NF SPECIAL RESERVE.	
WEDDERBURN	JOHN ROLAND	24 2 Lt	2/12/14					IN RANKS 9th NF, Lt 26/6/16.	AGE 23, TO 30th BN 1/12/15, A/CAPT TO 85th TR BN 1/9/16.
WELCH	OSWALD	30 2 Lt	5/8/16					JOINED 26th FOR DUTY 20/9/16, TO REGULAR BN 1918.	
WELTON	JAMES JOHN GRAHAM	24 2 Lt	26/7/15	1/7/16				BORN HUMESHAUGH ON TYNE. TO 30th BN 12/1/16	Lt 1/7/17 27th BN, TO REGULAR BN 14/10/17.
WEST	J W	27 2 Lt	27/6/17					TO REGULAR BN NOVEMBER 17.	
WESTTHORP	WILLIAM HAST	27 2 Lt	1/3/17		28/4/17	BROWNS COPSE		EX CADET.	
WHEELER	HUGH GRAHAM	25 2 Lt	2/4/17		28/4/17	ARRAS MEM		REP MISSING 28/4/17	LCPL FROM SERVICE BN EAST YORKSHIRE REGT.
WHITBY	WILLIAM JOSEPH	24 2 Lt	1/3/17					TO REGULAR BN DECEMBER 17, Lt 1/9/18.	
WHITE	HERBERT THOMAS	26 2Lt,A/Capt	8/4/15	1/7/16	4/10/16	TROIS ARBRES	MiD 2/1/17	BORN FELLING 1892, ATTACHED 103 LTMB, WITH BN 8/7/16	AGE 24.
WHITE	W J	26 Lt	14/6/15					COMMISSIONED 15th BN, TO 26th 22/6/16, Lt 1/7/17	EMPLOYED MINISTRY OF MUNITIONS 1917.
WHITLOCK	TOM OLIVER	30 2 Lt	8/11/15		29/8/16	ERQUINGHEM LYS		BORN BULWELL NOTTS 1896, TO 22nd BN JULY 1916.	
WHITWORTH	ARTHUR GEORGE RICHARD	24 2 Lt	19/12/16		30/3/18	DOULLENS EXT 1		TO 24/27th BN POSTED TO 19th BN 6/2/18, AGE 20.	
WILDING-JONES	C W	25 CAPT	11/1/15					DISAPPEARS FROM BATTALION STRENGTH SEPT 1915.	

SURNAME	FIRST_NAMS	BA RANK	COMMISION	WOUNDED	DIED	BUR_MEM	AWARDS	ADD_INFO	REMARKS
WILKINSON	HARTLEY	24 2 Lt	21/12/14	GAZ JUNE 17.				IN RANKS 7th NF, AGE 22, Lt 2/7/16, TO 24th BN 3/12/16.	TO REG BN 14/10/17, RELQ COMM DUE TO WOUNDS 3/10/19.
WILKINSON	JAMES HAYES	27 2 Lt	2/7/15					BORN FELLING, TO 30th BN 3/9/15, TO 24th BN IN FRANCE.	Oi/c REINFORCEMENTS 28/7/16, GEN LIST 3/12/16 ADJT 31 IBD.
WILKINSON	JOSEPH	27 2 Lt	28/5/15					BORN NORTON ON TEES 1893, ENLISTED 2/5th DURHAM LI 1914.	EDUCATED AT USHAW COLLEGE, Lt 1/7/17, TO REGULAR BN NOV 17.
WILLIAMS	GEORGE HENRY	34 2 Lt	5/8/16					FROM 34th BN TO SERVICE BN 20/10/16.	
WILLIAMS	MERYDITH ROBERT OWEN	25 2Lt	2/6/16		14/3/17	F.D.A. ARRAS		INNS OF COURT OTC TO 25th BN 24/8/16, AGE 22 FROM LUTON.	DEATH RECORDED IN BN WAR DIARY.
WILLIAMS	TREVOR LOTHERINGTON	25 CAPT	15/9/15				M.C.	WELCH REGT TO T.I.15/9/15, TO TRENCHES 12/2/16. C.O. 1/7/16	RELINQUISHED COMMISSION DUE TO ILL HEALTH 8/7/19.
WILLIAMSON	J M	27 Lt	26/10/16					TO REGULAR BN NOVEMBER 17.	
WOOD	N L	27 Lt	25/10/16					Lt 10/2/17	
WOODCOCK	VICTOR JOSEPH	26 2 Lt	15/1/16					CADET FROM OTC TO 32nd BN 15/1/16, TO 26th BN 8/7/16.	TO ROYAL FLYING CORPS 28/7/16.
WRIGHT	EDWARD FRANK MACER	4 2 Lt	11/7/16		2/4/17	F.D.A. ARRAS		ENL ARTIST RIFLES OTC NOV 1915, TO BEF 4/10/16 ATT 24th BN.	BORN 26/8/1890, MASTER AT AMERSHAM GRAMMAR SCHOOL.
WRIGHT	J	26 2 Lt	30/5/17						
WRIGHT	JAMES	25 CAPT	13/2/15					TO 30th BN 3/9/15, TO 85th TRB 1/9/16.	RELINQUISHED COMMISSION DUE TO WOUNDS 23/4/19.
WRIGHT	ROBERT WILLIAM	25 Lt	10/3/15				MiD	BORN HEWORTH 1889,ENL 16th NF 7/9/14,O.C. C+D COYS 11/4/17	Lt 1/9/15, CAPT 4/2/17.
WYKE	W H	26 2 Lt	5/3/16	SHELL SHOCK 11/5/16				TO 85th TRB 1/9/16, CQMS FROM DIV CYCLIST COY.	
YOUNG	F E	25 2 Lt	22/9/16						
YOUNG	JOHN LINDSEY	26 Lt	31/12/14				M.C.	BORN TYNEMOUTH 1894.TRANSPORT CSE 7/3/16.REJOINED 10/10/16	Lt 3/5/15

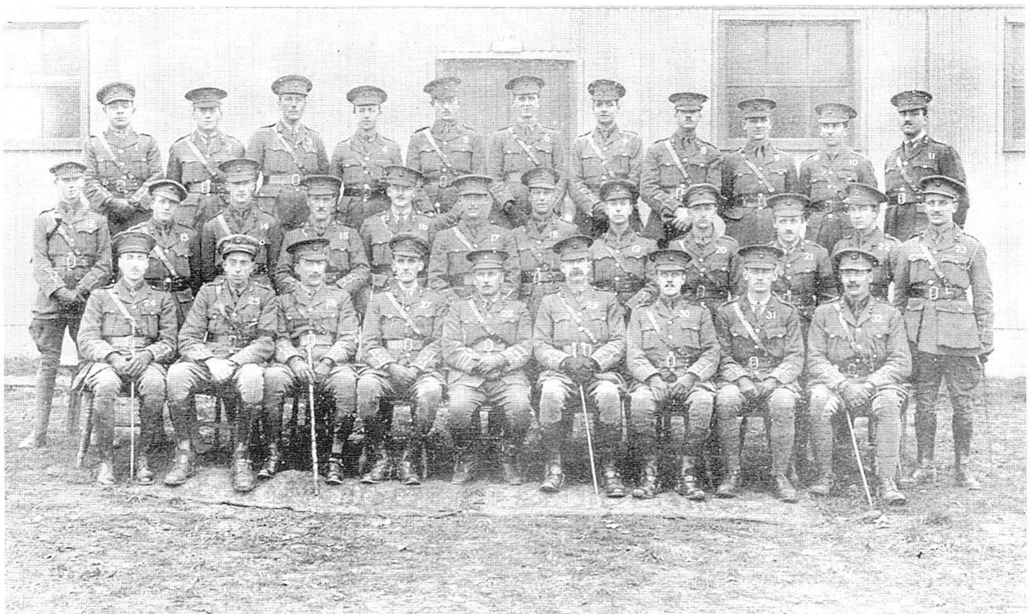

James Bacon and Sons.] OFFICERS, 4th Batt. Tyneside Irish Brigade. [27 (S) Batt. N.F.]. [*To face page* 205.

1. 2nd Lt. H. E. Crean.
2. ,, J. Wilkinson.
3. ,, J. B. Glass.
4. ,, D. J. O'Hanlon.
5. Lt. J. Woodall Marshall, M.C.
6. 2nd Lt. J. P. Connolly.
7. 2nd Lt. C. J. Ervine.
8. Lt. S. S. Scott.
9. Lt. J. J. Snailham.
10. 2nd Lt. H. R. H. Evered.
11. Lt. J. McIntyre.
12. 2nd Lt. G. J. Esmonde.
13. 2nd Lt. J. R. C. Burluraux.
14. Capt. R. B. Pritchard.
15. ,, W. H. Rigby.
16. ,, M. O'Connell.
17. Lt. F. A. Hobbs.
18. ,, J. H. Reid.
19. Lt. T. Simpson.
20. Capt. W. J. Morrogh.
21. ,, L. J. Donald.
22. 2nd Lt. J. P. Prior.
23. Capt. J. J. McCormack.
24. ,, A. K. Cosgrove, R.A.M.C.
25. Capt. W. H. Davey.
26. ,, M. Murtagh.
27. ,, R. D. Oliver.
28. Lt.-Col. G. R. V. Steward.
29. Capt. F. W. S. Buckman.
30. Major N. Lunn, M.C.
31. ,, J. V. Bibby.
32. Capt. G. S. Cosby.

Appendix III

ALHABETICAL NOMINAL ROLL
OTHER RANKS
24th NORTHUMBERLAND FUSILIERS
1st TYNESIDE IRISH

HIGHEST BATTALION NUMBER TRACED 24/1737
NUMBER ON ROLL **1298**
UNTRACED **439**
KILLED OR DIED OF WOUNDS **302**
WOUNDED **468**
DISCHARGED SICK, GASSED, TRENCH FOOT.
DEAFNESS, KR para 392 ETC **287**
TOTAL KNOWN CASUALTIES **1057**
CASUALTIES AS A % OF THOSE TRACED **81.4%**

NAME	INITI	RANK	BA	NUMBE	COMP	ADDRESS	TOWN_VILL	ENLISTED	DISCHARG	CAUSE_DIS	WOUNDED	BURIED	TRANSFER	ADD
ADAIR	Rob	PTE	24	/1660		12 NORTH VIEW	SHERBURN HILL			9 APRIL 1917		ROCLINCOURT VALLEY CEM	FROM 34 DIV CYC COY.	BORN MARYPORT CUMB, NOK 7 CROSS ROW LEAMSIDE.
ADAMS	E	CPL	24	/1081	C		WALLSEND			KR para 392	SEPTEMBER 16			
ADAMS	J	PTE	24	/1228						KR para 392			TO 1st GARRISON BN, 11th BNS.	
ADAMSON	Frncs	PTE	24	/1166	D	23 SHEPHERDSON ST	MURTON				OCTOBER 16		TO 27th, 16th, 1/5th, 14th BNS, CLASS Z RESERVE.	SPRINGBURN WOODSIDE HOSP GLASGOW 11/7/16.
AGNEW	J	PTE	24	/592	A		CONSETT	7/11/14	11/2/19	GUNSHOT WOUNDS	JULY 16		TO DEPOT.	AGE 31.
ALDONS	G	PTE	24	/1477	B									
ALLAN	John	PTE	24	/490	B	11 KING WILLIAM ST	GATESHEAD	12/11/14			SEPTEMBER 16			
ALLEN	Ed	PTE	24	/866	D	10 HIRST ST	WHEATLEY HILL	10/11/14		7 AUGUST 1916		CABERET ROUGE MIL CEM		AGE 37.
ALLEN	Mich	PTE	24	/1587	A	31 ABBOTT ST	GATESHEAD						TO ROYAL ENGINEERS.	77 ABBOT ST 1918.
AMBROSE	S	CPL	24	/1708				11/11/14	26/11/18	GUNSHOT WOUNDS			FROM 34 DIV CYC COY, TO DEPOT.	
ANDERSON	B	PTE	24	/512	A	28 POTTS ST	NEWCASTLE							ALSO ON D COY 30th BN ROLL.
ANDERSON	G	PTE	24	/613	D	28 BUCKINGHAM ST	NEWCASTLE						TO LABOUR CORPS.	LAB CORPS No 387913.
ANDERSON	H	CPL	24	/1084		WOODSIDE	WITTON PARK	10/11/14	2/3/17	WOUNDS	AUGUST 16		TO DEPOT.	WND R KNEE 34 CCS 2/7/16 EVAC 5/7/16 AGE 21.
ANDERSON	Isaac	PTE	24	/1011			ST IVES HUNTS			1 JULY 1916		THIEPVAL MEM		
ANDERSON	J	PTE	24	/1600	C									ALSO ON A COY 30th BN ROLL.
ANDERSON	Rich	PTE	24	/623	C	6 CLAVERING ST	GATESHEAD	11/11/14			JULY 16		TO CLASS Z RESERVE.	NEW NUMBER, 292109. BEAUFORT HOSP BRISTOL 12/7/16
ANDERSON	Sept	PTE	24	/1605	D	2 WAKEFIELDS YARD	WREKETON			1 JULY 1916		BECOURT MIL CEM		NOK 8 WEST VIEW WREKETON, AGE 35.
ANDERSON	T	PTE	24	/923	C									
ANDERSON	Thos	PTE	24	/1478	B	5 PERCY PLACE	NEWCASTLE	12/11/14			OCTOBER 16.		TO 12th, 12/13th, 22nd BNS, CLASS Z RESERVE.	
ANDERSON	Walt	PTE	24	/678	C	10 HAYMARKET	NEWCASTLE	11/11/14			MARCH 17		TO 2nd BN, CLASS Z RESERVE	AWOL 17/5/15 IN COURT 20/5/15.
ANGUS	J E	PTE		/478	A									No ALSO ALLOTED TO DIAMOND.
ANGUS	JohnE	CPL	24	/498	A	52 AVONDALE RD	BYKER	10/11/14						PHOTO IN IH. ALSO ON A COY 30th BN ROLL
ANGUS	T	PTE	24	/1485		10 HILLGATE	MORPETH	28/12/14	8/6/18	GUNSHOT WOUNDS			TO ARMY RESERVE CLASS W.	
APPLEBY	J	PTE	24	/999	C	122 VINE ST TEAMS	GATESHEAD			KR para 392.	SEPTEMBER 16			AWOL 7/6/15, VOLUNTARY AID HOSP CHELTENHAM 8/7/16
ARKLE	Wm	PTE	24	/1231		25 WATERLOOVALE	SOUTH SHIELDS	17/12/15	../6/15	BAD HEART				DID NOT SERVE OVERSEAS, AWOL
ARKLESS	Wm	PTE	24	/121	A	87 RAVENSWORTH RD	DUNSTON	28/10/14		1 JULY 1916		THIEPVAL MEM		MISSING AUGUST 16, BORN WHICKHAM.
ARMSTRONG	G	PTE	24	/273	C			4/11/14	23/11/17	WOUNDS			TO 9th BN, DEPOT.	
ARMSTRONG	J E	SGT	24	/916			NEWCASTLE				OCTOBER 16		TO CLASS Z RESERVE.	ACTING CSM.
ARMSTRONG	JohnR	PTE	24	/796	A	97 CRANK ROW	WEST MOOR	8/11/14	5/12/18				TO ARMY RESERVE CLASS P.	D COY 30th BN ROLL, BORN 1889, NEW No 88703 LCPL.
ARMSTRONG	Jos M	PTE	24	/129	A	NEWLANDS PLACE	PENRITH			30 JUNE 1916		HEILLY STATION CEM		IN LIEUT DAWSONS PLATOON.
ARNELL	H	LCPL	24	/1723				23/9/14	6/6/18	WOUNDS			FROM 34 DIV CYC COY, TO 3rd BN.	
ASHBURNER	H	LCPL	24	/1376			NEWCASTLE	19/12/14	14/3/18	GUNSHOT WOUNDS	JULY 16, MARCH 18.		TO DEPOT.	WND L BUTTOCK, AGE 28. 34 CCS 2/7/16 EVAC 5/7/16.
ASHMAN	E	PTE	24	/434	B									
ATHERTON	John	PTE	24	/669		14 ROWS EAST	PONTOP	29/10/14					TO 2nd GARRISON BN, CLASS Z RESERVE.	
ATKINS	T	PTE	24	/1512	C									ALSO ON D COY 30th BN ROLL.
ATKINSON	Adam	PTE	24	/1598	B	25 DUNSTON ST	HEBBURN			1 JULY 1916		GORDON DUMP CEM		MISSING NOVEMBER 16, IN 6 PLATOON.
ATKINSON	J T	PTE	24	/224	A		NEWCASTLE	4/11/14	10/4/18	GUNSHOT WOUNDS	NOVEMBER 16		TO 3rd BN.	3 CCS 2/7/16 EVAC 3/7/16.
ATKINSON	John	PTE	24	/449	B	ESLINGTON TERR	TEAMS COLLIERY				OCTOBER 16		TO 3rd BN, LABOUR CORPS.	LAB CORPS No 562300, M/G SECTION. BROTHER 18/839 D
ATKINSON	R	PTE	24	/1597	B									
ATKINSON	Wm	PTE	24	/196	A	7 MILBURNGATE	DURHAM CITY			1 JULY 1916	APRIL 16	THIEPVAL MEM		MISSING AUGUST 16, BORN SHEFFIELD.
ATTEY	Jas	PTE	24	/1595	A		OLD PENSHAW			23 MARCH 1918	JANUARY 18.	POZIERS MEM	TO 23rd, 1/5th BNS.	BORN NEW HERRINGTON.
BALDWIN	Robt	PTE	24	/527	B	87 CLAVERING AVE	DUNSTON	7/11/14	26/2/16				TO DEPOT.	DID NOT SERVE OVERSEAS.
BALL	T	PTE	24	/1604	A						MAY 16		TO 21st, 1/5th BNS, CLASS Z RESERVE.	
BALLENTINE	Adam	PTE	24	/1586	B	71 PLANTATION ST	LEADGATE	14/1/15		3 SEPT 1916	JUNE 16, JULY 16.	SERRE RD No 2+THIEPVAL		age 26,
BANKS	Thos	PTE	24	/622	D	3 RAILWAY ST	BLAYDON	6/11/14		16 SEPT 1916		THIEPVAL MEM		MISSING FEBRUARY 17.
BARKER	G D	PTE	24	/1302				19/12/14	4/10/18				TO 30th BN, DEPOT.	DID NOT SERVE OVERSEAS, ALSO ON D COY 30th BN ROLL
BARKER	W	PTE	24	/401	B									ALSO ON D COY 30th BN ROLL.
BARNES	Rich	PTE	24	/792	C	4 SMITH ST	WINGATE		31/1/19				TO 24/27th, 11th BNS, KOYLI(2/4th BN), Z RES	KOYLI No 63400.
BARNES	Richd	PTE	24	/1232	A 30		BRADFORD			4 SEPT 1916		THIEPVAL MEM	TO 30th, 27th BNS.	AWOL 8/5 1/8 COURT 10/5 18/8/15 DESERTED 12 FEBRUA
BARNES	T	PTE	24	/1561	C		LIVERPOOL				SEPTEMBER 16		TO 7th BN, ROYAL DEFENCE CORPS.	FRANCE 24 11/1/16 TO 16/7/16, 7th 15/9/17 TO 15/11
BARR	R	LCPL	24	/1702			CAMBUSLANG				SEPTEMBER 16		FROM 34 DIV CYC COY, TO CLASS Z RESERVE.	
BARRON	John	PTE	24	/689	D	CUMBERLEDGES BIULDIN	DIPTON	8/11/14					TO LABOUR CORPS(758 GAR GD COY) KRR CORPS(25th BN)	LAB CORPS No 397487.
BARRY	J	PTE	24	/1525	B	27 CAMDEN ST	SUNDERLAND							
BARTON	T	PTE	24	/1662									FROM 34 DIV CYC COY, TO 24/27th, 8th BNS, CLASS Z	
BARTON	Wm	PTE	24	/109						4 OCTOBER 1917		TYNE COT MEM	TO KINGS OWN YORKSHIRE LI(9th BN).	BORN BIRMINGHAM.
BATEY	J W	PTE	24	/1134	A	4 ROCK COTTAGE	HIGH USWORTH	2/11/14					TO SCOTTISH RIFLES.	
BATTY	Nich	CSM	24	/257		4 DURHAM RD	SUNDERLAND	6/11/14			SEPTEMBER 16		TO CLASS Z RESERVE.	AWO1
BATTY	R W	PTE	24	/1609									TO 2nd GARRISON BN, CLASS Z RESERVE.	
BAXTER	Wm	PTE	24	/144		14 BIRTLEY LANE	BIRTLEY	4/11/14	28/3/16	KR para 392			TO 1st GARRISON BN, DEPOT.	SERVED IN MALTA.
BAYLES	Mich	SGT	24	/811		12 STEPHENSON ST	FELLING	9/11/14	22/8/17	SICK			TO 85th TRAINING RESERVE BN.	

NAME	INITI	RANK	BA	NUMBE	COMP	ADDRESS	TOWN_VILL	ENLISTED	DISCHARG	CAUSE_DIS	WOUNDED	BURIED	TRANSFER	ADD
BAYLEY	C	PTE	24	/1154	B			10/1/15	10/1/19				TO 3rd BN, ROYAL INNISKILLING FUSILIERS.	WND R ELBOW, AGE 45. 34CCS 2/7/16 EVAC 5/7/16.
BEAMSON	A	PTE	24	/1603	D									
BEATTIE	J.	PTE	24	/342				5/11/14	8/6/15	SICK				DID NOT SERVE OVERSEAS.
BECK	Edgar	PTE	24	/1304	A	4 PRIMROSE HILL	WILLINGTON			1 JULY 1916		THIEPVAL MEM		BORN NENTHEAD CUMBERLAND. IN 2 PLATOON.
BECKETT	E	PTE	24	/23	A						MARCH 16			ALSO ON D COY 30th BN ROLL.
BELL	A W	PTE	24	/1616	A		WILLINGTON				AUGUST 16		TO LABOUR CORPS.	CPL, 3 CCS 2/7/16 EVAC 2/7/16
BELL	G W	PTE	24	/872	D		THORNLEY	9/11/14	13/6/17	WOUNDS	SEPTEMBER 16		TO DEPOT.	
BELL	Geo	PTE	24	/1377	B		SEAHAM			28 APRIL 1917	JULY 16	ARRAS MEM		BORN NEWCASTLE. DESERTED 14/6/15 COURT 12/7/15.
BELL	Geo W	PTE	24	/1514	D		HOUGHTON LE SPR			6 SEPT 1916		THIEPVAL MEM		WOUNDED AND MISSING FEBRUARY 17. BORN CARLISLE.
BELL	Henry	PTE	24	/270		18 CHAPEL ST	TANFIELD	4/11/14	11/9/18	GUNSHOT WOUNDS			TO 24/27th, 8th BNS, DEPOT.	
BELL	Isaac	PTE	24	/511	D	53 ALVINE ST BENWELL	NEWCASTLE	10/11/14			SEPTEMBER 16		TO 25th, 1/4th, 1/7th BNS, CLASS Z RESERVE.	NEW NUMBER 204578.SPRINGBURN HOS GLASGOW11/7/16
BELL	J	PTE	24	/603	B	30 QUEEN ST	CONSETT				JULY 16		TO LABOUR CORPS, ROYAL ENGINEERS.	
BELL	J	PTE	24	/860				19/12/14	29/12/16					
BELL	Mark	PTE	24	/244	B	5 LILY COTTAGES	DIPTON	6/11/14			SEPTEMBER 16		TO DURHAM LI(15th BN), 12th BN NF, 12/13th BN, Z R	
BELL	T M	PTE	24	/1520	C									
BELL	T W	PTE	24	/1384	C								TO 24/27th, 11th BNS, CLASS Z RESERVE.	
BELLWOOD	Alf	PTE	24										TO 30th BN.	AWOL REPEATEDLY FROM 24th + 30th BNS.
BELTON	Mich	PTE	24	/876	B	9 SOUTH ROW NEWFIELD	NEWCASTLE							ALSO ON D COY 30th BN ROLL.
BENNETT	JohnL	PTE	24	/922		37 BLANDFORD ST	NEWCASTLE			17 OCT 1915		ELSWICK		AGE 18.
BENTLEY	T E	PTE	24	/1646	A 30									
BERESFORD	JohnM	PTE	24	/1608	B			31/8/14	31/8/18				TO 30th BN.	DID NOT SERVE OVERSEAS.
BERRY	Alex	PTE	24	/358	D	11 HORSECROFT	BLAYDON	6/11/14	10/12/17	SICK			TO DEPOT.	LCPL
BEST	A	PTE	24	/1663			CLEETHORPES				OCTOBER 16.		FROM 34 DIV CYC COY, TO 16th BN, CLASS Z RESERVE.	
BEVERLEY	Her U	PTE	24	/670	B	11 GEORGE ST	DIPTON	9/11/14	27/2/17	WOUNDS	SEPTEMBER 16		TO DEPOT.	
BEWICK	Fenwk	PTE	24	/1029		5 EIGHT STREET	EASINGTON	11/11/14					TO 1st GARRISON BN, CLASS Z RESERVE.	
BEWLEY	J R	PTE	24	/627		WINDY NOOK	GATESHEAD	26/10/14					TO 1st GARRISON BN, CLASS Z RESERVE.	4 CARLTON TERR USWORTH 1918.
BINNINGTON	H	PTE	24	/431	B									ALSO ON A COY 30th BN ROLL.
BIRKETT	J	LCPL	24	/832	C	TOWER HOUSE CITY RD	NEWCASTLE	9/11/14	28/10/18	SICK			TO 24/27th, 3rd BNS.	
BIRKETT	J B	LSGT	24	/891	A 30	16 KENDAL STREET	BYKER							
BIRNEY	Rodr	PTE	24	/732	B	67 MANSFIELD ST	GATESHEAD	10/11/14		8 JULY 1916	1 JULY 16	GATESHEAD		BORN DURHAM.
BISHOP	Chas	PTE	24	/9	A	4 PROVIDENT PLACE	GATESHEAD	2/11/14	5/3/18	GUNSHOT WOUNDS	MARCH 16		TO 1st, 3rd BN.	REENLISTED 6th (TF) BN 15/4/20.
BLACK	A	PTE	24	/1198	D 30									
BLACKBURN	J	PTE	24	/1044	C		BLYTH				OCTOBER 16		TO LABOUR CORPS.	
BLACKETT	W	PTE	24	/1491	A	7 MELVILLE ST	CHESTER LE ST						TO 30th BN(D COY).	POS TRF TO R.E. 332245 FW&D.
BLACKWOOD	Jas	PTE	24	/747	B	5 REDBRICK ROAD	DIPTON	11/11/14		16 AUGUST 1918	AUGUST 16, OCTOBER 16.	RATHIEL FRENCH MIL CEM	TO 1st, 14th BNS.	POW AT TIME OF DEATH. 3 CCS 2/7/16 EVAC 2/7/16.
BLADES	F	PTE	24	/1602	C		WINGATE				5/6 JUNE 16		TO 9th, 23rd, 9th BNS, CLASS Z RESERVE.	BOMBER TOOK PART IN TRENCH RAID 5/6 JUNE 16.
BLAGDON	Geo	PTE	24	/1095	D	16 MILBURNGATE	DURHAM CITY	12/11/14			MARCH 16		TO ROYAL ARMY MEDICAL CORPS.	
BLANEY	H	PTE	24	/1381	B	31 MITCHELL ST	SOUTHMOOR						TO 8th BN, CLASS Z RESERVE.	
BLEWITT	Frank	PTE	24	/673	B	1 KELVIN GARDENS	DUNSTON				OCTOBER 16		TO ROYAL DEFENCE CORPS.	IN FRANCE 11/1/16 TO 16/3/17.
BONAS	A G	PTE	24	/1623	D			15/10/14	19/11/18	GUNSHOT WOUNDS			TO 24/27th, 9th BNS, DEPOT.	SEE ALSO 24/1601 BONAS A R. AGE 28
BONAS	And R	PTE	24	/1601	D	2 BROCKSIDE PLACE	BELLINGHAM	14/1/15		1 JULY 1916		THIEPVAL MEM		SEE 24/1623 BONAS A G, BORN LONDON.
BONNER	Jas	PTE	24	/395			MORPETH			1 JULY 1916		THIEPVAL MEM		AWOL 30/12/15 IN COURT BLYTH 3/1/16.
BOOTH	Rich	PTE	24	/579	B	218 SCHOOL ST	LANGLEY MOOR	9/11/14	2/5/18	GUNSHOT WOUNDS	OCTOBER 16		TO 8th, 16th, 3rd BNS.	BEAUFORT WAR HOSP BRISTOL 8/7/16.
BOOTH	S	PTE	24	/1177				12/11/14	8/3/15	SICK				DID NOT SERVE OVERSEAS.
BORROWS	T	PTE	24	/365	B									
BORTHWICK	ChasW	PTE	24	/1024	C	24 ASKEW RD	GATESHEAD			16 DEC 1916		RATION FARM CEM		AGE 22, LCPL
BOWEN	G	PTE	24	/1083	B	44 ALBION ST	WITTON PARK						TO ROYAL FUSILIERS.	
BOWES	John	PTE	24	/219	D	45 FRAMWELLGATE	DURHAM CITY	8/11/14		MUNITIONS WORK.				
BOWES	John	PTE	24	/658		5 ROBSONS BLDGS FRWG	DURHAM CITY			6 NOV 1915		ST CUTHBERTS DURHAM		AGE 26.
BOWES	Thos	PTE	24	/217	D	14 FRAMWELLGATE	DURHAM CITY				MAY 16		TO 21st BN, CLASS Z RESERVE.	
BOWLES	J N	PTE	24	/544	D	COCHRANE ST	BLAYDON	7/11/14	30/5/17	WOUNDS	OCTOBER 16		TO 3rd BN.	WOUNDED THIGH AND KNEE.
BOWMAN	Ant S	PTE	24	/991	C	20 BRINKBURN ST	BYKER	10/11/14	23/3/17	GUNSHOT WOUNDS	OCTOBER 16		TO DEPOT.	
BOWMAN	L	CPL	24	/1664		16 WILLOW ST	WASHINGTON STAT				AUGUST 16		FROM 34 DIV CYC COY TO 24th, 9th, 24th BNS, CLASS	PRISONER OF WAR JUNE 1918.
BOYD	J P	PTE	24	/253	C								TO 24/27th, 11th BNS, ROYAL FUSILIERS(24th BN).	FRANCE, 24 11/1/16, 24/27 10/8/17, 11 4/7/18,
BOYD	Jos	PTE	24	/1050	D	26 FREEHOLD ST	BLYTH	6/11/14	21/12/17	GUNSHOT WOUNDS			TO DEPOT.	
BOYLE	J	PTE	24	/628	D	42 BURN ST	GATESHEAD						TO LABOUR CORPS, ROYAL FUSILIERS, DURHAM LI.	LAB CORPS No 578026, R FUS GS/1028988.
BOYLE	Rich	CPL	24	/904	C	14 PUMP ROW WATERLOO	USWORTH			28 APRIL 1917		AGNY MIL CEM		RAID 25/26 JUNE 16, MISSING 8/17, BORN SSHIELDS.
BOYLE	ThosW	PTE	24	/725	C	19 LILBURN ST	BYKER	11/11/14		1 JULY 1916		THIEPVAL		MISSING AUGUST 16, BORN SEGHILL.
BOYNES	Jos	PTE	24	/120	A			3/11/14	27/2/18				TO 85th TRAINING RESERVE BN.	POSSIBLY BROTHER OF 24/124.
BOYNES	M	PTE	24	/124	A	12 STEPHENSON TERR	FELLING						TO 1st BN NF, LABOUR CORPS, ROYAL ENGINEERS.	

NAME	INITI	RANK	BA	NUMBE	COMP	ADDRESS	TOWN_VILL	ENLISTED	DISCHARG	CAUSE_DIS	WOUNDED	BURIED	TRANSFER	ADD
BRACKEN	Jos	PTE	24	/114	D 30	10 MOLINEAUX ST	HEATON	3/11/14	29/3/16				TO 30th BN	DID NOT SERVE OVERSEAS, AWOL 24th BN 3/6/15 IN COU
BRADLEY	Jas	PTE	24	/396	B	5 REDMAYNE ST	FELLING	2/11/14						ALSO ON D COY 30th BN ROLL.
BRADY	Wm	PTE	24	/766	C	94 PEARETH ST	GATESHEAD				NOVEMBER 16		TO MILITARY FOOT POLICE.	LCPL.
BRANNEN	Dan	PTE	24	/424	C	107 KENDAL ST	BYKER	6/11/14	14/11/17	SICK			TO DEPOT.	
BRANNEN	Mich	PTE	24	/1098	C	AUTON STYLE	DURHAM CITY	12/11/14					TO 25th, 12/13th BNS, CLASS Z RESERVE.	
BRENNAN	Edwd	PTE	24	/734	B	1 CHURCH ST	QUEBEC	11/11/14					TO 24/27th, 11th BNS, ATT 231 LAB COY, CLASS Z RES	
BRETT		WOII	24											CSM IN CAPT ARNOLD'S COY NEWCASTLE 1914.
BRIERLEY	Jos	PTE	24	/886	B	36 WEST ST	NEWCASTLE	10/11/14	7/3/18	SICK	NIGHT 5/6 JUNE 16			RAID 5/6 JUNE 16, 34CCS 2/7/16 WND JAW,BACK,HAND.
BRIGHT	T	PTE	24	/1123	D	92 KIRK ST	BYKER						TO ARMY SERVICE CORPS.	MISSING AUGUST 16, NOT MISSING NOVEMBER 16.
BRODIE	Alex	CPL	24	/220		14 FRAMWELLGATE	DURHAM CITY	6/11/14	18/3/19		OCTOBER 16		TO YORK AND LANCASTER REGT(8th BN).	D&D DURHAM 11/8/16 RAID 5/6 JUNE 16,
BROOKS	F	SGT	24	/1581	A 30									
BROUGHTON	W	PTE	24	/856									TO 1st GARRISON BN, CLASS Z RESERVE.	
BROWN	A	PTE	24	/1534	B 30		SWALWELL				FEB 17, APR 18			
BROWN	Albt	PTE	24	/1165		60 SILVER ST	MURTON						TO EAST YORKSHIRE REGT.	
BROWN	Andrw	PTE	24	/931	D	31 EDWARD ST	BLAYDON	12/11/14						59 JOHN ST 1914.
BROWN	Edwd	PTE	24	/351	B	10 SEVERS TERR	CALLERTON			1 JULY 1916		SERRE RD No 2 CEM		AGE 22, BORN BERWICK.
BROWN	J	PTE	24	/668			BEDLINGTON				AUGUST 16			3 CCS 2/7/16 EVAC 2/7/16, HOSP GOSFORTH 7/7/16.
BROWN	J R	PTE	24	/1639	D		HEBBURN COLLIER				OCTOBER 16.		TO CLASS Z RESERVE.	CPL.
BROWN	Olivr	PTE	24	/349	B	26 ARMSTRONG ST	WESTERHOPE	29/10/14			AUGUST 16		TO KINGS OWN YORKSHIRE LI, ROYAL ENGINEERS.	
BROWN	Thos	PTE	24	/48	B	EAST HOUSE FARM	USWORTH	2/11/14	12/8/16	WOUNDS	5/6th JUNE 16		TO DEPOT.	STRECHER BEARER, RAID 5/6 JUNE 16
BROWN	Thos	PTE	24	/194	A	13 GARDEN TERR	FELLING	4/11/14	24/10/17	WOUNDS	AUGUST 16		TO DEPOT.	
BROWN	Thos	PTE	24	/587	B	7 GEORGE ST	BLAYDON	12/11/14		1 JULY 1916		THIEPVAL MEM		BORN SWALWELL, ALSO ON A COY 30th BN ROLL.
BROWN	Thos	PTE	24	/1019	C		HASWELL PLOUGH				OCTOBER 16, MARCH 18.		TO 10th BN, CLASS Z RESERVE.	
BROWN	Thos	PTE	24	/1034	D								TO 24/27th, 23rd, 9th BNS, CLASS Z RESERVE.	
BROWN	Wm Bx	PTE	24	/1680		14 MITCHELL ST	DALKEITH			1 JULY 1916		THIEPVAL MEM	FROM R SCOTS & 34 DIV CYC COY.	MISSING AUGUST 16.
BRYDEN	G C	LCPL	24	/1647	B			21/9/15	15/9/16	SEPTIC FOOT			TO 30th BN.	
BUCKHAM	Jas	PTE	24	/182		52 OLD FORD RD	GATESHEAD	4/11/14	15/11/15				TO 30th BN.	DID NOT SERVE OVERSEAS.
BUCKLEY	G	PTE	24	/1380	C	TELLERS YARD QUBEC S	SPENNYMOOR						TO ROYAL FUSILIERS.	
BUDDLE	Robt	PTE	24	/1088	D	12 STEELE ST	CONSETT	10/11/14	19/3/18	GUNSHOT WOUNDS	AUGUST 16		TO ARMY RESERVE CLASS P.	
BULMER	Rob	LCPL	24	/1585	A		RYHOPE			23 OCT 1917		TYNE COT MEM	TO 24/27th BN.	ON BN ROLL AS K BULMER
BURDON		PTE	24											WON THREE LEGGED RACE ALNWICK 1915.
BURGESS	V	PTE	24	/397	A				6/1/19				TO 24/27th, 11th BNS, ROYAL FUSILIERS(24th BN).	FRANCE, 24 11/1/16, 24/27 10/8/17, 11 4/7/18,
BURKE	Jos	PTE	24	/750	D	31 FRAMWELLGATE	DURHAM CITY				OCT 16, NOV 16, NOV 18.		TO 9th BN, LABOUR CORPS.	21 AMB TRAIN, 18 GEN HOSP, CONV DEPOT 9/7/16SSHOCK
BURKE	M	PTE	24	/547	D	12 SOUTH ST	BLAYDON	7/11/14	22/10/17	SICK			TO DEPOT.	SEE 24/550 BROTHER SGT W.
BURKE	T	PTE	24	/520	D 30	99 JOHN ST	BLAYDON	7/11/14	4/4/16				TO DEPOT	DID NOT SERVE OVERSEAS.
BURKE	W	PTE	24	/1528	B		LIVERPOOL				AUGUST 16		TO 24th, 1st BNS, CLASS Z RESERVE.	WND R ARM+LEG, 34 CCS 2/7/16 EVAC 5/7/16
BURKE	Wm	SGT	24	/550		17 EVELYN TERR	BLAYDON	2/11/14		10 APRIL 1917	MAY 17	ST CATHERINES CEM		AGE 33,BROTHER M, 24/547.
BURN	J	PTE	24	/896	D									POS JAMES 27 HYLTON ST GATESHEAD S SHOCK JUL 16.
BURN	Jas W	PTE	24	/806	C	306 ST CUTHBERTS RD	GATESHEAD	12/11/14			OCTOBER 16		TO DURHAM LI(12th BN).	DLI NO 45888, AWOL 23/8/15 IN COURT GATESHEAD.
BURN	Wm J	PTE	24	/883	C	58 DAVISON ST	GATESHEAD	12/11/14		22 AUGUST 1918		MERVILLE COM CEM EXT	ATTACHED 103 LTMB, TO 24/27th, 9th(C COY) BNS.	CPL, AGE 22, 78 VINE ST 1918.
BURTON	A F	CPL	24	/1645	A 30	172 CANNING STREET	BENWELL							HOSP ROUEN 7/16, CQMS.
BURTON	J	PTE	24	/67	A	1 TWEED ST	NEWCASTLE						TO 27th, 24/27th, 9th BNS,ATT 183 LTMB, CLASS Z RE	ON BN ROLL AS BENTON
BUTLER	J W	PTE	24	/389	C									ALSO ON A COY 30th BN ROLL.
BUTLER	Pat	SGT	24	/348	D	5 LAMPTON COURT	NEWCASTLE	26/10/14		1 JULY 1916		OVILLIERS	TRENCH RAID 5/6th JUNE 16.	BORN CLONMEL CO TIPPERARY.FIRST MAN TO ENROL 21 OC
BUTTERFIELD	Alex	PTE	24	/298	A	1 POWELLS YARD, ANN	GATESHEAD				AUGUST 16		TO 11th, 10th BNS, CLASS Z RESERVE.	14 CARRICK ST 1916.
BYRNE	M	PTE	24	/1057	C	22 ADDISON ST EAST	SUNDERLAND	9/11/14	9/8/17	SICK	JULY 16		TO 85th TRAINING RESERVE BN.	34 CCS 2/7/16 EVAC 2/7/16
BYRNE	Mich	PTE	24	/1505			LIVERPOOL			3 JULY 1916		HEILLY STATION CEM		
CAIN	D	PTE	24	/1189	D		BLACKHALL	10/11/14	20/11/17	WOUNDS	JULY 16.		TO DEPOT.	RAID 5/6 JUNE 16. R VICTORIA HOSP NETLEY 11/7/16.
CAIN	Edwin	PTE	24	/364	C	18 ROSEHILL ST	SHIELDFIELD	6/11/14	7/6/18	WOUNDS	DECEMBER 17		TO 16th BN, DEPOT.	26 ELLISON ST WEST GATESHEAD 1918.
CAIRNS	Jas	PTE	24	/372	B				7/2/19				TO 24/27th, 1/4th BNS, KOYLI(2/4th BN). Z RES.	KOYLI No 63269.
CAIRNS	John	PTE	24	/370	B	27 BK HOWICK ST MNKW	SUNDERLAND	11/11/14						
CAIRNS	Owen	PTE	24	/1015	C	3 CHURCH ST	MARLEY HILL				AUGUST 16, DECEMBER 16		TO ROYAL DEFENCE CORPS.	RAIDS 5/6th, 25/26th JUNE 16.FRANCE UNTIL 22/10/17
CALDWELL	Wm	SGT	24	/799	C	1 BACK LIDDELL ST	GATESHEAD	12/11/14			OCTOBER 16		TO GREEN HOWARDS.	34CCS 1/7 EVAC VICTORIA HOSP NETLEY 11/7/16 AGE 40
CALLAGHAN	Thos	PTE	24	/1063	D		WILLINGTON QUAY			4 MAY 1917		ETAPLES	TO 10th, 9th, 24th BNS.	CPL.
CALLAN	Chas	SGT	24	/464		FRONT ST DAVEY LAMP	KELLOE	7/11/14	31/3/19		JULY 16		TO 10th BN, ARMY RESERVE CLASS P.	SEE 27/91 BROTHER N.
CALLERGHAN	Mich	PTE	24	/482		SMITHS YARD	DIPTON						TO 1st GARRISON BN, CLASS Z RESERVE.	STARTFORDS BIULDINGS PONTOP 1918.
CALVEY	W	PTE	24	/1007				10/11/14	20/3/17	GUNSHOT WOUNDS	OCTOBER 16		TO DEPOT.	
CAMSEY	J	LCPL	24	/1606	D 30									
CANNON	Anth	SGT	24	/119		2 GRENNEL TERR	NEWCASTLE	3/11/14	11/10/17	WOUNDS	APR 16		TO 9th, 3rd BNS.	
CARLIN	Thos	PTE	24	/1385									TO LABOUR CORPS.	LAB CORPS No 591542, AWOL 19/7/15 COURT GATESHEAD

NAME	INITI	RANK	BA	NUMBE	COMP	ADDRESS	TOWN_VILL	ENLISTED	DISCHARG	CAUSE_DIS	WOUNDED	BURIED	TRANSFER	ADD
CARNEY	Jos D	CQMS	24	/110		41 THIRD ST	GATESHEAD				AUGUST 16		TO CLASS Z RESERVE.	
CARR	Geo	PTE	24	/1235	D	5 CLIFTON RD	NETHERTON COLLI			1 JULY 1916		THIEPVAL MEM		BORN CALPER NORTHMBLD, MISSING AUGUST 16.
CARR	J	PTE	24	/1147	D								TO DURHAM LI.	
CARR	J	PTE	24	/1676				8/11/14	1/4/19	KR para 392			FROM 34 DIV CYC COY, ARMY RESERVE CLASS P.	
CARR	John	PTE	24	/1115	D		BLAYDON		23/1/19		JULY 16		TO 27th, 16th, 10th, 16th, 1/5th,YORK & LANCS(1/4t	Y&L No 57732.
CARR	M	CPL	24	/1227	A 30		NEWCASTLE	30/11/14	7/3/17	SICK	FEBRUARY 17.		TO 25th, 24th BNS, DEPOT.	ALSO ON B COMPANY 30th BN AS PTE.
CARR	Nelsn	PTE	24	/624	B	37 HARL ST MOUNT PLE	GATESHEAD	9/11/14	31/3/19	KR para 392			TO ARMY RESERVE CLASS P	Geo Hnry CARR 204456 SOUTH LANCS AT THIS ADDRESS 1
CARR	Thom	PTE	24	/400	D	66 BACK ROBINSON ST	BLAYDON	26/10/14			FEBRUARY 17		TO DURHAM LI, SUFFOLK REGT.	DLI No 481674.
CARR	Thos	PTE	24	/970	C	12 TYNE ST	WILLINGTON				SEPTEMBER 16		TO 11th, 16th, 8th BNS, CLASS Z RESERVE.	
CARR	ThosR	PTE	24	/575	C	7 STRATHMORE TERR	ROWLANDS GILL	10/11/14					TO 11th BN, ATTACHED 102nd FIELD AMB RAMC, Z RES.	
CARRICK	J	PTE	24	/728	C		DUNSTON	7/11/14	22/10/17	GUNSHOT WOUNDS	DECEMBER 16		TO 3rd BN.	
CARROLL	Jon P	PTE	24	/398	A	10 SOUTH ST	DURHAM CITY	8/11/14					TO 18th, 14th BNS CLASS Z RESERVE.	RAID 25/26th JUNE 16, AGE 27. AWOL 3/9/15.
CARROLL	Math	PTE	24	/143	B	983 WALKER RD	NEWCASTLE			1 JULY 1916		THIEPVAL MEM		BORN SACRISTON, MISSING AUGUST 16, AGE 40.
CARROLL	P	PTE	24	/314	A	55 CLYDESDALE RD	NEWCASTLE				OCTOBER 16.		TO LABOUR CORPS.	
CARROLL	Peter	SGT	24	/159		SUNDERLAND ST	BRANDON COLLIER							ALSO ON D COY 30th BN ROLL.
CARROLL	Peter	PTE	24	/1631	A	31 FRAMWELLGATE	DURHAM CITY	2/1/15	29/9/17	WOUNDS			TO DEPOT.	DRUNK AND DISORDERLY, AWOL, 11 APRIL 1915.
CARTER	JohnT	PTE	24	/617	B	72 CANNON ST ELSWICK	NEWCASTLE	8/11/14		1 JULY 1916		THIEPVAL MEM		MISSING SEPTEMBER 16, BORN FELLING.
CASE	Jas	LCPL	24	/443	B	4 WEST ROW	MIDDLE RAINTON			9 APRIL 1917		ARRAS MEM		BORN NORTH WALSHAM NORFOLK.
CASEY	O P	CPL	24	/1204									COMMISIONED 28 AUGUST 1917.	
CASS	JohnB	CPL	24	/340		46 ZETLAND ST MKWRMO	SUNDERLAND	3/11/14	22/8/17		OCTOBER 16		TO 85th TRAINING RESERVE BN.	
CASS	Tom R	PTE	24	/50		6 MILBURN ST	SUNDERLAND	13/11/14		11 FEB 1917		IN INDIA	TO 2nd GARRISON BN.	
CASSIDY	H	PTE	24	/1579	C	57 HEWITSON TERR	SOUTH FELLING				NOVEMBER 16		TO CLASS Z RESERVE.	WND SHOULDER. 34 CCS 2/7/16 EVAC 5/7/16 LCPL TRANSPORT SECTION.
CASSIDY	Thos	PTE	24	/22	B	52 PAINMURE ST	NEWCASTLE			18 OCTOBER 1918		TERLINCTHUN MIL CEM	TO 22nd, 24/27th,9th BNS.	
CASSIDY	Thos	PTE	24	/981	C	141 MAPLE ST	HIRST	10/11/14	27/12/17	GUNSHOT WOUNDS	OCTOBER 16		TO 85th TRAINING RESERVE BN.	
CAVANAGH	T	PTE	24	/1490	A		HALIFAX			KR para 392	MARCH 17.			
CHAPMAN	Albt	PTE	24	/18	A	104 COPELAND TERR	NEWCASTLE	26/10/14		6 NOVEMBER 1918		CITE BON JEAN MIL CEM		BORN MULLINGAR, AGE 22.
CHAPPLOW	H	PTE	24	/1674			HULL				OCTOBER 16.		FROM 34 DIV CYC COY, TO 23rd BN, CLASS Z RESERVE.	
CHARLTON	Geo	LSGT	24	/207		38 HARVEY ST	NEW BRANCEPETH						TO 85th TRAINING RESERVE BN, CLASS Z RESERVE.	
CHARLTON	Jacob	PTE	24	/173	A	FOSTERS YARD FLINTHI	DIPTON	5/11/14			MAY 16		TO 25th, 9th BNS, CLASS Z RESERVE.	
CHARLTON	Jn T	PTE	24	/302	A	CHURCH ST WALKER RD	NEWCASTLE	5/11/14		1 JULY 1916	NOVEMBER 16	THIEPVAL MEM		AWOL 27/4/15 IN COURT MORPETH 28/4/15.BORN WALKER.
CHARLTON	Robt	PTE	24	/501	B	8 CLEPHAN ST	DUNSTON	7/11/14	10/9/18	VDH	SEPTEMBER 16		TO EAST YORKSHIRE REGT, NORTHBLD FUSILIERS.	WND R KNEE. 34 CCS 2/7/16 EVAC 5/7/16
CHARLTON	Robt	PTE	24	/1038	C	13 HARPER ST	BLYTH			22 SEPT 1916	OCTOBER 16	THIEPVAL MEM	TO DURHAM LI(12th BN).	BORN SLEEKBURN, AGE 26, DLI No 45890.
CHARTERS	Pet A	LCPL	24	/884	C	20 GORDON ST	GATESHEAD	12/11/14		1 JULY 1916		THIEPVAL MEM		RAIDS 5/6th, 25/26th JUNE 16, BOMBER. 9 PLN
CHARTERS	Rob J	CPL	24	/882	C	20 GORDON ST	GATESHEAD	12/11/14		14 FEB 1917	OCTOBER 16, FEBRUARY 17.	ETAPLES	TO 16th BN.	GSW CHEST,THIGH,HAND AMPUTATED. 18 GEN HOSP 13/2/1
CHATT	J W	PTE	24	/962	C	15 BK WILLIAM ST	FELLING						TO MACHINE GUN CORPS.	MGC No 71009.
CHEESEMAN	J H	SGT	24	/1307	A 30	229 TAYLOR ST	SOUTH SHIELDS							
CHEESEMAN	J S	PTE	24	/1308	B	116 MARSHALL WALLIS	SOUTH SHIELDS	16/12/14	2/1/18	WOUNDS	JULY 16, AUG 16, JULY 17.		TO DEPOT.	
CHEESEMAN	L	PTE	24	/1387	A	200 JOHN WILLIAMSON	SOUTH SHIELDS				JULY 16.		TO LABOUR CORPS.	BEAUFORT WAR HOSP BRISTOL 12/7/16.
CHESSER	E	PTE	24	/809				9/11/14	10/4/16	SICK			TO 1st GARRISON BN, DEPOT.	
CHISHOLME	Geo	PTE	24	/1114	D	3 PROSPECT TERR	SUNNISIDE SWALW			17 APRIL 1917		GEZAINCOURT MIL CEM	FROM 34 DIV CYCLIST COY TO 19th BN.	BORN WHICKHAM, AGE 31, A CYC CORPS No 9666.
CHRISTIE	K	PTE	24	/296	B									ALSO ON D COY 30th BN ROLL.
CLARK	E	PTE	24	/1388	C			16/12/14	31/3/19	KR para 392			TO ARMY RESERVE CLASS P.	
CLARK	Frncs	PTE	24	/549		20 WEST ROW	BLACKHILL	28/10/14		KR para 392			TO 1st GARRISON BN.	
CLARK	Wm	PTE	24										TO 30th BN.	AWOL 5/4/15 COURT 8/4/15, AWOL 30th BN 5/9 COURT 8
CLARKE	John	PTE	24	/388	B	2 TRAFALGER ST	CONSETT	8/11/14		17 OCT 1917		TYNE COT MEM	TO 25th BN.	
CLARKE	Peter	PTE	24	/1170		25 KNITSLEY GDNS	CONSETT	10/11/14	24/11/16	KR para 392			TO 1st GARRISON BN.	
CLAUGHAN	Thos	PTE	24	/913	C	36 CROSS KEYS LANE	LOW FELL	12/11/14			OCTOBER 16		TO ARMY SERVICE CORPS(M T).	WND R LEG,34 CCS 2/7 EVAC 5/7/16 ASC No T/406567.
CLAYTON	Jas	PTE	24	/1543			EVERTON			1 JULY 1916				
CLIFF	J	PTE	24	/1673			NEWCASTLE	6/1/15	30/7/17	KR para 392	OCTOBER 16.		FROM 20th BN(A COY), 34 DIV CYC COY, TO DEPOT.	ORIGINAL 20th BN No 20/1243.
CLIFFORD	John	PTE	24	/379	A	FRONT ST	BURNHOPE							ALSO ON D COY 30th BN ROLL.
CLIFFORD	P	PTE	24	/377	A	FRONT ST	BURNHOPE				APRIL 16			ON B ROLL AS CUFFARD
CLOW	J	PTE	24	/21	D		NEWCASTLE				OCTOBER 16		TO LABOUR CORPS.	
COCHRANE	J W	PTE	24	/1588	B		SUNDERLAND				JUNE 17.		TO LABOUR CORPS.	LAB CORPS No 496361.
CODIA	J	PTE	24	/154	A	13 CARLIOL ST	NEWCASTLE	4/11/14	19/3/18	GUNSHOT WOUNDS	OCTOBER 16		TO ARMY RESERVE CLASS P.	RAID 25/26 JUNE 16. 34 CCS 2/7/16 EVAC 5/7/16
COLBY	Mich	PTE	24	/940	C	FRONT ST	DIPTON			17 JULY 1916		NUNHEAD LONDON.		BORN WIGAN, AGE 27.
COLEBY	G	CSM	24	/987									COMMISIONED NF.	
COLEMAN	ThosG	PTE	24	/805	C	13 OAK ST	GATESHEAD	12/11/14		26 OCT 1917	AUGUST 16	TYNE COT MEM	TO 25th, 1/4th BNS.	ALLOTED NEW NUMBER 204570, LCPL.
COLLINS	J P	PTE	24	/7	A	9 COLLEGE YARD	NEWCASTLE	2/11/14	8/4/19	KR para 392	OCTOBER 16		TO DEPOT.	
COLLINS	Mich	PTE	24			WALTONS ROW	BLACKHILL	31/10/14						LABOURER DESERTED 25/3/15, AGE 27, 5'7'', BORN BEN
COMERFORD	Jas	PTE	24	/57	A	MONUMENT COTTAGE	BIRTLEY	8/11/14					TO ROYAL DEFENCE CORPS.	FRANCE 11/1/16 TO 10/7/16, 7/2/17 TO 21/7/17

NAME	INITI	RANK	BA	NUMBE	COMP	ADDRESS	TOWN_VILL	ENLISTED	DISCHARG	CAUSE_DIS	WOUNDED	BURIED	TRANSFER	ADD
COMERFORD	Nich	PTE	24	/40		14 CLAVERING AVENUE	DUNSTON	2/11/14	27/12/16	SICK			TO 1st GARRISON BN, DEPOT.	
CONLIN	J	PTE	24	/422	D	16 HOPE ST	SUNDERLAND				OCTOBER 16		TO SCOTTISH RIFLES.	
CONLON	JohnJ	PTE	24	/241	A	32 ELSWICK EAST TERR	NEWCASTLE			3 JULY 1916		PUNCHVILLIERS MIL CEM		AWOL 29/11/15, 3/12/15. 3 CCS 2/7/16 DIED.BORN WIL
CONNELLY	Tom	CPL	24	/1574	C		DIPTON			1 JULY 1916		THIEPVAL MEM		BORN CARLISLE. IN 10 PLATOON.
CONNOLLY	Jas	PTE	24	/55		3 SHOT FACTORY LANE	NEWCASTLE	26/10/14		KR para 392			TO 1st GARRISON BN.	
CONNOLLY	Jerem	PTE	24	/1133	D	32 LUCKER ST	LEMINGTON ON TY	7/11/14	9/9/18	GUNSHOT WOUNDS	AUGUST 16		TO DEPOT.	BOMBER,RAID 5/6th JUNE 16, POW REPATRIATED 2/18.
CONNOLLY	John	SGT	24	/585		225 COMMERCIAL RD	BYKER	9/11/14	25/10/17	2 FEB 1918	AUGUST 16	HEATON	TO DEPOT.	WND SCALP.CQMS.34 CCS 2/7 HOSP SHEFFIELD, AGE 49.
CONNOLLY	John	PTE	24	/1151	D	120 MILBURNGATE	DURHAM CITY	11/11/14					TO LABOUR CORPS(101 LAB COY).	LAB CORPS No 397189, 107 MILBURNGATE 1918.
CONNOR	G	PTE	24	/973				9/11/14	10/3/16				TO 30th BN.	DID NOT SERVE OVERSEAS.
CONNOR	Hugh	SGT	24	/854		23 CHARLES ST	GATESHEAD						TO 12/13th BN, LABOUR CORPS.	LAB CORPS No 566210, AWOL 26/7/15 COURT 4/8/15.
CONNOR	J	PTE	24	/8	A		NEWCASTLE	2/11/14	3/6/18	26 JUNE 1918	MARCH 18	LONGBENTON	TO 3rd BN.	
CONNOR	Pat	PTE	24	/295	B	61 JOHN ST	HEBBURN NEWTOWN	2/11/14		21 MARCH 1918		ARRAS MEM	TO 22nd BN.	BORN CARLISLE. 52 GRACE ST HEBBURN 1918.
CONVERY	Hugh	PTE	24	/368	B	284 CHURCH ST	WALKER	27/10/14			JULY 16		TO LABOUR CORPS.	
CONWAY	Bernd	PTE	24	/1017	C	3 CURRY ST	CONSETT	12/11/14		KR para 392	AUGUST 16			3 CCS 2/7/16 EVAC 3/7/16 BORN MAGHERFELL
CONWAY	H	PTE	24	/548	B									ALSO ON D COY 30th BN ROLL.
CONWAY	W H	PTE	24	/5	A								TO LABOUR CORPS.	
COOK	J A	PTE	24	/1087			PENSHAW	9/11/14	24/10/17	WOUNDS	OCTOBER 16		TO & FROM 34 DIV CYCLIST COY, 3rd BN.	
COOK	Jas	PTE	24	/963	C	13 FRONT ST	BEBSIDE			1 JULY 1916		THIEPVAL MEM		MISSING SEPTEMBER 16.
COONEY	JohnP	PTE	24	/29	A	24 ATHOLL RD	SUNDERLAND	5/11/14			JUNE 18		TO 9th, 24/27th, 22nd BNS, CLASS Z RESERVE.	
COOPER	Sam	PTE	24	/1077	D	BIRDS NEST INN WALKE	NEWCASTLE	12/11/14			JULY 16, JUNE 18.		TO 9th, 22nd BNS, CLASS Z RESERVE.	AWOL 24/7/15. AGE 23, 34CCS 2/7/16 EVAC 5/7/16
CORRIGAN	John	PTE	24	/350	B	55 BEAUMONT TERR	WESTERHOPE	26/10/14		1 JULY 1916		THIEPVAL MEM		MISSING SEPTEMBER 16. BORN WESTPORT CO MAYO.
CORRIGAN	John	PTE	24	/1026	D	3 WALTERN ST	BLACKHILL	5/11/14						ALSO ON A COY 30th BN ROLL.
CORRIGAN	M	PTE	24	/332	A									DESERTED 28 MAY 1917
CORVEL		CPL	24											PHOTO IN IH.
COULSON	G	PTE	24	/432	B		BLYTH				JULY 16			3 CCS 2/7/16 EVAC 3/7/16
COULSON	James	PTE	24	/1499										DESERTED 25/5/15, AGE 23, 5'5'', LABOURER.
COWELL	Edwd	CPL	24	/614		16 WEBB ST	WHEATLEY HILL	11/11/14		KR para 392				
COX	S	SGT	24	/1233			EASINGTON			SHELLSHOCK	JULY 16.		TO 10th, 24th BNS.	
COYLE	John	SGT	24	/1214		8 BERNARD ST	HOUGHTON LE SPR	30/11/14	8/6/15	INEFFICIENT				DID NOT SERVE OVERSEAS.
CRAGGS	Jos	PTE	24	/1030	D	26 JOHN ST	WHEATLEY HILL	10/11/14	10/10/17	SICK			TO 85th TRAINING RESERVE BN.	HALF BROTHER PTE S HASTINGS 24/862.
CRAIG	Geo	PTE	24	/366			GATESHEAD							DESERTED 2/5/15, AGE 19, 5'4''.
CRAIGIE	A	PTE	24	/1666			SALFORD			KR para 392	AUGUST 16.		TO 25th, 1/5th BNS.	ALLOTED NEW NUMBER 243143.
CRAVEN	John	PTE	24	/403	D	130 VINE ST	GATESHEAD	28/10/14					TO 24/27th, 11th BNS, CLASS Z RESERVE.	
CRAWLEY	JohnW	PTE	24	/423	B	15 TENNYSON ST STHWI	SUNDERLAND	6/11/14						
CREIGHTON	JohnW	PTE	24	/541	D	71 THOMAS TERR	BLAYDON	10/11/14		1 JULY 1916		THIEPVAL MEM		RAID 5/6 JUNE 16, MISSING SEPTEMBER 16.
CROMPTON	Jas	PTE	24	/99	A	40 MARGARETS TERR	ROWLANDS GILL			1 JULY 1916		THIEPVAL MEM		BOMBER, TOOK PART IN TRENCH RAID 25/26 JUNE 16
CROSS		SGT		/461										34 CCS 2/7/16 EVAC 5/7/16,No ALSO ALLOTED TO LOCKE
CROSS	John	CPL	24	/608		22 WEAR ST	WILLINGTON	29/10/14		1 JULY 1916		THIEPVAL MEM		BORN WHITEHAVEN, AGE 38.
CROUDEN	Jas	PTE	24	/897	C	99 ASKEW RD	GATESHEAD			1 JULY 1916		THIEPVAL MEM		MISSING SEPTEMBER 16, LCPL.
CULLEN	Tom H	PTE	24	/1112	D	21 HILL ST	NEWCASTLE	12/11/14						
CUMESKEY	Corma	SGT	24	/855		227 PHILP ST	NEWCASTLE			29 AUGUST 1917	JULY 16	HOISEL COM CEM	TO 24/27th BN.	ALLOTED NEW NUMBER 42486.
CUMMINGS	Jn W	PTE	24	/1386	C	LONG ST	LITTLETOWN			1 JULY 1916		OVILLIERS		RAIDS 5/6, 25/26 JUNE 16. BORN SHERBURN HILL
CUNNINGHAM	Alf	CPL	24	/730		6 ELLISON PLACE	DUNSTON	28/10/14		KR para 392			TO 25th, 24th, 24/27th, 8th, 1st BNS.	3 CCS 2/7/16 EVAC 3/7/16
CUNNINGHAM	Peter	PTE	24	/729	A	98 CLAVERING AVENUE	DUNSTON	9/11/14	22/9/17	WOUNDS			TO DEPOT.	
CURRY	F	PTE	24	/559	D	78 ELSWICK ROW	NEWCASTLE				AUGUST 16		TO 1/4th BN, CLASS Z RESERVE.	NEW NUMBER 204572, WND SIDE, AGE 41 34 CCS 2/7/16.
CUTHBERT	B	PTE	24	/641	C	TYNE ST	FELLING SHORE							BILLQUAY HEWORTH 1918 ON A COY 30th BN ROLL.
DAGLISH	Wm	PTE	24	/1589	D		JARROW			1 JULY 1916		THIEPVAL MEM		MISSING SEPTEMBER 16.
DAVIES	Ed	PTE	24	/1569			LIVERPOOL			1 JULY 1916		THIEPVAL MEM		
DAVISON	Mich	CPL	24	/666	B	15 SCOTLAND ST	RYHOPE COLLIERY			9 APRIL 1917	JULY 16	FOCLINCOURT VALLEY CEM		WND HIP+BACK. 34 CCS 2/7/16 EVAC 5/7, BIRMINGHAM H
DAVISON	R	PTE	24	/1238	B		BEBSIDE	15/12/14	19/4/18	GUNSHOT WOUNDS	MARCH 16.		TO ARMY RESERVE CLASS P.	
DAWSON	J W	PTE	24	/1237	A			16/12/14	27/8/17	GUNSHOT WOUNDS			TO 3rd BN.	
DAWSON	Math	PTE	24	/953	D	47 JOHN ST	BLAYDON	12/11/14			OCTOBER 16		TO 23rd, 9th BNS, CLASS Z RESERVE.	
DEAN	Dan	PTE	24	/1549	D		WORKINGTON			1 JULY 1916		THIEPVAL MEM		MISSING SEPTEMBER 16.
DEAN	Nathn	PTE	24	/488	B	22 PARKINSON ST	FELLING	10/11/14						
DEEGAN	Mich	PTE	24	/1128		85 CHESTNUT ST	HIRST						TO 1st GARRISON BN, CLASS Z RESERVE.	
DELANEY	Tim	PTE	24	/814	C	5 DUNNES TERR	BYKER	28/10/14			OCT 16, SHELLSHOCK FEB 17		TO 16th, 1/6th BNS, CLASS Z RESERVE.	
DENNIS	L	PTE	24	/1476	B		LIVERPOOL				OCTOBER 16		TO 1/5th, 12/13th BNS, CLASS Z RESERVE.	WND ABDOMEN, AGE 20, SGT.25 AMB TRAIN,18 GEN HOSP
DERRICK	Pat	LCPL	24	/203		GALLONS YARD	FELLING SHORE	29/10/14		17 FEB 1918	JULY 16	HEWORTH ST MARYS CH YD	TO ROYAL ARMY MEDICAL CORPS(10th COY CHATHAM).	BOMBER, RAID 25/26 JUNE 16. 3CCS 2/7/16 GSW.
DEVINE	Hugh	PTE	24	/201	B	14 ARMSTRONG BLDGS	FELLING	4/11/14	3/11/17	SICK	APRIL 16		TO 30th BN	
DEVINE	Jas	PTE	24	/679	D	8 PACES BLDGS BACK L	NEWCASTLE	28/10/14		1 JULY 1916		THIEPVAL MEM		MISSING SEPTEMBER 16.

NAME	INITI	RANK	BA	NUMBE	COMP	ADDRESS	TOWN_VILL	ENLISTED	DISCHARG	CAUSE_DIS	WOUNDED	BURIED	TRANSFER	ADD
DEVINE	John	PTE	24	/907	D		BERWICK			1 OCT 1916		THIEPVAL MEM	TO 30th BN(B COY), KINGS OWN YORKSHIRE LI(8th BN).	AGE 23.34 CCS 2/7/16 EVAC 5/7/16 WND L ARM.
DEVLIN	Fcs J	PTE	24	/391	B	11 ARK ST	CONSETT	5/11/14	8/3/18	GUNSHOT WOUNDS	AUGUST 16		TO ARMY RESERVE CLASS P.	BORN CASTLE DAWSON.
DIAMOND	Mich	PTE	24	/6	A	27 ELDON ST	GATESHEAD	2/11/14	21/5/18	GUNSHOT WOUNDS				ENFIELD LODGE DURHAM RD 1918.
DIAMOND	V	SGT	24	/478		1 LIDDLE TERR	BENSHAM	7/11/14	3/1/18	SHELLSHOCK			TO 3rd BN.	INITIAL GIVEN AS C ON MR.
DIBDEN	F	PTE	24	/1389	A		GATESHEAD				JULY 16.		TO LABOUR CORPS.	
DILLON	J	PTE	24	/1046	D	68 CROFT RD	BLYTH						TO LABOUR CORPS.	
DIXON	G	PTE	24	/941	C	FRIEKS BLDGS HILLTOP	DIPTON	9/11/14	24/8/17	GUNSHOT WOUNDS	OCTOBER 16.		TO DEPOT.	
DIXON	G	PTE	24	/1000	D								TO 22nd BN, CLASS Z RESERVE.	
DIXON	Harry	PTE	24	/1069	D	32 ATTWOOD ST TUDHOE	SPENNYMOOR						TO 24/27th, 9th, 14th, 9th BNS.	16 PLN D COY 9th BN.
DIXON	John	PTE	24	/47	A 30	100 FRONT ST	LEADGATE	28/10/14						DICKSON WM ALSO AT THIS ADDRESS 28014 KOR LANCS.
DIXON	JohnW	CPL	24	/621			BLAYDON			9 APRIL 1917		ROCLINCOURT MIL CEM		
DIXON	Peter	PTE	24	/915	C	84 SANDYFORD RD	BYKER	12/11/14			AUGUST 16, OCTOBER 16.		TO 25th, 1/5th BNS, CLASS Z RESERVE.	NEW NUMBER 243146. HOSP LIECESTER 8/7/16
DIXON	W	PTE	24	/569	D		BLAYDON	6/11/14	31/7/17	WOUNDS	OCTOBER 16		TO 85th TRAINING RESERVE BN.	WND FOREARM, AGE 27.34 CCS 2/7/16 EVAC 5/7/16.
DOCHERTY	Chas	PTE	24	/709	C	YOUNGS BIULDINGS	TANTOBIE	27/10/14		2 JULY 1916	1 JULY 1916	PUNCHEVILLIERS MIL CEM		BORN DIPTON, AGE 24. 3 CCS 2/7/16 DIED IN CCS
DOCHERTY	G	SGT	24	/1311	A 30		USWORTH	19/12/14	31/3/19	KR para 392	OCTOBER 16, MARCH 18.		TO 30th BN, 24th BN(B COY), ARMY RESERVE CLASS P.	WND SCALP,BACK+THIGHS. 34 CCS 2/7/16 EVAC 5/7/16
DOCHERTY	J	PTE	24	/939	C		DIPTON				JULY 16, FEBRUARY 18.		TO 19th, 22nd BNS, CLASS Z RESERVE.	ACPL., 34CCS 2/7/16 EVAC 5/7/16 GSW L LEG.
DOCKERTY	Hugh	PTE	24	/636		TOWER HOUSE	NEWCASTLE	9/11/14	17/4/19	KR para 392			TO 1st GARRISON BN, DEPOT.	
DODDS	Jn T	PTE	24	/1313		COMMERCIAL COTTAGE	SHERBURN HILL			28 SEPT 1918		DUISANS BRIT MIL CEM	TO 26th, 8th, 2nd BNS.	BROTHERS R DODDS 26th BN, G DODDS KIA WITH DLI
DODDS	T	PTE	24	/1607	B		GATESHEAD				OCTOBER 16		TO KINGS OWN YORKSHIRE LI, ROYAL ENGINEERS.	
DODDS	T G	CQMS	24	/1641	A 30									
DODDS	Tom	PTE	24	/1672		12 BULLEN ST	FELLING			1 JULY 1916		THIEPVAL MEM	FROM 34 DIV CYC COY.	MISSING SEPTEMBER 16, BORN HEWORTH.
DODDS	Wm	PTE	24	/141	D	21 CUTHBERT ST	BLAYDON				OCTOBER 16			
DODSWORTH	Hen E	PTE	24	/97	D 30	225 JANET ST	BYKER	26/10/14					TO 30th BN.	AWOL 24th BN 21/5/15 IN COURT 22/5/15,AWOL 2/8/15
DONAGHY	J	LCPL	24	/1498	C		NEWCASTLE				OCTOBER 16		TO LABOUR CORPS.	
DONNELLY	F	LCPL	24	/436				29/10/14	30/1/18	ARTHRITIS			TO 24/27th, 3rd BNS.	
DONNELLY	J	PTE	24	/1218				10/11/14	14/3/18	VDH			TO 2nd GARRISON BN, 3rd BN.	
DONNELLY	J E	PTE	24	/466	A	12 WYNYARD ST	TUNSTALL				AUGUST 16		TO 1st, 10th BNS, CLASS Z RESERVE.	SCOUT, RAID 5/6 JUNE 16.
DONNELLY	Law P	SGT	24	/470		27 HOWARD ST	MORPETH	26/10/14		1 JULY 1916	JULY 16	THIEPVAL MEM		MISSING SEPTEMBER 16.
DONNELLY	Pat	PTE	24	/783	A	GALLONS YARD	FELLING SHORE	6/11/14						NOTE ON MR 'DIED'
DONOVAN	Corn	PTE	24	/588	D		CORK			19 JULY 1916	AUGUST 16	CORK ST JOSEPH'S CEM		
DORRIAN	John	PTE	24	/912		5 CARLTON ST	SHIELDFIELD			13 NOV 1916		AADDOLRATA MIL CEM MALTA	TO 1st GARRISON BN.	BORN DOWN IRELAND.
DOUGHERTY	Anth	PTE	24											AWOL 25/7/15 COURT 28/7/15.
DOUGHERTY	Jas	PTE	24	/176	A	QUEENS ROW	WALBOTTLE		7/1/19				TO 24/27th, 23rd BNS, 24th BN ROYAL FUSILIERS.	IN FRANCE 11/1/16, 24/27 10/8/17, 23NF 5/4/18 24RF
DOUGLAS	JohnJ	PTE	24	/928	C		GATESHEAD				JUNE 17, DECEMBER 17.		TO 8th, 12/13th, 1st BNS, CLASS Z RESERVE.	AWOL 19/8/15 IN COURT GATESHEAD, AGE 23.
DOUGLAS	T	PTE	24	/248	B	1 PATTERSONS COURT	NEWCASTLE	2/11/14						ALSO ON D COY 30th BN ROLL.
DOURISH	Jas	LCPL	24	/930	C	105 ABBOTT ST	GATESHEAD	10/11/14	11/4/17	WOUNDS	JULY 16.		TO DEPOT.	TOOK PART IN TRENCH RAID 25/26 JUNE 16.
DOURISH	JohnW	PTE	24	/46	A		GATESHEAD			1 JULY 1916		THIEPVAL MEM		MISSING SEPTEMBER 16
DOYLE	Henry	SGT	24	/101			NEWCASTLE			17 JANUARY 1917		RATION FARM MIL CEM	COMMISIONED 26th BN, TO 34th DIV CYC COY, TO 26th	MEDAL ROLL SHOWS 24th BN rank and number.
DOYLE	Thos	PTE	24	/652	B	95 ALBERT ST	GATESHEAD	28/10/14		8 JULY 1916	AUGUST 16	ABBEVILLE		DOYLE EDWARD IN AVL AT THIS ADDRESS ASC ATT RFC.
DOYLE	Wm	PTE	24	/1312		22 HUMBER ST	CHOPWELL						TO 1st GARRISON BN, CLASS Z RESERVE.	
DRYDEN	Rob O	PTE	24	/859	D	48 HIGH ST EAST	WALLSEND	28/10/14					TO LABOUR CORPS.	LAB CORPS No 401674.
DUFFY	Art A	PTE	24	/28	A	28 WILLIAM ST	NEWCASTLE	28/10/14			AUGUST 16		TO TANK CORPS.	3 CCS 2/7/16 EVAC 2/7/16. GSW.
DUFFY	J	PTE	24	/1239	D								TO LABOUR CORPS.	ON MR AS /1234, LABOUR CORPS No 397208.
DUFFY	J W	PTE	24	/1545	A	25 DOVER TERR	SOUTHMOOR	8/1/15	10/4/18	SICK			TO 24/27th BN, DEPOT.	
DUFFY	Jas	PTE	24	/188	A	7 QUAKING HOUSES	SOUTHMOOR	6/11/14		8 FEBRUARY 1917	OCTOBER 16	THIEPVAL MEM	TO 14th, 9th BNS.	WND L HAND, AGE 26, 34 CCS 2/76/16 EVAC 5/7/16.
DUFFY	Jas	PTE	24	/771		BROWNS BIULDINGS	ESH WINNING	26/10/14					TO 1st GARRISON BN, CLASS Z RESERVE.	
DUFFY	Jas	PTE	24	/1658	D								TO LABOUR CORPS, CLASS Z RESERVE.	ACPL, LAB CORPS No 571011, ST BEARER,RAID 25/26th
DUFFY	John	PTE	24	/238	A	12 BRUNEL ST	NEWCASTLE	2/11/14	2/6/18	SICK	MARCH 18		TO 24/27th, 3rd BNS.	AGE 38.
DUFFY	John	PTE	24	/325	D	78 CUTHBERT ST	BLAYDON	27/10/14			JAN 17		TO 5th TRAINING RESERVE BN.	TRES No TR5/590079.
DUFFY	Math	SGT	24	/558		5 THORNEHOLME TERR	STANLEY	26/10/14		1 JULY 1916		GORDON DUMP CEM		AGE 22.
DUFFY	Owen	SGT	24	/1155		7 MOUNT STEWART ST	DAWDON	9/11/14	14/10/16	VDH			TO 1st GARRISON BN, DEPOT.	
DUFFY	Rob	PTE	24	/794	D	24 YORKSHIRE ST	NEWCASTLE	28/10/14					TO COMMAND DEPOT NF, LABOUR CORPS.	AWOL 29/5/15 IN COURT 5/6/15.
DUFFY	Thom	PTE	24	/701	A	BROWNS BIULDINGS	ESH WINNING	26/10/14		28 APRIL 1917	OCTOBER 16	ARRAS MEM	TO 19th, 22nd BNS.	34 CCS 2/7 EVAC 5/7 2nd SOUTHERN HOSP BRISTOL 11/7
DUGGAN	Mich	PTE	24	/228	A	20 HOLLY ST	FELLING			1 JULY 1916		THIEPVAL MEM		NOK 46 WYLAM RD GATESHEAD. MISSING SEPTEMBER 16.BO
DUIGNAN	Philp	PTE	24	/945	D		COXHOE			1 JULY 1916		THIEPVAL MEM		
DUNCAN	Robt	PTE	24											AWOL 28/6/15 COURT SUNDERLAND
DUNN	Geo	PTE	24	/672	C	36 BURDON ST	GATESHEAD	28/10/14			OCTOBER 16		TO TANK CORPS.	TANK CORPS No 73715.
DUPREY	JohnA	SGT	24	/35		30 RAILWAY ST	NEWCASTLE	2/11/14	8/3/18		OCTOBER 16		TO 24th, 23rd, 24th, 19th, 24/27th BNS.	
DYKES	Thos	PTE	24	/125		109 EDWARD ST	BLAYDON	2/11/14	5/1/15	INEFFICIENT				DID NOT SERVE OVERSEAS.
EAGLESHAM	Math	PTE	24	/774	D	6 MARIA ST	NEWCASTLE	28/10/14			JULY 16		TO ROYAL ARMY MEDICAL CORPS.	

NAME	INITIAL	RANK	BN	NUMBER	COMP	ADDRESS	TOWN_VILL	ENLISTED	DISCHARG	CAUSE_DIS	WOUNDED	BURIED	TRANSFER	ADD
EDMONSTON	R	SGT	24	/1500				1/1/15	20/6/17	SICK			TO 1st GARRISON BN, DEPOT.	
EGAN	W	PTE	24	/803	D			6/11/14	8/12/18	SICK			ATTACHED 34th DIVISIONAL EMPLOYMENT COY, TO 3rd BN	
EGAN	W	PTE	24	/1150	D	74 GEORGE ST	BLAYDON				OCTOBER 16, JUNE 18.		TO 16th, 25th BNS, CLASS Z RESERVE.	TOOK PART IN TRENCH RAIDS 5/6th 25/26th JUNE 1916.
ELLIOTT	J	PTE	24	/749	A									ON D COY 30th BN ROLL, ON ROLL AS 732.
ELLIOTT	J	PTE	24	/785	C									ALSO ON D COY 30th BN ROLL.
ELLIOTT	J	PTE		/732	A									No ALSO ALLOTED TO BIRNEY R
ELLIS	Thos	PTE	24	/1620		111 JOHN ST	BLAYDON	12/11/14						CHEMICAL COTTAGE BLAYDON 1914.
EMBLETON	Edwd	PTE	24	/1071	D	47 SALVIN ST	SPENNYMOOR	28/10/14			JULY 16, DECEMBER 16.		TO LABOUR CORPS., ATTACHED DURHAM LI.	LAB CORPS No 389722.
EMMERSON	F W	PTE	24	/106	A	135 PARKER ST	BYKER			KR para 392				
ENGLISH	Alex	LCPL	24	/764	B	3 MADDISONS ROW	DIPTON	31/10/14		14 SEPT 1916		CONTALMAISON CHATEAU		SEE 24/765 BROTHER M.
ENGLISH	Mich	PTE	24	/765	B	3 MADDISONS ROW	DIPTON	31/10/14			JUNE 16, JULY 16.		TO 1/4th BN, CLASS Z RESERVE.	SEE 24/764 BROTHER A.
ENGLISH	W	PTE	24	/1488	B	9 GLADSTONE TERR	USWORTH COLLIER				AUGUST 16.		TO 11th BN.	DESERTED 9 NOVEMBER 1918. HOSP LEICESTER 8/7/16
BRETT	J	CSM	24	/618							MARCH 16		TO LABOUR CORPS(COMMISSIONED).	
ERSKINE	Adam	PTE	24	/1315	C	61 KING ST	BIRTLEY						TO LABOUR CORPS.	TRANSPORT SECTION.
ETHRINGTON	Geo	PTE	24	/1590	B	LONG ROW	COXHOE	13/1/15	12/7/18	WOUNDS			TO DEPOT.	
EYRE	Pat	LCPL	24	/462	A	16 STOCKTON RD	RYHOPE COLLIERY	2/11/14		2 SEPT 1916		THIEPVAL MEM		BORN HEBBURN.
FAIRHURST	Math	PTE	24	/1191			WHEATLEY HILL			1 JULY 1916		THIEPVAL MEM	TO & FROM 34 DIV CYCLIST COY.	MISSING SEPTEMBER 16, BORN EASINGTON.
FALCUS	Josh	PTE	24	/1504	A	54 COWPER ST	GATESHEAD	7/1/15			MARCH 16		TO 27th BN.	
FALCUS	Rob	PTE	24	/1507	A	6 NETTLE ST	DUNSTON	4/1/15	21/12/17	SICK			TO 3rd BN.	MISSING SEPTEMBER 16, NOT MISSING DECEMBER 16.
FALLON	Edw	PTE	24	/911	C	86 HIGH ST	NEWCASTLE	28/10/14		13 MARCH 1916		BREWERY ORCHARD CEM		
FALLON	J	PTE	24	/920	C	13 DERWENT ST	BLACKHILL						TO 8th, 1/7th BNS.	DESERTED 7 AUGUST 1918.
FALLON	Pat	PTE	24	/828	B	44 DAVIS ST	WALLSEND	28/10/14			OCTOBER 16		TO LABOUR CORPS.	BOLDON COLLIERY IN GAZ.
FALLOON	John	PTE	24											AWOL + ASSAULTS POLICE CONSTABLE 21/8/15.
FARRELL	J	PTE	24	/1470	B	16 BRIDGE ST	GATESHEAD							
FARRINGTON	Wm	PTE	24	/758		47 SPENCER ST	GATESHEAD	28/10/14					TO 12th, 12/13th, 20th, 18th BNS, CLASS Z RESERVE.	
FENNELLY	Jos	PTE	24	/1518	D		NEWCASTLE			14 NOV 1916	OCTOBER 16	ST SEVER CEM ROUEN		BOMBER,RAID 5/6 JUNE 16. DESERTED 16/2/15 COURT 1/
FENWICK	Arth	PTE	24	/1317		19 CHURCH ST	DURHAM CITY	28/10/14		1 JULY 1916		GORDON DUMP CEM		DRUNK AND DISORDERLY IN DURHAM 16 APRIL 1915.
FINLAY	Harry	PTE	24	/92	A	LONG RIGG	SWALWELL			KR para 392	OCTOBER 16		TO 18th BN.	HOSP FISHPONDS BRISTOL 8/7/16. DESERTED 7/5/17
FINLAY	Wm	PTE	24	/472	C	3 VICTORIA ST	PRUDHOE	26/10/14			OCTOBER 16			ALLOTED NEW NUMBER 292096
FINLEY	F	PTE	24	/63	A									WND SHLDER,AGE 41, 34 CCS 2/7/16 EVAC 5/7/16.
FINNERAN	T	SGT	24	/264		30 CHEVIOT VEIW	GOSFORTH	31/10/14			OCTOBER 16		TO 9th BN, CLASS Z RESERVE.	RAID 25/26 JUNE 1916.3 CCS 2/7/16 EVAC 2/7/16.
FISHER	J	PTE	24	/328	C	167 ST CUTHBERTS RD	GATESHEAD	5/11/14	1/3/19				TO 1st BN, ARMY RESERVE CLASS P.	
FISHER	Thos	PTE	24	/871	D	26 QUARRY ST	WHEATLEY HILL	9/11/14	31/3/19				TO 23rd BN, ARMY RESERVE CLASS P.	
FISK	Wm M	PTE	24	/769	C	31 SCHOOL TERR SOUTH	WEST STANLEY			16 JUNE 1917	AUGUST 16	SOUTHMOOR	TO 14th, 9th BNS.	BORN LOWESTOFT, AGE 30, ACCIDENTLY DROWNED.
FITZGERALD	G	PTE	24	/850	D								TO ROYAL ENGINEERS.	
FITZGERALD	Jas	PTE	24	/19		204 PILGRIM ST	NEWCASTLE	2/11/14		22 JANUARY 1916		HEATON		BORN BALLINA.
FITZPATRICK	Jas	PTE	24	/651	B	26 STEPNEY LANE	NEWCASTLE	28/10/14		8 AUGUST 1917	NOVEMBER 16	RAMSCAPPELLE	TO 8th, 16th BNS.	
FLANAGHAN	Thos	PTE	24	/420	B	19 DEAN TERR	SOUTHWICK	6/11/14			OCTOBER 16, NOVEMBER 18.		TO 21st, 8th, 1/5th BNS, SGT CLASS Z RESERVE.	MACHINE GUNNER, RAIDS 5/6, 25/26 JUNE 16
FLATT	Alf	CPL	24	/1182	D	6 JAMES ST	SEAHAM			6 AUGUST 1916		DIVION		DIED OF SELF INFLICTED WOUNDS.
FLEMING	J	PTE	24	/1678				9/12/14	7/1/18	KR para 392				
FLETCHER	J	PTE	24	/1316	B									ALSO ON D COY 30th BN ROLL.
FLINTHAM	Geo	PTE	24	/710	C	2 MOORE ST	DARLINGTON	29/10/14						
FLYNN	Jas	PTE	24	/576		16 FRAMWELLGATE	DURHAM CITY	28/10/14					TO 1st GARRISON BN, CLASS Z RESERVE.	
FLYNN	Jas	PTE	24	/702	B	21 EDWARD ST	TANFIELD						TO ROYAL ARMY MEDICAL CORPS.	RAMC No 135126.
FLYNN	T	PTE	24	/402	B	3 HOPPER SQUARE	HOUGHTON LE SPR	2/11/14			JULY 16		TO 9th BN, CLASS Z RESERVE.	
FOLEY	Edw	PTE	24	/753	D	25 LAWSON TERR	DURHAM CITY	12/11/14		16 SEPT 1916		THIEPVAL MEM		MISSING FEBRUARY 17.
FORD	Edwd	PTE	24	/105	A	26 PORTLAND RD	NEWCASTLE						TO MACHINE GUN CORPS(34th BN).	MGC No 151957.
FORD	Hugh	PTE	24	/163	A								TO LABOUR CORPS.	LAB CORPS No 710185, AWOL 9/3/15 IN COURT 10/3/15.
FORDY	John	PTE	24	/905	C	15 FOURTH ST SOUTH	EASINGTON COLLI	28/10/14	23/1/19				TO MACHINE GUN CORPS(34th BN), CLASS Z RESERVE.	MGC No 151958.
FORSTER	Hugh	PTE	24	/532		51 BURDON ST	GATESHEAD	10/11/14						RAID 25/26 JUNE 16.AWOL 4/8/15 AGE 25.
FORSTER	Jas	PTE	24	/570	C	43 EDGEWARE RD ELSWI	NEWCASTLE	6/11/14						
FORSTER	Jos	PTE	24	/239	A	10 ALBION ROW	BYKER	28/10/14		18 OCT 1917		TYNE COT MEM	TO 24/27th BN.	SCOUT,RAID 25/26 JUNE 16 MISSSING 9/16 REJOIN 12/1
FORSTER	Wm	PTE	24	/777	C	42 HOWARD ST	NEWCASTLE	6/11/14			APRIL 16			
FOSTER	Abrhm	PTE	24	/657	D	5 BACK LANE	DURHAM CITY	9/11/14	24/8/17	GUNSHOT WOUNDS	OCTOBER 16		TO DEPOT.	WND LEG, AGE 30. 2 GEN HOSP 4/7/16 EVAC 5/7/16
FOSTER	David	CPL	24	/1391		No 24	SHERBURN STATIO						TO 27th, 24/27th, 21st, 25th, 14th BNS, CLASS Z RE	
FOSTER	E	PTE	24	/309	A	HILL TOP	DIPTON							ALSO ON D COY 30th BN ROLL.
FOSTER	G	PTE	24	/1196	A	DURHAM ST	LANGLEY PARK							
FOSTER	Jas	PTE	24	/496			BRANDON			1 JULY 1916		THIEPVAL MEM		MISSING SEPTEMBER 16
FOSTER	Jas R	PTE	24											AWOL 11/8/15 IN COURT S SHIELDS.
FREMSON	Edw	PTE	24	/166	A	48 HENRY ST	NEWCASTLE	31/10/14			JULY 16			HOSP CHRIST CHURCH HANTS 15/7/16.

NAME	INITI	RANK	BA	NUMBE	COMP	ADDRESS	TOWN_VILL	ENLISTED	DISCHARG	CAUSE_DIS	WOUNDED	BURIED	TRANSFER	ADD
FRIELL	B	SGT	24	/102	D	30		3/11/14	24/5/16	SICK			TO 30th BN.	DID NOT SERVE OVERSEAS.
FRYER	John	PTE	24	/444	B	10 NORTH SIDE	BIRTLEY			1 JULY 1916		THIEPVAL MEM		MISSING SEPTEMBER 16, BORN NEWCASTLE. 7 PLN
GAFFNEY	Robt	PTE	24	/218	D	30 FRAMWELLGATE	DURHAM CITY	6/11/14		16 AUGUST 1917	OCTOBER 16	TYNE COT MEM	TO 8th BN.	SPRINGBURN HOSP GLASGOW 11/7/16.
GAFFNEY	T W	PTE	24	/135	B	64 WAPPING ST	SOUTH SHIELDS							
GALLAGHER	Dan	PTE	24	/616	A	7 BEACON LOUGH	GATESHEAD	9/11/14	21/9/18	GUNSHOT WOUNDS	JUNE 16, JULY 16,		TO 11th BN, DEPOT.	DANIEL SENIOR 64467 LCPL 52nd DLI.
GALLAGHER	H	PTE	24	/414	D	29 ALFRED ST	SOUTH SHIELDS	6/11/14	2/12/18	SICK			TO ARMY RESERVE CLASS W.	
GALLAGHER	J	PTE	24	/755	D	96 FRAMWELLGATE	DURHAM CITY	28/10/14			OCTOBER 16		TO ROYAL ARMY MEDICAL CORPS.	DESERTED 12/3/18, RAMC No 144078, HOLLIDAYS TERR S
GALLAGHER	John	CPL	24	/551		15 ELEVENTH ROW	ASHINGTON	7/11/14	15/12/17	GUNSHOT WOUNDS			TO 27th, 24th, DEPOT.	WND CHEST + ARM. 34 CCS 2/7/16 EVAC 5/7/16.
GARDENER	Aaron	PTE	24	/910	D	41 AMBERLEY ST TEAMS	GATESHEAD	12/11/14		17 JULY 1917		ACHIET LE GRAND	TO 19th, 14th BNS.	AWOL 13/7, 29/8/15 AGE 29 BORN BARRINGTON CAMBS.
GARDENER	Thos	PTE	24	/254	A	8 EASTBOURNE AVE	GATESHEAD	28/10/14			JULY 16		TO LABOUR CORPS.	6 HOWES COURT 1918. LAB CORPS No 654837. 3 CCS.
GARDNER	Jas	PTE	24	/988	C	101 VICTORIA RD TEAM	GATESHEAD	28/10/14		1 JULY 1916		THIEPVAL MEM		MISSING AUGUST 16, BORN DURHAM CITY, AGE 30.
GARDNER	Mich	PTE	24	/723	D	HORSECROFTS	BLAYDON				AUGUST 16		TO 3rd BN, LABOUR CORPS.	AGE 41,WND R LEG+BUTTOCK. LAB CORPS No 651859.
GARNER	E	PTE	24	/1467			CLEATOR MOOR			KR para 392	SEPTEMBER 16.		TO 27th BN.	
GARRAHAN	E	PTE	24	/1538	D		LIVERPOOL				JULY 16.		TO 16th, 19th(Z COY) BNS.	3 CCS 2/7/16 EVAC 2/7/16
GARRETT	Benj	PTE	24	/1241	C	3 LACKLAND ST	SOUTH SHIELDS			1 JULY 1916		THIEPVAL MEM		BORN NEWCASTLE.
GARSIDE	J	PTE	24	/489	C			7/11/14	22/3/19				TO ARMY RESERVE CLASS P	
GAULD	A	PTE	24	/964	C		NORTON ON TEES				OCTOBER 16		TO 23rd, 1/4th BNS, CLASS Z RESERVE.	ASGT.
GEE	ThosG	LCPL	24	/1654			NEW MILFORD PEM			5 JAN 1917		YPRES RESEVOIR CEM	TO 11th BN.	BORN NEYLAND PEMBROKE.
GERAGHTY	Pat	PTE	24	/817	C	5 PEARSON ST	WALKER	9/11/14	2/8/18	SICK	JANUARY 17		TO ROYAL DEFENCE CORPS, ARMY RESERVE CLASS P.	RDC No 69601, IN FRANCE 11/1/16 TO 4/9/16.
GETTINGS	Chas	PTE	24	/168	A	131 CLAVERING AVE	DUNSTON			23 OCTOBER 1917		TYNE COT MEM	TO 24/27th BN.	BORN CROOK.
GETTINGS	JohnW	PTE	24	/330	A	45 DONNISON ST	DUNSTON	6/11/14			OCTOBER 16		TO 10th BN, CLASS Z RESERVE.	LCPL.
GIBBON	R	PTE	24	/307	A	30								ON MR AS 24/, HALL I.S MAY BE 26/ BUT SHOWN AS 24/
GIBBONS	P	PTE	24	/1327	C		TRIMDON COLLIER				OCTOBER 16.		TO LABOUR CORPS.	LAB CORPS No 119837.
GIBLIN	Dan	PTE	24	/1618	B		WILLINGTON	8/3/15	14/3/18	VDH	OCTOBER 16.		TO 3rd BN.	
GIBSON	Henry	PTE	24	/1099	D	54 FRAMWELLGATE	DURHAM CITY	12/11/14		KR para 392	APRIL 16			
GIBSON	Jas	PTE	24	/674	C	219 SCHOOL ST	LANGLEY MOOR	12/11/14		1 JULY 1916		THIEPVAL MEM		NOK 61 PRINGLE PLACE NEW BRANCEPETH 1916, BORN SUN
GIBSON	Jas P	SGT	24	/473		24 PERCY ST	PRUDHOE	7/11/14	25/2/19	KR para 392			TO DEPOT.	
GIBSON	JohnE	PTE	24	/209	A	24 MARY ST	WEST STANLEY	4/11/14	20/12/17	WOUNDS	APRIL 16		TO 3rd BN.	LANGLEY PARK IN GAZETTE.
GIBSON	Wm	PTE	24	/887	B	39 OUTRAM ST	SUNDERLAND			20 MARCH 1917		BAILLEUL		
GILDEA	T C	PTE	24	/27	A		NEWCASTLE	2/11/14	7/3/18	SICK	JULY 16,OCTOBER 16.		TO ARMY RESERVE CLASS P	
GILLOONEY	John	PTE	24	/982		21 LEAZES PARK RD	NEWCASTLE	10/11/14					TO 24/27th, 14th, 12/13th BNS, CLASS Z RESERVE.	
GILPATRICK	J	PTE	24	/1116	D	24 CUTHBERT ST	BLAYDON							
GILROY	Hugh	PTE	24	/656	D	23 FRAMWELLGATE	DURHAM CITY	11/11/14		1 JULY 1916		THIEPVAL MEM		TRENCH RAID 5/6 JUNE 16. MISSING AUGUST 16.
GILROY	Jas	PTE	24	/230	D	8 CHARLES SQUARE	GATESHEAD	12/11/14					TO KINGS OWN YORKSHIRE LI.	
GOLDSBOROUGH	Edwd	PTE	24	/1142	D	78 ALEXANDER ST	ELSWICK	10/11/14					TO LABOUR CORPS.	
GOODE	E	ASGT	24	/1669			HUSSLINGFIELD				AUG 16, AUG 18.		FROM 34 DIV CYC COY, TO 26th BN, CLASS Z RESERVE.	
GORDON	Pat	PTE	24	/560	C	15 HELEN ST	BLAYDON	7/11/14	31/10/17	SHELLSHOCK	OCTOBER 16		TO DEPOT.	
GORMLEY	Wm	PTE	24	/216	A	40 STELLA RD	BLAYDON	5/11/14			OCTOBER 16		TO 27th BN, LABOUR CORPS.	LAB CORPS No 397969. 4 SKINNERY YARD 1918.
GOUGH	E	PTE	24	/1397	C	93 MAPLE ST HIRST	ASHINGTON						TO 8th BN, CLASS Z RESERVE.	
GOUNDRY	Jas	PTE	24	/174	A	21 HOLME ST	WEST STANLEY	4/11/14	16/5/18	GUNSHOT WOUNDS			TO DEPOT.	STRETCHER BEARER, TOOK PART IN TRENCH RAID 25/26 J
GOW	J S	PTE	24	/1657	A								TO 24/27th, 25th BNS, CLASS Z RESERVE.	SGT.
GRAHAM	Chas	PTE	24	/1396	D	MURTON VILLAGE	SHIREMOOR			5 JULY 1916		HEILLY STATION CEM		BORN BACKWORTH, age 21.
GRAHAM	J	PTE	24	/1067			NEWCASTLE	10/11/14	15/3/18	GUNSHOT WOUNDS	OCTOBER 16		TO DEPOT.	
GRAHAM	J T	CPL	24	/442				5/11/14	22/3/19	KR para 392			TO 1st BN, DEPOT.	TOOK PART IN TRENCH RAID 5/6 JUNE 16
GRAILEY	J	RSM	24	/1462									TO ROYAL FLYING CORPS.	SIGNALLER, RAID 5/6 JUNE 16
GRANT	John	PTE	24	/780		3 WATERLOO BIULDINGS	DIPTON	28/10/14		24 FEB 1915		LEADGATE		BORN BROOMS WORCESTERSHIRE, AGE 33.
GRANTHAM	Geo H	PTE	24	/1677		NEW FARM MARSHCHAPEL	THORSBY LINCONS			1 JULY 1916		THIEPVAL MEM		PROBABLY ORIGINALLY GRIMSBY CHUMS THEN 34 DIV CYC
GRAY	A	SGT	24	/1325									TO 24/27th, 8th BNS, ATTACHED WEST INDIES REGT, 11	
GRAY	J	LCPL	24	/761		83 RAILWAY ST	RYHOPE COLLIERY						TO 24/27th, 14th BNS, CLASS Z RESERVE.	SCOUT, TOOK PART IN TRENCH RAID 5/6 JUNE 16.
GRAY	Ralph	PTE	24	/1079	D	25 BYGATE ST	HEBBURN	28/10/14					TO LABOUR CORPS.	LAB CORPS No 446309.
GRAY	Thos	PTE	24	/632	C	238 HIGH ST	GATESHEAD	28/10/14						ALSO ON A COY 30th BN ROLL.
GRAY	Wm G	PTE	24	/1320		15 FORTH ST	CHOPWELL						TO 1st GARRISON BN, CLASS Z RESERVE.	
GREEN	H	PTE	24	/1157		28 ST ANNES TERR	STOCKTON			14 MAY 1917		DURHAM RD CEM STOCKTON		SERVED IN DURHAM LI DURING BOER WAR.
GREEN	J	PTE	24	/410	C								TO 24/27th, 11th BNS, CLASS Z RESERVE.	
GREEN	W	PTE	24	/1161	D	CURRY SQUARE	DIPTON				OCTOBER 16		TO LABOUR CORPS.	
GREENER	Thos	PTE	24	/1179		4 GEORGE ST	PONTOP	28/10/14		17 OCT 1918		ADDOLRATA MIL CEM MALTA	TO 1st GARRISON BN.	BORN LEADGATE.
GRIEVE	Tom	LCPL	24	/1650		BANK COTTAGE WHALTON	MORPETH			9 APRIL 1917		TILLOY	TO 1st BN NF.	BORN HAZELRIGG, AGE 43.
GRIMES	H	PTE	24	/653	A									
HAGAN	Domnc	PTE	24	/593	B		HOUGHTON LE SPR			1 JULY 1916		THIEPVAL MEM		MISSING AUGUST 16.
HALEY	Peter	PTE	24	/739	C		NEWCASTLE			1 JULY 1916		THIEPVAL MEM		MISSING AUGUST 16, MG SECTION.

										WOUNDED	BURIED	TRANSFER	ADD
HALFPENNY	H	PTE	24 /1400	A	5 WHORLTON TERR	SWALWELL	17/12/14	31/3/19	KR para 392			TO 25th BN, ARMY RESERVE CLASS P.	
HALFPENNY	John	PTE	24 /318	A	MARKET LANE	SWALWELL	6/11/14		28 APRIL 1917		ARRAS MEM		SEE 24/1400 PTE H.
HALL	Isaac	PTE	24 /307	B		HOUGHTON LE SPR			1 JULY 1916		THIEPVAL MEM		
HALL	J W	PTE	24 /242	A	11 ALMA PLACE	GRANGE VILLA						TO 18th, 14th BNS, CLASS Z RESERVE.	
HALL	Rich	PTE	24 /864	D		WHEATLEY HILL				OCTOBER 16		TO DURHAM LI.	DLI No 59321.
HALL	W	PTE	24 /895	D	200 PILGRIM ST	NEWCASTLE							
HALL	Wm	PTE	24 /1684		82 SOUTH ROW	WEST SLEEKBURN			1 JULY 1916		OVILLIERS	FROM 34 DIV CYC COY.	MISSING AUGUST 16, BORN CHOPPINGTON. ACC No 9744
HAMILTON	J D	PTE	24 /1242	B		BEBSIDE				OCTOBER 16.			
HAMILTON	R	PTE	24 /468	B	4 SECOND ROW	HASWELL PLOUGH	2/11/14			AUGUST 16		TO ROYAL DEFENCE CORPS.	IN FRANCE 11/1/16 TO 4/7/16.
HANLEY	Jos	PTE	24 /1091	D	16 LOVEGREEN ST SIDE	DURHAM CITY	12/11/14		5 JUNE 1921		REDHILLS RC CEM DURHAM	TO LABOUR CORPS(758 GAR GD COY) KRR CORPS(25th BN)	LAB CORPS No 397535, KRRC No 58385.
HANLEY	Mich	PTE	24 /661	D	126 MILBURNGATE	DURHAM CITY	28/12/14		1 JULY 1916		THIEPVAL MEM		MISSING AUGUST 16.
HANLEY	T	PTE	24 /746	C	28 HINDHAUGH ST	NEWCASTLE							ALSO ON D COY 30th BN ROLL.
HANN	J B	PTE	24 /1689			NEWBOTTLE				AUGUST 16.		TO 16th BN NF, ROYAL FUSILIERS.	
HANNAH	D	AWO2	24 /1670			NORTH LEITH				OCTOBER 16.		FROM 34 DIV CYC COY,TO 24/27th, 11th BNS ATT 8 WES	
HANSON	Cha W	PTE	24 /1688		114 HILYARD ST	GRIMSBY			2 JULY 1916		MEAULTE MIL CEM	FROM 34 DIV CYC COY.	ACC No 9512.
HANSON	J	PTE	24 /572	A		GATESHEAD				JULY 16			MISSING AUGUST 16, NOT MISSING NOVEMBER 16.
HARDCASTLE	Robt	PTE	24 /16	B	WILSON TERR	FOREST HALL	6/11/14			NOVEMBER 16			
HARDMAN	G	PTE	24 /1521	C	26 WILLIAM ST	SOUTHMOOR							
HARDY	Henry	PTE	24 /1401	C		SHILDON			1 JULY 1916		THIEPVAL MEM		IN 12 PLATOON MISSING NOVEMBER 16.
HARLAND	Adam	PTE	24 /249	A	5 LYONS LANE	HETTON LYONS				JULY 16		TO LABOUR CORPS.	LCPL, TOOK PART IN TRENCH RAID 25/26 JUNE 16.
HARMER	K B	PTE	24 /839	C	58 HARLE ST	GATESHEAD	9/11/14	2/11/17	WOUNDS	AUGUST 16		TO 20th BN, DEPOT.	ALSO ON D COY 30th BN ROLL.
HARRALD	C E	PTE	24 /1522		2 YORK RD	SEAHAM HARBOUR	.			NOVEMBER 16.			
HARRIS	Robt	CPL	24 /1402		7 MAY ST	BIRTLEY				JULY 16, JANUARY 18.		TO 34 DIV CYC COY, 25th, 24/27th, 14th, 9th BNS, C	SEE ALSO 26/333
HARRISON	Wm	PTE	24 /1593	D	24 BUCKINGHAM TERR	LEEHOLME			16 DEC 1917	OCTOBER 16.	DOCHY FARM NEW BRIT CEM	TO 1/6th BN.	BORN SPENNYMOOR.
HARROLD	John	LCPL	24 /1633	C		GRANGE VILLA			1 JULY 1916		THIEPVAL MEM		RAID 25/26 JUNE 16,BORN DURHAM MISSING AUGUST 16.
HART	Frank	SGT	24 /936		8 ROBSON ST	WHEATLEY HILL	9/11/14	30/1/17	WOUNDS	MARCH 17.		TO DEPOT.	FROM WIGAN.
HART	Hnry	LCPL	24 /1537	A		LIVERPOOL			20 APRIL 1918		LE GRD B/MART STEENWERK	TO 24/27th, 23rd BNS.	SIGNALLER TOOK PART IN TRENCH RAID 25/26 JUNE 16.
HARVEY	Ed	PTE	24 /1671		75 CAMBRIDGE ST	SOUTH SHIELDS			1 JULY 1916		THIEPVAL MEM	FROM 34 DIV CYC COY.	MISSING AUGUST 16,BORN EAST HARTLEPOOL.ACC No 9810
HARVEY	Jos	PTE	24 /1406										DESERTED 12/4/15, AGE 32, 5'9'', MINER.
HARWOOD	Jas G	PTE	24 /845		22 THOMAS TERR	BLAYDON	28/10/14					TO 1st GARRISON BN, CLASS Z RESERVE.	SON J G Junior SERVING IN 2/9 MANCHESTER REGT.
HASLEM	Jas	PTE	24 /990		15 TOWNLEY ST	BLAYDON	12/11/14					TO 23rd BN, CLASS Z RESERVE.	DESERTED 18/6/15 IN COURT 14/7/15.
HASTINGS	Sam	PTE	24 /862	D	22 PLANTATION ST	WHEATLEY HILL			1 JULY 1916		THIEPVAL MEM		MISSING AUGUST 16, BORN HARTLEPOOL. 24/1060 HALF B
HASTINGS	Wm	LSGT	24 /134	D		NEWCASTLE			KR para 392	SHELLSHOCK NOVEMBER 16			AWOL 5/4/15 IN COURT 8/4/15.
HATTLE	W	PTE	24 /1398	B								TO 24/27th, 8th BNS, CLASS Z RESERVE.	
HEALEY	Jas	SGT	24 /1201	D	6 PRIMROSE ST	DARLINGTON			1 JULY 1916		THIEPVAL MEM		BORN MOHALL CO LEITRIM, MISSING AUGUST 16.
HEATH	A	PTE	24 /1328						KR para 392			TO 1st GARRISON BN, 26th, 1st BNS.	
HEDLEY	Edmd	PTE	24 /1005	D	16 MAIDEN ST	NEWCASTLE	28/10/14		29 AUGUST 1917		ROISEL COM CEM	TO 24/27th BN.	RAID 25/26th JUNE 1916.DESERTED 6/1/16.AWOL 7/4/15
HENDERSON	Jn Ed	PTE	24 /70	A	16 STRATHMORE TERR	ROWLANDS GILL	10/11/14		KR para 392	OCTOBER 16			
HENDERSON	Thos	PTE	24 /334	D	C/O J WHITE ESQ DIPT	LANCHESTER	28/10/14		11 AUGUST 1916		CABERET ROUGE CEM		
HENNIGAN	Bernd	PTE	24 /146	A	4 VICTORIA TERR	WREKETON	28/10/14					TO 24/27th, 9th BNS, CLASS Z RESERVE.	IN DYCH AS HENNINGAM
HERBERT	Geo	PTE	24 /996	C	9 PRUDHOE COURT	NEWCASTLE	12/11/14			AUGUST 16		TO LABOUR CORPS, ROYAL FUSILIERS.	WND ABDOMEN. 3CCS 2/7/16 EVAC 2/7/16
HERWOOD	J	PTE	24 /56	A	19 TAYLOR ST	SOUTHMOOR		12/2/19				TO 10th BN, 2/4th BN KINGS OWN YORKSHIRE LI. CLASS	IN MR BOOK 703 AS DIS KR PARA 392.
HETHERINGTON	Robt	PTE	24	D									5th IN QUARTER MILE RACE ST PATRICKS DAY SPORTS AT
HIGGINS	J	PTE	24 /1208	D		BRANDON				JULY 16			
HIGGINS	Sam	PTE	24 /566	D	37 THERESA ST	BLAYDON	2/11/14		4 SEPT 1916		THIEPVAL MEM	TO 27th BN.	BORN WHITEHAVEN.
HIGGINS	T	PTE	24 /484		36 WILSON ST TEAMS	GATESHEAD	12/10/14	1/12/14	KR para 392iiic				DID NOT SERVE OVERSEAS.
HILL	A R	PTE	24 /1686			GRIMSBY	17/10/14	7/9/17	WOUNDS	SEPTEMBER 16		FROM 34 DIV CYC COY, DEPOT.	
HINDMORE	Thos	PTE	24 /1578	D	23 ROBINSON ST	BLAYDON			1 JULY 1916		CERISSY GAILLY CEM	FROM DURHAM LI.	BORN GATESHEAD,MISSING AUGUST 16,AGE 24.13 PLATOON
HOBBS	Wm	SGT	24 /808		GLEN BREA DEAN AVENU	ROWLANDS GILL	9/11/14	23/6/16	EAR INFLAMATION			TO 30th BN.	
HOBIN	M	PTE	24 /438	B	7 BRIDGE ROW	USWORTH			KR para 392	OCTOBER 16			
HODGENS	Henry	PTE	24 /80	A	63 CANNING ST	GATESHEAD	28/10/14					TO LABOUR CORPS(742 LAB COY),19th BN NF.	ALLOTED NEW NUMBER, 60255
HODGSON	John	PTE	24 /782	D	55 MORRISON ST	GATESHEAD	28/10/14					TO 24/27th, 11th BNS, CLASS Z RESERVE.	
HODGSON	Math	PTE	24 /117		5 OYSTERSHELL LANE	NEWCASTLE	3/11/14	29/11/15	VDH			TO 30th BN.	DID NOT SERVE OVERSEAS.
HODGSON	Ralph	PTE	24 /737	C	11 RAILWAY TERR	USWORTH	28/10/14		27 AUGUST 1918		H A C CEM ECOUST.	TO 10th BN, 2/4th BN KINGS OWN YORKSHIRE LI.	BORN LANGLEY MOOR, KOYLI No 63414.
HOGAN	Alex	PTE	24 /1335	C	BOTTLE BANK	LEADGATE	21/12/14	5/9/17		AUGUST 16			34 CCS 2/7/16 EVAC 5/7/16 COMPOUND FRAC L LEG.
HOGAN	T	PTE	24 /1471	D								TO LABOUR CORPS.	
HOGG	E	PTE	24 /1330	A			16/12/14	31/3/19				TO ARMY RESERVE CLASS P.	ALSO ON D COY 30th BN ROLL.
HOLDEN	Rich	PTE	24 /865	D	16 ASHMORE TERR	WHEATLEY HILL	10/11/14		1 JULY 1916		THIEPVAL MEM		MISSING AUGUST 16, BORN INGHAM LINCS.
HOLLINGTON	R	PTE	24 /1685		179 WILLINGHAM ST	GRIMSBY			1 JULY 1916		THIEPVAL MEM	FROM 34 DIV CYC COY.	MISSING AUGUST 16. ACC No 9519
HOLLOWAY	Fenwk	PTE	24 /1110	D	4 ELIZABETH ST	GATESHEAD			28 APRIL 1917		ARRAS MEM		LEWIS GUN SECTION MISSING AUGUST 17, LCPL, AGE 25.

NAME	INITI	RANK	BA	NUMBE	COMP	ADDRESS	TOWN_VILL	ENLISTED	DISCHARG	CAUSE_DIS	WOUNDED	BURIED	TRANSFER	ADD
HOLMES	Peter	PTE	24	/881	C	28 TRINITY ST	GATESHEAD	12/11/14		1 JULY 1916		THIEPVAL MEM		
HOPE	Jas	PTE	24	/1408						KR para 392				ALLOTED NEW NUMBER 365322.
HOPKINS	Jas J	PTE	24	/1068	D	110 TUDHOE COLLIERY	SPENNYMOOR	10/11/14					TO ROYAL DEFENCE CORPS.	IN FRANCE 11/1/16 TO 30/4/17. ASGT.
HORNSBY	J	PTE	24	/1404	B	37 JOICEY TERR OXHIL	STANLEY			KR para 392			TO 14th, 19th BNS.	DESERTED 15 NOVEMBER 1918.
HORNSBY	T	PTE		/1196	D	46 BOTTLE BANK	BLLACKHILL							No ALSO ALLOTED TO FOSTER.
HORWOOD	T	PTE	24	/1336				19/12/14	4/3/15	INEFFICIENT			TO DEPOT.	AGE 39.
HOWARD	S	PTE	24	/1550	C		LIVERPOOL				SEPTEMBER 16			BAYONET WND L ARM.34 CCS 2/7/16 EVAC 5/7/16
HOWARD	Wm	PTE	24	/696	B	365 NORTH CROSS ST	LEADGATE	9/11/14	26/12/17	GUNSHOT WOUNDS	OCTOBER 16		TO DEPOT.	HOWARD THOMPSON AT THIS ADDRESS 1918 7 Y&L.
HOWARTH	JohnW	PTE	24	/793	C		WHEATLEY HILL			1 JULY 1916		THIEPVAL MEM		BORN DURHAM CITY. MISSING AUGUST 16.
HOWEY	Alf	PTE	24	/1687		NEPTUNE HSE ALMA PLA	NORTH SHIELDS			22 MARCH 1918		ARRAS MEM	FROM 34 DIV CYC COY, TO 24/27th, 23rd BNS.	BORN TYNEMOUTH.
HOWEY	J	PTE	24	/1632	D									ALSO D COY 30th BN ROLL.
HOWEY	JohnT	PTE	24	/1180	B		ANNFIELD PLAIN			1 JULY 1916		THIEPVAL MEM		MISSING AUGUST 16.
HOWEY	W	LSGT	24	/1331	A	30								
HUBBARD	JohnG	PTE	24	/727	C	57 CLAVERING AVE	DUNSTON	9/11/14	20/12/17	FRACTURES	OCTOBER 16		TO 3rd BN.	TOOK PART IN TRENCH RAID 5/6 JUNE 16.
HUDDARD	J W	PTE	24	/1140	A	58 SCHOOL ST	GATESHEAD	11/11/14	27/11/17	WOUNDS	OCTOBER 16		TO DEPOT.	AWOL 11/7/15 IN COURT GATESHEAD, AGE 19.
HUGHES	A	PTE	24	/631	C		GATESHEAD				AUGUST 16, OCTOBER 16.			3 CCS 2/7/16 EVAC 2/7/16
HUGHES	Chas	PTE	24	/611	C	2 OWEN TERR	TANTOBIE	27/10/14		1 JULY 1916		OVILLIERS		SCOUT,RAIDS 5/6, 25/26 JUNE 16,BORN WHICKHAM.
HUGHES	F	PTE	24	/378	A	12 PRINCESS ST	CONSETT			KR para 392			TO 19th BN.	
HUGHES	Fredr	PTE	24	/997	C	8 TENTH ST	EASINGTON						TO LABOUR CORPS.	
HUGHES	J	PTE		/679	A	32 CASTLE ST CASTLET	LEEDS				AUGUST 16			No ALSO ALLOTED TO DEVINE.
HUGHES	John	PTE	24	/1575	A	81 RAVENSWORTH RD	DUNSTON			4 OCT 1918	OCTOBER 16.	SAILLY LA BOURSE	FROM BORDER REGT, TO 8th, 3rd, 22nd BNS.	BORN BLANTAIR LANARK. BORDER REGT No 17815.
HUGHES	Jos	PTE	24	/1070	D	40 SALVIN ST	SPENNYMOOR	11/11/14		5/6 JUNE 1916		BECOURT MIL CEM		KILLED DURING TRENCH RAID, BORN FERRYHILL.
HUGHES	M	PTE	24	/554										TOOK PART IN TRENCH RAID 5/6 JUNE 16.
HUMPHREY	ChasH	PTE	24	/985		14 ATHOL ST	NEWCASTLE	28/10/14		KR para 392			TO 1st GARRISON BN.	
HUMPHRIES	Hen	PTE	24	/1001	D	8 GIBB ST ST PETERS	NEWCASTLE	12/11/14			OCTOBER 16			AWOL 11/6/15 IN COURT 14/7/15.
HUNT	W	SGT	24	/1207				14/11/14	9/4/16	SICK			TO 30th BN.	ALSO ON D COY 30th BN ROLL.
HUNTER	G H	SGT	24	/287			WIDEOPEN						TO CLASS Z RESERVE.	MENTIONED IN BN WAR DIARY 2 SEPTEMBER 1916
HUNTER	Isaac	PTE	24	/1715		28 RIDGE TERR	BEDLINGTON			27 APRIL 1917		BEDLINGTON	TO 25th BN.	BORN MANSFIELD NOTTS, AGE 20.
HUNTER	Wm	PTE	24	/594			BISHOP AUKLAND			8 AUGUST 1915		WINGATE		
HUNTLEY	Edwd	PTE	24	/1399										DESERTED 1/5/15, AGE 22, 5'4'', HAWKER.
HURNEYMAN	Jas	PTE	24	/1729		20 BACK CHURCH ST	HASWELL	7/1/15			AUGUST 18.		FROM 34 DIV CYC COY. TO 25th, 23rd, 25th, 9th BNS,	5 FIELD HOUSE TERR HASWELL 1915.
HURSON	Phil	PTE	24	/390	B		DUNGANNON			19 APRIL 1917		ROCLINCOURT VALLEY CEM	TO 25th BN.	ALSO ON A COY 30th BN ROLL.
HURST	ChasG	PTE	24	/795	D	16 WILLIAM ST	CONSETT			22 NOV 1918	OCTOBER 16	BENFIELDSIDE	TO ROYAL DEFENCE CORPS, LABOUR CORPS.	RDC No 72956, LABOUR CORPS No 640206, AGE 29
HUTCHINSON	W	LCPL	24	/1226	A	73 STANHOPE ST	NEWCASTLE				OCTOBER 16.		TO KINGS OWN YORKSHIRE LI.	HOSP FRANCE 7/16
IGO	J	PTE	24	/557	C		GATESHEAD				DECEMBER 16		TO 21st, 24th BNS, ROYAL DEFENCE CORPS.	FRANCE 24 11/1/16 TO 9/7/16, 21 9/1/17 TO 12/1/17,
ILEY	John	PTE	24	/170	A	18 VICTORIA ST	DUNSTON			1 JULY 1916		THIEPVAL MEM		TOOK PART IN TRENCH RAID 25/26 JUNE 16, MISSING AU
IRVINE	C	PTE	24	/1690			NETHERTON COLLI	10/12/14	3/5/17	WOUNDS	OCTOBER 16		FROM 34 DIV CYC COY, TO DEPOT.	
ISAAC	W F	CSM	24	/1523				6/1/15	14/11/18	SICK			TO DEPOT.	
JACKSON	G	PTE	24	/1692			GORTON	3/10/14	21/6/18	GUNSHOT WOUNDS	OCTOBER 16		TO 8th, 16th, 3rd BNS.	AGE 27.
JACKSON	J	PTE	24	/256	A	30 WOOLSEY TERR	WEST STANLEY	29/10/14					TO NORTH STAFFORDSHIRE REGT.	
JACKSON	J E	PTE	24	/1414	A	29 BEWICK RD	BLACKHALL MILL	19/12/14	1/4/19	KR para 392			TO ARMY RESERVE CLASS P.	BROTHER IN 9 DLI(24788).
JACKSON	Jas W	PTE	24	/255	B	7 QUARRIE SQUARE	TANTOBIE	6/11/14		1 JULY 1916		THIEPVAL MEM		MISSING AUGUST 16, BORN EAST TANFIELD.
JACOBS	Wm	PTE	24	/1042	B	16 COWPEN SQUARE	BLYTH			1 JULY 1916		THIEPVAL MEM		MISSING AUGUST 1916.
JAMEISON	Jos	SGT	24	/1205	A	4 EVELYN TERR	WEST STANLEY			1 JULY 1916		GORDON DUMP CEM		RAID 25/26 JUNE 16, MISSING AUGUST 16. BORN SUNDER
JEFFERY	Chas	PTE	24	/1413	B	17 PELAW GRANGE	CHESTER LE STRE			1 JULY 1916		THIEPVAL MEM		MISSING AUGUST 16, BORN HOUGHTON LE SPRING.
JEFFERY	J	PTE	24	/1037	C	18 OYSTERSHELL LANE	NEWCASTLE							ALSO ON D COY 30th BN ROLL.
JENKINS	Ernst	PTE	24	/1412	D	LONG ST	LITTLETOWN		23/4/19				TO 24th, 24/27th, 25th BNS, KINGS OWN YORKSHIRE LI	KOYLI No 63372.
JOBLING	R W	PTE	24	/1222	A								TO ROYAL DEFENCE CORPS.	IN FRANCE 12/1/16 TO 18/4/17. ON BN ROLL AS COBLIN
JOHNS	Henry	PTE	24	/1340	C	1 EARL ST	GATESHEAD				OCTOBER 16, MARCH 18.		TO ROYAL ARMY MEDICAL CORPS.	WND L EYE, AGE 30. 34 CCS 2/7/16 EVAC 5/7/16
JOHNSON	Geo H	PTE	24	/1480	A		DIPTON			15 JULY 1916	NOVEMBER	DUNSTON		
JOHNSON	H	PTE	24	/1464	D	9 VICTORIA TERR	NEWBURN						TO 21st, 1st BNS, 12 N STAFFS REGT.	
JOHNSON	J	PTE	24	/992	B		NEWCASTLE				AUGUST 16, OCT 16, DEC 18		TO 27th, 26th, 23rd, 5th BN KINGS OWN YORKSHIRE LI	KOYLI No 63171. 3CCS 2/7/16 EVAC 3/7/16 GSW
JOHNSON	Jas W	PTE	24	/4	B		SPENNYMOOR			23 AUGUST 1918		MERVILLE COM CEM EXT	TO 24/27th, 9th BNS.	
JOHNSON	R	PTE	24	/1082	D	3 ESLINGTON TERR TEA	GATESHEAD	10/11/14	22/8/17	GUNSHOT WOUNDS	MARCH 16 –		TO 85th TRAINING RESERVE BN.	
JOHNSON	Rich	PTE	24	/369	B	103 FRAMWELLGATE	DURHAM CITY	6/11/14	6/6/18	TRENCH FOOT	OCTOBER 16		TO 3rd BN.	SEE 24/483 SGT T, BROTHER.
JOHNSON	S	PTE	24	/34	A	38 MERSEY ST	CHOPWELL	28/10/14						ALSO ON A COY 30th BN ROLL.
JOHNSON	T W	PTE	24	/1339	B	61 NEW ELVET	DURHAM CITY	28/10/14						ALSO ON A COY 30th BN ROLL.
JOHNSON	Thos	SGT	24	/483		103 FRAMWELLGATE	DURHAM CITY						TO 12th, 12/13th BNS, CLASS Z RESERVE.	SEE 24/369 BROTHER Rich, Edward R.F.A,Jos DLI.
JOHNSON	W	PTE	24	/1503										RAID 25//26 JUNE 1916, BAYONETMAN.
JOHNSON	W F	PTE	24	/1053	A	5 WAUGH ST	GATESHEAD				JULY 16		TO 16th, 1/7th BNS, CLASS Z RESERVE.	

												TRANSFER	ADD
JONES	C	SGT	24 /1527			LIVERPOOL				OCTOBER 16.		TO CLASS Z RESERVE.	
JONES	Wm	PTE	24 /480		14 DONNISON ST	DUNSTON	26/10/14					TO 1st GARRISON BN, CLASS Z RESERVE.	
JONES	Wm	PTE	24 /1411	C		NEWCASTLE				DECEMBER 16			RAID 5/6 JUNE 16,AWOL 27/7/15 CT 29/7/15 34 CCS
JOPLING	T	PTE	24 /1085	B								TO 24/27th, 9th BNS, CLASS Z RESERVE.	
JORDAN	J J	PTE	24 /822		41 SALOM ST	JARROW	9/11/14	30/1/15	INEFFICIENT				DID NOT SERVE OVERSEAS., AGE 29
JORDAN	Thom	PTE	24 /573	C	27 AIWELL TERR	SWALWELL	27/10/14						
JOYCE	John	PTE	24 /66	A	12 ALBION ROW	BYKER			1 JULY 1916	OCTOBER 16	THIEPVAL MEM		BORN CALDER MIDLOTHIAN.
JOYCE	Wm	PTE	24 /333	A	9 GRENVILLE ST	NEWCASTLE	2/11/14		1 JULY 1916		THIEPVAL MEM		MISSING AUGUST 16
KANE	John	PTE	24 /821	A								TO LABOUR CORPS.	LAB CORPS No 398150, AWOL 16/5/15 IN COURT 21/5/15
KAVENEY	Peter	PTE	24 /311	D	35 FRONT ST	EAST STANLEY			1 JULY 1916		THIEPVAL MEM		MISSING AUGUST 16, BORN GATESHEAD.
KEAN	Geo	SGT	24 /1541			LIVERPOOL			1 NOV 1916	30 OCTOBER 1916	BAILLEUL MIL CEM.		DIED 2.15am 1/11/16 AT No 2 CCS
KEARSLEY	Thos	PTE	24 /937	D		WHEATLEY HILL			8 SEPT 1917	AUGUST 16	TEMPLEUX	TO 23rd BN.	BORN WIGAN, AGE 23.
KEEBLE	Geo H	PTE	24 /1342	A									AWOL 13/6/15 IN COURT 7/7/15.
KEEGAN	Corn	PTE	24 /1580	C	20 THIRD ST	SOUTHMOOR						TO 24/27th, 19th(Z COY 12 PLTN) BNS, CLASS Z RESER	SGT
KEEGAN	John	PTE	24 /1341	C	32 MITCHELL ST	SOUTHMOOR			1 JULY 1916		THIEPVAL MEM		MISSING AUGUST 16, BORN USWORTH.
KEENAN	B	PTE	24 /841	B	15 CHARLES ST	SILKSWORTH							ALSO ON D COY 30th BN ROLL.
KEENAN	J	PTE	24 /1159	D	5 BOLDON LANE	BARTON COLLIERY							ALSO ON D COY 30th BN ROLL.
KEHOE	Owen	CPL	24 /1469	D		WREXFORD WARKS			27 APRIL 1917		ARRAS MEM		BOMBER,RAID 5/6th JUNE 16.MISSING AUGUST 17.
KELLET	Sam	PTE	24 /250	B	18 SMITH ST	WHEATLEY HILL	5/11/14	3/2/19	GUNSHOT WOUNDS	AUGUST 16		TO 23rd, 3rd BNS, ARMY RESERVE CLASS P..	LCPL
KELLY	J	PTE	24 /267	A		NEWCASTLE				NOVEMBER 16		TO LABOUR CORPS.	
KELLY	J	PTE	24 /694	B								TO LABOUR CORPS.	ALSO ON A COY 30th BN ROLL.
KELLY	J	SGT	24 /899	B		NEWCASTLE				JULY 16		TO LABOUR CORPS.	2nd IN QUARTER MILE RACE ON ST PATRICKS DAY SPORTS
KELLY	Jas	PTE	24 /1051	D								TO LABOUR CORPS.	LAB CORPS No 408412.
KELLY	Jas	LCPL	24 /1152		17 EILINGS COTTAGES	HEXAM			18 APRIL 1917		ETAPLES	FROM 34 DIV CYCLIST COY.	ARMY CYCLIST CORP No 9663.
KELLY	Jos R	PTE	24 /1343	C			19/12/14	4/4/16					ALSO ON D COY 30th BN ROLL, DID NOT SERVE OVERSEAS
KELLY	M	PTE	24 /93	A									ALSO ON D COY 30th BN ROLL.
KELLY	Pat	PTE	24 /225	A		FELLING		20/12/17		OCTOBER 16		TO ROYAL DEFENCE CORPS.	FRANCE 11/1/16 TO 7/7/16.HOSP LEICESTER 11/7/16.
KELLY	Pat	PTE	24 /441	D	8 SHIBDON RD	BLAYDON			1 JULY 1916	FEBRUARY 16	THIEPVAL MEM		BORN WINLATON, MISSING NOVEMBER 16.
KELLY	Sam	PTE	24 /113		18 TRINITY ST	GATESHEAD	5/11/14		1 JULY 1916		THIEPVAL MEM		MISSING AUGUST 16
KELLY	Terry	PTE	24 /1211		HANOVER HOUSE	WINLATON	28/10/14					TO 12/13th BN.	
KELLY	Thos	PTE	24 /693	D	FRAMWELLGATE	DURHAM CITY						TO LABOUR CORPS.	
KENDAL	Chas	PTE	24 /545	D	102 GEORGE ST	BLAYDON	26/10/14		1 MARCH 1916		ERQUINGHEM CEM		BORN FELLING, LCPL.
KENNEDY	Hugh	PTE	24 /1025	D	21 PITT ST	CONSETT	12/11/14					TO LABOUR CORPS(475 H.S.E COY).	D COY 30th BN ROLL, LAB CORPS No 263987.
KENNEDY	Wm	PTE	24 /596	C		GALWAY			1 JULY 1916		THIEPVAL MEM		MISSING AUGUST 16, LIVING KILRONAN.
KENWORTHY	Jas W	PTE	24 /477	B	427 BRANDON LANE	LANGLEY MOOR	7/11/14	28/7/17	GUNSHOT WOUNDS	JULY 16, OCTOBER 16.		TO 3rd BN.	34 CCS 2/7,21 AMB TRAIN 5/7,18 GEN HOSP 6/7 HSHIP
KETTLE	Alf	PTE	24 /1035		1 TWEEDY ST COWPEN	BLYTH			1 JULY 1916		THIEPVAL MEM		MISSING AUGUST 16, BORN GATESHEAD.
KEY	E	PTE	24 /762	B		DIPTON				JULY 16		TO 30th, 24th, 27th, 23rd BNS, ROYAL DEFENCE CORPS	WOUNDED IN THE FACE. IN FRANCE 24th 8/5/16 TO 6/7/
KEY	Edwd	PTE	24 /726	B	5 ST JOHNS TERR	DIPTON	28/10/14			JULY 16		TO 30th, 24th, 27th, 23rd BNS, ROYAL DEFENCE CORPS	IN FRANCE 24th 8/5/16 TO 6/7/16, 27th 6/2/17 TO 21
KIERNAN	M	PTE	24 /278	A		BILLQUAY	16/10/14	18/3/17	KR para 392	JANUARY 17			ALSO ON D COY 30th BN ROLL.
KILLGALLON	Edwd	LCPL	24 /946	D	COXHOE POTTERY	COXHOE	9/11/14	9/4/17	WOUNDS	OCTOBER 16		TO DEPOT.	
KILLGALLON	John	PTE	24 /943	D	COXHOE POTTERY	COXHOE				AUGUST 16, NOVEMBER 17.		TO LABOUR CORPS.	SEE 24/946 AND 24/1558
KILLGALLON	M	PTE	24 /1558	D									
KILLIAN	Mich	PTE	24 /1568		FRAMWELLGATE	DURHAM CITY	3/9/14	28/2/18	GUNSHOT WOUNDS	OCTOBER 16.		TO ARMY RESERVE CLASS P.	HOSP ROUEN 7/16
KING	Thos	PTE	24 /731	B	8 CHRISTOPHER ST	GATESHEAD	28/10/14		8 APRIL 1917		FABOURG D'AMIENS ARRAS		MISSING AUGUST 16,AGE 45, NOT MISS NOVEMBER 16.
KIRKUP	John	PTE	24 /698		4 BARKER ST	SHIELDFIELD	9/11/14	22/11/15	DEAFNESS			TO 30th BN.	DID NOT SERVE OVERSEAS.
KIRTON	Jas	PTE	24		2 SUNDERLAND STREET	NEWCASTLE	6/11/14						AWOL 19/5, 19/7, 31/7, 31/8 COURT 25/5, 21/7, 6/8,
KITCHING	J J	PTE	24 /1516									TO 1st GARRISON BN, CLASS Z RESERVE.	
KNEEBONE	E	PTE	24 /867	C									
KNIGHT	Con	PTE	24 /687	C	1 CURRYS SQUARE	DIPTON	28/10/14						
KNIGHTON	W	PTE	24 /1513			FENCEHOUSES				OCTOBER 16		TO LABOUR CORPS.	R VICTORIA HOSP NETLEY 11/7/16
KNOX	Thos	PTE	24 /984	C	107 SALISBURY ST	BYKER	12/11/14			OCTOBER 16		TO TRAINING RESERVE BN, ROYAL ENGINEERS.	DESERTED 14/4/15 COURT 11/6/15. AWOL 28/7, 21/9/15
KNOX	Wm	PTE	24 /221	A		LEAMSIDE			1 JULY 1916		THIEPVAL MEM		BORN DURHAM CITY, MISSING AUGUST 16.
LACEY	Geo W	PTE	24 /1162	D	7 MOUNT STEWART ST	DAWDON	28/10/14			JULY 16, JULY 17.			LSGT.
LAGGAN	J J	PTE	24 /111	B					KR para 392				ALSO ON D COY 30th BN ROLL.
LALLY	A	PTE	24 /680	D			9/11/14	9/6/16	WOUNDS	MARCH 16		TO DEPOT.	PHOTO IN IC.
LALLY	M	PTE	24 /969	C	13 LAMB ST	RYHOPE COLLIERY	10/11/14	28/3/17	WOUNDS	OCTOBER 16		TO DEPOT.	LEG AMPUTATED. LAY ON FIELD FOR THREE DAYS.
LALLY	Mich	SGT	24 /33		10 WELLINGTON ST	NORTH SHIELDS	27/10/14					TO ROYAL ARMY ORDNANCE CORPS	
LAMB	E	SGT	24 /1496		6 SIXTH STREET	SHOTTON COLLIER						TO ROYAL FUSILIERS.	ON AVL AS /1469.
LAMB	Lawr	PTE	24 /107	A	124 JEFFERSON ST	NEWCASTLE			1 JULY 1916		THIEPVAL MEM		MISSING AUGUST 16, BORN WESTGATE Co DURHAM.
LAMB	Peter	PTE	24 /1348	A	DOUGLAS TERR	USWORTH	19/12/14	29/1/18	WOUNDS	OCTOBER 16.		TO 19th, 20th BNS, DEPOT.	BOMBER,RAID 25/26 JUNE 16.34 CCS 2/7/16 EVAC 5/7/1

NAME	INITI	RANK	BA	NUMBE	COMP	ADDRESS	TOWN_VILL	ENLISTED	DISCHARG	CAUSE_DIS	WOUNDED	BURIED	TRANSFER	ADD
LAPPING	Geo S	PTE	24	/1656	A									AWOII, PHOTO IN IH AS A CPL.
LARGUE	Wm Hy	PTE	24	/677	C	4 CLOUGH DENE	BURNHOPEFIELD	9/11/14	13/2/19	KR para 392			TO 3rd BN, ARMY RESERVE CLASS P.	LCPL, LOW FRIARSIDE ROWLANDS GILL 1914.
LAVELLE	F	PTE	24	/1020	C									
LAVERICK	John	PTE	24	/563	C	ANDERSONS BLDGS	BURRADON	7/11/14	29/3/16				TO 30th BN.	DID NOT SERVE OVERSEAS.
LAWLER	J	CPL	24	/191		14 NEALE ST	ANNFIELD PLAIN				JULY, AUGUST 16		TO 5th TRAINING RESERVE BN.	SIGNALLER, TOOK PART IN TRENCH RAID 5/6 JUNE 16
LAWLER	Wm	PTE	24	/352	C		WALLSEND	28/10/14						
LAWSON	T	PTE	24	/423	A									ON A COY AND D COY 30th BN, No ALSO ALLOTED TO CRA
LEACH	Jas	PTE	24	/921	B	228 PILGRIM ST	NEWCASTLE	12/11/14			OCTOBER 16			AWOL 30/7 COURT 6/8/15,AWOL 16/4/15 COURT 22/4/15.
LEE	D	PTE	24	/171		9 SEYMOUR ST	DUNSTON						TO 24/27th BN.	
LEIGHTON	Jas	LSGT	24	/630		43 WOLSELEY ST	GATESHEAD			KR para 392	NOVEMBER 16		TO 51st BN.	TOOK PART IN TRENCH RAIDS 5/6, 25/26 JUNE 16.
LEWINS	Wm	PTE	24	/768	C	7 JOHN ST	TANTOBIE	31/10/14					TO 24/27th, 11th BNS, ATTACHED 34 DIVISIONAL HQ, Z	
LEWIS	JohnH	PTE	24	/744	C	54 MILLFIELD CRES	NEWBURN	28/10/14			AUGUST 1916			
LIDDELL	T	PTE	24	/1349	D								TO 30th BN(A COY).	ALSO ON A COY 30th BN ROLL.
LIDDLE	Thos	PTE	24	/626	B	14 ORVEN HOUSE	TANTOBIE			1 JULY 1916		THIEPVAL MEM		MISSING AUGUST 16, BORN SOUTH MOOR.
LISTER	Geo	PTE	24	/712		5 ROBSON ST	WHEATLEY HILL	28/10/14					TO 2nd GARRISON BN, CLASS Z RESERVE.	BROTHER IN THE NAVY.
LOCKEY	Harry	PTE	24	/461	B	8 CASTLE VW FRAMWELL	DURHAM CITY	28/10/14					TO LABOUR CORPS(949 LAB COY).	LAB CORPS No 398597
LOCKEY	John	PTE	24	/1145	D	120 FRONT ST	LANGLEY MOOR	11/11/14	9/11/17	5 OCT 1919		ALL SAINTS NEWCASTLE	TO DEPOT.	No GIVEN AS 445 IN WGR.
LOCKWOOD	Allan	PTE	24	/662	D	GILESGATE	DURHAM CITY	9/11/14	31/12/17	FOOT WOUND				SGT
LOFTHOUSE	Wm Hy	CPL	24	/1668		193 GILESGATE	DURHAM CITY			5 JULY 1916	1 JULY 16	ST NICHOLAS' DURHAM CITY	FROM TYNESIDE SCOTTISH(29th BN), 34 DIV CYC COY.	DIED ON BOARD HOSP SHIP ST GEORGE, AGE 24,BORN LAN
LOFTUS	J	PTE	24	/1347	A		GATESHEAD			KR para 392	JULY 16.		TO 21st, 24th BNS.	BEAUFORT WAR HOSP BRISTOL 11/7/16
LONG	G	PTE	24	/1420	B									
LOVE	Mat W	SGT	24	/1197		20 HARVEY ST	CONSETT	12/11/14			AUGUST 16		TO 23rd, 24th, 24/27th BNS, CLASS Z RESERVE.	
LOWDEN	J T	PTE	24	/1497	B	5 PUMP ROW	USWORTH		15/5/19		OCTOBER 16.		TO 25th BN, KOYLI(2/5th BN), CLASS Z RES.	KOYLI No 63305.
LOWRIE	M	PTE	24		A									4th IN QUARTER MILE RACE ST PATRICKS DAY SPORTS AT
LUKE	Wm	PTE	24	/1013	D		THORNLEY			24 FEB 1916		RATION FARM CEM		
LUMLEY	T	PTE	24	/909									TO 1st GARRISON BN, CLASS Z RESERVE.	
LYDONN	Wm W	PTE	24	/831	D	25 HINSON ROAD	BYKER	28/10/14					TO 30th BN(A COY).	ALSO ON A COY 30th BN ROLL.
LYNCH	Hugh	PTE	24	/1061	D		WALLSEND			1 JULY 1916		THIEPVAL MEM		MISSING AUGUST 16.
LYNN	Hugh	PTE	24	/79	A	187 PILGRIM ST	NEWCASTLE	28/10/14			JULY 16, AUGUST 16.		TO 27th, 20th, 25th BNS CLASS Z RESERVE.	TOOK PART IN TRENCH RAID 25/26 JUNE 16.
LYONS	T	PTE	24	/1199	A		WALLSEND	11/11/14	26/10/17	SHELLSHOCK	JUNE 16		TO DEPOT.	
LYONS	Wm	PTE	24	/210	B	60 VIOLET ST	BENWELL	5/11/14						ALSO ON D COY 30th BN ROLL.
MACHIN	J	SGT	24	/1104			GATESHEAD	11/11/14	10/8/17	WOUNDS	OCTOBER 16		TO 3rd BN.	
MACKIE	Rob	CPL	24	/118	C		GATESHEAD			1 JULY 1916		OVILLIERS		MISSING SEPTEMBER 16. SGT ON B ROLL. IN 12 PLATOON
MACKIN	J	PTE	24	/200	B	16 GARDEN PLACE	FELLING							ALSO ON D COY 30th BN ROLL.
MACKIN	Peter	PTE	24	/1049			GATESHEAD			9 APRIL 1917		ROCLINCOURT MIL CEM		
MALIA	G	PTE	24	/222	A		NEWCASTLE				JULY 16		TO NORTH STAFFORDSHIRE REGT	
MALIA	JohnH	PTE	24	/130	A	158 WALKER RD	NEWCASTLE	5/11/14					TO LABOUR CORPS.	MISSING SEPTEMBER 16. NOT MISSING NOVEMBER 16
MALIA	Martn	PTE	24	/272	B	75 CALTON ST	NEWCASTLE	5/11/14			JUNE 16, JULY 16.		TO LABOUR CORPS.	
MALIA	Pat	PTE	24	/1059	D	6 GREENMAN BANK LIDD	NORTH SHIELDS			1 JULY 1916		THIEPVAL MEM		MISSING SEPTEMBER 16, BORN MORPETH.
MALLOY	P	PTE	24	/1040	B	10 TYNE ST	NORTH SHIELDS	7/11/14	1/4/19	KR para 392			TO 27th, 21st, 10th BNS, ARMY RESERVE CLASS P.	
MALLY	Mart	PTE	24	/53	A	11 HEUTE ST	FELLING	26/10/14			DECEMBER 16			
MALONE	John	PTE	24	/823	C	268 ST CUTHBERTS RD	GATESHEAD			1 JULY 1916		THIEPVAL MEM		MISSING SEPTEMBER 16, LCPL.
MALONEY	L	PTE	24	/95		33 RABY ST	BYKER	3/11/14	3/12/15	UNFIT				DID NOT SERVE OVERSEAS.
MALONEY	Pat	PTE	24	/226	A		DURHAM CITY			1 JULY 1916		THIEPVAL MEM		MISSING SEPTEMBER 16
MALONEY	Pat	PTE	24	/263	C30								TO 30th BN.	AWOL 29/5/15 IN COURT NEWCASTLE 2/6/15
MALONEY	R	PTE	24	/956	C		SUNDERLAND				OCTOBER 16		TO 25th, 1/4th, 22nd, 2nd BNS, CLASS Z RESERVE.	ALLOTED NEW NUMBER 204616.
MALPAS	Jothn	LSGT	24	/754		95 FRAMWELLGATE	DURHAM CITY	12/11/14			FEBRUARY 16		TO CAMERON HIGHLANDERS.	WOUNDED IN THE ARM, 40 NEW ELVET IN 1918.
MANNING	J	PTE	24	/286	A	34 CHARLOTTE ST	GATESHEAD	5/11/14	7/12/16	WOUNDS	OCTOBER 16		TO DEPOT.	LCPL, WND HEAD+L ARM, AGE 34. 34 CCS 2/7 -5/7/16
MANNING	Steph	PTE	24	/1027	D	55 WAUGH ST	GATESHEAD	12/11/14			OCTOBER 16		TO LABOUR CORPS.	
MANSFIELD	A	PTE	24	/888	C	32 CLEPHAN ST	WHICKHAM				AUGUST 16		TO 23rd, 22nd, 19th, 1/5th BNS, CLASS Z RESERVE.	
MARKHAM	Wm	PTE	24	/756	D	16 SUNDERLAND RD GIL	DURHAM CITY	11/11/14					TO 24/27th, 1st BNS, CLASS Z RESERVE.	5 SUNDERLAND RD 1914
MARLTON	W	PTE	24	/1421				18/12/14	23/5/18				TO 1st GARRISON BN, ARMY RESERVE CLASS W.	ON MEDAL ROLL AS 25/1421 MARTIN.
MARRON	JohnT	PTE	24	/1426	C	50 WARWICK ST	MIDDLESBOROUGH			9 APRIL 1917		ST LAURENT BLAGNY		SIGNALLER TOOK PART IN TRENCH RAID 25/26th JUNE 16
MARSHALL	Jos	PTE	24	/323	D	63 CUTHBERT ST	BLAYDON	27/10/14					TO LABOUR CORPS.	LABOUR CORPS No 617006.
MARTIN	G H	PTE	24	/599									TO 2nd GARRISON BN, CLASS Z RESERVE.	AWOL 21/7/15, 29/7/15 23/1/16 COURT SUNDERLAND.
MARTIN	Geo W	PTE	24	/1546	D	GILES BUILDINGS	HETTON LE HOLE				JULY 16			
MARTIN	J	PTE	24	/890	D		LOW TEAMS	9/11/14	14/4/17	GUNSHOT WOUNDS	OCTOBER 16		TO DEPOT.	3CCS 3/7 EVAC 4/7, 2nd SOUTHERN BRISTOL 11/7/16.
MARTIN	Thos	PTE	24	/600	B	4 FOURTH ST NORTH	EASINGTON COLLI	28/10/14		1 JULY 1916		THIEPVAL MEM		BORN RYHOPE COLLIERY.
MARTIN	Thos	PTE	24	/900	C	3 EAST VIEW HOME HIL	EASINGTON YORKS			2 SEPT 1918		VIS EN ARTOIS MEM	TO 24/27th, 25th BNS, KOYLI(2/4th BN).	KOYLI No 63310, BORN WALDRIGE.
MASON	R	PTE	24	/788	B	ROBINSONS BLDGS	DIPTON				JULY 16		TO LABOUR CORPS.	LAB CORPS No 397265, LIVING CAUSEY MILL.

					ADDRESS	TOWN_VILL	ENLISTED	DISCHARG	CAUSE_DIS	WOUNDED	BURIED	TRANSFER	ADD
MASSITER	W	CSM	24 /237		50 WOODBINE ST	SUNDERLAND	6/11/14					TO LABOUR CORPS.	LAB CORPS No 401789.
MASTERS	Sid	PTE	24 /1617	A	13 DEAN ST	HEMLINGTON ROW	4/3/15	31/8/18	GUNSHOT WOUNDS	JUNE 18.		TO 25th, 3rd BNS(D Coy).	
MATHEWS	Jas J	PTE	24 /127	A	9 SUNDERLAND ST	NEWCASTLE	31/10/14					TO 24/27th, 11th, 1st BNS, CLASS B RESERVE	
MATHEWSON	Wm	PTE	24 /1694			BLYTH			1 JULY 1916		O'VILLIERS		
MAUGHAN	John	LSGT	24 /517		7 WIDDRINGTON RD	BLAYDON			28 APRIL 1917		A'RRAS MEM	FROM 7th, 14th, 34 DIV CYC COYS.	ACC No 679.
MAVIN	Harle	PTE	24 /205	A	142 FRONT ST	LANGLEY MOOR				OCTOBER 16, DECEMBER 17.		TO 20th, 21st, 25th, 12/13th BNS CLASS Z RESERVE.	IN GAZETTE AUGUST 18, BORN WINLATON. 3CCS 2/7/16 EVAC 2/7, HOSP NOTTINGHAM 17/7/16.
MAY	JohnT	PTE	24 /399	A	31 BEAUFORT ST	GATESHEAD	6/11/14	30/10/17	WOUNDS	AUGUST 16		TO 85th TRAINING RESERVE BN.	RAID 25/26 JUNE 16. AWOL 23/8 22/9 10/11/15
MAY	Mart	PTE	24 /10	D		GATESHEAD			1 JULY 1916		T'HIEPVAL MEM		MISSING SEPTEMBER 16
MEAKIN	Stan	CPL	24 /1495	A 30		FLINTHILL						TO 30th, 19th, 14th, 12/13th, 14th BNS, CLASS Z RE	
MEARMAN	Thos	PTE	24 /514	B	1630 WALKER RD	WALKER	10/11/14						ALSO ON D COY 30th BN ROLL.
MEE	Thos	PTE	24 /1163	D	15 WALTON ROW	BLACKHILL	10/11/14	16/11/17	WOUNDS			TO 10th, 3rd BNS.	
MEEGAN	JohnT	PTE	24 /1169	D	24 ELTRINGHAM ST	BLACKHILL	12/11/14						ALSO ON A COY 30th BN ROLL.
MEEHAN	John	PTE	24 /640	C	9 SALISBURY ST	SUNDERLAND				NOVEMBER 16		TO LABOUR CORPS.	LAB CORPS No 399883, WND 2 JULY 16.
MEEHAN	Pat	PTE	24 /189	A	2 DERBY RD	WEST STANLEY	5/11/14			OCTOBER 16		TO TF BN NF.	WND R SHD, AGE 23.NEW NUMBER 292093.34 CCS 2/7
MEEK	Henry	PTE	24 /1016	B	31 CUTHBERT ST	MARLEY HILL	10/11/14	31/3/19	KR para 392			TO 1st BN, ARMY RESERVE CLASS P.	
MELLON	C	PTE	24 /925	B									
MEREDITH	W	PTE	24 /976						KR para 392			TO 1/7th BN.	
METCALF	Wm	PTE	24										AWOL 16/4/15 COURT 22/4/15.
MIDDLEMASS	Wilf	PTE	24 /980	C	50 FRONT ROW	BEBSIDE COLLIER	29/10/14		1 JULY 1916		T'HIEPVAL MEM		BORN COWPEN.
MILBURN	Ern A	PTE	24 /879		80 ELSWICK RD ELSWIC	NEWCASTLE	10/11/14		1 JULY 1916	NOVEMBER 16	T'HIEPVAL MEM		WOUNDED AND MISSING DECEMBER 16.
MILES	W	PTE	24 /1264	D 25									MISSING 1 JULY 1916. REQUIRES CONFIRMATION. ******
MILLER	Cuthb	LSGT	24 /86	D	124 CUTHBERT ST	BLAYDON	3/11/14	20/12/17	SHELLSHOCK	AUGUST 16		TO 3rd BN.	
MILLER	J	SGT	24 /820				10/11/14	15/9/16				TO 30th BN.	DID NOT SERVE OVERSEAS, ALSO ON D COY 30th BN ROLL
MILLER	J W	PTE	24 /439	B		HIGH FELLING				OCTOBER 16		TO DURHAM LI(12th BN).	WND R ARM,34 CCS 2/7 EVAC 5/7/16 DLI No 45889.
MILLER	John	PTE	24 /1101	D		DURHAM CITY			30 MARCH 1917	SEPTEMBER 16	P'ERONNE COM CEM EXT	TO WEST YORKSHIRE REGT(2nd BN).	WEST YORKS No 41012, BORN DURHAM CITY.
MILLER	JohnW	PTE	24 /1358		9 ATHOLL ST	DUNSTON						TO 1st GARRISON BN, CLASS Z RESERVE.	
MILLER	Wm N	PTE	24 /1246	B	21 ILCHESTER ST	DAWDON			1 JULY 1916	OCTOBER 16	T'HIEPVAL MEM	TO 30th, 25th BNS.	ALSO ON A COY 30th BN ROLL, BORN LUDWORTH.
MILLWARD	Geo	PTE	24 /1074	D	25 OLD POST OFFICE S	SPENNYMOOR	10/11/14	22/8/17	WOUNDS	OCTOBER 16		TO DEPOT.	
MIRLEY	Thos	PTE	24 /180	A	100 LANE ROW	WEST MOOR	6/11/14		8 AUGUST 1917	OCTOBER 16	R'AMSCAPPELLE RD MIL CEM	TO 1st, 16th BNS.	GSW R THIGH, BORN NORWICH.34 CCS 2/7/16 5/7/16.
MITCHELL	Jas	PTE	24 /39	A	THE BLACK BULL	BELLINGHAM			1 JULY 1916		T'HIEPVAL MEM		MISSING SEPTEMBER 16, BORN ST ANDREWS NB.
MITCHELL	P J	PTE	24 /1012	D									
MOCHREE	P	PTE	24 /1696			EDINBURGH	28/11/14	26/9/17	WOUNDS	JANUARY 17.		FROM 34 DIV CYC COY, TO DEPOT.	
MOLLOY	JohnT	PTE	24 /776	D	233 SCHOOL ST	LANGLEY MOOR	11/11/14		1 JULY 1916		S'IERRE RD NO 2 CEM		MISSING SEPTEMBER 16. AGE 35.
MONAGHAN	Hugh	PTE	24 /878		12 ELSWICK ROW	NEWCASTLE	11/11/14			OCTOBER 16			3CCS 2/7, 2 GEN HOSP 4/7/16 EVAC HSHIP ASTURIAS
MONOGHAN	J P	SGT	24 /1080		29 PHILIP ST	HEBBURN COLLIER						TO 8th, 24th, 1st, 8th BNS, CLASS Z RESERVE.	
MONTGOMERY	Rob T	PTE	24 /531	A	19 CARRVILLE RD	NEWCASTLE	10/11/14		KR para 392				27 DENMARK ST HEATON 1914.
MOODY	Wm	PTE	24 /213	A	93 ADDISON COTTAGES	CROOKHILL				OCTOBER 16		TO 16th, 12th, 12/13th, 25th, 12/13th BNS, CLASS Z	
MOONEY	Wm	PTE	24 /89	A				25/4/19				TO WEST YORKSHIRE REGT, CLASS Z RESERVE.	
MOORE	Jermi	PTE	24 /522	D	39 EDWARD ST	BLAYDON	6/11/14	28/4/19		OCTOBER 16		TO 31st COMMAND DEPOT, ARMY RESERVE CLASS P.	34 CCS 2/7, 21 AMB TRAIN, 18 GEN HOSP, SHIP CALAIS
MOORE	Mich	PTE	24 /283	B	57 BUCKINGHAM ST	NEWCASTLE	5/11/14						
MORALEE	Andrw	PTE	24 /393	B	24 MART ST	WALLSEND	29/10/14			OCTOBER 16		TO LABOUR CORPS.	
MORAN	John	PTE	24 /156	A	FRAMWELLGATE	DURHAM CITY	31/10/14		1 JULY 1916		T'HIEPVAL MEM		TOOK PART IN TRENCH RAID 25/26 JUNE 16
MORDY	Geo	PTE	24 /665	B	15 DARLINGTON RD	FERRYHILL			30 OCT 1917		B'OULOGNE	TO 24/27th BN.	BORN SOUTHWICK.
MORGAN	Geo	PTE	24 /476		62 ROCHESTER ST	WALKER ON TYNE			21 NOV 1914		L'ONGBENTON		AGE 28.
MORGAN	H	PTE	24 /12	B		HARTON COLLIERY							
MORLEY	W H	SGT	24 /1734				30/12/14	2/10/16	SICK			FROM 34 DIV CYC COY, TO DEPOT.	
MORRISON	J	PTE	24 /486				10/10/14	1/12/14	DROPSY				DID NOT SERVE OVERSEAS. AGE 37
MOUNTJOY	Wm	PTE	24 /525	D	14 ALGERNON TERR	NEWBURN	7/11/14	17/6/18	WOUNDS	OCTOBER 16		TO DEPOT, ROYAL ENGINEERS.	WND L FOOT, AGE 20.34 CCS 2/7/16 EVAC 5/7/16.
MUIR	Peter	PTE	24 /138	A	93 SANDYFORD RD	NEWCASTLE	27/10/14					TO ROYAL DEFENCE CORPS.	IN FRANCE 11/1/16 TO 31/5/17. ASGT
MULDOON	P	PTE	24 /705	B		SUNDERLAND						TO 24/27th, 11th BNS, CLASS Z RESERVE.	MISSING SEPTEMBER 16, NOT MISSING NOVEMBER 16.
MULKEEN	W	CPL	24 /467		39 HUME ST	BORDEN COLLIERY	4/11/14	3/4/18	VDH	OCTOBER 16		TO 10th, 24/27th, DEPOT.	SGT
MULLARKEY	M	PTE	24 /463	B	30 FRAMWELLGATE	DURHAM CITY	6/11/14	26/2/19				TO ARMY RESERVE CLASS P.	CPL. 1st HOP STEP JUMPS ALNWICK SPORTS
MULLEN	Edwd	PTE	24 /1190	D	15 THOMAS ST	CONSETT	12/11/14			JANUARY 18.		TO 22nd, 8th, 25th BNS, CLASS Z RESERVE.	
MULLEN	Jn Wm	PTE	24 /445	B	41 ASKEW RD EAST	GATESHEAD	6/11/14			OCTOBER 16		TO 25th, 1/4th BNS, CLASS Z RESERVE.	ALLOTED NEW NUMBER 204609.
MULLENDER	J	PTE	24 /1245									TO 2nd GARRISON BN, CLASS Z RESERVE.	
MULLIGAN	Dan	PTE	24 /518	A	62 DERWENT ST	BLACKHILL	6/11/14		1 JULY 1916		T'HIEPVAL MEM		MISSING NOVEMBER 16
MULVEY	Jas	PTE	24 /615	C	4 TWEDDLES BLDGS	WHICKHAM	11/11/14		1 JULY 1916		T'HIEPVAL MEM		MISSING SEPTEMBER 16. BORN HAWICK
MUNROE	Jas	PTE	24 /1357	D		BLYTH			KR para 392				AWOL 16/8/15 IN COURT BLYTH 24/8/15.
MURDY	Geo	PTE	24 /552	B	21 BRICK ROW	NEWSHAM	27/10/14			OCTOBER 16		TO LABOUR CORPS.	
MURDY	Thos	PTE	24 /553	B	32 SOUTH ROW	NEW DELAVAL	27/10/14					TO 24/27th, 25th, 14th BNS, CLASS Z RESERVE.	

NAME	INITI	RANK	BA	NUMBE	COMP	ADDRESS	TOWN_VILL	ENLISTED	DISCHARG	CAUSE_DIS	WOUNDED	BURIED	TRANSFER	ADD
MURPHY	A M	PTE	24	/211			SHIREMOOR				JULY 16			3 CCS 2/7/16 EVAC 2/7/16.
MURPHY	Edwd	PTE	24	/17	A	HUSTLE DOWN	SOUTHMOOR				OCTOBER 16		TO DURHAM LI, LABOUR CORPS,ROYAL ENGINEERS.	HORDEN?
MURPHY	F	PTE	24	/1530	C		WILLINGTON QUAY				JULY 16.		TO ROYAL ARMY ORDNANCE CORPS.	SSHOCK,AGE 54.34CCS EVAC 5/7/16, HOSP BRISTOL 12/7
MURPHY	J E	PTE	24	/1425	B		NEWCASTLE				OCTOBER 16, DECEMBER 17.		TO 8th, 16th, 22nd BNS, CLASS Z RESERVE.	BEAUFORT WAR HOSP BRISTOL 8/7/16
MURPHY	Jos J	PTE	24	/460		4 DOUBLE BARDON	RYHOPE COLLIERY				JULY 16		TO 1st, 24th, 24/27th, 11th BNS, CLASS Z RESERVE.	AWOII
MURPHY	Pat	PTE	24	/411	B	16 HIGH FRIAR ST	NEWCASTLE	6/11/14			OCTOBER 16, DECEMBER 17.		TO 16th, 3rd BN, CLASS Z RESERVE.	34 CCS 2/7/16 EVAC 5/7/16, 69 HIGH FRIAR ST 1914.
MURPHY	Peter	PTE	24	/1529	C		KIRKDALE LANCS			2 JULY 1916		HEILLY STATION CEM		
MURRAY	E	PTE	24	/807	D								TO LABOUR CORPS.	
MURRAY	J	SGT	24	/1554									TO 1st GARRISON BN, CLASS Z RESERVE.	
MURRAY	Mich	PTE	24	/877	C	7 CRAWCROOK TERR	RYTON	10/11/14		23 NOV 1918		LES BARAQUES, SANGATTE.	TO 11th BN, LABOUR CORPS(54 POW COY).	ST BEARER,RAID 25/26th JUNE 16. BORN SOUTHWICK
MURRAY	O	PTE	24	/1553	D								TO 30th BN(A COY), ROYAL ENGINEERS	ON 24th BN ROLL AS /1550.
MURRAY	Wm Fl	PTE	24	/20	A	ERRINGTON TERR	SWALWELL	31/10/14		2 JULY 1916		WARLOY		BORN FERRYHILL.
MURTHWAITE	H	PTE	24	/345	D	39 HERBERT ST	NEWCASTLE				OCTOBER 16		TO LABOUR CORPS.	34 CCS 2/7 EVAC 5/7/16, LONDON HOSP 12/7/16
MYHILL	J	PTE	24	/1356	B		NEWBURN				OCTOBER 16		TO ROYAL ARMY MEDICAL CORPS.	21 AMBTRAIN,18 GEN HOSP,6 CONV DEPOT,SSHOCK,AGE 40
McADAM	J	PTE	24	/1540										DESERTED 13/5/15, AGE 22, 5'5'', FIREMAN, TATTOOES
McALLISTER	Frank	PTE	24	/609		6 BEDA COTTAGES	TANTOBIE			1 JULY 1916		BAPAUME POST CEM		MISSING AUGUST 16, BORN RYHOPE.
McALLISTER	Rob	PTE	24	/246	A	16a CHAPEL ST	TANTOBIE			25 OCT 1918		AWOINGT BRIT CEM	TO 22nd, 9th, 1st BNS.	NOK 17 QUARRY SQUARE TANTOBIE.
McALLISTER	W W	LCPL	24	/1615			JARROW	26/2/15	27/7/17	GUNSHOT WOUNDS	OCTOBER 16.		TO 3rd BN.	WND THIGH, AGE 19, 34 CCS 1/7/16 EVAC 5/7/16
McANDREW	Owen	PTE	24	/465			SLIGO			1 JULY 1916		THIEPVAL MEM		
McARDLE	P	PTE	24	/381	B	2 KING ST	CONSETT	5/11/14	14/11/17	WOUNDS	OCTOBER 16		TO 8th, 16th BNS, DEPOT.	3rd IN THREE LEGGED RACE AT ALNWICK SPORTS.
McARTHUR	G	PTE	24	/1651	C		NEWCASTLE				OCTOBER 16		TO ARMY SERVICE CORPS.	
McAVOY	Arth	PTE	24	/1430	A	26 SMITHFIELD	EGERMONT			2 JULY 1916		HEILLY STATION CEM		BORN CLEATOR MOOR, AGE 32.
McCABE	Bernd	PTE	24	/453		TOWER HOUSE	NEWCASTLE	10/11/14		16 SEPT 1917		JESMOND	TO 1st GARRISON BN, 11th BN.	BORN EDINBURGH, LCPL.
McCABE	P	PTE	24	/94				3/11/14	1/5/18	SICK			TO 1st GARRISON BN, 2nd BN, ARMY RESERVE CLASS P.	ENTERED THEATRE OF WAR (BALKANS) 31/12/15. AWARDED
McCABE	Pat	PTE	24	/1353	B	60 DOCTOR ST	SEAHAM COLLIERY			1 JULY 1916		OVILLIERS+THIEPVAL MEM		MISSING AUGUST 16.
McCABE	T	PTE	24	/11				2/11/14	19/12/14	INEFFICIENT				DID NOT SERVE OVERSEAS.
McCABE	W	PTE	24	/1250	B	11 CAROLINE ST	HETTON LE HOLE						TO 24/27th, 11th BNS, CLASS Z RESERVE.	
McCARDLE	Edwd	PTE	24	/380	A	30 2 BATH ST	CONSETT	6/11/14						
McCARTNEY	Rob	SGT	24	/112		30 DERBY ST	NEWCASTLE			9 APRIL 1917		ROCLINCOURT VALLEY CEM		
McCARTY	Bernd	PTE	24	/595	B	23 CUTHBERT ST	BIRTLEY	10/11/14			OCTOBER 16		TO 22nd, 8th BNS.	DESERTED 2 DECEMBER 1916.
McCOMB	John	PTE	24	/262	B	36 BURN ST	GATESHEAD			7 SEPT 1916		FLAT IRON COPSE CEM		BORN GLASGOW, PARENTS LIVING GROSEVNOR ST GATESHEA
McCONVILLE	H	SGT	24	/786		2 CHURCH ROW	GATESHEAD	9/11/14	15/11/17	SICK			TO 3rd BN.	
McCOY	Alex	PTE	24	/1149		15 PRINCE CONSORTS R	HEBBURN	11/11/14	23/10/17	WOUNDS	OCTOBER 16		TO DEPOT.	CPL, AGE 24. SPRINGBURN HOSP GLASGOW 11/7/16
McCOY	Thos	PTE	24	/497	B	7 CROFT STAIRS	NEWCASTLE			1 JULY 1916		THIEPVAL MEM		MISSING SEPTEMBER 16.
McCUE	Jas	PTE	24	/212	A	9 RAMSEY ST	WEST STANLEY	5/11/14						ALSO ON D COY 30th BN ROLL.
McDONALD	P	PTE	24	/1431	C	28 NOBLE ST	NEWCASTLE				APRIL 16, DECEMBER 17.		TO 8th, 16th, 14th, 9th BNS.	DESERTED 15 AUGUST 1916.
McDONALD	T	PTE	24	/938	D		WHEATLEY HILL				AUGUST 16		FROM 34 DIV CYCLIST COY TO 10th, 1st BNS, CLASS Z	1st IN THREE LEGGED RACE ALNWICK SPORTS 1915.
McDONNELL	F	PTE	24	/1624	B									
McDONNELL	Jothn	SGT	24	/583		1 VICTORIA RD	HEBBURN	6/11/14			AUGUST 16		TO LABOUR CORPS.	34 CCS, 21 AMB TRAIN, 18 GEN HOSP, H SHIP 7/7/16.
McDONOUGH	Jas	PTE	24	/181	B	14 PANDON ST	NEWCASTLE	14/11/14	28/12/17	SICK			TO 3rd BN.	DESERTED 5/7/15 IN COURT 29/7/15.
McELPHONE	M	SGT	24	/813		979 WALKER RD	NEWCASTLE						TO 24/27th, 25th, 9th BNS, CLASS Z RESERVE.	SIGNALLER, TOOK PART IN TRENCH RAID 25/26 JUNE 16.
McGARR	Wm	PTE	24	/1097	D	6 SOUTH ST	DURHAM CITY	12/11/14			JULY 16, OCTOBER 16.		TO CLASS Z RESERVE,	RAID 5/6th JUNE 1916. 34CCS 2/7 EVAC 5/7/16 AGE 28
McGARRITY	P G	CPL	24	/646		13 LONDONDERRY ST	EASINGTON						TO 24/27th, 11th BNS, ATTACHED 17 CORPS SCHOOL, CL	
McGEAREY	W J	PTE	24	/1056				10/11/14	10/10/17	SICK			TO 85th TRAINING RESERVE BN.	
McGEE	M	PTE		/554	B									ALSO ON D COY 30th BN ROLL, No ALSO ALLOTED TO HUG
McGEE	T	PTE	24	/137	D		HIRST				AUGUST 16		TO ROYAL DEFENCE CORPS.	34 CCS 1/7/16 EVAC 5/7/16. RDC No 65684..
McGILL	James	PTE	24	/261	A	4 PRIOR ST	GATESHEAD	6/11/14		23 MARCH 1918	OCTOBER 16	ARRAS MEM	TO MACHINE GUN CORPS(3rd BN).	SEE 25/1166 ALSO 24/1129, MGC No 139529.
McGILL	John	PTE	24	/1129	A	114 ABBOTT ST	GATESHEAD			1 JULY 1916		THIEPVAL MEM		IN 2 PLATOON.
McGINN	F	PTE	24	/1135	A		DIPTON				JANUARY 18		TO 19th, 22nd, 18th BNS, CLASS Z RESERVE.	
McGINTY	P	PTE	24	/69	A	15 BOLIVAR PLACE	GATESHEAD	2/11/14	29/7/16				TO D COY 30th BN	DID NOT SERVE OVERSEAS.
McGINTY	Rich	PTE	24	/284	C	5 PRIOR ST	GATESHEAD						TO CATTERICK BASE DEPOT, CLASS Z RESERVE.	
McGRATH	Mich	PTE	24	/1118		37 BOLSOVER ST	ASHINGTON	6/11/14		15 SEPT 1917	MARCH 17	ZUYDCOOTE MIL CEM	TO 1st, 16th BNS.	BORN BALLYMULLETT Co MAYO, AGE 29.
McGRATH	Thos	PTE	24	/247	A	C/O J WHITE ESQ DIPT	BALLINSLOE CO G	28/10/14		1 JULY 1916		THIEPVAL MEM		MISSING SEPTEMBER 16
McGRATH	Wm	PTE	24	/1106	C	32 QUEBEC ST	LANGLEY PARK	12/11/14		1 JULY 1916		THIEPVAL MEM		BORN NEW DURHAM.
McGUINESS	John	PTE	24	/240	A	354 ASKEW RD	GATESHEAD						TO 11th BN, ROYAL ENGINEERS.	SON JOHN JUNIOR 202929 1/7th DLI, RE No 615201.
McGUMMERS	John	PTE	24											AWOL 3/8/15 COURT GATESHEAD.
McGURK	J	PTE	24	/1089	D			9/11/14	1/4/18	SHELLSHOCK			TO 3rd BN.	
McGURK	Thos	PTE	24	/1127	D	2 EMMERSON VILLA	SCOTSWOOD	11/11/14	4/4/16	HERNIA			TO 30th BN(D COY).	
McHUGH	Jos	PTE	24	/30	A		BEDLINGTON			1 JULY 1916		THIEPVAL MEM		MISSING SEPTEMBER 16
McINTYRE	Jas	PTE	24	/339	B	3 BRANDLING TERR	FELLING	5/11/14					TO 12th BN.	

NAME	INITL	RANK	BN	NUMBER	COMP	ADDRESS	TOWN_VILL	ENLISTED	DISCHARG	CAUSE_DIS	WOUNDED	BURIED	TRANSFER	ADD
McINTYRE	Wm H	PTE	24	/1508		40 ELSWICK ST	GATESHEAD						TO 1st GARRISON BN, CLASS Z RESERVE.	
McKAY	Jas	PTE	24	/715	D	13 LYNWOOD ST	BLAYDON	11/11/14		12 JULY 1917		NIEUPORT MEM	TO 16th BN.	AGE 25.BORN GOSFORTH, NOK 2 STORE ST BLAYDON.
McKAY	Peter	PTE	24	/714	D	13 LYNWOOD ST	BLAYDON	11/11/14			AUGUST 16		TO 1/7th, 1/5th BNS, CLASS Z RESERVE.	
McKEATING	John	PTE	24	/1562	B		WORKINGTON			1 JULY 1916		GORDON DUMP CEM		
McKENNA	Chas	PTE	24	/367		70 HEITSON TERR	FELLING	10/11/14						DESERTED 2/5/15, AGE 19, 5'3'', MINER COAL MARKS O
McKENNA	Jas	PTE	24	/493	B	10 EDWARD ST	HEBBURN	5/11/14			JANUARY 17		TO ROYAL FUSILIERS.	
McKEOWN	J J	PTE	24	/294		14 FOURTH ST	EASINGTON						TO 2nd GARRISON BN, CLASS Z RESERVE.	
McKEOWN	John	SGT	24	/610	D	30 LABURNUM HOUSE	WALKER	29/10/14						
McKEVER	Thos	PTE	24	/510	A	47 HOWARD ST	NEWCASTLE	7/11/14	4/3/18	GUNSHOT WOUNDS	DECEMBER 16		ATTACHED 103rd LIGHT TRENCH MORTAR BTY, ARMY RESER	3 CCS 2/7/16 EVAC 3/7/16
McKIE	G A	PTE		/1622	A									No ALSO ALLOTED TO PITTS T SAME Coy.
McKIE	Wm	PTE	24	/1122	A		GATESHEAD			27 OCT 1917	MARCH 16, SEPTEMBER 16.	TYNE COT MEM	TO KINGS OWN YORKSHIRE LI(8th BN).	LCPL, AGE 30. SSHOCK JUL 16,KOYLI No 37809.
McKINLEY	H	PTE	24	/1539	A								TO 24/27th, 8th BNS, CLASS Z RESERVE.	
McKITTERICK	Wm	PTE	24	/165	A	70 WORSLEY ST	NEWCASTLE	2/11/14		9 APRIL 1917		ROCLINCOURT MIL CEM		BORN CORK.
McKIVITT	W	PTE	24	/842	C					KR para 392				MG SECTION, RAIDS 5/6th, 25/26th JUNE 16.
McLANAGHAN	ChasF	PTE	24	/521	B	22 OLD FOLD COTTAGES	GATESHEAD	7/11/14	2/5/17	15 NOV 1918		GATESHEAD	TO DEPOT.	DIED OF GAS POISONING, AGE 43.
McLANE	Jos	PTE	24	/456									TO LABOUR CORPS.	LAB CORPS No 219947.
McLAUGHLIN	Jas	PTE	24	/235	D	35 THOMPSON ST	WALLSEND	29/10/14		1 JULY 1916		THIEPVAL MEM		BORN MAHARA CO DERRY, MISSING SEPTEMBER 16
McLAUGHLIN	P	LCPL	24	/718		1 PATTERSON ST	BLAYDON	9/11/14	27/12/17	GUNSHOT WOUNDS	OCTOBER 16		TO ARMY RESERVE CLASS W.	WND FOOT, AGE 35.34 CCS 1/7/16 EVAC 5/7/16
McLAUGHLINN	How	SGT	24				SEAHAM							NICK NAMED 'PUNCHY' AT ALNWICK WITH L SHAUGHNESSY.
McLOUGHLIN	D	PTE	24	/24	A	PILGRIM ST	NEWCASTLE				OCTOBER 16		TO HIGHLAND LI.	BORN BALLYCOLEY.
McMAHON	John	PTE	24	/198		5 ROBERT TERR	SHIELDROW	3/11/14	1/6/17	WOUNDS	AUGUST 16		TO DEPOT.	AWOL 19/10/15 IN COURT 20/10/15.
McMANUS	John	PTE	24	/1187	D	11 VICTORIA ST		12/11/14						ALSO ON A COY 30th BN ROLL.
McNALLY	F	PTE	24	/1047	D			7/11/14	23/8/18				TO DEPOT.	
McNAMARA	Thos	PTE	24	/584			MOHILL CO LEITR			1 JULY 1916		GORDON DUMP CEM		LCPL.
McNULTY	J	SGT	24	/437				3/11/14	8/6/15	UNFIT				DID NOT SERVE OVERSEAS.
McPARLIN	B	LCPL	24	/1251	C	512 JOHN WILLIAMSON	TYNE DOCK				MARCH 17, JUNE 18.		TO 24/27th, 25th, 9th BNS, CLASS Z RESERVE.	
McQUILLAN	J	PTE	24	/1351	D		USWORTH	18/12/14	31/12/17	DEBILITY	JULY 16.		TO 30th BN.	SWB 3134 GIVES DATES 18/12/14 TO 19/8/16.
McROY	Geo W	PTE	24	/581	B	11 TATES BIULDINGS	BROOMPARK	11/11/14		11 APRIL 1918	JULY 16, AUGUST 18.	PLOEGSTEERT MEM	TO 8th, 16th, 10th, 22nd BNS.	BORN SOUTH SHIELDS, 11 HILL VIEW BROOMPARK 1918.
McSHANE	Domnc	SGT	24	/619		6 OAK ST	LANGLEY PARK	11/11/14		1 JULY 1916	OCTOBER 16	THIEPVAL MEM		BORN SUNDERLAND.
McSHERRY	Jas	PTE	24	/1428	A		BEDLINGTON			1 JULY 1916		THIEPVAL MEM		MISSING SEPTEMBER 16.
McSLOY	John	PTE	24	/994	C	65 WATERLOO RD	BLYTH		14/2/19				TO MACHINE GUN CORPS(34th BN), CLASS Z RESERVE.	MGC No 152015, SGT.
McTAGGART	A	PTE	24	/978	C		NEWCASTLE				OCTOBER 16		TO LABOUR CORPS.	3 CCS 2/7/16 EVAC 2/7/16 GSW
McVEIGH	Jos	PTE	24	/384		1 KNITSLEY GARDENS	CONSETT	3/11/14	14/11/17	WOUNDS	OCTOBER 16		TO 3rd BN.	WND CHEST. 3CCS 2/7/16 EVAC 2/7/16
McVEIGH	Pat	PTE	24	/650	D	6 FURNACE TERR	CHESTER LE ST	26/10/14		KR para 392				
NELSON	John	PTE	24	/861			HIGH FELLING						TO 1st GARRISON BN, 24/27th, 1st, 14th BNS, CLASS	A COY 4 PLATOON 14 BN.
NESBIT	JohnW	PTE	24	/1435	A	12 SWINBURN PLACE	BIRTLEY							
NEVINS	W	PTE	24	/1253	B		SEAHAM				JULY 1916		TO DURHAM LI.	DLI 59329.
NEWTON	E	PTE	24	/1440				10/1/15	26/12/17	GUNSHOT WOUNDS			TO 3rd BN.	
NEWTON	W	PTE	24	/1434				19/12/14	17/6/16	ARTERITIS			TO 30th BN.	DID NOT SERVE OVERSEAS.
NICHOL	W	PTE	24	/136	A	41 BUCKINGHAM ST	NEWCASTLE							
NICHOLSON	Norm	PTE	24	/1006	D	48 DELAVAL RD BENWEL	NEWCASTLE	11/11/14		29 AUGUST 1917		THIEPVAL MEM	TO 24/27th BN.	DESERTED 9/11/15 IN COURT 24/12/15.
NICHOLSON	Rob H	PTE	24	/450	B	72 MILLING ST TEAMS	GATESHEAD	10/11/14						ALSO ON D COY 30th BN ROLL.
NICHOLSON	Scott	PTE	24	/1436	B	53 DIXON ST	GATESHEAD		11/3/19		APRIL 16, JANUARY 17.		TO MACHINE GUN CORPS.	MGC No 139042.
NIGHTINGALE	Andrw	PTE	24	/1577	B		WASHINGTON				OCTOBER 16.		TO ROYAL INNISKILLING FUSILIERS.	TOOK PART IN TRENCH RAID 5/6th JUNE 16.
NIGHTINGALE	Mark	PTE	24	/1576	B									CORPORAL DESERTED 14 AUGUST 1917.
NIGHTINGALE	Math	PTE	24	/556	B	50 WARWICK ST MNKWRM	SUNDERLAND			8 SEPT 1916		FLAT IRON COPSE CEM		AGE 32.
NIGHTINGALE	Wm	PTE	24	/555	B	SOUTHWICK	SUNDERLAND	4/11/14	30/11/17	WOUNDS	OCTOBER 16		TO DEPOT.	SEE ALSO 24/556, 24/1576, 24/1577.
NIMMONS	W	PTE	24	/983	C		LEADGATE				JULY 16, AUGUST 18.			RAIDS 5/6, 25/26 JUNE 16, BOMBER. 34CCS 2/7-5/7/16
NIXON	R	PTE	24	/290	B		WEST RYTON			KR para 392	OCTOBER 16			
NOBLE	F	PTE	24	/741		26 WAKEFIELD TERR	GATESHEAD						TO 1st GARRISON BN, 12/13th BN, CLASS Z RESERVE.	
NOBLE	John	PTE	24	/721	D	83 MORRISON ST TEAMS	GATESHEAD						TO 24/27th, 11th BNS, ATTACHED 103rd BDE HQ, Z RES	NOBLE JOHN & GEO IN AVL AT THIS ADDRESS RM LAB COY
NOLAN	James	LCPL	24	/204	A		LANGLEY MOOR	4/11/14	13/8/17	GUNSHOT WOUNDS	MAY 16, NOVEMBER 16.		TO DEPOT.	MG SECTION RAIDS 5/6, 25/26 JUNE 16
NOON	P	SGT	24	/59			WALLSEND	2/11/14	24/11/17	WOUNDS	AUGUST 16		TO DEPOT.	WND LEG,CHEST. SCOTTISH RX CARDONALD GLASGOW.
NOON	R	PTE	24	/546	D			7/11/14	26/10/16	WOUNDS			TO DEPOT.	34 CCS 2/7/16 EVAC 5/7/16 FRAC FOREARM.
NORMAN	W	PTE	24	/1252	D	170 PALMERSTON ST	SOUTH SHIELDS	19/12/14	15/9/16	SICK			TO 30th BN.	
NORTON	John	PTE	24	/1153			POPLAR LONDON							DESERTED 4/3/15, AGE 19, 5'9'', CLERK.
NORTON	Wm	PTE	24	/1124		63 PONT ST HIRST	ASHINGTON	11/11/14	14/9/15	INEFFICIENT				DID NOT SERVE OVERSEAS. AGE 29.
O'BRIEN	P	PTE	24	/305		46 BERWICK ST	GATESHEAD						TO 1st GARRISON BN, CLASS Z RESERVE.	JAMES OBRIEN ASC ALSO AT THIS ADDRESS IN AVL.
O'CONNER	P	PTE	24	/152		118 EAGLESFIELD RD	SOUTH SHIELDS	3/11/14	21/12/17	SICK			TO DEPOT.	
O'CONNER	Pat	PTE	24	/153	A	3 BOUNDARY HOUSES	WREKETON	28/10/14		KR para 392				

NAME	INITI	RANK	BA	NUMBE	COMP	ADDRESS	TOWN_VILL	ENLISTED	DISCHARG	CAUSE_DIS	WOUNDED	BURIED	TRANSFER	ADD
O'CONNOR	J	PTE	24	/1524	C		SEAHAM	15/1/15	24/11/17	WOUNDS	OCTOBER 16		TO 3rd BN.	WND L LEG AGE 28, 34 CCS EVAC 5/7/16
O'DONNELL	H	PTE	24	/1360	B		ASHINGTON	19/12/14	3/11/17	WOUNDS	JULY 16.		TO DEPOT.	
O'FARRELL	M	PTE	24	/1078	D			11/11/14	21/2/17	MYALGIA			TO 3rd BN.	
O'HALLORAN	Wm Hy	SGT	24	/236		12 JEFFERSON ST	NEWCASTLE	26/10/14		1 JULY 1916	OCTOBER 16	THIEPVAL MEM		BORN ALDERSHOT, AGE 28, MISSING DECEMBER 16
O'HARE	Jas	SGT	24	/707		51 WELLINGTON ST	LEMINGTON			3 SEPT 1916		THIEPVAL MEM		PRIVATE WHEN KILLED, AGE 37, BORN LIVERPOOL.
O'KANE	Pat	ACPL	24	/474		10 BURNVILLE	NEWCASTLE	6/11/14					TO 2nd GARRISON.BN, CLASS Z RESERVE.	AWOL 27/5/15 IN COURT 1/6/15.
O'KELLY	Jas	PTE	24	/234	C	ROWTON HOUSE PILGRIM	NEWCASTLE	6/11/14						
O'MARA	M	PTE	24	/977	C	5 SHORT ROW	JARROW				OCTOBER 16		TO LABOUR CORPS.	
O'NIELE	C.F	PTE	24	/1557										DESERTED 6/4/15, AGE 19, 5'6'',TRIMMER,No 1558?
O'NIELL	Alf E	PTE	24	/654	D	16 NEWCOMBE ST ELSWI	NEWCASTLE	6/11/14		28 APRIL 1917	MARCH 17	BROWNS COPSE CEM ROUEX		
O'NIELL	C	PTE	24	/1185	D								TO LABOUR CORPS.	
O'NIELL	Jos F	PTE	24	/85	A	15 ELDON ST	GATESHEAD	26/10/14		1 JULY 1916		THIEPVAL MEM		BORN KILKENNY.
O'NIELL	Mich	PTE	24	/1195	C	14 RANDLE ST	NEWCASTLE	6/11/14						ALSO ON A COY 30th BN ROLL.
O'NIELL	Steph	SGT	24	/251		39 HECTOR ST	GATESHEAD			9 APRIL 1917	OCTOBER 16	BAILLEUL RD ST LAURENT BLAGNY		HOSP 8 JULY 16 WOUNDED,
O'NIELL	Thos	PTE	24	/353									TO ARMY SERVICE CORPS.	ASC No M/381093
O'REILLY	Thos	PTE	24	/745	C	27 11 SUNDERLAND ST	NEWCASTLE	11/11/14		23 MARCH 1918		ARRAS MEM	TO 27th, 24th, 21st, 25th BNS.	BORN LONDON
OAKLEY	S	PTE	24	/1255				18/12/14	28/3/18	BRONCHITIS			TO 1st GARRISON BN, DEPOT.	
ORD	J G	PTE	24	/979	C	EWART TERR COWPEN	BLYTH				OCTOBER 16		TO CLASS Z RESERVE.	SEE 25/1198.
ORD	W	PTE	24	/1018	C		HASWELL PLOUGH				AUGUST 16, OCTOBER 16.		TO ROYAL FLYING CORPS.	
ORRICK	E	PTE	24	/116	A									
OTOOLE	J	PTE	24	/870	C		SEATON DELAVAL	9/11/14	8/4/18	GUNSHOT WOUNDS	AUGUST 16		TO ARMY RESERVE CLASS P.	34 CCS 2/7/16 EVAC 5/7/16 GSW R LEG.
OTOOLE	J L	PTE	24	/1564	A	53 HEYWORTH ST	EVERTON	9/1/15	12/12/17	14 JAN 1918	OCTOBER 16.	FORD RC CEM LIVERPOOL	TO LABOUR CORPS.	LAB CORPS No 130519, AGE 39 BORN 6/7/1878.
OTOOLE	P	WO1	24	/100				30/10/14	29/4/16	OLD AGE (60)				DID NOT SERVE OVERSEAS, FIRST DRILL SGT.
OUGHTON	Andrw	PTE	24	/1160	D	28 NEW ELVET	DURHAM CITY						TO LABOUR CORPS(913 LAB COY), ROYAL FUSILIERS.	LAB CORPS No 387253. AWOL 4/8/15 TO 9/8/15.
OWENS	Thos	LCPL	24	/1096	D	FRAMWELLGATE	DURHAM CITY						TO LABOUR CORPS.	LIVING CLAYPATH 1918
OXLEY	J	PTE	24	/759	B	8 CHESTER RD	EAST STANLEY		15/5/19				TO 24/27th, 11th BNS, KINGS OWN YORKSHIRE LI(2/4th	KOYLI No 63401, CHARLTON OXLEY 17123 198 LAB COY I
OXNARD	T	PTE	24	/819	A	99 NORFOLK RD	BYKER	9/11/14	4/4/16	VDH			TO 30th BN.	DID NOT SERVE OVERSEAS. ALSO ON D COY 30th BN ROLL
PADDEN	John	PTE	24	/232	A	1 ST MARYS ST	NEWCASTLE	6/11/14		1 JULY 1916		THIEPVAL MEM		MISSING SEPTEMBER 16, AGE 19.
PAISLEY	S	PTE	24	/1548	B			8/1/15	19/2/18	KNEE WOUND			TO DEPOT.	
PALLAN	G	LCPL	24	/1649	C								TO CLASS Z RESERVE.	TOOK PART IN TRENCH RAID 25/26 JUNE 16.
PALMER	J	PTE	24	/586	C									
PALMER	M	PTE	24	/2	D	RAMSEY COTTAGE	SWALWELL	2/11/14	22/12/17	SICK			TO DEPOT.	
PALMER	Wm	PTE	24	/1698		LYNN RD	LITTLEPORT CAMB			1 JULY 1916		THIEPVAL MEM	FROM SUFFOLK REGT, 34 DIV CYC COY.	MISSING SEPTEMBER 16, AGE 19.
PARKIN	ChasT	CPL	24	/713		2 TWEDDLES BLDGS	WHICKHAM	9/11/14	31/3/19	KR para 392	OCT 16		TO 19th BN, ARMY RESERVE CLASS P.	
PARKIN	Thom	PTE	24	/1173									TO & FROM 34th DIV CYC COY, TO TANK CORPS.	ACC No 9686, TANK CORPS No 302495.
PATT	P	PTE	24	/1363	B									
PAYTON	Pat	PTE	24	/949	D		KELLOE			1 JULY 1916		THIEPVAL MEM		MISSING SEPTEMBER 16.
PEARS	Jos	PTE	24	/1526	C	19 POPLAR ST	SOUTHMOOR						TO LABOUR CORPS(EASTERN COMMAND LAB CENTRE).	LAB CORPS No 459703
PEARSON	C E	PTE	24	/408		6 GEORGE STAIRS PILG	NEWCASTLE	5/11/14	25/7/19				TO 2nd GARRISON BN, DEPOT.	
PEPPER	John	PTE	24	/190		VIOLA ST	USWORTH	31/10/14		30 JUNE 1916		HEILLY STATION CEM		BORN DURHAM CITY.
PERRY	A	PTE	24	/1573			GOSFORTH	28/8/14	18/4/17	WOUNDS	AUGUST 16.		TO DEPOT.	
PERRY	C	PTE	24	/1442	D			17/12/14	15/9/16				TO 30th BN(D COY).	DID NOT SERVE OVERSEAS.GAVE PUPPET DISPLAY AT ALNW
PERRY	Hnry	CPL	24	/91		5 BACK STEPNEY ST	NEWCASTLE	31/10/14					TO 1st GARRISON BN, CLASS Z RESERVE.	44 CITY RD NEWCASTLE 1914.
PHILBIN	Wm	PTE	24	/849	C	7 BROUGHAM ST	SUNDERLAND	28/10/14		1 JULY 1916		THIEPVAL MEM		MISSING SEPTEMBER 16, BORN SWINFORD Co MAYO.
PHILIPSON	Geo W	PTE	24	/1039	B		CONSETT			2 JULY 1916		MEAULTE MIL CEM		BORN HEXAM.
PHILIPSON	Tos H	PTE	24	/955	D	44 THOMAS TERR	BLAYDON	12/11/14					TO 24/27th, 23rd BNS CLASS Z RESERVE.	
PIPKIN		CPL	24											CPL PHOTO IN IRISH HEROES UNABLE TO TRACE ON MR.
PITT	B	PTE	24	/1699			NEWCASTLE	5/12/14	5/1/17	WOUNDS	AUGUST 16.		FROM 34 DIV CYC COY, TO COMMAND DEPOT.	
PITTS	G S	PTE	24	/1364	A	21 HUMBER ST	CHOPWELL	18/12/14	24/4/18	SICK	OCTOBER 16		TO ARMY RESERVE CLASS W.	
PITTS	Tom L	PTE	24	/1622	A		ALL HALLOWS CUM			1 JULY 1916		THIEPVAL MEM	FROM BORDER REGT.	MISSING SEPTEMBER 16. BORDER REGT No 13551.
PORTEOUS	J	PTE	24	/447	B									ALSO ON D COY 30th BN ROLL.
POWELL	J T	PTE	24	/629	C		GATESHEAD				OCTOBER 16			
POWER	M	PTE	24	/76	B		NEWTON SANDS				OCTOBER 16, DECEMBER 17.		TO 16th, 1/6th BNS, CLASS Z RESERVE.	
POWTON	J G	PTE	24	/1259	B		CROOK			KR para 392	SEPTEMBER 16, DECEMBER 16			
PREST	J T	PTE	24	/38	A		NEWCASTLE				OCTOBER 16		TO LABOUR CORPS.	
PRESTON	T	PTE	24	/324	B	9 WALLACE ST	DUNSTON							ALSO ON D COY 30th BN ROLL.
PRICE	Math	PTE	24	/873	C	1 FOURTH ST	WHEATLEY HILL	12/11/14			JULY 16		TO 22nd BN.	DESERTED 5 OCTOBER 1917.
PRICE	Tom A	PTE	24	/1721	D	3 STATION ROW PARKGA	ROTHERHAM			1 JULY 1916	DECEMBER 16.	THIEPVAL MEM	FROM 10, 34 DIV CYC COY.	ENTERED THEATRE OF WAR BALKANS 28 JULY 1915.AGE 22
PRINCE	G	PTE	24	/1146	D								TO LABOUR CORPS.	
PRIOR	H	PTE	24	/1441	C		SUNDERLAND				OCTOBER 16.		TO 16th, 1/5th BNS, CLASS Z RESERVE.	WND L FOOT, AGE 29.34 CCS 2/7/16 EVAC 5/7/16

NAME	INITL	RANK	BN	NUMBER	COMP	ADDRESS	TOWN_VILL	ENLISTED	DISCHARG	CAUSE_DIS	WOUNDED	BURIED	TRANSFER	ADD
PRUDHOE	J	CQMS	24	/857			GATESHEAD						TO LABOUR CORPS.	PROBATION OFFICER COUNTY COURT GATESHEAD.
PUNSHON	R	PTE	24	/519	D	23 CROSS ROW STARGAT	RYTON				SHELLSHOCK DECEMBER 16		TO ROYAL ENGINEERS.	
PURDY	Geo W	PTE	24	/1697		12 ELLISON TERR	RYTON	14/1/15			JANUARY 1917		FROM 20th BN,34 DIV CYC COY,TO 16th,19th(W COY)BNS	ORIGINAL 20th BN No 20/1350.
PURDY	Wm	PTE	24	/1258	B		GATESHEAD			2 JULY 1916	OCTOBER 16.	WARLOY MIL CEM		
PURVIS	G	PTE	24	/540	C		CHOPWELL							MISSING SEPTEMBER 16, NOT MISSING FEBRUARY 17.
PURVIS	Sam W	ACPL	24	/185		14 BUCKINGHAM ST	NEWCASTLE	6/11/14					TO 1st GARRISON BN, CLASS Z RESERVE.	
PYE	Jn Js	PTE	24	/1055	D	68 PEARETH ST	GATESHEAD	12/11/14					TO 2nd BN, CLASS Z RESERVE.	ALSO ON A COY 30th BN ROLL.
PYLE	Math	PTE	24	/1014	C	8 LOUGHWALL CRES	ASHINGTON						TO 85th TRAINING RESERVE BN.	
QUIGG	P	PTE	24	/827	C									ALSO ON D COY 30th BN ROLL.
QUIGLEY	Jos	PTE	24	/787	C		GATESHEAD			1 JULY 1916		THIEPVAL MEM		
QUIGLEY	Jos	PTE	24	/1126	A	18 ATHOL ST	DUNSTON				JANUARY 17		TO 12/13th BN, CLASS Z RESERVE.	
QUINN	D	PTE	24	/1262	A	124 CHURCHWAY	NORTH SHIELDS				OCTOBER 16			
QUINN	Domnc	PTE	24	/51	A	2 COLLING SQUARE	SUNDERLAND	2/11/14	2/11/18				TO 30th BN, DEPOT.	DID NOT SERVE OVERSEAS. ALSO ON D COY 30th BN ROLL
QUINN	Isaac	PTE	24	/1443	C	20 SUSSEX ST	SUNDERLAND			27 MAY 1918		SOISSONS MEM	TO 12/13th BN.	BORN RYHOPE, NOK 17 SUSSEX ST SUNDERLAND.
QUINN	Jas W	PTE	24	/1176	D	8 ASYLUM SQUARE	SHERRIFF HILL				SEPTEMBER 16.			same address 1918 QUINN Wm 397618 25 GAR BN KRRC.
QUINN	Pat	PTE	24	/506	B	21 EIGHTON TERR	WREKETON	28/10/14		9 JULY 1916		ST SEVER CEM ROUEN		AGE 28, BORN BALLINDERRAN Co GALWAY, NOK ORANMORE
QUINN	Wm	PTE	24	/1261	A 30	12 ASYLUM SQUARE	SHERRIFF HILL						TO LABOUR CORPS, KRRC(25th GAR BN).	LAB CORPS No 397618, SEE ALSO 24/1176.
RAFFERTY	H	PTE	24	/995	C									ALSO ON A COY 30th BN ROLL.
RAFFLE	R	PTE	24	/1737				31/10/14	1/4/19	KR paras 392			FROM 34 DIV CYC COY, TO 23rd BN, ARMY RESERVE CLAS	
RAILTON	Alex	PTE	24	/625	A	42 HARLE ST MNT PLEA	GATESHEAD			1 JULY 1916		THIEPVAL MEM		MISSING SEPTEMBER 16, EMPLOYED AT G/HEAD STN BY NE
RAINEY	R	PTE	24	/643	C	16 NORTH TERR	BEDLINGTON				OCTOBER 16		TO MACHINE GUN CORPS.	
RAINEY	T	PTE	25	/1445	B									ALSO ON A COY 30th BN ROLL.
RAMSEY	Alex	CPL	24	/1703			NEWCASTLE			1 JULY 1916		THIEPVAL MEM	FROM 34 DIV CYC COY.	MISSING AUGUST 16. ACC No 9641.
RAMSHAW	D	PTE	24	/1136	A		JARROW							MISSING AUGUST 16, NOT MISSING NOVEMBER 16.
REARDON	Jack	CPL	24	/373			THORNLEY			KR para 392	JULY 16, OCTOBER 16.			RAID 5/6th JUNE 16, HOSP LEICESTER 11/7/16.
REARDON	P	PTE	24	/526	A									
RECHALL	J	PTE	24	/187	B									
REED	Geo	PTE	24	/1175	D	32 ESHWOOD ST	NEW BRANCEPETH	11/11/14	31/3/19				TO LABOUR CORPS(GRN GUARD COY), ARMY RESERVE CLASS	RDC No 62196, SEE 24/1105 BROTHER JOHN
REED	John	PTE	24	/1105	D	32 ESHWOOD ST	NEW BRANCEPETH	12/11/14					TO ROYAL AIR FORCE(14 SECTION).	SEE 24/1175 BROTHER GEORGE.
REED	W	PTE	24	/1551	C									
REGAN	Edwd	PTE	24	/607	B	5 BURN PLACE	WILLINGTON	29/10/14					TO LABOUR CORPS.	LAB CORPS No 397070.
REGAN	John	PTE	24	/172	A		LANGLEY MOOR			1 JULY 1916		THIEPVAL MEM		STRECHER BEARER, TOOK PART IN TRENCH RAID 25/26 JU
REID	D L	PTE	24	/1728		5 HUNTER ST	WHITE LE HEAD	14/11/14	31/3/19	KR para 392			FROM 34 DIV CYC COY, TO 24/27th BN, ARMY RESERVE C	
REID	J	PTE	24	/1621										
REIDY	J	WO1	24	/62		4 WELLESLEY TERR	NEWCASTLE	2/11/14	11/1/19	SICK			TO 3rd BN.	AGE 50.
RENWICK	Jos	PTE	24	/360	C	2 CHAPEL ST	GOSFORTH	26/10/14		31 MARCH 1916		BAILLEUL MIL CEM		BORN ADDINGTON SURREY, AGE 35.
REYNOLDS	M	PTE	24	/889	C		SUNDERLAND	9/11/14	21/12/17	SICK	NOVEMBER 16		TO 3rd BN.	
REYNOLDS	Rob	PTE	24	/816	C	19 LESTER AVE	GREENSIDE			12 JANUARY 1918		WANCOURT	TO 24/27th BN.	ON ROLL AS /876, BORN LEADGATE.
REYNOLDS	ThosA	PTE	24	/1103	D	COUNCIL SCHOOLS	HIGH FELLING	6/11/14					TO LABOUR CORPS.	LAB CORPS No 397956
REYNOLDS	W	PTE	24	/929	C	106 PARKER ST	BYKER	10/11/14	22/7/16	VDH			TO DEPOT.	
RICHARDS	A	PTE	24	/1642	A 30									
RICHARDS	C	PTE	24	/738	C	38 JOHNSON TERR STN	USWORTH				JUNE 18		TO 26th, 18th, 1/6th BNS, CLASS Z RESERVE.	
RICHARDS	Hen W	PTE	24	/706	C	6 BOYNE ST	BRANCEPETH COLL			29 AUGUST 1918		LIGNY-SUR-CANCHE CEM	TO 25th BN, 2/4th BN KINGS OWN YORKSHIRE LI.	KOYLI No 63323, BORN RODIMOOR CROOK Co DURHAM..
RICHARDS	Wm	CPL	24	/847	A 30	96 CLAYPATH	DURHAM CITY	10/11/14	26/6/17	WOUNDS	JANUARY 17		TO 25th, 12th BNS, DEPOT.	
RICHARDSON	A	PTE	24	/1215	A						MAY 16		TO LABOUR CORPS.	
RICHARDSON	J	PTE	24	/1487	C	25 SOUTH VIEW AUTON	DURHAM CITY	28/12/14	10/10/17	AO 267/17	AUGUST 16		TO DURHAM LI, DEPOT DLI.	DLI 59328. 34 CCS 2/7/16 EVAC 5/7/16
RICHARDSON	J	PTE	24	/1722			CHOPPINGTON	10/12/14	24/8/17	GUNSHOT WOUNDS	AUGUST 16		FROM 34 DIV CYC COY, TO DEPOT.	
RICHARDSON	T	PTE	24	/157	A	15 THORPE TER	RYTON							
RICHARDSON	Tom	PTE	24	/1479	C		SUNDERLAND			1 JULY 1916		THIEPVAL MEM		
RICHES	E	PTE	24	/108	D	55 THOMAS TERR	BLAYDON	3/11/14	30/3/18	SICK			TO ARMY RESERVE CLASS P	
RICHES	S C	SGT	24	/103		14 JOHN ST	BLAYDON				OCTOBER 16			STILL SERVING MARCH 1920
RICKARDS	Chas	PTE	24											AWOL 8/5, 6/6, COURT 10/5, 10/6.DESERTER 31/7 COUR
RIDDELL	Wm	PTE	24	/1004	D		NEWCASTLE			10 APRIL 1918		PLOEGSTEERT MEM	TO 20th, 9th BNS.	
RIDLEY	John	PTE	24	/1225	C	7 CRAWCROOK TERR	RYTON			10 MARCH 1918	JULY 16.	RYTON	TO 3rd BN.	AGE 45.
RIDLEY	T	PTE	24	/1041	B									
RIGG	Wm	PTE	24	/671		1 LEAZES ST	GATESHEAD			9 SEPT 1918		PIETA MIL CEM MALTA	TO 1st GARRISON BN.	
RILEY	F	PTE	24	/1570				18/1/15	29/3/16	SICK			TO 30th BN.	DID NOT SERVE OVERSEAS.
RILEY	T	PTE	24	/184	A									ALSO ON D COY 30th BN ROLL.
RILEY	W	PTE	24	/638	D	10 NICHOLSONS BLDGS	CHESTER LE STRE	9/11/14	31/3/19	KR para 392			TO 23rd, 16th, 19th BNS, ATTACHED R ENGINEERS, ARM	
RIMINGTON	Tom	PTE	24	/1681			GATESHEAD			1 JULY 1916		THIEPVAL MEM		MISSING AUGUST 16.

NAME	INITI	RANK	BA	NUMBE	COMP	ADDRESS	TOWN_VILL	ENLISTED	DISCHARG	CAUSE_DIS	WOUNDED	BURIED	TRANSFER	ADD
ROBERTSON	J	PTE	24	/695	D 30			9/11/14	29/3/16				TO DEPOT.	DID NOT SERVE OVERSEAS.
ROBINSON	B	CPL	24	/1644	A 30								TO WEST YORKSHIRE REGT.	WEST YORKS No 63949.
ROBINSON	Chas	SGT	24	/892		40 PRINCESS ST	CONSETT	5/11/14			DECEMBER 16		TO 24/27th, 11th BNS, ATT 8th WEST INDIES REGT, CL	COLOUR SGT.
ROBINSON	J	PTE	24	/1726		117 SEVENTH ST	SHOTTON COLLIER	23/11/14	1/4/19	KR para 392			FROM 34 DIV CYC COY, ARMY RESERVE CLASS P.	
ROBINSON	Rob D	PTE	24	/1711	A	19 STAVORDALE ST	DAWDON			1 JULY 1916		THIEPVAL MEM	FROM 23rd BN, 34 DIV CYC COY.	MISSING AUGUST 16, ORIGINAL 23rd BN No 23/6.AGE 18
ROBSON	A W	PTE	24	/975	C		COXHOE	9/11/14	11/5/17	GUNSHOT WOUNDS	OCTOBER 16, JANUARY 17.		TO 3rd BN.	WOUNDED BACK AND ABDOMEN.
ROBSON	Hen T	CPL	24	/1148		7 TURRET PLACE	BLAYDON	11/11/14	1/4/19		MARCH 16		TO ARMY RESERVE CLASS P.	
ROBSON	John	PTE	24	/1267	A	53 NEWCASTLE ST	BRANDON				JULY 16.		TO ROYAL ENGINEERS.	ALSO ON D COY 30th BN ROLL, RE No 403518.
ROBSON	Math	PTE	24	/271	A 30		BYERNS NTHBLD			1 JULY 1916		THIEPVAL MEM	TO 30th BN(A COY), 24th BN.	
ROBSON	S	PTE	24	/1710			HOWDEN ON TYNE	4/9/14	30/1/17	WOUNDS	OCTOBER 16		FROM 17, 34 DIV CYC COY, TO DEPOT.	
ROBSON	T	LCPL	24	/1700			ASHINGTON	11/11/14	3/2/19		OCTOBER 16		FROM 34 DIV CYC COY, TO 22nd, 1/5th BNS, DEPOT.	AGE 34.
ROBSON	Wm	PTE	24											AWOL 27/7/15 COURT SUNDERLAND.
ROCHE	Peter	PTE	24	/71		39 GORDON RD	BYKER	2/11/14	8/6/15	KR para 392 iii				DID NOT SERVE OVERSEAS.
RODGERS	FredT	PTE	24	/321	B	18 BRIDGE ST	BLAYDON			7 SEPT 1916	JULY 16	FLAT IRON COPSE CEM		AGE 44, BORN MORPETH.
RODGERS	J	SGT	24	/824			SUNDERLAND	7/11/14	2/8/18	GUNSHOT WOUNDS	APR 16, JANUARY 18		TO 23rd, 24th, 24/27th, 19th BNS, DEPOT.	
RODGERS	J	PTE	24	/1634	B								TO LABOUR CORPS.	
RODGERS	Jos	PTE	24	/158	A	1 PARK TERR	NEWCASTLE	31/10/14	19/5/19				TO MACHINE GUN CORPS(34th BN), CLASS Z RESERVE.	MGC No 152009.
ROGAN	J	PTE	24	/1265	A 30									
ROGAN	Mart	PTE	24	/193	A		FELLING			1 JULY 1916		THIEPVAL MEM		
ROGERS	John	PTE	24	/1369	A	1 REGENT TERR	NEWCASTLE				1 JULY 16			WND L THIGH, AGE 30. 34 CCS 2/7/16 EVAC 5/7/16
RONAN	W	PTE	24	/1563	A	58 PALMER TERR	WILLINGTON QUAY			KR para 392	OCTOBER 16.			
ROONEY	Geo	PTE	24	/335	B	SYKE RD	BURNHOPEFIELD			19 MAY 1916		MERICOURT CEM		NOK 10 MADDISON ROW DIPTON.
ROONEY	T	PTE	24	/356	B		WALLSEND				AUG 16,JAN 18,NOV 18.		TO LABOUR CORPS.	34 CCS 2/7 EVAC 5/7/16, 1/5th NTHN GEN HOSP 7/7/16
ROSS	E	PTE	24	/405	B		WALKER				OCTOBER 16		TO HIGHLAND LI.	VOLUNTARY AID HOSP CHELTENHAM 8/7/16
ROSS	JohnW	PTE	24	/140		132 CLAVERING AVE	DUNSTON			1 JULY 1916		THIEPVAL MEM	TO 1st GARRISON BN, 26th BN.	MISSING OCTOBER 16, BORN WHICKHAM, AGE 35.
ROUGHT	Geo	PTE	24	/971	C		PELTON FELL			19 MAY 1916		BECOURT MIL CEM		
ROURKE	Jas W	PTE	24	/577	C	6 JOHN ST	KIMBLESWORTH			1 JULY 1916		THIEPVAL MEM		MISSING AUGUST 16, AGE 25, BRTHR/FATHER PATRICK DI
ROWELL	Frank	PTE	24	/833	C	2 MIRK LANE	GATESHEAD						TO 24/27th, 25th, 12/13th BNS, CLASS Z RESERVE.	STRETCHER BEARER RAIDS 5/6th, 25/26th JUNE 16.
ROWELL	T B	PTE	24	/742	D	SIMPSONS BIULDINGS	FELLING SHORE				JULY 16			LCPL
ROWELL	W	SGT	24											ON BN ROLL & PHOTO IN IH NO OTHER TRACE.
ROWELL	Wm	PTE	24	/942	B	16 RAILWAY ST	NEWCASTLE			1 JULY 1916		THIEPVAL MEM		MISSING AUGUST 16.
RUANE	P	SGT	24	/1266			SUNDERLAND				AUGUST 16, JANUARY 17.		TO 11th, 24th BNS.	WND L EAR,HEAD.34 CCS 2/7/16 EVAC 5/7/16,
RUSE	Reg	CPL	24	/1712		36 BERMUDA ST	CAMBRIDGE			1 JULY 1916		THIEPVAL MEM	FROM SUFFOLK REGT, 34 DIV CYC COY.	BORN CHESTERTON CAMBS, AGE 36.
RUSK	Rob H	SGT	24	/880		51 BROUGHTON ST	DARLINGTON	6/11/14		KR para 392	OCTOBER 16			CSM STILL SERVING 1920.
RUSSELL	T H	PTE	24	/491	B	52 RAVENSWORTH RD	DUNSTON						TO LABOUR CORPS.	LAB CORPS No 577363.
RUTTER	M	PTE	24	/1102	C		QUEBEC				AUGUST 16		TO LABOUR CORPS.	GSW L KNEE AGE 28, 4CCS 2/7/16 EVAC 5/7/16.
RUTTER	T	PTE	24	/733	B	12 BYRNE ST	QUEBEC			KR para 392	AUGUST 16		TO 25th, 1/5th, 12/13th BNS.	ALLOTED NEW NUMBER 243187.
RYAN	J W	PTE	24	/412	C	126 HERBOTTLE ST	NEWCASTLE	6/11/14	2/11/17	WOUNDS	NOVEMBER 16		TO DEPOT.	40 PRUDHOE ST NEWCASTLE 1916.
RYAN	John	PTE	24	/663	D	6 FOWLERS TERR FRWGA	DURHAM CITY	12/11/14					TO LABOUR CORPS(797 AE COY).	LAB CORPS No 518929.
RYAN	Mich	PTE	24	/1368	B	4 CROSSGATE	DURHAM CITY			1 JULY 1916		THIEPVAL MEM		MISSING AUGUST 16, BORN BRANDON.
RYAN	P	PTE	24	/972		8 BELL ST	RYHOPE COLLIERY						TO 1st GARRISON BN, CLASS Z RESERVE.	
RYAN	Steph	PTE	24	/810	A	45 DENTON GARDENS	WEST BENWELL	31/10/14			DECEMBER 17		TO LABOUR CORPS.	
RYAN	W	PTE	24	/1137	A		GATESHEAD				OCTOBER 16		TO 25th, 1/5th, 9th BNS, CLASS Z RESERVE.	NEW NUMBER 243171.3rd SCOTTISH GEN GLASGOW 11/7/16
RYDER	J	PTE	24	/268	A	59 STARSET ST	NEWCASTLE	4/11/14	31/10/17	WOUNDS	MARCH 16		TO 85th TRAINING RESERVE BN.	
SAMPSON	J	PTE	24	/1045	D		HIRST				JULY 16		TO LABOUR CORPS.	34 CCS 1/7/16 EVAC 5/7/16, WND L HAND AGE 38.
SAUNDERS	Jas	PTE	24	/1705			DUNDEE			18 JULY 1916		BOULOGNE	FROM 34 DIV CYC COY.	
SAVAGE	H	PTE	24	/90	A 30								TO 30th BN(A COY).	
SAXBY	W G	PTE	24	/1719			WHEATLEY HILL	7/11/14	31/3/19	KR para 392	JULY 16.		FROM 34 DIV CYC COY, ARMY RESERVE CLASS P.	PHOTO IN CC 2/3/16 RANK GIVEN AS CYCLIST, WEARING
SCANLON	Mich	PTE	24	/149	C	40 PALMERSVILLE	FOREST HALL	5/11/14			JULY,OCT,DEC, 16 MARCH 18		TO 10th BN, CLASS Z RESERVE.	
SCOTT	J T	PTE	24	/1648	B	HILLHEAD FARM	WHALTON NTHMBLD						TO 24/27th BN.	
SCOTT	Jas	PTE	24	/1131	A		GATESHEAD				OCTOBER 16		TO ROYAL INNISKILLING FUSILIERS.	VOLUNTARY AID HOSP CHELTENHAM 8/7/16
SCOTT	John	PTE	24	/329	B	15 POPLAR ST	MEDMOMSLEY							
SCULLION	Jas	PTE	24											AGE 45 AWOL 2/9/15 COURT GATESHEAD
SCULLION	John	PTE	24			44 ANN STREET	GATESHEAD	10/11/14						AWOL 7/7/15 COURT GATESHEAD
SEAGRAVE	J	PTE	24	/675	B									
SEDGEWICK	J	PTE	24	/1280	C	FRAMWELLGATE MOOR	DURHAM CITY	19/12/14	13/3/18	WOUNDS	JULY 16		TO ARMY RESERVE CLASS W.	HOSP KENT 7/16.
SHANNON	M	PTE	24	/451	B									ALSO ON D COY 30th BN ROLL.
SHEA	W L	PTE	24	/699	A 30	48 MIDDLE ST	WALKER	11/11/14						
SHEARER	J	PTE	24	/1276				21/12/14	8/6/15	SICK				DID NOT SERVE OVERSEAS.
SHEEN	Edw	PTE	24	/1100	D	11 NEVILLE TERR	DURHAM CITY	10/11/14	20/2/18	BRONCHITIS(GAS)			TO DEPOT.	BROTHER JAMES 9 GREEN HOWARDS.

NAME	INITI	RANK	BA	NUMBE	COMP	ADDRESS	TOWN_VILL	ENLISTED	DISCHARG	CAUSE_DIS	WOUNDED	BURIED	TRANSFER	ADD
SHEFFIELD	A	LCPL	24	/1447									TO 1st, 2nd, 8th BNS.	
SHEPARDSON	A	LSGT	24	/1625	C		GATESHEAD				OCTOBER 16			RAID 25/26th JUNE 16.34CCS 2-5/7/16 NETLEY 11/7/16
SHEPARDSON	John	PTE	24	/918	C	362 LEWIS ST	GATESHEAD	10/11/14	28/11/16	WOUNDS	JULY 16		TO DEPOT.	
SHERIDAN	T	PTE	24	/1021	D	19 UNION ST	SHIELDFIELD						TO LABOUR CORPS.	
SHIELD	H	PTE	24	/965				18/11/14	29/7/15					DID NOT SERVE OVERSEAS.
SHIELDS	E	PTE	24	/43	B	26 DONNISON ST	DUNSTON				OCTOBER 16		TO LABOUR CORPS.	3 CCS 2/7/16 EVAC 2/7/16. GSW
SHREEVE	Chas	PTE	24	/568	D	7 NORTH ST	BLAYDON	11/11/14	19/3/19				TO 24/27th, KINGS OWN YORKSHIRE LI(15th BN), CLASS	KOYLI No 64148.
SIMPSON	J	PTE	24	/288	A	4 MALTON ROW	BENWELL				JULY 16, OCTOBER 16			
SIMPSON	T	PTE	24	/528				6/11/14	15/11/15				TO 30th BN.	DID NOT SERVE OVERSEAS.
SIMPSON	W	PTE	24	/537		4 MALTON ROW	BENWELL	7/11/14	28/4/16				TO DEPOT	DID NOT SERVE OVERSEAS.
SINCLAIR	A	PTE	24	/133	A	70 ELSWICK EAST TER	NEWCASTLE						TO 24/27th, 11th BNS, CLASS Z RESERVE.	
SINCLAIR	John	PTE	24											AWOL 16/7/15 COURT GATESHEAD AGE 31.
SKELTON	J W	PTE	24	/1448	C		NEWCASTLE	21/12/14	26/4/17	SICK	JULY 16		TO DEPOT.	TOOK PART IN TRENCH RAIDS 5/6 25/26 JUNE 16.
SKINNAN	Frank	SGT	24	/310			LIMERICK			23 OCT 1917		TYNE COT MEM	TO 24/27th BN.	
SLASOR	E	PTE	24	/1635	D									ALSO ON A COY 30th BN ROLL.
SLATER	F	LCPL	24	/927	C			10/11/14	13/11/17	WOUNDS			TO DEPOT.	
SLATER	Thos	PTE	24	/1065	C	10 DERWENT VIEW	ROWLANDS GILL	10/11/14	17/5/18	SICK	JULY 16		TO 8th, 16th BNS, DEPOT.	
SLOAN	Leond	PTE	24	/1277	A	20 CROW ST	SUNDERLAND			28 DEC 1916	OCTOBER 16.	BAILLEUL COM CEM EXT		BORN HEBBURN ON TYNE. NOT WOUNDED DECEMBER 16 GAZE
SLOWTHER	J	PTE	24	/313	B		BLACKHALL MILL			KR para 392	JULY 16		TO 25th, 1/5th BNS.	ALLOTTED NEW NUMBER 243170.
SLOWTHER	S	PTE	24	/902	D	5 DERWENT ST	BLACKHALL MILL	9/11/14	10/5/19	KR para 392	JULY 16		TO 27th, 16th, 1/5th BNS, DEPOT.	
SMITH		PTE		/764										TOOK PART IN TRENCH RAID 5/6 JUNE 16 BAYONETMAN.
SMITH	A	PTE	24	/1636	D		GATESHEAD				OCTOBER 16.		TO 24/27th, 8th, 14th, CLASS Z RESERVE.	
SMITH	A T	PTE	24	/1373	B	60 WORDSWORTH ST	GATESHEAD				NOVEMBER 16			SIGNALLER RAID 5/6th JUNE 16.34 CCS 2/7-5/7/16
SMITH	Frank	PTE	24	/1450	B		BLAYDON			16 FEB 1916		RATION FARM CEM		
SMITH	J	PTE	24	/167				2/11/14	15/2/18	SICK			TO ARMY RESERVE CLASS W.	DID NOT SERVE OVERSEAS.
SMITH	J	PTE	24	/303	A									ALSO ON A COY 30th BN ROLL. INITIAL T
SMITH	J R	SGT	24	/155		3 JUBILEE TERR	LANGLEY MOOR	2/11/14	28/6/16	3 JANUARY 1919		BLAYDON	TO DEPOT.	PIONEER SGT.
SMITH	J T	PTE	24	/1107	A	30 106 FRONT ST	LEADGATE	11/11/14	15/11/17	WOUNDS			TO 3rd BN.	RAIDS 5/6th 25/26th JUNE 1916, A COY 30th BN
SMITH	John	PTE	24	/223	A	5 GRENVILLE TERR	NEWCASTLE	5/11/14			OCTOBER 16		TO LABOUR CORPS, ROYAL FUSILIERS.	
SMITH	JohnG	PTE	24	/567	D	8 THOMAS TERR	BLAYDON	11/11/14					TO LABOUR CORPS(193 LAB COY).	LAB CORPS No 421413.
SMITH	Pat	SGT	24	/562		70 JAMES ST	BYKER	3/11/14	2/11/15				TO 30th BN.	DID NOT SERVE OVERSEAS.
SMITH	T	PTE	24	/791	C		DIPTON			KR para 392	SEPTEMBER 16		TO 11th, 1/5th BNS.	NEW NUMBER 243138,CORPORAL DESERTED 2/12/16.
SNEE	Pet A	PTE	24	/644	B	38 TARSET ST	NEWCASTLE			9 SEPT 1916		HEILLY STATION CEM		AGE 22
SNOWBALL	J T	PTE	24	/374	C	2 NORTH TERR	WILLINGTON						TO 24/27th BN, LABOUR CORPS.	BROTHER Wm IN R.E.
SNOWDON	E E	PTE	24	/692	C									ALSO ON D COY 30th BN ROLL.
SPENCE	Alex	PTE	24	/322		19 ASKEW RD WEST	GATESHEAD						TO 24/27th, 14th, 12/13th BNS, CLASS Z RESERVE.	
SPENCER	Aaron	PTE	24	/495	B				1/5/19				TO MACHINE GUN CORPS(34th BN), CLASS Z RESERVE.	
SPINDLOE	J W	PTE	24	/944	D					KR para 392			TO 8th BN.	
SPINKS	Edw	PTE	24	/192	A	30 MITCHELL ST	SOUTHMOOR	6/11/14		21 MARCH 1918	JULY 16	ARRAS MEM	TO 26th, 25th BNS.	NOK 87 PINE ST SOUTHMOOR 1918, BORN CONHOE.
SPINKS	W	PTE	24	/320	A	WHEATLEY HOUSE	DIPTON	2/11/14					TO 9th, 24/27th, 23rd, 9th BNS, CLASS Z RESERVE.	
SPOORS	Andrw	PTE	24	/720	D	27 VICTORIA ST	BLAYDON				JULY 1916			
SPOWART	W	PTE	24	/1701									FROM 34 DIV CYC COY, TO 19th, 25th, 11th BNS, CLAS	
STAFF	John	PTE	24	/676	C	141 FRONT ST	LANGLEY MOOR	12/11/14		21 JULY 1916	1 JULY 16	ABBEVILLE		
STANLEY	Rich	PTE	24	/1502	A	2 MONTAGUE ST	SCOTSWOOD			1 JULY 1916		OVILLIERS		MISSING AUGUST 16.
STAPLETON	R	PTE	24	/1048	D								TO 24/27th, 11th BNS, ROYAL FUSILIERS(24th BN).	FRANCE, 24 11/1/16, 9/8/17, 10/8/17 11th 4/7/18,
STEPHENSON	T	PTE	24	/1002	D	2 RIVER ST	NEWCASTLE			KR para 392	DECEMBER 16			
STEPHENSON	ThosD	CQMS	24	/858		46 PINE ST	NEWCASTLE			1 JULY 1916		THIEPVAL MEM		MISSING NOVEMBER 16, BORN HASWELL MOOR.
STEWART	A S	PTE	24	/299	C	79 LAMPTON ST	SHERBURN HILL	5/11/14	31/10/16	SICK	JULY 16		TO 16th, 26th, 1/7th BNS, CLASS Z RESERVE.	
STOBBART	John	PTE	24	/1132	A	22 FORSTER ST	GATESHEAD				AUGUST 16		TO 25th, 1/5th BNS, CLASS Z RESERVE.	ALLOTED NEW NUMBER 243176.
STOCKHILL		LCPL	24	/1683			GRIMSBY				JULY 16.			TOOK PART IN TRENCH RAID 5/6 th JUNE 16.
STOKER	T	PTE	24	/300	B		WHITE LE HEAD			KR para 392	JULY 16			ALLOTED TWO NEW NUMBERS, 243192, 89562.
STOKOE	Wm	PTE	24	/1224	A	357 ALBERT ST	BROOMPARK				JULY 16.		TO ROYAL ARMY MEDICAL CORPS.	459 GARDEN ST 1918, RAMC No 130750.
STRAKER	A	PTE	24	/1274	B	79 LAMPTON ST	SHERBURN HILL				JULY 16, NOVEMBER 17.		TO 16th, 26th, 1/7th BNS, CLASS Z RESERVE.	
SULLIVAN	Jas	SGT	24	/280		1 BROWNS TERR	LANGLEY PARK	5/11/14	4/11/16	WOUNDS	OCTOBER 16		TO DEPOT.	
SULLIVAN	John	ASGT	24	/844		NEW SOUTH TERR	BIRTLEY	12/11/14					TO 1st GARRISON BN, CLASS Z RESERVE.	
SULLIVAN	Pat	PTE	24	/852	A	29 NORTH TERR	NEW SEAHAM	31/10/14						
SULLIVAN	W	CPL	24	/778									TO 1st GARRISON BN, CLASS Z RESERVE.	
SUMMERS	G	PTE	24	/304	C	12 SUNDERLAND ST	NEWCASTLE						TO 9th, 1/5th BNS, CLASS Z RESERVE.	
SUMMERVILLE	Wm	PTE	24	/724		14 COWEN ST	BLAYDON	12/11/14		27 SEPT 1918	OCTOBER 16	GOUZEAUCOURT NEW BRIT CEM	TO 14th, 19th, 12/13th BNS.	DESERTED 2/1/18
SUTHERLAND	Geo	PTE	24	/1720			EDINBURGH			9 APRIL 1917		ROCLINCOURT VALLEY CEM	FROM 20th BN(D COY), 34 DIV CYC COY.	ORIGINAL TS No 20/928.

NAME	INITI	RANK	BA	NUMBE	COMP	ADDRESS	TOWN_VILL	ENLISTED	DISCHARG	CAUSE_DIS	WOUNDED	BURIED	TRANSFER	ADD
SWALES	Thos	PTE	24	/950	D	COXHOE POTTERY	COXHOE						TO CLASS Z RESERVE.	
SWAN	Jas F	PTE	24	/392	A	12 QUEEN ST	CONSETT	5/11/14	21/1/19	WOUNDS,			TO 23rd BN, DEPOT.	12 SPENCER ST CONSETT 1918. WND R HAND,AGE 37.
SWEENEY	Jas	PTE	24	/252		29 CHURCH WALK	GATESHEAD	5/11/14	5/6/18				TO 3rd BN, DEPOT.	DID NOT SERVE OVERSEAS.
TAIT	Mich	PTE	24	/659	C	32 JUBILEE TERR	ANNITSFORD	29/10/14		9 JULY 1917	AUGUST 16	DICKEBUSCH NEW MIL CEM	TO KINGS OWN YORKSHIRE LI, MACHINE GUN CORPS(70th	BORN SEGHILL.3CCS EVAC 3/7/16 MGC No 72709.
TAIT	T	PTE	24	/1484	C									
TALBOT	JohnJ	PTE	24	/1285	A	31 MITCHELL ST	SOUTHMOOR			5 APRIL 1917		SAVY BRIT MIL CEM	TO 16th BN.	AGE 31.
TAYLOR	A	PTE	24	/132				3/11/14	21/12/17	WOUNDS			FROM 34 DIV CYCLIST COY, TO 3rd BN.	
TAYLOR	E	PTE	24	/1709			BINNINGTON LINC				SEPTEMBER 16		FROM 34 DIV CYC COY, TO 12th, 12/13th BNS, CLASS Z	
TAYLOR	Ralph	PTE	24	/1120	D	34 WOLSELEY ST TEAMS	GATESHEAD	10/11/14	9/3/17		SEPTEMBER 16		TO DEPOT.	BOMBER TOOK PART IN TRENCH RAID 5/6th JUNE 16.
TAYLOR	W H	PTE	24	/1032	D		GATESHEAD	10/11/14	3/1/18	SHELLSHOCK	OCTOBER 16		TO 3rd BN.	
TELFORD	N	PTE	24	/1556	B	11 PARK ST BLACKFINE	BLACKHILL	23/12/14	7/12/17	WOUNDS	JULY 16		TO DEPOT.	
TEMPLE	A	PTE	24	/697	B	7 FORTH ST	CHOPWELL	10/11/14	11/12/17	INJURIES			TO DEPOT.	
THEW	T	SGT	24	/1652									TO 24th BN, CLASS Z RESERVE.	
THIRKELD		PTE	24											4th IN HOP, STEP AND LEAP, ALNWICK 1915.
THOMAS	Sam	PTE	24	/1156	D	11 ROSEBERRY TERR	CONSETT	6/11/14		1 JULY 1916		THIEPVAL MEM		BORN THORNABY, MISSING OCTOBER 16.
THOMPSON	Bruce	PTE	24	/245	D	HILL TOP	DIPTON	28/10/14		30 SEPT 1916		BAILLEUL		AWOL 7/6/15 IN COURT GATESHEAD, AGE 33.
THOMPSON	G	PTE	24	/31	C		TANTOBIE				AUGUST 16,OCTOBER 16.		TO 5th TRAINING RES BN, STILL SERVING 1920.	
THOMPSON	G H	PTE	24	/686		13 ATHOLL ST	DUNSTON				JULY 16		TO 1st BN.	BEAUFORT HOSP BRISTOL 12/7/16,CPL STILL SERVING 20
THOMPSON	Geo H	PTE	24	/1283	A 30	28 CROSSGATE	DURHAM CITY				MAY 18.		TO 12th, 12/13th BNS, CLASS Z RESERVE.	AWOL 27 JULY 1915 IN COURT DURHAM.
THOMPSON	J	LCPL	24	/933	D			11/11/14	1/1/18	WOUNDS	MARCH 16		TO DEPOT.	
THOMPSON	Pat J	PTE	24	/779	C	30 HENRY ST	GOSFORTH			1 JULY 1916		THIEPVAL MEM		BORN WASHINGTON.
THOMPSON	T A	PTE	24	/789									TO 24/27th, 19th BNS.	DESERTED 28 JULY 1918.
THOMPSON	ThosI	PTE	24	/227	A		FRIZINGTON			20 MAY 1916		BECOURT MIL CEM.		
THORNTON	Jos	PTE	24	/580	B	477 WHITWELL TERR	LANGLEY MOOR	9/11/14	10/3/19	KR para 392	NOVEMBER 16		TO 9th, 1/4th BNS, ARMY RESERVE CLASS P.	3 CCS 2/7/16 EVAC 3/7/16.
THORPE	F	PTE	24	/535	D								TO LABOUR CORPS.	
THUBRON	Thos	PTE	24	/948	D	COXHOE POTTERY	COXHOE			KR para 392	JULY 16			AGE 25. 34CCS 1/7/16 EVAC 5/7/16 WND R ARM
THURLAWAY	Edw	PTE	24	/1724		24 RAILWAY ST	CRAGHEAD	10/12/14		1 JULY 1916		THIEPVAL MEM	FROM 34 DIV CYC CUY.	MISSING AUGUST 16, ACC No 10053.
TIERNEY	P	CSGT	24	/1626		48 PRINCE CONSORTS R	JARROW						TO 24/27th, 11th BNS, CLASS Z RESERVE.	SEE ALSO 30/111 TIERNEY J SAME ADDRESS.
TIERNEY	Pat	PTE	24	/54	A	15 DAVIDSON ST	FELLING	2/11/14	30/10/17	WOUNDS	JULY 16		TO 3rd BN.	
TIGHE		PTE	24	/162	D30									
TILLEY	John	PTE	24	/206	A	16 MARGARET ST	NEW BRANCEPETH						TO 27th, 24/27th, 10th, 4th BNS, CLASS Z RESERVE.	MISSING JULY 16, NOT MISSING NOVEMBER 16.
TIMLIN	Wm	PTE	24	/868	C	22 BAXTER PLACE	SEATON DELAVAL						TO 19th BN, LABOUR CORPS.	
TIMMINS	E	PTE	24	/446	C									
TINDLE	R	PTE	24	/1286	C	5 MAY ST	BIRTLEY						TO 11th, 1/7th, 12/13th, 1st BNS, CLASS Z RESERVE.	
TODD	Dan	PTE	24	/1287	B	56 DOUGLAS TERR	USWORTH COLLIER			19 AUGUST 1917		VILLERS FAUCON	ATTACHED 103rd LTMB.	BORN WASHINGTON.
TODD	Olivr	PTE	24	/959	C	37 DIBBLY ST	BYKER	12/11/14					TO KINGS OWN SCOTTISH BORDERERS.	
TOMAN	H	PTE	24	/416	D			6/11/14	27/10/17	SICK			TO ROYAL WELCH FUSILIERS.	
TONER	Geo	PTE	24	/458	A		SUNDERLAND			9 APRIL 1917	OCTOBER 16	ROCLINCOURT VALLEY CEM	TO 21st BN.	BORN LIVERPOOL.3CCS 2/7/16 EVAC 2/7/16
TOWARD	Geo	PTE	24	/1054	D	12 GORDON ST	GATESHEAD				MARCH 17		TO 8th BN, CLASS Z RESERVE.	
TOWNSLEY	Isaac	PTE	24	/1519										DESERTED 5/4/15, AGE 29, 5'6'', GROOM, SCARS ON CH
TRAYNOR	Thos	PTE	24	/417	C	22 NEWBOLD RD	ELSWICK	10/11/14					TO LABOUR CORPS, ROYAL FUSILIERS.	TOOK PART IN TRENCH RAID 5/6 JUNE 16.
TROTTER	J	SGT	24	/199			NEWCASTLE	4/11/14	3/2/19	KR para 392	JULY 16		TO ARMY RESERVE CLASS P.	
TROTTER	Jn Tm	PTE	24	/800	C	8 CARNABY YARD GALLO	NEWCASTLE	9/11/14	3/1/18	WOUNDS	JULY 16		TO DEPOT.	CPL, WND FACE+MOUTH, AGE 23.34 CCS EVAC 5/7/16
TRUEMAN	Thos	PTE	24	/1452	C	7 JOICEY TERR OXHILL	STANLEY		2/2/20		OCTOBER 16.		TO KOYLI(8th BN),TANK CORPS, KOYLI(2,10 BNS)	TOOK PART IN TRENCH RAID 25/26th JUNE 16.
TUNLEY	Wm	LCPL	24	/543		1 MARCH TERR	BLAYDON	5/11/14		1 JULY 1916		THIEPVAL MEM		MISSING AUGUST 16, BORN WHITEHAVEN.
TURNBULL	J M	SGT	24	/1713				21/1/15	5/6/18	GUNSHOT WOUNDS			FROM 34 DIV CYC COY, TO 3rd BN.	
TURNBULL	Jos S	PTE	24	/1282	A 30	188 GILESGATE	DURHAM CITY	12/11/14					TO 30th, 26th BNS.	GSW FACE+L HAND. 34 CCS 2/7/16 EVAC 5/7/16
TURNBULL	W	PTE	24	/1547	B	WILLIS ST	HETTON LE HOLE				AUGUST 16, NOVEMBER 17.		TO 24th, 16th BN, CLASS Z RESERVE.	
TURNBULL	W J	PTE	24	/274	A	7 GULLOCH ST	WHEATLEY HILL	5/11/14	12/12/17	WOUNDS	OCTOBER 16		TO 16th BN, DEPOT.	
TURNBULL	Wm	PTE	24	/3		BREWERY BANK	SWALWELL	31/10/14		15 MAY 1915		WHICKHAM ST MARY		AGE 42.
TURNBULL	Wm	CPL	24	/1111	D	7 OLD DISPENSARY YAR	GATESHEAD			KR para 392			TO 24/27th, 11th, 10th BNS.	
TURNER	E R	PTE	24	/989	D			10/11/14	21/2/17	KR para 392			TO DEPOT.	
TURNER	J	PTE	24	/523	B	173 BOLINGBROKE ST	HEATON			1 JULY 1916		THIEPVAL MEM		MISSING AUGUST 16.
TURNER	Math	PTE	24	/260	A	23 MULGRAVE ST	GATESHEAD	4/11/14	15/9/16	SICK			TO 30th BN(D COY).	AWOL 11/7/15 COURT GATESHEAD AGE 50.
VASEY	M E	PTE	24	/1365	C	FRAMWELLGATE MOOR	DURHAM CITY	11/11/14	30/1/18	SHELLSHOCK	MARCH 16.		TO 3rd BN.	
VINCENT	V	PTE	24	/427	B									
VINTON	Geo	PTE	24	/924	C	35 DORNEY ST	GATESHEAD	12/11/14			OCTOBER 16		TO 13TH, 36th BNS, CLASS Z RESERVE.	34 CCS 2/7/16 EVAC 5/7/16 WND R LEG. 105 DORNEY ST
VOUT	S	PTE	24	/1289	C		NEWCASTLE	21/12/14	3/11/16	GUNSHOT WOUNDS	AUGUST 16		TO 85th TRAINING RESERVE BN.	
WADHAM	John	PTE	24	/1655		33 ABBEY ST	GATESHEAD	30/3/15	25/10/18	SICK			TO COMMAND DEPOT CATTERICK.	CPL PHOTO IN IRISH HEROES.
WAINWRIGHT	Alb	PTE	24	/1718		13 CLAYTON ST	DUDLEY NTHMBLND			1 JULY 1916		THIEPVAL MEM	FROM 20th BN(C COY), 34 DIV CYC COY.	BORN LONG BENTON, TS No 20/680, ACC No 9465.

NAME	INITI	RANK	BN	NUMBE	COMP	ADDRESS	TOWN_VILL	ENLISTED	DISCHARG	CAUSE_DIS	WOUNDED	BURIED	TRANSFER	ADD
WAISTLE	I	PTE	24	/1458	B									
WAKE	Math	PTE	24	/435	C	10 DOUBLE ROW	ISABELLA PIT			1 JULY 1916		OVILLIERS		ALSO ON D COY 30th BN ROLL.
WAKE	W	PTE	24	/1457	C		SHILDON				OCTOBER 16			BORN BLYTH.
WALES	Luthr	PTE	24	/767	B	8 JUBILEE PLACE	LANGLEY MOOR	12/11/14			OCTOBER 16		TO 24/27th, 14th, 12/13th BNS, CLASS Z RESERVE.	
WALKER	Fred	PTE	24	/1481	C		NEWCASTLE				JULY 16.		TO LABOUR CORPS(525 LAB COY)	LAB CORPS No 454677.
WALKER	G M	PTE	24	/1667									TO 26th BN, LABOUR CORPS.	AWOL 17/5/15 COURT 26/5/15, 9/6/15 COURT 11/6/15.
WALLACE	J	PTE	24	/64	A			2/11/14	4/4/16	SICK			FROM 34 DIV CYC COY, TO CLASS Z RESERVE.	SGT.
WALSH	J	PTE	24	/1465										DID NOT SERVE OVERSEAS. AGE 32
WALTON	Arth	PTE	24	/49	A	257 BENSHAM RD	GATESHEAD	26/10/14			OCTOBER 16		TO 1st GARRISON BN, CLASS Z RESERVE.	
WALTON	R,T	SGT	24	/917			NEWCASTLE				OCTOBER 16			SIGNALLER, TRENCH RAID 25/26 JUNE 16
WARD	R	PTE	24	/1310						KR para 392				3 CCS 2/7/16 EVAC 2/7/16.
WARDLE	G	PTE	24	/123	A	19 BK HIGH ST	FELLING	28/10/14		2 DECEMBER 1918	OCTOBER 16	HEWORTH ST MARYS CH YD	TO 1st GARRISON BN.	
WARREN	JohnT	PTE	24	/479		ROBSON TERR FLINTHIL	DIPTON	28/10/14					TO 25th, 1/4th, 4th RESERVE BNS.	NEW NUMBER,204581, AGE 30, HOSP CHELTENHAM 8/7/16.
WARWICK	J	PTE	24	/419	B		BLYTH				JULY 16, AUGUST 16.		TO 1st GARRISON BN, CLASS Z RESERVE.	
WATERS	T	PTE	24	/571	B		ROWLANDS GILL				OCTOBER 16		TO TRAINING RESERVE BN.	TRG RES BN No TR/5/41406
WATSON	J H	SGT	24	/169		35 KELVIN GARDENS	DUNSTON						TO CLASS Z RESERVE.	
WAUGH	R H	PTE	24	/1643	A 30								TO 22nd, 18th, 14th BNS, CLASS Z RESERVE.	
WEBSTER	A	PTE	24	/740	D		BACKWORTH				JULY 16			
WELSH	Jas	PTE	24	/375		18 CLYDE ST	CHOPWELL							WD R THIGH+SHELLSHOCK, AGE 24.18 GEN HOSP 3/7.
WELSH	Jas	CPL	24	/834	C	119 CLARENCE ST	NEWCASTLE	10/11/14	31/3/19				TO 1st GARRISON BN, CLASS Z RESERVE.	
WELSH	Mich	PTE	24	/177	A	11 DELAVAL ST	BENWELL	26/10/14					TO 21st, 25th, 4th(RES) BNS, ARMY RESERVE CLASS P.	STRETCHER BEARER, RAID 5/6 JUNE 16
WELSH	Pat	PTE	24	/122	A		NEW HERRINGTON				OCTOBER 16		TO 24/27th, 19th(W COY) BNS, CLASS Z RESERVE.	
WELSH	Pat	PTE	24	/326	B	47 BATH ST	WALKER	6/11/14					TO LABOUR CORPS.	LAB CORPS No 183756.
WELSH	W	PTE	24	/835	D		NORTH SHIELDS				AUGUST 16		TO LABOUR CORPS.	LCPL. LAB CORPS No 16097.
WELSH	Waltr	PTE	24	/338	B	16 LITTE BLAYDON ST	NEWCASTLE						TO MILITARY FOOT POLICE.	
WEST	J	SGT	24	/1682				3/9/14	19/3/18	SICK				ALSO ON D COY 30th BN ROLL.
WHARTON	Edwd	PTE	24	/1003	C	2 ROMULUS ST	GATESHEAD	12/11/14					FROM 34 DIV CYC COY, TO 1/7th BN, DEPOT ARMY RESER	
WHEATLEY	J H	PTE	24	/1630	A	5 RIPPONDEN ST	BYKER				OCTOBER 16		TO LABOUR CORPS.	LAB CORPS No 386437.
WHITE	Geo W	PTE	24	/1141		5 ASYLUM SQUARE	SHERRIFF HILL							
WHITE	H	PTE	24	/1290	A	22 DINSDALE ST	RYHOPE	21/12/14	22/10/18	KR para 392	OCTOBER 16, DECEMBER 17		TO 2nd GARRISON BN, CLASS Z RESERVE.	14 ASYLUM SQUARE 1918.
WHITE	J	PTE	24	/1453	B		HEBBURN	7/12/14	30/5/17	GUNSHOT WOUNDS	OCTOBER 16.		TO 1st, 16th, 1/5th BNS, COMMAND DEPOT CATTERICK.	WND THIGH. 34 CCS 2/7/16 EVAC 5/7/16 AGE 28.
WHITE	Jothn	PTE	24	/383	B	23 WILLIAM ST	CONSETT	6/11/14			JULY 16		TO 3rd BN.	
WHITEFIELD	J W	PTE	24	/1299	B	10 VIOLA ST	USWORTH COLLIER						TO 16th, 19th BNS.	ALLOTED NEW NUMBER 89557.
WHITTLE	W	PTE	24	/784	B	13 GLADSTONE TERR	USWORTH COLLIER	11/11/14			NOVEMBER 16		TO LABOUR CORPS.	ALSO ON D COY 30th BN ROLL.
WIDDOWSON	Wm	PTE	24	/1295	B	26 LONG ROW	FENCEHOUSES			26 DEC 1915		WEST RAINTON	TO LABOUR CORPS.	
WILKES	C	PTE	24	/1455	C	LONG ROW	LITTLETOWN							NOT SERVE OVERSEAS,BORN HOUGHTON LE SPRING, AGE 37
WILKES	Geo H	PTE	24	/183	A	9 CRANTH ROW	FOREST HALL	6/11/14			OCTOBER 16		TO MACHINE GUN CORPS.	
WILKINSON	C	PTE	24	/993	C		NEWCASTLE			KR para 392	OCTOBER 16		TO SOUTH LANCASHIRE RRGT	21 AMB TRAIN, 18 GEN HOSP 6/7, 6 CONV DEPOT 7/7/16
WILKINSON	J	PTE	24	/32	A	40 CLIFTON ST	HARTLEPOOL	2/11/14	31/1/19				TO 11th BN.	2nd SOUTHERN GEN HOSP BRISTOL 11/7/16.
WILLIAMS	A	PTE	24	/644	C								TO ARMY RESERVE CLASS P.	
WILLIAMS	Thom	PTE	24	/371		94 DYKE ST	THORNLEY COLLIE	6/11/14	29/11/15	SICK				ALSO ON D COY 30th BN ROLL.
WILLIAMSON	J	PTE	24	/1203	C									DID NOT SERVE OVERSEAS., AGE 34
WILLIAMSON	T	PTE	24	/509	D	27 WELLINGTON ST	NEWCASTLE			KR para 392				
WILLIAMSON	Thos	PTE	24	/1297	B		GATESHEAD		9/2/19		OCTOBER 16.			
WILLIAMSON	Wm	SGT	24	/382		24 BOTTLE BANK	BLACKHILL						TO 23rd BN, KINGS OWN YORKSHIRE LI(5th BN).	HOSP SHIP 9/7/16. WOUNDED L ARM. KOYLI No 63246
WILSON	G	PTE	24	/1461	B								TO 24/27th, 12/13th, 14th, 9th BNS, CLASS Z RESERV	COMPANY SERGEANT MAJOR.
WILSON	G	PTE		/821	A		FOREST HALL				SEPTEMBER 16			ALSO ON D COY 30th BN ROLL.
WILSON	Geo	PTE	24	/1463	B	3 NORTHUMBERLAND RD	LEMINGTON ON TY			1 JULY 1916		THIEPVAL MEM		3rd CCS 2/7/16 EVAC 5/7/16 WND R KNEE.
WILSON	H	PTE	24	/633	B	4 KING GEORGE RD	NEWBIGGIN	7/11/14	2/6/18	KR para 392	JANUARY 17			MISSING AUGUST 16, BORN BELL CLARE NTHMBLD.
WILSON	J	PTE	24	/846				10/11/14	6/2/18	WOUNDS			TO DEPOT.	
WILSON	J	PTE	24	/1130	A								TO 25th BN, DEPOT.	
WILSON	J W	PTE	24	/1168	D	15 DERWENT ST	BLACKHILL				JULY 16, DECEMBER 16.		TO ROYAL ENGINEERS.	
WILSON	John	P Mj	24	/1629	D		BACKWORTH	15/5/15	31/3/19	KR para 392			TO LABOUR CORPS.	HOSP DEVONPORT 12/7/16.
WILSON	P	PTE	24	/1492	B			29/12/14	7/9/17	INJURIES			TO 24/27th, 26th, 25th BNS, ARMY RESERVE CLASS P.	SGT, AGE 52, 3 SONS IN TS.
WILSON	R	PTE	24	/1300	B	26 CALIFORNIA ST	SEAHAM COLLIERY				OCTOBER 16		TO DEPOT.	
WILSON	W	PTE	24	/503	C	5 COLLIERY ROW	DUNSTON	7/11/14	11/10/17	WOUNDS	OCTOBER 16		TO 18th, 22nd BNS.	
WILSON	Wm	PTE	24	/243	A	40 PRINCESS ST	CONSETT	4/11/14	17/9/18	GUNSHOT WOUNDS			TO 3rd BN.	
WINN	T	PTE	24	/1293	B	1 WEST VIEW	SHERBURN HILL						TO 25th BN, DEPOT.	
WOODS	F	SGT	24	/1725										ALSO ON A COY 30th BN ROLL.
WOODS	J	PTE	24	/1559	A		LIVERPOOL				OCTOBER 16.		FROM 34 DIV CYC COY, TO 22nd BN, CLASS Z RESERVE.	

NAME	INITI	RANK	BA	NUMBE	COMP	ADDRESS	TOWN_VILL	ENLISTED	DISCHARG	CAUSE_DIS	WOUNDED	BURIED	TRANSFER	ADD
WOOF	R	PTE	24	/1158	A	9 BOUNDARY COTTAGE	LOW FELL	12/11/14	15/3/17	WOUNDS			TO DEPOT.	
WRANGHAM	Osmnd	PTE	24	/281	A	10 HILL TOP	ESH	5/11/14					TO 1st, 14th BNS, CLASS Z RESERVE.	
WRIGHT	Fred	RQMS	24	/1571	A	30 60 DENTON GARDENS	BENWELL			31 MAY 1917		ST NICHOLAS CEM	TO 30th, 24th BNS.	AGE 37.
WRIGHT	G	PTE	24	/601	D									
WRIGHT	J	PTE	24	/1291	A								TO 24/27th, 11th BNS, ROYAL FUSILIERS(24th BN).	FRANCE 24 11/1/16 TO 8/8/17, 24/27 9/8/17 TO 2/7/1
WRIGHT	Wm	PTE	24											AWOL 26/6/15 IN COURT 20/7/15.
WYLIE	Chas	PTE	24	/869	D	5 FOURTH ST	WHEATLEY HILL			1 JULY 1916		THIEPVAL MEM		MISSING AUGUST 16, BORN LUDWORTH.
YALLOP	Chas	PTE	24	/538	D	2 PATTERSON ST	BLAYDON	5/11/14		5 APRIL 1917	OCTOBER 16	SAVY BRITISH MIL CEM	TO 27th, 16th BNS.	WOUNDED L ARM, SEE ALSO 24/539
YALLOP	Fred	PTE	24	/539	D	2 PATTERSON ST	BLAYDON	6/11/14	29/3/19		OCT 16, DEC 17, MARCH 18.		TO 24th,27th,16th BNS, YORK AND LANCASTER REGT, CL	WOUNDED L HAND+ L LEG.
YOUNG	Edw	PTE	24	/1092	D	123 MILBURNGATE	DURHAM CITY	12/11/14			AUGUST 16		TO LABOUR CORPS(790 AE COY).	LAB CORPS No 398895 3rd NTHRN SHEFFIELD 10/7/16
YOUNG	Geo	PTE	24	/266	A	C/O J WHITE ESQ	DIPTON	28/10/14			APRIL 16			
YOUNG	Geo	PTE	24	/748	B	ALMA PLACE WEST KYO	ANNFIELD PLAIN	11/11/14			DECEMBER 16		TO ROYAL DEFENCE CORPS.	IN FRANCE 11/1/16 TO 24/5/17.
YOUNG	Rob W	PTE	24	/513	A	11 DERWENT ST	BLACKHILL	6/11/14					TO 18th, 8th BNS.	2 DOBSON ST 1918, AWOL 4/8/15 COURT 20/8/15.
YOUNGER	J	PTE	24	/45	A		GATESHEAD				JULY 16			

Gale and Polden, Ltd.] CORPORALS, 1st Batt. Tyneside Irish Brigade. [24 (S) Batt. N.F.]. [*To face page* 155.

1. Malpac.
2. Connor.
3. Shephardson.
4. Sullivan.
5. O'Neill.
6. Oraham.
7.
8. Williamson.
9. O'Halloran.
10. McGarrity.
11.
12. Wardle.
13.
14.
15.
16. Kettle.
17. Duffy.
18. McArdle.
19. Brown.
20. Davison.
21. Pipkin.
22. Connor.
23. Bowes.
24. Casey.
25. McAlister.
26.
27. Campbell.
28. Joyce.
29. Corvel.
30. Kean.
31. Lacey.
32. Summerville.
33.
34. Coleby.
35. Birkett.
36. Bonner.
37. McAndrew.
38. Rodgers.
39. Mackin.
40. Bell.
41. Cross.
42. Dixon.
43. Burke.
44. Davison.
45. McIntyre.
46. Timlin.
47. Cassidy.
48. Callon.
49. Brodie.
50. Diamond.
51. Bowes.
52. R. S. M. Grierley.
53. Major Prior.
54. Col. Howard.
55. Adj. (2nd. Lt.) Waring.
56. McNamara.
57. Angus.
58. Bayles.
59. Hunter.
60. Lawler.
61. Murphy.
62. Kilgallon.
63. Wadham.
64. Lapping.
65. Arnott.
66. Donnelly.

Appendix IV

ALHABETICAL NOMINAL ROLL
OTHER RANKS
25th NORTHUMBERLAND FUSILIERS
2nd TYNESIDE IRISH

HIGHEST BATTALION NUMBER TRACED 25/1547
NUMBER ON ROLL **1266**
UNTRACED **281**
KILLED OR DIED OF WOUNDS **283**
WOUNDED **386**
DISCHARGED SICK, GASSED, TRENCH FOOT.
DEAFNESS, KR para 392 ETC **256**
TOTAL KNOWN CASUALTIES **925**
CASUALTIES AS A % OF THOSE TRACED
73.06%

NAME	INITI	RANK	BA	NUMBE	COMP	ADDRESS	TOWN_VILL	ENLISTED	DISCHARG	CAUSE_DIS	WOUNDED	BURIED	TRANSFER	ADD
ABBOTT	Jos	SGT	25	/56	A	102 VICTOR ST MONKWM	SUNDERLAND			28 APRIL 1917	AUGUST 16	ARRAS MEM	TO 23rd, 25th BNS.	3 CCS 2/7/16 EVAC 2/7/16 BORN ALABAMA USA.
ADAMS	Albt	LCPL	25	/748	B	30 HOWICK ST MNKWRMT	SUNDERLAND	26/11/14		1 JULY 1916		THIEPVAL MEM		
ADAMS	W	PTE	25	/5	A	45 VICTORIA RD	HEBBURN							ALSO ON B COY 30th BN ROLL.
ALLAN	Rob	PTE	25	/55	A	16 GILESGATE	HEXAM						TO AGHR UNFIT.	
ALLISON	J	PTE	25	/758	A								TO CLASS Z RESERVE.	ACPL.
ANDERSON	G W	PTE	25	/747									TO 19th, 9th BNS, CLASS Z RESERVE.	
ANDREWS	J	PTE	25	/58	A	HEDLEY HILL TERR	WATERHOUSES	9/11/14	2/5/18	GUNSHOT WOUNDS			ATTACHED 179 TUNNELLING COY ROYAL ENGINEERS, 3rd B	
ANNFIELD	J	LCPL	25	/753	B		FRIZINGTON COLL				OCTOBER 16, MARCH 18		TO TF BN, CLASS Z RESERVE.	ALLOTED NEW NUMBER 292109, CPL, ASGT.
APPLEBY	T J	PTE	25	/57	A	16 GILESGATE	HEXAM						TO 24th, 8th BNS, CLASS Z RESERVE.	
APPLEBY	W	PTE	25	/6	C								TO CLASS Z RESERVE.	COLOUR SERGEANT.
ARKLE	J	PTE	25	/1543			BARRINGTON				JUNE 18		TO CLASS Z RESERVE.	
ARMSTRONG	J	SGT	25	/4	A		HOUGHTON LE SPR				JULY 16		TO CLASS Z RESERVE.	ALLOTED NEW NUMBER 42496
ARMSTRONG	John	LCPL	25	/755	D	5 DELTA HOUSE	SWALWELL			22 MAY 1916		BECOURT MIL CEM		BORN DERWENTHAUGH COUNTY DURHAM, AGE 26.
ARMSTRONG	P	PTE	25	/756	D			14/11/14	3/1/17	EPILEPSY			TO 30th BN(B COY), DEPOT.	
ARMSTRONG	R	SGT	25	/3	C		CONSETT	3/11/14	29/9/17	KR para 392	SEPTEMBER 16		TO DEPOT.	2 GEN HOSP 5/7/16 EVAC 10/7/16 FOOT WND
ARMSTRONG	Thos	PTE	25	/751			NEWCASTLE	18/11/14						LABOURER DESERTED 1/3/15 AGE 28, 5'3''.
ASHBRIDGE	Jas	PTE	25	/1	A	62 RYHOPE ST	RYHOPE COLLIERY			20 AUGUST 1920	JULY 16	RYHOPE	TO ROYAL DEFENCE CORPS.	RDC No 75920, AGE 47.
ASPINALL	John	PTE	25	/53	A	7 OFFICE SQUARE	LINTZ COLLIERY						TO CLASS Z RESERVE.	
ATHERTON	John	PTE	25	/750	A	14 ROWS YARD	PONTOP	29/10/14			AUGUST 16		TO DURHAM LI.	
ATKINSON	J	SGT	25	/8	C		KESWICK	16/11/14	15/3/18	GUNSHOT WOUNDS	SEPTEMBER 16			ALLOTED NEW NUMBER 42495.
ATKINSON	J	PTE	25	/1437	D			7/7/15	5/5/16				TO 30th BN(D COY).	DID NOT SERVE OVERSEAS.
ATKINSON	J F	PTE	25	/749	A	185 A ST WEST	PELTON						TO 30th BN(B COY), CLASS Z RESERVE.	CPL.
ATKINSON	Jothn	PTE	25	/752	B		GATESHEAD			20 SEPT 1916		LONSDALE CEM	TO KINGS OWN YORKSHIRE LI(1/4th BN).	KOYLI No 7004, AGE 28.
ATWELL	Wm	PTE	25	/54	D	21 DRYDENS BLD BERTR	SHIREMOOR			1 JULY 1916		THIEPVAL MEM	TO 30th(D COY), 24th BNS.	MINER, BORN GATESHEAD, MISSING NOV 16.
BAGGS	A H	PTE	25	/775	A									
BAIN	Robt	SGT	25	/64	A	70 ARTHUR ST	GATESHEAD	6/11/14			AUGUST 16		TO EAST YORKSHIRE REGIMENT.	LCPL IN 1918.
BAIN	Wm R	LSGT	25	/20	A	61 JAMES ST	BLAYDON						TO LABOUR CORPS.	LAB CORPS No 610145
BAKER	Arth	PTE	25	/777	B	18 HALGARTH ST ELVET	DURHAM CITY	26/11/14		1 JULY 1916		THIEPVAL MEM		
BALDRY	A	LSGT	25	/65	D		HAZELRIGG				SEPTEMBER 16		TO LABOUR CORPS.	3 CCS 2/7/16 EVAC 2/7/16.
BANKS	John	PTE	25	/14	A	15 THOMAS ST MONKWMT	SUNDERLAND	28/10/14						
BARKER	John	PTE	25											AWOL 14/6/15 COURT SUNDERLAND
BARKER	Thos	PTE	25	/798		4 SIXTH ST EAST	EASINGTON	9/12/14						
BARKHAM	Henry	PTE	25	/22	A	HILLTOP FLINTHILL	DIPTON	16/11/14	31/1/19	KR para 392	OCTOBER 16		TO ARMY RESERVE CLASS P.	
BARLOW	WalnJ	PTE	25	/76	A	3 HEDLEY ST	SOUTH SHIELDS	26/11/14					TO 12/13th BN, CLASS Z RESERVE.	
BARNETT	D	PTE	25	/15	A	137 ROSE ST	GATESHEAD							
BARRON	David	PTE	25	/810	B	23 DALE ST	BLYTH			1 JULY 1916		THIEPVAL MEM		MISSING OCTOBER 16, LCPL IN 5 PLATOON.
BARRON	Jos	PTE	25	/785	B		CHESTER LE ST			1 JULY 1916		THIEPVAL MEM		MISSING OCTOBER 16.
BARTON	Tom	PTE	25	/94	D	67 JOHN ST	BLAYDON			1 JULY 1916		THIEPVAL MEM		MISSING OCTOBER 16, BORN ASPATRIA AGE 37.
BATEY	E	CPL	25	/92	A			11/11/14	18/12/17	SICK			TO DEPOT.	DID NOT SERVE OVERSEAS. ON D COY ROLL 30TH BN.
BATEY	J J	PTE	25	/70		4 CANDY BANK	USWORTH						TO 1st GARRISON BN, CLASS Z RESERVE.	
BATEY	Thos	PTE	25	/21	A	14 BRIDGE ST	BLAYDON				SEPTEMBER 16		TO LABOUR CORPS.	3 CCS 2/7/16 EVAC 2/7/16. A/SGT
BATIE	W C	PTE	25	/769		64 HOWE ST	GATESHEAD							
BELL	F	PTE	25	/96	C	WHITE COTTAGE HOLLY	FELLING	11/11/14	9/2/17	GUNSHOT WOUNDS	SEPTEMBER 16		TO 85th TRAINING RESERVE BN.	3 CCS 2/7/16 EVAC 2/7/16 HOSP BRISTOL 11/7/16.
BELL	Fred	PTE	25	/782	A	14 SARAH ST	GATESHEAD						TO 10th BN, CLASS Z RESERVE.	SEE ALSO 25/771.
BELL	J	PTE	25	/83	D			17/11/14	31/1/19	KR para 392			TO ARMY RESERVE CLASS P.	CORPORAL
BELL	J	PTE	25	/792	B	HALF MOON YARD ELVET	DURHAM CITY	18/11/14	3/11/15					AWOL 10/9/15 COURT 16/9, DESERTED 17 SEPTEMBER 191
BELL	J W	PTE	25	/19	A			14/11/14	1/6/18	SICK			ATTACHED HQ 34th DIVISION, TO 3rd BN.	
BELL	S	PTE	25	/77	A	ELDON ST	SOUTH SHIELDS			KR para 392	OCTOBER 16			
BERRIGAN	J W	PTE	25	/794	B								TO 30th BN(D COY).	
BERRY	Jas G	PTE	25	/768	A	7 HAWK ST	GATESHEAD			1 JULY 1916		OVILLIERS MIL CEM		TRANSFERRED TO C COY.
BERRYMAN	J	PTE	25	/78	A	13 AGNES ST	SOUTH SHIELDS	19/11/14	31/1/19	KR para 392			TO ARMY RESERVE CLASS P.	LCPL
BEWICK	J	PTE	25	/71	A									
BEWLEY	M	PTE	25	/86	D		WOLSINGHAM				SEPTEMBER 16		TO LABOUR CORPS.	
BING	John	PTE	25	/767			GREENWICH KENT	20/11/14						SHIPS FIREMAN DESERTED 19/2/15, AGE 29 5'8''.
BINNIE	G	PTE	25	/764	B	14 HARRISONS COURT	SOUTH SHIELDS						TO ROYAL FUSILIERS(24th BN).	FRANCE 25th,11/1/16 TO 30/8/18, 24RFUS 31/8/18 TO
BISHOP	F	CSM	25	/1411	A		MURTON COLLIERY				AUGUST 16			
BISHOP	Walt	PTE	25	/24	A	23 FIRST ST	WHEATLEY HILL	11/11/14					TO LABOUR CORPS.	ALBERT TERR SHOTTON COLLIERY 1918.
BLACK	Andrw	PTE	25	/61	A	21 PENREUL ST SCOTSW	NEWCASTLE	11/11/14					TO 9th, 8th BNS, CLASS Z RESERVE.	

NAME	INITI	RANK	BA	NUMBE	COMP	ADDRESS	TOWN_VILL	ENLISTED	DISCHARG	CAUSE_DIS	WOUNDED	BURIED	TRANSFER	ADD
BLACK	Geo	PTE	25	/765	A		GATESHEAD			4 JUNE 1917		BAILLEUL RD ST LAURENT BLAGNY		
BLACKBURN	Jos	LCPL	25	/73	A	17 HARVEY ST	CONSETT	29/10/14					TO CLASS Z RESERVE.	ACTING WOII. 10 HARTINGTON STREET 1918 CQMS.
BLAND	T	PTE	25	/799	B	COUNCIL SCHOOLS	HIGH SPEN						TO CLASS Z RESERVE.	ATTESTED WITH TYNESIDE SCOTTISH 27/10/14
BLYTH	Jothn	PTE	25	/88	D	15 COMMERCIAL RD	JARROW	6/11/14		KR para 392	AUGUST 16			34 CCS 1/7/16 EVAC 1/7/16 WND RLEG,AGE 37.
BLYTH	T	PTE	25	/791	B	1 ALMA PLACE	GRANGE VILLA				SEPTEMBER 16			
BLYTHE	J	SGT	25	/770	D			21/11/14	10/4/18	VDH			ATTACHED 103 LTMB, 3rd BN.	
BLYTHE	Peter	PTE	25	/82	D	29 LAWRENCE ST	HENDON			1 JULY 1916		THIEPVAL MEM		BORN WASHINGTON.
BOLAM	E	PTE	25	/804	B		NORTH SHIELDS	15/11/14	28/12/17	GUNSHOT WOUNDS	AUGUST 16		TO DEPOT.	3 CCS 2/7/16 EVAC 2/7/16.
BOND	E	PTE	25	/808	B	3 GIBSIDE TERR	BURNHOPEFIELD							
BONES	M	PTE	25	/62	A	14 WILKINSON ST	HESLEDENE	12/11/14			JUNE 18		TO LABOUR CORPS.	
BOOTH	Isaac	PTE	25	/28									TO 1st GARRISON BN, 11th, 11th, 1st GARR BN, CLASS	
BOOTH	J W	PTE	25	/59	A		NEWCASTLE	23/11/14	1/1/18	WOUNDS	JULY 16		TO DEPOT.	
BOWEN	W	PTE	25	/793	A		WHICKHAM	12/11/14	6/9/16	8 JUNE 1920	APRIL 16	WHICKHAM	TO 30th, 3rd BNS.	
BOYCE	J	LCPL	25	/95	D									
BOYLE	F	PTE	25	/17	A		HASWELL				OCTOBER 16		TO 10th BN, CLASS Z RESERVE.	
BRABAN	J	PTE	25	/13	A	22 HAROLD ST	WASHINGTON STAT							ALSO ON D COY 30th BN ROLL.
BRADDICK	C H	PTE	25	/778	B	23 HIRST ST	WHEATLEY HILL	9/11/14	19/2/18	SICK			TO 3rd BN.	
BRADLEY	John	PTE	25	/67	A	MURRAYS BLDGS FRONT	DIPTON	21/11/14	28/3/18	SHELLSHOCK	MARCH 17		TO 3rd BN.	
BRADLEY	John	PTE	25	/787	B		NORTH SHIELDS			28 AUGUST 1918		WARLOY COM CEM.	TO 24th, 24/27th, 19th BNS.	AGE 27.
BRADY	P J	LCPL	25	/801	B		FRIZINGTON COLL				OCTOBER 16		TO CLASS Z RESERVE.	CSGT.
BRANNEN	Mich	PTE	25	/760	B	3 NEWCASTLE RD CROSS	DURHAM CITY				MARCH 18		TO 9th, 2nd, 3rd BNS, CLASS Z RESERVE.	
BRANNIGAN	T	PTE	25	/1485	A									
BREHANY	John	PTE	25	/75	A	4 ARMSTRONGS BLDGS	WEST BOLDON	26/11/14						ALSO ON D COY 30th BN ROLL.
BRENNAN	James	PTE	25	/795	D		GATESHEAD			22 MAY 1916		BECOURT MIL CEM		
BRENNAN	Mich	PTE	25	/60	A	100 PALMERSTON ST	SOUTH SHIELDS			1 JULY 1916		BAPAUME POST CEM		961/2 PORCHESTER ST.
BRESMAN	JohnW	LCPL	25	/773	B	55 SWINBANK COTTAGES	DAWDON			1 JULY 1916		THIEPVAL MEM		MISSING JULY 16, BORN SUNDERLAND.
BRIGGS	F C	PTE	25	/80	D									
BRIGGS	W	PTE	25	/781		16 PEEL STREET	WEST STANLEY			KR para 392			TO 1st GARRISON BN.	
BROOKS	J	PTE	25	/1508	D	127 ELDON ST	SOUTH SHIELDS	30/7/15	9/3/16				TO 30th BN.	DID NOT SERVE OVERSEAS.
BROOKS	Robt	PTE	25	/766	A		NEWCASTLE		31/1/19		SHELLSHOCK JUNE 17		TO KINGS OWN YORKSHIRE LI 2/4 BN, CLASS Z RESERVE.	SGT, KOYLI No 63247.
BROOKS	S	PTE	25	/68	A		WASHINGTON	21/11/14	8/8/17	SICK	JULY 16		TO DEPOT.	
BROPHY	Jas	LCPL	25	/11	A	17 NEVILLE TERR	DURHAM CITY	12/11/14	24/10/17	SICK			TO DEPOT.	
BROWELL	W	PTE	25	/25	A					KR para 392				
BROWN	Chas	SGT	25	/18	A	25 NORTH ST	BLAYDON			25 OCTOBER 1918	JUNE 18	AWOINGT MIL CEM	TO 9th BN.	
BROWN	David	PTE	25	/762			AMBLE	18/11/14						MINER DESERTED 21/2/15, AGE 33, 5'8'' POCK MARKED
BROWN	E	PTE	25	/802	A	20 MARLEBOROUGH ST	SUNDERLAND						TO 30th BN(D COY).	
BROWN	JohnG	PTE	25	/761	A	13 EMMERSONS BLDGS S	NEWCASTLE			6 APRIL 1916		BOULOGNE		BORN DIPTON, AGE 37.
BROWN	JohnG	PTE	25	/779	D	20 RAVENSWORTH RD	DUNSTON			18 JULY 1916		ST SEVER CEM ROUEN		3 CCS 2/7/16 EVAC 2/7/16, WND LEG.
BROWN	Jos	PTE	25	/16			NORTH SHIELDS	14/11/14						SEAMAN DESERTED 28/3/15, AGE 32, 5'5''.
BROWN	Mich	PTE	25	/788	A	11 PRINCESS ST	JARROW	12/11/14						ALSO ON D COY 30th BN ROLL.
BROWN	R	PTE	25	/79	A	17 HOWARD ST	NORTH SHIELDS							ALSO ON D COY 30th BN ROLL.
BROWN	R	PTE	25	/784	B	21 EAST TERR	NEW KYO							ACPL ALLOTED NEW NUMBER 88664.
BROWN	Thos	PTE	25	/805	B	7 GEORGE ST	BLAYDON	12/11/14					TO 19th, 1st BNS, CLASS Z RESERVE.	DESERTED 30/9/1918.
BROWN	Wm	PTE	25											AWOL 29/11/15 COURT 4/12/15.
BROWN	Wm G	PTE	25	/797			NEWCASTLE	13/11/14						RIGGER DESERTED 1/3/15 AGE 38, 5'6''.
BROWNS	J	PTE	25	/780	B									
BRUCE	J	PTE	25	/74	A									
BRYSON	J T	PTE	25	/63	A	29 ROBERTS PLACE	GATESHEAD	19/11/14	9/9/18	GUNSHOT WOUNDS	AUGUST 16		TO ARMY RESERVE CLASS W.	34 CCS 1/7/16 EVAC 5/7/16, AGE 30.
BUCKNALL	Tom W	PTE	25	/90		12 NORTH ST	JARROW	6/11/14		19 APRIL 1917		JARROW		AGE 42.
BULMAN	R	PTE	25	/10	A	21 VICTORIA ST	BLAYDON				SEPTEMBER 16		TO 23rd BN, CLASS Z RESERVE.	34 CCS 1/7/16 EVAC 5/7/16 WND HEEL AGE 29
BURKE	Edw	PTE	25	/776	D	9 EDWARD ST	HEBBURN						TO LABOUR CORPS.	
BURKE	John	PTE	25	/89	A	26 FRONT ST	BURNHOPEFIELD			23 JUNE 1917	JANUARY 17	COXYDE MIL CEM	TO 16th BN(D COY).	BORN DIPTON.
BURKE	Peter	PTE	25	/783	A	77 TARSETT ST	BATTLEFIELD			24 SEPT 1918	OCTOBER 16	RETHEL FRENCH MIL CEM	TO 27th, 16th, 1/5th BNS.	3 CCS 2/7/16 EVAC 2nd SOUTHERN GEN 11/7/16, TAKEN
BURLINSON	James	CPL	25	/27	A	11 BUXTON ST	NEWCASTLE			23 AUGUST 1918	OCTOBER 16	ALL SAINTS NEWCASTLE	TO 23rd, 25th, 1/5th, 3rd BNS.	34CCS 1/7 EVAC 5/7 HOSP BRISTOL 8/7/16.AGE 24.
BURLINSON	T	PTE	25	/806	A		NETTLESWORTH				JULY 16		TO ARMY SERVICE CORPS.	
BURN	Tom E	PTE	25	/803	B	146 MORTON ST	SOUTH SHIELDS			26 OCT 1917	SEPTEMBER 16	TYNE COT MEM	TO 14th, 1/7th BNS.	34 CCS 2/7 EVAC 5/7/16 WND L KNEE, AGE 23.
BURNETT	T	LSGT	25	/772	A			21/11/14	27/7/17	SICK			TO 3rd BN.	
BURNS	J	PTE	25	/72	A	18 ELM ST	HEBBURN	2/11/14	7/2/18	WOUNDS	OCTOBER 16		TO ARMY RESERVE CLASS W.	

NAME	INITI	RANK	BA	NUMBE	COMP	ADDRESS	TOWN_VILL	ENLISTED	DISCHARG	CAUSE_DIS	WOUNDED	BURIED	TRANSFER	ADD
BURNS	J	PTE	25	/786				13/11/14	28/3/18	KR para 392			TO 1st GARRISON BN, 3rd BN.	DID NOT SERVE OVERSEAS.
BURNS	T	PTE	25	/26	A		NEWCASTLE				OCTOBER 16(SHELLSHOCK)		TO ROYAL DEFENCE CORPS.	IN FRANCE 11/1/16 TO 5/3/17.
BURRELL	John	PTE	25	/771			WINLATON	21/11/14						LABOURER DESERTED 6/5/15, AGE 16, 5'2''.
BURRELL	T	PTE	25	/1470	A	37 HAMPDEN STREET	GATESHEAD	20/7/15	17/6/18	WOUNDS	APRIL 18		TO DEPOT.	
BURTON	Jas W	PTE	25	/796	B		SUNDERLAND	13/11/14						LABOURER,DESERTED 10/3/15,COURT SLAND 25/10/15. AG
BUSSEY	R	PTE	25	/790	B		BIRTLEY				OCTOBER 16		TO LABOUR CORPS.	
BUTLER	R	PTE	25	/85	D		SOUTH SHIELDS				AUGUST 16		TO 11th, 26th, 12/13th BNS, CLASS Z RESERVE.	34 CCS 2/7/16 EVAC 5/7/16.
BUXTON	J R	PTE	25	/66	A		WINGATE	21/11/14	26/10/16	SICK	JULY 16		TO 24th BN, DEPOT.	ALSO ON D COY 30th BN ROLL.
CABLE	J	PTE	25	/873	B			12/11/14	10/10/18	GUNSHOT WOUNDS			TO 8th BN, DEPOT, ARMY RESERVE CLASS P.	AGE 23.
CAFFERY	J	PTE	25	/109	A					KR para 392				
CAIN	Geo	PTE	25	/122	D	1 ALBANY ST SOUTHWIC	SUNDERLAND			1 JULY 1916		THIEPVAL MEM		NOK 4 SCHOOL ST DAWDON.
CAIN	Math	PTE	25	/30	D	GATESHEAD HOUSE	BONNERSFIELD	26/11/14						ALSO ON D COY 30th BN ROLL.
CAIRNS	Mathe	PTE	25	/893	B	13 EDEN ST	BURNHOPEFIELD			26 APRIL 1917		ARRAS MEM		AGE 36, BORN WHICKHAM.
CALLAGHAN	J T	PTE	25	/1442	D		CONSETT	12/7/15	11/12/17	WOUNDS	SEPTEMBER 16		TO 27th BN, DEPOT.	34 CCS 2/7/16 EVAC 5/7/16 WND ARM.
CALLAGHAN	Jos	LCPL	25	/862	B	8 ENID ST	DINNINGTON			24 OCT 1918		ROMERIES COM CEM EXT	TO 9th BN.	SGT, BORN NEWCASTLE. BROTHER 18/752
CAMBELL	J	PTE	25	/138	D		NEWCASTLE	17/11/14	20/8/18	GUNSHOT WOUNDS	JUNE 18		TO 3rd BN.	
CAMBELL	J	PTE	25	/833	D		HEBBURN COLLIER	31/11/14	18/3/17	KR para 392	JUNE 16		TO DEPOT.	
CAMBELL	Jas	PTE	25	/850	B		SUNDERLAND			1 JULY 1916		THIEPVAL MEM		MISSING OCTOBER 16.
CAMBELL	JohnT	SGT	25	/822	B		WALLSEND			6 SEPT 1916		THIEPVAL MEM		
CAMPBELL	A	PTE	25	/127	B			9/11/14	23/1/16	MEDICALLY UNFIT				AWOL 6/5/15 COURT 2/6/15, NOT SERVE OVERSEAS.
CAMPBELL	J W	SGT	25	/44										ALSO ON B COY 30th BN ROLL.
CANNING	Hugh	CPL	25	/878	D		DURHAM CITY			1 JULY 1916		THIEPVAL MEM		MISSING OCT GAZ
CANNON	M	PTE	25	/819		37 ALBION ST	JARROW						TO 2nd GARRISON BN, CLASS Z RESERVE.	
CAPSTICK	G	PTE	25	/870	B									
CAREY	E	PTE	25	/136	D								TO 2nd GARRISON BN, CLASS Z RESERVE.	
CAREY	N	PTE	25	/844	D	9 SHAMROCK ST	HEBBURN NEW TOW	12/11/14						
CARITHNESS	J	PTE	25	/838	D									
CARLING	Geo	PTE	25	/131	A	81 COMMERCIAL RD	JARROW			1 JULY 1916		THIEPVAL MEM		MISSING OCTOBER 16, BORN BACKJARROW.
CARLING	R	PTE	25	/815		27 HIGH ST	JARROW			KR para 392			TO 11th, 25th, 12/13th BNS.	
CARR	E	PTE	25	/845				23/11/14	3/7/15	VDH				DID NOT SERVE OVERSEAS.
CARR	Geo	LCPL	25	/50	D		DURHAM CITY			9 APRIL 1917		BAILLEUL RD ST LAURENT BLAGNY		
CARR	Jas	PTE	25	/861	B		BLAYDON			1 JULY 1916		THIEPVAL MEM		MISSING OCTOBER 16.
CARR	M	PTE	25	/142	D		WEST STANLEY				NOVEMBER 16			
CARR	Mason	PTE	25	/143	D	8 SOUTH VIEW	WEST RYTON	28/10/14		1 JULY 1916		THIEPVAL MEM		MISSING OCTOBER 16, BORN BLAYDON.
CARR	T	PTE	25	/40				12/11/14	21/4/15	INNEFFICIENT			TO DEPOT.	DID NOT SERVE OVERSEAS, AGE 31.
CARR	T	PTE	25	/137	A	24 PALMER ST	GATESHEAD						TO ARMY SERVICE CORPS.	ASC No 389705.
CARROLL	J	PTE	25	/32	A	COWPEN	BLYTH			17 DEC 1917		BLYTH		
CARROLL	J	CPL	25	/132	A			19/11/14	18/12/17	KR para 392			TO 85th TRAINING RESERVE BN.	
CARROLL	John	PTE	25	/146	D	12 LOVE ST NEW DURHA	DURHAM CITY	19/11/14	18/12/17				TO 85th TRAINING RESERVE BN, LABOUR CORPS, 22 PoW	
CARROLL	Wm	PTE	25	/120		10 ALBERT ST	SUNDERLAND			28 SEPT 1915		BISHOPWEARMOUTH		SERVED IN BOER WAR, AGE 41.
CARRUTHERS	S	PTE	25	/126	B		GATESHEAD				AUGUST 16			
CARSON	J	PTE	25	/890	A	7 HEWORTH ST	HIGH FELLING	16/11/14	12/9/18	GUNSHOT WOUNDS	APRIL 17		TO 3rd BN.	AGE 26.
CARSON	JohnR	PTE	25	/843	B	20 FIELD ST	FELLING	12/11/14		14 SEPT 1917	NOVEMBER 16	HENIEL COM CEM EXT	TO 1/4th BN.	ALLOTED NEW NUMBER 204569, LCPL, AGE 25.
CARTER	Stan	PTE	25	/852	B	36 FAWCETT ST	SOUTH SHIELDS			10 APRIL 1918	JULY 16	PLOEGSTEERT MEM	TO 1/4th BN.	ALLOTTED NEW NUMBER 204576.
CASEY	Dougl	PTE	25	/880			NEWCASTLE	13/11/14						DRAUGHTSMAN DESERTED 15/1/15, AGE 17, 5'2''.
CASH	J	PTE	25	/128	D	2 CLEADON ST	CONSETT			KR para 392				34CCS 2/7/16 EVAC 22 AMB TRN 9/7/16,SICK.
CASSELL	A	PTE	25	/1441	D								TO 1st, 14th, 12/13th BNS, CLASS Z RESERVE.	
CASSIDY	M	PTE	25	/876	B	32 WESTERN RD	WILLINGTON QUAY	15/5/15	20/12/18	GUNSHOT WOUNDS	AUGUST 16		TO 1st BN, DEPOT.	LCPL DESERTED 15 MAY 1918. AGE 28
CASSIDY	Rob	CPL	25	/866	B		SUNDERLAND			1 JULY 1916		THIEPVAL MEM		MISSING OCTOBER 16, IN 10 PLATOON.
CASSIDY	W	LCPL	25	/103	D	64 CALIFORNIA ST	NEW SEAHAM	16/11/14	6/2/18				TO DEPOT.	DID NOT SERVE OVERSEAS.
CAVANAGH	John	PTE	25	/832			NEWCASTLE			1 JULY 1916		THIEPVAL MEM		MISSING OCTOBER 16. DESERTED JULY 15 IN COURT 25/1
CAVENEY	Math	PTE	25	/818		28 CARLISLE ST	NEWCASTLE	19/11/14	27/4/15	SICK				DID NOT SERVE OVERSEAS.
CHAMBERS	J	PTE	25	/147	D									
CHAPMAN	P	PTE	25	/875									TO 2nd GARRISON BN, CLASS Z RESERVE.	
CHARLTON	Aaron	PTE	25	/101	A	9 NORTH ST	WHITBURN COLLIE	11/11/14		23 MARCH 1918	OCTOBER 16	POZIERES MEM	TO 14th, 12/13th, 14th BNS.	AGE 44.
CHARLTON	Math	PTE	25	/830	B		SUNDERLAND							AWOL 7/7/16 UNTIL 30/7/16 IN COURT SUNDERLAND.
CHARLTON	R	CQMS	25	/1525	B	8 CLAPHAM ST	DUNSTON						COMMISSIONED, TO PRISONER OF WAR GUARD COY.	
CHARLTON	Thos	PTE	25	/145			NEWCASTLE	12/11/14						IRON MOULDER, DESERTED 1/3/15, AGE 23, 5'7''.

NAME	INITI	RANK	BA	NUMBE	COMP	ADDRESS	TOWN_VILL	ENLISTED	DISCHARG	CAUSE_DIS	WOUNDED	BURIED	TRANSFER	ADD
CHESTER	H	CPL	25	/864	B	11 SOUTH STREET	DURHAM CITY							
CHRISTOPHER	J	PTE	25	/36	A									ALSO ON D COY 30th BN ROLL.
CLARK	Ben E	PTE	25	/882	B	4 LOGAN ST	SOUTH HETTON			12 JULY 1917		ARRAS MEM	TO 27th, 1/6th BNS.	BORN KNIGHTTOWN Co MAYO, AGE 24.
CLARK	John	PTE	25	/1475	A	5 THOMPSON ST	BYKER BANK			26 APRIL 1917		HEATON	TO 8th, 16th BNS.	AGE 39.
CLARK	P	LCPL	25	/871	B	TOWER HOUSE CITY RD	NEWCASTLE							
CLARK	Peter	PTE	25	/1375			CONSETT	10/11/14						IRON WORKER DESERTED 15/1/15, AGE 38, 5'9''.
CLARK	Wm	PTE	25	/884	B	13 DODDS TERR	LOW FELL			9 APRIL 1917		ST CATHERINES CEM		BORN DURHAM CITY, AGE 37.
CLARKE	J	PTE	25	/859	B	50 BOTTLE BANK	BLACKHILL	17/11/14	15/3/18	WOUNDS	AUGUST 16		TO DEPOT.	
CLARKE	Jas	PTE	25	/41	D	25 KNITSLEY GARDENS	CONSETT	5/11/14					TO 21st, 11th ATTACHED 68th LTMB, CLASS Z RESERVE.	
CLARKE	John	PTE	25	/1419	D	HIGH HOPE ST	CROOK	13/4/15	1/8/17	GUNSHOT WOUNDS	OCTOBER 16		TO 3rd BN.	VOLUNTEERED 29/10/14.
CLARKE	JohnM	PTE	25	/110	D	16 POLONAIZE ST	EAST STANLEY			17 MAY 1916	MARCH 16	BECOURT MIL CEM		AGE 35.
CLARKSON	Wm	PTE	25	/1482	C			22/7/15	5/10/17	SICK			TO DEPOT.	AGE 40.
CLELLAND	John	PTE	25	/816	B		NEWCASTLE			1 JULY 1916		CERISSY GAILLY	TO 24th BN.	MISSING SEPTEMBER 16.
CLEMENTS	J T	PTE	25	/46	D	38 FLAG LANE	SUNDERLAND				NOVEMBER 16			
CLIMPSON	Rich	PTE	25	/820	B	37 JOHNSON ST	SUNDERLAND			9 APRIL 1917		ROCLINCOURT VALLEY CEM		
CLOSE	R	PTE	25	/1472									TO 1st GARRISON BN, CLASS Z RESERVE.	
CLOUGH	F R	PTE	25	/115	A		GATESHEAD							AWOL 15/7/15,GATESHEAD.8/6/15 S SHIELDS AGE 32.
CLOUGH	Wm	PTE	25	/150	C	60 CARTERS YD OAKWEL	GATESHEAD			1 JULY 1916		THIEPVAL MEM		MISSING OCTOBER 16.
CLYDESDALE	W	PTE	25	/129	B									ALSO ON D COY 30th BN ROLL.
COLE	P	PTE	25	/856	B					KR para 392				
COLLINS	D	PTE	25	/38	B	30 22 MILL ST SCOTSWOOD	NEWCASTLE							
COLLINS	Edw	PTE	25	/869	B	28 AMY ST SOUTHWICK	SUNDERLAND			1 JULY 1916		THIEPVAL MEM		MISSING OCTOBER 16.
COLLINS	M	PTE	25	/853	B	4 BOWMAN TERR	NEWCASTLE						TO 30th BN(D COY), KINGS OWN YORKSHIRE LI.	KOYLI No 63385.
COLLINS	M	PTE	25	/867	B	28 AMY ST SOUTHWICK	SUNDERLAND	10/11/14	18/1/19	GUNSHOT WOUNDS	SEPTEMBER 16, NOVEMBER 18		TO 1st, 23rd, 8th, 12/13th, DEPOT.	25 AMB TRAIN 5/7/16,18 GEN HOSP, HOSP SHIP 9/7/16,
COLLINS	Mich	PTE	25	/807				10/11/14	18/1/19	AO 6/18 GSW				
COLPITTS	Tom E	PTE	25	/813	B	1 SHINEY ROW	BEDLINGTON	8/11/14		1 JULY 1916		THIEPVAL MEM		MISSING, DIARY IN IWM BODY MUST HAVE BEEN FOUND.
CONNELLY	John	PTE	25	/886	B	79 NINTH ROW	ACKLINGTON	31/10/14						
CONNER	John	PTE	25	/841	B		HEBBURN			1 JULY 1916		THIEPVAL MEM		MISSING OCTOBER 16,IN MACHINE GUN SECTION.
CONNOLLY	Bernd	PTE	25	/35		205 HIGH ST EAST	WALLSEND	12/11/14	24/4/15	INEFFICIENT				DID NOT SERVE OVERSEAS, AGE 47.
CONNOLLY	F	PTE	25	/114	D			23/11/14	14/12/18				TO DEPOT.	DID NOT SERVE OVERSEAS.
CONNOLLY	P	PTE	25	/837	A									ALSO ON B COY 30th BN ROLL.
CONNOLLY	Rob	PTE	25	/831	B	19 ELM ST	SOUTHMOOR	26/11/14			JUNE 16, AUGUST 16.			
CONNOR	J	PTE	25	/827	B								TO LABOUR CORPS.	
CONNOR	J	PTE	25	/1440	D								TO CLASS Z RESERVE.	
CONNOR	John	PTE	25	/29			BELTURBET CAVAN	9/11/14						MINER, DESERTED 16/2/15 AGE 38, 5'7''.
CONROY	John	PTE	25	/107	D	67 WILLOW POND TERR	SUNDERLAND	26/11/14		1 JULY 1916		THIEPVAL MEM		MISSING OCTOBER 16, BORN FERMOY Co CORK.
CONROY	M	PTE	25	/858	D		NEWCASTLE	17/11/14	10/8/17	GUNSHOT WOUNNDS	OCTOBER 16		TO 3rd BN.	
CONROY	Wm	PTE	25	/826	D	15 BK CUTHBERT ST	HEBBURN	10/11/14		14 MARCH 1917		FABOURG DE AMIENS CEM ARRAS		LCPL
CONVERY	H	PTE	25	/824	A		NEWCASTLE				AUGUST 16		TO LONDON REGT(33rd BN).	
CONVEY	John	PTE	25	/43	A	67 WILLOW POND TERR	MILLFIELD	29/10/14					TO ROYAL ARMY MEDICAL CORPS, LABOUR CORPS.	
CONWAY	A	PTE	25	/855	B		SOUTH SHIELDS				OCTOBER 16		TO 1/4th BN, CLASS Z RESERVE.	NEW NUMBER 204571. FITTER HIGH DOCKS(SMITHS)
CONWAY	C	PTE	25	/39	D	JOICEY TERR	OXHILL				MARCH 16			PHOTO IN CC 2/3/16 INVALIDED HOME 3/16.
COOK	Andrw	PTE	25	/894	D		SOUTH SHIELDS			3 JULY 1916		ALBERT COM CEM		MISSING OCTOBER 16.
COOK	John	PTE	25	/102	D	190 MILE END ROAD	SOUTH SHIELDS	15/11/14	22/8/17	WOUNDS	OCTOBER 16		TO 3rd BN.	
COOKE	Chas	PTE	25	/847	B	15 PRINCESS ST	JARROW	29/10/14		KR para 392			TO 20th, 10th BNS.	
COOKE	J T	LCPL	25	/821	A								TO 18th, 8th BN, CLASS Z RESERVE.	
COOPER	Geo	PTE	25	/865	B		NEWCASTLE			1 JULY 1916		THIEPVAL MEM		MISSING OCTOBER 16, BORN STRATFORD ESSEX.
COOPER	R	PTE	25	/134		72 GRACE ST	NEWCASTLE						TO 2nd GARRISON BN.	
CORLESS	J	PTE	25	/1529	A									
CORR	Denn	PTE	25	/113	D	4 CROSS ST FARRINGTO	SUNDERLAND	26/11/14						
CORSBIE	T D	PTE	25	/118	D	8 RIVER VIEW	WASHINGTON						TO CLASS Z RESERVE.	SERGEANT.
CORVEN	P	PTE	25	/1495	A		WASHINGTON	26/5/15	26/2/17		SHELLSHOCK MARCH 17			
COSGRAVE	T	PTE	25	/140	A									
COUGHLAN	Rob	PTE	25	/105	D	37 CLYDE ST	CHOPWELL			25 APRIL 1917		DUISANS	TO 21st BN.	BORN BLACKHILL.
COULEY	Wm	PTE	25	/42	B		NEWCASTLE			1 JULY 1916		THIEPVAL MEM		MISSING AUGUST 16.CONLEY ON MR.
COULSON	Alex	PTE	25	/1489	D		NEWCASTLE			1 JULY 1916		THIEPVAL MEM	TO 30th, 24th BNS.	ALSO ON B COY 30th BN ROLL.
COULSON	W E	PTE	25	/857	A					KR para 392				LCPL.
COUNSELL	Alb J	PTE	25	/825	A		CONSETT	26/11/14			12 FEBRUARY 16			

NAME	INITI	RANK	BA	NUMBE	COMP	ADDRESS	TOWN_VILL	ENLISTED	DISCHARG	CAUSE_DIS	WOUNDED	BURIED	TRANSFER	ADD
COURTNEY	Pat	SGT	25	/31	D	27 TAYLOR ST COWPEN	BLYTH			1 JULY 1916		THIEPVAL MEM		MISSING OCTOBER 16, BORN MULLINGAR.
COWLEY	Wm	LCPL	25	/48		34 TALBOT TERR ST PE	NEWCASTLE	7/11/14					TO 1st GARRISON BN, 12/13th BN, CLASS Z RESERVE.	SPECIAL CONSTABULARY MEDAL GVI.
COXFORD	W	PTE	25	/104	D		HASWELL	16/11/14	30/11/18	GUNSHOT WOUNDS	SEPTEMBER 16		TO DEPOT.	
COYLE	W	PTE	25	/849	B								TO 12/13th BN, CLASS Z RESERVE.	
COYNE	C	PTE	25	/1487	A									ALSO D COY 30th BN.
COYNE	James	PTE	25	/1486	A		BLYTH			9 APRIL 1917		ROCLINCOURT VALLEY CEM	TO 24th BN.	
COYNE	Jas P	PTE	25	/108	D	35 SIMPSON ST	SOUTH SHIELDS			1 JULY 1916		THIEPVAL MEM		MISSING OCTOBER 16, LCPL, BORN JARROW.
COYNE	T	PTE	25	/141	A	35 BEWICK ST	HEBBURN				SEPTEMBER 16		TO LABOUR CORPS.	
CRAGGS	W	PTE	25	/1454	D	95 FAIRLESS ST	NEWCASTLE						TO 2nd GARRISON BN, CLASS Z RESERVE.	
CRAIG	W	LCPL	25	/829	B	58 ROBINSON ST	BLAYDON	21/11/14	18/6/18	WOUNDS	AUGUST 16		TO ARMY RESERVE CLASS W.	CPL,34 CCS 2/7 EVAC 5/7/16 WND R ARM, AGE 22.
CRANNY	Pat	PTE	25	/848			GATESHEAD	11/11/14						LABOURER DESERTED 14/3/15 AGE 42, 5'4''.
CRAWFORD	Edmd	PTE	25	/139	A		NEWCASTLE	18/11/14	24/1/18	SICK	MARCH 17		TO 19th, 14th BNS, DEPOT.	DESERTED 22/5/15 COURT 18/6/15 NEWCASTLE.
CRAWFORD	J J	CPL	25	/144		912 SCOTSWOOD RD	NEWCASTLE						TO 3rd BN.	
CRONEY	J	PTE	25	/846	B	32 MITCHELL ST	SOUTHMOOR			KR para 392	MAY 16, MARCH 18.			
CROPP	RichF	LCPL	25	/828	B		ASHINGTON			1 JULY 1916		THIEPVAL MEM		MISSING OCTOBER 16.
CROSS	J	PTE	25	/111	A	42 BYKER BANK	NEWCASTLE				AUGUST 16		TO 23rd, 26th, 25th, 12/13th BNS, CLASS Z RESERVE.	34 CCS 1/7/16 EVAC 5/7/16,WND LLEG,AGE 31.
CROSSLEY	J	PTE	25	/1378	A	RICHARDSONS YD JOHN	SEAHAM				APRIL 16			
CROUDACE	J	PTE	25	/49	A	17 PORTLAND PLACE	NEWCASTLE						TO 27th, 24th, 23rd, 9th BNS, CLASS Z RESERVE.	
CUDDEN	John	PTE	25	/33		19 BERRYEDGE RD	CONSETT	12/11/14		KR para 392				
CULLEN	J	PTE	25	/1484	C	27 DERWENT ST	BLACKHILL				NOVEMBER 16			LCPL, HOSP COVENTRY 12/7/16.
CULLERTON	H	PTE	25	/45	D			14/11/14	22/10/17	VARICOSE VEINS			TO DEPOT.	
CUMMINGS	Wm	PTE	25	/149	A	42 SOUTH ST	BRANDON	12/11/14			NOVEMBER 16		TO 26th, 22nd BNS, CLASS Z RESERVE.	WOUNDED RIGHT ARM, HOSP STOCKPORT.
CUNNINGHAM	W	PTE	25	/823	B		JARROW				NOVEMBER 16			
CURRAN	C	PTE	25	/125	A					KR para 392				
CURRAN	M	PTE	25	/840	B				12/2/19				TO KINGS OWN YORKSHIRE LI 2/4 BN, CLASS Z RESERVE.	KOYLI No 63404.
CURRAN	T	PTE	25	/119	C		GATESHEAD	23/11/14	4/10/16	SICK	AUGUST 16		ATTACHED 103 LTMB, DEPOT.	3 CCS 2/7/16 EVAC 4/7/16 MULTIPLE INJURIES.
CURRIE	J E	PTE	25	/1464	A									ALSO ON B COY 30th BN ROLL.
CURRY	John	PTE	25	/814	B	4 SOUTH ST	DURHAM CITY			28 APRIL 1917		ARRAS MEM	TO 24th BN.	NOK 20 CROSSGATE 1917
CURRY	R H	PTE	25	/117	B30		USWORTH				AUGUST 16			
CURTIS	Robt	PTE	25	/1527	A	STARFORDS BLDGS	DIPTON			28 MARCH 1918	OCTOBER 16	POZIERES MEM	TO 20th, 21st, 12/13th BN.	
DACK	R H	PTE	25	/157	C	163 HARBOTTLE ST	NEWCASTLE						TO 9th, 8th BNS, CLASS Z RESERVE.	
DALE	Geo	PTE	25	/179	D		WARDLEY COLLIER			17 MAY 1916		BECOURT MIL CEM		NOK 2 SALISBURY RD KILBURN LONDON, AGE 40.
DALEY	J	PTE	25	/905	A		NEWCASTLE	16/11/14	1/1/18	WOUNDS	JULY 17		TO DEPOT.	
DALEY	J J	PTE	25	/183	C		NEWCASTLE				JULY 16		TO LABOUR CORPS.	
DALEY	W	PTE	25	/908	B									ALSO ON D COY 30th BN ROLL.
DALTON	R	PTE	25	/904	B	10 BERWICK ST	SOUTH SHIELDS	21/11/11	23/8/18	SICK			TO DEPOT.	
DANE	Peter	PTE	25	/187	D		WALLSEND			1 JULY 1916		THIEPVAL MEM		MISSING OCTOBER 16, BORN WOOLER.
DARBY	H	PTE	25	/1383	B	2 RAILWAY ST	KELLOE	12/1/15	31/7/17	GUNSHOT WOUNDS	OCTOBER 16		TO 3rd BN.	LCPL, 3CCS 2/7/16 EVAC 2/7/16 PARALYSED.
DARWOOD	Rob	PTE	25	/152	D	40 LADYSMITH TERR	CRAGHEAD	21/11/14	1/2/19		JANUARY 17		TO ARMY RESERVE CLASS P.	SEE 25/909 BROTHER. OTHER BROTHER IN 6 RIF
DARWOOD	Saln	PTE	25	/909	B	36 LADYSMITH TERR	CRAGHEAD	26/11/14		1 JULY 1916		THIEPVAL MEM		INNELIGIBLE MEDALS, SELF INFLICTED WOUNDS 6/4/16.
DAVEY	Jos W	PTE	25	/932	D	50 DEAN ST	LOW FELL			1 JULY 1916		THIEPVAL MEM		AWOL 8/9/15, MIS OCT 16, BORN WREKETON. AGE 19.
DAVIDSON	F	PTE	25	/181	B									ALSO ON D COY 30th BN ROLL.
DAVIDSON	Robt	PTE	25	/1494	B		NEWCASTLE			3 NOV 1916		CITE BON JEAN CEM		
DAVIDSON	Thos	PTE	25	/940	B	33 DORNEY ST	GATESHEAD			19 OCT 1917		TYNE COT MEM	TO 22ND BN.	
DAVIS	B	PTE	25	/180	A									ALSO ON D COY 30th BN ROLL.
DAVIS	J W	PTE	25	/1497	A			28/7/15	15/10/17	SICK			TO 85th TRAINING RESERVE BN.	
DAVIS	S	CQMS	25	/1379	B 30									
DAVISON	J	PTE	25	/165	D			17/11/14	8/11/16	GUNSHOT WOUNDS			TO DEPOT.	
DAVISON	W	SGT	25	/160	B 30									
DAVISON	W	PTE	25	/175	D	BALIANS GATE	HEXAM	14/11/14	11/10/18	SICK			TO ARMY RESERVE CLASS W.	
DAWSON	Ant B	CPL	25	/1376	D	130 BRINKBURN ST	NEWCASTLE			2 JULY 1916		WARLOY		
DAWSON	Rob	PTE	25	/1547		21 BEECHGROVE TERR	EDMONDSLEY			1 JULY 1916		THIEPVAL MEM	FROM ARMY CYCLIST CORPS.	BORN SOUTHMOOR.
DAY	G E	SGT	25	/1424	A									
DEACON	R	PTE	25	/185	D	9 DOUGLAS ST	DIPTON							POS ROBT WM 30099 RE. ON AVL.
DEARY	J	PTE	25	/900	A									
DEIGHAN	Mich	PTE	25	/917	A	85 CHESTNUT ST	HIRST					BRESLE MIL CEM		59 MAPLE ST HIRST NOK, AGE 38.
DEIGHAN	W	PTE	25	/941	C	19 PENNY ST	JARROW				AUGUST 16			
DELANEY	Edwd	PTE	25	/919			WEST STANLEY	17/11/14						MINER DESERTED 15/1/15, AGE 34.

NAME	INITI	RANK	BA	NUMBE	COMP	ADDRESS	TOWN_VILL	ENLISTED	DISCHARG	CAUSE_DIS	WOUNDED	BURIED	TRANSFER	ADD
DELANEY	Jas	PTE	25	/896		169 WILLINGTON LANE	HEBBURN			1 JULY 1916	JULY 16	THIEPVAL MEM		BORN GATESHEAD.
DEMPSEY	J	PTE	25	/926	A	11 DAVISON ST	FELLING							
DEMPSEY	T	PTE	25	/901	C		THORNLEY COLLIE	6/10/14	1/4/18	GUNSHOT WOUNDS	AUGUST 16		TO ARMY RESERVE CLASS P.	3 CCS 2/7/16 EVAC 2/7/16.
DEMPSTER	F	PTE	25	/922	B								REENLISTED 6th DRAGOON GUARDS 1920.	CPL, RETURNED WITH THE COLOURS.
DEMPSTER	J	PTE	25	/921	B		BLYTH						TO CLASS Z RESERVE.	PRISONER OF WAR DECEMBER 1917.
DENEVAN	J	PTE	25	/1380	B		SUNDERLAND				SEPTEMBER 16		TO 27th, 16th, 8th BNS, CLASS Z RESERVE.	
DESMOND	Dan	PTE	25	/927			SOUTH SHIELDS	11/11/14						LABOURER DESERTED 23/2/15, AGE 44, 5'8''.
DEVANNEY	Jas	PTE	25	/903	D		GATESHEAD						TO CLASS Z RESERVE.	AWOL 9/9/15, MIS OCT 16, POW FEB 1917.AGE 18.
DEVENISH	A	LCPL	25	/943			CORNSAY COLLIER				JULY 16, MARCH 18.		TO ROYAL FLYING CORPS.	
DEVINE	B	PTE	25	/161	D	18 CHAPEL CHARE	WINGATE				DECEMBER 16		TO TANK CORPS.	TANK CORPS No 302673.
DEVITT	Wm	PTE	25	/933	C	102 MAPLE ST	HIRST						TO 8th, 1/7th BNS, CLASS Z RESERVE.	
DEVLIN	J	PTE	25	/1382	D		SEAHAM				18 JUNE 16			ALLOTED NEW NUMBER 267655.
DIAMOND	J	PTE	25	/906	A								TO LABOUR CORPS.	SIX J DIAMONDS IN NEWSPAPER LISTS.
DICKENSON	G	CPL	25	/192	C		NEWCASTLE			KR para 392	OCTOBER 16			
DINNING	W	PTE	25	/934	C	HIGH ST	SHINCLIFFE	6/1/15	24/5/18	GUNSHOT WOUNDS	JUNE 17		TO 3rd BN, ARMY RESERVE CLASS P.	
DIX	R	LCPL	25	/930	D								TO LABOUR CORPS.	
DIX	Sam	LCPL	25	/928	D	79 ROBINSON ST	SOUTH SHIELDS			1 JULY 1916		THIEPVAL MEM		
DIXON	A	PTE	25	/895	D			18/11/14	4/10/19	KR para 392			TO DEPOT.	AWOL 21/8/15 IN COURT 27/8/15.
DIXON	G	PTE	25	/920	B			18/11/14	31/8/17	WOUNDS			TO DEPOT.	
DIXON	Jas	PTE	25	/188	D	11 DEAN CRES	SHOTTON COLLIER				AUGUST 16		TO 9th, 1/5th BNS, CLASS Z RESERVE.	
DIXON	John	PTE	25	/174	A									ON B ROLL AS DISCON.
DIXON	T	PTE	25	/191	B									
DOBBY	Henry	PTE	25	/159	D	20 EMMAVILLE	RYTON						TO LABOUR CORPS.	
DOCHERTY	Frank	LCPL	25	/923	B		JARROW			1 JULY 1916		THIEPVAL MEM		MISSING OCTOBER 1916.
DOCHERTY	Peter	LCPL	25	/911	B		WALLSEND			6 APRIL 1916		BREWERY ORCHARD CEM		
DODDS	Ambrs	PTE	25	/1545		22 FOWLER GDNS	DUNSTON							
DODDS	J	PTE	25	/176	B	4 SOUTH ST	SEAHAM HARBOUR							ALSO ON B COY 30th BN ROLL.
DODDS	JohnR	PTE	25	/1439	D	9 GREENLAND VILLAS	SOUTHMOOR							
DODGESON	T	PTE	25	/902				19/11/14	12/6/15	ONLY ONE EYE				DID NOT SERVE OVERSEAS.
DODGSON	Wm	PTE	25	/1381	B	75 LAWRENCE RD	BYKER			1 JULY 1916		THIEPVAL MEM		
DOLAN	Mich	PTE	25	/936	A	39 UNION ST	NORTH SHIELDS				12 FEBRUARY 1916		TO LABOUR CORPS, ROYAL FUSILIERS.	
DONAGHY	R	PTE	25	/189	A		BEDLINGTON				APRIL 16, SEPTEMBER 16.			
DONNELLY	Dan	CPL	25	/924	C	64 CALIFORNIA ST	NEW SEAHAM	31/10/14		28 APRIL 1917		ARRAS MEM		3 CCS 2/7/16 EVAC 2/7/16.
DONNELLY	F	PTE	25	/915	B		COXHOE POTTERY				AUGUST 16		TO 20th, 18th, 14th BNS, CLASS Z RESERVE.	
DONNELLY	J	PTE	25	/162	D									
DONNELLY	J	CPL	25	/925	C		REDCAR	10/11/14	23/8/17	GUNSHOT WOUNDS	OCTOBER 16		TO DEPOT.	
DONNELLY	John	PTE	25	/153	A		GATESHEAD			1 JULY 1916		THIEPVAL MEM		MISSING OCTOBER 16.
DONNELLY	Jos	PTE	25	/182	D	6 LION ST BACK	HEBBURN	6/11/14		KR para 392				MISSING OCTOBER 16, NOT MISSING DECEMBER 16.
DOOLEY	Jas	PTE	25	/164		5 HOLY ISLAND	HEXAM						TO 1st GARRISON BN, CLASS Z RESERVE.	
DORAN	C B	CQMS	25	/186	D								TO 12/13th BN, CLASS Z RESERVE.	REDUCED TO LCPL.
DORAN	JohnW	LCPL	25	/177	D	132 EDWARD ST	BLAYDON				AUGUST 16		TO LABOUR CORPS, ROYAL DEFENCE CORPS.	34 CCS EVAC 5/7, 3rd GEN HOSP SHEFFIELD 10/7/16.
DORIAN	Thos	PTE	25	/916	B	4 FARRINGDON RD	SUNDERLAND	26/11/14						
DOUGHERTY	J	PTE	25	/938	A	16 FONT HOUSE	LEADGATE						TO 22nd BN, CLASS Z RESERVE.	
DOVEY	J	PTE	25	/167	C									
DOW	M	PTE	25	/1542			NEWCASTLE			KR para 392	OCTOBER 16		TO 8th, 16th BNS.	
DOWLING	P	PTE	25	/912	B									ALSO ON D COY 30th BN ROLL.
DOWSON	RobtB	PTE	25	/168		39 THORPE AVE CROOKH	RYTON						TO 2nd GARRISON BN, CLASS Z RESERVE.	
DOYLE	J	PTE	25	/155				23/11/14	3/5/18	DYSENTRY			TO 1st GARRISON BN, 3rd BN.	
DOYLE	Jos M	PTE	25	/910	B	10 CRONE ST	EARSDON						TO 1st BN, CLASS Z RESERVE.	
DOYLE	Pat	PTE	25	/918	A	3 WASH HOUSES	BIRTLEY				JUN 16, JULY 16.		TO 25th, 20th, 21st, 25th, 24th BN ROYAL FUSILIERS IN FRANCE 11/1/16 TO 12/6/16, 20 8/1/17 TO 11/1/17	
DRAKE	G	LCPL	25	/931	A	163 SUNDERLAND RD	GATESHEAD							
DRENNON	T	PTE	25	/163	D		TANFIELD LEA				OCTOBER 16		TO ROYAL JERSEY GARRISON BN.	
DRIVER	J	PTE	25	/913	B 30									
DRYDEN	C	PTE	25	/897	B									ALSO ON B COY 30th BN ROLL.
DRYDEN	W	PTE	25	/939	B 30									
DUFFY	Arth	PTE	25	/898			SUNDERLAND	10/11/14						RIVETTER DESERTED 15/1/15, AGE 19,5'5''.
DUFFY	James	PTE	25	/935	C			13/11/14	1/4/19	KR para 392			TO ARMY RESERVE CLASS P.	SGT.
DUFFY	John	PTE	25	/169									TO 1st GARRISON BN, CLASS Z RESERVE.	

NAME	INITI	RANK	BA	NUMBE	COMP	ADDRESS	TOWN_VILL	ENLISTED	DISCHARG	CAUSE_DIS	WOUNDED	BURIED	TRANSFER	ADD
DUFFY	Martn	PTE	25	/170	D	HILL TOP	DIPTON	5/11/14					TO LABOUR CORPS.	
DUFFY	P	PTE	25	/151	D		BEDLINGTON	19/11/14	21/8/17	GUNSHOT WOUNDS	OCTOBER 16		TO DEPOT.	3 CCS 2/7/16 EVAC 2/7/16
DUFFY	Pat	PTE	25	/154		32 PEARETH ST	GATESHEAD	6/11/14					TO 1st GARRISON BN, CLASS Z RESERVE.	38 FRANKLIN ST 1914.
DUFFY	T M	PTE	25	/190	D									ALSO ON D COY 30th BN ROLL.
DUGGAN	Thos	PTE	25	/929	C	1 RYTON TERR WEST AL	BACKWORTH			9 APRIL 1917		ROCLINCOURT VALLEY CEM		BORN CRAMLINGTON.
DURKIN	M	PTE	25	/171	D					KR para 392				
DURKIN	Mart	PTE	25	/942	C	11 THIRD ST	WHEATLEY HILL			1 JULY 1916		THIEPVAL MEM		MIS OCT 16, BORN TRIMDON GRANGE.BROTHER JOHN KIA 2
DURRANT	Chas	PTE	25	/1364	D	2 PRICE ST	SOUTH SHIELDS	26/11/14		1 JULY 1916		THIEPVAL MEM		MISSING OCTOBER 16, IN 14 PLATOON.
DUXFIELD	A	PTE	25	/184	D									
DUXFIELD	Clarn	PTE	25	/1425	D	18 CHURCH ROW	HOLYWELL						TO CLASS Z RESERVE.	TAKEN POW ACCORDING TO AVL.
EADE	J	PTE	25	/196	D		SUNDERLAND				NOVEMBER 16		TO KINGS OWN YORKSHIRE LI.	
ECCLES	John	PTE	25	/193	D	FOSTERS YARD FLINTHI	DIPTON			15 JULY 1918	AUGUST 16	GIAVERA MEM ITALY	TO 21st, 10th BNS.	3 CCS 2/7/16, HOSP LEICESTER 8/7/16. AGE 28 1918.
EDMONDS	G M	SGT	25	/944	C	2 PRIMROSE CRES FULW	SUNDERLAND				NOVEMBER 16.		COMMISSIONED, CAPTAIN NF.	SGT NCO i/c STRETCHER BEARERS, CSM.
EDWARDS	L D	SGT	25	/1412	D								TO 30th BN(D COY).	DRUM MAJOR IN BN BAND.
EDWARDS	T	PTE	25	/197	C	10 WELLINGTON ST	HIGH FELLING						TO 9th, 1st BNS, CLASS Z RESERVE.	
EDWARDS	Tom	PTE	25	/945	D	35 OAK ST TEAMS	GATESHEAD			1 JULY 1916		THIEPVAL MEM		MISSING OCTOBER 16, BORN HOUGHTON LE SPRING.
EGAN	M T	PTE	25	/1384				11/1/15	6/5/16				TO 30th BN(D COY).	DID NOT SERVE OVERSEAS, ON 30th ROLL AS HAGAN.
EKE	WaltG	PTE	25	/1414		7a NEWMARKET ROAD	NORWICH	4/1/15						COACH BUILDER DESERTED 8/4/15 AGE 37, 5'3''.
ELCOAT	W H	PTE	25	/200	D	6 MARY ST	LUDWORTH				DECEMBER 16, JANUARY 17.		TO 3rd BN, LABOUR CORPS.	
ELDER	J	PTE	25	/195	B	8 CROFT STAIRS	NEWCASTLE				NOVEMBER 16		TO CLASS Z RESERVE.	
ELDERFIELD	Henry	SGT	25	/194	D	FRONT ST	ANNFIELD PLAIN			11 NOV 1918	JULY 16	ABBEVILLE COM CEM EXT	COMMISSIONED, 2LT ATTACHED 163 CHINESE LABOUR COMP	AGE 33.
ELLIOTT	J	SGT	25	/1430	A									
ELLIOTT	James	LCPL	25	/201	D	9 SOUTH VIEW	TANTOBIE				OCTOBER 16(SHELLSHOCK)		TO 1/4th BN, CLASS Z RESERVE.	CORPORAL, ALLOTED NEW NUMBER 204564.
ELWOOD	Wm	PTE	25	/198	B	8 MONK ST	NEWCASTLE	21/11/14	11/7/17	12 JUNE 1919		ELSWICK	TO 30th BN.	AWOL 4/15, 8/15 11/15 COURT 2/6 26/8 2/12/15.
ENGLISH	T H	PTE	25	/1420	C			15/4/15	20/8/18	GASSED			TO 3rd BN.	STRETCHER BEARER, LETTER PUBLISHED IN COUNTY CHRON
EVANS	A E	PTE	25	/946	C									
EWART	J	PTE	25	/199	B	28 LUCY ST	WEST STANLEY	23/11/14	3/1/18	WOUNDS	SEPTEMBER 16		TO 3rd BN.	HOSP MANCHESTER
FALLON	A	PTE	25	/206	C									ALSO ON D COY 30th BN ROLL.
FALLON	M	PTE	25	/966	C									EMPLOYED BY SMITHS DOCKS, HEATER BULLRING.
FALLON	Thos	PTE	25	/967	A	HIGH FLAT	CROOK	26/11/14					TO 24th BN, CLASS Z RESERVE.	SGT, ALSO ON D COY 30th BN ROLL.
FANON	T	PTE	25	/205						KR para 392			TO 1st GARRISON BN.	
FARRELL	H	PTE	25	/1498	A									
FARRELL	H	LCPL	25	/1519			SPENNYMOOR	24/7/15	14/5/17	WOUNDS	AUGUST 16		TO 3rd BN.	3 CCS 2/7/16 EVAC 2/7/16.
FARRELL	M	PTE	25	/210	C	22 CHARLES ST	GATESHEAD	20/11/14	2/4/17	WOUNDS	AUGUST 16		TO DEPOT.	
FAWCETT	C G	PTE	25	/221	D		SOUTH SHIELDS			KR para 392	SEPTEMBER 16		TO 1/4th BN.	ALLOTED NEW NUMBER 204632.
FAWCETT	Jos	PTE	25	/218	D	14 SOUTH VIEW	TANFIELD				AUGUST 16		TO 25th, 10th, 1/5th BNS, CLASS Z RESERVE.	
FEENEY	J	PTE	25	/959	B								TO ROYAL AIR FORCE.	
FEENEY	T C	PTE	25	/946	B	10 KINGS RD	SUNDERLAND							
FENWICK	E	CPL	25	/216	D								TO LABOUR CORPS.	LAB CORPS No 403118.
FINNIGAN	ThosJ	PTE	25	/964	B	30 CROSS ST	CROOK	29/10/14		26 MARCH 1918		POZIERES MEM	TO DURHAM LI(22nd BN).	SGT, DLI No 43992, BORN CONSETT.
FISHER	G	PTE	25	/957	C								TO 12th, 12/13th, 9th BNS, CLASS Z RESERVE.	
FISHER	ThosR	PTE	25	/203	D	23 GEORGE ST	TANFIELD LEA		24/1/19				TO KINGS OWN YORKSHIRE LI 2/4 BN, CLASS Z RESERVE.	KOYLI No 63281.
FISHER	Wm	PTE	25	/956	C	7 HALLGARTH TERR	DURHAM CITY	26/11/14		1 JULY 1916		THIEPVAL MEM		MISSING OCTOBER 16.
FLANAGHAN	John	PTE	25	/1520	B	18 HILL ST	SOUTH SHIELDS			14 MARCH 1917		FABOURG DE AMIENS CEM ARRAS		AGE 33
FLANAGHAN	Thos	PTE	25	/219	B	21 OYSTERSHELL LANE	NEWCASTLE	17/11/14	17/5/16	EPILEPSY			TO 30th BN.	D COY 30th BN ROLL, DID NOT SERVE OVERSEAS.
FLORENTINE	P V	PTE	25	/220	C	6 CORN RIGGS BONDGAT	DARLINGTON	17/11/14	3/2/19	KR para 392	AUGUST 16, JANUARY 18.		TO 9th, 1st, 1/5th BNS, ARMY RESERVE CLASS P.	
FLYNN	J C	PTE	25	/208	A					KR para 392				
FLYNN	J J	SGT	25	/1539									TO 14th, 12/13th BNS, CLASS Z RESERVE.	
FOLEY	B	PTE	25	/213	D	30		23/11/14	25/10/17				TO 85th TRAINING RESERVE BN.	CORPORAL, DID NOT SERVE OVERSEAS.
FOLEY	J	PTE	25	/209		9 WESLIAN CHAPEL ROW	SHOTTON COLLIER						TO 1st GARRISON BN, CLASS Z RESERVE.	
FONT	F	PTE	25	/1445	D			13/7/15	18/4/16				TO 30th BN.	DID NOT SERVE OVERSEAS
FORD	Thos	PTE	25	/962			BELFORD	13/11/14						LABOURER DESERTED 19/2/15 AGE 25, 5'6''.
FOSTER	J	PTE	25	/958	D	30								
FOSTER	R E	SGT	25	/955	C	OFFICE ROW	EAST CASTLE						COMMISSIONED, NF	CSM.
FOSTER	Wm J	PTE	25	/950	C		SOUTHMOOR			1 JULY 1916		THIEPVAL MEM		MISSING OCTOBER 16.
FOX	J	PTE	25	/212	D			23/11/14	19/2/18	DAH			TO DEPOT.	
FOX	J	PTE	25	/214	B									ALSO ON D COY 30th BN ROLL.
FOX	J	PTE	25	/968	A		NEWCASTLE				JULY OCT 16			3 CCS 2/7/16 EVAC 2/7/16.

NAME	INITI	RANK	BA	NUMBE	COMP	ADDRESS	TOWN_VILL	ENLISTED	DISCHARG	CAUSE_DIS	WOUNDED	BURIED	TRANSFER	ADD
FOX	Peter	PTE	25	/953	C	3 SHAKESPEARE ST	JARROW			21 MARCH 1918		ARRAS MEM		
FRAIN	D	PTE	25	/1388	B	THORNLEY RD ENDS	TOW LAW	11/1/15	18/5/18	GUNSHOT WOUNDS	AUGUST 16			
FRAIN	D orJ	PTE	25	/202	D	28 DOUGLAS TERR	USWORTH	11/1/15	18/5/18					
FRAIN	T	PTE	25	/963	A			13/11/14	24/12/17	VDH			TO DEPOT.	
FRENCH	Alb	PTE	25	/960	D 30	14 POST OFFICE ST	LOW SPENNYMOOR	11/11/14	12/8/16					DID NOT SERVE OVERSEAS.
FROOME	W	PTE	25	/969	D								TO 27th BN, CLASS Z RESERVE.	
GAFFNEY	Jas W	PTE	25	/234	D	7 FISHBURN TERR	FISHBURN			1 JULY 1916		THIEPVAL MEM		ASGT MISSING OCTOBER 16, BORN COWPEN NTHBLND.
GAINES	P	PTE	25	/242	D		WALLSEND	17/11/14	19/6/17	GUNSHOT WOUNDS	SEPTEMBER 16, APRIL 17.		TO DEPOT.	SERGEANT
GALL	E J	PTE	25	/979	D		GATESHEAD				OCTOBER 16		TO 24th, 24/27th, 8th BNS, CLASS Z RESERVE.	LCPL.
GALLAGHER	M	PTE	25	/224	D	8 RYHOPE ST	HOUGHTON LE SPR						TO LABOUR CORPS.	
GALLAGHER	Thos	PTE	25	/981	C		SUNDERLAND			17 APRIL 1918		MONT NOIR CEM		
GALLAGHER	Tom	PTE	25	/982	C		EASINGTON			1 JULY 1916		THIEPVAL MEM		MISSING OCTOBER 16, BORN SWINFORD Co MAYO.
GARDNER	W	SGT	25	/978	B 30									
GARRITY	W	PTE	25	/243	A									
GIBBONS	M	PTE	25	/246	D	99 HEDLEY ST	SOUTH SHIELDS			KR para 392	SEPTEMBER 16			
GIBBONS	Theo	CSM	25	/232	B	SPOORS COTTAGES	WHICKHAM	16/11/14	3/2/19	KR para 392	OCTOBER 16		TO 85th TRAINING RES BN, ARMY RESERVE CLASS P.	SERGEANT.
GIBBS	J	PTE	25	/229				13/11/14	27/6/17	SICK			TO DEPOT.	
GIBSON	Fredk	PTE	25	/1392	B	28 BARING ST	TOW LAW	11/1/15	23/4/17	WOUNDS	AUGUST 16		TO 85th TRAINING RESERVE BN.	SEE 25/1389
GIBSON	Geo	PTE	25	/1389	B	28 BARING ST	TOW LAW	14/1/15			AUGUST 16			SEE ALSO 25/1392
GIBSON	Jas	PTE	25	/228	D	6 JACKS ROW	BACKWORTH			2 SEPT 1918	OCTOBER 16	ECOUSTE ST MEIN BRIT CEM	TO 1st BN.	LCPL, BORN EARSDON.
GIBSON	T	PTE	25	/976	C			23/11/14	7/8/16				TO 30th BN(D COY).	DID NOT SERVE OVERSEAS. AGE 47.
GILBERT	W	PTE	25	/988	B	115 PARKER ST	BYKER				MARCH 16		TO 16th, 1/5th BNS, CLASS Z RESERVE.	LCPL.
GILES	W H	PTE	25	/231	D	3 WEST TERR	BIRTLEY	14/11/14	22/3/18	GUNSHOT WOUNDS	AUGUST 16		TO DEPOT.	
GILL	E	PTE	25	/1544				4/1/15	26/6/17	SICK			TO DEPOT.	
GILL	J	PTE	25	/240	D		JARROW				AUGUST 16			
GILL	T	PTE	25	/980	D		SOUTH SHIELDS				NOVEMBER 16		TO ROYAL DEFENCE CORPS.	IN FRANCE 11/1/16 TO 11/8/16.
GILROY	John	PTE	25	/970				19/11/14						MINER DESERTED 16/5/15 AGE 37, 5'5''.
GLANCY	Jas	PTE	25	/233	D	2 COUNCIL TERR	WASHINGTON	6/11/14					TO CLASS Z RESERVE.	FARRIER, TRANSPORT SECTION.
GOLDSBURY	Jos	PTE	25	/237	A	49 FOURTH ROW	ASHINGTON	12/11/14		1 JULY 1916		THIEPVAL MEM		MISSING OCTOBER 16, BORN WILLINGTON QUAY.
GOODWIN	Jas	PTE	25	/230	B	24 BLAGDON ST	NEWCASTLE			23 APRIL 1917		ETAPLES		DRUNK & DISORDERLY CITY RD 3/5/15, PROM CPL.
GORDON	James	PTE	25	/972	B		NEWCASTLE			7 SEPT 1916	SEPTEMBER 16	FLAT IRON COPSE CEM	TO 24th BN.	
GORMLEY	Jas	PTE	25	/977		17 CUTHBERT ST	BLAYDON	23/11/14	21/4/15	INJURED				DID NOT SERVE OVERSEAS, INJURED DURING TRAINING.
GOUGH	R	PTE	25	/244	C									ALSO ON D COY 30th BN ROLL.
GOWAN	J	PTE	25	/226	A	16 WALKER ST	DINNINGTON COLL	12/11/14	26/12/17	SICK			TO 3rd BN.	
GRADY	P	PTE	25	/236		15 EAST VIEW	HUTTON HENRY						TO 1st GARRISON BN, CLASS Z RESERVE.	
GRAHAM	J B	PTE	25	/986	B	47 FRONT ST	SOUTH SHIELDS							
GRAHAM	James	PTE	25	/983	C	44 PIKE ST	PONTOP				JUNE 18		TO CLASS Z RESERVE.	
GRAHAM	W	PTE	25	/971	A	20 FRANKLIN ST	NEWCASTLE				APRIL 16			
GRANT	Geo R	PTE	25	/245	D	7 ORMONDE ST	JARROW			1 JULY 1916		THIEPVAL MEM	ATTACHED 2 SQUADRON ROYAL FLYING CORPS FOR A SHORT	BORN NORTH SHIELDS.
GRANVILLE	W	PTE	25	/227	D								TO 9th BN	
GRAVELING	W	PTE	25	/1435	B	54 HIGH ST NORTH	LITTLEBURN				APRIL 16, AUGUST 16.		TO 1st, 25th, 24th, 1st, 17th, CLASS Z RESERVE.	
GRAY	J	PTE	25	/1391	C									ALSO ON D COY 30th BN ROLL.
GRAY	W	PTE	25	/973	C					KR para 392			TO 12/13th BN.	
GRAY	W	SGT	25	/975				20/11/14	14/4/19	KR para 392			TO DEPOT.	
GREEN	E	PTE	25	/225	A		SHADFORTH	12/11/14	27/2/18	10 MAY 1920	AUGUST 16	SHADFORTH	TO ARMY RESERVE CLASS W.22/5/17, ARMY RES P, 27/2/	
GREENER	J	PTE	25	/984	C	135 FRONT ST	LANGLEY MOOR	14/11/14	30/7/17	TRENCH FEET			TO 3rd BN.	
GREY	JohnW	PTE	25	/222	C		BLYTH			1 JULY 1916		THIEPVAL MEM		ALSGT MISSING OCTOBER 16, BORN NEWCASTLE.
GRIFFITHS	W	PTE	25	/238				21/11/14	31/8/17	SICK			TO 1st GARRISON BN, DEPOT.	
GRIMES	Jos	PTE	25	/1514	B		WALLSEND			1 JULY 1916		THIEPVAL MEM		MISSING OCTOBER 16.
GRIMES	P J	PTE	25	/223	C	156 TAYLOR ST	SOUTH SHIELDS	12/11/14	20/12/18	GUNSHOT WOUNDS	OCTOBER 16		TO ARMY RESERVE CLASS W.	
GROGHAN	F	PTE	25	/987	C	2 LANGDALE TERR	GREENCROFT						TO ROYAL FUSILIERS(24th BN).	FRANCE 25th,11/1/16 TO 30/8/18, 24RFUS 31/8/18 TO
GROGHAN	P	PTE	25	/985	C	12 ROSEBERRY TERR	CONSETT				SEPTEMBER 16		TO NORTH STAFFORDSHIRE REGT(8th BN).	3 CCS 2/7/16 EVAC 2/7/16.
GRUGAN	Jn Jo	PTE	25	/235	D		HAMSTERLEY			1 JULY 1916		THIEPVAL MEM		MISSING OCTOBER 16, BORN CONSETT.
GUTTERIDGE	C	WO2		/794									TO 1/4th BN.	STILL SERVING 1921.
HABERSHAW	John	PTE	25	/273	A	2 HENRY TERR	SOUTH SHIELDS			1 JULY 1916		OVILLIERS MIL CEM		MISSING OCTOBER 16,MG SECTION.
HADDRICK	W	PTE	25	/291	A	33 FRONT ST	EAST STANLEY			KR para 392			TO EAST YORKS(12th, 6th BNS).	17 MIDDLE ST 1918. E YORKS No 36690.
HAGAN	Edw	PTE	25	/247	D	18 ALICE ST	RYHOPE COLLIERY	6/11/14		2 JULY 1916		WARLOY		BORN USWORTH.AGE 36.
HAGGERTY	John	PTE	25	/989	D		NEWCASTLE			14 JUNE 1918	SEPTEMBER 16	ABBEVILLE COM CEM	TO 11th BN, LABOUR CORPS.	LAB CORPS No 398776,34 CCS 1/7 EVAC 5/7/16 WND L L

NAME	INITI	RANK	BA	NUMBE	COMP	ADDRESS	TOWN_VILL	ENLISTED	DISCHARG	CAUSE_DIS	WOUNDED	BURIED	TRANSFER	ADD
HALL	Geo	PTE	25	/1013	A	109 MILLING ST TEAMS	GATESHEAD			28 APRIL 1917		BROWNS COPSE CEM	ATTACHED 103 LTMB.	AGE 27. ALSO ON D COY 30th BN ROLL.
HALL	J T	PTE	25	/293	A			16/11/14	15/11/16	WOUNDS	APRIL 16		TO DEPOT.	
HALL	Jas H	PTE	25	/260	A		CHESTER LE ST			9 APRIL 1917		ROCLINCOURT VALLEY CEM		
HALL	R	PTE	25	/1399						KR para 392			TO 1st GARRISON BN.	
HALL	S	PTE	25	/284	A	72 STARGATE	RYTON			KR para 392	MARCH 17			
HALL	W	PTE	25	/1431	C								TO 12/13th BN, CLASS Z RESERVE.	
HALL	Wm	PTE	25	/1014	D		BLAYDON			1 JULY 1916		THIEPVAL MEM		MISSING OCTOBER 16.
HAMMIL	J	PTE	25	/1005	D		DURHAM CITY							D&D AND AWOL IN DURHAM 15/10/15
HAND	Fred	PTE	25	/282			BLYTH			15 OCTOBER 1915		SUTTON VENY WILTSHIRE		BORN WALLSEND.
HANLEY	Edwd	PTE	25	/1510	B		DIPTON			12 OCT 1917		TYNE COT MEM		
HANLEY	R	PTE	25	/295	D 30									
HANLEY	Ridly	PTE	25	/1012	A		GATESHEAD		24/5/19		OCTOBER 16		TO MACHINE GUN CORPS, CLASS Z RESERVE.	MGC No 138872.
HARDY	T	PTE	25	/278	A	17 HIGH ST	LANGLEY MOOR							
HARGREAVES	Tom W	PTE	25	/1395	D 30	FRONT ST	COXHOE			1 JULY 1916		THIEPVAL MEM	TO 30th, 25th BNS.	BORN SEDGEFIELD.
HARKNESS	Arthu	PTE	25	/1010	B	13 HUITT ST	GATESHEAD						TO 12/13th BN, CLASS Z RESERVE.	AWOL 1/9/15, 13/9/15 IN COURT GATESHEAD, AGE 17.
HARRINGTON	Rob	PTE	25	/996	B		GATESHEAD			1 JULY 1916		THIEPVAL MEM		AWOL 25/11/15 COURT GATESHEAD MIS OCT 16.
HARRISON	Denni	PTE	25	/1001	C		SUNDERLAND			21 JAN 1918	JULY 16	WANCOURT MIL CEM		SHOWN IN WGR AS 23rd BN.
HARRISON	Jos	PTE	25	/277	D		FELLING			1 JULY 1916		THIEPVAL MEM		MISSING OCTOBER 16, BORN HUNWICK.
HARRISON	Tom G	PTE	25	/248	D	17 STEVENSON ST	SOUTH SHIELDS			1 JULY 1916		THIEPVAL MEM		MISSING OCTOBER 16, BORN STOCKTON.
HARRISON	W	LCPL	25	/271	A	186 HANLON LANE	WINGATE	19/11/14	20/6/17	WOUNDS	JULY 16, AUGUST 16,		TO DEPOT.	
HART	J E	PTE	25	/1016	C	39 CORONATION ST	SOUTH SHIELDS				SEPTEMBER 16		TO ROYAL DEFENCE CORPS.	IN FRANCE 11/1/16 TO 8/7/16.EVAC HOSP NOTTINGHAM 1
HARVEY	Jas	PTE	25	/1397	B	BACK HOPE ST	CROOK	9/1/15	17/10/18	SICK	18 JUNE 16, MARCH 17.		TO COMMAND DEPOT CATTERICK.	DIED OF WOUNDS 1924, EX REGULAR SOLDIER.
HAUGHIN	G	PTE	25	/1396									TO 1st GARRISON BN, CLASS Z RESERVE.	
HAWLEY	J	PTE	25	/262	C									
HEALY	D	CSM	25	/1469	A 30									
HEALY	J	SGT	25	/1003	C	82 DURHAM RD	SPENNYMOOR				JULY 16		TO CLASS Z RESERVE.	NCO i/c LEWIS GUNS 5 NOVEMBER 16.
HEARTY	Owen	PTE	25	/249	D	25 MONK ST	GATESHEAD			23 JULY 1916		GATESHEAD	TO DEPOT.	3 CCS 2/7/16 EVAC 3/7/16 AGE 39.
HEDLEY	T H	PTE	25	/1398	B								TO CLASS Z RESERVE.	
HEIER	F T	LCPL	25	/265	A	1 BLUE HOUSE NEWCAST	SUNDERLAND							
HENDERSON	Thos	PTE	25	/1015	D	SPENCERS BANK	SWALWELL				DECEMBER 16		TO 19th, 9th BNS, CLASS Z RESERVE.	
HENRY	John	PTE	25	/999	D	38 ANNE ST	HEBBURN	5/11/14		20 JULY 1916		ST SEVER CEM ROUEN		BORN GLASGOW.
HERDMAN	A	PTE	25	/1367	C									
HERRON	J	PTE	25	/1006	A									
HERRON	Rob W	PTE	25	/264	A	10 CORVAN HSE WHITE	STANLEY	12/11/14		26 FEB 1916		X FARM CEM		
HETHRINGTON	P	PTE	25	/1452	D		WALKER				SEPTEMBER 16			
HIGGINS	Jn Dv	PTE	25	/259	D	9 RUSSEL ST	BRANDON	10/11/14			OCTOBER 16,MARCH 18.		TO 21st, 10th, 19th, 12/13th BNS, CLASS Z RESERVE.	LCPL,NTHN GEN HOSP LEEDS ,WND R LEG.
HILTON	Tom	PTE	25	/290	D	34 WILLIAM ST	HEBBURN	6/11/14		1 JULY 1916		THIEPVAL MEM		ACPL MISSING OCTOBER 16, BORN BILLQUAY.
HIND	T	PTE	25	/1522	B		DARLINGTON				SHELLSHOCK NOVEMBER 16		TO 1st, 25th BNS, CLASS Z RESERVE.	
HINDMARSH	Jos H	PTE	25	/1011	C	48 ALFRED ST	SOUTH SHIELDS	10/11/14						
HINDSON	E	PTE	25	/1000	C	2 SEVENTH ST	SHOTTON COLLIER						TO 12/13th BN.	
HOBSON	A V	PTE	25	/1490	B	130 MARIA ST	NEWCASTLE				AUGUST 16		TO 1st, 12/13th, 14th BNS, CLASS Z RESERVE.	
HOEY	J	PTE	25	/1009	C		SUNDERLAND	11/11/14	26/7/17	GUNSHOT WOUNDS	JULY 16		TO DEPOT.	
HOFFMAN	Jos	PTE	25	/286	A	60 FLEMING ST	GATESHEAD	19/11/14	9/3/18	GUNSHOT WOUNDS	JULY 16		TO ARMY RESERVE CLASS W.	LCPL.
HOGAN	E	PTE	25	/279	A	27 CORONATION ST	NEW KYO				APRIL 16		TO LINCOLNSHIRE REGT, LABOUR CORPS.	
HOGG	Jos	PTE	25	/276	A	69 DOUGLAS TERR	NEWCASTLE	12/11/14						
HOLLINGSWORT	Geo	PTE	25	/1393	B		NEWCASTLE			1 JULY 1916		THIEPVAL MEM		MISSING OCTOBER 16.
HOLMES	Thops	PTE	25	/261	D		KESWICK	14/11/14					TO 30th(B COY), 26th, 12th, 12/13th, 8th, 12/13th,	STOKER, DESERTED 5/5/15
HOOD	David	PTE	25	/287	A	173 ROSE ST TEAMS	GATESHEAD			29 DEC 1916		BREWERY ORCHARD CEM		ACPL, AGE 41, ALSO ON B COY ROLL 30th BN.
HOOD	J	PTE	25	/252	D 30			12/11/14	17/6/16	SICK			TO 30th BN.	AGE 24.
HOPE	John	PTE	25	/257		74 RYE HILL	NEWCASTLE	5/11/14		KR para 392			TO 1st GARRISON BN.	
HOPE	Tom	PTE	25	/255	D		BROOMSIDE			5 JULY 1916		HEILLY STATION CEM		
HOPPER	E	PTE	25	/1400	B									
HOPPER	John	PTE	25	/994	C	38 JOHN ST	BLAYDON			1 JULY 1916		THIEPVAL MEM		MISSING OCTOBER 16.
HOPPER	Ralph	PTE	25	/1467	B								TO 12/13th BN.	AWOL 24/7/15 IN COURT 21/8/15, DESERTED 8 JULY 191
HORAN	Mich	PTE	25	/1002	D	1 DIPTON ST	BISHOP AUKLAND			28 APRIL 1917		ARRAS MEM		BORN STANFORDHAM.
HORN	Fred	PTE	25	/1394	D		MIDDLESBOROUGH			1 JULY 1916	18 JUNE 16	THIEPVAL MEM		
HOUGHTON	J	PTE	25	/294	A			12/11/14	13/3/18	SICK			TO ARMY RESERVE CLASS P.	
HOWE	JohnJ	PTE	25	/1017			WALLSEND	16/11/14						LABOURER DESERTED 8/5/15 AGE 19,5'4''.AWOL 6/3/15

NAME	INITI	RANK	BA	NUMBE	COMP	ADDRESS	TOWN_VILL	ENLISTED	DISCHARG	CAUSE_DIS	WOUNDED	BURIED	TRANSFER	ADD
HOWE	Rich	PTE	25	/1008	C	16 COUSIN ST	SUNDERLAND			1 JULY 1916		THIEPVAL MEM		MISSING OCTOBER 16.
HOWGEGO	J R	PTE	25	/266	A	27 BACK LIDDLE ST MN	SUNDERLAND						TO LABOUR CORPS.	
HUGHES	A	CPL	25	/1018	C								COMMISSIONED.	ACSM.
HUGHES	F	PTE	25	/997	C	8 TENTH ST	EASINGTON COLLI							
HUGHES	J	PTE	25	/250	D		TYNEDOCK				JULY 16		TO 1/4th BN, CLASS Z RESERVE.	LCPL, ALLOTED NEW NUMBER 204627.
HUGHES	J	PTE	25	/253	D									
HUGHES	J	PTE	25	/258						KR para 392			TO 1st GARRISON BN, 26th BN.	
HUGHES	J	PTE	25	/1401	B		SEAHAM				OCTOBER 16			
HUGHES	Peter	PTE	25	/992	C	13 COURT LANE	DURHAM CITY			18 MARCH 1916		BREWERY ORCHARD CEM		BORN SEAHAM HARBOUR.
HUMBERSTONE	Wm	PTE	25	/269	A	THE GREEN	GAINFORD			1 JULY 1916		BAPAUME POST CEM		MISSING OCTOBER 16, BORN ESTON YORKS.
HUMBLE	Rob E	PTE	25	/254	A	FLAG ROW SUNNISIDE	TOW LAW	12/11/14	14/1/18	GUNSHOT WOUNDS			TO DEPOT.	
HUMBLE	Thos	PTE	25	/251	D	13 SHERBURN RD GILES	DURHAM CITY				AUGUST 16	ST GILES WAR MEMORIAL	TO KINGS OWN YORKSHIRE LI, ROYAL ENGINEERS.	10 EDWARD ST 1918. ON WM DEATH UNCONFIRMED.
HUME	G	PTE	25	/289	A									
HUMES	John	PTE	25	/275	D	24 HEWORTH VILLAGE	FELLING	10/11/14		1 JULY 1916		THIEPVAL MEM		MISSING OCTOBER 16, BORN HEWORTH.
HUNT	Wm	PTE	25	/256	D	17 PITT ST	CONSETT			1 JULY 1916	MARCH 16	THIEPVAL MEM		MISSING OCTOBER 16, BORN GATESHEAD.
HUNTER	Ernst	ACPL	25	/270	A		BISHOP AUKLAND			22 JUNE 1917		ARRAS MEM		BORN SUNDERLAND.
HUNTER	J A	PTE	25	/1533	B	4 STONE ST	HAMSTERLEY COLL	16/8/15	22/8/16				TO 34th BN.	DID NOT SERVE OVERSEAS.
HURST	Thos	PTE	25	/998	C	LOVES HOTEL	BROOMPARK	12/11/14		3 JULY 1916		THIEPVAL MEM		WOUNDED AND MISSING DECEMBER 16, AGE 21.
HUTCHINSON	G	PTE	25	/292	D 30			16/11/14	24/3/16				TO 30th BN.	DID NOT SERVE OVERSEAS.
HUTCHINSON	R	PTE	25	/1402	B	2 CLIFFE TERR	SUNDERLAND				OCTOBER 16		TO ROYAL DEFENCE CORPS.	IN FRANCE 11/1/16 TO 19/7/16, 3 CCS 2/7 EVAC 2/7/1
HUTTON	J	PTE	25	/281	C			23/11/14	24/3/16	SICK			TO 30th BN.	DID NOT SERVE OVERSEAS.
HYMERS	Joe	PTE	25	/993	C	38 GEORGE ST	BLAYDON	12/11/14			MARCH 17		TO 11th, 23rd BNS.	
INGLEBY	R G	PTE	25	/1020	C	35 NEW ELVET	DURHAM CITY	23/11/14	24/10/18	GUNSHOT WOUNDS	JUNE 18		TO TYNESIDE SCOTTISH, DEPOT.	
INGLIS	P	PTE	25	/296	A	49 HUNTER ST	WALLSEND							
IVERS	W	SGT	25	/1019	B 30			13/11/14	15/9/16				TO DEPOT.	DID NOT SERVE OVERSEAS.
IVESON	R	PTE	25	/1021	C	11 BELLES VILLE GILE	DURHAM CITY				JANUARY 17		TO 14th, 24th, 24/27th, 8th BNS, CLASS Z RESERVE.	
JACKSON	F	PTE	25	/1037				15/11/14	8/2/19	SICK			TO 1st GARRISON BN, 2nd, 3rd BNS.	ENTERED SALONIKA 20/12/15, 1914/15 STAR. AGE 43
JACKSON	J	PTE	25	/305						KR para 392			TO 2nd GARRISON BN.	
JACKSON	J	PTE	25	/1023	C			17/11/14	14/8/17	SICK			TO 3rd BN.	
JACKSON	W	PTE	25	/1032			NEWCASTLE	16/11/14						HEATER DESERTED 21/5/15 AGE 18, 5'4''.
JAGGERS	JohnW	PTE	25			83 EDWARD STREET	NORTH SHIELDS	26/11/14						AWOL 26/4/15 COURT SOUTH SHIELDS
JAMES	R	PTE	25	/1025	D			8/11/14	1/12/17	WOUNDS			TO DEPOT.	
JAMES	T	PTE	25	/319	A	262 SOUTH ELDON ST	SOUTH SHIELDS						TO LABOUR CORPS.	
JARVIS	A	PTE	25	/1038	B	29 WELLINGTON ST	FELLING				SEPTEMBER 16, DECEMBER 16		TO 11th, 8th, 25th, 12/13th BNS, CLASS Z RESERVE.	3 CCS 2/7/16 EVAC 3/7/16 SHELL SHOCK.
JEFFERY	J	PTE	25	/311	A	27 WOODLAND TERR	WASHINGTON						TO LABOUR CORPS.	
JEFFRIES	J	PTE	25	/302	B 30	100 FOURTH ST	SHOTTON	16/11/14	19/3/19	KR para 392			TO 24th, 24/27th, 8th BNS, DEPOT.	
JEMISON	J	SGT	25	/315	A	14 LAMBERTS PLACE	WASHINGTON							
JENNINGS	Jothn	PTE	25	/1022	C	44 HIGH ST	JARROW	6/11/14			APRIL 16		TO ROYAL SCOTS, ARMY SERVICE CORPS.	
JEWITT	E	PTE	25	/309	A									
JOBES	Archi	PTE	25	/317	A	26 ANNE ST	WHEATLEY HILL			KR para 392			TO 1/4th BN.	ALLOTED NEW NUMBER 204626.
JOBLING	J	PTE	25	/1035	C		GATESHEAD	14/11/14	26/3/18		JULY 18		TO 24th, 26th BNS, ARMY SERVICE CORPS.	
JOBSON	R	PTE	25	/313	C		GATESHEAD				AUGUST 16		TO ROYAL ARMY MEDICAL CORPS.	
JOHNSON	C	SGT	25	/301	D	81 MORGAN ST SOUTHWI	SUNDERLAND	14/11/14	31/8/18	CONTUSIONS OF T			TO ARMY RESERVE CLASS W.	
JOHNSON	F	PTE	25	/308				18/11/14	29/10/15	SICK				
JOHNSON	Henry	PTE	25	/312	A	13 ASH TERR	TANTOBIE	21/11/14	31/3/19	KR para 392			TO 25th, 13th, 12/13th, 26th BNS, ARMY RESERVE CLA	
JOHNSON	J	PTE	25	/1488	B		BYKER				APRIL 16, DECEMBER 17.		TO 16th, 1/7th BNS, CLASS Z RESERVE.	
JOHNSON	J W	PTE	25	/316	A	23 SIXTH ST	EASINGTON						TO CLASS Z RESERVE.	
JOHNSON	Wilf	PTE	25	/1030	C	45 NORTH TERR	WATERHOUSES			8 JULY 1916		WIMEREUX		BORN CHESTER LE ST, IN BAND AT BIRTLEY, FIRST OF B
JOHNSTONE	J J	CPL	25	/318	A		WASHINGTON	23/11/14	11/6/17	GUNSHOT WOUNDS	SEPTEMBER 16		TO 3rd BN.	SGT.
JOHNSTONE	Rob	PTE	25	/310	D	10 CHURCH WALK	GATESHEAD			9 APRIL 1918	APRIL 16, OCTOBER 16.	PLOEGSTEERT MEM	TO 20th, 26th, 9th BNS.	3 CCS 2/7/16 EVAC 3/7/16. BORN STATION TOWN.
JONES	E	PTE	25	/303	A	30 CARNATION ST	BIRTLEY							ALSO ON D COY 30th BN ROLL.
JONES	R	PTE	25	/1024	B	5 CURRY SQUARE	DIPTON	18/11/14	1/12/17	GUNSHOT WOUNDS			TO DEPOT.	
JONES	Reg G	PTE	25	/1033	C		MANNINGTREE			18 MAY 1917		ST SEVER CEM ROUEN		LCPL.
JOPLING	H	PTE	25	/307	A		HORDEN	17/11/14	26/3/18	SICK	JULY 16		TO ARMY RESERVE CLASS P.	
JOPLING	John	PTE	25	/1456	D	9 CUMBERLAND TERR	WILLINGTON				JULY 16		TO ROYAL AIR FORCE.	RAF No 136452.
JORDAN	M	PTE	25	/299	D			14/11/14	29/11/15				TO 30th BN.	DID NOT SERVE OVERSEAS.
JORDAN	T	PTE	25	/1036	D	33 EDITH AVENUE	USWORTH				MAY 17		TO CLASS Z RESERVE.	
JORDAN	W	PTE	25	/320	A	9 HIGH ST	AMBLE				AUGUST 16		TO LABOUR CORPS.	MILLBANK HOSP 5/7 - 18/7/16 AGE 48.SHRAPNEL WND.

NAME	INITI	RANK	BA	NUMBE	COMP	ADDRESS	TOWN_VILL	ENLISTED	DISCHARG	CAUSE_DIS	WOUNDED	BURIED	TRANSFER	ADD
JORDINSON	W	LCPL	25	/1034	A		GATESHEAD				JULY 16			BEAUFORT WAR HOSP BRISTOL 12/7/16
JOYCE	P	PTE	25	/1031	C									
JOYCE	T S	PTE	25	/1507	C	TOWER HOUSE PILGRIM	NEWCASTLE						TO 22nd, CLASS Z RESERVE.	
KANE	Robt	LCPL	25	/331	A	3 JOHN STREET	CONSETT				JULY 16		TO NORTH STAFFORDSHIRE REGT(1st GARR BN).	CPL, NORTH STAFFS No 43138 .
KATE	P B	PTE	25	/1050		5 JAMES ST	WHICKHAM	12/11/14	23/3/15					DID NOT SERVE OVERSEAS.
KAVANAGH	J	PTE	25	/336									TO 1st GARRISON BN, CLASS Z RESERVE.	
KEEFE	J	PTE	25	/1040	A									ALSO ON D COY 30th BN ROLL.
KEEGAN	Jos	PTE	25	/330	A	19 BEATRICE ST	HIRST	10/11/14						ALSO ON D COY 30th BN ROLL.
KEEGAN	Thos	PTE	25	/343		ONIELLS BLDGS FLINTH	DIPTON	12/11/14					TO 1st GARRISON BN, CLASS Z RESERVE.	
KEELER	Claud	PTE	25	/335	A		BLYTH			9 APRIL 1917		BAILLEUL RD ST LAURENT BLAGNY		BORN SIXTHORPE NORFOLK, AGE 27.
KEENAN	Dan	PTE	25	/322	A	62 SOUTH ST	BRANDON	12/11/14					TO LABOUR CORPS.	
KEENAN	Dan	CPL	25	/325	A	28 ALFRED ST	SOUTH SHIELDS	28/10/14		KR para 392	SEPTEMBER 16			
KEENAN	Jas	PTE	25	/324	A	5 BOLDON LANE	SOUTH SHIELDS			1 JULY 1916		THIEPVAL MEM		MISSING OCTOBER 16, BORN RYHOPE COLLIERY.
KEENAN	P	PTE	25	/323	A	50 DURHAM ST	BRANDON						TO LABOUR CORPS.	
KEENAN	Wm	PTE	25	/321	D	1 EDWARDS ST	HEBBURN	6/11/14		KR para 392				
KELLY	D	CPL	25	/338	D	21 BULLER ST	HIGH FELLING	21/11/14					TO 9th BN, CLASS Z RESERVE.	AWOII, COALMINER AGE 28 IN 1916,PAYBOOK IN RNF MUS
KELLY	Felix	PTE	25	/333		42 ELLISON ST WEST	GATESHEAD						TO 1st GARRISON BN, CLASS Z RESERVE.	
KELLY	H	PTE	25	/339	A		SEAHAM	21/10/14	11/10/17		JULY 16		TO DURHAM LI.	DLI 59322.
KELLY	J	PTE	25	/1366	C	2 PROVIDENCE PLACE	GATESHEAD							
KELLY	Jas	PTE	25	/334	A	6 QUARRY ST	WHEATLEY HILL			1 JULY 1916		THIEPVAL MEM		MISSING OCTOBER 16.BORN ELDON COLLIERY.
KELLY	P	PTE	25	/1054	D			11/11/14	17/5/16				TO 30th BN(D COY).	DID NOT SERVE OVERSEAS.
KELLY	T	PTE	25	/341	A								TO LABOUR CORPS.	
KELLY	Wm J	PTE	25	/1043	C	6 RUBY TERR	TUDHOE	10/11/14					TO 191 LABOUR COY, 25th, 12/13th BNS, CLASS Z RESE	
KENNEDY	J T	PTE	25	/1404	C	25 CLARENCE TERR	WILLINGTON						TO 9th BN, CLASS Z RESERVE.	
KENNEDY	John	PTE	25	/1042	C		BLYTH			1 JULY 1916		THIEPVAL MEM		MISSING OCTOBER 16.
KENNEY	Dan	PTE	25	/342	A	39 LYMINGTON TERR	ESH WINNING	5/11/14					TO ROYAL DEFENCE CORPS.	IN FRANCE 11/1/16 TO 15/8/17. A/CPL
KENNICK	Frank	PTE	25	/1041	C	72 SUNDERLAND ST	BRANDON COLLIER	26/11/14			NOVEMBER 16			SEE 26/1278+26/1281 COUSINS.
KIDD	J	PTE	25	/1049	C								TO CLASS Z RESERVE.	
KING	Chas	PTE	25	/1052	D	4 RIDLEY CT GROATMAR	NEWCASTLE			24 APRIL 1917		ARRAS MEM		
KING	F	PTE	25	/1434	A		TYNEMOUTH	8/6/15	12/4/17	22 DEC 1918		TYNEMOUTH		
KING	Peter	PTE	25	/340	A	15 WILLIAM ST	HEBBURN	23/11/14	6/3/18	GUNSHOT WOUNDS	JULY 16		TO ARMY RESERVE CLASS P.	
KING	T	PTE	25	/1051	B				28/5/19				TO KINGS OWN YORKSHIRE LI 2/4 BN, CLASS Z RESERVE.	KOYLI No 63302.
KIRKUP	Mich	PTE	25	/1045	A	10 WILLIAM ST	CONSETT	10/11/14	29/3/16				TO 30th BN(D COY).	DID NOT SERVE OVERSEAS.
KNIGHT	Geo	PTE	25	/337	A	24 MAUD ST	NEWCASTLE			1 JULY 1916		THIEPVAL MEM		MISSING OCTOBER 1916, BORN TROWBRIDGE WILTS.
KNIPE	J	PTE	25	/1046	C		MILLOM				AUGUST 16			21 AMB TRAIN 6/7, 18 GEN HOSP, HOSP SHIP 7/7/16 AG
KNOX	J	PTE	25	/1048	B				10/4/19				TO KINGS OWN YORKSHIRE LI 2/4 BN, CLASS Z RESERVE.	KOYLI No 63305.
KNOX	Jos	PTE	25	/332	B	1 OAK ST	NEWCASTLE			14 MARCH 1917		FAUBOURG DE AMIENS CEM ARRAS		LCPL.
LALLY	P Jos	PTE	25	/1058			WOLSINGHAM			12 AUGUST 1915		WOLSINGHAM		
LAMB	J	PTE	25	/1443	D	17 ATHOL ST	DUNSTON						TO LABOUR CORPS.	
LAMP	P	PTE	25	/368	D			18/11/14	9/4/16				TO 30th BN(D COY).	DID NOT SERVE OVERSEAS.
LAMPTON	Peter	PTE	25	/366	D	230 RABY ST	BYKER			5 JULY 1916		HEATON		AWOL 12/4,8/5,5/6 COURT 14/4,24/5,8/6/15.AGE 45
LAMPTON	Rob	PTE	25	/367	D		BYKER			12 OCT 1916		CITE BON JEAN CEM		AWOL 8/5,18/6,31/7 COURT 22/5,30/6,9/8/15.
LANCASTER	W	PTE	25	/365	D								TO ROYAL FUSILIERS(24th BN).	FRANCE 11/1/16 TO 28/8/18, 29/8/18 TO 11/11/18.
LANGWELL	T	PTE	25	/354	C									
LARGUE	Wm H	CPL	25	/355	A	25 LOW FRIARSIDE	ROWLANDS GILL	16/11/14	24/7/16	WOUNDS	APRIL 16		TO DEPOT.	
LARKIN	M	PTE	25	/1479	C								TO DURHAM LI, ARMY SERVICE CORPS.	
LARMOUTH	Josh	PTE	25	/373	A	1 STARFORD BUILDINGS	DIPTON	28/10/14					TO LABOUR CORPS(21 LAB COY).	LAB CORPS No 12272.
LAVENDER	J	PTE	25	/1075	C					KR para 392				
LAVIN	Chas	CPL	25	/374		22 HODGSON ST	WILLINGTON QUAY			30 MARCH 1916		BIAILLEUL		BORN FELLING SHORE.
LAWLER	W	PTE	25	/1491	D		NEWCASTLE	26/7/15	23/12/16	WOUNDS	SEPTEMBER 16		TO DEPOT.	3 CCS 2/7/16 EVAC 2/7/16.
LAWSON	G	PTE	25	/1077	A	SOUTH VIEW WAGGS LAN	WINLATON						TO 12/13th BN, CLASS Z RESERVE.	
LAWSON	J	PTE	25	/347	D	9 ETON ST	GATESHEAD	13/11/14	25/3/18	GUNSHOT WOUNDS	NOVEMBER 16		TO ARMY RESERVE CLASS P.	
LEE	Alb A	PTE	25	/346	D	37 ATHOL ST	DUNSTON				OCTOBER 16		TO 27th BN, CLASS Z RESERVE.	
LEE	J J	PTE	25	/345		30 WOLESLEY ST	GATESHEAD						TO 1st GARRISON BN, CLASS Z RESERVE.	
LEE	Wm	PTE	25	/363	A		HOWDEN LE WEAR			29 MARCH 1916		BIAILLEUL		
LEIGH	Geo	CPL	25	/360	D		STALYBRIDGE			26 MARCH 1918		POZIERES MEM	TO 1/4th BN, 1/5th BN.	
LEIGHTON	J	PTE	25	/364	A									
LENIHAN	E	PTE	25	/1072				11/11/14	7/4/17	WOUNDS			TO DEPOT.	

NAME	INITI	RANK	BA	NUMBE	COMP	ADDRESS	TOWN_VILL	ENLISTED	DISCHARG	CAUSE_DIS	WOUNDED	BURIED	TRANSFER	ADD
LENNARD	Mich	PTE	25	/1070	C	57 GRANARY TERR	WEST STANLEY			15 APRIL 1918	MARCH 17	PLOEGSTEERT MEM	TO 13th BN.	BORN KELLOE.
LEONARD	JohnE	PTE	25	/1060	C	104 POPLAR ST	HIRST			26 OCT 1917	NOVEMBER 16	TYNE COT MEM	TO 14th, 1/7th BNS.	
LERTORIA	J	PTE	25	/1064	C								TO YORK AND LANCASTER REGT.	
LEVITT	F	PTE	25	/372	A	8 WILLIAM ST	SEAHAM	16/11/14	4/3/19	KR para 392			TO ARMY RESERVE CLASS P.	5 BACK CHURCH ST DAWDON 1918.
LEWIS	R J	SGT	25	/361	C		CHESTER LE ST	21/11/14	19/10/17	WOUNDS			TO 85th TRAINING RESERVE BN.	LCPL.
LEWIS	Wm	PTE	25	/1079	C		SOUTHMOOR			1 JULY 1916		THIEPVAL MEM		MISSING OCTOBER 16, BORN WIGAN.
LIDDELL	R	PTE	25	/1056	C	4 PATTISON TERR	HEBBURN COLLIER	19/11/14	31/3/19	KR para 392			TO ARMY RESERVE CLASS P.	
LISGO	G	PTE	25	/1067	C		PELTON	18/11/14	7/3/18	SHELLSHOCK	AUGUST 16		TO ARMY RESERVE CLASS P.	3 CCS 2/7/16 EVAC 3/7/16.
LISHMAN	H	PTE	25	/1524	C		BARLOW	9/8/15	10/1/17	WOUNDS			TO DEPOT.	
LISLE	W Jas	PTE	25	/358	B 30	69 MILL LANE	NEWCASTLE	20/11/14	13/7/16				TO 30th BN, DEPOT.	DID NOT SERVE OVERSEAS.
LIVINGSTONE	J	PTE	25	/1074	C					KR para 392				
LOAN	J	PTE	25	/356	A		WALLSEND	6/11/14	20/12/17	TRENCH FEVER	SEPTEMBER 16		TO 1st BN, DEPOT.	
LOBBAN	J	CPL	25	/353	A	20 ROBBINSON TERR	SUNDERLAND							ALSO ON D COY 30th BN ROLL.
LODGE	Wm	PTE	25	/344		5 NINTH ST EAST	EASINGTON COLLI	6/11/14					TO 1st GARRISON BN, CLASS Z RESERVE.	
LOUGHRAN	H J	PTE	25	/1068	D	41 TAYLOR ST	CONSETT	11/11/14	8/3/18	KR para 392	JULY 16			BORN TYRONE.
LOVELLE	John	PTE	25	/1061	C		NEWCASTLE	20/11/14		1 JULY 1916		THIEPVAL MEM		MINER DESERTED 8/5/15, AGE 37,5'8'',MISSING OCT 16
LOWERY	MichJ	PTE	25	/350	A	22 CLARENCE ST	BOWBURN			1 JULY 1916		THIEPVAL MEM		MISSING OCT 16, BORN SLIGO. BROTHER IN LAW 25/1145
LOWERY	Thos	LCPL	25	/348	D	23 MANOR CHARE	NEWCASTLE	28/10/14			OCTOBER 16, JANUARY 18.		TO ROYAL ENGINEERS.	CPL.
LOWERY	W	PTE	25	/1078	B		NEWCASTLE				SEPTEMBER 16			
LOWES	T	PTE	25	/1369	C					KR para 392				
LUKE	R W	LCPL	25	/1365	A	21 REGENT TERR	SUNDERLAND						TO 1/4th BN, CLASS Z RESERVE.	CSM.
LUMLEY	Ernst	PTE	25	/1062	A	36 NORTHBOURNE ST	GATESHEAD				SEPTEMBER 16		TO 14th, 1/7th BNS.	34 CCS 2/7/16 EVAC 5/7/16 STILL SERVING 1921.
LUMSDEN	Chas	PTE	25	/357		264 CONYERS RD	NEWCASTLE	10/11/14						LABOURER DESERTED 23/2/15 AGE 28, 5'4''.
LYDON	Mich	PTE	25	/351		3 CO-OP BLDGS	HOLYWELL	28/10/14					TO 2nd GARRISON BN, CLASS Z RESERVE.	
LYNCH	J	PTE	25	/352	A	16 MORGAN ST	SUNDERLAND	11/11/14	27/1/17	WOUNDS	OCTOBER 16		TO DEPOT.	
LYNCH	James	PTE	25	/1073	C	5 PRINCE CONSORTS LA	HEBBURN			1 APRIL 1916		BAILLEUL COM CEM EXT		AGE 20.
LYNCH	Peter	PTE	25	/1069	C	3 ST MARKS TERR	SOUTH SHIELDS			18 JULY 1916	NOVEMBER 16	HARTON ST PETERS STH SHIELDS		AGE 21, BORN NORTH SHIELDS.
LYNCH	W	PTE	25	/349	A		SEDGEFIELD	14/11/14	4/8/17	GUNSHOT WOUNDS	26/27 JUNE 16, OCT 16.		TO DEPOT.	
LYNN	J	LCPL	25	/362	A	STATION RD	USHAW MOOR				NOVEMBER 16			
MACKEY	R	PTE	25	/425	B									
MADDEN	J	SGT	25	/387	A	HIRST	ASHINGTON	14/11/14	25/2/19	KR para 392	NOVEMBER 16		TO ARMY RESERVE CLASS P.	
MAGEE	E J	PTE	25	/1111	C	34 LORD ST	TRIMDON				SHELLSHOCK OCTOBER 16		TO DURHAM LI(12th, 15th BNS).	DLI No 45894. 3 CCS 2/7/16 EVAC 3/7/16 S SHOCK.
MAIN	W	PTE	25	/400	A		DURHAM CITY			KR para 392	JULY 16			3 CCS 2/7/16 EVAC 3/7/16.
MALLET	T	PTE	25	/1082	D		DUNSTON	19/11/14	4/4/17	WOUNDS	AUGUST 16		TO 26th BN, DEPOT.	
MALLON	J	PTE	25	/423	B									
MALLOWS	J L	PTE	25	/421	A			17/11/14	31/3/19	KR para 392	APRIL 16		TO 26th BN, ARMY RESERVE CLASS P.	LCPL.
MANLEY	J H	LCPL	25	/1540	A 30								COMMISSIONED	LCPL.
MANNERS	Chas	PTE	25	/413	A		BLYTH		14/12/19		OCTOBER 16		TO KINGS OWN YORKSHIRE LI, CLASS Z RESERVE.	KOYLI No 48272.
MANNERS	J R	PTE	25	/411	A	94 FERRY ST	JARROW	19/11/14	19/7/17	KR para 392	JULY 16		TO 3rd BN.	HOSP CHATHAM 17/7/16.
MANNING	J	PTE	25	/380	A								TO CLASS Z RESERVE.	
MAQUIRE	J	PTE	25	/1122	C	12 EDWARD ST	MORPETH				MARCH 17			
MAQUIRE	J W	PTE	25	/406	D		BLAYDON	23/11/14	30/10/17	KR para 392	AUGUST 16		TO 85th TRAINING RESERVE BN.	
MAQUIRE	Roger	PTE	25	/1094	C		SACRISTON			9 APRIL 1917	MARCH 17	ROCLINCOURT VALLEY CEM		
MARCH	Joe	PTE	25	/1102	B	21 THERESA ST	BLAYDON			12 FEB 1916		BREWERY ORCHARD CEM		BORN WINLATON, AGE 31.
MARCH	Wm	PTE	25	/1131	C		OUSTON			28 APRIL 1917		ARRAS MEM		BROTHER IN TS 22/273 JAS MARCH KIA 1/7/16
MARLEY	A	PTE	25	/1101	C	FRONT ST	ESH						TO 12/13th BN, CLASS Z RESERVE.	
MARR	Wm	PTE	25	/1097	C		SHOTTON COLLIER			1 JULY 1916		THIEPVAL MEM		MISSING OCTOBER 16, BORN MURTON.
MARRINER	Geo	PTE	25	/1406	C		BISHOP AUCKLAND			16 APRIL 1917	JULY 16	THIEPVAL MEM	TO 8th, 16th BNS.	
MARSDEN	J	PTE	25	/1374		27 CUTHBERT ST	HEBBURN	8/1/15	21/12/17	SICK			TO 1st GARRISON BN, 2nd BN, 3rd GARRISON BN(HOME S	ENTERED SALONIKA 20/12/15, 1914/15 STAR.
MARSHALL	G H	PTE	25	/376	A									
MARSHALL	W	PTE	25	/422	B									
MARTIN	H	PTE	25	/1104	C	7 COVENT GARDEN ST	SUNDERLAND						TO ROYAL DEFENCE CORPS.	IN FRANCE 11/1/16 TO 21/7/16.
MARTIN	J	PTE	25	/415	A	11 WILLIAM ST	TANFIELD						TO CLASS Z RESERVE.	77 GEORGE ST NEWCASTLE 1918.
MARTIN	John	PTE	25	/378	A		SUNDERLAND				MARCH 17		TO LABOUR CORPS.	LAB CORPS No 565769.
MARTIN	W	PTE	25	/1421						KR para 392			TO 1stGB, 2nd BNS.	NUMBER ALSO ALLOCATED TO RSM STEVENS.
MASON	J	PTE	25	/390	C	6 CHURCH VIEW	QUEBEC						TO CLASS Z RESERVE.	
MATHEWS	T	PTE	25	/1528	C	1 HAVANNAH TERR	WASHINGTON			KR para 392			TO 1/4th BN.	ALLOTTED NEW NUMBER 204610.
MATHEWSON	W P	PTE	25	/1132	C		DUNSTON	16/11/14	30/1/18	SICK	NOVEMBER 16		TO DEPOT.	ASGT, EMPLOYED AT DUNSTON STN BY NE RAILWAY.

NAME	INITI	RANK	BA	NUMBE	COMP	ADDRESS	TOWN_VILL	ENLISTED	DISCHARG	CAUSE_DIS	WOUNDED	BURIED	TRANSFER	ADD
MATTISON	T	LCPL	25	/414	C			13/11/14	5/9/17	SICK			TO 3rd BN.	CPL.
MAUGHAN	H	PTE	25	/397	A						APRIL 16		TO LABOUR CORPS.	
MAUGHAN	Wm	PTE	25	/412	C		FELLING			2 JULY 1916		WARLOY		
MEDD	Thos	PTE	25	/379	C	28 LEONARDS COURT	GATESHEAD	10/11/14	14/2/18	GUNSHOT WOUNDS	JULY 16		TO 3rd BN.	
MEDDIES	E	PTE	25	/1105	C	31 WILFRED ST PALLIO	SUNDERLAND	23/11/14	13/9/18	KR para 392			TO 1st BN, DEPOT.	
MEDHURST	Fred	PTE	25	/1090	C	63 DURHAM ST	SPENNYMOOR						TO CLASS Z RESERVE.	AWOL 23/10/15 IN COURT GATESHEAD, AGE 27.
MEEHAN	John	PTE	25	/1091	C	STANLEY COTTAGE	WESTERHOPE			28 APRIL 1917		ARRAS MEM		AGE 29.
METCALF	R	PTE	25	/434	A	2 WELLINGTON ST	NEWCASTLE						TO 8th, 24th, 8th BNS, CLASS Z RESERVE.	
METCALFE	J	PTE	25	/1080	C	FRONT ST	BROOMPARK						TO CLASS Z RESERVE.	LCPL.
MIDDLETON	Wm	PTE	25	/1123	C		SOUTH SHIELDS			10 FEB 1917		SIERRE RD NUMBER 1 CEM	TO 8th, 16th BNS.	34 CCS 2/7/16 EVAC 5/7/16 WND L ARM AGE 34.
MILBURN	R	PTE	25	/377	A								TO 9th BN, CLASS Z RESERVE.	
MILBURN	W	PTE	25	/1092	D			21/11/14	13/12/17	WOUNDS			TO 3rd BN.	
MILBURN	W	PTE	25	/1125		24 ALBERT ST	NEWCASTLE						TO 1/5th BN, CLASS Z RESERVE.	
MILBURN	Wm	PTE	25											AWOL 26/8/15 COURT GATESHEAD, AGE 35.
MILEY	J	PTE	25	/393	A			16/11/14	11/7/17	SICK			TO DEPOT.	LCPL
MILEY	J	PTE	25	/1096	A			21/11/14	8/1/18	WOUNDS			TO DEPOT.	
MILLER	H J	CPL	25	/375	D									
MILLER	J	PTE	25	/429	A			18/11/14	25/1/18	KR para 392			ATTACHED 179 TUNNELLING COY ROYAL ENGINEERS, TO 3r	
MILLER	J	PTE	25	/433	A									ALSO ON D COY 30th BN ROLL.
MILLER	J H	PTE	25	/403	D									ALSO ON D COY 30th BN ROLL.
MILLER	T	PTE	25	/1418	C		EASINGTON						TO CLASS Z RESERVE.	
MILLICAN	John	PTE	25	/1126	D	55 BLANFORD ST	NEWCASTLE	13/11/14		16 JUNE 1917	MARCH 17	ARRAS MEM	TO 30th(D COY), 12th BNS.	LABOURER DESERTED 13/3/15 AGE 20,5'5'', COURT 18/9
MILLIGAN	Rob	PTE	25	/420	A	80 ELSWICK RD	NEWCASTLE	17/11/14	1/11/17	KR para 392	AUGUST 16			
MILLIGAN	T	PTE	25	/1098	D									ALSO ON D COY 30th BN ROLL.
MILLION	R	PTE	25	/417	A		THORNLEY COLLIE				AUGUST 16			
MILLS	Jos	PTE	25	/1100	A		NEWCASTLE			1 JULY 1916		THIEPVAL MEM		MISSING OCTOBER 16, BORN GATESHEAD.
MILNER	Jos	PTE	25	/1121			CROOK	17/11/14						COOK DESERTED 31/12/14 AGE 31, 5'3''.
MITCHELL	Jos	CSM	25	/1099	C	35 KEELMANS HOSPITAL	NEWCASTLE			17 APRIL 1918		MONT NOIR CEM		ORGANIZED AMMO FROM THE DUMP ETC, AGE 31.
MITCHINSON	Andrw	PTE	25	/1093	C	47 MARY ST	BLAYDON			5 JUNE 1917		ARRAS MEM	TO 20th, 21st BNS.	AGE 24.
MITCHINSON	JohnG	PTE	25	/1089	B	22 CHARLES ST	GATESHEAD						TO 30th BN(D COY), LABOUR CORPS(1851 EMP COY).	LAB CORPS No 401692.
MITCHINSON	W	PTE	25	/432	D		FELLING				OCTOBER 16			34 CCS 1/7/16 EVAC 5/7/16, WND R LEG, AGE 29.
MOFFIT	W	PTE	25	/402	C	14 BLAGDON ST	GATESHEAD						TO 12/13th BN, CLASS Z RESERVE.	
MOLYNEUX	H	PTE	25	/1116	C	17 RAILWAY ST	LITTLEBURN	16/11/14	23/7/17	GUNSHOT WOUNDS	AUGUST 16		TO 3rd BN.	3 CCS 2/7/16 EVAC TO 3rd NTH HOSP SHEFFIELD 8/7/16
MONOGHAN	H	PTE	25	/1106	C	106 AYTON ST	NEWCASTLE				JUNE 17		TO CLASS Z RESERVE.	LCPL. SEE ALSO 24/878 H MONAGHAN
MONOGHAN	P	PTE	25	/1405	C	35 STEPHENSON ST	NORTH SHIELDS						TO ROYAL DEFENCE CORPS.	IN FRANCE 11/1/16 TO 4/1/18.
MONTGOMERY	Peter	PTE	25	/396	A	22 WESLEY TERR	FELLING	5/11/14						
MOODY	R W	CPL	25	/404			CONSETT	23/11/14	15/4/17	KR para 392	JULY 16		TO DEPOT.	
MOONEY	J	PTE	25	/1081	C									
MOORE	J	PTE	25	/1130	D		BELFAST				MARCH 17, JUNE 18.		TO 1st BN, CLASS Z RESERVE.	POS LIVING 58 MORRIS ST TEAMS GATESHEAD 1914
MORALEE	Wm	PTE	25	/435	C	223 PARKER ST	BYKER				JUNE 16		TO 12th, 12/13th BNS, CLASS Z RESERVE.	3 CCS 2/7/16 EVAC 2/7/16, SHELLSHOCK.
MORAN	Sam	PTE	25	/405	C	35 VIOLET ST	NEWCASTLE				JULY 16		TO LABOUR CORPS(68th POW COY).	
MORLAND	Wm	PTE	25	/389									TO 1st GARRISON BN, CLASS Z RESERVE.	
MORPETH	Sam	PTE	25	/1124	D	22 CLAVERING AVE	DUNSTON			20 NOV 1917	SEPTEMBER 16	ARRAS MEM	TO 1st BN.	34 CCS 2/7/16 EVAC 5/7/16 WND L LEG.BORN FELLING.
MORRIS	D	PTE	25	/1127	A		DUNSTON	14/11/14	1/4/19	KR para 392	DECEMBER 16		TO ARMY RESERVE CLASS P.	
MORRIS	T	PTE	25	/408	C									ALSO ON D COY 30th BN ROLL.
MORTON	E	PTE	25	/1086	A									
MORTON	T S	PTE	25	/1088	C		NEWCASTLE				SEPTEMBER 16			
MORTON	W A	PTE	25	/391	A									
MOWBRAY	J	PTE	25	/426	B	44 QUEBEC ST	LANGLEY PARK						TO 9th BN, CLASS Z RESERVE.	
MULKERN	Mich	PTE	25	/1128	D		WREKETON			23 MARCH 1918	DECEMBER 16	HAC CEM ECOUSTE ST MEIN		
MULLARKEY	A	PTE	25	/398	A								TO CLASS Z RESERVE.	
MULLARKEY	Mich	PTE	25	/395	A	78 ASTLEY TERR	SEATON DELAVAL	11/11/14		15 JULY 1916		ABBEVILLE MIL CEM		BORN KILHOAN ARGYLE.
MULLEN	C	PTE	25	/407		38 ELLISON SQUARE	GATESHEAD	23/11/14	11/2/18	SICK			TO 1st GARRISON BN, DEPOT.	AGE 56.
MULLEN	F	PTE	25	/1407	C	FRONT ST NEVILLES CR	DURHAM CITY						TO 8th, 16th, 20th, 16th, 1/7th, 12/13th BNS, CLAS	
MULLEN	Jas	PTE	25	/383	A	23 HIRST ST	WHEATLEY HILL	13/11/14	23/5/18	WOUNDS	OCTOBER 16		TO ARMY RESERVE CLASS P.	
MULLEN	M	PTE	25	/409	A	9 EAST PARADE	CONSETT	19/11/14	3/1/18	SHELLSHOCK			ATTACHED 1/1st LONDON REGT, DEPOT NF.	
MULLEN	Thos	PTE	25	/1112	C	42 DILYON LANE	HEBBURN	6/11/14					TO 12/13th BN, CLASS Z RESERVE.	54 FERRY ST JARROW 1918.
MULLHOLLAND	M	PTE	25	/1110	D									

NAME	INITI	RANK	BA	NUMBE	COMP	ADDRESS	TOWN_VILL	ENLISTED	DISCHARG	CAUSE_DIS	WOUNDED	BURIED	TRANSFER	ADD
MULVANNEY	Peter	PTE	25	/1119	C	59 JOHN ST COWPEN	BLYTH			1 JULY 1916		THIEPVAL MEM		MISSING OCTOBER 16, BORN RYHOPE.
MUNDY	Rob J	PTE	25	/386	D	1 TYNEMOUTH ENTRY	NORTH SHIELDS			6 APRIL 1916		BREWERY ORCHARD CEM		AGE 28.
MUNROE	P	PTE	25	/1106	C			11/11/14	12/1/18	GUNSHOT WOUNDS			TO DEPOT.	
MURPHY	B J	PTE	25	/431	A		JARROW				OCTOBER 16			STILL SERVING 1920.
MURPHY	James	PTE	25	/382	A								TO ARMY SERVICE CORPS.	ASC No M/375862.
MURPHY	James	PTE	25	/419	A			17/11/14	16/8/17	WOUNDS			TO 85th TRAINING RESERVE BN.	
MURPHY	John	PTE	25	/1120			SUNDERLAND	10/11/14						LABOURER DESERTED 4/2/15 AGE 22, 5'10''.
MURPHY	Jos	CPL	25	/1117	D		SACRISTON			1 JULY 1916		THIEPVAL MEM		MISSING OCTOBER 16.
MURPHY	Robt	PTE	25	/394	A	16 SOUTH BENWELL RD	NEWCASTLE	5/11/14						
MURRAY	E	PTE	25	/410	A									
MURRAY	F	PTE	25	/401	A	73 CASTLE TERR	ASHINGTON				JULY 16		TO LABOUR CORPS.	
MURRAY	M	SGT	25	/427	B		LOW SPENNYMOOR	14/11/14	15/4/17	WOUNDS	JULY 16		TO DEPOT.	34 CCS 2/7/16 EVAC 5/7/16 WND L LEG+R ARM.
MURRAY	M	PTE	25	/1493	B		NEWCASTLE				OCTOBER 16			ALSO ON B COY 30th BN ROLL.
MURRAY	Rob	PTE	25	/388	A	4 ISLE ST WHITHORN	WIGTOWN			24 APRIL 1917		BROWNS COPSE CEM		BORN WHITEHAVEN, AGE 39.
MaCAULEY	Jas	PTE	25	/1084		17 AKENSIDE HILL	NEWCASTLE	19/11/14						LABOURER DESERTED 19/2/15 AGE 28, 5'6'', BORN LIVE
McALLISTER	J	PTE	25	/446	A	83 MARSHALL WALLIS R	SOUTH SHIELDS				JULY 16			CPL, 3 CCS 2/7/16 EVAC 2/7/16.
McALLISTER	J	SGT	25	/1146	A		LESBURN				JULY 16			LCPL IN 1916.
McANDREWS	A	PTE	25	/1147	C								TO 12/13th, 1st BNS, CLASS Z RESERVE.	
McANDREWS	J	CSM	25	/1377	D		AMBLE	8/1/15	7/4/17	SICK	SHELLSHOCK DECEMBER 16		TO DEPOT.	IN 3rd SCOTTISH GEN HOSP GLASGOW 18/7/16.
McAVINNIE	P	PTE	25	/441									TO 1st GARRISON BN, CLASS Z RESERVE.	
McCABE	Fred	PTE	25	/493	B	24 MAPLE ST	SOUTHMOOR	6/11/14					TO CLASS Z RESERVE.	SGT.
McCABE	M	PTE	25	/445	A	8 FENWICK ST	OLD PENSHAW	13/11/14	16/10/17	SICK			TO DEPOT.	
McCAFFERTY	E	PTE	25	/1173	C									
McCALLUM	JohnD	PTE	25	/1179	C	2 NEWHOUSES RD	ESH WINNING	21/11/14	10/5/18	GUNSHOT WOUNDS			TO DEPOT.	
McCANN	John	PTE	25	/1158	C	4 WEST ST	EAST STANLEY			1 JULY 1916		BAPAUME POST CEM		BORN WARDLEY.
McCARTHY	D	PTE	25	/452	D	22 BACK GEORGE ST	NEWCASTLE						TO CLASS Z RESERVE.	
McCARTHY	Jas	PTE	25	/490	C	3 WILLIAM ST	HEBBURN	6/11/14		1 JULY 1916		WARLOY		BORN GATESHEAD
McCARTHY	John	PTE	25	/439	B	12 WESTMORLAND LANE	NEWCASTLE	11/11/14	30/1/17	SICK			TO DEPOT.	
McCARTHY	John	PTE	25	/1151	B	16 EGERTON RD	TYNE DOCK	10/11/14		1 JULY 1916		THIEPVAL MEM		MISSING OCTOBER 16, BORN CONSETT.
McCARTNEY	John	PTE	25	/494		52 CALIFORNIA ST	NEW SEAHAM			1 JULY 1916		THIEPVAL MEM		SEE 27/1096.
McCARTNEY	Ralph	PTE	25	/486		51 EDITH AVENUE	USWORTH	10/11/14					TO 1st GARRISON BN, CLASS Z RESERVE.	
McCAY	T	PTE	25	/1143	D									
McCERERY	W	PTE	25	/479	D	52 BACK NORMAN ST	SUNDERLAND	18/11/14	29/8/16	WOUNDS			TO DEPOT.	
McCLAIN	John	PTE	25	/444	C	9 KING WILLIAM ST	GATESHEAD	12/11/14		KR para 392				
McCLUSKER	Thos	PTE	25	/468	B	NEWCASTLE HOUSE	DIPTON				OCTOBER 16		TO DURHAM LI, LABOUR CORPS.	
McCLUSKEY	B	PTE	25	/476	D									
McCLUSKEY	Chas	PTE	25	/1165	C	119 VICTORIA ST	SHOTTON COLLIER	23/11/14	16/9/18	GUNSHOT WOUNDS				CPL
McCLUSKEY	D	PTE	25	/462	B			20/11/14	30/10/17	WOUNDS			TO 85th TRAINING RESERVE BN.	3 CCS 2/7/16 EVAC-1st SCOTTISH GEN ABERDEEN, 8/7/1
McCOLL	Jas	PTE	25	/1170	C	21 RAILWAY ST	BRANDON COLLIER	26/11/14			NOVEMBER 16		TO KINGS OWN YORKSHIRE LI.	KOYLI No 203372.
McCOLL	Mich	PTE	25	/1178	D	61 WEST HOLBORN	SOUTH SHIELDS			1 JULY 1916		THIEPVAL MEM		LCPL, MISSING OCTOBER 16, BORN DONEGAL.
McCORMACK	Jas	PTE	25											AWOL 5/4/15 COURT 8/4/15
McCORMACK	P	CPL	25	/1185	C		SUNDERLAND				JULY 16		ATTACHED KINGS AFRICAN RIFLES, CLASS Z RESERVE.	
McCOURT	Steph	PTE	25	/437	D	34 LAWSON ST	WORKINGTON			1 JULY 1916		THIEPVAL MEM		MISSING OCTOBER 16, BORN CONSETT, LIVING COWPEN.
McCOY	A	PTE	25	/465	B	15 PRINCE CONSORTS L	HEBBURN						TO 3rd BN.	
McCOY	J	PTE	25	/1492	C									
McDONALD	Arth	PTE	25	/1184	B	20 LYONS ST	HEBBURN	6/11/14						
McDONALD	H	PTE	25	/448				14/11/14	3/9/17	SICK			TO 1st GARRISON BN.	
McDONALD	John	PTE	25	/488	B	1 VICTORIA RD EAST	HEBBURN	10/11/14	13/8/16	SICK			TO 30th BN.	
McDOUGALL	Wm	PTE	25	/1174			NEWCASTLE	19/11/14						FIREMAN DESERTED 4/2/15 AGE 32, 5'9''.
McENEANEY	J	PTE	25	/477	B									ALSO D COY 30th BN.
McENEANEY	John	PTE	25	/1159	C	3 JAMES ST KIPHILL	STANLEY	11/11/14		1 JULY 1916		THIEPVAL MEM		MISSING OCTOBER 16, BORN HEXAM.
McENEANEY	P	PTE	25	/1169	C		NEWCASTLE				NOVEMBER 16			
McEVOY	John	PTE	25	/1135	C	13 SOUTH VIEW	CHESTER LE ST			28 AUGUST 1917	AUGUST 16	TYNE COT MEM	TO 21st, 8th BNS.	3 CCS 2/7/16 EVAC 3/7/16 AGE 44, BORN B/AUKLAND
McFALL	W	PTE	25	/471	C	28 HENRY ST	GOSFORTH							ALSO ON D COY 30th BN ROLL.
McFARLANE	Jas	PTE	25	/447	D	203 SHIPLEY RD	BYKER	10/11/14		1 JULY 1916		THIEPVAL MEM		MISSING OCTOBER 16.
McGARRITY	J	PTE	25	/451	B	MONKWEARMOUTH	SUNDERLAND				JULY 16			
McGARRY	P	PTE	25	/436	B			9/11/14	8/3/18	SICK			TO ARMY RESERVE CLASS P.	IN VOLUNTARY AID HOSP CHELTENHAM 8/7/16.
McGEAREY	E	PTE	25	/1448	D 30			13/7/15	11/5/16				TO 30th BN.	DID NOT SERVE OVERSEAS.

NAME	INITI	RANK	BA	NUMBE	COMP	ADDRESS	TOWN_VILL	ENLISTED	DISCHARG	CAUSE_DIS	WOUNDED	BURIED	TRANSFER	ADD
McGEE	Dan	PTE	25	/1164	A		WALKER			1 JULY 1916		THIEPVAL MEM		AWOL 6/6/15 COURT NEWCASTLE BORN FELLING.
McGEE	G	PTE	25	/484	B	16 BUDDELL ST	WALLSEND							
McGEE	J	PTE	25	/443	B	58 MITCHELL ST	LOW WALKER	11/11/14						ALSO D COY 30th BN ROLL.
McGILL	Mich	PTE	25	/1166	C	4 PRIOR ST	GATESHEAD			11 JUNE 1917		ARRAS MEM	TO 12th, 25th BNS.	SEE BROTHER JAMES AND JOHN IN 24th BN.
McGILLVARY		PTE	25	/1463	D	9 STATION TERR	EAST BOLDON	17/7/15	23/8/18	GUNSHOT WOUNDS	DECEMBER 17		TO 27th, 16th BNS, DEPOT.	
McGINLEY	H	PTE	25	/483	B					KR para 392			TO 2nd BN.	
McGLYNN	Tom	PTE	25	/1162	C		WEST STANLEY			1 JULY 1916		THIEPVAL MEM		MISSING OCTOBER 16, BORN CONSETT.
McGONEGAL	J	SGT	25	/492		32 DUCHESS ST	WHITLEY BAY	17/11/14	5/3/18	DEBILITY			TO 1st GARRISON BN, 3rd BN.	
McGONNEL	H	PTE	25	/481	B									
McGRANAGHAN	J	PTE	25	/474	D	98 CITY RD	NEWCASTLE			KR para 392	SEPTEMBER 16		TO 20th, 21st BNS.	
McGREAVEY	James	LCPL	25	/1175	C		SUNDERLAND			28 APRIL 1917	MARCH 16	ARRAS MEM		
McHUGH	F	PTE	25	/464	B									ALSO ON D COY 30th BN ROLL.
McHUGH	Mich	PTE	25	/1150	D	8 SQUARE	USWORTH COLLIER	29/10/14		17 JUNE 1917	OCTOBER 16	GREVILLES BRIT CEM	TO 30th(B COY), 22nd, 12th, 25th BNS.	BORN LEADGATE, AGE 32.
McHUGH	W	PTE	25	/470									TO 2nd GARRISON BN, CLASS Z RESERVE.	
McHUGH	W	PTE	25	/1148	D			14/11/14	4/2/19	GUNSHOT WOUNDS			TO 12/13th BN, DEPOT.	AGE 27.
McINTYRE	John	LCPL	25	/1168	B 30	4 KIRKSOP ST JESMOND	NEWCASTLE						TO 30th BN(B COY), 25th BN(A COY).	34 CCS 2/7/16 EVAC 5/7/16 WND HEAD/SHLDR, AGE 40.
McKABE	J E	PTE	25	/454	A		NEWCASTLE	16/11/14	11/4/18	GUNSHOT WOUNDS	DECEMBER 17		TO DEPOT.	AWOL 7/8/15 IN COURT 26/8/15.
McKENNA	Chas	PTE	25	/1160	D	8 EDWARD ST	HEBBURN	6/11/14						
McKENNA	J	LCPL	25	/450	B									
McKENNA	Sam W	RQMS	25	/1152	C	16 TUNSTALL TERR	SUNDERLAND			10 OCT 1918		DUNDALK ST PATRICKS(C of I)		BORN DUNDALK, DIED AT SEA, AGE 26
McKENNA	Walt	PTE	25	/1180	A		NEWCASTLE			16 AUGUST 1917	OCTOBER 16	TYNE COT MEM	TO 24th, 8th BNS.	34 CCS 1/7/16 EVAC 5/7/16 WND ANKLE, AGE 19.
McKEOWN	Jas	LCPL	25	/1145	C	22 CLARENCE ST	BOWBURN			1 JULY 1916		THIEPVAL MEM		MISSING OCTOBER 16.BROTHER IN LAW 25/350.
McKIE	R	PTE	25	/1523	C									
McLANE	John	PTE	25	/456	D	62 ALEXANDER ST	NEWCASTLE				MARCH 16			POS LIVING 20 ETON ST GATESHEAD 1914.
McLANE	Jos	PTE	25											AWOL 21/7/15, 24/8/15 COURT GATESHEAD AGE 38.
McLEAN	Mich	PTE	25	/489		83 WALKER ST	GATESHEAD						TO 2nd GARRISON BN, CLASS Z RESERVE.	
McLOUGHLIN	J R	PTE	25	/463	D	2 BK LYLE ST	BYKER BANK	11/11/14			JUNE 17			
McMAHON	J	PTE	25	/1156	B	22 DEAN ST	FERRYHILL							
McMAHON	P	PTE	25	/1137	C								TO 1/5th BN, CLASS Z RESERVE.	
McMAHON	T	PTE	25	/495	B									ALSO ON D COY 30th BN ROLL.
McMANN	B	PTE	25	/1134	C									
McMANUS	J	PTE	25	/472				19/11/14	6/8/17	SICK			TO 3rd BN.	
McMENEMEY	J	PTE	25	/487	B		GATESHEAD				AUGUST 16			3 CCS 2/7/16 EVAC 2/7/16
McMILLAN	Jhn E	PTE	25	/1140	C	FANCY COTTAGE CROSS	LOW FELL			1 JULY 1916		OVILLIERS MIL CEM		MISSING OCTOBER 16, BORN STANHOPE.
McMULLEN	John	PTE	25	/458		24 ROSEDALE ST	NEWCASTLE			KR para 392			TO 1st GARRISON BN.	
McNALLY	J	PTE	25	/1139	D									
McNALLY	J	PTE	25	/1177	C								TO LABOUR CORPS.	
McNALLY	T	PTE	25	/440	D	5 BALMORAL ST	WALLSEND							ALSO ON D COY 30th BN ROLL AS J McNALLY.
McNALLY	Wm	PTE	25	/453	B	34 QUEEN ST	CONSETT	16/11/14					TO 12/13th BN, CLASS Z RESERVE.	LABOURER DESERTED 4/4/15 AGE 28, 5'3''.
McNAMARA	J L	CPL	25	/1087	A	c/o DONNELLYS SANDHI	NEWCASTLE				MARCH 17			CPL, DESERTED 30 JULY 1918.
McNAMARA	M	PTE	25	/461	C	8 COLLIERY VIEW	NEW BRANCEPETH							ALSO ON D COY 30th BN ROLL.
McNULTY	J	LCPL	25	/1141	C						SHELLSHOCK JULY 16		TO 21st, 1st BNS, CLASS Z RESERVE.	3 CCS 2/7/16 EVAC 3/7/16.
McNULTY	T	PTE	25	/491	B									ALSO ON D COY 30th BN ROLL.
McNULTY	T	PTE	25	/1182	A		GATESHEAD				NOVEMBER 16		TO 11th BN, CLASS Z RESERVE.	21 AMB TRAIN 6/7, 18 GEN HOSP, No 6 CONV DEPOT 7/7
McPARTLIN	Peter	PTE	25	/1181	B		NEWCASTLE						TO 16th, 1/6th BNS, STILL SERVING 1920.	3 CCS 2/7, 2 GEN HOSP 5/7 HOSP SHIP 10/7/16.
McPEAK	John	PTE	24	/457	D	9 WANSBECK ST	NEWCASTLE	5/11/14		1 JULY 1916		THIEPVAL MEM		MISSING OCTOBER 16, BORN GATESHEAD.
McQUADE	P	PTE	25	/475	B	1 HODGSONS BIULDINGS	SUNDERLAND							
McQUIRE	J	PTE	25	/463	B									THIS No ALLOTED TO McLOUGHLIN J R. POS /473?
McTAGGART	Jas	PTE	25											AWOL 24/4 9/5 6/6 25/7 15/8 COURT 28/4 22/5 7/6 27
McTEER	A	SGT	25	/449	B	23 ROBINSON ST	BLAYDON						TO 85th TRAINING RESERVE BN, CLASS Z RESERVE.	AWOII, ATTESTED WITH TYNESIDE SCOTTISH 17/11/14.
McVAY	J	PTE	25	/460	B	162 CLEVELAND ST	SOUTH SHIELDS				OCTOBER 16		TO 24th BN, CLASS Z RESERVE.	125 BATH ST 1916.
McVAY	J	PTE	25	/1476	D	8 MIDDLE ST	BLACKHILL				APRIL 16			
McVAY	P	SGT	25	/1183	C								ATTACHED KINGS AFRICAN RIFLES.	CSGT.
McWILLIAMS	Edw	PTE	25	/1142	A		NEWCASTLE			1 JULY 1916		THIEPVAL MEM		MISSING OCTOBER 16, BORN GATESHEAD.
McWILLIAMS	J	PTE	25	/1161	D		GOSFORTH			KR para 392	AUGUST 16			
NATTRESS	H	PTE	25	/1188	C	EAST HOUSE COT DRGN	DURHAM CITY		13/1/19		OCTOBER 16		TO 23rd BN, KINGS OWN YORKSHIRE LI 5th BN, CLASS Z	KOYLI No 63084.
NEAL	J	PTE	25	/497	D		NEW WASHINGTON	14/11/14	9/11/16	SICK	AUGUST 16		TO DEPOT.	CPL
NEALONS	M	PTE	25	/495	D	26 THORNBERRY ST	BYKER	11/11/14		KR para 392	AUGUST 16		TO 1/5th BN.	3 CCS 2/7/16 EVAC 2/7/16,LCPL,NUMBER 243179.

NAME	INITI	RANK	BA	NUMBE	COMP	ADDRESS	TOWN_VILL	ENLISTED	DISCHARG	CAUSE_DIS	WOUNDED	BURIED	TRANSFER	ADD
NEE	Frc J	PTE	25	/1190	C		SUNDERLAND			5 JUNE 1917		ARRAS MEM	TO 20th BN.	BORN GRANGETOWN.
NELSON	G	PTE	25	/501	B	31a SOUTH VIEW	TANFIELD				OCTOBER 16		TO 8th, 16th, 26th, 25th, 12/13th BNS, CLASS Z RES	LCPL.
NEVINS	A	PTE	25	/1186	C	4 HARDYS BLDGS CAMPE	BURRADON	11/11/14						ALSO ON D COY 30th BN ROLL.
NICHOLETTE	P	PTE	25	/503	A		NEWCASTLE	17/11/14	28/8/17	GUNSHOT WOUNDS	JULY 16		TO 85th TRAINING RESERVE BN.	SIGNALLER, BEAUFORT HOSP BRISTOL 12/7/16.
NICHOLSON	G	PTE	25	/502	B									ALSO ON D COY 30th BN ROLL.
NICHOLSON	T	PTE	25	/1503	B			27/7/15	10/10/17	SICK				AGE 27.
NIELL	P	PTE	25	/1189	D		KILKENNY				JULY 16			
NOBLE	C	SGT	25	/499	B	59 MAPLE ST	SOUTHMOOR	21/11/14	28/2/17	MYALGIA			TO ARMY RESERVE CLASS W.	
NORMAN	T	PTE	25	/1187	A		NEWCASTLE				JULY 1916			VOLUNTARY AID HOSP CHELTENHAM 11/7/16.
NUTTNEY	Henry	PTE	25	/498	C	25 FOX ST	GATESHEAD	12/11/14					TO LABOUR CORPS(442 A E COY).	ALSO ON D COY 30th BN ROLL,LAB CORPS No 246082.
O'BRIEN	M	PTE	25	/515	B		SOUTH SHIELDS	10/11/14	3/6/18	GUNSHOT WOUNDS	OCTOBER 16		TO ARMY RESERVE CLASS W.	CPL.
O'BRIEN	P	PTE	25	/1370	C									
O'CONNER	Arth	PTE	25	/1194	C		TYNE DOCK			28 APRIL 1917		ARRAS MEM		IN AUGUST 18 GAZ, BORN B/AUKLAND.
O'DOWD	B	PTE	25	/1196	D								TO 1/4th BN, CLASS Z RESERVE.	ALLOTED NEW NUMBER 204602.
O'DOWD	P	PTE	25	/509		70 BACK STATION RD	HEBBURN						TO 1st GARRISON BN, CLASS Z RESERVE.	ON AVL AS DOWD.
O'HAGAN	T	LCPL	25	/505	D									
O'HARA	B	PTE	25	/507	C	3 WALL ST	SUNDERLAND							ALSO ON B COY 30th BN ROLL.
O'HARA	J	PTE	25	/504	B								TO LABOUR CORPS.	
O'HARE	J	PTE	25	/1192	A	12 CAMPERDOWN ST	GATESHEAD	12/11/14	17/12/18	GUNSHOT WOUNDS			TO DEPOT.	AGE 35
O'LEARY	WmPat	SGT	25	/1193	D	15 STURGE ST	LONDON			6 JULY 1916	AUGUST 16	WARLOY		REDUCED TO LCPL, AGE 41 BORN MULLINGAR.
O'MALLEY	T	PTE	25	/514	B	12.........ST	NEW HARTLEY							ALSO ON D COY 30th BN ROLL.
O'NIELL	J H	PTE	25	/506	C		GATESHEAD	16/11/14	6/3/18	SHELLSHOCK	OCT 16, DEC 17, MAR 18.		TO DEPOT.	
OLIVER	J	PTE	25	/510	D	30 HARBOTTLE BIULDINGS	SWALWELL							
OLIVER	R	PTE	25	/511						KR para 392			TO 1st GARRISON BN.	
OPENSHAW	J	PTE	25	/1197	A		SUNDERLAND				JULY 16		TO CLASS Z RESERVE.	
ORD	Wm B	PTE	25	/1198	C	EWART TERR	COWPEN VILLAGE	2/11/14			SEPTEMBER 16		TO CLASS Z RESERVE.	
OSBORNE	F J	LCPL	25	/1433	C								COMMISSIONED IN LIECESTER REGT.	ACPL.
OWENS	Alex	PTE	25	/1199	C	72 LYONS ST	HEBBURN QUAY			9 NOV 1916		CITE BON JEAN CEM		BORN JARROW AGE 20.
PALLACE	John	PTE	25	/530	D	66 THAMES ST EAST	WALLSEND			1 JULY 1916		THIEPVAL MEM		MISSING OCTOBER 16, BORN SUNDERLAND.
PALMER	Thos	PTE	25	/518	B			10/11/14	18/2/18	SICK			TO ARMY RESERVE CLASS W.	AWOL 30/11/15 IN COURT 2/12/15.
PARKER	Wm	PTE	25	/521	D	19 BARNES RD	SOUTH SHIELDS	5/11/14						ON D COY 30th BN ROLL AS HARKER W 521.
PARKIN	Tom	PTE	25	/535	A	48 PEARETH ST	GATESHEAD				OCTOBER 16, DECEMBER 16.		TO 1st BN.	
PARKS	C	PTE	25	/546		10 JAMES ST	STANLEY	7/11/14	17/2/19	SICK			TO 2nd GARRISON BN, DURHAM LI(1st BN), 2nd GAR BN	AGE 26.
PARKS	T	PTE	25	/545	B		STANLEY	17/11/14	12/11/17	WOUNDS	OCTOBER 16		TO 85th TRAINING RESERVE BN.	IN BEAUFORT WAR HOSP FISHPONDS BRISTOL 8/7/16.
PARNELL	E	PTE	25	/534	B		GRANGETOWN						TO 1/5th BN.	MISSING OCTOBER 16, STILL SERVING 1920.
PARR	W	PTE	25	/1213	C		NEWCASTLE				JUNE 18		TO CLASS Z RESERVE.	
PARRY	Edw	PTE	25	/1205	C		MARSDEN			18 JULY 1917	OCTOBER 16	WHITBURN	TO LABOUR CORPS(498 LAB COY).LAB CORPS No 261020.	34 CCS, 21 AMB TRAIN, 18 GEN HOSP, 26 GEN HOSP 6/7
PATTERSON	Geo	PTE	25	/1217	C	2 PROVIDENCE PL GILE	DURHAM CITY		21/3/19		AUGUST 16		TO YORK AND LANCASTER REGT(18th BN).	
PATTERSON	Henry	PTE	25	/1207	C		EAST SLEEKBURN			1 JULY 1916		THIEPVAL MEM		
PATTERSON	Tom J	PTE	25	/531	B	11 DOUBLE ROW	COWPEN COLLIERY			1 JULY 1916		THIEPVAL MEM		MISSING OCTOBER 16, BORN BLYTH.
PATTISON	R	PTE	25	/1224	C	VICTORIA TER	BLACKFYNE	18/11/14	21/9/17	WOUNDS	JULY 16		TO DEPOT.	LCPL.
PAUL	R	PTE	25	/1226	C	MARMADUKE ST	SPENNYMOOR	18/11/14			SEPTEMBER 16		TO YORK AND LANCASTER REGT.	DESERTED 2/5/15, 5'6''.3 CCS 2/7/16 EVAC 2/7/16.
PEACOCK	G	PTE	25	/544	B	8 DAVISON ST	SACRISTON							
PEARSON	J	PTE	25	/542	D		FELLING	18/11/14	22/8/17	GUNSHOT WOUNDS	AUGUST 16		TO DEPOT.	
PEARSON	J E	LCPL	25	/538	B	12 RIVER VIEW	WASHINGTON				AUGUST 16, JUNE 18.		TO 19th, 25th BNS, CLASS Z RESERVE.	SGT.
PEART	J	PTE	25	/1209	C	172 MARSDEN ST	SOUTH SHIELDS	19/11/14	31/3/19				TO ARMY RESERVE CLASS P.	
PEAT	JohnR	PTE	25	/522	D	38 HINDHAUGH ST	NEWCASTLE	5/11/14			MARCH 17			
PEET	John	PTE	25	/1532	D		KESWICK			1 JULY 1916		THIEPVAL MEM		MISSING OCTOBER 16, BORN CROSTHWAITE CUMBERLAND.
PEMBERTON	Rich	PTE	25	/1218	C		SUNDERLAND			21 MARCH 1918		ARRAS MEM		CPL.
PENALUNA	Tom	SGT	25	/527	A	9 MUNICIPAL TERR	WASHINGTON	10/11/14		1 JULY 1916		THIEPVAL MEM		MISSING OCTOBER 16, SEE 26/549 W PENALUNA.
PENNY	J	PTE	25	/528	B	16 NELSON ST	WILLINGTON							
PENTLAND	John	CPL	25	/525	A	18 RENDALSHAM ST MNK	SUNDERLAND			28 APRIL 1917		ARRAS MEM		
PERCIVAL	C	PTE	25	/1204	A									ALSO ON D COY 30th BN ROLL.
PERCIVAL	J	PTE	25	/524	D	7 BARKER ST	SHIELDFIELD				OCTOBER 16		TO ROYAL ENGINEERS.	2nd SOUTHERN GEN HOSP 11/7/16, 5 PINK LANE NEWCAST
PERCY	Robt	PTE	25	/1211		21 CALIFORNIA ST	NEW SEAHAM			20 APRIL 1920		SEAHAM	TO LABOUR CORPS.	LAB CORPS No 219625, AGE 45.
PERRY	J	PTE	25	/1201				12/11/14	6/3/15	SICK				DID NOT SERVE OVERSEAS.
PHELAN	F	LCPL	25	/1206	C									ALSO ON D COY 30th BN ROLL.
PHILIPS	J W	PTE	25	/526	B	30		16/11/14	15/9/16	SICK			TO 30th BN(B COY).	DID NOT SERVE OVERSEAS.

						TOWN_VILL	ENLISTED	DISCHARG	CAUSE_DIS	WOUNDED	BURIED	TRANSFER	ADD
PICKARD	G	SGT	25 /529	B	30 ROSEHILL TERR	WILLINGTON QUAY	11/11/14					TO 24th, 25th BNS, CLASS Z RESERVE.	WOII
PINKNEY	M	PTE	25 /539	B								TO CLASS Z RESERVE.	
PORTEOUS	W	LCPL	25 /537	A	15 MIRK LANE	GATESHEAD	23/11/14	1/4/17	ARTHRITIS			TO DEPOT.	ON BN ROLL AS /535.
PORTER	Wilf	PTE	25 /520	B	3 PIT ROW AUKLAND TE	SHILDON			1 JULY 1916		THIEPVAL MEM		MISSING OCTOBER 16, BORN BARNARD CASTLE.
PORTHOUSE	J	PTE	25 /543	D	10 LOWERYS LANE	LOW FELL							
POTTER	John	PTE	25 /1225	A		NEWCASTLE			22 MARCH 1918		POZIERES MEM	TO 1/5th BN.	
POTTER	Thos	PTE	25 /1212			SUNDERLAND	20/11/14						DESERTED 19/2/15 AGE 38, 5'6''.
POTTS	Dav F	PTE	25 /549	D	312 CHURCH ST	NEWCASTLE				OCTOBER 16			
POTTS	J	PTE	25 /550	D		NEWCASTLE	11/11/14	27/8/17	GUNSHOT WOUNDS	SEPTEMBER 16		TO 85th TRAINING RESERVE BN.	ACPL.
POTTS	W	PTE	25 /1210	B									ALSO ON D COY 30th BN ROLL.
POWER	Thos	PTE	25 /541	D		HEBBURN			19 OCT 1918	DECEMBER 16	COLOGNE SOUTHERN CEM	TO MACHINE GUN CORPS(21st BN).	LCPL, MGC No 71840, BORN GREENCASTLE Co ANTRIM.
POWNEY	Jas	PTE	25 /547	B	FRAMWELLGATE	DURHAM CITY			1 JULY 1916		THIEPVAL MEM		MISSING OCTOBER 16.
PRENDERGAST	P	PTE	25 /548	B									
PRICE	Robt	PTE	25 /523	B	33 QUEEN ST	CONSETT	14/11/14	9/3/16				TO 30th BN.	DID NOT SERVE OVERSEAS, ALSO ON D COY 30th BN ROLL
PRINGLE	Andrw	PTE	25 /1222	D		NEWCASTLE			17 FEB 1918		BISHOPWEARMOUTH	TO 85th TRAINING RESERVE BN.	ALSO ON D COY 30th BN ROLL.
PRINGLE	C	PTE	25 /517	B								TO ROYAL ENGINEERS.	
PROSSER	H	PTE	25 /1219	C			23/11/14	23/1/16				TO DEPOT.	DID NOT SERVE OVERSEAS.
PROUD	Jos	PTE	25 /1220	A		TOW LAW			19 AUGUST 1917	MARCH 17	TEMPLEUX - LE -GUERARD BRIT		IN JAN 18 GAZ.
PULFER	Rich	PTE	25 /1215			SHAW LANCS	20/11/14						LABOURER DESERTED 21/2/15 AGE 35, 5'8''.
PURCELL	Jas	SGT	25 /516	B	3 THAMES ST WEST	BYKER			1 JULY 1916		THIEPVAL MEM		MISSING OCTOBER 16. ALSO ON B COY 30th BN ROLL AS
PURCELL	John	SGT	25 /1413	B	26 KITTY BREWSTER SQ	COWPEN BLYTH			14 OCT 1917	JULY 16	BARD COTTAGE CEM YPRES	TO 30th BN(B COY), 8th BN.	3 CCS 2/7/16 EVAC 3/7/16,AWOL 27/12/15 COURT BLYTH
PURDY	T		25 /1202	B 30									
PURVIS	J	LCPL	25 /1534	A	17 TARMAC ST	BATTLEFIELD						TO CLASS Z RESERVE.	CSGT.
PURVIS	R E	PTE	25 /1223	C	20 PIONEER ST	BLAYDON				OCTOBER 16		TO 24th, 8th BNS, CLASS Z RESERVE.	WND LEFT FOREARM.
PYLE	C W	PTE	25 /1208	C		ASHINGTON	19/11/14	25/4/17	WOUNDS	JULY 16, APRIL 17.		TO DEPOT.	
PYLE	Geo A	PTE	25 /533	B	16 TINDLE ST WESTGAT	NEWCASTLE			13 NOV 1917	JULY 16, DECEMBER 17.	OXFORD RD CEM YPRES	TO 16th BN.	SEE 25/532, 24/1014 BROTHERS, BORN MONKWEARMOUTH.
PYLE	H	PTE	25 /532	B		NEWBIGGIN	19/11/14	25/4/17	WOUNDS	MARCH 16, SEPTEMBER 16		TO DEPOT.	SEE 25/533, 24/1014 BROTHERS.
PYLE	Jhn T	PTE	25 /1203	D	19 ATHOL ST	DUNSTON			1JULY 1916		THIEPVAL MEM		MISSING OCTOBER 16, BORN NEWCASTLE.
QUINN	Chas	PTE	25 /1228	D	8 GLEN ST	HEBBURN	6/11/14						
QUINN	H	PTE	25 /553	A		DURHAM CITY	19/11/14	1/1/18	GUNSHOT WOUNDS	OCTOBER 16		TO 3rd BN.	BEAUFORT HOSP BRISTOL 11/7/16.
QUINN	H	PTE	25 /554	D 30									CHECK SWB LISTS****
QUINN	H	PTE	25 /1227									TO 1st GARRISON BN, CLASS Z RESERVE.	
QUINN	J	PTE	25 /552	B	STANLEY VILLA	TOWNLEY						TO 9th BN, CLASS Z RESERVE.	
QUINN	Jacob	PTE	25 /551	B	4 KETTLEDRUM ST	WEST STANLEY	11/11/14		1 JULY 1916		THIEPVAL MEM		MISSING OCTOBER 16, BORN SPENNYMOOR.
QUINN	P	PTE	25 /1230	D	1 WOOD ROW	SOUTH WYLAM				SEPTEMBER 16		TO LABOUR CORPS.	BORN CROSSMAGLEN, LAB CORPS No 403513.
QUIRK	M	PTE	25 /1231	C	6 ROBSONS TERR	DIPTON				DECEMBER 16			LSGT.
RAMSEY	JohnW	CPL	25 /587	B	8 LONG ROW	LITTLETOWN			1 JULY 1916		THIEPVAL MEM		LSGT MISSING OCTOBER 16, BORN BROOMSIDE.
RAMSEY	W	PTE	25 /591	B		TANTOBIE	11/11/14	21/12/17	WOUNDS	MARCH 16, SEPTEMBER 16.		TO 85th TRAINING RESERVE BN.	
RATCLIFFE	R	LCPL	25 /1255	C	4 LIDDLE ST	SUNDERLAND						TO CLASS Z RESERVE.	
REA	A	PTE	25 /1478	D									
REA	W	SGT	25 /1430	A			21/515	3/7/18	SICK			TO ARMY RESERVE CLASS W.	
REDDY	Chas	PTE	25 /1496	D		NEWCASTLE			1 JULY 1916		BAPAUME POST CEM		MISSING OCTOBER 16.
REDHEAD	David	PTE	25 /567	B	16 CLEVELAND ST	SOUTH SHIELDS	26/11/14						
REED	G	PTE	25 /585	B						12 FEBRUARY 16, 1 JULY 16			3 CCS 2/7/16 EVAC 3/7/16.
REILLY	P	PTE	25 /590			NEWCASTLE			KR para 392			TO 2nd GARRISON BN.	MISSING OCTOBER 16.
RENDELL	F	PTE	25 /1237				19/11/14	12/3/18	DEBILITY			TO 1st GARRISON BN.	
RENSHAW	JohnG	PTE	25 /1458	D	22 JOHN STREET	CONSETT		14/12/18		S,SHOCK JUN16,SEP16,MAR18		TO KINGS OWN YORKSHIRE LI.	3 CCS 2/7/16 EVAC 2/7/16, KOYLI No 54025.
REYNOLDS	E J	PTE	25 /1259	D	COUNCIL SCHOOLS	FELLING	6/11/14	5/10/17	WOUNDS	DECEMBER 16		TO 80th TRAINING RESERVE BN.	SGT.
REYNOLDS	HughJ	CPL	25 /1251	C	34 SPELTER WORKS RD	SUNDERLAND	7/1/15		27 JAN 1918		BUCQUOY ROAD CEM		BORN CROMUNGAN Co LEITRIM, AGE 23.
REYNOLDS	J	PTE	25 /595				11/11/14	16/4/19	KR para 392			TO 1st GARRISON BN, DEPOT.	
REYNOLDS	J	PTE	25 /1256	D	25 PENSHAW VIEW	USWORTH	14/11/14	4/10/18	SICK	SEPTEMBER 16		TO ARMY RESERVE CLASS W.	
RHODES	J	LCPL	25 /1247	C	43 POST OFFICE ST	SPENNYMOOR				JULY 16			3 CCS 2/7/16 EVAC 2/7/16.
RICHARDS	Edgar	PTE	25 /583	B	11 PRINCESS ST	DALTON IN FURNE			12 OCT 1917		TYNE COT MEM		
RICHARDSON	D	PTE	25 /1261	C	63 HIGH ST NORTH	LANGLEY MOOR				JULY 16			34 CCS 2/7/16 EVAC 5/7/16, WND SHLDR,AGE 22.
RICHARDSON	Dan	PTE	25 /576	B		LEMINGTON ON TY			1 JULY 1916		THIEPVAL MEM		MISSING OCTOBER 16, BORN OVINGHAM.
RICHARDSON	Jas T	PTE	25 /1238			ST JOHNS NEWCAS	20/11/14						CARTMAN DESERTED 8/5/15 AGE 40, 5'3''.
RIDLEY	J	PTE	25 /1511	D		CONSETT	3/8/15	20/12/17	SICK	OCTOBER 16		TO DEPOT.	
RIDLEY	John	PTE	25 /1250	C	16 MILITARY RD	SOUTH SHIELDS			5 NOV 1917	OCTOBER 16	ST STEPHEN SOUTH SHIELDS		AGE 20,RV HOSP NETLEY, MINER ST HILDA COLLIERY.

NAME	INITI	RANK	BA	NUMBE	COMP	ADDRESS	TOWN_VILL	ENLISTED	DISCHARG	CAUSE_DIS	WOUNDED	BURIED	TRANSFER	ADD
RIED	J	PTE	25	/559	A	14 JOHN ST	COWPEN	10/11/14	24/2/17	WOUNDS	MARCH 16		TO DEPOT.	
RIGBY	W	PTE	25	/1254	B	7 CHARLETON ROW	HIGH FELLING		7/2/19				TO KINGS OWN YORKSHIRE LI 2/4 BN, CLASS Z RESERVE.	KOYLI No 63325.
RILEY	J	PTE	25	/584		31 BACK EDWARD ST	HEBBURN						TO 1st GARRISON BN, CLASS Z RESERVE.	
RIPLEY	T	CPL	25	/568	B	CAPE VILLA ORCHARD A	ROWLANDS GILL	11/11/14						ALSO ON D COY 30th BN ROLL.
RIPPON	J	PTE	25	/560	B	6 ALBERT TERR	ESH WINNING	11/11/14						ALSO ON D COY 30th BN ROLL.
ROBERTS	E	PTE	25	/1235	C			18/11/14	30/10/17	WOUNDS			TO 3rd BN.	
ROBERTS	H	PTE	25	/572	A									
ROBINSON	J	PTE	25	/582	B		WHITTON PARK				JULY 1916			
ROBINSON	J	PTE	25	/1239	C	19 SUNDERLAND ST	BRANDON COLLIER						TO 12/13th BN, CLASS Z RESERVE.	5 HERBERT ST LANGLEY MOOR 1914.
ROBINSON	J	PTE	25	/1461	D									
ROBINSON	J G	PTE	25	/577	D		FELLING				JULY 16			
ROBSON	G	PTE	25	/1415	C	14 SUCCESS COTTAGES	NEWBOTTLE						TO CLASS Z RESERVE.	BANDSMAN.
ROBSON	G W	LCPL	25	/565	B									EMPLOYED AT SMITHS DOCK, RIVETER PONTOONS.
ROBSON	Geo J	PTE	25	/579	B	161 MARSDEN ST	WESTOE			23 OCT 1916		SOUTH SHIELDS(WESTOE)	TO 2nd GARRISON BN EAST YORKSHIRE REGT.	ALSO ON B COY 30th BN ROLL, EAST YORKS No 24157.
ROBSON	J	PTE	25	/1233	C	74 ADDISONS COTTAGES	CROOKHALL						TO CLASS Z RESERVE.	
ROBSON	J	PTE	25	/1245	B		GATESHEAD	18/11/14	21/6/18	ARM+LEG AMPUTAT	JUNE 18		TO DEPOT.	CPL.
ROBSON	J	PTE	25	/1416	C								TO ARMY SERVICE CORPS.	
ROBSON	J C	CPL	25	/593	B		NEWCASTLE				OCTOBER 16			
ROBSON	R R	PTE	25	/1258	C	JUBILEE AVE	LAMESLY	16/11/14	1/4/19		JULY 16		TO ARMY RESERVE CLASS P.	
ROBSON	Robt	PTE	25	/566	B	10 QUEEN ST	CONSETT			1 JULY 1916		THIEPVAL MEM		
ROBSON	T M	PTE	25	/569	B		WALLSEND	23/11/14	18/7/17	SICK	FEBRUARY 16		TO DEPOT.	
ROBSON	Tom W	PTE	25	/570		9 MAYNARDS ROW GILES	DURHAM CITY			15 JANUARY 1915		HARTON ST PETERS STH SHIELDS		NOK 7 SHAKESPEARE ST SOUTH SHIELDS, BORN DURHAM CI
ROGAN	H	PTE	25	/1248	C		BISHOP AUKLAND				DECEMBER 16			
ROGAN	J	PTE	25	/575									TO 1st GARRISON BN, CLASS Z RESERVE.	
ROGERSON	JohnJ	PTE	25	/1426	A			18/5/15	12/10/17	SICK			TO 3rd BN.	AGE 40.
ROGERSON	Wm	PTE	25	/574	B	67 BACK ROBERTSON ST	BLAYDON	12/11/14		1 JULY 1916		THIEPVAL MEM		MISSING OCTOBER 16.
ROONEY	M	PTE	25	/581	D	11 SPLIT CROW LANE	FELLING	19/11/14	31/3/19	KR para 392			TO ARMY RESERVE CLASS P.	
ROSEBERRY	G	PTE	25	/1473	B									
ROSS	D	PTE	25	/592	C									ALSO ON D COY 30th BN ROLL.
ROSS	Geo	PTE	25	/1260	C	14 MORTON ST	SOUTH SHIELDS			3 JULY 1916		ST SEVER CEM ROUEN		ROUEN GEN HOSP 3/7/16
ROSS	John	PTE	25	/1243	A		GATESHEAD			26 AUGUST 1918	JUNE 18	COLOGNE SOUTHERN CEM	TO 8th, 1/5th BNS.	DIED IN GERMANY WHILST A PRISONER OF WAR.
ROUND	E	PTE	25	/580	D		NEWCASTLE				JANUARY 17			
ROWAN	John	PTE	25	/562	A	28 RAWLING RD	BENSHAM			19 OCT 1915		SALTWELL		
RUDDY	Edwd	CPL	25	/589	D 30	16 THOMAS ST	BLAYDON	12/11/14					TO 30th BN(D COY), MACHINE GUN CORPS(24th BN).	MGC No 58550. 1 MIDDLE COURT BLAYDON 1918.
RUDDY	H	PTE	25	/561									TO 1st GARRISON BN, CLASS Z RESERVE.	
RUDGE	J	PTE	25	/1253	C									
RUSSELL	James	PTE	25	/1234			MULLINGAR	18/11/14						LABOURER DESERTED 5/3/15 AGE 38, 5'5''.
RUTTER	A	PTE	25	/1241	C									
RUTTER	H	PTE	25	/573	C									ALSO ON D COY 30th BN ROLL.
RYAN	D	PTE	25	/588	A	4 CONSETT TERR	ESH COLLIERY							
RYAN	E	PTE	25	/1244	C	6 SOUTH ST	BRANDON COLLIER				SEPTEMBER 16		TO 24th, 8th BNS.	
RYAN	M	PTE	25	/556	B			16/11/14	19/8/18	SICK			TO ARMY RESERVE CLASS W.	CPL.
RYOTT	Elish	PTE	25	/563	B	11 HECTOR ST	GATESHEAD			26 APRIL 1917		ARRAS MEM		BORN NEWCASTLE.
SALKELD	Tom	PTE	25	/645	B	30 ROSEBERRY ST	WEST STANLEY			1 JULY 1916		THIEPVAL MEM		MISSING OCTOBER 16, BORN CHESTER LE STREET.
SANDERSON	T W	PTE	25	/1466		9 LEIGHTON ST	NEWCASTLE						TO 1st GARRISON BN, CLASS Z RESERVE.	
SANGER	T	PTE	25	/1462	C									
SAVAGE	P	PTE	25	/606		69 QUARRY ST	HUTTON HENRY			3 MARCH 1919		THORNLEY	TO 1st GARRISON BN, CLASS Z RESERVE.	AGE 39.
SAVAGE	W	PTE	25	/1291	C	6 BELLES VILLE GILES	DURHAM CITY	21/11/14	28/9/17	WOUNDS	OCTOBER 16		TO DEPOT.	
SAYERS	T	PTE	25	/646	B	4 POLONAISE ST	EAST STANLEY	17/11/14	28/3/18	GUNSHOT WOUNDS			TO ARMY RESERVE CLASS P.	3 CCS 2/7/16 EVAC 2/7/16.
SAYERS	W	PTE	25	/1263	C	22 FRY ST	EAST STANLEY			KR para 392				
SCORER	F	PTE	25	/650	B	4 CARR ROW	LEAMSIDE				APRIL 16, OCTOBER 16.		TO 12/13th BN.	DESERTED 25 NOVEMBER 1918.
SCOTT	Andrw	PTE	25	/1283	C	3 BLACKMILL HOUSE ST	SUNDERLAND			1 JULY 1916		THIEPVAL MEM		MISSING OCTOBER 16.
SCOTT	Ebezr	PTE	25	/1436	D	41 GLANTON STREET	BYKER			3 OCT 1918		PROSPECT HILL CEM GOUY	TO ROYAL INNISKILLING FUSILIERS(6th BN).	R INNIS F No 21590.
SCOTT	G W	PTE	25	/1270	D								TO CLASS Z RESERVE.	CPL.
SCOTT	JohnW	PTE	25	/598	A		BLAYDON			1 JULY 1916		THIEPVAL MEM		MISSING OCTOBER 16, BORN TRIMDON.
SCOTT	Tom R	PTE	25	/625	D		GATESHEAD			1 JULY 1916		THIEPVAL MEM	TO 24th BN.	MISSING AUGUST 16.
SCULLY	T	PTE	25	/1280	C								TO 14th, 9th BNS, CLASS Z RESERVE.	
SEDGEWICK	J	PTE	25	/1268	C	2 DOBSONS BUILDINGS	SPENNYMOOR				SEPTEMBER 16			3CCS 2/7/16 EVAC 3/7/16.

						TOWN_VILL				WOUNDED	BURIED	TRANSFER	ADD
SEWELL	J H A	PTE	25 /1480	C									
SEYMOUR	Henry	LCPL	25 /621	B	14 ALGERNON TERR	NEWBURN	12/11/14			JANUARY 17.		TO 10th, 9th BNS, CLASS Z RESERVE.	
SHARKEY	Geo	PTE	25 /1265	D	44 FULLERTON PLACE	GATESHEAD						TO 26th BN.	
SHARKEY	J	PTE	25 /1449	D		CONSETT	13/7/15	8/11/16	GUNSHOT WOUNDS	NOVEMBER 16		TO DEPOT.	
SHEPHERD	J	PTE	25 /1296	B								TO CLASS Z RESERVE.	
SHIELDS	J	PTE	25 /620	B		BLYTH			KR para 392	AUGUST 16			
SHIPLEY	J R	PTE	25 /1465	C									
SHOTTON	R	PTE	25 /1459	D	18 DOBSON STREET	BLACKHILL	20/7/15						
SIMPSON	H	PTE	25 /1271	D	3 WALKER ST LOW TEAM	GATESHEAD	14/11/14	22/12/17	GUNSHOT WOUNDS	NOVEMBER 16		TO DEPOT.	ALSO ON B COY 30th BN ROLL.
SIMPSON	J	PTE	25 /624	B		WARDLEY	21/11/14	12/9/17	GUNSHOT WOUNDS	JULY 16		TO 85th TRAINING RESERVE BN.	3 CCS 2/7/16 EVAC 2/7/16.
SIMPSON	J	PTE	25 /648	D	27 PORTUGAL PLACE	WALLSEND	11/11/14						ALSO ON D COY 30th BN ROLL.
SIMPSON	J H	PTE	25 /1276	D					KR para 392				
SIMPSON	JohnE	PTE	25 /616	A		SUNDERLAND			1 JULY 1916		THIEPVAL MEM		MISSING OCTOBER 16.
SKIDMORE	A	PTE	25 /633				18/11/14	27/4/15	OLD AGE, AGE 57				DID NOT SERVE OVERSEAS.
SKIRVING	J	PTE	25 /1515	C		BYKER				JULY 16		TO 20th, 10th BNS, CLASS Z RESERVE.	SEE 25/1264 BROTHER.
SKIRVING	Math	PTE	25 /1264	A	31 BOTHAL ST	BYKER				SEPTEMBER 16, JUNE 18.		TO 26th, 18th, 8th, CLASS Z RESERVE.	3 CCS 2/7/16 EVAC 2/7/16, 25/1515 BROTHER.
SLATER	John	PTE	25 /602	A	16 WILKIE ST	NEWCASTLE	16/11/14	24/2/16				TO 30th BN.	ALSO ON B COY 30th BN ROLL, DID NOT SERVE OVERSEAS
SLOAN	Edwd	PTE	25 /618	B	101 PALMERSTON ST	SOUTH SHIELDS	14/11/14	23/9/16	SICK			TO 30th BN.	
SLOAN	J H	PTE	25 /1275	C		SOUTH SHIELDS	15/11/14	8/11/16	WOUNDS	JUNE 16		TO DEPOT.	LCPL.
SLOAN	L H	PTE	25 /1288	D	2 CROW ST	SUNDERLAND							
SLOWTHER	A	PTE	25 /631	B									
SLOWTHER	Tom G	PTE	25 /607	B	35 RAVENSIDE TERR	CHOPWELL			1 JULY 1916		WARLOY		BORN GATESHEAD.
SMAILES	Robt	PTE	25 /1281	A	65 BRIGHTON RD	GATESHEAD							
SMITH	A	CPL	25 /643	A		BYKER	18/11/14	28/9/18	GUNSHOT WOUNDS	JULY 16		TO ARMY RESERVE CLASS P.	3 CCS 2/7/16 EVAC 2/7/16.
SMITH	Andrw	PTE	25 /1266	C		SOUTH SHIELDS			1 JULY 1916		THIEPVAL MEM		MISSING OCTOBER 16.
SMITH	Bernd	PTE	25 /1269	B	41 WOLESLEY ST TEAMS	GATESHEAD			1 JULY 1916		THIEPVAL MEM		SMITH Wm IN AVL 43751 PTE 1/4th LONDON REGT
SMITH	E	PTE	25 /1287	C		DARLINGTON				OCTOBER 16, DECEMBER 17.			
SMITH	G	PTE	25 /627	B		WASHINGTON STAT				JULY 16, SEPTEMBER 16			3 CCS 2/7/16 EVAC 3/7/16.
SMITH	H	PTE	25 /1501	A									
SMITH	J	PTE	25 /1282	C								TO 19th, 1st BNS, CLASS Z RESERVE.	
SMITH	J	PTE	25 /1460	D									ALSO ON B COY 30th BN ROLL.
SMITH	J	PTE	25 /1474	B	47 GERALD ST	WALLSEND	13/7/15	[illegible]/3/19	KR para 392	SEPTEMBER 16, JUNE 18.		TO 8th, 10th BNS, ARMY RESERVE CLASS P.	
SMITH	J C	PTE	25 /647	C								TO CLASS Z RESERVE.	
SMITH	R	PTE	25 /1451	D		NEWCASTLE				JANUARY 17		TO CLASS Z RESERVE.	
SMITH	R J	PTE	25 /603	C									ALSO ON D COY 30th BN ROLL.
SMITH	Rob	PTE	25 /1471	B		CHESTER LE ST			1 JULY 1916		THIEPVAL MEM		
SMITH	T	PTE	25 /600	B		TANTOBIE	16/11/14	10/12/17	GUNSHOT WOUNDS	OCTOBER 16		TO 12th BN, DEPOT.	
SMITH	T D	PTE	25 /632	B			18/11/14	28/8/17	SICK			TO DEPOT.	
SMITH	Thos	LCPL	25 /623	A	17 WOODBINE TERR	NEW KYO	26/11/14		1 JULY 1916		THIEPVAL MEM		MISSING OCTOBER 16, BORN STANLEY.
SMITH	Wm	PTE	25 /637	B	78 PEARETH ST	GATESHEAD			1 JULY 1916		THIEPVAL MEM		MISSING OCTOBER 16, BORN 8/2/1876, MAR 31 DEC 1900
SNELL	F W	RQMS	25 /1422	A								COMMISSIONED.	
SNELL	Thos	PTE	25 /634	B	39 WINDSOR ST GRANGE	SUNDERLAND	19/11/14					TO 30th BN(D COY).	MINER DESERTED 4/4/15 AGE 33, 5'6''.COURT SUNDLD 1
SOUGHAM	Nich	PTE	25 /1267	C	C/o J WHITE HILL TOP	DIPTON	6/11/14			NOVEMBER 16		TO ROYAL DEFENCE CORPS.	IN FRANCE 11/1/16 TO 6/9/16.
SOWERBY	P	LCPL	25 /1541									COMMISSIONED.	
SOWERBY	Ralph	PTE	25 /614	A	75 CATHERINE AVE	DUNSTON				JULY 16			34 CCS 2/7/16 EVAC 5/7/16, WND L HAND, AGE 40.
SPALDING	E	PTE	25 /641	D	51 KITCHENER TERR	WALLSEND							ALSO ON D COY 30th BN ROLL.
SPARKES	J	PTE	25 /1294	D			23/11/14	11/1/19	SICK			TO DEPOT.	AGE 24.
SPENCE	H	PTE	25 /619	D	162 PARKER ST	NEWCASTLE				JUNE 16,DEC 17, NOV 18.		TO LABOUR CORPS(119 LAB COY).	
SPENCE	J	PTE	25 /1285	D									
SPENCER	Tom	PTE	25 /599	B	36 HOWARD ST	NEWCASTLE			12 APRIL 1916	APRIL 16	BOULOGNE		
SPRAGGON	W	PTE	25 /626	B	14 HARDWICK ST	SUNDERLAND						ATTACHED 103 MG COY, ROYAL FUSILIERS(24th BN).	FRANCE 25 TO 22/2/17 103 MGC 23/2/17 TO 30/8/18
STAFFORD	P G	PTE	25 /1499	A			29/7/15	28/9/18	GUNSHOT WOUNDS	12 FEBRUARY 16		TO 27th, 24/27th, 9th BNS.	
STAFFORD	Wm	SGT	25 /596	B	3 VANE TERR	SUNDERLAND			1 JULY 1916		THIEPVAL MEM		MISSING ON 1 JULY, BORN BARROW IN FURNESS.
STALLARD	Rob H	PTE	25 /611	B	23 REID ST	DARLINGTON			1 JULY 1916		CERISSY GAILLY		IN 5 PLATOON.
STARKEY	J	PTE	25 /630									TO 1st GARRISON BN, CLASS Z RESERVE.	
STEELE	F R	LCPL	25 /1537				21/10/15	25/1/18	WOUNDS			TO DEPOT.	
STEPHENSON	D	PTE	25 /622	D	8 WATERLOO VALE LANE	SOUTH SHIELDS							ALSO D COY 30th BN ROLL.
STEPHENSON	P	SGT	25 /640	A									

NAME	INITI	RANK	BA	NUMBE	COMP	ADDRESS	TOWN_VILL	ENLISTED	DISCHARG	CAUSE_DIS	WOUNDED	BURIED	TRANSFER	ADD
STEPHENSON	Rob	PTE	25	/1295	C	5 WATER LANE	DURHAM CITY	26/11/14		26 OCT 1917		TYNE COT MEM	TO 19th BN,ATTACHED 185 TUN COY RE, 1/5th BN.	FATHER KILLED WITH 26th BN.
STEPHENSON	W	PTE	25	/1277	B		DUNSTON	16/11/14			JULY 16		TO 30th(D COY), 24th, 1st, 16th BNS.	WAGGON GREASER DESERTED 19/4/15 AGE 20, 5'4''.
STEVENS	T W	RSM	25	/1421	C								COMMISSIONED.	
STEWART	Alf	PTE	25	/1457	D		DARLINGTON			1 JULY 1916		THIEPVAL MEM		
STEWART	C	PTE	25	/652	A						APRIL 16			
STEWART	Geo	PTE	25	/609	D	68 ATHOL ST	NEWCASTLE	11/11/14	13/1/19	GUNSHOT WOUNDS	AUGUST 16, DECEMBER 17.		TO 16th, 1/4th, 3rd BNS.	30 RAILWAY ST ELSWICK 1914, AGE 38.
STEWART	John	PTE	25	/605	B	9 JAMES STREET	STOCKTON ON TEE			2 OCTOBER 1916		PLOEGSTEERT MEM		KILLED WHILST ON PATROL IN NO MANS LAND. AGE 27.
STEWART	Jos	PTE	25	/1289	C	11 HOLY ISLAND	HEXAM			26 OCT 1917	OCTOBER 16	TYNE COT MEM	TO 1st, 14th, 1/7th BNS.	
STEWART	W	PTE	25	/638	D	21 THIRD ST NORTH	EASINGTON	11/11/14						ON D COY 30th BN ROLL AS /630.
STEWART	W	PTE	25	/1526	D		NORTH SHIELDS			17 FEB 1916		ERQUINGHEM - LYS CEM		LCPL,ACCIDENTLY KILLED.
STOREY	A	PTE	25	/608	D	38 DOLPHIN ST	BENWELL			KR para 392	AUGUST 16			
STOUT	H	PTE	25	/615	B		DURHAM CITY				DECEMBER 16		TO CLASS Z RESERVE.	
STRIBLING	H	PTE	25	/644	D									
STRIKE	W J	PTE	25	/1371	C		HIRST	21/11/14	8/3/17	SICK			TO DEPOT.	MISSING OCTOBER 16,BELIEVED DEAD DECEMBER 16.
SUMMERS	Jos	PTE	25	/639	D		GATESHEAD			22 MAY 1916		BECOURT MIL CEM		
SUMMERVILLE	J	PTE	25	/636	B	2 LARCH ST	NEWCASTLE	19/11/14	1/4/19	KR para 392	JULY 16, JUNE 18.		TO 12th BN, ATTACHED 257 TUN COY RE,3rd BN, ARMY R	LOW FELL IN 1916.
SUMMERVILLE	Wm	PTE	25	/1417	D	3 TURRET PLACE	BLAYDON						TO 30th BN(D COY).	CPL,HOSP BIRMINGHAM WND ARM.
SUTTON	Geo R	LCPL	25	/612	B	16 ROCKLIFFE RD	LINTHORPE			1 JULY 1916		THIEPVAL MEM		BORN INGLETON.
SWADDLE	Geo	PTE	25	/597	D		DUNSTON			1 JULY 1916		THIEPVAL MEM		IN 16 PLATOON, MISSING 1 JULY.
SWALLOW	Hnry	CPL	25	/1292	C	16 SIMPSON ST	STANLEY	26/11/14					COMMISSIONED, Lt NF.	SGT.
SWEENEY	F	PTE	25	/1284	D		NEWCASTLE	19/11/14	20/9/16	WOUNDS	SEPTEMBER 16		TO DEPOT.	
SWEENEY	Normn	PTE	25	/1273	D		GATESHEAD							AWOL 29/7/15, 13/9/15 IN COURT GATESHEAD, AGE 17.
SWEENEY	Tom	PTE	25	/610	B	27 ARNOLD ST	BOLDON COLLIERY			1 JULY 1916		THIEPVAL MEM		MISSING OCTOBER 16. IN 7 PLATOON, BORN WARDLEY.
SWEENEY	Wm	PTE	25	/1274	C	4 BLAST ROW	WASHINGTON	10/11/14					TO CLASS Z RESERVE.	LCPL.
SWIFT	P	PTE	25	/635	B		SHOTTON COLLIER	20/11/14	13/3/18	GUNSHOT WOUNDS	OCTOBER 16		TO DEPOT.	3 CCS 2/7/16 EVAC 2/7/16
TAIT	John	PTE	25	/661		17 THE SIDE	NEWCASTLE	18/11/14	16/4/16	SICK			TO 1st GARRISON BN, DEPOT.	
TALBOT	Pat	PTE	25	/673	A	CURRYS SQUARE	DIPTON	28/10/14			DECEMBER 16		TO LABOUR CORPS.	
TAQUE	J	PTE	25	/1307	C	63 KING ST	WHITTON PARK						TO 12/13th BN, CLASS Z RESERVE.	
TAYLOR	Hubrt	PTE	25	/1299	C	26 HENRY ST	SUNDERLAND			28 OCT 1917	DECEMBER 16	TYNE COT MEM	TO 12th, 12/13th BN(C COY).	
TAYLOR	R	PTE	25	/1438	D	24 JAMES ST	JARROW	12/7/15	24/2/16	SICK			TO 30th BN.(B COY)	DID NOT SERVE OVERSEAS.
TAYLOR	R R	PTE	25	/667	B	1 BESTS YARD	WITTON GILBERT	23/11/14	28/10/18				TO 30th BN(D COY),ROYAL ENGINEERS, NORTHUMBERLAND	1914/15 STAR.
TEASDALE	R	PTE	25	/678	B	2 CROSS ST	LITTLETOWN	17/11/14	25/10/17	WOUNDS	OCTOBER 16		TO DEPOT.	51 LONG ROW, 1916
TELFORD	J	RQMS	25	/676	A			18/11/14	5/12/17	SICK			TO DEPOT.	
THOM	J M	PTE	25	/1319	D	44 LYON ST	HEBBURN			1 MAY 1917		ETAPLES		AGE 19.
THOMAS	H	PTE	25	/665	B	19 MITCHELL ST	SOUTHMOOR							
THOMAS	J W	SGT	25	/670	A									
THOMAS	W H	PTE	25	/1306	C	10 PERCY AVENUE	CATCHGATE			KR para 392				17 PERCY AVE 1918.
THOMPSON	J	PTE	25	/659	D 30		NEWCASTLE				JUNE 16			
THOMPSON	J	PTE	25	/662	A									
THOMPSON	J W	PTE	25	/675	A	45 CLARENCE ST	SHIELDFIELD	18/11/14	4/8/17	SICK	OCTOBER 16		TO 85th TRAINING RESERVE BN.	
THOMPSON	Jas	PTE	25		B									AWOL 18/5, 8/9/15 COURT S SHIELDS. POS /659?
THOMPSON	Jas B	PTE	25	/654	B	74 DENMARK ST	SOUTH SHIELDS	10/11/14	5/2/19		MARCH 16		TO 25th, 8th, 25th BNS, 2/4 BN KO YORKSHIRE LI, CL	KOYLI No 63347.
THOMPSON	Thos	PTE	25	/658	B	42 FRONT ST	LINTZ COLLIERY	5/11/14			JUNE 16			
THOMPSON	W	PTE	25	/1304	C									
THORNTON	J	PTE	25	/672	A		ELSWICK	18/11/14	8/10/17	SICK			TO DEPOT.	STOKE WAR HOSP 13/7/16
THUBRON	G	PTE	25	/1317	C		COXHOE POTTERY						TO 12/13th BN.	SEE 24/948 THUBRON T.
THWAITES	W	SGT	25	/683	B		LANCHESTER				NOVEMBER 16		TO ROYAL DEFENCE CORPS.	IN FRANCE 11/1/16 TO 9/7/16.
TINNION	Pat	PTE	25	/1313	C	47 IMEARY ST	SOUTH SHIELDS			1 JULY 1916		THIEPVAL MEM		MISSING OCTOBER 16, BORN WHITEHAVEN, AGE 33.
TOASE	W	LCPL	25	/666	B			23/11/14	18/3/19	KR para 392			TO ARMY RESERVE CLASS P.	
TONER	Frank	PTE	25	/1509	B		BIRTLEY			1 JULY 1916		THIEPVAL MEM		MISSING OCTOBER 16, BORN FELLING.
TONGE	Benj	PTE	25	/669	B									AWOL 29/11/15 IN COURT 4/12/15.
TONGE	Sam	PTE	25	/656	B	42 BENSON RD	BYKER	18/11/14	29/1/16				TO 30th BN(D COY), DEPOT.	DID NOT SERVE OVERSEAS. AWOL 29/11/15 COURT 4/12/1
TONOTHEY	Henry	PTE	25	/1315	A		GATESHEAD			29 MARCH 1916		ERQUINGHEM - LYS CEM		AWOL 10/7/15 IN COURT GATESHEAD AGE 19.
TOOHEY	J	PTE	25	/679	A									ALSO ON B COY 30th BN ROLL.
TOPHAM	Albt	PTE	25	/1305	C		LEEDS			25 JUNE 1917	APRIL 17, DECEMBER 18.	ST SEVER CEM EXT ROUEN	TO 25th, 19th, 16th, 1/4th BNS.	LCPL.
TOWELL	John	PTE	25	/674	B	1/23 BERKLEY ST	JARROW	5/11/14		1 JULY 1916		THIEPVAL MEM		MISSING OCTOBER 16, BORN CARLTON DURHAM ?.
TOWEY	J	PTE	25	/682	B		SOUTH SHIELDS				DECEMBER 16			
TREWICK	Chas	PTE	25	/671	B	36 LORD ST	JARROW	26/11/14			OCTOBER 16		TO 1st BN.	

NAME	INITI	RANK	BA	NUMBE	COMP	ADDRESS	TOWN_VILL	ENLISTED	DISCHARG	CAUSE_DIS	WOUNDED	BURIED	TRANSFER	ADD
TROTTER	J	PTE	25	/1300	C		NEWCASTLE	13/11/14	2/1/18	WOUNDS	SEPTEMBER 16		TO DEPOT.	3 CCS 2/7/16 EVAC 2/7/16.
TROTTER	Jas H	PTE	25	/1316	C	7 GORDON TERR	SHIELDROW	21/11/14	9/3/16				TO 30th BN(D COY).	DID NOT SERVE OVERSEAS.
TUCKER	Frank	PTE	25	/677	B			17/11/14	29/1/16				TO 30th BN.	DID NOT SERVE OVERSEAS. AWOL 16/5/15 COURT 31/5/15
TUCKERMAN	R	PTE	25	/663	B						APRIL 16			
TULLY	Wm	PTE	25	/1290	D	24 19 HENRY ST	STANLEY	12/11/14			OCTOBER 16		TO 1st, 18th, 1/6th, 2nd BNS, CLASS Z RESERVE.	MINER DESERTED 9/4/15 AGE 27, 5'5''.
TUMULTY	Jos M	SGT	25	/681	B	5 DURHAM ST	BRANDON COLLIER	6/11/14		1 JULY 1916		THIEPVAL MEM		MISS OCTOBER 16, BORN SHINCLIFFE. BOER WAR + LSGC.
TURNBULL	Alex	PTE	25	/1303	D	135 ASKEW RD WEST	GATESHEAD	14/11/14						MINER DESERTED 5/3/15 AGE 19, 5'9''.
TURNBULL	C	PTE	25	/660	B	476 PILGRIM ST	NEWCASTLE							AWOL 2/5/15 DRUNK & DISORDERLY MELBOURNE ST 4/5/15
TURNBULL	H	PTE	25	/1302	D			13/11/14	23/10/18	SICK			TO 3rd BN.	DESERTED 1/2/19.
TURNER	J J	PTE	25	/668	B		EASINGTON COLLI				JANUARY 17		TO 8th BN, CLASS Z RESERVE.	
TURNER	John	PTE	25	/664		24 SIMPSON ST CHIRTO	NORTH SHIELDS	26/11/14					TO 1st GARRISON BN, CLASS Z RESERVE.	
TWEDDLE	JohnC	PTE	25	/1320	D	7 ROMULUS ST	GATESHEAD						TO 27th BN, CLASS Z RESERVE.	TAKEN PRISONER OF WAR MAY 1917.BROTHER 18/67.
TWEDDLE	Rol S	PTE	25	/1301	B	30 64 MITCHELL ST	WALKER			24 APRIL 1917		ARRAS MEM	TO 25th BN.	SGT.
TWEMPLETON	Thos	PTE	25	/1312			GATESHEAD	19/11/14						SHOEING SMITH DESERTED 15/1/15 AGE 30, 5'6''.
UNSWORTH	R	PTE	25	/684		10 ALBERT PLACE	SUNDERLAND	12/11/14	2/10/15				TO DEPOT.	DID NOT SERVE OVERSEAS.
URWIN	C	PTE	25	/1321	C		GATESHEAD				AUGUST 16		TO LABOUR CORPS.	3 CCS 2/7/16 EVAC 2/7/16 TO 3rd NTHN HOSP SHEFFIEL
URWIN	R	CPL	25	/686	B	30 3 CURRYS BLDGS	WHITE LE HEAD				OCTOBER 16		TO LABOUR CORPS.	
VALLELY	F H	PTE	25	/1325	D			14/11/14	27/2/18	SICK			TO ARMY RESERVE CLASS P.	
VARTY	J	PTE	25	/1530	D		FELLING				OCTOBER 16.		TO LABOUR CORPS, ROYAL FUSILIERS.	
VAUGHAN	Thos	PTE	25											DESERTER 26/4/15 COURT SUNDERLAND
VEST	Wm	PTE	25	/1323	C	75 NEW ELVET	DURHAM CITY	26/11/14			APRIL 16		TO CLASS Z RESERVE.	LCPL.
WALKER	A	PTE	25	/1360	C	97 FRAMWELLGATE	DURHAM CITY				OCTOBER 16		TO LABOUR CORPS.	
WALKER	E	PTE	25	/691		33 RED ST	NORTH SHIELDS						TO 1st GARRISON BN, 11th, 16th, 1/4th BNS, CLASS Z	
WALKER	John	PTE	25	/734	C	2 STABLE ST	CORNSAY COLLIER	5/11/14		23 OCT 1916		CITE BON JEAN CEM	TO B COY.	BORN KILKENNY, AGE 34.
WALKER	R R	PTE	25	/1355	C	8 HUDSON RD	SUNDERLAND				OCTOBER 16			BEAUFORT WAR HOSP BRISTOL 12/7/16.
WALKER	T	LCPL	25	/709	C	22 LANSDOWN RD	FOREST HALL	16/11/14	9/-/18	WOUNDS	SEPTEMBER 16		TO 85th TRAINING RESERVE BN.	CPL.
WALKER	Tom	CPL	25	/1352	C	12 REID ST SPRINGWEL	GATESHEAD			1 JULY 1916		THIEPVAL MEM		MISSING OCTOBER 16, BORN FATFIELD.
WALLACE	John	PTE	25	/1335				23/11/14	8/10/17	WOUNDS			TO 36th BN.	AGE 39.
WALSH	A	PTE	25	/700	B		DURHAM CITY	12/11/14	20/11/17	SHELLSHOCK	OCTOBER 16		TO 24th, 3rd BNS.	34 CCS 2/7/16 EVAC 5/7/16, WND R ARM, AGE 27.
WALSH	F	PTE	25	/719	D	12 KNIGHT ST	JARROW		24/2/19		OCTOBER 16		TO WEST YORKSHIRE REGT.	
WALSH	J	PTE	25	/1356	C	14 SECOND ST	EASINGTON	11/11/14	22/6/18	SICK			TO DEPOT.	
WALSH	Jos	PTE	25	/1329	C	21 WATSON ST PALLION	SUNDERLAND			6 JULY 1916		ST SEVER CEM ROUEN		2 BROTHERS ALSO SERVED.
WALTERS	G	PTE	25	/708	C		WHICKHAM	14/11/14	30/10/17	GUNSHOT WOUNDS	SEPTEMBER 16		TO 85th TRAINING RESERVE BN.	
WALTON	Hry B	PTE	25	/728	D	WALTON HOUSE	TRIMDON GRANGE			8 MARCH 1917	JUNE 17	FABOURG DE AMIENS CEM ARRAS		AGE 28, KILLED WITH C COY, WYNYARD HOUSE.
WALTON	J	PTE	25	/730	C			21/11/14	17/10/18	WOUNDS			TO LABOUR CORPS, EASTERN COMMAND LAB COY.	AGE 39. LAB CORPS No 397317.
WALTON	J	PTE	25	/731	A								TO 30th BN(D COY).	
WALTON	T	PTE	25	/727	C	GEORGE AND DRAGON	FORTH BANKS			KR para 392			TO LABOUR CORPS.	
WASTEL	J	PTE	25	/696	B									
WATERS	J	PTE	25	/715	C								TO LABOUR CORPS.	
WATERS	J	PTE	25	/1347	D								TO LABOUR CORPS.	
WATERS	M	PTE	25	/721	D									
WATSON	Fred	PTE	25	/1344			EDINBURGH	19/11/14						COOK DESERTED 9/5/15 AGE 32, 5'3''.
WATSON	R	PTE	25	/690	B		SOUTH SHIELDS				S SHOCK DECEMBER 16.		TO DURHAM LI(12th BN).	DLI 45893.
WATSON	Thos	LCPL	25	/1351	C	37 THERESA STREET	BLAYDON			KR para 392	JANUARY 17		ATTACHED KINGS AFRICAN RIFLES.	ACPL 1917, ASGT 1918.
WEATHERITT	J	PTE	25	/1535	D									
WEBB	G	PTE	25	/1345	C	8 OAKEYS COTTAGES	STANLEY	17/11/14	1/4/19	KR para 392			TO ARMY RESERVE CLASS P.	1 ALFRED ST 1918. CPL.
WELCH	J E	PTE	25	/739	D		GATESHEAD				SEPTEMBER 16		TO KINGS OWN YORKSHIRE LI 2/4 BN, CLASS Z RESERVE.	SGT, 3 CCS 2/7/16 EVAC 2/7/16, KOYLI No 63255.
WELDON	Thos	PTE	25	/694	C	18 NORMANBY ST MNKWR	SUNDERLAND	5/11/14			DECEMBER 16			3 CCS 2/7/16 EVAC 2/7/16.
WELDON	Wm	PTE	25	/701	C	37 FRONT ST	EAST STANLEY	12/11/14	14/8/18	GUNSHOT WOUNDS				
WELSH	J	SGT	25	/718	C								TO 11th, 25th, 9th BNS, CLASS Z RESERVE.	
WELSH	J	PTE	25	/1339	D									ALSO ON D COY 30th BN ROLL.
WELSH	Math	PTE	25	/1338			CORK	12/11/14						LABOURER DESERTED 15/1/15 AGE 29, 5'10''.
WENSLEY	R E	PTE	25	/1343	D			19/11/14	19/3/18	SICK			TO ARMY RESERVE CLASS W.	SGT.
WHEATLEY	J	PTE	25	/1444	D	80 ALEXANDER ST	NEWCASTLE	11/11/14						HOSP FRANCE, FEBRUARY 16
WHEATLEY	Wm K	PTE	25	/702	C	9 MILBURNGATE	DURHAM CITY	17/11/14		1922	APRIL 16	KILLED IN PIT ACCIDENT	TO EAST YORKS(12th, 6th BNS).	E YORKS No 36687, HOSP FAVERSHAM 4/16.
WHIEGHTMAN	T	PTE	25	/705	C			14/11/14	28/12/17	SICK			TO 3rd BN.	
WHILES	J C	PTE	25	/729	A								TO 1st BN, CLASS Z RESERVE.	
WHITE	J C	PTE	25	/732	C	2 GERTRUDE ST	HOUGHTON LE SPR	23/11/14	10/2/17	WOUNDS	JULY 16		TO DEPOT.	SGT.

NAME	INITI	RANK	BA	NUMBE	COMP	ADDRESS	TOWN_VILL	ENLISTED	DISCHARG	CAUSE_DIS	WOUNDED	BURIED	TRANSFER	ADD
*WHITE	T	PTE	25	/723	B								TO 30th BN(D COY).	
WHITE	W	PTE	25	/1328	A	17 EDWARD ST	NEWCASTLE				AUGUST 16		TO 8th, 22nd, CLASS Z RESERVE.	34 CCS 2/7/16 EVAC 5/7/16 WND R SIDE FACE.
WHITEMAN	Ern J	PTE	25	/698	B		WEST STANLEY			1 JULY 1916		THIEPVAL MEM		MISSING OCTOBER 16, BORN BISHOP AUKLAND.
WHITEMAN	W	PTE	25	/1353	C	6 BRADLEY TERR	HETTON LYONS						TO CLASS Z RESERVE.	
WHITFIELD	Henry	PTE	25	/695	B	1 POTTS COURT	SOUTH SHIELDS			23 OCT 1917		CEMENT HOUSE CEM, LANGEMARCK		
WHITFIELD	J	PTE	25	/1340	C	5 ELLESMERE ST	SOUTH SHIELDS						TO 12/13th BN, CLASS Z RESERVE.	
WHITTEN	J T	PTE	25	/1331	C									
WHITTON	G R	SGT	25	/692	A		SOUTH SHIELDS	10/11/14	20/3/18	GUNSHOT WOUNDS	SEPTEMBER 16		TO ARMY RESERVE CLASS W.	
WILKINSON	John	CPL	25	/689	B	34 EAST ROW	ISABELLA PIT	6/11/14		1 JULY 1916		THIEPVAL MEM		MISSING OCTOBER 16, BORN BLYTH.
WILKINSON	John	PTE	25	/1332	C	4 NORTH ST	BLAYDON						TO 9th BN, CLASS Z RESERVE.	
WILKINSON	R	PTE	25	/720	C	GILESGATE	DURHAM CITY	12/11/14	28/3/18	GUNSHOT WOUNDS	SEPTEMBER 16		TO 12th BN, DEPOT.	
WILKINSON	Thos	PTE	25	/1521		3 CORN RIGGS	DARLINGTON	5/11/14						
WILKINSON	Wm	PTE	25	/740	C		DURHAM CITY	16/11/14	20/10/17	WOUNDS	SEPTEMBER 16		TO DEPOT.	3 CCS 2/7/16 EVAC 3/7/16, AGE 35.
WILLIAMS	Austn	PTE	25	/1333	C		BLAYDON	23/11/14	28/3/18	GUNSHOT WOUNDS	OCTOBER 16		TO ARMY RESERVE CLASS W.	BEAUFORT WAR HOSP BRISTOL 8/7/16
WILLIAMS	Ernst	SGT	25	/1349	D		NEWCASTLE			1 JULY 1916		THIEPVAL MEM		MISSING OCTOBER 16, BORN CARDIFF.
WILLIAMS	J	PTE	25	/1346	C		JARROW	18/11/14	7/1/19		OCTOBER 16, FEBRUARY 18.		TO 24th, 2nd BNS, DEPOT.	LCPL.
WILLIAMS	J P	LCPL	25	/1372	C	12 WEAR ST	SUNDERLAND						TO CLASS Z RESERVE.	
WILLIAMSON	G	PTE	25	/713	C	9 PITT ST	CONSETT						TO CLASS Z RESERVE.	
WILSON	Colin	PTE	25	/744	D	13 FRAMWELLGATE	DURHAM CITY						TO CLASS Z RESERVE.	53 ARTHUR ST GATESHEAD 1918.
WILSON	D	PTE	25	/706	C		SCOTSWOOD	14/11/14	1/4/17	WOUNDS	OCTOBER 16		TO DEPOT.	
WILSON	Ed	PTE	25	/717	C	35 FRANKLIN ST	SOUTH SHIELDS	26/11/14		KR para 392	JUNE 18			
WILSON	Geo	PTE	25	/712	D	59 PONT ST	ASHINGTON	11/11/14	25/10/17	SICK			TO ARMY RESERVE CLASS W.	
WILSON	J	PTE	25	/704	A									ALSO ON D COY 30th BN ROLL.
WILSON	J	PTE	25	/737	C		GATESHEAD				SEPTEMBER 16			
WILSON	J	LCPL	25	/743	A									
WILSON	J G	PTE	25	/1354	A		NEWCASTLE	14/11/14	1/7/18	SICK	MARCH 17		TO DEPOT.	
WILSON	Peter	PTE	25	/1342	D		GATESHEAD							AWOL 21/7/15 IN COURT GATESHEAD, AGE 49.
WILSON	Tom	PTE	25	/703	C	15 BEAMISH ST	WEST STANLEY			1 JULY 1916		THIEPVAL MEM		BORN CONSETT.
WILSON	W	PTE	25	/711	C	65 GEORGE ST	NEWCASTLE	16/11/14	18/9/18	KR para 392				AWOL 22/5 9/8 26/11/15 IN COURT 31/5 26/8 30/1
WILTON	Wm R	PTE	25	/733	C		BEBSIDE			1 JULY 1916		THIEPVAL MEM		MISSING OCTOBER 16, BORN SOUTH SHIELDS.
WINFIELD	Edwd	PTE	25	/1453	D	8 PIONEER ST	BLAYDON						TO 1st, 12/13th BNS, CLASS Z RESERVE.	
WINTER	Tom	PTE	25	/1359	C	23 JOHN ST	CONSETT	26/11/14		1 JULY 1916		THIEPVAL MEM		MISSING OCTOBER 16, BORN CONSETT.
WIPER	A	PTE	25	/722	A		NEWCASTLE	19/11/14	22/2/18	BRONCHITIS	JANUARY 18		TO DEPOT.	
WOOD	F J	PTE	25	/716	C	COX GREEN	WASHINGTON							CPL.
WOOD	J	PTE	25	/724	D								TO LABOUR CORPS(287 AE COY), ROYAL DEFENCE CORPS.	IN FRANCE 11/1/16 TO 25/9/17, 287 LAB COY 26/9/17
WOOD	W	PTE	25	/707	C		NORTH SHIELDS				SEPTEMBER 16			
WOOD	W H	PTE	25	/710	D		NEWCASTLE				JUNE 16			AWOL 12/4, 11/7, 19/7, 22/8/15.COURT 19/4, 14/7, 2
WRIGHT	G W	LCPL	25	/725	D	37 WALWORTH RD	SUNDERLAND	20/11/14	13/8/18	SICK	JANUARY 17		TO DEPOT.	ACPL.
WRIGHT	J	PTE	25	/1327	C			17/11/14	17/5/16				TO 30th BN(D COY).	DID NOT SERVE OVERSEAS.
WRIGHT	Math	PTE	25	/1330	D		BYKER			27 MAY 1918	OCTOBER 16	LA VILLE-HAUX-BOIS BRIT CEM	TO 8th, 16th, 1/5th BNS.	
WRIGHT	Wm	PTE	25	/1357	D	24 LIME ST	NEWCASTLE	5/11/14		KR para 392	JULY 16		TO 16th, 20th, 2nd BNS.	LIVING 49 SANDHILL NEWCASTLE 1914.
YOUNG	C	PTE	25	/746	D								TO 30th BN(D COY).	
YOUNG	Mark	PTE	25	/1362	C	BARKER ST MERRINGTON	SPENNYMOOR	14/11/14	31/3/19	KR para 392			TO DEPOT.	PHOTO IN CC 6/4/16
YOUNG	W	PTE	25	/745	D									AWOL 21/6/15 8/8/15 IN COURT 12/7/15 10/8/15.

James Bacon and Sons.]

[*To face page* 169.

THE SERGEANTS' MESS, 2nd Batt. Tyneside Irish Brigade. [25 (S) Batt. N.F.].

1. Sgt. Healey, J.
2. ,, Bain, R.
3. ,, Foster, R.
4. ,, Marr, J.
5. ,, Abbot, J.
6. ,, Stevenson, J.
7. ,, Armstrong, J.
8. Sgt. Stafford, W.
9. ,, Noble, C.
10. ,, Tailor.
11. ,, Quirk, M.
12. ,, Welsh, J.
13. ,, Bell, J.
14. ,, Johnson, C.
15. Sgt. Williams, E.
16. ,, Atkinson, J.
17. ,, Lynn, W.
18. ,, Wallace, J.
19. ,, McAllister, C.
20. ,, Peniluna, T.
21. ,, Lewis, R.
22. Sgt. McTeer, A.
23. ,, McVay, P.
24. ,, Day, J.
25. ,, Murray, M.
26. ,, Pickard, G.
27. ,, Campbell, J.
28. ,, Walton, R.
29. Sgt. Madden, J.
30. ,, Rae, W.
31. ,, Blythe, J.
32. ,, O'Leary, W. P.
33. C.Q.M.S. Doran, C.
34. ,, McKenna, C.
35. Staff Instr. Murrell, J.
36. C.S.M. McAndrews, J.L.
37. ,, Nichalls, C.
38. ,, Bishop, F.
39. ,, Gibbons, T.
40. C.Q.M.S. Telford J.
41. ,, Pearson, J.
42. ,, Charlton, R.
43. Sgt. Whitton, R.

Appendix V

ALHABETICAL NOMINAL ROLL
OTHER RANKS
26th NORTHUMBERLAND FUSILIERS
3rd TYNESIDE IRISH

HIGHEST BATTALION NUMBER TRACED 26/1489
NUMBER ON ROLL **1163**
UNTRACED **326**
KILLED OR DIED OF WOUNDS **285**
WOUNDED **456**
DISCHARGED SICK, GASSED, TRENCH FOOT.
DEAFNESS, KR para 392 ETC **276**
TOTAL KNOWN CASUALTIES **1017**
CASUALTIES AS A % OF THOSE TRACED
87.4%

NAME	INITI	RANK	BATTA	NUMBE	COMP	ADDRESS	TOWN_VILL	ENLISTED	DISCHARG	CAUSE_DIS	WOUNDED	BURIED	TRANSFER	ADD
ABBOTT	J	PTE	26	/1340	B		FENCEHOUSES	15/12/14	11/5/17		JULY 16, SEPTEMBER 16.		TO DURHAM LI(12th BN).	DLI No 45897.
ADAMS	H	PTE	26	/1	A						APRIL 16		TO ARMY SERVICE CORPS.	
ADAMS	J	PTE	26	/2	D30			28/11/14	17/6/16	SICK			TO 30th BN.	
ADAMSON	Math	PTE	26	/22	A	13 BEECH ST	COWPEN			10 MAY 1918	JUNE 17	HINGES MIL CEM	TO 1st BN.	BORN HINDERWELL YORKS.
ADDISON	Edwd	PTE	26	/15	A		RAINTON			1 JULY 1916	APRIL 16	THIEPVAL MEM		
AGNEW	P	PTE	26	/1337	B		BLACKSHAW ?	19/12/14	28/3/18	GUNSHOT WOUNDS	JUNE 16, JULY 16		TO ARMY RESERVE CLASS P.	
ALCOCK	Edwd	PTE	26	/16	A	11 ORMOND ST	SOUTH SHIELDS	3/12/14	3/7/19		OCTOBER 16, JUNE 17.		TO 25th, 1/4th BNS, YORK AND LANCASTER REGT(5th BN	ACPL.
ALDERSON	Chris	PTE	26	/17	B	13 GARDINER CRES	PELTON FELL			1 JULY 1916		THIEPVAL MEM		BORN TOPCLIFFE YORKS.
ALDERSON	J	PTE	26	/1338	C	22 GEORGE ST	SHILDON							ALSO ON D COY 30th BN ROLL.
ALEXANDER	B	PTE	26	/30	D	104 SOMERSET ST	GATESHEAD							ALSO ON C COY 30th BN.
ALLEN	C	PTE	26	/23	A			9/12/14	10/12/17	BRONCHITIS			TO DEPOT.	
ALLEN	Ed	PTE	26	/3	A	4 SPENCERS BLDGS	RYTON	26/11/14					TO LABOUR CORPS.	
ALLEN	P	PTE	26	/753	A		NEWCASTLE				SEPTEMBER 16			DESERTED 17/7 CT 23/8/15,AWOL 30/11/15 CT 6/12/15.
ALLISON	Thos	PTE	26	/12		13 ALDIN GRANGE	DURHAM CITY	10/12/14		23 JUNE 1918		DUEVILLE MIL CEM ITALY	ATTACHED 34th DIV HEADQUARTERS, TO 10th BN.	BORN THORNABY.
ALSOP	R W	RQMS	26	/1483	A								TO MACHINE GUN CORPS.	
AMOS	W T	PTE	26	/1474	C		NORTH SHIELDS	4/7/15	30/6/17	GUNSHOT WOUNDS	JULY 16		TO DEPOT.	
ANDERSON	M	PTE	26	/1466	A									
ANDERSON	Ralph	PTE	26	/1334	B	16 SMITH ST	WHEATLEY HILL			20 SEPT 1917	AUGUST 16, OCTOBER 16.	DICKEBUSH	TO 1st, 14th BNS.	BORN KELLOE.
APPLEGATE	G W E	PTE	26	/4	A	7 JOHN ST	CONSETT	25/11/14	23/4/16	VDH, 14/3/1921		BENFIELDSIDE	TO 30th BN(D COY).	DID NOT SERVE OVERSEAS., AGE 44.
ARCHER	W	PTE	26	/761	D	58 PARKINSON ST	FELLING						TO LABOUR CORPS.	LAB CORPS No 119594.
ARMSTRONG	F	PTE	26	/5	D30			25/11/14	17/5/16				TO 30th BN.	DID NOT SERVE OVERSEAS.
ARMSTRONG	G	LCPL	26	/28	B								TO LABOUR CORPS.	SGT.
ARMSTRONG	J T	PTE	26	/21	A		WEST STANLEY				NOVEMBER 16 SHELLSHOCK			
ARMSTRONG	Jas	PTE	26	/11	D		WASHINGTON			1 JULY 1916		THIEPVAL MEM		MISSING OCTOBER 16, BORN USWORTH.
ARMSTRONG	John	PTE	26	/6	B	171 HARRIET ST	BYKER			1 JULY 1916		THIEPVAL MEM		BORN BEDLINGTON.
ARMSTRONG	John	PTE	26	/754	D		GATESHEAD				JANUARY 17, JUNE 17.			AWOL 2/9/15 IN COURT GATESHEAD, AGE 17.
ARMSTRONG	L	PTE	26	/7	A		GATESHEAD	27/11/14	24/10/16	WOUNDS	OCTOBER 16		TO DEPOT.	BEAUFORT WAR HOSP BRISTOL 8/7/16.
ARMSTRONG	M	PTE	26	/755				25/11/14	23/4/15	INNEFFICIENT			TO DEPOT.	DID NOT SERVE OVERSEAS.
ARTHUR	C C	PTE	26	/8		6 ALNWICK ST	NEWBURN						TO 1st GARRISON BN, CLASS Z RESERVE.	
ASHTON	J	PTE	26	/1339	D	56 BK WELLINGTON ST	FELLING	19/12/14	23/6/16	VDH				
ASHURST	J	PTE	26	/20	B		WINGATE				JULY 16			
ASKEW	GeoWm	PTE	26	/766	D	12 CHAPEL ROW	TANTOBIE			1 JULY 1916		THIEPVAL MEM		MISSING OCTOBER 16, BORN SOUTH SHIELDS.
ATCHISON	R E P	SGT	26	/26	A	6 HARTLEY ST	SUNDERLAND	10/12/14	25/4/17	WOUNDS	JULY 16		TO DEPOT.	3 CCS 2/7/16 EVAC 3/7/16 TO HOSP LONDON 7/16.
ATKINSON	Archi	PTE	26	/762	A	21 MADRAS ST	SOUTH SHIELDS	10/12/14			APRIL 18		TO 1st, 12/13th BNS, CLASS Z RESERVE.	
ATKINSON	Edwd	PTE	26	/9	A	73 HAWICK CRES	NEWCASTLE			1 JULY 1916	OCTOBER 16	THIEPVAL MEM		
ATKINSON	J	PTE	26	/759	B	15 GROSVENOR ST	GATESHEAD				JANUARY 18		TO 11th, 20th, 22nd, 12/13th BNS, CLASS Z RESERVE.	25 ALBERT ST 1914.
ATKINSON	J	PTE	26	/1402	C									
ATKINSON	Rich	PTE	26	/25	A		USWORTH				NOVEMBER 16 SHELLSHOCK		TO ARMY SERVICE CORPS.	3 CCS 2/7/16 EVAC 2/7/16, ASC No M/354186.
ATKINSON	ThosF	PTE	26	/10	D	12 NOEL TERR	STANLEY	2/12/14	19/10/18	SICK			TO ARMY RESERVE CLASS W.	
BAGLEY	Wm	LCPL	26	/87	C	MARSDENS BLDGS	NEW SEAHAM			1 JULY 1916		THIEPVAL MEM		MISSING OCTOBER 16, BORN EASINGTON LANE.
BAILEY	G W	LCPL	26	/768	D	47b WESLEY TERR	FELLING			24 NOV 1918	SEPTEMBER 16	CAUDRY BRIT CEM	TO 1st, 14th(D COY) BNS.	AGE 24.
BAILEY	John	PTE	26	/69	B	69 QUEEN ST	NORTH SHIELDS			1 JULY 1916	OCTOBER 16	THIEPVAL MEM		MISSING DECEMBER 16, BORN WEST STANLEY.
BAINBRIDGE	R	PTE	26	/1462				16/6/15	20/6/16	SICK			TO 1st GARRISON BN, 3rd BN.	
BAINBRIDGE	Wm	PTE	26	/58		21 CROSSGATE	DURHAM CITY	10/12/14					TO 2nd GARRISON BN, CLASS Z RESERVE.	QUEENS HEAD YARD DURHAM 1918.
BAKER	J	PTE	26	/31	A	3 HIGH FRIARSIDE	BURNHOPEFIELD	28/11/14	17/6/16	KR para 392			TO 30th BN(D COY).	DID NOT SERVE OVERSEAS.
BAKER	Wm	PTE	26	/66	C	27 FRAMWELLGATE	DURHAM CITY	1/12/14	12/9/17	GUNSHOT WOUNDS	SEPTEMBER 16		TO 3rd BN.	
BALL	JohnW	PTE	26	/32	C	1 SMITHS YARD	PONTOP	26/11/14			OCTOBER 16, JANUARY 18.		TO 20th, 21st BNS, ROYAL DEFENCE CORPS.	3rd SCOTTISH GEN HOSP GLASGOW 11/7/16, CPL
BALMFORTH	Sam	PTE	26	/57	C	2 QUEEN ST	SACRISTON	9/12/14		23 MARCH 1918		GREVEVILLIERS MIL CEM	TO LABOUR CORPS(198 LAB COY).	BORN NORMANTON, LABOUR CORPS No 118358.
BARF	E R	SGT	26	/1432	A								TO CLASS Z RESERVE.	AWOII.
BARFIELD	J W	PTE	26	/33	D	35 NEW ELVET	DURHAM CITY	28/11/14						NEW NUMBER 1843671.
BARKAS	E	PTE	26	/34	C		NEWCASTLE				OCTOBER 16		TO 9th, 23rd, 9th BNS, CLASS Z RESERVE.	
BARKER	T	PTE	26	/798	D	4 SIXTH ST	EASINGTON	10/12/14	31/3/19	KR para 392	OCTOBER 16, NOT WND DEC.		TO 25th BN, ARMY RESERVE CLASS P.	
BARNES	Frd H	PTE	26	/78	B	9 SHERBURN RD	DURHAM CITY	7/12/14	16/8/17	WOUNDS	OCTOBER 16		TO DEPOT.	
BARNES	G	PTE	26	/800	C	CHURCH STREET	BLAYDON				OCTOBER 16		TO ROYAL DEFENCE CORPS.	
BARNES	Robt	PTE	26	/792		4 SMITH ST	WINGATE						TO 11th BN.	
BARNES	W	PTE	26	/84				15/12/14	8/3/15	INNEFFICIENT			TO DEPOT.	DID NOT SERVE OVERSEAS, AGE 41.
BARRASS	D	PTE	26	/76	B		WASHINGTON STAT	3/12/14	14/12/17	WOUNDS	OCTOBER 16		TO 3rd BN.	
BARRETT	Peter	LCPL	26	/92	C	11 HOLLINS TERR	CHOPWELL	5/11/14	3/4/19	KR para 392	AUGUST 16, NOVEMBER 18.		TO 21st, 26th, 19th, 2nd, 3rd BNS.	CPL, HOSP WIGAN 20/7/16-18/9/16.
BARROW	JohnC	PTE	26	/791	B	54 WATERWORKS RD	SUNDERLAND			1 JULY 1916	OCTOBER 16.	THIEPVAL MEM		MISSING OCTOBER 16, BORN SUNDERLAND.
BATES	G	PTE	26	/67	D		NEWCASTLE	1/12/14	28/6/17	GUNSHOT WOUNDS	AUGUST 16		TO DEPOT.	

NAME	INITI	RANK	BATTA	NUMBE	COMP	ADDRESS	TOWN_VILL	ENLISTED	DISCHARG	CAUSE_DIS	WOUNDED	BURIED	TRANSFER	ADD
BATEY	A A	PTE	26	/53	B	18 AGNES ST	SOUTH SHIELDS			KR para 392				
BATEY	R	PTE	26	/65	C		GATESHEAD				SEPTEMBER 16		TO ROYAL ENGINEERS.	
BATIE	Wm C	PTE	26	/769	A		GATESHEAD			17 OCT 1918		BEAULENCOURT MIL CEM	TO 20th, 25th, 17th, 12/13th BNS.	CPL.
BAYLIE	Wm Js	SGT	26	/35	C	7 CHARLES ST	GATESHEAD	29/10/14					TO 30th BN(D COY), NORFOLK REGT(12th BN).	AWOL 11/8/15 COURT GATESHEAD AGE 30.
BECK	Wm	LCPL	26	/62	C		SOUTHMOOR			20 APRIL 1918	JULY 16, JUNE 17.	PLOEGSTEERT MEM	TO 23rd BN.	SGT ON MR, BORN SEATON DELAVAL.
BELL	A	PTE	26	/1343	B	10 PUMP ROW	USWORTH				SEPTEMBER 16		TO SOUTH LANCASHIRE REGT.	HOSP FISHPONDS BRISTOL 7/16.
BELL	F	PTE	26	/46	C	119 ASTLEY RD	SEATON DELAVAL				AUGUST 16		TO 8th, 16th, 1/5th BNS, CLASS Z RESERVE.	SGT.
BELL	G	PTE	26	/45	A		GATESHEAD				AUGUST 16		TO LABOUR CORPS.	3 CCS 2/7/16 EVAC 2/7/16 GSW.
BELL	J G	PTE	26	/771	D	14 SARAH STREET	GATESHEAD						TO 25th, 9th BNS, CLASS Z RESERVE.	
BELL	Jhn H	PTE	26	/47	A		BISHOP AUKLAND			8 DEC 1916		BOULOGNE		ACPL.
BELL	W D	PTE	26	/794	D		NEWCASTLE				OCTOBER 16, MARCH 18.		TO 10th, 8th BNS.	LCPL, DESERTED 2 JUNE 1918.
BENDELOW	JohnR	PTE	26	/37	C	12 LOW POTTERY YARD	NEWBOTTLE	24/11/14	3/5/18	GUNSHOT WOUNDS	JUNE 17		TO 30th BN(D COY), 3rd BN.	
BENNET	W	PTE	26	/63									TO 1st GARRISON BN, CLASS Z RESERVE.	
BENNETT	John	PTE	26	/797	D	PEARSONS BLDGS DRINK	DARLINGTON			2 MARCH 1916		ERQUINGHEM - LYS CHYD EXT		PHOTO EVEN DESP 6/4/16
BENTLEY	Jas	PTE	26	/93	B	16 ELEVENTH ST SOUTH	EASINGTON COLLI			23 JULY 1916	AUGUST 16	EASINGTON		WND FOOT,HOSP SUNDERLAND,BATMAN CAPTAIN MULLALLY.
BERRY	W	PTE	26	/38	C	3 STONE ROW TEAMS	GATESHEAD	25/11/14	11/10/17	SICK			TO 3rd BN.	
BEST	J	PTE	26	/1434	A		DUNSTON	25/5/15	19/3/18	GUNSHOT WOUNDS	OCTOBER 16		TO ARMY RESERVE CLASS W.	
BEWICKE	Thos	RQMS	26	/64	C								TO KINGS LIVERPOOL REGT.	KINGS REGT No 90970.
BIRD	W	PTE	26	/785	C	30 FRAMWELLGATE	DURHAM CITY				JULY 16		TO ROYAL ARMY MEDICAL CORPS.	VOLUTARY AID HOSP CHELTENHAM 11/7/16.
BIRTLE	W	PTE	26	/68	C		CROOK			GUNSHOT WOUNDS	OCTOBER 16			34CCS 2/7 EVAC 21 AT, 18 G HOSP 6/7 SHIP 11/7/16
BLACKBURN	Thos	PTE	26	/54	B		NEW SEATON			1 JULY 1916	OCTOBER 16	THIEPVAL MEM		BORN ASHINGTON
BLAGDON	Thos	PTE	26	/784	D	40 MILBURNGATE	DURHAM CITY				OCTOBER 16		TO LABOUR CORPS(487 LAB COY).	LAB CORPS No 502901.
BLAIR	Robt	PTE	26	/1345	B		GLASGOW			1 JULY 1916		THIEPVAL MEM		LCPL.
BLAKEY	J E	CPL	26	/72	A		NEWCASTLE				SEPTEMBER 16			
BLEWITT	J	PTE	26	/1440	A		SHIREMOOR				JANUARY 17		TO LABOUR CORPS.	
BLIGH	John	PTE	26	/799	D	JOHNSONS LDG HSE S S	KILMER CO MEATH			17 MARCH 1918		JESMOND ST ANDREWS	TO LABOUR CORPS(783 LAB COY).	LAB CORPS No 396904, AGE 51.
BOLAM	J	PTE	26	/775	A	11 MAKEPEACE TERR	HIGH FELLING						TO 14th, 1st BNS, CLASS Z RESERVE.	LCPL.
BOLT	Wm	PTE	26	/79	B	HEYS BLDGS WEST MOOR	FOREST HALL	11/12/14		KR para 392	OCTOBER 16		TO 25th, 1/4th BN.	NEW No 204614, 34 CCS 2/7 EVAC 5/7/16 AGE 31.
BONNER	Math	PTE	26	/40	C	17 PARK PLACE	NEWCASTLE			21 MARCH 1918		ARRAS MEM	ATTACHED 9th ENTRENCHING BN.	BORN GREAT YARMOUTH, DESERTED 3/7/15.
BONNER	W	PTE	26	/1342	B		NEWCASTLE				OCTOBER 16		TO 24th, 24/27th, 14th, 12/13th BNS, CLASS Z RESER	
BOWES	John	PTE	26	/59	C	RAILWAY ST	BROOMPARK	12/11/14		1 JULY 1916		THIEPVAL MEM		MISSING OCTOBER 16, BORN LANGLEY MOOR.
BOYLE	F	PTE	26	/60	B	6 CHARLTON ST	GATESHEAD				NOVEMBER 16		TO 23rd BN, CLASS Z RESERVE.	ASGT.
BOYLE	Thos	PTE	26	/55		52 DOCK ST	TYNE DOCK	8/12/14	23/4/15	INEFFICIENT			TO DEPOT.	DID NOT SERVE OVERSEAS, AGE 38.
BRADY	John	PTE	26	/41		2 CHAPEL ST	TRIMDON	25/11/14	5/2/19	SICK			TO 1st GARRISON BN, DEPOT.	AGE 42 ON DIS.
BRADY	John	LCPL	26	/82		3 COUNCIL ST	STANLEY	5/12/14	23/11/17	SICK			TO DEPOT.	DID NOT SERVE OVERSEAS.
BRANNEN	J	PTE	26	/80	B	ATKINSONS BLDGS	BIRTLEY	7/12/14	9/4/18	INJURIES	JUNE 16, AUGUST 16.		TO ARMY RESERVE CLASS P.	
BRENNAN	Mich	PTE	26	/43	A	22 FOURTH ST	EASINGTON COLLI	10/11/14						
BREW	J	SGT	26	/1344	C30	4 WELLINGTON SQUARE	WALLSEND	19/12/14	31/3/19	KR para 392			TO 8th, 25th BNS, ARMY RESERVE CLASS P.	PALLBEARER AT THE FUNERAL OF SGT FINAN.
BRIGGS	Jos	PTE	26	/783	D								TO LABOUR CORPS, ROYAL FUSILIERS.	LAB CORPS No 404708, R FUS No GS/101455.
BRITTON	JohnR	LCPL	26	/781	D		NEWCASTLE			1 JULY 1916	OCTOBER 16	THIEPVAL MEM		LSGT.
BROCKSBANK	Clar	PTE	26	/94	A	28 NORTH ST	SOUTH SHIELDS						TO LABOUR CORPS, ROYAL ENGINEERS.	LAB CORPS No 380904, RE No 606696.
BROWN	G D	PTE	26	/1469	B									ALSO ON D COY 30th BN ROLL.
BROWN	H	LCPL	26	/85	B	9 LAMPTON PLACE	NEWCASTLE	10/1/15	25/4/18	GASSED	OCTOBER 16, JANUARY 18.		TO 3rd BN.	
BROWN	J E	PTE	26	/802	B	17 WATSON ST	GATESHEAD						TO 23rd BN, CLASS Z RESERVE.	SGT.
BROWN	Rich	PTE	26	/787	D	37 NEW ELVET	DURHAM CITY	8/12/14		1 JULY 1916	OCTOBER 16	THIEPVAL MEM		AWOL 6 AUGUST 1915 H/O TO ESCORT 12/8/15.
BROWN	Steph	PTE	26	/796	D		SACRISTON			1 JULY 1916	OCTOBER 16	THIEPVAL MEM		BORN FRAMWELLGATE MOOR.
BROWN	T	PTE	26	/51				30/11/14	2/12/15	UNFIT				DID NOT SERVE OVERSEAS, AGE 57 ON DIS.
BROWN	ThosE	SGT	26	/790	D	6 BELFORD ST	SUNDERLAND	10/12/14			AUGUST 16		TO CLASS Z RESERVE.	
BROWN	ThosM	PTE	26	/50	C 30		NEWCASTLE			21 SEPT 1917		TYNE COT MEM	TO DURHAM LI(13th BN).	DLI No 44116.
BRUCE	Robt	PTE	26											AWOL 25/5/15 COURT NEWCASTLE 3/6/15.
BUCHAN	J	PTE	26	/776	A			27/11/14	4/12/17	KR para 392			TO 30th BN(D COY), DEPOT.	DID NOT SERVE OVERSEAS.
BUGLASS	N	PTE	26	/793	C									
BULLOCK	Fred	PTE	26	/74	D		NEWCASTLE			8 NOV 1917		ST MARTIN CAVALRIE MIL CEM		BORN ESSEX.
BULLOCK	Wm	PTE	26	/73	B	37 ROBINSON ST	BLAYDON				AUG 16, OCT 16, MAR 17.		TO 27th, 18th, 1st BNS, CLASS Z RESERVE.	
BURBRIDGE	John	PTE	26	/1487	C		BENWELL			1 JULY 1916	OCTOBER 16			BORN ST HELENS LANCS, IN 11 SECTION.
BURBRIDGE	W	PTE	26	/90	B		NEWCASTLE				JULY 16		TO LABOUR CORPS.	
BURGESS	Wm	PTE	26	/1458	B		BLYTH			25 JUNE 1916		THIEPVAL MEM		MISSING DURING TRENCH RAID 25/26 JUNE.
BURKE	T	CPL	26	/81	D		MIDDLESBOROUGH	7/12/14	3/12/17	WOUNDS	JUNE 16, JULY 16.		TO DEPOT.	SGT.
BURNS	H	PTE	26	/777	C	70 POTTER ST	WILLINGTON QUAY							
BURNS	John	PTE	26	/779	D		NEWCASTLE			1 JULY 1916		THIEPVAL MEM		MISS OCTOBER 16, AWOL 24/5/15 CT 31/5/15.

NAME	INITI	RANK	BATTA	NUMBE	COMP	ADDRESS	TOWN_VILL	ENLISTED	DISCHARG	CAUSE_DIS	WOUNDED	BURIED	TRANSFER	ADD
BURNS	Rob	PTE	26	/778	D		HIGH WALKER			27 FEB 1916		X FARM CEM ARMENTIERES		
BURNS	W	LCPL	26	/75				8/12/14	12/9/18	KR para 392			TO 2nd GARRISON BN, DEPOT.	
BUSHBY	John	PTE	26	/780	B		SCOTSWOOD			1 JULY 1916		SERRE RD NO 2 CEM.		AGE 19.
BUTLER	M G	PTE	26	/782	D	13 WHITBURN ST	SUNDERLAND			KR para 392	APRIL 16, OCTOBER 16.			21 AMB T, 18 G HOSP 6/7, SHIP 9/7/16 SSHOCK AGE 19
BUTLER	M J	PTE	26	/52	C			1/12/14	18/8/17	DAH			TO 26th, 18th, 14th, 36th BNS.	
BUTTERFIELD	John	PTE	26	/1448	A	WATER LANE	DURHAM CITY	APRIL 19				COMELY BANK EDINBURGH	TO 30th BN(D COY), ROYAL DEFENCE CORPS.	AWOL 28/7, 20/8/15. RDC No 43264.AGE 48.
BYRNE	Cavin	PTE	26	/1395	C	10 POTTER STREET	WILLINGTON QUAY							
BYRNE	P	LSGT	26	/56	C	14 ATKINSONS BLDGS	BIRTLEY				JULY 18		TO 11th, 24th, 26th, 8th BNS, CLASS Z RESERVE.	NORTH EVINGTON HOSP LEICESTER 11/7/16
CALLAGHAN	Den T	PTE	26	/1346	C	37 CLOSE	NEWCASTLE						TO 9th, 1/5th, 3rd BNS, CLASS Z RESERVE.	
CALLAGHAN	Jas	PTE	26	/823	D	19 MILTON ST	JARROW	6/11/14						
CALLAGHAN	John	PTE	26	/100	B		MIDDLESBOROUGH				JULY 16			AWOL 3/8/15 IN COURT GATESHEAD.
CALLAGHAN	Mich	PTE	26	/101	C	42 JACKSON ST	ANNITSFORD	27/11/14	2/7/16				TO 30th BN(D COY).	DID NOT SERVE OVERSEAS.
CALLAGHAN	Thos	PTE	26											AWOL 1/8/ 16/8/15 COURT NEWCASTLE 6/8 20/8/15
CALVERT	Issac	PTE	26	/131	C		WALKER	3/12/14	16/11/17	GUNSHOT WOUNDS	JULY 16, MARCH 17		TO DEPOT.	AWOL 15/11/15 IN COURT 25/11/15.
CALVERT	J	PTE	26	/107		2 SOUTH THORN	STANLEY	28/11/14	9/4/19	KR para 392			TO 1st GARRISON BN(B COY).	
CALVERT	W	PTE	26	/134	A			4/12/14	15/3/18	ARTHRITIS			TO 3rd BN.	
CAMBELL	R	LCPL	26	/825	B	HIGH HOPE ST	CROOK				JUNE 17		TO 18th BN.	SGT, BORN LONGFORD.
CAMNOCK	J T	CPL	26	/116	B	73 SEVENTH ST	HORDEN	15/1/15	1/4/19	KR para 392			TO ARMY RESERVE CLASS P.	SGT, BROTHER STOKER R.N..
CAMPBELL	A	PTE	26	/840	B		CHESTER LE ST	10/12/14	11/12/17	SHELLSHOCK	MAY 16, AUGUST 16.		TO DEPOT.	
CAMPBELL	A	PTE	26	/1463	A		NEWCASTLE				JULY 16		TO CLASS Z RESERVE.	ACPL.
CAMPBELL	A E	PTE	26	/803	D	27 BLENHEIM ST	NEWCASTLE	24/11/14	5/5/17	WNDS 12/11/18	SEPTEMBER 16	WESTGATE HILL NEWCASTLE	TO DEPOT.	3 CCS 2/7 EVAC 2/7, 2 G HOSP 4/7, SHIP 5/7.
CAMPBELL	J	PTE	26	/1423	D	33 MONK ST	GATESHEAD	17/5/15	17/12/17	GUNSHOT WOUNDS	OCTOBER 16		TO 3rd BN.	
CAMPION	Edwd	PTE	26	/827	A	66 ELDON ST	SOUTH SHIELDS			1 JULY 1916	OCTOBER 16	SERRE RD NO 2 CEM		BORN WALLSEND
CANDLISH	Mich	PTE	26	/124	B		GATESHEAD			9 APRIL 1917		ST CATHERINES MIL CEM		AWOL 7/7 7/8 22/8 3/12/15 COURT GATESHEAD AGE 32.
CANNING	C	PTE	26	/841	A	42 MAINSFORTH TERR	SUNDERLAND				NOVEMBER 16		TO LABOUR CORPS.	
CAREY	J	PTE	26	/833	B		WILLINGTON	7/12/14	12/10/18	GUNSHOT WOUNDS	JULY 16, FEBRUARY 18.		TO 20th BN, DEPOT.	LCPL.
CAREY	T A	PTE	26	/1481	A	74 NORAH ST	TYNE DOCK	13/7/15	24/4/18	VDH	OCTOBER 16		TO 3rd BN.	
CARLISLE	J	PTE	26	/159									TO 1st GARRISON BN, CLASS Z RESERVE.	
CARR	G	PTE	26	/103	D	16 BACK STATION RD	HEBBURN						TO 24th, 24/27th, 14th, 1st BNS, CLASS Z RESERVE.	14 STATION LANE 1914.
CARR	J	PTE	26	/147	C	1 FARROW ROW	SHOTTON COLLIER	10/12/14	1/4/19	KR para 392	JULY 16		TO ARMY RESERVE CLASS P.	SGT.
CARR	John	PTE	26	/848	C	LAMPTON ST	SHERBURN HILL			10 APRIL 1917	OCTOBER 16	AUBIGNY COM CEM		HOSP CHESHIRE 13/7/16
CARR	R	PTE	26	/145	C	5 CROFT TERR	ANNFIELD PLAIN	14/12/14	26/7/17	WOUNDS	OCTOBER 16		TO DEPOT.	
CARR	Tom	PTE	26	/1405	B		CRAGHEAD			1 JULY 1916	JUNE 16, OCTOBER 16.	THIEPVAL MEM		
CARROL	John	PTE	26											AWOL 23/8/15 COURT GATESHEAD AGE 39.
CARROLL	J	PTE	26	/96	C		GATESHEAD	2/12/14	8/3/18	GUNSHOT WOUNDS	JULY 16		TO ARMY RESERVE CLASS P, ARMY SERVICE CORPS.	VOLUNTARY AID HOSP CHELTENHAM 11/7/16
CARROLL	T	PTE	26	/95	B		GATESHEAD				OCTOBER 16		TO LABOUR CORPS.	
CARROLL	W	PTE	26	/130	A	3 CHATHAM PLACE	NEWCASTLE	8/12/14					TO COMMAND DEPOT NF.	
CASEY	J	PTE	26	/1347	B	2 BK REAY ST BILLQUA	HEWORTH				JUNE 16		TO LABOUR CORPS.	
CASSIDY	Dan	PTE	26	/849	D	FRONT ST	DIPTON			1 JULY 1916	OCTOBER 16	THIEPVAL MEM		
CATNEY	T	PTE	26	/806	D		HILLSBOROUGH	25/11/14	8/10/17	GUNSHOT WOUNDS	OCTOBER 16		TO 36th BN.	
CAULFIELD	J	PTE	26	/152	C		WEST STANLEY				OCTOBER 16		TO LABOUR CORPS.	34 CCS 2/7/16 EVAC 5/7/16, WND R SLDR, AGE 23
CAVANAGH	Wm	PTE	26	/123	A	27 PRESS ST	GATESHEAD			1 JULY 1916	OCTOBER 16	THIEPVAL MEM		BORN STOCKTON.
CHADWICK	John	PTE	26	/127	C								TO TRAINING RES BN.	TRG RES No TR/5/59078.
CHAMBERS	M B	PTE	26	/135	A	27 WILSON ST	GATESHEAD						TO ROYAL DEFENCE CORPS.	IN FRANCE 10/1/16 TO 11/10/17. POSTED TO IRELAND.
CHARLTON	J	PTE	26	/150	A		BLYTH				MARCH 17			
CHARLTON	Tom A	PTE	26	/99	C	7 WOODSIDE BANK TOP	RYTON WOODSIDE				OCTOBER 16, DECEMBER 16.		ATTACHED DURHAM LI(DEC 16), TO DWR, LABOUR CORPS.	
CLARK	Alf	PTE	26	/148	C	COURT LANE	DURHAM CITY						ATTACHED 103 LTMB, 9th BN, CLASS Z RESERVE.	CPL.
CLARK	David	PTE	26	/847	B	6 FIFTH ST EAST	EASINGTON COLLI	9/12/14					TO 1st, 24th, 26th, 25th, 12/13th BNS, CLASS Z RES	SGT, SIGNAL SECTION.
CLARK	J	PTE	26	/850	B		NEWCASTLE			KR para 392	OCTOBER 16			CPL, 3 CCS 2/7/16 EVAC 3/7/16.
CLARK	J W	PTE	26	/128	C		BYKER				DECEMBER 18		TO 21st, 20th, 8th, 1/7th BNS, CLASS Z RESERVE.	IN 11 SECTION.
CLARK	MichB	LCPL	26	/854	B	21 RAGLAN ST	SOUTH SHIELDS			8 JULY 1916		ETAPLES		
CLARK	R	PTE	26	/133	A								TO 19th BN(Z COY), CLASS Z RESERVE.	
CLARKE	Mich	PTE	26	/132	C	13 SHAWS RD	HETTON LE HOLE	8/12/14		1 JULY 1916		THIEPVAL MEM		MISSING OCTOBER 16, IN MACHINE GUN SECTION.
CLARKSON	Wm	PTE	26	/146	C	MAIN ENGINE	LITTLETOWN	10/12/14						
CLEMMY	Geo L	PTE	26	/108	B								TO 30th BN(C COY).	AWOL 6/6/15 IN COURT 15/6/15.
COCKBURN	Wm H	PTE	26	/140	A	53 KIMBERLEY TERR	CRAGHEAD				JULY 16		TO 25th, 9th, 22nd BNS, CLASS Z RESERVE.	BATMAN TO LT SHACKLETON AT SUTTON VENY.
COLE	Dan	PTE	26	/118	B	FRONT ST CHIRTON	SOUTH SHIELDS			1 JULY 1916		THIEPVAL MEM		MISSING OCTOBER 16.
COLEMAN	Jos	CQMS	26	/828	A		MIDDLESBOROUGH						TO EAST LANCASHIRE REGT.	EAST LANCS No 33530.
COLLINS	Henry	PTE	26	/808	A		THROCKLEY			8 APRIL 1916		BREWERY ORCHARD CEM		
COLLINS	M	PTE	26	/105	D30			21/11/14	4/4/16	KR para 392			TO 30th BN.	DID NOT SERVE OVERSEAS.

NAME	INITI	RANK	BATTA	NUMBE	COMP	ADDRESS	TOWN_VILL	ENLISTED	DISCHARG	CAUSE_DIS	WOUNDED	BURIED	TRANSFER	ADD
COLLINS	M J	PTE	26	/155	B	40 BRUNSWICK ST	NEWCASTLE							ALSO ON D COY 30th BN ROLL.
COLLINS	P	PTE	26	/112	C	23 WALKERS BLDGS	WASHINGTON				JUNE 18		TO LABOUR CORPS.	POSSIBLY LIVING 29 WALTON ROW BLACKHILL 1914.
CONLAN	Andw	PTE	26	/1443	C	75 ALEXANDRA ST	NEWCASTLE					CABARET ROUGE BRIT CEM		BORN DONAGHMORE CO TYRONE, AGE 38.
CONLAN	P	PTE	26	/844	D30			9/12/14	2/3/16				TO 30th BN.	DID NOT SERVE OVERSEAS.
CONLIN		PTE	26	/161	B			15/12/14	7/6/17	SICK			TO 30th BN(C COY), DEPOT.	DID NOT SERVE OVERSEAS.
CONLON	B	PTE	26	/817	B		WILLINGTON				MARCH 17		TO 1/4th, 12/13th BNS, CLASS Z RESERVE.	CPL.
CONNELL	M	PTE	26	/855	B	3 DALE ST	SOUTH SHIELDS	15/12/14	1/11/18	GUNSHOT WOUNDS	SEPTEMBER 16		TO 8th, 16th BNS, DEPOT.	LCPL.
CONNOLLY	J	LCPL	26	/119	D	1 SYCAMORE ST	NEWCASTLE							
CONNOLLY	J E	SGT	26	/1386	B		JARROW				OCTOBER 16		COMMISIONED IN LEINSTER REGT	TOOK PART IN TRENCH RAID 25/26 JUNE 16.
CONNOLLY	M	CPL	26	/160	B	7 BACK RAILWAY ST	JARROW						TO CLASS Z RESERVE.	SEE 26/1394 BROTHER.
CONNOLLY	Peter	CPL	26	/1394	B		SHOTTON			1 JULY 1916		THIEPVAL MEM		SGT, MISSING OCTOBER 16, 26/160 BROTHER.
CONNOR	James	PTE	26	/838	B	BULMERS YARD PARKGAT	DARLINGTON				AUGUST 16, DEC 17, JUN 1		TO ROYAL FUSILIERS(24th BN).	RFUS No 93120.
CONNOR	P	PTE	26			45 CARLISLE STREET	JARROW							
CONWAY	Dan	PTE	26	/810		8 MARY ST	STANLEY	26/11/14					TO 1st GARRISON BN, CLASS Z RESERVE.	CLIFFORD RD SOUTHMOOR 1918.
CONWAY	J H	PTE	26	/109	D30									
COOK	Jas	PTE	26	/836	B		EIGHTON BANKS			15 JAN 1918	AUGUST 16	EIGHTON BANKS		
COOK	John	PTE	26	/829	C	14 ARMSTRONG STREET	DUNSTON				OCTOBER 16		TO KINGS OWN YORKSHIRE LI(2nd BN).	
COOPER	ArthF	PTE	26	/143	C	52 NEW MITCHELL ST	BIRTLEY			1 JULY 1916		THIEPVAL MEM		
COOPER	N	PTE	26	/820	A	52 NEW MITCHELL ST	BIRTLEY	7/12/14	31/10/16	VDH			TO 3rd BN.	
COPE	John	PTE	26	/853	B	17 PERCY ST	TYNEMOUTH				AUGUST 16		TO LABOUR CORPS.	LAB CORPS No 600446.
CORBETT	Andrw	PTE	26	/1480	D		STANLEY			1 JULY 1916	OCTOBER 16	THIEPVAL MEM		MISSING DECEMBER 16, BORN CROOK.
CORRIGAN	Geo	PTE	26											AWOL 30/11 COURT NEWCASTLE 6/12/15
CORRIGAN	John	PTE	26	/122	C		SUNDERLAND			1 JULY 1916		THIEPVAL MEM		MISSING OCTOBER 16.
COSGROVE	Pat	PTE	26	/138	A		NEWCASTLE	5/12/14	8/9/17	SICK	NOVEMBER 16		TO 3rd BN.	AWOL 24/5/15 IN COURT 25/5/15.
COULSON	J W	PTE	26	/97	D	17 DOUGLAS ST	WEST STANLEY	9/12/14					TO 23rd BN, CLASS Z RESERVE.	
COULSON	John	PTE	26	/98	C		DURHAM CITY				JULY 16		TO TANK CORPS.	3 CCS 2/7/16 EVAC 3/7/16, TANK CORPS No 302513.
COWAN	David	PTE	26	/154	A	5 NEW ST	SHERBURN HILL				OCTOBER 16		TO LABOUR CORPS.	3 CCS 2/7/16 EVAC HOSP BOURNEMOUTH 13/7 STOMACH WN
COWAN	J	PTE	26	/126	A		LANGLEY MOOR				JULY 16		TO 10th BN, CLASS Z RESERVE.	
COX	C	PTE	26	/151	B		WOLSINGHAM			8 DEC 1919		WOLSINGHAM RC CEM	TO LABOUR CORPS.	
COX	R	PTE	26	/1426	D		SUNDERLAND				OCTOBER 16		TO ROYAL WELCH FUSILIERS.	RW FUS No 57392.
COYLE	J	PTE	26	/139						KR para 392			TO 1st GARRISON BN.	
COYNE	F	PTE	26	/120	A		SOUTH SHIELDS	12/10/14	29/8/17	WOUNDS	JULY 16		TO DEPOT.	LCPL.
COYNE	P	PTE	26	/1418	A		JARROW				OCTOBER 16			DESERTED 2 NOVEMBER 16.
CRANE	Pat	SGT	26	/843		33 GILESGATE	DURHAM CITY	9/12/14	15/9/16	UNFIT			TO 30th BN.	
CRAWFORD	Jas W	PTE	26	/819	B	2 BK HIBERNIAN RD	JARROW	12/11/14					TO 8th, 16th, 1/5th, 17th, 12/13th BNS, CLASS Z RE	SGT.
CREIGHTON	Wm	PTE	26	/141	C	5 CRAWFORD RD	OUSEBURN			1 JULY 1916		THIEPVAL MEM		BORN NEWCASTLE.
CRESSWELL	H	CPL	26	/114	D	5 WESTGARTH TERR	USWORTH				AUGUST 16		TO 3rd BN, ROYAL DEFENCE CORPS.	IN FRANCE 10/1/16 TO 4/7/16.
CRINNION	Nich	PTE	26	/106		6 THORN LEA RD	TOW LAW			10 OCTOBER 1918		ADDOLRATA MIL CEM MALTA	TO 1st GARRISON BN.	ACCIDENTLY KILLED.
CRONEY	J	PTE	26	/846	B	32 MITCHELL ST	SOUTHMOOR			KR para 392	MAY 16, MARCH 18.			
CROOK	C	PTE	26	/129	D			2/12/14	7/7/16	SICK			TO DEPOT.	
CROSSEN	John	PTE	26	/839		9 PRINCES ST	CONSETT						TO 1st GARRISON BN, CLASS Z RESERVE.	
CULLEN	H	PTE	26	/831	B	21 HILL ST	NEWCASTLE				JULY 16		TO 12th, 12/13th BNS, ROYAL DEFENCE CORPS.	FRANCE 26 10/1/16TO6/9/16, 12BN 7/9/16TO18/8/17,
CULLER	Benj	PTE	26	/158	A	20 WILSON ST TEAMS	GATESHEAD	11/12/14		1 JULY 1916		THIEPVAL MEM		MISSING OCTOBER 16, SGT BORN GATESHEAD.
CUNNINGHAM	D	PTE	26	/834	A		GATESHEAD	7/12/14	16/11/18	GUNSHOT WOUNDS	JULY 16		TO 23rd, 26th, 9th, 3rd BNS.	
CUNNINGHAM	G	PTE	26	/137	D	2 THOMPSON ST	NEWCASTLE				JUNE 18		TO 8th, 22nd BNS.	
CUNNINGHAM	J	PTE	26	/136	A	15 LIEGHTON ST	SOUTH SHIELDS	4/12/14	1/2/19	KR para 392			TO 22nd, 26th, 25th BNS, ARMY RESERVE CLASS P.	SGT.
CUNNINGHAM	Peter	PTE	26	/812	A	68 HOPE ST	JARROW	2/12/14		1 JULY 1916	OCTOBER 16	SERRE RD NO 2 CEM		LCPL.
CURRAN	E	PTE	26	/852	D30			15/12/14	6/5/16	KR para 392			TO 30th BN.	DID NOT SERVE OVERSEAS.
CURRY	Jas	PTE	26	/115	D30	20 CROSSGATE	DURHAM CITY	24/11/14	2/7/16	AO 265/17			TO 30th BN(D COY).	AAWOL 20/8/15, ESCORT 6/9/15. AGE 58.
CURRY	K	PTE	26	/818	B									
CURTIS	Chas	PTE	26	/157	A	13 CLAYPATH	DURHAM CITY				JULY 16		TO ARMY SERVICE CORPS(978 MT COY).	ASC No T/389940.
CUTTER	Anthy	PTE	26	/816	A	4 RAILTONS COURT	SOUTH SHIELDS	26/11/14			OCT 16, DEC 17, W+M JAN1		TO 27th, 16th BNS.	34 CCS 2/7/16 EVAC 5/7/16 WND R EAR,CPL,POW 1/18.
CUTTER	R H	PTE	26	/117	B	18 ORMONDE ST	SOUTH SHIELDS	26/11/14	16/11/17	GUNSHOT WOUNDS	OCTOBER 16		TO DEPOT.	SEE 26/816.
DALE	John	PTE	26	/164	A	30 ERNEST PLACE GILE	DURHAM CITY	26/11/14			JANUARY 17		ATTACHED 17 CORPS HEADQUARTERS, TO LABOUR CORPS.	
DALE	Tom	PTE	26	/195	B	30 CUTHBERT ST	BLAYDON			26 OCT 1917	APR 16	TYNE COT MEM	TO 25th, 1/4th BNS.	ALLOTTED NEW NUMBER 204630.
DANCE	J T	PTE	26	/165			LEMINGTON ON TY			KR para 392	AUGUST 16		TO 1st GARRISON BN, 26th BN.	18 GEN HOSP 3/7/16, SHIP 5/7/16 WND THIGH AGE 41.
DARLING	P	LCPL	26	/874	D		NEWCASTLE			KR para 392	OCTOBER 16		TO 19th BN.	HOSP FRANCE MARCH 16.
DAVIES	C	PTE	26	/192	B	34 NOBLE ST	NEWCASTLE	10/12/14	28/6/18	GUNSHOT WOUNDS	SEPTEMBER 16		TO DEPOT.	
DAVIS	David	PTE	26	/166	C	BYMBRO	DENBIGH			1 JULY 1916		THIEPVAL MEM		
DAVISON	C	PTE	26	/181	C									

NAME	INITI	RANK	BATTA	NUMBE	COMP	ADDRESS	TOWN_VILL	ENLISTED	DISCHARG	CAUSE_DIS	WOUNDED	BURIED	TRANSFER	ADD
DAVISON	J T	PTE	26	/175	C			2/12/14	3/2/19	KR para 392			TO 23rd, 22nd BNS, ARMY RESERVE CLASS P.	
DAVISON	John	PTE	26	/172	A	10 THOMAS STREET	CRAGHEAD				OCTOBER 16		TO LABOUR CORPS.	LAB CORPS No 168410 A SSGT.
DAVITT	F	PTE	26	/1459	C									ALSO ON D COY 30th BN ROLL.
DAWSON	J W	PTE	26	/876	B					KR para 392			TO 18th BN.	
DAWSON	M	PTE	26	/197	B	4 SUNNY TERR	STANLEY						TO 25th BN, CLASS Z RESERVE.	CPL, 44 JOICEY TERR STANLEY 1918.
DAYKIN	J	PTE	26	/189	C		SACRISTON				NOVEMBER 16 SHELLSHOCK		TO 25th, 1/4th BNS, CLASS Z RESERVE.	3 CCS 2/7/16 EVAC 3/7/16 SHELLSHOCK.
DEAN	Wm	PTE	26	/859	B	10a BUCKINGHAM ST	NEWCASTLE			4 JULY 1916		THIEPVAL MEM		MISSING OCTOBER 16, BORN CHESTER LE ST.
DEMPSEY	W	PTE	26	/866	B					KR para 392	MAY 16		ATTACHED 9th ENTRENCHING BN, 23rd, 22nd BNS.	
DEVINE	Jas	PTE	26	/857	B	1 NORFOLK ST	NORTH SHIELDS	2/12/14		1 JULY 1916	OCTOBER 16	THIEPVAL MEM		
DEVINE	John	PTE	26	/188	C									AWOL 1/5/15, 22/7/15, 25/8/15 IN COURT BEDLINGTON.
DEVLIN	Edwd	PTE	26	/858	B		NEWCASTLE			1 JULY 1916		THIEPVAL MEM		
DIAMOND	J	LCPL	26	/167	A	21 WILLIAM ST BK	HEBBURN COLLIER						TO KINGS OWN YORKSHIRE LI, ARMY ORDNANCE CORPS.	ALSO ON C COY 30th BN ROLL.
DICKSON	Jas A	PTE	26	/174	C	9 ANTHONY ST	EASINGTON			1 JULY 1916		THIEPVAL MEM		MISSING OCTOBER 16, BORN ROCHESTER KENT.
DITCHBURN	Frncs	PTE	26	/191	B	37 CHURCH ST	NORTH SHIELDS	10/12/14					TO ARMY SERVICE CORPS.	
DIXON	Chas	SGT	26	/864		6 HEMMING ST	GRANGETOWN			7 SEPT 1917		TEMPLEUX	TO 1st, 26th BNS.	AWOII,LIVING 7 LEECHMORE ST GRANGETOWN 1914,AGE 35
DIXON	J	PTE	26	/860	C					KR para 392				
DIXON	J	PTE	26	/877	D									
DIXON	Wm	PTE	26	/183	D	9 WATSONS BLDGS HEWO	FELLING	11/12/14			OCTOBER 16, NOVEMBER 17		TO 16th BN, CLASS Z RESERVE.	
DOBSON	T	PTE	26	/1476	D			6/7/15	2/4/18	SICK			TO 19th, 10th ENTRENCHING BN, 14th, 1/7th BNS ATT	ALSO ON C COY 30th BN ROLL.
DOCHERTY	W	PTE	26	/168									TO 1st GARRISON BN, CLASS Z RESERVE.	
DODD	T	PTE	26	/884	B									
DODD	W	PTE	26	/180	C									
DODDS	J C	PTE	26	/169	A	16 JUBILEE ST	MEDOMSLEY						TO 14th BN, LABOUR CORPS.	3 CCS 2/7/16 EVAC 2/7/16 SHELLSHOCK.
DODDS	R	SGT	26	/179	A								TO 11th, 26th, 1/4th BNS, CLASS Z RESERVE.	
DODDS	R	CPL	26	/186	C								TO CLASS Z RESERVE.	SGT ALLOTED NEW NUMBER 88652.
DODDS	Robt	PTE	26	/878	C	2 CO-OP TERR	SHERBURN HILL						TO 1/7th BN, CLASS Z RESERVE.	SGT.
DODDS	Wm	PTE	26	/872	B	39 PRIOR TERRACE	HEXAM				OCTOBER 16		TO LABOUR CORPS(395 EMP COY).	LAB CORPS No 441292. REQ CONFIRMING.
DONALDSON	Wm	PTE	26	/198	A	29 GROSVENOR ST	GATESHEAD						TO 25th BN, CLASS Z RESERVE.	
DONNELLY	MichE	PTE	26	/871	B	6 PRINCES STREET	NEWCASTLE			27 AUGUST 1918		HAC CEM ECOUST ST MEIN	TO 10th BN, KINGS OWN YORKSHIRE LI(2/4th BN).	KOYLI No 63316, AGE 21.
DONNELLY	W H	PTE	26	/193		192 JOHN WILLIAMSON	SOUTH SHIELDS	11/12/14	11/6/15	SICK				DID NOT SERVE OVERSEAS.
DONOHOE	Wm Ed	PTE	26	/173	C		NORTH SEATON			1 JULY 1916		THIEPVAL MEM		MISSING OCTOBER 16, BORN ASHINGTON
DORAN	P	PTE	26	/883	D	1 WYLAM ST	STANLEY				OCTOBER 16		TO 11th, 26th, 22nd, 9th BNS, CLASS Z RESERVE.	34 CCS 2/7/16 EVAC 5/7/16 WND R THIGH AGE 21.
DORNER	John	PTE	26	/1411	B	58 COOKS BLDGS	NEWCASTLE			5 AUGUST 1916		CABERET ROUGE BRIT CEM		AGE 25.
DOWIE	David	PTE	26	/196	B	408 JOHN WILLIAMSON	SOUTH SHIELDS	11/12/14						ALSO ON D COY 30th BN ROLL.
DOYLE	E	PTE	26	/865	B	353 JOHN WILLIAMSON	SOUTH SHIELDS	30/11/14	21/2/18	GUNSHOT WOUNDS	OCTOBER 16		TO LINCOLNSHIRE REGT, ARMY RESERVE CLASS P.	3 CCS 2/7/16 EVAC 2/7/16 GSW
DOYLE	Mich	PTE	26	/163	A	19 STROTHERS TERR	HIGH SPEN			1 JULY 1916		THIEPVAL MEM		SGT, MISSING OCTOBER 16, BORN WOLF HILL PERTH.
DOYLE	Rich	LSGT	26	/162	C		NORTH ORMSBY			1 JULY 1916		THIEPVAL MEM		SGT.
DRUMMOND	Jas	PTE	26	/185	C		USWORTH			1 JULY 1916		THIEPVAL MEM		MISSING OCTOBER 16, BORN SHOTWITH CHESHIRE.
DRYDEN	John	DRUM	26	/862	B		NORTH SHIELDS			8 JULY 1916	MAY 16, 1 JULY 16.	ST SEVER CEM ROUEN		34 CCS 2/7/16 EVAC 5/7/16 HEAD WND, AGE 30.
DUDDY	J	PTE	26	/170	A		BLAYDON BURN	28/11/14	5/3/18	GUNSHOT WOUNDS	OCTOBER 16		TO DEPOT.	
DUFFY	J	PTE	26	/879	B									
DUFFY	James	LCPL	26	/190	B	87 MITFORD ST	NEWCASTLE	14/12/14	25/8/18	SICK	AUGUST 16		TO 3rd BN, ATTACHED 85th TRAINING RESERVE BN.	ASGT.
DUFFY	James	PTE	26	/194	B		NORTH SHIELDS				SEPTEMBER 16, NOVEMBER 1		TO LABOUR CORPS.	LAB CORPS No 396946.
DUNBAR	A	PTE	26	/171	D	LOVETTS YARD	GATESHEAD							ALSO ON D COY 30th BN ROLL.
DUNLOP	J	PTE	26	/873	B	SKINNERGATE	DARLINGTON				OCTOBER 16		TO ROYAL ENGINEERS.	34 CCS 2/7/16 EVAC 5/7/16 WND R THIGH.
DUNN	John	PTE	26	/886	D	12 BYKER BANK	NEWCASTLE	10/12/14			OCTOBER 16		TO LABOUR CORPS.	
DUNN	Pat	PTE	26	/184		60 CLAYPATH	DURHAM CITY						TO 1st GARRISON BN, CLASS Z RESERVE.	
DUPEAR	H	PTE	26	/875				11/12/14	31/8/16	SICK			TO 1st GARRISON BN.	
DYER	P	PTE	26	/881	B		NEWCASTLE	14/12/14	25/1/18	SICK			TO 10th, 3rd BNS.	MISSING OCTOBER 16, AGE 54.
DYKE	Edwd	LSGT	26	/880	D	6 ST HILDA LANE	SOUTH SHIELDS	11/12/14	18/2/19	KR para 392	AUGUST 16		TO 14th BN.	3 CCS 2/7 EVAC 3/7 TO 18 G HOSP 3/7 TO SHIP 5/7/16
DYSON	H	SGT	26	/870	B									ALSO ON C COY 30th BN ROLL.
DYSON	Thos	PTE	26	/867	B	BLACK HOUSE	EDMONDSLEY			20 APRIL 1918		PLOEGSTEERT MEM	TO 10th, 26th, 23rd BNS.	LCPL, MEMBER OF WASHINGTON METHODIST CHURCH BROTHE
EAGLE	Dav		26	/212		103 FRAMWELLGATE	DURHAM CITY						TO 1st GARRISON BN, CLASS Z RESERVE.	ALSO LIVING 3 SOUTH ST TANFIELD.
EASTON	J	PTE	26	/207	B			1/12/14	6/3/18	TRENCH FEET			TO DEPOT.	
EDWARDS	D	PTE	26	/209	B			4/12/14	6/8/17	SICK			TO 30th BN.	ALSO ON D COY 30th BN ROLL.
EGLON	T	PTE	26	/211	B		NEWCASTLE	7/12/14	17/7/17	GUNSHOT WOUNDS	JUNE 16		TO DEPOT.	
ELLIOT	C	PTE	26	/199	B		BIRTLEY			18 JULY 1916	NOVEMBER 16	ETAPLES		STONEMAN AT BURNHOPE COLLIERY.
ELLIS	E	SGT	26	/201	B	55 SIXTH ST	HORDEN	30/11/14	3/2/19				ATTACHED 179 TUN COY RE, 141 POW COY, ARMY RESERVE	
ELLISON	Frank	PTE	26	/206	B	34 STANDERTON TERR	CRAGHEAD	1/12/14	4/3/19		OCTOBER 16		TO ARMY SERVICE CORPS(374 Siege Bty Amm Col).	3 CCS 2/7/16 EVAC 4 GEN HOSP 3/7/16, GSW.
ELLSENDER	E	PTE	26	/889	A				4/10/19				TO 10th BN, KINGS OWN YORKSHIRE LI(8th BN).	

NAME	INITI	RANK	BATTA	NUMBE	COMP	ADDRESS	TOWN_VILL	ENLISTED	DISCHARG	CAUSE_DIS	WOUNDED	BURIED	TRANSFER	ADD
ELSE	Andrw	PTE	26	/200	D30		GATESHEAD	25/11/14	29/3/16	SICK				NOT SERVE OVERSEAS, AGE 42 AWOL 20/8/15.
ELVES	A	PTE	26	/202	B	CASTELREAGH ST	TUNSTALL						TO 1st BN, CLASS Z RESERVE.	
EMBLETON	S	PTE	26	/214	B	7 BROUGH BLDGS	BYKER						TO KINGS OWN YORKSHIRE LI.	
EMMERSON	T	PTE	26	/208	B	20 WEST ST	GRANGE VILLA						TO 19th BN(Z COY), CLASS Z RESERVE.	25 COLLIERY ROW 1914.
ETHRINGTON	E	LCPL	26	/213	B		BISHOP AUKLAND	7/12/14	9/7/17	GUNSHOT WOUNDS	AUGUST 16		TO 3rd BN.	CPL.
EVANS	E	CPL	26	/205	B									
EVANS	J	PTE	26	/204	B		COWPEN QUAY				OCTOBER 16		TO 12th, 12/13th BNS.	
EVANS	J B	PTE	26	/203	B	119 MILBURNGATE	DURHAM CITY							ALSO ON C COY 30th BN ROLL.
EVANS	Jos	PTE	26	/890	B	1 SCHOOL ROW	SHOTTON COLLIER							
EVANS	P	PTE	26	/891	C	16 KELVIN GARDENS	DUNSTON			1 JULY 1916		THIEPVAL MEM		MISSING OCTOBER 16, BORN COATBRIDGE LANARK.
EXLEY	JohnJ	PTE	26	/888	B	20 ST JAMES RD	GATESHEAD	7/12/14	23/8/17	GUNSHOT WOUNDS	NOVEMBER 16		TO 85th TRAINING RESERVE BN.	AWOL 7/8/15 COURT GATESHEAD AGE 29.
EXLEY	Thos	PTE	26	/210	B	7 OLD ROW PITY ME	DURHAM CITY	11/12/14		1 JULY 1916		THIEPVAL MEM		BORN BARNSLEY.
FAGAN	M	PTE	26	/225	D									ALSO ON D COY 30th BN ROLL.
FAIRLEY	Henry	PTE	26	/911	D	49 DEVONSHIRE ST	TYNE DOCK			1 JULY 1916	OCTOBER 16	THIEPVAL MEM		MISSING DECEMBER 16, BORN GATESHEAD.
FAIRNESS	J	PTE	26	/215				26/11/14	27/6/16	SICK			TO 1st GARRISON BN.	
FALCUS	James	PTE	26	/227	C	28 THORNBOROUGH ST	BYKER			16 OCT 1917	AUGUST 16	TYNE COT MEM	TO 9th, 18th, 23rd BNS.	
FALLON	D	PTE	26	/900	B	31 VICTORIA ST	WITTON LE WEAR						TO 10th, 25th, 12/13th BNS, CLASS Z RESERVE.	LCPL.
FALLON	Thos	PTE	26	/218	C	HIGH FLATS	CROOK	26/11/14			MARCH 17		TO ROYAL ARMY MEDICAL CORPS.	
FARRELL	Peter	SGT	26	/228	A								TO DURHAM LI.	DLI No 56437.
FEARON	Peter	PTE	26	/233	C	BULMER ST	MIDDLESBOROUGH						TO 4th BN, ROYAL FUSILIERS.	R FUS No GS/79723.
FEENAN	D	PTE	26	/906	B		CRAGHEAD				OCTOBER 16		TO LABOUR CORPS.	
FENNELLY	Tim	LSGT	26	/216	C	111 STOCKTON RD	HARTLEPOOL							
FENWICK	Rich	PTE	26	/914	C	45 MOORSLEY TERR	LOW PITTINGTON						TO 1st, 17th BNS, CLASS Z RESERVE.	914 D LINES 35 I.B.D.
FERGUSON	Jos	PTE	26	/901	B	14 KITTY BREWSTER SQ	BLYTH			5 OCT 1916	JUNE 16, OCTOBER 16.	ADANAC MIL CEM	TO 11th BN.	3 CCS 2/7/16 EVAC 2/7/16, BORN ALNWICK, AGE 25.
FERONS	Frc A	PTE	26	/222	C		WILLINGTON			1 JULY 1916		THIEPVAL MEM		SGT.
FERRY	Thos	PTE	26	/229	A	27 THOMAS ST	CRAGHEAD			KR para 392			TO 23rd BN.	CPL, 1918 SGT LIVING 37 LADYSMITH TERR CRAGHEAD.
FINAN	Mich	SGT	26	/893		14 MILBURNGATE	DURHAM CITY			22 JAN 1916		ST BEDES RC CEM DURHAM CITY	TO 3rd BN, DEPOT.	DLI,16 YEARS IN INDIA,AGE 56,5530 E COY 2DLI 1897
FINN	John	PTE	26	/894	B	28 WILLIAM ST	SUNDERLAND	27/11/14	2/8/16	WOUNDS			TO DEPOT.	AWOL IN COURT SUNDERLAND 28/6/15.
FISHER	Harry	PTE	26	/905	B	4 SOUTH ST	BRANDON COLLIER	11/12/14		11 APRIL 1918		PLOEGSTEERT MEM	TO 9th BN.	LSGT, AGE 23 NOK 49 PARK ST BRANDON COLLIERY.
FISHER	J G	PTE	26	/1376		38 SUNNISIDE NORTH	NEWBOTTLE							
FLEETHAM	R	PTE	26	/230	A	3 WATERLOO ST	HUTTON HENRY						ATTACHED DIV,AD, TO LABOUR CORPS.	
FLEMING	John	PTE	26	/895	D	32 MELBOURNE ST	GATESHEAD				OCTOBER 16, NOT W DEC 16		TO LABOUR CORPS(750 EMP COY).	
FLETCHER	Jothn	PTE	26	/908	A	6 SIXTH ST EAST	EASINGTON COLLI	9/12/14					TO ROYAL FUSILIERS(24th BN).	IN FRANCE 26 9/1/16 TO 30/8/18, 24 RFUS 31/8/18 TO
FLOOD	Arth	PTE	26			5 TREWITTS BLDGS	SUNDERLAND	10/12/14						AWOL 15/4/15, DESERTER 10/7/16 CT S/LAND AGE 18
FLOWERS	Geo	PTE	26	/219	C	33 FRAMWELLGATE	DURHAM CITY	2/12/14			AUGUST 16		TO LABOUR CORPS.	LAB CORPS No 570421.
FLYNN	T	PTE	26	/896	B		HOUGHTON				AUGUST 16		TO LABOUR CORPS.	3 CCS 2/7/16 EVAC 7/7/16 No 4 AMB TRAIN.
FORD	J	PTE	26	/904	B	24 WINDSOR TERR NEW	ANNFIELD PLAIN	9/12/14			AUGUST 16, MARCH 18.		TO EAST YORKSHIRE REGT.	
FORESTER	John	PTE	26	/232	C	20 THOMAS ST	CRAGHEAD		7/2/19				TO 10th BN, KINGS OWN YORKSHIRE LI(2/4th BN), CLAS	
FORSTER	Jas W	PTE	26	/897		31 JOHN ST	BLAYDON			29 SEPT 1918	1 JULY 1916	UNICORN CEM VEND'HUILE	TO 1/4th BN, ROYAL FUSILIERS(11th BN).	3 CCS 2/7/16 EVAC 2/7/16 GSW. R FUS No 79648.
FORTH	F	PTE	26	/899	B									
FOSS	Geo W	PTE	26	/1453	D		GATESHEAD	7/6/15	4/3/19	SICK			TO LABOUR CORPS.	AWOL 25/8/15 CT G/HEAD,AGE 18,LAB CORPS No 474194
FOSTER	T	LCPL	26	/913	A		GATESHEAD	16/12/14	27/2/18	RHEUMATISM			TO ARMY RESERVE CLASS W.	AWOL 2/7/15 IN COURT GATESHEAD, AGE 19.
FOWLIE	H	PTE	26	/234	C	14 AGNES ST	SOUTH SHIELDS	24/11/14	9/10/16	WOUNDS	OCTOBER 16		TO DEPOT.	34 CCS 1/7/16 EVAC 5/7/16, WND L HAND, AGE 23
FOX	R	PTE	26	/909	D		NEWCASTLE			KR para 392	AUGUST 16, MARCH 18.		TO 21st, 10th BNS.	
FRANCES	G W	PTE	26	/223		10 WALKER TERR	NEWCASTLE							
FRANKLIN	Geo	PTE	26	/226	A	59 PINE ST	GRANGE VILLA	9/12/14		25 APRIL 1917		LEVEL CROSSING CEM FAMPOUX		BORN BRANDON, AGE 26.
FRANKLIN	Wm	PTE	26	/217	C	50 STANTON TERR	CRAGHEAD	2/12/14					TO 3rd BN.	
FULTHORPE	Robt	PTE	26	/1398	A		GATESHEAD			1 JULY 1916		THIEPVAL MEM		MISSING OCTOBER 16.
GAFFNEY	E	PTE	26	/260		ITALY ST	MIDDLESBOROUGH						TO 1st GARRISON BN, CLASS Z RESERVE.	
GAFFNEY	P	PTE	26	/268		14 FOURTH ST	EASINGTON						TO 1st GARRISON BN, CLASS Z RESERVE.	
GALLAGHER	Thos	PTE	26	/1391	A	23 LONDONDERRY ST	DAWDON			1 JULY 1916		THIEPVAL MEM		MISSING OCTOBER 16, BORN THORNLEY.
GALLAGHER	W	PTE	26	/266		38 STONE ROW SUNNISI	NEWBOTTLE	9/12/14					TO 1st GARRISON BN, CLASS Z RESERVE.	
GALLOGLY	Felix	PTE	26	/924		8 UPPER ARCHER ST	DARLINGTON	11/12/14					TO 1st GARRISON BN, CLASS Z RESERVE.	COULD HAVE BEEN LIVING 9 SPRING LANE SOUTH SHIELDS
GALLOWAY	John	CPL	26	/936	C	5 DURHAM ROW	SHERBURN HILL	11/12/14	1/4/19	KR para 392	OCTOBER 16		TO ARMY RESERVE CLASS P.	SGT, HOSP GUILFORD 13/7/16 WND LEFT ARM.
GALLOWAY	Rob J	PTE	26	/235	D		GATESHEAD	25/11/14	23/8/17	GUNSHOT WOUNDS	OCTOBER 16		TO DEPOT.	AWOL 19/8/15 IN COURT GATESHEAD, AGE 25.
GANNON	T	PTE	26	/930				4/12/14	21/6/18	KR para 392			TO 1st GARRISON BN.	
GARNETT	Lawr	PTE	26	/271	B	51 GROSVENOR ST	GATESHEAD				MARCH 18		TO ?BN NF(3rd COY).	AWOL 6/8/15 IN COURT GATESHEAD.
GARRETTY	Pat	PTE	26	/253	B	1545 WALKER RD	NEWCASTLE	2/12/14	16/2/18	GUNSHOT WOUNDS	MARCH 18		TO 3rd BN.	SGT.
GARRITTY	W	PTE	26	/254	A		BYKER				AUGUST 16		TO 10th BN, CLASS Z RESERVE.	3 CCS 2/7/16 EVAC 3/7/16
GARSIDE	Wm	PTE	26	/276	B	5 WEST ST	SHERBURN COLLIE						TO 30th BN(D COY), 3rd BN, LABOUR CORPS.	LAB CORPS No 619461.

NAME	INITI	RANK	BATTA	NUMBE	COMP	ADDRESS	TOWN_VILL	ENLISTED	DISCHARG	CAUSE_DIS	WOUNDED	BURIED	TRANSFER	ADD
GASH	JohnT	PTE	26	/927	B		BISHOP AUKLAND			26 SEPT 1916		CITE BON JEAN CEM		ASGT.
GATES	M	SGT	26	/1435	A		WEST STANLEY	26/5/15	30/3/18	GUNSHOT WOUNDS	AUGUST 16.		TO DEPOT.	
GATTENBY	S	PTE	26	/920	C30	8 FIRST ST	WARDLEY						TO 30th BN(C COY), 3rd BN.	
GAUGHAN	G	PTE	26	/918	C		BALLINA				AUGUST 16		TO ROYAL DEFENCE CORPS.	IN FRANCE 10/1/16 TO 6/7/16.
GEARY	John	PTE	26	/919	B	7 SHERBURN TERR	CONSETT	2/12/14			SHELLSHOCK JUNE 16.		TO 8th BN, CLASS Z RESERVE.	10 EAST PARADE CONSETT 1918.
GEORGE	J C	PTE	26	/237	D30									
GETTINGS	J	PTE	26	/265	B		DUNSTON				OCTOBER 16		TO CLASS Z RESERVE.	
GIBBON	Jos S	PTE	26	/257		47 GRAINGER'S TERR	LEAMSIDE	8/12/14	21/8/18	SICK			TO 3rd BN.	AGE 50.
GIBBON	R	PTE	26	/238	D30	8 ALLERGATE	DURHAM CITY	28/11/14						
GIBBS	R	PTE	26	/255	B									
GIBSON	A	CPL	26	/248	D30	23 SOUTH ELDON ST	SOUTH SHIELDS							
GIBSON	R	PTE	26	/246	B								TO 10th BN, ROYAL FUSILIERS(24th BN).	FRANCE 26th,9/1/16 TO 3/7/16, 10 4/7/18 TO 29/8/18
GIBSON	Wm	PTE	26	/249	C 24	68 COBURG ST	GATESHEAD	30/11/14	31/7/18	DEAF			TO 24th, 3rd BNS.	
GILBERT	W H	PTE	26	/239	B									SGT.
GILLESPIE	Jos	PTE	26	/935	B	815 WALKER RD	NEWCASTLE	12/12/14			OCTOBER 16			
GILLESPIE	Wm	PTE	26	/915	B	13 DIXON ST	SOUTH SHIELDS			9 AUGUST 1916		THIEPVAL MEM	TO 30th BN(C COY) 9th BN.	BORN NEWCASTLE, REPEATEDLY AWOL THROUGH 1915.
GILMORE	J	PTE	26	/270									TO 1st GARRISON BN, CLASS Z RESERVE.	NAME IN DYCH BUT NO ADDRESS.
GILMORE	W	CPL	26	/934	B	20 FRONT ST	NETTLESWORTH	9/12/14					TO 8th, 26th, 9th BNS, CLASS Z RESERVE.	SGT.
GLEASON	Geo	SGT	26	/274	A	2 OLD ELVET	DURHAM CITY			1 JULY 1916		THIEPVAL MEM		SERVED 16 YRS 1st BN ROYAL SCOTS, BOER WAR.
GLENDENNING	Rob	PTE	26	/937	A	3 NINTH ST EAST	EASINGTON COLLI	12/12/14	3/11/17	WOUNDS	JULY 16		TO 24th BN, DEPOT.	
GONE	W	PTE	26	/263				7/12/14	11/6/15				TO DEPOT.	DID NOT SERVE OVERSEAS.
GORDON	R	PTE	26	/252	B	5 MAIDEN ST	SCOTSWOOD	/11/14		27 JAN 1920		ELSWICK	TO 30th BN(C COY).	DIED FROM APPENDICITIS, AGE 44.
GORMAN	J	PTE	26	/247	C									ALSO ON D COY 30th BN ROLL.
GORMAN	Jas	PTE	26	/932	A	73 BK ABBOTT ST	GATESHEAD			1 JULY 1916		THIEPVAL MEM		LSGT, MISSING OCTOBER 16.
GOUGH	Tom	PTE	26	/929	B	98 MAPLE ST HIRST	ASHINGTON				OCTOBER 16			RENUMBERED 292087, VOL AID HOSP CHELTENHAM 8/7/16.
GOUNDRY	J	PTE	26	/256	B			7/12/14	7/8/17	SICK			TO DEPOT.	AGE 30 ON DIS.
GOURLEY	R	PTE	26	/917	D								TO 10th BN, ROYAL FUSILIERS(24th BN).	FRANCE 26th, 10/1/16to3/7/18, 10th 4/7/18to30/8/18
GOWRIE	Alb	PTE	26	/933	A	14 LEOPOLD ST	GATESHEAD	9/12/14	20/6/18	GUNSHOT WOUNDS	OCTOBER 16, AUGUST 18.		TO DEPOT.	
GRAHAM	Frs J	PTE	26	/928	B	39 ALICE ST SOUTHWIC	SUNDERLAND	10/12/14		17 MARCH 1916		BREWERY ORCHARD		LCPL.
GRAHAM	JohnR	PTE	26	/262	B	26 HIGH ST	SOUTH HYLTON						TO ROYAL ARMY ORDNANCE CORPS.	RAOC No 039314.
GRAHAM	Wm A	PTE	26	/251	C	22 WELLINGTON ST	NORTH SHIELDS			1 JULY 1916		THIEPVAL MEM		LSGT, BORN TYNEMOUTH.
GRAINGER	David	PTE	26	/921	C		GATESHEAD			10 JULY 1916	OCTOBER 16	BOULOGNE EAST MIL CEM		
GRANT	Maur	PTE	26	/240	B	21 BAIRD AVE	EAST HOWDEN			1 JULY 1916	OCTOBER 16	THIEPVAL MEM		MISSING OCTOBER 16, BORN WATERFORD.
GRAY	G W	LCPL	26	/245	B									
GRAY	J	PTE	26	/1488	B									LSGT DESERTED 2 JANUARY 1917.
GRAY	R	PTE	26	/267									TO 1st GARRISON BN, CLASS Z RESERVE.	
GRAY	Thos	PTE	26	/931	A	56 RAILWAY ST	HEBBURN COLLIER	10/12/14			APRIL 16, NOVEMBER 18		TO 1st, 23rd BNS, CLASS Z RESERVE.	
GREAVES	J	PTE	26	/925	B								TO LABOUR CORPS.	LAB CORPS No 376624.
GREEN	Fred	PTE	26	/258	D30			8/12/14	30/1/17	AO/29/17 Para 3			TO DEPOT.	SERVED OVERSEAS.
GREEN	H	PTE	26	/940									TO 1st GARRISON BN, CLASS Z RESERVE.	
GREEN	J	PTE	26	/922	B								TO 25th BN, CLASS Z RESERVE.	
GREEN	T	PTE	26	/243	B	54 EDMUND ST	HEBBURN	27/11/14	16/9/16	WNDS 22 NOV 16	MAY 16, JULY16.	HEBBURN	TO DEPOT.	AGE 45.
GREEN	W	PTE	26	/242	B	6 BEECH GROVE TERR	EDMONDSLEY				JUN 16, AUG 16, MAR 17.		TO 1/7th BN, CLASS Z RESERVE.	CPL.
GREEN	Wm	PTE	26	/241	C		WINGATE			16 APRIL 1918		HOUGHTON LE SPRING RC CEM	TO 30th BN(D COY), EAST YORKS REGT(2nd GAR BN).	DIED HOME.
GREENGRASS	M	PTE	26	/916	B								TO 10th, 12/13th BNS, CLASS Z RESERVE.	
GREENWELL	Geo	PTE	26	/244	B		WASHINGTON				OCTOBER 16		TO LABOUR CORPS.	LAB CORPS No 222806.
GREGORY	Edwd	PTE	26	/250	B		SUNDERLAND						TO ARMY SERVICE CORPS.	AWOL CT SUNDLND 20/5/15, ASC No MT/54793,DESERTED.
GRIEVSON	Geo	PTE	26											AWOL 1/7/15 COURT NEWCASTLE 21/7/15
GRUNDY	Wm	PTE	26	/923	B		CRAGHEAD			1 JULY 1916	JUNE 16	OVILLIERS MIL CEM		BORN ANNITSFORD.
GUSTARD	Wm	PTE	26	/269	B	11 FIFTH ST NORTH	EASINGTON COLLI	10/12/14	28/2/19	KR para 392			TO 10th BN, ARMY RESERVE CLASS P.	
HAGAN	JohnJ	PTE	26	/989	C		GATESHEAD	14/12/14	4/10/17	WOUNDS	OCTOBER 16		TO 85th TRAINING RESERVE BN.	AWOL 7/7/15 IN COURT GATESHEAD.
HAGGERTY	Fred	PTE	26	/965	B	57 WOODHORNE RD	ASHINGTON			5 JUNE 1917		BAILLEUL RD ST LAURENT BLAGNY		AGE 21.
HAILS	C	PTE	26	/277	C	43 VICTORIA TERR	WINLATON	26/11/14	5/10/18	SICK			TO DEPOT.	
HALEY	John	PTE	26	/311	C	9 TEES ST	SHOTTON COLLIER	9/12/14			OCTOBER 16		TO 25th, 9th BNS, CLASS Z RESERVE.	SGT.
HALEY	Sam	SGT	26	/963	B		NEWCASTLE			5 JUNE 1917		ARRAS MEM		ACTING COLOUR SERGEANT.
HALL	ChasE	PTE	26	/317	C	54 RAILWAY TERR	GATESHEAD	11/12/14			AUGUST 16			ALSO ON C COY 30th BN ROLL, LIVING STANLEY 1916?
HALL	Geo	SGT	26	/323	B	BARMSTON FERRY LANDI	WASHINGTON	15/12/14	31/3/19	KR para 392			TO ARMY RESERVE CLASS P.	MEMBER OF WASHINGTON METHODIST CHURCH BROTHERHOOD.
HALL	J	PTE	26	/944	B									ALSO ON D COY 30th BN ROLL.
HALL	J H	PTE	26	/978	A		GATESHEAD				OCTOBER 16, DECEMBER 17.		TO 16th BN, ROYAL DEFENCE CORPS.	FRANCE 26th 10/1/16 TO 6/7/16, 16th 7/2/17 TO 16/7
HALL	J J	PTE	26	/943	B			30/11/14	11/10/17	GUNSHOT WOUNDS			TO DEPOT.	

NAME	INITI	RANK	BATTA	NUMBE	COMP	ADDRESS	TOWN_VILL	ENLISTED	DISCHARG	CAUSE_DIS	WOUNDED	BURIED	TRANSFER	ADD
HALL	J W	PTE	26	/986	C				15/5/19				TO 10th BN, KINGS OWN YORKSHIRE LI(2/4TH BN), Z RE	
HALL	T	PTE	26	/278	C	1 ERNEST PLACE GILES	DURHAM CITY	25/11/14	27/3/17	SICK			TO DEPOT.	
HALL	T	PTE	26	/1425	C		SUNDERLAND				NOVEMBER 16			
HALL	W	PTE	26	/942	D		SHILDON COLLIER				OCTOBER 16			
HALLORAN	Dan	PTE	26	/297		44 STANLEY ST	JARROW	6/11/14					TO 1st GARRISON BN, CLASS Z RESERVE.	
HAMIL	Pat	PTE	26	/308			OLD ESH VILLAGE	1/12/14	22/8/17	SICK			TO 1st GARRISON BN, DEPOT.	
HANLON	Edwd	PTE	26	/328	C	9 RECTORY TERR	HETTON LE HOLE				OCTOBER 16		TO LABOUR CORPS.	LAB CORPS No 604473.
HANNAH	G R	PTE	26	/946	B	DEAN COTTAGE	HEWORTH	8/1/15	11/10/18	GUNSHOT WOUNDS	MARCH 16		TO ARMY RESERVE CLASS W.	DESERTED 9/8/15.
HANNEY	F	PTE	26	/947	B	68 STARGATE	RYTON ON TYNE	28/11/14	24/4/18	TRENCH FEVER	AUGUST 16		TO 3rd BN.	
HANNEY	Hugh	PTE	26	/979	C	5 SLINGSBY TERR SHIE	STANLEY	12/12/14		1 JULY 1916		THIEPVAL MEM		BORN BEDLINGTON.
HANNEY	P	PTE	26	/945	B									
HANZELL	Geo O	PTE	26	/1428	C								TO 30th BN(D COY), COMMISSIONED 32nd BN TO 27th BN	
HANZELL	Gibsn	PTE	26	/1427	C								TO LABOUR CORPS.	LAB CORPS No 457210.
HARDCASTLE	M	PTE	26	/1467	D	73 PINE ST	SOUTHMOOR						ATTACHED 34th DIV EMPLOYMENT COY, TO 10th BN, CLAS	
HARDY	D	PTE	26	/1400						KR para 392				
HARDY	J	PTE	26	/280	C	8 CANADA	CHESTER LE ST	25/11/14	23/11/17	GUNSHOT WOUNDS			TO DEPOT.	
HARDY	Thos	PTE	26	/319	B		GATESHEAD	8/12/14	1/8/17	GUNSHOT WOUNDS	OCTOBER 16		TO 3rd BN.	
HARDY	Thos	PTE	26	/948	B		GATESHEAD				JULY 16		TO 25th, 1/4th BNS, CLASS Z RESERVE.	ALLOTED NEW NUMBER 204565.
HARKINS	J	SGT	26	/303	A			30/11/14	20/9/18	SICK			TO 30th BN(C COY), DEPOT.	DID NOT SERVE OVERSEAS, AGE 47.
HARPER	T	PTE	26	/330	C	17 PUMP ROW FRAMWELG	DURHAM CITY	14/12/14	26/10/17	WOUNDS	NOVEMBER 16		TO 85th TRAINING RESERVE BN.	3rd NORTHN GEN HOSP SHEFFIELD 7/16.
HARRIS	A	PTE	26	/333	D	7 MAY ST	BIRTLEY				OCTOBER 16		TO LABOUR CORPS.	LAB CORPS No 396983, SEE ALSO 24/1402
HARRIS	RichO	PTE	26											AWOL 16/2 COURT NEWCASTLE 5/2/15
HARRISON	C	SGT	26	/329	C					KR para 392				
HARRISON	Frank	PTE	26	/281	C	11 MAYNARDS ROW GILE	DURHAM CITY	26/11/14		1 JULY 1916	OCTOBER 16	BAPAUME POST CEM		BORN KIMBLESWORTH.
HARRISON	G	PTE	26	/282	A	FLINT HILL	DIPTON							
HARRISON	J	PTE	26	/316	D									
HARRISON	JohnE	PTE	26	/976	B		TANTOBIE			1 JULY 1916	OCTOBER 16	THIEPVAL MEM		BORN WHITE LE HEAD.
HARWOOD	Henry	PTE	26	/341	D	28 GORDON ST	GATESHEAD						TO 1/4th, 1st BNS, CLASS Z RESERVE.	AWOL 5/9/15 IN COURT GATESHEAD AGE 23.
HARWOOD	J	PTE	26	/283	A	8 VICTORIA PLACE	WASHINGTON						TO 23rd, 10th BNS, CLASS Z RESERVE.	MURDOCHS YARD 1914.
HASTINGS	Thos	PTE	26	/327	C	8 LAMPTON PLACE	NEWCASTLE			1 JULY 1916		THIEPVAL MEM		AWOL 10/7 COURT 22/7/15,53 GARTH HEADS NEWCASTLE.
HAVER	James	CPL	26	/284	C	17 WILLIAM ST	LINTZ COLLIERY				OCTOBER 16		TO 1st, 26th, 23rd BNS, CLASS Z RESERVE.	SGT.
HAWKINS	John	PTE	26	/950	B	72 HALLGARTH ST	DURHAM CITY			12 DEC 1917	JANUARY 17	BUCQUOY RD MIL CEM FICHEUX		
HAWTHORNE	Wm	SGT	26	/326	C	42 HIGH MARKET ST	ASHINGTON	11/12/14					TO 30th BN(C COY).	
HEAD	Arth	PTE	26											AWOL 7/4/15 COURT SUNDERLAND
HEADS	T	PTE	26	/987	A	21 BOLINGSBROKE ST	NEWCASTLE				JULY 1916		TO 23rd, 21st, 25th BNS, CLASS Z RESERVE.	CPL.
HEAL	C	PTE	26	/339	A	6 THE SHUTTLES	GATESHEAD							
HEAL	J	PTE	26	/285				25/11/14	15/11/15	KR para 392			TO 30th BN.	DID NOT SERVE OVERSEAS.
HEAL	Math	PTE	26	/951	A		GATESHEAD			1 JULY 1916		THIEPVAL MEM		AWOL 2/9/15 IN COURT GATESHEAD, AGE 29.
HEAL	Rich	PTE	26											AWOL 2/9/15 COURT GATESHEAD AGE 35.
HEATON	Peter	PTE	26	/338	B	5 LOWER GRAHAM ST	SACRISTON	10/12/14					TO 9th BN, CLASS Z RESERVE.	15 IVESON ST 1914
HEGAN	T	PTE	26	/286	C		EASINGTON	24/11/14	12/9/16	WOUNDS	OCTOBER 16		TO DEPOT.	
HENDERSON	Adam	PTE	26	/962	B	18 WHITEHOUSE TERR	USHAW MOOR	2/12/14						ALSO ON D COY 30th BN.
HENDERSON	James	PTE	26	/298	C	19 WANSBECK ST	CHOPWELL				SHELLSHOCK DEC 16			
HENDERSON	W	PTE	26	/287	C									
HENDRY	J	PTE	26	/320	C									ALSO ON C COY 30th BN ROLL.
HENRY	J W	PTE	26	/970	D									ALSO ON D COY 30th BN ROLL.
HENRY	M	PTE	26	/966	B	183 HIGH ST EAST	SUNDERLAND							
HENRY	T	PTE	26	/300	C	TOWER HOUSE	NEWCASTLE	12/12/14						ALSO ON D COY 30th BN ROLL.
HERDMAN	W L	PTE	26	/1422	A			14/5/15	9/3/16				TO 30th BN(D COY).	DID NOT SERVE OVERSEAS.
HERON	JohnT	PTE	26	/313	C	BEECHGROVE TERR	EDMONDSLEY			6 JULY 1916		BOULOGNE		BORN HETTON, AGE 41.
HERRON	Phil	PTE	26	/967	B	85 HIGH ST	LANGLEY MOOR	7/12/14	31/3/19	KR para 392	SHELLSHOCK NOVEMBER 16		TO 24th, 24/27th, 8th BNS, DEPOT.	ALSO ON C COY 30th BN ROLL.
HESLOP	J	PTE	26	/340	C	21 PADDYS ROW ELDON	SHILDON	15/12/14	5/6/18	SHELLSHOCK			TO ARMY RESERVE CLASS W.	
HEWITSON	W	PTE	26	/343	C	14 CLAYPATH	DURHAM CITY	15/12/14	22/8/17	GUNSHOT WOUNDS	OCTOBER 16		TO 85th TRAINING RESERVE BN.	WATER LANE NEW ELVET 1916.
HICKSON	G	PTE	26	/290	C	SOUTH VIEW	WHICKHAM				JULY 16		TO 2nd BN, CLASS Z RESERVE.	LCPL, ATTESTED WITH TYNESIDE SCOTTISH 2/11/14.
HIGGINS	F	PTE	26	/952	B	41 DOCKWAY SQUARE	NORTH SHIELDS						TO 22nd, 8th BNS, CLASS Z RESERVE.	
HILL	E	PTE	26	/1441	B		TANTOBIE				OCTOBER 16			
HILL	JohnA	PTE	26	/309	C	37 ANGUS ST	WEST HARTLEPOOL	11/12/14						11 SECTION.
HILL	Wilf	PTE	26	/954	D		NEWCASTLE			1 JULY 1916		THIEPVAL MEM		MISSING OCTOBER 16.
HILLARY	M	SGT	26	/292	C			26/11/14	18/4/17	SICK			TO DEPOT.	CPL 11 SECTION.
HILLARY	Mark	PTE	26	/291	C								TO TRAINING RES BN.	AWOL 25/7/15 COURT 11/8, TRG RES BN No TR/5/41405.

NAME	INITI	RANK	BATTA	NUMBE	COMP	ADDRESS	TOWN_VILL	ENLISTED	DISCHARG	CAUSE_DIS	WOUNDED	BURIED	TRANSFER	ADD
HIND	J	DRUM	26	/968	C		GATESHEAD				AUGUST 16		TO CLASS Z RESERVE.	1/5th NORTHERN GEN HOSP LEICESTER 7/7/16.
HINDMARSH	R	PTE	26	/314	C					KR para 392				
HIRST	J	PTE	26	/331	A	41 DURHAM ST	BRANDON	8/12/14		KR para 392				
HODGESON	Aaron	PTE	26	/306	C		BURRADON COLLIE			26 APRIL 1918		BOULOGNE	TO 18th BN.	AGE 37.
HODGSON		PTE	26	/1454	B									ALSO ON D COY 30th BN ROLL.
HODGSON	Miles	PTE	26	/321	A	44 STEPHENSON ST	NORTH SHIELDS	26/11/14					TO 14th BN, CLASS Z RESERVE.	
HODGSON	W	PTE	26	/975	B	11 MILBURNGATE	DURHAM CITY	8/12/14	29/11/17	WOUNDS	MAY 16, JUNE 16, DEC 17.		TO DEPOT.	
HOGG	WilfA	PTE	26	/293	C	18 ROBINSON ST	BLAYDON						TO LABOUR CORPS.	LAB CORPS No 119587, ASGT.
HOGG	Wm A	PTE	26	/971	B		SOUTHWICK	27/11/14	15/12/17	GUNSHOT WOUNDS	AUGUST 16		TO DEPOT.	
HOLDEN	R	CSM	26	/295	A			25/11/14	11/10/18	SHELLSHOCK			TO ARMY RESERVE CLASS W.	LSGT.
HOLDEN	R M	PTE	26	/335	B		CHESTER LE ST	10/12/14	7/3/18	SICK	APRIL 16		TO ARMY RESERVE CLASS P.	
HOLLIDAY	T	SGT	26	/955	B								TO LABOUR CORPS.	LAB CORPS No 613455.
HOLT	R D	PTE	26	/296		47 CHIRTON ST	NEWCASTLE						TO 1st GARRISON BN, CLASS Z RESERVE.	
HOPE	ThosD	PTE	26	/310	C	105 FRAMWELLGATE	DURHAM CITY	2/12/14			AUGUST 16		TO 10th BN, CLASS Z RESERVE.	AWOL 8/8/15 ESCORT 15/8/15.IN 11 SECTION.
HORNSBY	T M	PTE	26	/342	D	935 WALKER RD	NEWCASTLE	14/12/14	15/3/17	WOUNDS	AUGUST 16		TO DEPOT.	
HOUSTON	Jas	PTE	26	/977	C	5 BEDES BLDGS	HEBBURN	12/12/14	14/4/17	GUNSHOT WOUNDS	OCTOBER 16		TO DEPOT.	34 CCS 2/7 EVAC 5/7/16 WND L THIGH, AWOL 15/8/15 C
HOWARD	A A	PTE	26	/302	C		SELBY	30/11/14	27/10/16	CONCUSION OF TH	SEPTEMBER 16		TO DEPOT.	
HOWDEN	T H	LCPL	26	/315	A	14 DOUGLAS ST	WEST STANLEY	2/12/14	4/1/18	GUNSHOT WOUNDS	SEPTEMBER 16		TO ARMY RESERVE CLASS W.	CPL.
HOWELL	Den C	SGT	26	/973	C	31 DUKE ST	NORTH SHIELDS	11/12/14			APRIL 16		TO TRAINING RES BN.	TRG RES No TR/5/61551
HOWGATE	Thos	PTE	26	/322	C		GATESHEAD						TO LABOUR CORPS.	AWOL 8/8, 1/9/15 IN COURT GATESHEAD, AGE 39
HUDSPETH	W	PTE	26	/346	A	91 CANTERBURY ST	BYKER						TO 1st BN, CLASS Z RESERVE.	111 PARKER ST 1918.
HUGGINS	T	PTE	26	/1414	B									
HUGHES	B	LCPL	26	/989		1 EMBLETON ST	DAWDON							
HUGHES	Chris	PTE	26	/958	B	13 HAMPDEN RD	SUNDERLAND			26 OCT 1917		TROIS - ARBRES MIL CEM		
HUGHES	O	PTE	26	/959	B		SPENNYMOOR				SHELLSHOCK AUGUST 16		TO 1/7th, 8th BNS, CLASS Z RESERVE.	SGT.
HUME	W	PTE	26	/343	C	8 FRONT ST	USWORTH			KR para 392	JULY 16, DECEMBER 17.		TO 25th BN.	LCPL 10 PLN C COY 25th BN REP MISSING 21/3/18.
HUNTER	Chas	PTE	26	/1473	C	PROCTORS YARD	MORPETH			1 JULY 1916		THIEPVAL MEM	TO 30th BN.	BORN PRUDHOE.REPEATED AWOL AUGUST 15.
HUNTER	Henry	PTE	26	/961	A	6 GROSVENOR ST	GATESHEAD	2/12/14			OCTOBER 16		TO LABOUR CORPS.	34CCS 1/7 EVAC 5/7/16 WND L ARM,AGE 16 AWOL22/7/15
HUNTER	John	PTE	26	/985	C	23 CLARENCE ST	BOWBURN			1 JULY 1916	APRIL 16	THIEPVAL MEM		KILLED DRAGGING CQMS WILD INTO A SHELLHOLE.
HUNTER	Jos	PTE	26	/1471	D		GATESHEAD				SEPTEMBER 16			AWOL 4/8,14/8,18/8/15 CT 4/8,16/8,21/8/15
HURLEY	Jos	PTE	26	/299	C	1 BRYSON ST	SHIELDFIELD			18 MARCH 1918		ARRAS MEM	TO 23rd, 26th, 1st BNS.	SGT.
HURST	Henry	PTE	26											DESERTER 23/2/15 COURT SUNDERLAND
HUTCHINSON	Alf Y	LCPL	26	/972	B	18 CECIL ST	NORTH SHIELDS	10/12/14		9 MARCH 1916		SAILLY SUR LYS CANADIAN CEM		LSGT, BORN HEBBURN.
HUTCHINSON	John	PTE	26	/305	C	26 PLANTATION ST	WINGATE			13 APRIL 1918		PLOEGSTEERT MEM	TO 25th BN(10 PLTN).	REP MISSING 21/3/18 BORN WIGAN.
HUTCHINSON	W	PTE	26	/1450	A		AUKLAND PARK				MAY 17			
HUTTON	C	PTE	26	/337				10/12/14	15/11/15	KR para 392			TO 30th BN.	DID NOT SERVE OVERSEAS.
HYDE	J	AWO1	26	/345									TO 1st GARRISON BN, CLASS Z RESERVE.	
IBBETSON	Mich	PTE	26	/352	C	20 TEES ST	CHOPWELL			1 JULY 1916		THIEPVAL MEM		LCPL, BORN B/AUKLAND. MISSING OCTOBER 16.
ICETON		PTE	26	/355									TO 14th BN, CLASS Z RESERVE.	DESERTED 17/9/17.
INGLIS	Will	PTE	26	/351	B		GATESHEAD			10 SEPT 1916		ADANAC MIL CEM		ACPL.
INGRAM	A	PTE	26	/999	C	60 STATION RD	EASINGTON COLLI	10/12/14	31/3/19	KR para 392	JANUARY 1917		TO ARMY RESERVE CLASS P.	
IREDALE	Geo	PTE	26	/990	A		GATESHEAD			5 JUNE 1917		ARRAS MEM		
IRVINE	JohnW	PTE	26											AWOL 1/12 COURT NEWCASTLE 4/12/15
IRVING	J	PTE	26	/991	D		DARLINGTON	30/11/14	15/10/17	WOUNDS	AUGUST 16		TO 85th TRAINING RESERVE BN.	
IRVING	J W	PTE	26	/357	B	11 BARKER ST	NEWCASTLE						TO 3rd BN, ROYAL ARMY MEDICAL CORPS	RAMC No 205951.
IRVING	R	PTE	26	/358	C	21 WILLIAM ST	LINTZ COLLIERY				JULY 16		TO LABOUR CORPS.	3 CCS 2/7/16 EVAC 2/7/16 GSW.
IRVING	ThosF	PTE	26	/353	B	268 JOHN WILLIAMSON	SOUTH SHIELDS	2/12/14		1 JULY 1916		THIEPVAL MEM		MISSING OCTOBER 16, BORN HEBBURN.
IRWIN	H	PTE	26	/1385	C	6 HEWORTH TERR	PENSHAW				OCTOBER 16		TO 20th, 26th, 25th BNS, ROYAL FUSILIERS(24th BN).	21 AMB TR,18 G HOSP 6/7,6 CONV DEPOT 13/7/16.
JACKSON	Chas	PTE	26	/365	C	5 SEASIDE LANE GLEBE	EASINGTON COLLI	9/12/14			OCTOBER 16		TO LABOUR CORPS.	
JACKSON	J	PTE	26	/1003	C30		GATESHEAD				NOVEMBER 16		TO 25th, 1/5th, 1st BNS.	AWOL 7/4/15, DESERTED 1/8/18.
JACKSON	Wm	PTE	26											AWOL 14/5/15 COURT GATESHEAD
JAMES	S	PTE	26	/359	D									ALSO ON D COY 30th BN ROLL.
JARVIS	Edwin	PTE	26	/382		6 KIRKSOP ST JESMOND	NEWCASTLE							
JEFFERSON	G	PTE	26	/1005	C									IN 11 SECTION, CROSSED OFF ROLL. ALSO ON C COY 30t
JEFFERY	N	PTE	26	/998	C		CHESTER LE ST	12/12/14	26/9/17	KR para 392	OCTOBER 16		TO DEPOT.	
JEFFERY	Thos	PTE	26	/363	C		WASHINGTON			1 JULY 1916		THIEPVAL MEM		
JENNINGS	JohnE	PTE	26	/360	B		FELLING			11 MAY 1916		BECOURT MIL CEM		
JENNINGS	Tom	CPL	26	/1006	B	20 RAILWAY ST	LITTLEBURN COLL			9 APRIL 1916	8 APRIL 16	BAILLEUL		SGT.
JOBLING	E	SGT	26	/362	D	18 CHANDLER LANE	NORTH SHIELDS						TO CLASS Z RESERVE.	CSGT.
JOBSON	C	PTE	26	/995	C		BOLDON COLLIERY	8/12/14	18/4/17	WOUNDS	JUNE 16		TO DEPOT.	CPL.

NAME	INITI	RANK	BATTA	NUMBE	COMP	ADDRESS	TOWN_VILL	ENLISTED	DISCHARG	CAUSE_DIS	WOUNDED	BURIED	TRANSFER	ADD
JOHNSON	A	PTE	26	/1001	D	25 VICTORIA ST	GATESHEAD							
JOHNSON	Geo	PTE	26	/993	C	13 EAST ST	BRANDON COLLIER	11/12/14		1 JULY 1916		THIEPVAL MEM		
JOHNSON	J	PTE	26	/369	C	9 MOODYS BLDGS GILES	DURHAM CITY	26/11/14					TO TRAINING RES BN.	
JOHNSON	John	PTE	26	/361	B	CROSSGATE	DURHAM CITY			12 MAY 1916		BECOURT MIL CEM		
JOHNSON	Thos	PTE	26	/367	A	131 STAFFORDSHIRE ST	SACRISTON	9/12/14		1 JULY 1916		THIEPVAL MEM		MISSING OCTOBER 16, NICKNAMED TOSSER.
JOHNSTON	J	PTE	26	/1410	B									
JONES	Chas	PTE	26	/1007	D	14 FOURTH ST EAST	EASINGTON COLLI	9/12/14		31 MARCH 1916		BREWERY ORCHARD		BORN WAPPING, ACCIDENTLY KILLED.
JONES	Dvd J	LCPL	26	/997	C	13 SOUTH VIEW	SHERBURN HILL						TO 10th BN, ROYAL FUSILIERS(24th BN).	FRANCE 26th, 10/1/16 to 3/7/18, 10th 4/7/18 to 29/
JONES	J W	PTE	26	/364		64 WEST ST	GRANGE VILLA						TO 39 POW COY.	
JONES	J W	SGT	26	/368	D	12 WEAR TERR	WASHINGTON	9/12/14	1/3/19	KR para 392	SEPTEMBER 16		TO 3rd BN, ARMY RESERVE CLASS P.	
JORDAN	J	PTE	26	/366	A								ATT 109,112 RAIL CONST COYS R.E. 10th BN, Z RES.	
KANE	P	PTE	26	/1013	C	12 STANLEY ST	JARROW							ALSO ON D COY 30th BN ROLL.
KEARNEY	Rob	PTE	26	/1021		47 BUDDLE RD	BENWELL	12/12/14					TO 1st GARRISON BN, CLASS Z RESERVE.	
KEATING	T	PTE	26	/1375	C		NEWCASTLE	12/1/15	4/11/16	SICK	OCTOBER 16		TO DEPOT.	IN 11 SECTION, BATH WAR HOSP 11/7/16.
KEGG	Nelsn	PTE	26	/1024	D	3 FORESTER CT PILGRI	NEWCASTLE				OCTOBER 16		TO 27th, 24/27th, 14th, 12/13th, 14th BNS, Z RES.	AWOL 17/4 CT 23/5/15, 195 PILGRIM ST 1918.
KELLS	Thos	PTE	26	/1356	A								TO ROYAL ARMY MEDICAL CORPS.	RAMC No 135431.
KELLY	Aaron	PTE	26	/1011	A		GATESHEAD	28/11/14	13/7/18	WOUNDS	APRIL 16, APRIL 18.		TO DEPOT.	
KELLY	E	PTE	26	/1019									TO 1st GARRISON BN, CLASS Z RESERVE.	
KELLY	Jas	PTE	26											AWOL 7/7 29/7 28/10 COURT GATESHEAD AGE 43.
KELLY	L	PTE	26									? UNABLE TO TRACE	TO 1st GARRISON BN, UNKNOWN REGT.	SERVANT TO CAPT FALKOUS AT WOOLSINGTON
KELLY	M	PTE	26	/1336	A		DIPTON						TO LABOUR CORPS.	ALSO ON C COY 30th BN ROLL.
KELLY	Thos	PTE	26	/1012	C	105 STATION RD	EASINGTON COLLI	9/12/14	10/5/18		OCTOBER 16		TO ROYAL JERSEY GARRISON BN.	BATH WAR HOSP 11/7/16, BORN DUNDEE.
KENNEDY	G S	PTE	26	/1020	B								TO LABOUR CORPS.	LAB CORPS No 260026.
KENNEDY	J	PTE	26	/377	B						MAY 16			
KENNEDY	J	PTE	26	/1369	B									ALSO ON C COY 30th BN ROLL.
KENNEY	G S	PTE	26	/378	B		NEWCASTLE				JULY 16			
KENT	G	PTE	26	/1016	A									COULD BE ON D COY 30th BN ROLL AS /1216.
KETTLE	David	PTE	26	/1009	D		GATESHEAD	30/11/14	31/8/18	GUNSHOT WOUNDS	OCTOBER 16		TO LABOUR CORPS, ARMY RESERVE CLASS W.	LAB CORPS No 702230,BEAUFORT WAR HOSP BRISTOL 8/7/
KEYLAND	Dan	PTE	26	/1014	C	48 GEORGE ST	SPENNYMOOR	8/12/14					TO LABOUR CORPS.	IN 11 SECTION, LAB CORPS No 371427.
KILTY	Rich	PTE	26	/1023	A	64a SCOTSWOOD RD	NEWCASTLE	12/12/14					TO 30th BN(C COY).	AWOL 25/7, 28/8 CT 29/7, 2/9/15.
KIMMETT	Andrw	PTE	26	/1015	C	CHURCH ST	HASWELL COLLIER				JULY 16		TO ROYAL ENGINEERS 30th LABOUR BN, CLASS Z RESERVE	
KING	J	PTE	26	/373	D	27 STROTHERS TERR	HIGH SPEN				JULY 16		TO 10th BN, CLASS Z RESERVE.	
KIRBY	David	PTE	26	/1018	C	6 RUSSELL ST TEAMS	GATESHEAD	10/12/14			DECEMBER 16		TO LABOUR CORPS.	LAB CORPS No 418112, SEE 27/1059 BROTHER.
KITCHEN	T	PTE	26	/372	A	21 PARK TERR	TANFIELD		7/2/19				TO 10th BN, KINGS OWN YORKSHIRE LI(2/4th BN), Z RE	
KNOWLES	Jas	PTE	26	/376	A	43 DOUGLAS TERR	USWORTH COLLIER						TO ROYAL ARMY ORDNANCE CORPS.	RAOC No 039305.
KNOWLES	Robt	PTE	26	/381	A	8 ARCHERS HILL	SOUTH SHIELDS	9/12/14	13/3/18	TRENCH FEET	AUGUST 16		TO 3rd BN.	
KNOX	Andrw	PTE	26	/375		2 WEATHERLEY ST	NEWCASTLE			26 AUGUST 1917		HAGRICOURT CEM	TO 19th, 22nd BNS.	DESERTED 2 JUNE 1917, age 33.
LAKE	J	PTE	26	/392	B	21 CAMDEN LANE	NORTH SHIELDS	5/12/14	1/12/17	SICK			TO 3rd BN.	DID NOT SERVE OVERSEAS. AGE 33.
LAMB	JohnG	PTE	26											AWOL 17/7/15 COURT GATESHEAD AGE 24.
LAMPH	H	PTE	26	/398	A			2/12/14	2/1/18				TO DEPOT.	ALSO ON D COY 30th BN ROLL.
LANAHAN	John	PTE	26	/1039	A		JARROW			1 JULY 1916		THIEPVAL MEM		MISSING OCTOBER 16.
LANCASTER	Arthr	LSGT	26	/1046	A	FRONT ST	CRAGHEAD	10/12/14		29 APRIL 1917	AUGUST 16	ARRAS MEM	TO 23rd BN.	BROTHER J 26/406 BROTHER CHARLES ALSO KILLED.
LANCASTER	James	LCPL	26	/406	C	53 KIMBERLEY TERR	CRAGHEAD	10/12/14		1 JULY 1916	OCTOBER 16	SERRE RD NO2 CEM		26/1046 BROTHER LSGT A,BROTHER CHARLES ALSO KILLED
LANGFORD	John	PTE	26	/399	D		NEWCASTLE			1 JULY 1916	OCTOBER 16	OVILLIERS MIL CEM		LCPL. BORN BERWICK.
LANGTON	J M	PTE	26	/388	B	80 DEPTFORD RD	SUNDERLAND	24/11/14	22/5/17	WOUNDS	AUGUST 16		TO DEPOT.	
LARGUE	Isaac	PTE	26	/383	C		BURNHOPEFIELD			1 JULY 1916		OVILLIERS MIL CEM		MISSING OCTOBER 16.
LAWS	M	LCPL	26	/1041	D								TO LABOUR CORPS.	LAB CORPS No 6155009.
LAWSON	Geo	PTE	26	/1366	B		SOUTH SHIELDS			27 SEPT 1918		VIS-EN-ARTOIS MEM	TO 25th, 12/13th BNS.	ALSO ON C COY 30th BN ROLL.
LAWSON	Wm	SGT	26	/391	A	15 LIME ST OUSEBURN	NEWCASTLE	10/12/14			OCTOBER 16			
LAYDON	Chas	PTE	26	/1045	D		NEWCASTLE			31 DEC 1917	OCTOBER 16	TYNE COT MEM	TO 14th, 1/7th BNS.	
LEADBITTER	Wm	PTE	26	/396									TO LABOUR CORPS.	LAB CORPS No 475950. AWOL 29/8/15 CT G/HEAD AGE 29
LEE	Jos	LCPL	26	/389	B	35 BLOEMFONTEIN TERR	CRAGHEAD				JULY 16		TO 12th, 26th, 28th BNS, DURHAM LI(15th BN), Z RES	SGT DLI No 46514.
LESSELLS	Alex	PTE	26	/1044	C		BLYTH				OCTOBER 16		TO LABOUR CORPS.	LAB CORPS No 478076.
LEVITT	P	PTE	26	/1368	C									ALSO ON D COY 30th BN ROLL.
LEWCOCK	J	PTE	26	/1055	C		GATESHEAD				OCTOBER 16		TO 25th, 8th BNS.	DESERTED 31 MAY 1917.
LEWINS	Henry	PTE	26	/1048	C		OLD PENSHAW			1 JULY 1916		OVILLIERS MIL CEM		
LEWINS	Mart	PTE	26	/395		THOMPSONS BLDGS	HUTTON HENRY			KR para 392			TO 2nd GARRISON BN.	
LEWIS	J W	PTE	26	/385				30/11/14	3/9/16	KR para 392			TO 1st GARRISON BN, DEPOT.	
LEWIS	Ternc	LCPL	26	/1038	A	1 RED BARNS TERR	NEWCASTLE			1 JULY 1916		THIEPVAL MEM		SGT, MISSING OCTOBER 16,TRENCH RAIDS 5/6, 25/26/16
LIDDLE	T W	PTE	26	/1367	C	66 FRANK ST	BENWELL						TO LABOUR CORPS.	LAB CORPS No 407696.

NAME	INITI	RANK	BATTA	NUMBE	COMP	ADDRESS	TOWN_VILL	ENLISTED	DISCHARG	CAUSE_DIS	WOUNDED	BURIED	TRANSFER	ADD
LIGHTFOOT	W	PTE	26	/1030	D		FELLING	27/11/14	15/1/19	KR para 392	DECEMBER 16		TO ARMY RESERVE CLASS W.	
LINCOLN	Jas	SGT	26	/402	B	27 VESPASIAN AVE	SOUTH SHIELDS	15/12/14	28/3/16	VDH			TO 30th BNS.	DID NOT SERVE OVERSEAS, BOROUGH ENGRS DEPT SSHIELD
LISTER	Ralph	PTE	26	/1047	C	7 SHERATON ST	SHOTTON COLLIER	12/12/14		1 JULY 1916		THIEPVAL MEM		
LITTLEWOOD	Wm	CPL	26	/400	B	10 SHERATON ST	SHOTTON COLLIER	9/12/14	31/12/17	GUNSHOT WOUNDS			TO 3rd BN.	
LIVETT	John	PTE	26	/1034	C		SPENNYMOOR			27 OCT 1917	AUGUST 16	SOLFERINO FARM CEM YPRES	TO 1st, 1/7th BNS.	3rd SOUTHERN GEN HOSP EXETER 8/7/16.
LOCKERON	James	PTE	26	/1043	C	17 FRAMWELLGATE	DURHAM CITY						TO LABOUR CORPS, ROYAL FUSILIERS.	IN 11 SECTION.
LOCKERON	John	PTE	26	/387	C	119 MILBURNGATE	DURHAM CITY	26/11/14	30/7/17	FRACTURES			TO 3rd BN. CONSCRIPTED INTO RAOC.	IN 11 SECTION.
LOCKEY	J	PTE	26	/1424	D									ALSO ON D COY 30th BN ROLL.
LOGAN	Jas	PTE	26	/1040	C30	56 BENWELL DENE TERR	BENWELL	7/12/14	25/1/19	KR para 392			TO DEPOT.	DID NOT SERVE OVERSEAS.
LOGAN	P	PTE	26	/394	B	5 WALTON TERR	BEDLINGTON STAT						TO 10th BN, ROYAL FUSILIERS(24th BN).	FRANCE 26th,10/1/16to3/7/18,10th 4/7/18to30/8/18,
LONGDON	T	PTE	26	/1436									TO 1st GARRISON BN, CLASS Z RESERVE.	
LORIMER	AlexG	PTE	26	/1057			DARLINGTON			13 JULY 1915		JESMOND		BORN BRADFORD.
LOWCOCKS	John	PTE	26											AWOL 19/10 COURT NEWCASTLE 10/11/15
LOWERY	RichH	PTE	26	/1035	A		BENWELL			24 APRIL 1917		ARRAS MEM		
LOWERY	Thos	PTE	26	/1365	B	ELVET	DURHAM CITY				AUGUST 16		TO LABOUR CORPS(930 LAB COY).	LAB CORPS No 418229,AWOL 3rd BN 30/1/17 H/O 8/2/17
LUCAS	Alf	PTE	26	/407	C	1 NORTH VIEW	ASHINGTON	12/12/14		KR para 392				CPL
LUCY	John	PTE	26	/404	C	3 WHITWELL ST	EAST STANLEY						TO LABOUR CORPS.	LAB CORPS No 570410.
LUKE	Geo	PTE	26	/403	C	13 BACK STONE ST	BENFIELDSIDE				JANUARY 1917		TO 27th, 24/27th, 25th, 12/13th BNS, CLASS Z RESER	
LUKE	J	PTE	26	/1527										34 CCS 1/7/16 EVAC 5/7/16 WND L SIDE. AGE 47.
LUKE	Syd	PTE	26	/1049	C	LAMPTON ST	SHERBURN HILL	12/12/14		19 MAY 1917		ETAPLES		CPL.
LUNN	Fred	PTE	26	/401	B		OUSEBURN				JUNE 16, OCTOBER 16.		TO LABOUR CORPS, ARMY SERVICE CORPS.	AWOL 23/5 CT 10/6/15, LC No 425096,ASC No M/332206
LUNN	G	PTE	26	/1029	D	348 STANHOPE RD	TYNE DOCK	26/11/14	9/4/17	GUNSHOT WOUNDS	OCTOBER 16		TO 85th TRAINING RESERVE BN.	3 CCS 2/7/16 EVAC 3/7/16.
LYNAS	T	PTE	26	/397	B	24 JACKSON ST	WEST HARTLEPOOL							
LYNCH	H	SGT	26	/1032	A	6 MOUNT PLEASANT	NEWBURN						TO 85th TRAINING RESERVE BN, CLASS Z RESERVE.	
LYNCH	John	PTE	26	/390	A	13 PRINCE CONSORT RD	HEBBURN	9/12/14		5 MAY 1917		ETAPLES		BORN GLASGOW.
LYNCH	John	SGT	26	/1033	B	33 YORK ST	GATESHEAD				AUGUST 16		TO 14th, 1/7th BNS, CLASS Z RESERVE.	3 CCS 2/7/16 EVAC 2/7/16 GSW, ACTING CSM.
LYNCH	Mich	PTE	26	/1054	C	35 SUNDERLAND ST	BRANDON COLLIER			1 JULY 1916		THIEPVAL MEM		MISSING OCTOBER 16.
LYNCH	T	PTE	26	/1053				15/12/14	25/9/16	UNFIT			TO 1st GARRISON BN, DEPOT.	AGE 40.
MACKELL	Thos	PTE	26	/1409	B		GATESHEAD	11/5/15	11/4/17	NEURATHASIA			TO DEPOT.	AWOL 24/8/15 COURT GATESHEAD AGE 41.
MACKIN	F	PTE	26	/419	D	86 CHARLES ST	HEBBURN	25/11/14	4/8/17	KR para 392			TO DEPOT.	
MACKIN	Thos	PTE	26	/449	A	19 BLAKE ST	EASINGTON			1 JULY 1916		THIEPVAL MEM		MISSING OCTOBER 16, BORN FELLING.
MADDEN	J	PTE	26	/420	C	6 WOODSIDE	WASHINGTON				DECEMBER 16		TO 21st, 25th BNS, 24th ROYAL FUSILIERS.	FRANCE 26 11/1/16 TO 4/7/16, 21 10/1/17 TO 13/2/18
MADDEN	Nich	PTE	26	/421	A	34 GROSVENOR ST	GATESHEAD	12/11/14			OCTOBER 16		TO LABOUR CORPS.	LAB CORPS No 368588. REPEATED AWOL.
MADDISON	JohnA	PTE	26	/1390	C	FIRE BRICK COTTAGE	WASHINGTON			1 MARCH 1916		BREWERY ORCHARD		LCPL, AGE 20, BORN CHESTER LE ST.
MADDISON	Jos	PTE	26	/415	C	12 RIVER VIEW	WASHINGTON	7/12/14	31/3/19	KR para 392	OCTOBER 16		TO ARMY RESERVE CLASS P.	SGT, SPRINGBURN HOSP GLASGOW 11/7/16.
MADDOX	John	PTE	26	/1085	A	2 HEPWORTH ST	NEW BRANCEPETH	11/12/14		1 JULY 1916		THIEPVAL MEM		LCPL, BORN DURHAM.
MAGEE	J	PTE	26	/433	D		EASINGTON LANE	15/12/14	4/8/17	GUNSHOT WOUNDS	AUGUST 16		TO 85th TRAINING RESERVE BN.	
MAINS	W	SGT	26	/417	A	31 HEBBURN ST	HEBBURN						TO LABOUR CORPS.	LAB CORPS No 417960, AWOL 22/8 CT G/HEAD, AGE 45,
MALIN	P	PTE	26	/422				28/11/14	15/2/16	KR para 392			TO 2nd GARRISON BN, 30th BN.	
MALOY	P	PTE	26	/1081									TO 1st GARRISON BN, ROYAL DEFENCE CORPS.	IN MALTA 17/8/15 TO 11/6/17.
MANLEY	A	PTE	26	/428	C	8 BACK ST	DINNINGTON	30/11/14	15/11/18	TRENCH FEVER			TO 3rd BN.	
MANLEY	Mich	PTE	26	/1064	C	8 LUCY ST	STANLEY	2/12/14				STANLEY	TO 9th, 12/13th BNS, CLASS Z RESERVE.	104 YEARS OLD.
MANN	W	PTE	26	/1065	C	ALBION HOUSE	WILLINGTON	24/11/14	10/12/17	GUNSHOT WOUNDS	OCTOBER 16		TO DEPOT.	
MARCH	Thos	PTE	26	/458	D	61 BIRCHAM ST	SOUTHMOOR	12/12/14			JUNE 16		TO 16th BN, CLASS Z RESERVE.	120 BEAMISH ST 1914.
MARR	Dan	PTE	26	/1104	D	21 WILFRED ST	BYKER			8 JULY 1916	NOVEMBER 16	WIMEREUX		1/8/15 IN COURT 23/8/15.
MARRINGTON	A	PTE	26	/1066	A								TO 10th BN, CLASS Z RESERVE.	
MARSHALL	Geo	PTE	26	/457	D	81 THOMAS TERR	BLAYDON			1 JAN 1917		FORCEVILLE COM CEM		
MARSHALL	J	SGT	26	/1097	C		CARLISLE	14/12/14	8/8/17	WOUNDS	OCTOBER 16		TO DEPOT.	
MARSHALL	Jos	PTE	26	/1102	C	81 THOMAS TERR	BLAYDON			1 APRIL 1916		BREWERY ORCHARD		
MARTIN	Jas	PTE	26	/455	D		SUNDERLAND			1 JULY 1916		THIEPVAL MEM		MISSING OCTOBER 16.
MARTIN	John	PTE	26	/1086	A	22 BLOOMFIELD ST	SUNDERLAND	10/12/14			JULY 16		TO LABOUR CORPS.	LAB CORPS No 18876.
MARTIN	Pat	LCPL	26	/1077	A	20 NELSON ST	WILLINGTON	30/11/14	3/1/18	GUNSHOT WOUNDS	OCTOBER 16		TO 85th TRAINING RESERVE BN.	BROTHERS FELIX IN DLI AND FRANK IN RFA.
MARTIN	Thos	PTE	26											DESERTED 26/4/15 COURT NEWCASTLE 3/6/15.
MASON	J	PTE	26	/427	C		CHOPWELL				OCTOBER 16		TO ROYAL DEFENCE CORPS.	IN FRANCE 10/1/16 TO 5/7/16.
MASON	J	PTE	26	/447	D30			10/12/14	9/3/16				TO 30th BN.	DID NOT SERVE OVERSEAS.
MASON	Math	PTE	26	/426	C		LEEDS			28 AUGUST 1917	OCTOBER 16	ARRAS MEM	TO 11th, 1st BNS.	IN 11 SECTION.
MATHEWS	J	PTE	26	/1362	D		SOUTH SHIELDS	12/1/15	27/7/17	GUNSHOT WOUNDS	JULY 16		TO 3rd BN.	SGT.
MEEK	Sam	PTE	26	/1068	A		NEWCASTLE			1 JULY 1916	OCTOBER 16	THIEPVAL MEM		MISSING DECEMBER 16, BORN WEST HARTLEPOOL.
MEGAN	Thos	PTE	26	/412	C	18 WELDON TERR	WASHINGTON			20 SEPT 1917	OCTOBER 16.	TYNE COT MEM	TO 11th BN.	BORN LANCASTER. POS LANCHESTER ?
MERRINER	James	CPL	26	/432	A	16 QUEEN ST	RYHOPE	8/12/14		20 FEB 1916		SUTTON VENY	TO 30th BN ?.	DID NOT SERVE OVERSEAS, BORN WASHINGTON.

NAME	INITI	RANK	BATTA	NUMBE	COMP	ADDRESS	TOWN_VILL	ENLISTED	DISCHARG	CAUSE_DIS	WOUNDED	BURIED	TRANSFER	ADD
METCALFE	JohnT	PTE	26	/416	A	8 SIXTH ST	EASINGTON	10/12/14		5 AUGUST 1916		CABERET ROUGE BRIT CEM		BORN HOUGHTON LE SPRING.
MEUSE	J	PTE	26	/464	D				17/3/19				TO 18th BN, KINGS OWN YORKSHIRE LI(2/4th BN), Z RE	
MIDDLEMAS		CPL	26	/409	C30									
MIDDLEMASS	T	LCPL	26	/405	B									
MILEY	T	PTE	26	/443	A		WASHINGTON	1/12/14	23/12/18	SICK	OCTOBER 16		TO ARMY RESERVE CLASS W.	AGE 39.
MILLAR	R H	PTE	26	/1103	C		SUNDERLAND				JUNE 18		TO 19th, 2nd BNS, CLASS Z RESERVE.	
MILLAR	T	CSM	26	/1439	D30			28/5/15	28/8/16	VARICOSE VEINS			TO 30th, 34th BNS.	DID NOT SERVE OVERSEAS.
MILLER	Wm	PTE	26	/418	A	8 CHATHAM PLACE	NEWCASTLE	12/12/14					TO BEDFORDSHIRE REGT, BEDFDS & HERTS REGT.	BEDFDS No 43776.
MILLER	Wm	PTE	26	/454	D		RYHOPE	10/12/14	20/4/17	GUNSHOT WOUNDS	AUGUST 16		TO DEPOT.	
MILLIGAN	R	PTE	26	/1412	D	80 ELSWICK RD	NEWCASTLE				OCTOBER 16			
MILLS	R	SGT	26	/463	A		BEDLINGTON	7/12/14	31/3/19	KR para 392	OCTOBER 16		TO ARMY RESERVE CLASS P.	
MILTON	G	PTE	26	/446										ALSO ON C COY 30th BN ROLL.
MILTON	W	PTE	26	/1413	C		SOUTH SHIELDS				DECEMBER 16		TO LABOUR CORPS.	LAB CORPS No 401353.
MINTO	Geo	PTE	26	/1090	C	14 THIRD ST EAST	EASINGTON COLLI	10/12/14	31/12/17	GUNSHOT WOUNDS	OCTOBER 16		TO 3rd BN.	
MINTO	Wm	PTE	26	/1096	C	18 VICTOR ST	BEARPARK	10/12/14	25/8/16	14 AUGUST 1916		BEARPARK		DIED OF GAS POISONING, BRO JOHN IN T/SIDE SCOTTISH
MOAN	T	CPL	26	/429	A								TO LABOUR CORPS.	LAB CORPS No 442630.
MONOGHAN	Jas	PTE	26	/1099	C		WESTGATE Co DUR			1 JULY 1916		THIEPVAL MEM		
MONTAGUE	John	PTE	26	/1101	B	65 ORTON ST	GATESHEAD				OCTOBER 16		TO LABOUR CORPS(743 A E COY).	CPL. LAB CORPS No 421097.
MOOR	Walte	PTE	26	/410	A	79 LICHFIELD ST	GATESHEAD			27 SEPT 1918		RIBECOURT ROAD CEM	TO 25th BN, KINGS OWN YORKSHIRE LI(2/4th BN).	BORN PENRITH, KOYLI No 63420.
MOORE	Wm	PTE	26	/430	A	11 FRAMWELLGATE	DURHAM CITY	28/11/14		5 JUNE 1918		BRANDON	TO 1st, 3rd BNS.	FELL FROM EXPRESS TRAIN ON DURHAM VIADUCT 5/6/18.
MORALEE	M	PTE	26	/1070				23/11/14	9/10/15	MEDICALLY UNFIT				
MORAN	J	PTE	26	/1091	C	3 GIBSIDE TERR	BURNHOPEFIELD	9/12/14	10/7/16	SICK			TO DEPOT.	
MORAN	M	PTE	26	/459		44 CHARLTON ST	GATESHEAD						TO 2nd GARRISON BN.	
MORELAND	Jhn W	PTE	26	/461	D	14 BROOM LANE	USHAW MOOR	8/12/14						
MORGAN	F	PTE	26	/1060	D	36 FRAMWELLGATE	DURHAM CITY	26/11/14	18/5/17	FRACTURES			TO COMMAND DEPOT RIPON.	
MORGAN	Frcis	PTE	26	/1059	C		WITTON PARK			1 JULY 1916		THIEPVAL MEM		11 SECTION.
MORGAN	W	PTE	26	/431	D									ALSO ON D COY 30th BN ROLL.
MORPETH	John	PTE	26	/413			HEWORTH			1 JULY 1916		THIEPVAL MEM		IN 11 SECTION.
MORRIS	Bernd	PTE	26	/1095	C	15 BLACKETT ST	SACRISTON	10/12/14		23 JUNE 1916		BOIS GUILLAME MIL CEM		HEWER AT SACRISTON PIT, BORN TRIMDON COLLIERY.
MORRIS	W	PTE	26	/411	D	26 BLENHEIM ST	NEWCASTLE			KR para 392				
MORROW	A	PTE	26	/1076	A								TO ROYAL ENGINEERS.	RE No 359878.
MORTON	T	PTE	26	/444	C		EDMONDSLEY				JULY 16, DEC 16, DEC 17.		TO LABOUR CORPS.	LCORPS No 421042 WND RSHLDR 34 CCS 2/7/16 EVAC 5/7
MOSS	H	PTE	26	/1082	C						MAY 16		TO GREEN HOWARDS.	GREEN HOWARDS No 39823.
MOSSOP	G	PTE	26	/1071	A		WHEATLEY HILL	24/11/14	24/8/17	GUNSHOT WOUNDS	JULY 16		TO 85th TRAINING RESERVE BN.	VOLUNTARY AID HOSP CHELTENHAM 11/7/16.
MUCKIAN	Ternc	PTE	26	/436	A	14 DUNNS BLDGS HILLG	GATESHEAD				OCTOBER 16		TO RES BN IN SCOTLAND, LABOUR CORPS.	LAB CORPS No 472254.
MULLEN	Isaac	PTE	26	/456	D30		GATESHEAD	11/12/14	7/5/16				TO 30th BN.	DID NOT SERVE OVERSEAS, AWOL 5/8, 31/8/15 AGE 43.
MULLEN	J	PTE	26	/1456	C									
MULLHOLLAND	Thos	PTE	26	/450	D	132 STATION RD	ASHINGTON	12/12/14			MARCH 16, APR 16, OCT 16		TO 12/13th BN, CLASS Z RESERVE.	LCPL, RV HOSP NETLEY 11/7/16
MULLVANEY	Thos	PTE	26	/438	A	4 JAMES ST	BLAYDON			4 NOV 1918		RUESNES COM CEM	TO 10th BN, KINGS OWN YORKSHIRE LI(2/4th BN).	BORN KELLO CO MEATH, KOYLI No 63419.GEORGE ST BLAY
MUDIE	John	PTE	26	/1451		6 THIRLEWELL TERR ST	SUNDERLAND					SOUTHWICK	TO 85th TRAINING RESERVE BN?	BORN GATESHEAD.
MURDY	R	PTE	26	/445	C								TO LABOUR CORPS.	
MURPHY	J	PTE	26	/1074	B	41 BK CHARLES ST	JARROW	4/12/14						
MURPHY	T	PTE	26	/1075	D		BLACKHALL MILL				JULY 16			
MURPHY	Tom	PTE	26	/1080		23 SUNDERLAND STREET	NEWCASTLE			20 NOV 1916		HULL HEDON ROAD CEM	TO 30th BN.	
MURRAY	B	PTE	26	/460	D	1 NEW ROW NORTH	WASHINGTON						TO ROYAL FLYING CORPS 22/1/18.	
MURRAY	J W	PTE	26	/1062				30/11/14	15/3/15	INNEFFICIENT				DID NOT SERVE OVERSEAS.
MURRAY	P	PTE	26	/439	C	57 BK ROSE ST	HEBBURN NEWTOWN						TO 30th BN(C COY).	
MURRAY	R	PTE	26	/408	B	36 GOSFORTH ST	SUNDERLAND							
MURTHWAITE	Robt	PTE	26	/1094	D	123 SYCAMORE ST	NEWCASTLE	10/12/14						
MUSGROVE	Jas	PTE	26	/462	A	1 VICTORIA ST	SACRISTON	9/12/14			JULY 16		TO 1/5th BN, TO ROYAL FUSILIERS.	R FUS No GS/83706, 114 PITFIELD ST 1914.
MUSGROVE	Robt	CPL	26	/440	C		GATESHEAD			1 JULY 1916	OCTOBER 16	THIEPVAL MEM		BORN RYHOPE.
MUSGROVE	W	PTE	26	/448	A		SACRISTON			KR para 392	AUGUST 16			
MUSTARD	H	PTE	26	/1083	C	38 MARLBOROUGH ST	SUNDERLAND						TO 25th, 9th BNS, CLASS Z RESERVE.	
MYLER	Chas	PTE	26	/1079	C	72 SOUTHEY ST	GATESHEAD				AUGUST 16, JUNE 18.		TO 1st, 14th BNS, CLASS Z RESERVE.	3 CCS 2/7/16 EVAC 2/7/16.
McALLISTER	Tom	PTE	26	/1125	C	55 FLORENCE AVE	GATESHEAD				OCTOBER 16		TO 8th BN, CLASS Z RESERVE.	
McATOMONEY	Henry	PTE	26	/1129	A	122 SHORT ROW	WEST MOOR	10/12/14			DECEMBER 16		TO LABOUR CORPS.	LAB CORPS No 369215.
McAVOY	D	PTE	26	/1122	B		ABBEYLEIX				OCTOBER 16			
McCABE	P	PTE	26	/1137	D		NEWCASTLE	14/12/14	19/4/17	WOUNDS			TO DEPOT.	
McCAFFERY	James	LSGT	26	/487		20 DARCY PLACE	MURTON			1 JULY 1916		THIEPVAL MEM		BORN SHILDON.
McCARRICK	J	PTE	26	/484	A	NEWHOUSE RD	ESH WINNING							

NAME	INITI	RANK	BATTA	NUMBE	COMP	ADDRESS	TOWN_VILL	ENLISTED	DISCHARG	CAUSE_DIS	WOUNDED	BURIED	TRANSFER	ADD
McCARTHY	Jn Js	CPL	26	/488	D	30 SHAKESPEARE ST	NORTH SHIELDS	7/12/14	10/4/18	GUNSHOT WOUNDS	JANUARY 17		TO 3rd BN.	LSGT.
McCLEER	W	PTE	26	/1130	B		GATESHEAD				JULY 16			
McCORMACK	Enry	PTE	26	/490	B	1 ESPLANIS AVE	FOREST HALL	7/12/14	17/6/18	SICK			TO ARMY RESERVE CLASS W.	POS 16 LOW LIGHTS N SHIELDS.
McCORMACK	J	PTE	26	/1110	D	728 WELBECK RD	BYKER		23/3/19				TO 10th BN, KINGS OWN YORKSHIRE LI, CLASS Z RESERV	
McCOY	JohnW	PTE	26	/1121	C								TO ROYAL ENGINEERS.	IN 11 SECTION, RE Nos 338837, WR/205513.
McCULLOCK	R	PTE	26	/1127	A									ALSO ON C COY 30th BN ROLL.
McDERMOTT	Edwd	PTE	26	/470		42 NEW ROWS	WASHINGTON			5 JAN 1917		WASHINGTON	TO 1st GARRISON BN.	
McDONALD	Edwd	PTE	26	/500		97 LAMBTON ST	SHERBURN HILL			11 APRIL 1917		WARLINCOURT HALT BRIT CEM	TO DURHAM LI(10th BN).	DLI No 42254, AGE 27. TWO BROTHERS IN R.F.A.
McDONALD	J	PTE	26	/468	A			29/11/14	29/11/17	SICK			TO DEPOT.	
McDONALD	James	PTE	26	/469	C	38 DONNISON STREET	DUNSTON	29/11/14	29/1/17	AO 265/17	AUGUST 16		TO LABOUR CORPS.	25 AMBTR,18 GEN HOSP 5/7 SHIP 7/7/16,LC No 183184.
McDONALD	John	PTE	26	/494	D								TO ROYAL ARMY MEDICAL CORPS.	RAMC No 135131.
McDONALD	Math	PTE	26	/1126	B		GATESHEAD			1 JULY 1916		THIEPVAL MEM		MISSING OCTOBER 16, BORN JARROW.
McDONALD	Pat	PTE	26											AWOL 27/6/15 COURT NEWCASTLE 8/7/15
McDUNNAGH	Jos	PTE	26	/492	B	53 JOHNS LANE	HEBBURN NEWTOWN						TO ARMY SERVICE CORPS.	ASC No T/312584
McELVOY	T A	PTE	26	/478	A			1/12/14	12/10/17	SICK	MARCH 16		TO 3rd BN.	
McFARLANE	Nich	PTE	26	/497	D	4 KNIGHT ST	JARROW			1 FEB 1917		JARROW	TO 30th BN(D COY), DEPOT.	BORN BELFAST.
McGEEVER	Alex	PTE	26	/477	A		RYHOPE			1 JULY 1916	OCTOBER 16	THIEPVAL MEM		
McGEEVER	John	PTE	26	/471	B		RYHOPE			16 OCT 1916		CITE BON JEAN CEM.		
McGETTAGAN	J	PTE	26	/480	A									ALSO ON D COY 30th BN ROLL.
McGIBBON	Robt	PTE	26	/1134	C	5 BRIGHTON TERR	SHERBURN HILL			KR para 392	JANUARY 18		TO 25th, 9th BNS.	
McGLONE	Jos	PTE	26	/489	A			8/12/14	21/1/19	KR para 392 xvi				ALSO ON C COY 30th BN ROLL,DID NOT SERVE OVERSEAS.
McGORRIGAN	J	PTE	26	/479	B	11 HIGH HOWLETT	PELTON FELL				JUNE 16		TO 24th, 26th, 1st, 11th BNS, CLASS Z RESERVE.	
McGOUGH	C	PTE	26	/493	A									
McGOVERN	J	PTE	26	/1118	C		NEWCASTLE	1/12/14	31/3/19	KR para 392	JANUARY 17		ATTACHED 13th ENTRENCHING BN, 16th BN, ARMY RESERV	
McGOWAN	John	PTE	26	/1132	C	45 STATION RD	EASINGTON COLLI	9/12/14		1 JULY 1916		THIEPVAL MEM		11 SECTION.
McGOWAN	Mark	PTE	26	/1139	C	45 STATION RD	EASINGTON COLLI	9/12/14		1 JULY 1916		THIEPVAL MEM		LCPL, MISSING FEBRUARY 17, BORN NEWBURN NTHBLND.
McGRADY	Hugh	CSM	26	/1138	D	3 CRAWHILL TERR CITY	NEWCASTLE						TO LABOUR CORPS.	LAB CORPS No 419276.
McGRATH	Pat	PTE	26	/1482	A		WILLINGTON			1 JULY 1916		THIEPVAL MEM		MISSING OCTOBER 16.
McGUIRE	John	PTE	26	/498	A	14 STANDERTON TERR	CRAGHEAD	10/12/14			OCTOBER 16		TO MANCHESTER REGT.	MANC REGT No 78637, 3 CCS 2/7/16 EVAC 3/7/16 GSW.
McGURK	John	PTE	26	/1136	C	23 THIRD ST NORTH	EASINGTON COLLI	9/12/14		3 JULY 1916		ST SEVER CEM ROUEN.		BORN BERKLEY GLOUCESTERSHIRE.
McHALE	M	PTE	26	/1128	A			8/12/14	27/12/17	SICK			TO 3rd BN.	
McINTYRE	J	PTE	26	/495				11/12./1	14/1/18	SICK			TO 1st GARRISON BN.	
McIVER	Jas	PTE	26	/483									TO ROYAL ENGINEERS.	RE No 102715, ENTERED FRANCE 20/6/15, AWOL 24/5/15
McIVOR	Pat	PTE	26											DESERTER 28/4/15 COURT NEWCASTLE 10/6/15.
McKENARY	J B	PTE	26	/1133	A		DUNSTON				OCTOBER 16, DECEMBER 17		TO 8th, 22nd BNS.	34 CCS 2/7 EVAC 5/7/16 WND L ANKLE DEST 27/6/18.
McKENNA	Thos	PTE	26	/474	D	1 CHADWICK ST	CORNSAY COLLIER			9 APRIL 1916		BREWERY ORCHARD CEM		LCPL, AGE 41.
McKINNELL	J	PTE	26	/1364	B	96 WILFRED ST	SUNDERLAND	5/1/15	24/12/17	GUNSHOT WOUNDS	DECEMBER 16		TO DEPOT.	
McLAUGHLIN	G	PTE	26	/1131	C									IN 11 SECTION.
McLENNAN	Alex	PTE	26	/475	A	19 BELLS COURT PILGR	NEWCASTLE			1 JULYY 1916		THIEPVAL MEM		LCPL, BORN EDINBURGH.
McMAHON	Geo E	PTE	26	/1124	C		ANNFIELD PLAIN			1 JULY 1916		THIEPVAL MEM	TO 24th BN.	
McMANUS	H	PTE	26	/485	C		KILLINGWORTH	3/12/14	28/9/17	SICK	OCTOBER 16		TO 85th TRAINING RESERVE BN.	34 CCS 1/7/16 EVAC 5/7/16, WND L FOOT, AGE 33.
McMANUS	Hugh	PTE	26	/1112	C	20 CROSSGATE	DURHAM CITY			1 JULY 1916		THIEPVAL MEM	FROM ROYAL NAVAL DIVISION.	MIS OCT 16.MINER AT WALLSEND COLLIERY.BORN TOW LAW
McMULLEN	J	PTE	26	/1461	A		NEWCASTLE				APRIL 16, OCTOBER 16.			DESERTED 26 AUGUST 1918.
McNALLY	D	PTE	26	/1115	C	5 MONKTON RD	JARROW	30/11/14	21/12/17	SICK			TO DEPOT.	
McNAMARA	J	PTE	26	/1363	B									
McPHAIL	Wm W	PTE	26	/1120	D	153 SUNDERLAND RD	GATESHEAD				MARCH 16		TO 25th, 10th BNS, CLASS Z RESERVE.	
McPHERSON	A	PTE	26	/476	D	37 VEITCHES BLDGS	GATESHEAD	24/11/14	31/12/17	DEBILITY			TO 13th, 3rd BN.	LCPL.
McSWEENEY	P	PTE	26	/482	D	13 FENWICK ROW	SEAHAM							ALSO ON D COY 30th BN ROLL.
McTERNON	J	PTE	26	/1406	D30			10/5/15	24/5/16	KR para 392			TO 30th BN.	DID NOT SERVE OVERSEAS.
NASH	Math	PTE	26			MULGRAVE TERR	GATESHEAD						TO ROYAL AIR FORCE(2nd PTE).	AWOL 2/7/15 COURT GATESHEAD AGE 37, RAF No 275106.
NEE	John	PTE	26	/502	A		FELLING			1 JULY 1916		THIEPVAL MEM		MISSING OCTOBER 16, LCPL
NEESHAM	W	PTE	26	/501	A		MURTON	5/12/14	23/10/16	GUNSHOT WOUNNDS	OCTOBER 16		TO 85th TRAINING RESERVE BN.	8 AMBTR,18 GHOSP 10/7,SHIP 16/7 ABDOMEN WND.AGE 42
NESBIT	W	PTE	26	/509	B			4/12/14	31/3/19	KR para 392			TO 20th, 18th BNS, ARMY RESERVE CLASS P.	
NETTLETON	J A	PTE	26	/1141	D30	28 BK CHURCH ST ELVE	DURHAM CITY	24/11/14			AUGUST 16		TO ROYAL NAVAL DIVISION	AWOL 28/7/15 TO ESCORT 5/8/15. RND No 117497.
NETTLETON	Ths W	PTE	26	/1142	C	28 BK CHURCH ST ELVE	DURHAM CITY	24/11/14	6/6/17	GUNSHOT WOUNDS	OCTOBER 16		TO 85th TRAINING RESERVE BN.	WOUNDED R ARM.
NEVAN	Chart	PTE	26	/507	A	8 HIGH FRIARSIDE	BURNHOPEFIELD	12/12/14					TO 12/13th BN, CLASS Z RESERVE.	
NEWLEY	John	PTE	26	/508		JAMES ST	PONTOP						TO 1st GARRISON BN, CLASS Z RESERVE.	AGE 33.
NEWTON	G	PTE	26	/513	B	36 DELVES TERR	CONSETT	25/11/14	22/1/19	SICK			TO ARMY RESERVE CLASS W.	
NICHOLLS	C	PTE	26	/504	C	20 THIRD ST	WALLSEND	26/11/14	31/3/19	KR para 392	OCTOBER 16, JUNE 18.		TO 1st, 24th, 26th BNS, ARMY RESERVE CLASS P.	
NICHOLSON	F	PTE	26	/1145	C		DURHAM CITY				OCTOBER 16			

NAME	INITI	RANK	BATTA	NUMBE	COMP	ADDRESS	TOWN_VILL	ENLISTED	DISCHARG	CAUSE_DIS	WOUNDED	BURIED	TRANSFER	ADD
NICHOLSON	R	PTE	26	/512	C30			24/11/14	13/7/16	SICK			TO 30th BN(C COY).	DID NOT SERVE OVERSEAS.
NICHOLSON	Robt	PTE	26	/1148	D		CHOPWELL				DECEMBER 16		TO ROYAL DEFENCE CORPS.	FRANCE 10/1/16 TO 3/12/16.RDC No 65390.AWOL 10/8/1
NICHOLSON	Thpsn	PTE	26	/510	B		SEATON DELAVAL			24 SEPT 1916		POZIERES MIL CEM	TO DURHAM LI(12th BN).	DLI No 45895.
NIEL	ChasT	PTE	26	/514	B	39 DOUGLAS TERR	USWORTH			1 JULY 1916	OCTOBER 16	THIEPVAL MEM		MISSING DECEMBER 16, BORN PARKHEAD LANARK.
NILES	John	PTE	26	/1143	A						APRIL 16		TO ROYAL DEFENCE CORPS.	IN FRANCE 10/1/16 TO 1/4/16.
NIXON	Math	PTE	26	/506		93 FRAMWELLGATE	DURHAM CITY	2/12/14					TO 2nd GARRISON BN, CLASS Z RESERVE.	
NIXON	R	PTE	26	/503	D								TO LABOUR CORPS.	LAB CORPS No 238006.
NOBLE	T Wm	PTE	26	/1146	A	37 FIRST ST	GATESHEAD			11 JULY 1916		ST SEVER CEM ROUEN		
NOLAN	M	PTE	26	/511	B	10 BK STATION LANE	HEBBURN NEWTOWN						TO 30th BN(C COY).	
NYE	Wm Hr	PTE	26	/1144	C		NEWCASTLE			1 JULY 1916		THIEPVAL MEM		MISSING OCTOBER 16, BORN BRIGHTON SUSSEX.
O'BRIAN	J	PTE	26	/528	A	7 BK LEIGHTON ST	BYKER BANK							
O'BRIEN	H	PTE	26	/1157	D									ALSO ON D COY 30th BN ROLL.
O'BRIEN	J	PTE	26	/1153		28 FELT ST ST PETERS	NEWCASTLE	7/12/14	11/6/15	HIP DISORDER			TO 3rd BN.	DID NOT SERVE OVERSEAS.
O'BRIEN	L W	PTE	26	/1154	A		SUNDERLAND				JULY 1916		TO 20th, 21st, 1/5th BNS, CLASS Z RESERVE.	
O'BRIEN	Wm	PTE	26	/1156	D	39 RUSSELL ST TEAMS	GATESHEAD	12/12/14		1 JULY 1916	OCTOBER 16	THIEPVAL MEM		AWOL 22/8, 13/9/15 IN COURT GATESHEAD, AGE 20.
O'CONNOR	Henry	PTE	26	/1151	C		THORNLEY			1 JULY 1916		THIEPVAL MEM		MISSING OCTOBER 16, BORN HOUGHTON LE SPRING.
O'CONNOR	J	PTE	26	/1150	C	22 SECOND ST	SHOTTON COLLIER				JULY 16		TO 25th, 1/4th, 1/5th, 12/13th BNS, CLASS Z RESERV	3 CCS 2/7/16 EVAC 3/7/16 GSW. NEW No 204601.
O'DONNELL	P	PTE	26	/516	D	5 HIGH ST	JARROW						TO 30th BN(D COY).	
O'HARA	Thos	PTE	26	/517	A	153 SHIPLEY ST	NEWCASTLE						TO 26th, 18th, 14th(A COY) BNS, CLASS Z RESERVE.	
O'HARE	Jas D	PTE	26	/1442	D	6 LUMSDENS LANE	MORPETH			16 JUNE 1917		ARRAS MEM	TO 12th BN.	
O'NIELL	Andrw	PTE	26	/521	D	14 ATKINSONS BLDGS	BIRTLEY	4/12/14		28 APRIL 1917		BROWNS COPSE CEM ROUEX		SGT, BORN KILKENNY
O'NIELL	Isaac	PTE	26	/527	C		GATESHEAD	15/12/14	24/5/16	KR para 392			TO 30th BN(C COY).	NOT SERVE OVERSEAS,AWOL 19/7/15 CT G/HEAD AGE 38.
O'NIELL	J	PTE	26	/518	A		BEDLINGTON				OCTOBER 16		TO 11th BN, CLASS Z RESERVE.	LCPL, 3CCS 2/7/16 EVAC 3/7/16 GSW.
O'NIELL	J	PTE	26	/530	D	1 STRATHMORE TERR	ROWLANDS GILL				APRIL 16		TO LABOUR CORPS.	
O'NIELL	T	PTE	26	/520	A		NEWBOTTLE				OCTOBER 16			LCPL, 34 CCS 1/7/16 EVAC 5/7/16 WND R THIGH, AGE 2
O'RIELLY	Ed	PTE	26	/526	D	35 DUKE ST	NEWCASTLE	11/12/14	22/5/16		MARCH 16		TO DEPOT.	CPL.
O'RIELLY	Jos	PTE	26	/519	D		NEWCASTLE			1 JULY 1916		THIEPVAL MEM		MISSING OCTOBER 16, LCPL.
OLDFIELD	E	PTE	26	/522						KR para 392			TO 1st GARRISON BN.	
OLIVER	John	PTE	26	/1158	C	21 WEST VIEW TERR	DUNSTON			1 JULY 1916		THIEPVAL MEM		BORN BLACKHILL.
OLIVER	R	PTE	26	/525	B		PENSHAW				OCTOBER 16		TO LONDON REGT(16th BN).	
OPIE	Wm	PTE	26	/1155	C	5 OAK TERR	TANTOBIE				OCTOBER 16, JUNE 18.		TO 10th, 26th, 9th ENTRENCHING BN, 1/7th BNS, CLAS	REP MISS DEC 16, REPORTED REJOINED FEB 17.
ORD	JohnG	PTE	26	/515	D	ROGERSONS BLDGS	WEST CORNFORTH	2/12/14					TO 25th BN, CLASS Z RESERVE.	
OSWALD	Fenwk	PTE	26	/523	A	7 WILLIAM ST	CHOPWELL			1 JULY 1916		THIEPVAL MEM		BORN PRUDHOE.
OTTO	W	PTE	26	/1393	B			19/3/15	1/6/18	SICK			TO 3rd BN.	
OWENS	Thos	PTE	26	/1152	C	30 LONG ROW BURNMOO	FENCEHOUSES			1 JULY 1916		THIEPVAL MEM		CPL, MISSING OCTOBER 16, BORN BANKHEAD DURHAM.
PALMER	J	PTE	26	/541	A	67 STAINTON ST	SOUTH SHIELDS	28/11/14	10/6/18	WOUNDS	OCTOBER 16		TO 3rd BN.	LCPL.
PARK	H	PTE	26	/542	A									ALSO ON D COY 30th BN ROLL.
PARK	J	PTE	26	/1166	C		WASHINGTON STAT			KR para 392	AUGUST 16		TO 25th, 1/4th BNS.	ALLOTED NEW NUMBER 204606.
PARK	Thos	PTE	26	/1180	C	66 ELDON ST	SOUTH SHIELDS			1 JULY 1916	OCTOBER 16	SERRE RD NO 2 CEM		LCPL MISSING DECEMBER 16, BORN THORNLEY AGE 23.
PARKIN	Ern	PTE	26	/1174	A	14 HARDWICK ST	SUNDERLAND	10/12/14			OCTOBER 16		TO ROYAL INNISKILLING FUSILIERS, ROYAL ENGINEERS.	34 CCS 2/7/16 EVAC 5/7/16 WND BUTTOCKS, AGE 24.
PARKIN	Geo	PTE	26	/544	D		DIPTON			1 JULY 1916		THIEPVAL MEM		DESERTED 18/4/15 IN COURT 10/6/15. BORN LANCHESTER
PARKIN	H	PTE	26	/1159	D								TO 1st, 17th BNS, CLASS Z RESERVE.	
PARKIN	Nath	PTE	26	/1179	C		EASINGTON			1 JULY 1916		THIEPVAL MEM		LCPL MISSING FEBRUARY 17, BORN COPLEY.
PARKIN	T	PTE	26	/545	A									ALSO ON D COY 30th BN ROLL.
PARRY	J	PTE	26	/534	D	121 HARVEY ST	BYKER				AUGUST 16		TO 27th, 24/27th, 11th BNS, CLASS Z RESERVE.	ATTACHED No 3 REST CAMP BOULOGNE 1919.
PARRY	JohnW	PTE	26	/539	A	CANNON ST	MIDDLESBOROUGH							
PATRICK	Wm Hy	PTE	26	/546	A	30 DIANA ST	NEWCASTLE			1 JULY 1916		THIEPVAL MEM		LCPL, BORN ADELAIDE SHROPSHIRE.
PATTERSON	J T	PTE	26	/1165	C		NEWCASTLE	1/12/14	11/6/18	SICK	AUGUST 16		TO DEPOT.	
PATTISON	Robt	CPL	26	/532	B	1 PEASES ST	SOUTH CHURCH BI			1 JULY 1916	OCTOBER 16	THIEPVAL MEM		MISSING DECEMBER 16, BORN CROOK.
PATTISON	Wm	PTE	26	/1404		9 ROSE AVENUE	OXHILL						TO 1st GARRISON BN, CLASS Z RESERVE.	
PAXTON	Archi	PTE	26	/1172	C	CRAWFORD ST	LITTLETOWN	8/12/14		28 SEPT 1918	SHELLSHOCK JULY 17	GREVILLERS BRIT CEM	TO 10th BN, KINGS OWN YORKSHIRE LI(2/4th BN).	BN TRANSPORT SECTION, KOYLI No 63403.
PAXTON	T W	PTE	26	/1392	B	5 RIVER VIEW	WASHINGTON STAT							MEMBER OF WASHINGTON METHODIST CHURCH BROTHERHOOD.
PAYTON	ThosW	PTE	26	/548	D		DARLINGTON			9 APRIL 1917		ORCHARD DUMP CEM		
PAYTON	T	PTE	26	/1178									TO 1st GARRISON BN, CLASS Z RESERVE.	
PEAKER	J	PTE	26	/531	D		OLD SHILDON	4/12 14	31/3/19	KR para 392	NOVEMBER 18		TO 20th, 26th BNS, ARMY RESERVE CLASS P.	
PEARCE	Geo	PTE	26	/554	D		SOUTH SHIELDS				OCTOBER 16		TO DURHAM LI.	34 CCS 2/7 EVAC 5/7 BEAUFORT HOSP BRISTOL 9/7/16.
PEARSON	J T	PTE	26	/1460	B								TO CLASS Z RESERVE.	ALSO ON C COY 30th BN ROLL.
PEARSON	Thos	PTE	26	/558	A	4 COPELANDS LANE	CHESTER LE ST			1 JULY 1916	OCTOBER 16	THIEPVAL MEM		LCPL, BORN USWORTH.
PEARSON	W	PTE	26	/1433	D		NEWCASTLE				OCTOBER 16		TO ROYAL ENGINEERS.	21 AMB TR, 18 G HOSP 6/7, TO 6 CONV DEPOT 7/7/16.
PEEL	Nich	PTE	26	/562	D	3 SIXTH ST SOUTH	EASINGTON COLLI	9/12/14		1 JULY 1916		THIEPVAL MEM		MISSING OCTOBER 16, BORN NEW SEAHAM.

NAME	INITI	RANK	BATTA	NUMBE	COMP	ADDRESS	TOWN_VILL	ENLISTED	DISCHARG	CAUSE_DIS	WOUNDED	BURIED	TRANSFER	ADD
PENALUNA	W	PTE	26	/549	D		WASHINGTON	25/11/14	6/8/17	GUNSHOT WOUNDS	OCTOBER 16		TO DEPOT.	3 CCS 2/7/16 EVAC 2/7/16 AGE 29.
PETCH	John	PTE	26	/1168	C	24 DUNNS BLDGS	GATESHEAD						TO 13th, 10th BNS, CLASS Z RESERVE.	
PHELAN	Frank	PTE	26	/550	D	201 TRINITY ST	NORTH SHIELDS			1 JULY 1916		THIEPVAL MEM		BORN WATERFORD,LCPL, WND + MISS DECEMBER 16.
PICKERING	B W	PTE	26	/1360	A			12/1/15	11/2/19	GUNSHOT WOUNDS			TO 1/5th, 8th BNS, DEPOT.	AGE 23.
PICTON	JohnP	LSGT	26	/551	D	100 BLENHEIM ST	NEWCASTLE			1 JULY1916		BAPAUME POST CEM		BORN READING BERKS.
PLANT	Rolnd	SGT	26	/1175	C	86 SCOTSWOOD RD	NEWCASTLE			1 JULY 1916		THIEPVAL MEM		AWOII MISSING OCTOBER 16.BORN WESTMINISTER.
PORTER		PTE	26	/1171										IN 11 SECTION.
PORTER	J	PTE	26	/1176	C			9/12/14	10/7/18	SICK			TO ARMY RESERVE CLASS W.	
POTTS	A	PE	26	/1163	D		NEWCASTLE				AUGUST 16		TO 21st, 24th, 24/27th, 9th BNS, CLASS Z RESERVE.	
POTTS	Frank	LCPL	26	/559	A		FELLING				OCTOBER 16		TO TANK CORPS.	AWOL 23/8/15 CT G/HEAD, AGE 31,T CORPS No 302661.
POTTS	G M	PTE	26	/1444	A			31/5/15	8/9/17	TRENCH FEET			TO 85th TRAINING RESERVE BN.	
POULSON	Robt	PTE	26	/536	A	4 HIRST ST	WHEATLEY HILL			1 JULY 1916	OCTOBER 16	THIEPVAL MEM		MISSING DECEMBER 16, BORN WHITBURN.
POULSON	W R	PTE	26	/538	B									ALSO ON D COY 30th BN ROLL.
POWELL	R	PTE	26	/537	D	8 BRISCOE ST	GATESHEAD				MISS OCT 16, JUNE 18		TO CLASS Z RESERVE.	LCPL.
PRINGLETON	J G	PTE	26	/556	D	1 LUMSDENS BLDGS	SACRISTON	10/12/14	10/4/17	GUNSHOT WOUNDS	AUGUST 16		TO DEPOT.	SHOWN AS LIVING DARLINGTON IN GAZ.
PROCTER	T	PTE	26	/533	A									
PROCTER	Thos	PTE	26	/552	B								TO LABOUR CORPS.	LAB CORPS No 398043.
PRUDHOE	C	PTE	26	/535	A	2 JACKSON SQ WEST KY	STANLEY	9/12/14	6/2/19				TO KINGS OWN YORKSHIRE LI(5th BN), CLASS Z RESERVE	ASGT.
PRUDHOE	E	LCPL	26	/547	D		WASHINGTON STAT				OCTOBER 16.		TO 26th BN B COY, SOUTH STAFFORDSHIRE REGT.	34 CCS 2/7/16 EVAC 5/7/16, WND L THIGH AGE 32.
PUNTIN	R	PTE	26	/553	A		GATESHEAD	24/11/14	21/10/16	SHELLSHOCK	S SHOCK OCTOBER 16		TO ARMY RESERVE CLASS W.	TO W RES 19/2/18.
PUNTON	Geo	PTE	26	/557	D	22 CUMBERLAND ST	GATESHEAD	10/12/14	19/6/17	WOUNDS	OCTOBER 16		TO DEPOT.	3 CCS 2/7/16 EVAC 2/7/16 COMPOUND FRAC R FEMUR.
PYLE	H	PTE	26	/1177	C	31 BARTON ST	GOSFORTH				JUNE 18		TO 23rd BN, STILL SERVING DECEMBER 1920.	
QUINN	Chas	PTE	26	/563	A	70 WALKER ST LOW TEA	GATESHEAD			26 SEPT 1916		ETAPLES		
QUINN	J	PTE	26	/564	C		BLYTH	2/12/14	3/7/18	WOUNDS	DECEMBER 16		ATT TUNNELLING COY R ENGINEERS, ARMY RESERVE CLASS	
QUINN	J	PTE	26	/1181				3/12/14	31/7/15	SICK				DID NOT SERVE OVERSEAS.
QUINN	John	PTE	26	/566	D		PENSHAW			7 NOV 1918	OCTOBER 16	TERLINCTHUN BRIT CEM	TO 10th BN.	BORN WASHINGTON, COMPANY SERGEANT MAJOR.
QUINN	M	LCPL	26	/565	D	1 HEPWORTH ST	NEW BRANCEPETH	8/12/14			MAY 16			LSGT.
RACE	J H	LCPL	26	/601						KR para 392				
RAFFLE	Thos	PTE	26	/582	D	9 EAST BRIDGE ST	PENSHAW						TO LABOUR CORPS.	IN Y COY BN UNKNOWN 1918, LAB CORPS No 649226 CPL.
RAINE	Math	PTE	26	/1198	C	DOVECOTE ST	LITTLETOWN	10/12/14					TO 23rd BN, CLASS Z RESERVE.	
RAITT	Alex	PTE	26	/1197	A		WALKER				MARCH 17		TO ROYAL ARMY MEDICAL CORPS.	DESERTED 21/8/15 CT 14/9/15, RAMC No 205841.
RAMSHAW	Harry	PTE	26	/1188	C	LUMLEY HOUSE	SHOTTON COLLIER				AUGUST 16		TO 25th BN, CLASS Z RESERVE.	LIVING CRAGHEAD 1916? HOSP BIRMINGHAM 7/16.
RAMSHAW	Ralph	PTE	26	/603	D		BEBSIDE FURNACE				OCTOBER 16		TO ROYAAL ARMY MEDICAL CORPS.	RAMC No 256282.
RAMSHAW	Ruebn	PTE	26	/596	B	4 COWAN ST	DUNSTON	10/12/14					TO 25th BN, CLASS Z RESERVE.	LCPL.
RAMSHAW	Thos	PTE	26	/591	D		CRAGHEAD			1 JULY1916		THIEPVAL MEM		MISSING OCTOBER 16, BORN CHESTER LE STREET
RAYNHAM	W W	CSM	26	/1396	B									
REARDON	E	SGT	26	/1183	C		SOUTH SHIELDS						ATTACHED 103 LTMB, D COY 26th BN, LABOUR CORPS.	LAB CORPS No 397390.
REAY	John	PTE	26	/1212	D	35 NOEL ST	WEST STANLEY				OCTOBER 18		TO LABOUR CORPS.	LAB CORPS No 618420.
REAY	Wm	PTE	26	/1211	A	2 HAVELOCK TERR	TANTOBIE			1 JULY 1916		THIEPVAL MEM		MISSING OCTOBER 16.
REDDEN	Geo	PTE	26	/590	A	3 LOVEGREEN ST FRAM/	DURHAM CITY	2/12/14			APRIL 16		TO 1st, 21st, 25th, 1st BNS, CLASS Z RESERVE.	3 SIDEGATE IN 1914.
REDDEN	Thos	PTE	26	/577	A	4 LOVEGREEN ST FRAM/	DURHAM CITY	11/12/14					TO 1/4th BN, CLASS Z RESERVE.	
REED	Alex	PTE	26	/1184	D	6 CARNABYS YARD GALL	NEWCASTLE			1 JULY 1916	OCTOBER 16	THIEPVAL MEM		
REED	Jas	PTE	26	/593	D	24 EAST BRIDGE ST	PENSHAW	10/12/14		20 FEB 1916		X FARM CEM ARMENTIERES		BORN FENCEHOUSES.
REED	W G	PTE	26	/587	A	20 JOICEY TERR OXHIL	STANLEY		23/1/19		JULY 16		TO YORK AND LANCASTER REGT(18th BN).	
REED	Wm	PTE	26	/592	B	5 WEST BRIDGE ST	PENSHAW			1 JULY 1916	JULY 16	THIEPVAL MEM		MISSING DECEMBER 16. BORN BANKHEAD.
REGAN	P	PTE	26	/574		27 ELEVENTH ST	SHOTTON	5/12/14	8/10/17	SICK			TO 1st GARRISON BN, 2nd, 36th BNS.	ENTERED SALONIKA 20/12/15. 1914/15 STAR.
REID	Alex	PTE	26											AWOL17/5,1/7,26/8,12/12 CT N/CASTLE 31/5,9/7,2/9,1
REILLY	J	PTE	26	/1196	B								TO LABOUR CORPS.	
REILLY	MichT	PTE	26	/597	D30	1 POST OFFICE ROW	SEGHILL	10/12/14		KR para 392			TO 30th, 25th, 11th, 24th BNS.	
REYNOLDS	Rodrk	PTE	26	/1187	B			30/11/14	7/5/17	WOUNDS	APRIL 16		TO EAST YORKSHIRE REGT.	EAST YORKS No 34638.
RICE	J T	PTE	26	/613	A	109 MILL LANE	NEWCASTLE				AUGUST 16		TO LABOUR CORPS, ROYAL ENGINEERS.	LAB CORPS No 19715 RE No 323402, WR/30676.
RICHARDSON	A	PTE	26	/594	A	9 MAKEPEACE TERR	HIGH FELLING	8/12/14	4/3/19	KR para 392			TO ARMY RESERVE CLASS P.	
RICHARDSON	Jos	PTE	26	/607	A	120 MILLING ST	GATESHEAD						TO 18th BN, LABOUR CORPS.	RICHARDSON Arth Wm ENL TI 120 MILLING ST,AWOL 22/8
RICHARDSON	Palmy	PTE	26	/586	D	4 VICTORIA ST	FELLING			1 JULY 1916	OCTOBER 16	THIEPVAL MEM		
RICHARDSON	R	PTE	26	/569	A		HIGH USWORTH	3/12/14	27/8/17	SICK	DECEMBER 16		TO 3rd BN.	21 AMBTR, 18 GHOSP 6/7 SHIP 7/7/16 S/SHOCK. AGE 45
RICHIE	Wm	LSGT	26	/580		48 TWEED ST	CHOPWELL						TO 1st GARRISON BN, CLASS Z RESERVE.	
RICKLETON	A	PTE	26	/570	C									
RIDGE	Pat	PTE	26											AWOL 9/7/15 COURT GATESHEAD AGE 29.
RIDLEY	Henry	PTE	26	/1186	A	21 CLIFFORD STREET	BLAYDON			11 JULY 1917	OCTOBER 16	COXYDE MIL CEM	TO 16th BN.	34 CCS 2/7/16 EVAC 5/7/16 S SHOCK. AGE 24.
RIDLEY	Thos	PTE	26	/610									TO LABOUR CORPS.	LAB CORPS No 601097. AWOL 10/6 17/8/15 CT SNDLAND

NAME	INITI	RANK	BATTA	NUMBE	COMP	ADDRESS	TOWN_VILL	ENLISTED	DISCHARG	CAUSE_DIS	WOUNDED	BURIED	TRANSFER	ADD
RILEY	J	PTE	26	/581	A									
RILEY	John	PTE	26	/1359									TO ROYAL ENGINEERS.	ENTERED FRANCE 10/1/15 RE No WR/301448.
RILEY	Thos	PTE	26	/1210	D	10 JAMES ST	WEST STANLEY			1 JULY 1916	OCTOBER 16	THIEPVAL MEM		
RITCHIE	T	PTE	26	/1189	A		SACRISTON			KR para 392				
RITSON	J D	PTE	26	/595	A		HEXAM				OCTOBER 16			
ROACH	J W	PTE	26	/1203	A		SUNDERLAND			KR para 392	OCTOBER 16			3rd SCOTTISH GEN HOSP GLASGOW 11/7/16.
ROACH	Wm	PTE	26	/1199	B		GATESHEAD			1 JULY 1916	OCTOBER 16	THIEPVAL MEM		MISSING DECEMBER 16.
ROBINSON	F C	PTE	26	/583	A	16 TENT ST	GATESHEAD						TO LABOUR CORPS, ROYAL FUSILIERS.	LAB CORPS No 517422, R FUS No 110613.
ROBINSON	G	PTE	26	/571	A	THE SQUARE	ESH VILLAGE						TO 30th BN(D COY).	COULD POS LIVE WOOD VIEW LANGLEY PARK.
ROBINSON	G	PTE	26	/1213	D	59 CROSSGATE	DURHAM CITY				FEBRUARY 16			
ROBINSON	H W L	PTE	26	/572	A		COCKFIELD			8 OCT 1917		DOZINGHEM MIL CEM	TO 19th, 21st BNS.	3 CCS 2/7/16 EVAC 2/7/16. IN MAY 18 GAZ.
ROBINSON	J	PTE	26	/584	A									
ROBINSON	J	PTE	26	/1206	A		SUNDERLAND				OCTOBER 16			
ROBINSON	P F	CPL	26	/1389	C	HAWTHORN HOUSE	RYTON GREENSIDE	5/3/15	26/2/18	GUNSHOT WOUNDS	OCTOBER 16		ATTACHED 179 TUNNELLING COY RE, TO ARMY RESERVE CL	ROBINSON JOHN 13446 RFA AT THIS ADDRESS IN AVL.
ROBINSON	Thos	PTE	26	/568	A	14 ALLENDALE RD	STOCKTON	26/11/14						
ROBINSON	W	PTE	26	/598	A	6 FOURTH ST	EASINGTON						TO 1/6th BN, CLASS Z RESERVE.	
ROBSON	Ed	PTE	26	/588	D		NEWCASTLE			1 JULY 1916	OCTOBER 16	THIEPVAL MEM		
ROBSON	G	PTE	26	/589	B		WARDLEY	27/11/14	14/12/17	WOUNDS	OCTOBER 16		TO DEPOT.	
ROBSON	James	PTE	26	/1200	D	CARRS COTTAGE SCOTSW	NEWCASTLE			1 JULY 1916		THIEPVAL MEM		MISSING OCTOBER 16.
ROBSON	Jhn G	SGT	26	/1193	C30	30 CLAYTON ST	GATESHEAD			26 MARCH 1918		HEATH CEM HARBONIERS	TO 1/4th BN.	AGE 23.
ROBSON	John	PTE	26	/1201	D	24 FAR WEST ST	EAST STANLEY			27 MARCH 1916		BOULOGNE		BORN SHOTTON.
ROBSON	Robt	PTE	26	/1194	A	10 CROSS STREET	SACRISTON	9/12/14		1 JULY 1916	OCTOBER 16	THIEPVAL MEM		
ROBSON	Wm	PTE	26	/1202	B	23 CORONATION ST	SHERBURN HILL	12/12/14		3 OCT 1918	OCTOBER 16	TEMPLEUX LE GUERARD BRIT CEM	TO ROYAL INNISKILLING FUSILIERS(6th BN).	2 G HOSP 5/7 SHIP 10/7 HOSP PLYMOUTH 13/7/16.WOUND
RODGERS	P	PTE	26	/579	A	5 BURNVILLE RD	SUNDERLAND	9/12/14			OCTOBER 16			HOSP EDINBURGH 7/16 WND CHEST + ARM
ROGAN	J	PTE	26	/599	A									ALSO ON D COY 30th BN ROLL.
ROGERSON	Henry	PTE	26	/605	A	PEMBERTON ST	HETTON LE HOLE			1 JULY 1916		THIEPVAL MEM		MISSING OCTOBER 16, BORN BLAYDON.
ROONEY	P	PTE	26	/1358	A									
ROPER	Jhn G	PTE	26	/1205	C	12 JACKSON ST	ANNITSFORD	9/12/14		1 JULY 1916		THIEPVAL MEM		BORN BEDLINGTON.
ROSS	Frank	PTE	26	/573	A	31 SEYMOUR ST	DUNSTON						TO 27th, 26th, 9th BNS, CLASS Z RESERVE.	
ROSS	Jas	PTE	26	/612	B	101 QUEEN ST	GATESHEAD				OCTOBER 16		TO 3rd BN.	AWOL 25/8/15 IN COURT GATESHEAD, AGE 48.
ROUTLEDGE	J	PTE	26	/606	A	12 WARDLE ST	SOUTHMOOR	9/12/14						
ROWAN	J J	PTE	26	/1204	C	38 RAWLING RD	GATESHEAD							
ROWE	J W	PTE	26	/1207	A	57 CORONATION ST	SUNDERLAND				OCTOBER 16, DECEMBER 16			
ROWELL	Jas	PTE	26	/1195	D	3 HOLLOW MEADOW	HEXAM	1/12/14	24/1/18	WOUNDS	JULY 16		TO DEPOT.	
RUSSELL	G	PTE	26	/1419	D									ALSO ON C COY 30th BN ROLL.
RUTHERFORD	Wm	PTE	26	/611	A	64 WEST ST	GRANGE VILLA			4 SEPT 1916		WEST PELTON ST PAULS CHYD YD		34 CCS 2/7/16 EVAC 5/7/16, WND R SHLDR+CHEST.
RYAN	T	PTE	26	/609	D			14/12/14	31/10/17	SICK			TO 85th TRAINING RESERVE BN.	
RYANS	John	PTE	26	/1209	C	64 LAMPTON ST	SHERBURN HILL	14/12/14	5/3/19	KR para 392			TO 18th BN, DEPOT.	C WARD LEITH HOSP 1918.
RYANS	Thos	PTE	26	/1208	C	64 LAMPTON ST	SHERBURN HILL	14/12/14		1 JULY 1916	MARCH 16	THIEPVAL MEM		
RYOTT	Rob S	PTE	26	/604	D	3 ALBIONS BLDGS	NEWCASTLE	12/12/14		1 JULY 1916		OVILLIERS MIL CEM		MISSING OCTOBER 16.AWOL 25/7/15 COURT 11/8/15.
SADLER	Geo	PTE	26	/1239	A		NEWCASTLE			1 JULY 1916	OCTOBER 16	THIEPVAL MEM		
SALKELD	Jos	LCPL	26	/1252	D	231 SOUTH TAYLOR ST	SOUTH SHIELDS			1 APRIL 1916		BREWERY ORCHARD		CPL, AGE 20.
SAMPLE	J	PTE	26	/672	B									ALSO ON C COY 30th BN ROLL.
SAUNDERS	C	PTE	26	/657	A			14/12/14	4/8/16	SICK			TO DEPOT.	
SAUNDERS	E	PTE	26	/639	B	7 ILCHESTER ST	DAWDON COLLIERY						TO LABOUR CORPS.	LAB CORPS No 400797.
SAXBY	Chas	PTE	26	/614	D	40 NEW ELVET	DURHAM CITY	26/11/14		1 SEPT 1918	JULY 16, OCTOBER 18.	GWALIA CEM POPERINGE	TO 24th, 8th BNS, YORK AND LANCASTER REGT(18th BN)	34 CCS 1/7/16 EVAC 5/7/16 Y & L No 62454, AGE 33.
SCHOFIELD	B	LCPL	26	/1215	D	5 EDWARD ST GILESGAT	DURHAM CITY				JULY 16		TO CLASS Z RESERVE.	3CCS 2/7 EVAC 5/7/16 WND HEAD+CHEST HOSP B/GHAM.
SCHOFIELD	J	PTE	26	/634	C									ON BN ROLL AS /436.
SCOLLINS	A	PTE	26	/631		59 CARNABY TERR	GATESHEAD						TO 1st GARRISON BN, CLASS Z RESERVE.	
SCOTLAND	John	PTE	26	/620	B	24 GROSEVNOR STREET	GATESHEAD						TO 11th INFANTRY BDE HQ, LABOUR CORPS.	LAB CORPS No 432789, IN BN TRANSPORT SECTION.
SCOTT		LSGT	26	/624	D30									LSGT ON D COY 30th BN ROLL.
SCOTT	A	PTE	26	/621	A	5 GRIFFITHS TERR	WEST ALLOTMENT		25/2/19				TO 25th BN, KINGS OWN YORKSHIRE LI(2/4th BN),CLASS	
SCOTT	E E	PTE	26	/1251	A	75 PRINCESS ST	SOUTH SHIELDS				MAY 16			
SCOTT	Edw	PTE	26	/667	B	1 HIGH ROW	PERCY MAIN	10/12/14						
SCOTT	F	PTE	26	/656	A	4 EAST ST	SHERBURN COLLIE						TO ROYAL DEFENCE CORPS.	IN FRANCE 10/1/16 TO 21/8/16.
SCOTT	J	PTE	26	/1421	A			17/5/15	16/3/18	SICK			TO 3rd BN.	ALSO ON C COY 30th BN ROLL.
SCOTT	J H	PTE	26	/625	B		EDMONDSLEY				OCTOBER 16, MARCH 18.		TO 11th, 1/7th BNS, CLASS Z RESERVE.	LCPL, 3 CCS 2/7/16 EVAC 2/7/16 SSHOCK.
SCOTT	J W	PTE	26	/622	D									
SCOTT	Jacob	PTE	26	/623			BYKER			19 OCT 1918		INDIA	TO 2nd GARRISON BN.	
SCOTT	Sam	PTE	26	/1236	C	2 NORTH ST	SHERBURN HILL	12/12/14			MARCH 18		TO 18th BN, CLASS Z RESERVE.	CPL, 5 CROSS ROW HASWELL 1918.

NAME	INITI	RANK	BATTA	NUMBE	COMP	ADDRESS	TOWN_VILL	ENLISTED	DISCHARG	CAUSE_DIS	WOUNDED	BURIED	TRANSFER	ADD
SCOTT	Wm H	PTE	26	/650	D		SOUTH SHIELDS			1 JULY 1916	OCTOBER 16	THIEPVAL MEM		
SCURFIELD	W	PTE	26	/658	A			5/12/14	27/12/17	GUNSHOT WOUNDS	APRIL 16		TO 3rd BN.	
SEDDON	L	PTE	26	/664									TO 2nd GARRISON BN, CLASS Z RESERVE.	
SEERY	Thos	PTE	26	/632	D	31 BACK BOLDON LANE	HARTON						TO LABOUR CORPS.	AWOL 28/8/15 CT S SHIELDS, LAB CORPS No 397091.
SEWELL	J	PTE	26	/1446	B	60 SOUTH ST	DURHAM CITY				AUGUST 16, MARCH 17.		TO 8th BN.	3 CCS 2/7/16 EVAC 2/7/16 GSW.
SHARP	W	PTE	26	/1455	D		MORPETH	10/6/15	20/6/16	KR para 392			TO DEPOT.	AWOL 4/8, 18/8/15 CT MORPETH 4/8, 21/8/15.
SHAW	J	PTE	26	/633	C			24/11/14	10/4/17	GUNSHOT WOUNDS			TO 85th TRAINING RESERVE BN.	WOUNDED L LEG.
SHAW	J	PTE	26	/653							1 JULY 16			3 CCS 2/7/16 EVAC 2/7/16 GSW
SHAW	J R	LCPL	26	/1240	D								TO 10th BN, CLASS Z RESERVE.	
SHEARER	ThosD	PTE	26	/666	A		DUNDEE			1 JULY 1916		THIEPVAL MEM		
SHEPHERD	JohnJ	PTE	26	/668	B	120 CLOSE ROW FRAM M	DURHAM CITY	12/12/14		KR para 392	SHELLSHOCK JUNE 16			HOSP CARLISLE 7/16.
SHORT	Jes R	PTE	26	/626	A	11 PARKINSON ST	FELLING			4 OCT 1917		BOULOGNE	TO 24th, 24/27th, 8th BNS.	SENTENCED TO BE SHOT BY FGCM FOR MUTINOUS CONDUCT
SHORT	P	PTE	26	/1234	D		USWORTH	9/12/14	7/6/17	WOUNDS	AUGUST 16		TO DEPOT.	
SILCOX	Moses	PTE	26	/628	C	5 LONG ST	LITTLETOWN			25 APRIL 1917		LEVEL CROSSING CEM FAMPOUX		BORN WHEATLEY HILL, AGE 39.
SILL	Simon	PTE	26	/670	B	26 ILCHESTER ST	DAWDON	9/12/14	18/9/16	FRACTURES	DECEMBER 16		TO DEPOT.	
SIMPSON	G	PTE	26	/1226	C	10 GEORGE ST	BILLQUAY				JULY 16.		ATTACHED 231 LABOUR COY, TO 25th, 12/13th BN.	
SIMPSON	John	PTE	26	/660	D	52 WYLAM ST	CRAGHEAD	10/12/14		2 SEPT 1918		FAULX HILL CEM	TO 10th BN, KINGS OWN YORKSHIRE LI(2/4th BN).	KOYLI No 63260, BORN EDMONDSLEY.
SIMPSON	Jos	LCPL	26	/630	A	16 THOMAS STREET	CRAGHEAD	10/12/14			OCTOBER 16		TO ROYAL DEFENCE CORPS.	IN FRANCE 10/1/16 TO 8/7/16, SGT.
SKELTON	ChasW	PTE	26	/629	B	26 VICTORIA ST	DUNSTON			KR para 392				
SLATER	James	PTE	26	/661	B	40 PRUDHOE ST	NEWCASTLE						TO 3rd BN, ROYAL DEFENCE CORPS.	IN FRANCE 10/1/16 TO 6/12/17.
SMITH	A	PTE	26	/618	D									ALSO ON C COY 30th BN ROLL.
SMITH	A	PTE	26	/1238	D									
SMITH	F	SGT	26	/616	A	7 BRAINBRIDGE AVE	WILLINGTON						TO 10th BN.	
SMITH	F	PTE	26	/1379	D	10 ERNEST PLACE GILE	DURHAM CITY	12/1/15	28/8/17	GUNSHOT WOUNDS	JULY 16		TO DEPOT.	SMITH Fred W 5911 MGC AT SAME ADDRESS IN 1918.
SMITH	G	PTE	26	/1242	D			14/12/14	25/10/17	SICK			TO 1/7th BN, 85th TRAINING RESERVE BN.	
SMITH	H	PTE	26	/1222	B								TO 10th BN, ROYAL FUSILIERS(24th BN).	FRANCE 26th 10/1/16to3/7/18, 10th 4/7/18to29/8/18,
SMITH	J	PTE	26	/648	A									
SMITH	J	PTE	26	/1241	C30								TO LABOUR CORPS.	
SMITH	Jos	PTE	26	/619	A	23 PRIOR ST	GATESHEAD		29/1/19				TO KINGS OWN YORKSHIRE LI(10th BN), CLASS Z RESERV	
SMITH	R	PTE	26	/1220		9 WEALE ST	FERRYHILL	27/11/14	1/12/19	SICK			TO 1st GARRISON BN, DEPOT.	AGE 50.
SMITH	R	PTE	26	/1221	A	22 MILITARY RD	SOUTH SHIELDS				SEPTEMBER 16			
SMITH	R	PTE	26	/1235	D		LANGLEY PARK	9/12/14	6/8/17	GUNSHOT WOUNDS	SEPTEMBER 16		TO 27th BN, DEPOT.	
SMITH	R W	PTE	26	/1249	A		DARLINGTON				OCTOBER 16			
SMITH	T C	PTE	26	/1243	D	1 RAILWAY TERR	MEDOMSLEY						TO 1/7th BN, CLASS Z RESERVE.	
SMITH	W E	PTE	26	/1218	D									
SMITH	Wm	PTE	26	/617	B		CARRICKFERGUS			1 JULY 1916	OCTOBER 16	THIEPVAL MEM		
SMITH	Wm	LCPL	26	/649	A	11 VINE ST EAST END	SUNDERLAND			1 JULY 1916		THIEPVAL MEM		BORN WHITEHAVEN.
SMITH	Wm L	PTE	26	/615	D		SOUTH SHIELDS	28/11/14	19/3/18	GUNSHOT WOUNDS	JULY 16		TO ARMY RESERVE CLASS P.	AWOL 10/5, 29/7 CT 18/5/15 SOUTH SHIELDS.
SNOWDON	J H	PTE	26	/1224	D	119 GILESGATE	DURHAM CITY				OCTOBER 16			
SOLAN	Pat	PTE	26	/1237	D	1 SECOND ST NORTH	EASINGTON COLLI	9/12/14		1 JULY 1916		THIEPVAL MEM		MISSING OCTOBER 16. BORN BIRTLEY.
SOULSBY	Robt	PTE	26	/643	B	8 COOPERS TERR	THORNLEY COLLIE			1 JULY 1916	OCTOBER 16	THIEPVAL MEM		BORN EASINGTON LANE.
SOULSBY	Thos	PTE	26	/1472	D	34 STEAD ST	JARROW				APRIL 16		TO 25th, 23rd, 9th BNS, CLASS Z RESERVE.	AWOL 18/8/15 IN COURT MORPETH 21/8/15.
SOWERBY	James	PTE	26	/1246	A	ONIELLS BLDGS HILLTO	DIPTON			1 JULY 1916		THIEPVAL MEM		MISSING OCTOBER 16, BORN GATESHEAD.
SPURGEON	A	PTE	26	/636	B			28/11/14	30/7/17	GUNSHOT WOUNDS	APRIL 16		TO 3rd BN.	
STABLES	W	PTE	26	/652	A	1 RAILWAY ST	WASHINGTON STAT						TO ROYAL ARMY MEDICAL CORPS.	RAMC No 520012.
STANE	J	PTE	26	/635	A									ON ROLL AS 365.
STEAD	Rich	SGT	26	/669		7 BANNERMAN TERR	SHERBURN HILL	12/12/14		KR para 392			TO 1st GARRISON BN, 1st BN NF.	
STEPHENSON	Edwd	PTE	26	/637	A	17 SOUTH ST	BIRTLEY			4 SEPT 1916	NOVEMBER 16	THIEPVAL MEM	TO 27th(B COY) BN.	BORN NEWCASTLE, DESERTED 22/7/15 CT 2/9/15.
STEPHENSON	Geo	PTE	26	/1248	D	37 DOUGLAS TERR	USWORTH				JULY 16			12 GEN HOSP 2/7/16 WND R EYE, DESERTED 25/9/16
STEPHENSON	J	PTE	26	/638	A		NEWCASTLE	24/11/14	7/8/17	GUNSHOT WOUNDS	OCTOBER 16		TO DEPOT.	AGE 37.
STEPHENSON	Rob	PTE	26	/654	A	WATER LANE	DURHAM CITY			1 JULY 1916		THIEPVAL MEM		MISSING OCTOBER 16, SON KiA WITH 25th BN
STEWART	Dan J	PTE	26											AWOL 9/6/ 30/6/15 COURT GATESHEAD AGE 22.
STEWART	Robt	PTE	26											AWOL 1/6/15 COURT NEWCASTLE 10/6/15.
STIRLING	G	PTE	26	/640	A		GATESHEAD				DECEMBER_16			3 CCS 2/7/16 EVAC 3/7/16.
STONEHOUSE	E W	PTE	26	/647	A	16 GARBUTT ST	BISHOP AUKLAND						TO 22nd, 9th, 3rd BNS, CLASS Z RESERVE.	
STOTT	W W	PTE	26	/671				15/12/14	4/5/15	KR para 392iii				DID NOT SERVE OVERSEAS.
STRONG	JohnR	PTE	26	/655	B	40 JOICEY ST	SHERBURN HILL			2 JULY 1916		SHADFORTH		ACCOUNT OF FUNERAL IN DC, BORN EASINGTON LANE.
STUBBS	Peter	PTE	26	/642	A	120 FRAMWELLGATE	DURHAM CITY						TO LABOUR CORPS(783 LAB COY).	LAB CORPS No 397109.
SUMMERS	Dav H	PTE	26	/665	C	97 LAMPTON ST	SHERBURN HILL	9/12/14	12/4/18	SICK	SHELLSHOCK OCTOBER 16		TO 3rd BN.	AWOL 14/5/15,BRTHR Wm 21/1301 BUR PENSHAW Dd 27/11
SUMMERS	John	CPL	26	/644	A	211 KENDAL ST	BYKER	21/12/14	6/5/18	VDH			TO 3rd BN.	AWOL 7/8/15 CT 10/8/15, ACTING WOII.

NAME	INITI	RANK	BATTA	NUMBE	COMP	ADDRESS	TOWN_VILL	ENLISTED	DISCHARG	CAUSE_DIS	WOUNDED	BURIED	TRANSFER	ADD
SUMMERS	Wm	PTE	26	/1225	B	11 WALKER ST TEAMS	GATESHEAD				JULY 16		TO ROYAL ARMY MEDICAL CORPS.	3 CCS 2/7 EVAC No 16 AMB TR 11/7/16. BLACKPOOL 19
SWANNEL	Albt	PTE	26	/627	B		WANDSWORTH			24 APRIL 1917		BROWNS COPSE CEM		LCPL.
SWEENEY	Frank	PTE	26	/1229	D	5 QUEENS RD	JARROW			1 OCT 1916	DECEMBER 16	PLOEGSTEERT MEM		AGE 35.
SWEENEY	M	PTE	26	/1230	C		GATESHEAD				OCTOBER 16		TO ROYAL DEFENCE CORPS.	IN FRANCE 10/1/16 TO 3/7/16.
SYKES	C H	PTE	26	/645	A	WEST ALLOTMENT	BACKWORTH						TO CLASS Z RESERVE.	ACTING WOII
SYMM	JohnW	PTE	26	/1231	D		GATESHEAD			5 DEC 1917	OCTOBER 18	ST MARTIN CALVARIE MIL CEM		SGT, AGE 19.
TAGGART	D	CQMS	26	/674	D	1 WILLIAM ST	HEBBURN	2/12/14	4/3/19		DECEMBER 16		TO ARMY RESERVE CLASS P.	
TAGGART	J	PTE	26	/1266	D		DUNSTON			KR para 392	MAY 17		TO 27th BN.	
TAIT	J	PTE	26	/1420	C									IN 11 SECTION, IN BN BAND.
TANNEY	Dan	PTE	26	/1271	C		ASHINGTON			1 JULY 1916		THIEPVAL MEM		
TATE	Geo W	CPL	26	/700	B	111 SALISBURY ST	COWPEN QUAY			1 JULY 1916		THIEPVAL MEM		BORN BLYTH.
TATE	Wm	PTE	26	/1381		CHURCH ST	HASWELL COLLIER			28 APRIL 1917		ARRAS MEM		
TAYLOR	J	PTE	26	/1253	C								TO 25th BN, CLASS Z RESERVE.	ALSO ON C COY 30th BN ROLL.
TAYLOR	J	PTE	26	/1282	C									
TAYLOR	J	PTE	26	/1447	A									
TAYLOR	J	PTE	26	/1477	A								TO 25th BN, ROYAL FUSILIERS(24th BN).	FRANCE 26 10/1/16 TO 4/2/18, 25 5/2/18 TO 28/8/18.
TAYLOR	JohnT	PTE	26	/1254	D		SOUTH SHIELDS			1 JULY 1916		THIEPVAL MEM		
THIRKLE	B M	CPL	26	/1267	D	5 JAMES SQ HUDSON ST	NORTH SHIELDS		17/3/19		JULY 16		TO 1st, 25th, KINGS OWN YORKSHIRE LI(2/4th BN). CL	3CCS 2/7/16 EVAC 2/7/16 GSW, HOSP ABERDEEN 7/16.
THOMPSON	C	PTE	26	/1270				4/12/14	4/5/15	EYESIGHT				DID NOT SERVE OVERSEAS.
THOMPSON	Chas	PTE	26	/1259	D	24 AGNES ST	SOUTH SHIELDS			1 JULY 1916	W+M DECEMBER 16	THIEPVAL MEM		AWOL 10/5/15 IN COURT 18/5/15 SOUTH SHIELDS.
THOMPSON	D	CPL	26	/701	C		SOUTH SHIELDS	12/12/14	31/3/19	KR para 392			TO ARMY RESERVE CLASS P.	SGT
THOMPSON	F W	PTE	26	/1255	B	22 GRAHAMSLEY ST	GATESHEAD				NOVEMBER 16, SSHCK JUL 1		TO 8th, 16th, 1/7th BNS, CLASS Z RESERVE.	LSGT.
THOMPSON	Geo	PTE	26	/695	D30	380 ASKEW RD	GATESHEAD	12/12/14	4/4/16	MYALGIA			TO 30th BN.	CHRIS THOMPSON 45220 RFN 1/5th LONDON RIFLE BDE.
THOMPSON	J	PTE	26	/687	D			1/12/14	29/3/16	BRIGHTS DISEASE			TO 30th BN(D COY).	DID NOT SERVE OVERSEAS.
THOMPSON	J	PTE	26	/690	D	50 ALFRED ST	SOUTH SHIELDS				SHELLSHOCK OCTOBER 16			
THOMPSON	J	PTE	26	/1382	D			11/1/15	22/12/17	SICK			TO 3rd BN.	
THOMPSON	James	PTE	26	/693	A		BENWELL			1 JULY 1916	OCTOBER 16	THIEPVAL MEM		
THOMPSON	Sam J	PTE	26	/1273	A		WORKINGTON			28 APRIL 1917		ARRAS MEM	TO KINGS OWN YORKSHIRE LI(9th BN).	KOYLI No 43088 LCPL.
THOMPSON	Steve	PTE	26	/1371	C	COMMERCIAL STREET	CROOK		18/2/19		OCTOBER 16		TO 9th, 20th, 9th, 22nd, YORK & LANCS REGT(2/4th B	CPL.
THOMPSON	Thos	PTE	26	/1269	D	11 ROBERTS PLACE	GATESHEAD			11 OCT 1916	OCT 16.	FELLING	TO 8th BN.	AGE 34. AWOL 19/8/15 COURT GATESHEAD
THOMPSON	W	PTE	26	/692	A	15 LEIGHTON ST	BYKER	8/12/14		12 MAY 1919	OCTOBER 16	ALL SAINTS NEWCASTLE	TO LABOUR CORPS.	AGE 38, LAB CORPS No 605760.
THOMPSON	W	PTE	26	/696	D	28 HERON ST	SOUTH SHIELDS	10/12/14						
THOMPSON	Wm	PTE	26	/1408	A		ALNWICK			1 JULY 1916	OCTOBER 16	THIEPVAL MEM		NAME ADDED TO THIEPVAL MEM 1996.
THORNTON	A	PTE	26	/702	B	26 ANNFIELD PLACE	ANNFIELD PLAIN	15/12/14	9/1/18	SICK			TO DEPOT.	
THORNTON	Fred	PTE	26	/1260			NEWCASTLE			25 APRIL 1915		ELSWICK		REAL NAME WILSON F.A, AGE 27.
THORNTON	P	PTE	26	/1261	D	26 PITT ST	NEWCASTLE				OCTOBER 16			
THWAITES	R	LCPL	26	/681		3 CHURCH VIEW	LANCHESTER						TO 2nd GARRISON BN, CLASS Z RESERVE.	SEE ALSO 25/683 SGT THWAITES, FROM LANCHESTER.
TIERNEY	J	PTE	26	/679	B	23 GEORGE ST SOUTHWI	SUNDERLAND	9/12/14			JULY 16			
TIGHE	Chas	PTE	26	/683	D		WITTON GILBERT				OCTOBER 16		TO LABOUR CORPS, ARMY SERVICE CORPS.	LAB CORPS No 478119, ASC No M/379882.
TIGHE	John	PTE	26											AWOL 3/7/15 COURT GATESHEAD AGE 27.
TIMINEY	P	PTE	26	/684		4 QUEENS COURT QUEEN	NORTH SHIELDS						TO 1st GARRISON BN, CLASS Z RESERVE.	
TODD	J	PTE	26	/697	B		BEDLINGTON			KR para 392	JULY 16		TO 25th, 12/13th BNS.	
TOMLINSON	J	PTE	26	/1272	D		NEWCASTLE				OCTOBER 16			R VIC HOSP NETLEY 11/7/16.
TOMLINSON	L	PTE	26	/1256	C 27	12 CHURCH STREET	DURHAM CITY							
TOMLINSON	W	PTE	26	/685	B									ALSO ON C COY 30th BN ROLL.
TONES	John	PTE	26	/694	D	10 MILBURNGATE	DURHAM CITY				JULY 16		TO MACHINE GUN CORPS.	BATH WAR HOSP 7/16, MGC No 71029.
TOOLE	A	PTE	26	/698	B	70 DUNNS TERR	BYKER				MAY 16, JULY 16		TO CLASS Z RESERVE.	LCPL.
TOOLE	Arth	PTE	26	/691	D		MIDDLESBOROUGH			1 JULY 1916		THIEPVAL MEM		MISSING OCTOBER 16.
TOOLE	T	PTE	26	/1263	D									ALSO ON C COY 30th BN ROLL.
TROTTER	A	SGT	26	/675	A								TO 10th, 8th BNS, CLASS Z RESERVE.	
TUNNEY	James	PTE	26	/1278	D	72 SUNDERLAND ST	BRANDON COLLIER	9/12/14			OCTOBER 16		TO 12/13th BN.	
TUNNEY	Jos	PTE	26	/1281	D	72 SUNDERLAND ST	BRANDON COLLIER	9/12/14		6 MARCH 1916		BAILLEUL		
TURNER	Chas	PTE	26	/1280	D	11 ELEVENTH ST EAST	EASINGTON COLLI	9/12/14			OCTOBER 16		TO TRAINING RES BN.	TRG RES No TR/5/59076.
TURNER	Jos	CPL	26	/1370	C	42 COMMERCIAL ST	CROOK			1 JULY 1916		THIEPVAL MEM		IN 11 SECTION, MISSING OCTOBER 16.
TURNER	W	CPL	26	/682	A	1 WELL YARD	TYNEMOUTH	30/11/14	5/1/18	SICK			TO DEPOT.	
TURNER	W	PTE	26	/689				1/12/14	29/1/16				TO 30th BN.	DID NOT SERVE OVERSEAS.
TYDESLEY	Geo	PTE	26	/680	B		WHEATLEY HILL			11 MAY 1916		BECOURT MIL CEM		BORN BOLTON LANCS.
TYMAN	Mich	PTE	26	/1275	A	1 EIGTH ST	EASINGTON COLLI	9/12/14		1 JULY 1916		OVILLIERS MIL CEM		LCPL BORN WEST AUKLAND.
TYSON	Jas	PTE	26	/699	A	53 NORFOLK ST	NORTH SHIELDS	10/12/14					TO LABOUR CORPS.	LAB CORPS No 603883, CSGT.
USHER	T	PTE	26	/1284		17 NEW ELVET	DURHAM CITY	16/12/14	3/8/16	SICK			TO 1st GARRISON BN, 2nd BN, DEPOT.	ENTERED BALKANS 26/12/15, 14/15 STAR.

NAME	INITI	RANK	BATTA	NUMBE	COMP	ADDRESS	TOWN_VILL	ENLISTED	DISCHARG	CAUSE_DIS	WOUNDED	BURIED	TRANSFER	ADD
VALLEY	J	PTE	26	/705	A			26/11/14	25/10/17	SHELLSHOCK	MAY 16		TO 30th BN.	
VINCENT	Robt	PTE	26	/1285	D		NEWCASTLE			1 JULY 1916	OCTOBER 16	THIEPVAL MEM		WNDED+MISSING DECEMBER 16.
VOSE	John	PTE	26	/703	D		BANKHEAD			9 APRIL 1917		ORCHARD DUMP CEM		
WAITE	Chas	PTE	26	/731	B	44 STEPNEY LANE	NEWCASTLE			1 JULY 1916		THIEPVAL MEM		MISSING OCTOBER 16, BLACKBURN.
WAKE	John	PTE	26	/1468	C	15 BRECON HILL	FENCEHOUSES			1 JULY 1916		THIEPVAL MEM		BORN WINGATE.
WAKE	W	PTE	26	/727	D	6 COOPERATIVE TERR	WEST STANLEY	7/12/14	9/5/17	WOUNDS	OCTOBER 16		TO DEPOT.	3 CCS 2/7/16 EVAC 3/7/16.
WAKENSHAW	J	PTE	26	/711	D		NORTH SHIELDS	24/11/14	14/3/19	WOUNDS	OCTOBER 16		TO 26th,12th,12/13th,25th, KOYLI(2/4th),DEPOT KOYL	LCPL.
WALKER	A M	PTE	26	/1286	D		NEWCASTLE				FEBRUARY 17, MARCH 18.		TO 10th BN, CLASS Z RESERVE.	
WALKER	Cliff	PTE	26	/746	B	127 MARSDEN ST	SOUTH SHIELDS						TO ROYAL ENGINEERS.	RE No 306653, WR/23239.
WALKER	Jas M	PTE	26	/710	B	13 WALL KNOWLES	NEWCASTLE			20 FEB 1916		X FARM CEM ARMENTIERES		AGE 38.
WALKER	R H	PTE	26	/733	D	20 BOLIVAR PLACE	GATESHEAD				OCTOBER 16		TO ROYAL DEFENCE CORPS.	IN FRANCE 10/1/16 TO 8/7/16.
WALKINGTON	Thos	PTE	26	/1323	D	6 SEASIDE LANE GLEBE	EASINGTON COLLI	9/12/14		31 JULY 1916		THIEPVAL MEM		NOK 20 ATKINSON RD FULWELL, BORN SUNDERLAND.
WALLACE	W	PTE	26	/747	B	23 AUSTRALIA ST	NEW SEAHAM	14/12/14	29/8/17	SHELLSHOCK			TO DEPOT.	
WALSH	M	PTE	26	/738	D	5 GIBSIDE TERR	TANFIELD						ATTACHED 34th DIV BAND, TO 10th BN, CLASS Z RESERV	
WALTON	J L	PTE	26	/712	D	99 UNION ST	NEWCASTLE		20/4/19				TO 10th BN, KINGS OWN YORKSHIRE LI(2/4th BN), Z RE	
WALTON	Thos	PTE	26	/1329	D	3 GEORGE ST	BROOMPARK			1 JULY 1916		THIEPVAL MEM		MISSING OCTOBER 16. BORN ELDON.
WALTON	W	PTE	26	/1321		FRONT ST	WITTON GILBERT	10/12/14	11/6/16	UNFIT				DID NOT SERVE OVERSEAS.
WARD	H	PTE	26	/724	D								TO 9th, 1st, 9th, CLASS Z RESERVE.	
WARD	Pat	PTE	26	/713	B	GREEN ST	CONSETT	28/11/14					TO LABOUR CORPS(783 LAB COY).	LAB CORPS No 397130 D&D 23/4/15, AWOL 4/7 COURT 12
WARD	Thos	PTE	26	/1311	C	60 LAMPTON ST	SHERBURN HILL	11/12/14					ATTACHED 9th ENTRENCHING BN, 1/4th BN, CLASS Z RES	CPL, IN 4 PLATOON A COY 1/4th BN.
WARDLE	R	PTE	26	/1287				30/11/14	8/5/18	SICK			TO 1st GARRISON BN, 12/13th BN, DEPOT.	NOT OVERSEAS WITH TI.
WARMAN	H E	PTE	26	/742									TO ROYAL DEFENCE CORPS.	IN FRANCE 10/1/16 TO 15/2/17
WARREN	Silas	PTE	26	/732	D	23 OLIVER ST	SOUTHMOOR	9/12/14			OCTOBER 16, DECEMBER 16.		TO 12th, 12/13th BNS, CLASS Z RESERVE.	CPL.
WASS	Jn Go	PTE	26	/729		6 DUNELM TERR	DALTON LE DALE	5/12/14	24/8/18	SICK			TO 1st GARRISON BN, 11th, 31st? BNS, DEPOT.	31st MAY HAVE BEEN 30th.
WATSON	E	SGT	26	/737	D		SEAHAM HARBOUR				SEPTEMBER 16		TO CLASS Z RESERVE.	RENUMBERED IN NORTHBD FUS 42499.
WATSON	J	PTE	26	/1294	B		GATESHEAD				OCTOBER 16, NOVEMBER 16.			
WATSON	M	PTE	26	/1316	B									
WATSON	Thos	PTE	26	/728			WREKETON			7 APRIL 1916		GATESHEAD	TO 30th BN.	
WATTS	Fred	PTE	26	/1403	C		SWALWELL			1 JULY 1916		THIEPVAL MEM		
WEATHERBURN	E	PTE	26	/741	D									
WEDDLE	R S	PTE	26	/739	D		LANGLEY PARK	9/12/14			JULY 16			
WEIGHELL	J	CQMS	26	/714				28/11/14	15/1/15	KR para 392 xvi				DID NOT SERVE OVERSEAS.
WELSH	M	PTE	26	/1308	D						APRIL 1916			
WELSH	Robt	PTE	26	/1303	D		SPENNYMOOR			28 APRIL 1917		BROWNS COPSE CEM	TO 24th BN.	
WELSH	W	PTE	26	/707	D	119 FRAMWELLGATE	DURHAM CITY							
WEST	Jas L	PTE	26	/715	D	30 CUTLERS RD	BLACKHILL			1 JULY 1916	OCTOBER 16	THIEPVAL MEM		BORN CLAY NEXT THE SEA NORFOLK,AWOL 22/8/15 AGE 28
WHARTON	T	PTE	26	/1296	A		CHOPPINGTON			KR para 392	OCTOBER 16, MARCH 17.		TO 14th BN.	3 CCS 2/7/16 EVAC 3/7/16.
WHEATLEY	Geo	PTE	26	/1300	D	12 WILFRED ST	BYKER			1 JULY 1916	OCTOBER 16	THIEPVAL MEM		MISSING DECEMBER 16.
WHELAN	Math	BDSM	26	/1297	A	8 CHAPEL SQUARE	HEWORTH COLLIER			2 SEPT 1917		HAGRICOURT MIL CEM		CPL, BORN WATERFORD, AGE 37 POS FROM CLEATOR MOOR.
WHITE	J W	PTE	26	/734									TO 1st GARRISON BN, CLASS Z RESERVE.	
WHITE	Jas W	PTE	26	/1445		27 WELLINGTON ST	SOUTH SHIELDS	31/5/15	10/3/19	KR para 392			TO 1st GARRISON BN, 25th, 9th BNS, DEPOT.	Died age 72. MINER ST HILDA'S COLLIERY.
WHITFIELD	S	PTE	26	/716	D									
WIDDRINGTON	Jas	PTE	26	/1306	D		NEWCASTLE		9/6/19		OCTOBER 16		TO 24th, 21st, 14th BNS, YORK & LANCS(18th BN) CLA	HOSP CHELTENHAM 7/16
WILD	Gavin	CQMS	26	/1310	C	4 FRONT ST	LITTLETOWN				JULY 16		TO LABOUR CORPS(732 LAB COY).	HOSP STOURBRIDGE 7/16.
WILD	Wm	CQMS	26	/725	B	5 LONG ST	LITTLETOWN	10/12/14			JULY 16		TO 27th, 26th BNS, COMMISSIONED ARGYLL & SUTH HIGH	
WILD	Wm D	PTE	26	/1309	C	4 NORTH VIEW	SHERBURN HILL		7/2/19				TO 10th BN, KINGS OWN YORKSHIRE LI(2/4th BN), CLAS	IN 11 SECTION.
WILKES	W	PTE	26	/1327	C	1 VICTORIA ST	LOW PITTINGTON							
WILKINSON	G	PTE	26	/717				26/11/14	23/7/18	SICK			TO 1st GARRISON BN, DEPOT.	
WILKINSON	J	PTE	26	/1317	C								TO LABOUR CORPS.	
WILKINSON	James	PTE	26	/1305	C	3 THE GREEN	SUNDERLAND	8/12/14			OCTOBER 16, FEBRUARY 18.		TO 24th, 21st, 14th BNS, CLASS Z RESERVE.	
WILKINSON	Jos K	PTE	26	/1407	D	OFFICE YARD WHITE LE	TANTOBIE			3 APRIL 1916		BREWERY ORCHARD		AGE 19.
WILLIAMS	John	PTE	26	/1304	B		MIDDLESBOROUGH	1/12/14	19/11/17	WOUNDS	JUNE 16,SEPTEMBER 16		TO DEPOT.	RAID 5/6/16, 3 CCS 2/7/16 EVAC 2/7/16.
WILLIAMSON	E	LCPL	26	/1320	C	2 BRIGHTON TERR	SHERBURN HILL	11/12/14	21/12/17	WOUNDS	OCTOBER 16		TO DEPOT.	CPL.
WILLIAMSON	R	PTE	26	/1315	B	45 DERWENT ST	BLACKHILL				1 JULY 16			HOSP EPSOM 7/16.
WILSON	E	PTE	26	/1464	C			21/6/15	17/5/16	SICK				DID NOT SERVE OVERSEAS.
WILSON	F	PTE	26	/748	D	12 HAWK YARD	GATESHEAD				OCTOBER 16		TO 12/13th, 23rd, 9th BNS, CLASS Z RESERVE.	SGT.
WILSON	G	PTE	26	/1289	D									
WILSON	H	PTE	26	/1322	A	7 ANDERSON ST	SOUTH SHIELDS				DEC 16, MAR 17, JUN 18.		TO EAST YORKSHIRE REGT.	
WILSON	JohnG	PTE	26	/718	D	139 VIOLET ST	NEWCASTLE						TO 11th, 24th, 25th, 12/13th BNS, CLASS Z RESERVE.	
WILSON	Robt	PTE	26	/719		31 WALKER ST LOW TEA	GATESHEAD			4 MAY 1915		GATESHEAD EAST CEM		

NAME	INITI	RANK	BATTA	NUMBE	COMP	ADDRESS	TOWN_VILL	ENLISTED	DISCHARG	CAUSE_DIS	WOUNDED	BURIED	TRANSFER	ADD
WINSHIP	A N	PTE	26	/730	D		FENCEHOUSES				OCTOBER 16, NOT WND DEC]			
WINTER	Jos	SGT	26	/721	D	43 CLYDE ST	CHOPWELL	28/11/14	24/8/17	SHELLSHOCK	OCTOBER 16		TO 85th TRAINING RESERVE BN.	
WINTHORPE	J	PTE	26	/1417	A								ATTACHED 9th ENTRENCHING BN, 10th BN, CLASS Z RESE	
WOOD	Geo	PTE	26	/1312	A	13 THIRD ST EAST	EASINGTON COLLI	9/12/14			OCTOBER 16, DECEMBER 16.		TO 25th, 1/7th BNS, CLASS Z RESERVE.	LCPL.
WOOD	J	PTE	26	/750		12 CHURCH ST	DARLINGTON						TO 1st GARRISON BN, CLASS Z RESERVE.	
WOOD	Jas	PTE	26	/1325	D	5 HILL ST	HEMLINGTON ROW				AUGUST 16		TO 14th BN, CLASS Z RESERVE.	
WOOD	John	PTE	26	/1291	D	19 WALKER ST TEAMS	GATESHEAD	2/12/14			OCTOBER 16		TO ROYAL DEFENCE CORPS.	IN FRANCE 10/1/16 TO 6/7/16.
WOOD	R	PTE	26	/709	B		GATESHEAD	24/11/14	22/5/18	SICK	OCTOBER 16		TO DEPOT.	
WOOD	R B	PTE	26	/1484	B27	LONGFORD ST	MIDDLESBOROUGH			KR para 392			TO 27th, 24/27th, 25th BNS.	COLOUR SGT 27th BN, WO11 25th BN.
WOOD	W	PTE	26	/708	A	1 QUALITY ROW	BYKER	2/12/14	17/9/18	SICK			TO 1/7th, DEPOT.	SGT.
WOOD	W C	PTE	26	/1292	D		WASHINGTON STAT				OCTOBER 16, JANUARY 18.		TO 23rd, 24th, 21st, 23rd BNS, CLASS Z RESERVE.	3 CCS 2/7/16 EVAC 2/7/16.
WOODCOCK	J	PTE	26	/744	D	9 THOMAS ST	SOUTH SHIELDS				MARCH 16			
WRAY	J	LCPL	26	/1465	D	36a THERESA ST	SOUTHMOOR							
WRIGHT	Jas W	PTE	26	/722	D		SOUTH SHIELDS	2/12/14		12 OCT 1917		CEMENT HOUSE LANGEMARCK	TO 25th BN.	LCPL. ALSO ON C COY 30th BN ROLL.
WRIGHT	M H	PTE	26	/743	C		GATESHEAD	10/12/14	25/10/17	SICK			TO 16th BN, DEPOT.	
WRIGHT	W	PTE	26	/723	D	49 SANDHILL	NEWCASTLE				OCTOBER 16			LCPL, AWOL 19/6, DESERTED 26/6/15, COURT 19/7/15.
WYNN	J	LCPL	26	/740	D	1 SEVENTH ST SOUTH	EASINGTON COLLI	9/12/14		KR para 392	OCTOBER 16			SGT.
WYNN	J	PTE	26	/1299	B								TO ROYAL DEFENCE CORPS.	IN FRANCE 10/1/16 TO 14/4/17.
WYNN	J P	CQMS	26	/1485	A								TO CLASS Z RESERVE.	
YOUNG	J	PTE	26	/1475	A								ATTACHED 257 TUNNELLING COY RE, TO 19th, 1/5th BN,	
YOUNG	JohnT	PTE	26	/1332	D	10 HOLY ISLAND	HEXAM				FEBRUARY 16		TO 19th BN, CLASS Z RESERVE.	
YOUNG	Wilf	PTE	26	/1331	B		NEWCASTLE			1 JUNE 1917		BAILLEUL RD ST LAURENT BLAGNY		SGT.
YOUNGHUSBAND	W	SGT	26	/751	D	9 ALBERT PLACE	WASHINGTON		28/1/19				TO 25th BN, KINGS OWN YORKSHIRE LI(5th BN), Z RES.	WOII

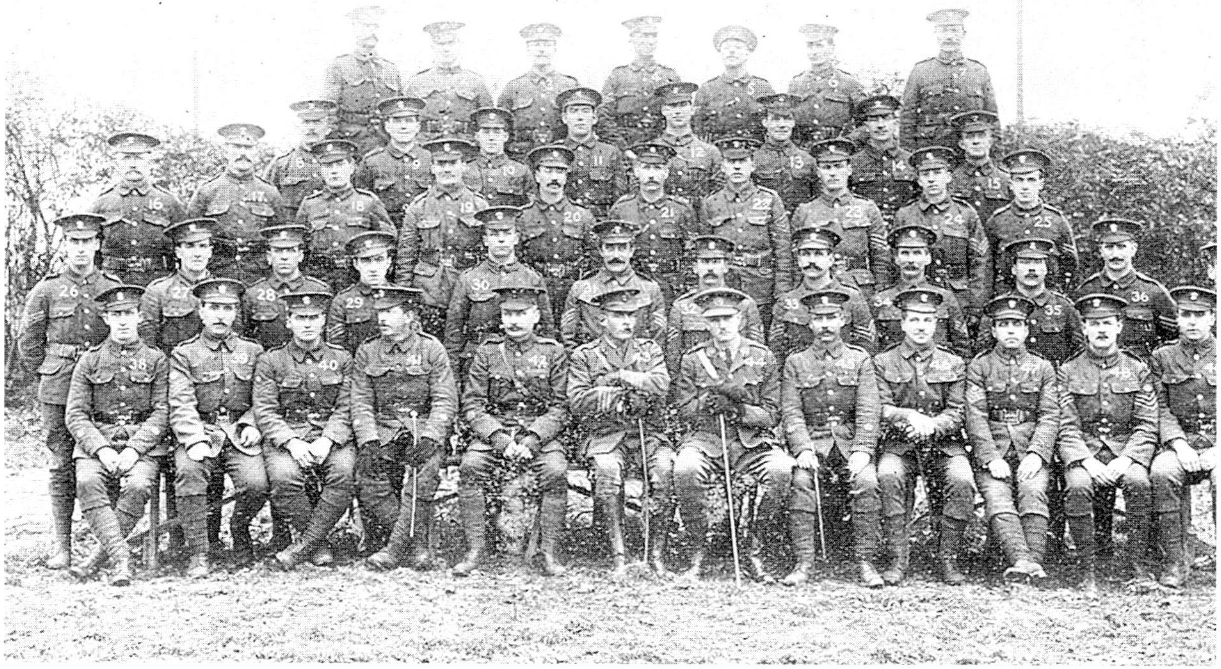

James Bacon and Sons.]

[*To face page* 189.

OFFICERS AND NON-COM. OFFICERS, 3rd Batt. Tyneside Irish Brigade. [26 (S) Batt. N.F.].

1. Sgt. Harkins.
2. ,, Lincoln.
3. ,, Jones.
4. ,, Mills.
5. ,, Lawson.
6. ,, Dodds.
7. ,, Hillary.
8. ,, Dixon.
9. Sgt. Dyson.
10. ,, Yates.
11. ,, Aitchison.
12. ,, Harrison.
13. ,, Thompson.
14. ,, Plant.
15. ,, Byron.
16. ,, Gleeson.
17. C.S.M. Raynham.
18. Sgt. Hawthorne.
19. ,, Baylie.
20. ,, Joblin.
21. ,, Mains.
22. ,, Younghusband.
23. ,, Hall.
24. ,, Thirlaway.
25. Sgt. Connolly.
26. ,, Lynch.
27. ,, Haley.
28. ,, Doyle.
29. ,, Winn.
30. ,, Brown.
31. ,, Marshall.
32. ,, Winter.
33. Sgt. Howell.
34. ,, Smith.
35. ,, Ellis.
36. ,, Fennelly.
37. ,, Farrell.
38. R.Q.M.S. Bewick.
39. C.Q.M.S. Wilde, W., D.C.M.
40. ,, Coleman, ,,
41. C.S.M. McGrady.
42. R.S.M. Steel.
43. Major Chichester, C.O.
44. Capt. Cobb, Adj., D.S.O.
45. C.S.M. Holden.
46. ,, Dyke.
47. C.Q.M.S. Taggart.
48. Allsopp, O.S.
49. C.Q.M.S. Wilde, G.

Appendix VI

ALHABETICAL NOMINAL ROLL
OTHER RANKS
27th NORTHUMBERLAND FUSILIERS
4th TYNESIDE IRISH

HIGHEST BATTALION NUMBER TRACED 27/1560
NUMBER ON ROLL **1260**
UNTRACED **300**
KILLED OR DIED OF WOUNDS **321**
WOUNDED **482**
DISCHARGED SICK, GASSED, TRENCH FOOT.
DEAFNESS, KR para 392 ETC **283**
TOTAL KNOWN CASUALTIES **1086**
CASUALTIES AS A % OF THOSE TRACED
86.1%

NAME	INITI	RANK	BA	NUMBE	COMP	ADDRESS	TOWN_VILL	ENLISTED	DISCHARG	CAUSE_DIS	WOUNDED	BURIED	TRANSFER	ADD
ABBOTT	J	PTE	27	/1532	D	49 PRUDHOE ST	NEWCASTLE				SEPTEMBER 16, JANUARY 17.			21AMBTR,18 GHOSP 6/7, 6 CONV DEPOT 7/7/16 SSHOCK A
ADAMS	Thos	PTE	27	/16	D	SOUTH ST	NORTH SHIELDS	9/1/15	2/8/17	GUNSHOT WOUNDS	JULY 16		TO 85th TRAINING RESERVE BN.	VOLUNTARY AID HOSP CHELTENHAM 11/7/16.
ADAMSON	W S	PTE	27	/9		12 SHERATON ST	SHOTTON COLLIER						TO 1st GARRISON BN, CLASS Z RESERVE.	
AGNEW	Mich	PTE	27	/792	A	9 PROSPECT TERR	BLACKHILL			1 JULY 1916		T HIEPVAL MEM		
ALDERSON	Geo W	PTE	27	/6	B	64 NEW FOURTH ST	HORDEN	29/12/14	4/4/16				TO 30th BN.	DID NOT SERVE OVERSEAS.
ALLAN	F	SGT	27	/7	B	9 HIGH ST WEST	WALLSEND	29/12/14	8/4/18	GUNSHOT WOUNDS	AUGUST 16		TO DEPOT.	3 CCS 2/7/16 EVAC 2/7/16 GSW
ALLEN	Jn Hy	PTE	27	/2	A	4 SINGLE ROW	SOUTH NEWSHAM			6 JULY 1916		W IMEREUX		BORN HINFRENHAM NORFOLK.
ALLISON	J	PTE	27	/1470	B								TO 24/27th, 19th, 11th BNS, CLASS Z RESERVE.	IN BN BAND
ANDERSON	Henry	PTE	27	/797		PRIMROSE COTTAGE	SHOTTON COLLIER						TO 2nd GARRISON BN, CLASS Z RESERVE.	
ANDERSON	JohnJ	PTE	27	/21	D	20 BELL ST	RYHOPE	7/1/15						
ANDERSON	Wm	PTE	27	/793	B	18 FRONT ST MILBURN	NORTH SHIELDS	7/1/15			SEPTEMBER 16.		TO SCOTTISH RIFLES(10th BN), NORTHUMBERLAND FUSILI	ALLOTTED NEW NUMBER 97798.
ANGUS	G	PTE	27	/18	D									ALSO ON D COY 30th BN ROLL.
APPLETON	A	PTE	27	/1453	B								TO 24/27th, 9th, 10th BNS, CLASS Z RESERVE.	
ARMSTRONG	Edw	PTE	27	/14	C	9 SPENCER ST	NORTH SHIELDS			KR para 392	SEPTEMBER 16			
ARMSTRONG	Edw	PTE	27	/17	D	50 BENSHAM AVE	GATESHEAD	14/1/15			SEPTEMBER 16		ATT 17 CORPS SCHOOL, TO 24/27th, 11th BNS, CLASS Z	LCPL.
ARMSTRONG	G	PTE	27	/12	C									
ARMSTRONG	H	PTE	27	/1	A		BEBSIDE FURNACE				SEPTEMBER 16		TO 10th, 9th BNS, CLASS Z RESERVE.	
ARMSTRONG	J	SGT	27	/15	D	25 STONE ROW	GRANGE VILLA						TO 30th BN(D COY), 22nd BN.	SERVED OVERSEAS WITH 22nd BN ONLY.
ARNOTT	Jos T	PTE	27	/795	D	4 USWORTH AVE	PELAW	9/1/15	23/4/18	GUNSHOT WOUNDS	AUGUST 16.		TO DEPOT.	
ASHWORTH	Geo	PTE	27	/5	A	16 FRANK ST FULWELL	SUNDERLAND	28/12/14	12/5/18	WOUNDS			TO 27th, BASE NF, 24/27th, 11th BNS, DEPOT.	
ASKEW	Math	PTE	27	/13	C	30 NOEL ST	EAST STANLEY	7/1/15					TO LABOUR CORPS.	7 PALMER ST OXHILL 1918.
ATKIN	T	LCPL	27	/8	B									
ATKINSON	Ed	SGT	27	/796	A	BRAMPTON HOUSE	USHAW MOOR	14/1/15		1 JULY 1916		T HIEPVAL MEM		MISSING OCT 16, BORN LANGLEY MOOR, CPL IN BAND
ATKINSON	J	PTE	27	/3	C									
ATKINSON	J	PTE	27	/4	A	22 MORRIS ST	BIRTLEY						TO 8th, 1/4th, 1/7th, 3rd BNS, CLASS Z RESERVE.	DESERTED 28 JANUARY 1918.
ATKINSON	J	PTE	27	/19	A									
BAGLEY	Wm	PTE	27	/823	C	BYRON ST	SOUTH SHIELDS	10/1/15	8/2/17	PHTHISIS			TO DEPOT.	
BAINBRIDGE	Rob	PTE	27	/74	D	23 ILCHESTER ST	DAWDON	7/1/15			OCTOBER 16		TO LABOUR CORPS.	
BAINES	J	PTE	27	/808			SOUTH SHIELDS	22/12/14						LABOURER DESERTED 24/4/15 AGE 26, 5'4''.
BAKER	Tos H	PTE	27	/35		HARTON	SOUTH SHIELDS			27 JAN 1915		H ARTON ST PETERS		
BALL	Jos	PTE	27	/55	C	30 DOUGLAS TERR	USWORTH			6 FEB 1916		U SWORTH HOLY TRINITY		AGE 33, NOK 3 BRANDY ROW WASHINGTON.
BALL	Jos	PTE	27	/68		27 NITH STREET	HORDEN	30/1/15						MINER DESERTED 24/5/15 AGE 31, 5'5'' BORN BUCKLEY
BALMETT	G	SGT	27	/834									TO 1st GARRISON BN, CLASS Z RESERVE.	
BARBER	Jas	PTE	27	/73	D	6 OBAN ST	NEWCASTLE	9/1/15	16/9/18	GUNSHOT WOUNDS			TO 24/27th BN, DEPOT.	
BARKELL	A	PTE	27	/822	C		DURHAM CITY			KR para 392	DECEMBER 16.			
BARKER	Isaac	PTE	27	/27	A		SOUTH HETTON				SEPTEMBER 16, MARCH 18.		TO 26th, 18th, 22nd BNS, CLASS Z RESERVE.	
BARKHOUSE	Jas	PTE	27	/829	A	BRICKGARTH	EASINGTON COLLI	12/1/15			APRIL 16, JULY 16, DEC 17		TO 8th BN, CLASS Z RESERVE.	
BARNES	J W	PTE	27	/833	D		EASINGTON	6/1/15	8/4/17	WOUNDS	FEBRUARY 16.		TO DEPOT.	
BARNES	John	PTE	27	/90	B	38 STATION ROAD	EASINGTON COLLI							
BARNES	Tom W	PTE	27	/59		38 STATION RD	EASINGTON COLLI	29/12/14	5/5/18	SICK			TO 2nd GARRISON BN, 3rd BN.	PHOTO IN CC 13/4/16.
BARNINGHAM	J	PTE	27	/839	A		NEWCASTLE				AUGUST 16.		TO LABOUR CORPS.	ENTERED FRANCE 30/11/15, NOT NOTED ON 14/15 STAR R
BARRASS	Henry	PTE	27	/41	B	7 SOUTH ST	SHERBURN COLLIE	21/12/14	12/7/17	WOUNDS	SEPTEMBER 16		TO 85th TRAINING RESERVE BN.	2 GHOSP 4/7 SHIP 5/7 HOSP PLYMOUTH 7/16 WND L FOOT
BARRASS	T	PTE	27	/82	D	1 QUALITY ROW	SHOTTON COLLIER	8/1/15			JULY 16,APR 17, DEC 17.		TO 16th BN, RIF BDE(DEPOT), ATT 1/5th LONDON REGT.	RIFLE BDE No 45139.
BARRASS	Wm	PTE	27	/40	B	22 SOUTH ST	SHERBURN COLLIE			23 MARCH 1918	SEPTEMBER 16	A RRAS MEM	TO 11th, 24th, 23rd BNS.	BORN DURHAM, HOSP MANCHESTER 7/16.
BARRETT	Jas A	PTE	27	/815	B	26 ROSA ST	SPENNYMOOR	5/1/15		1 JULY 1916		T HIEPVAL MEM		LCPL.
BARROW	Geo W	PTE	27	/50	C	17 SCHOOL STREET	DAWDON	23/12/14	7/1/19				TO 24/27th, 14th BNS, CLASS Z RESERVE.	BORN 1890. DISCHARGED AT WINCHESTER 9/12/18.
BATEY	John	PTE	27	/1444	B	185 BUDDLE RD	NEWCASTLE						TO 14th BN, CLASS Z RESERVE.	
BAYLES	Robt	PTE	27	/83	D	18 QUARRY ROW	TANTOBIE			1 JULY 1916		T HIEPVAL MEM		BORN WEST AUKLAND.
BEAN	JohnR	PTE	27	/38	B	4 TYNE ST	NORTH SHIELDS			1 JULY 1916		T HIEPVAL MEM		BORN TYNEMOUTH.
BEARDSMORE	G	PTE	27	/72	D	23 SIXTH ST	EASINGTON COLLI				SEPTEMBER 16		TO LABOUR CORPS, EAST LANCASHIRE REGT.	
BEATTIE	G E	LCPL	27	/85	A		FELLING				AUGUST 16.		TO 20th, 23rd BNS, CLASS Z RESERVE.	34 CCS 2/7/16 EVAC 5/7/16 WND L THIGH.
BECKWITH	T	PTE	27	/847	D		MIDDLESBOROUGH				SEPTEMBER 16.			
BEECROFT	Math	LCPL	27	/25	B	38 THISTLE ST	HEBBURN NEWTOWN	12/1/15	31/1/19		JULY 16		TO DUKE OF WELLINGTONS REGT.	
BEEVER	Wm	PTE	27	/76	C	124 DURHAM RD	BLACKHILL				JUNE 16.		TO LABOUR CORPS(A E COY).	LAB CORPS No 368976.
BELL	Ernst	PTE	27	/809	B		GATESHEAD			1 JULY 1916		T HIEPVAL MEM		MISSING OCTOBER 16.
BELL	Fred	PTE	27											DESERTER 1/8/15 COURT NEWCASTLE 26/8/15.
BELL	G T	PTE	27	/61	D			29/12/14	13/12/15					DID NOT SERVE OVERSEAS.
BELL	J	PTE	27	/87	D	75 QUEEN ST	NORTH SHIELDS	8/1/15			SEPTEMBER 16		TO LABOUR CORPS.	3 CCS 2/7/16 EVAC 2/7/16 S SHOCK.
BELL	J	PTE	27	/800	A		NEWSHAM	19/12/14	29/12/16	WOUNDS	JULY 16.		TO DEPOT.	
BELL	J	PTE		/790	A	27								

NAME	INITI	RANK	BA	NUMBE	COMP	ADDRESS	TOWN_VILL	ENLISTED	DISCHARG	CAUSE_DIS	WOUNDED	BURIED	TRANSFER	ADD
BELL	J R	PTE	27	/29	D								TO CLASS Z RESERVE.	ALLOTED NEW NUMBER 97931.
BELL	Jn Ts	PTE	27	/31	A	42 REDHEAD ST	SOUTH SHIELDS	14/1/15		31 JULY 1916		LA PUGNOY CEM		BORN ANNFIELD PLAIN, MINER AT ST HILDA COLLIERY.
BELL	M	PTE	27	/820	C									
BELL	T	PTE	27	/832	D		NEWCASTLE	5/1/15	26/7/18	GUNSHOT WOUNDS	SEPTEMBER 16.		TO 3rd BN, DEPOT.	FINAL DISCHARGE 4/12/18.
BENFOLD	Chas	PTE	27	/811			SPENNYMOOR	24/12/14						HORSE DEALER DESERTED 1/5/15 AGE 23, 5'4''.
BENNETT	R	PTE	27	/84	D								TO 24/27th, 11th BNS, CLASS Z RESERVE.	
BERTRAM	Jhn H	PTE	27	/24	B	43 PRINCESS ST	GATESHEAD	8/1/15	16/11/18	SICK	SEPTEMBER 16		TO 11th, 27th, 3rd BNS.	CPL, 7 DOROTHY STREET 1918.
BEWICK	E	PTE	27	/60	D								TO 24/27th, 8th BNS, CLASS Z RESERVE.	
BEWICK	R W	PTE	27	/65	D	22 OLD SCHOOL ROW	SHOTTON COLLIER	30/12/14	16/12/18	GUNSHOT WOUNDS	AUGUST 16.		TO 3rd BN.	
BEWSHAW	Thos	PTE	27	/837	D	4 FYLANDS BRIDGE	BISHOP AUKLAND			9 JULY 1916		BOULOGNE EAST CEM		BORN MIDDLETON IN TEASDALE.
BLACK	Wm	PTE	27	/799	A		SOUTH SHIELDS	14/1/15		KR para 392				AWOL IN COURT SOUTH SHIELDS 17/8/15.
BLACKBURN	W	LCPL	27	/37	B		BLYTH				AUGUST 16		TO 24/27th, 11th BNS, CLASS Z RESERVE.	21 AMBTR,18 GHOSP 6/7 CONV DEPOT 7/7SSHOCK AGE 34,
BLACKMORE	Edwd	PTE	27	/46	C	17 ALISON ST	SOUTH SHIELDS			11 MAY 1916		BECOURT MIL CEM		BORN MURTON COLLIERY, AGE 31.
BLAIR	C	PTE	24	/63	A		WORKINGTON				NOVEMBER 16, MAY 17.			
BLAIR	Geo	PTE	27	/814	C		WORKINGTON			2 JULY 1916		THIEPVAL MEM		
BLAKEY	G	PTE	27	/57	A	4 LITTLE VANE TERR	SUNDERLAND				AUGUST 16		TO ROYAL ENGINEERS.	34 CCS 2/7 EVAC 5/7 BATH WAR HOSP 11/7/16, AGE 36
BOLAM	JohnR	CPL	27	/89	A		BLAYDON			2 APRIL 1917	1 JULY 16	SAVY BRITISH MIL CEM	TO 16th BN.	34 CCS 1/7 EVAC 5/7/16 WND RLEG+LFOOT, AGE 27.
BOND	G	LCPL	27	/824	C									
BOND	Mich	PTE	27	/827	D	24 THE AVENUE	HETTON DOWNS	12/1/15		29 MARCH 1918		POZIERES MEM	TO 24/27th, 19th BNS.	COMPANY SERGEANT MAJOR 19NF.
BOOTH	T	PTE	27	/817	B									
BORTHWICK	JohnW	PTE	27	/52	C	34 WILSON ST	GATESHEAD							NEW NUMBER 258204, TYNESIDE IRISH FRANCE.
BORWICK	G	PTE	27	/826	C								TO 20th, 1/4th BNS, CLASS Z RESERVE.	
BOWERBANK	P	SGT	27	/1412	B									
BOWES	Jos L	PTE	27	/62	A		NEW SHILDON			1 JULY 1916		THIEPVAL MEM		
BOWES	Rob	PTE	27	/78	D	17 DEAN ST LOW DOWNS	HETTON LE HOLE	12/1/15						
BOWEY	E	PTE	27	/39	A			15/12/14	1/8/16	SICK			TO 24th BN, DEPOT.	
BOWMAN	JohnT	PTE	27	/75	D	7 HARRINGTON PLACE	NEWCASTLE	5/1/15					TO 24/27th, 19th(W COY), 23rd BNS, CLASS Z RESERVE	3 PORTERS HILL 1919 AWOL 6/7/15 COURT 12/7/15.
BOWMAN	W	PTE	27	/801	A		SUNDERLAND				SEPTEMBER 16		TO 84th TRG RES BN, ROYAL ENGINEERS.	
BOYACK	W H	PTE	27	/840	B									
BOYD	JohnF	PTE	27	/802	A	4 FINSBURY ST MNKWRM	SUNDERLAND			1 JULY 1916		THIEPVAL MEM		MISSING OCTOBER 16.
BOYLE	Wm	PTE	27	/32	A	10 RAILWAY ST	LITTLEBURN						TO 12/13th BN, CLASS Z RESERVE.	ALSO ON AVL FOR 7 GEORGE ST TANFIELD.
BRACEBRIDGE	J W	PTE	27	/22	B	21 ROSE ST	SUNDERLAND							
BRADFORD	Thos	PTE	27	/48	C	4 THOMAS ST	RYHOPE COLLIERY			1 JULY 1916		THIEPVAL MEM		NOK 28 CASTLEREAGH ST SILKSWORTH, BORN NEWBOTTLE.
BRADLEY	P	PTE	27	/1502	C	5 DACRE ST	MIDDLESBOROUGH			KR para 392				
BRADY	Tom S	PTE	27	/77	B		STATION TOWN			1 JULY 1916		THIEPVAL MEM		
BRANCH	H	PTE	27	/804	A	64 COMMERCIAL RD	SOUTH SHIELDS				SEPTEMBER 16.		TO 24th, 24/27th, 14th BNS.	DESERTED 16 JUNE 1917.
BRAY	A	PTE	27	/71	C	12 THIRD ST SOUTH.	EASINGTON COLLI						TO R.A.F. BALLOON SECTION.	RAF No 107033.
BRENNAN	John	PTE	27	/841	B	34 LIVINGSTONE ST	SOUTH SHIELDS	4/1/15	10/4/18	DAH 26 JAN 1919		HARTON ST PETERS	TO 24/27th BN, DEPOT.	
BRENNAN	Jos	PTE	27	/45		9 SCHOOL ST	LINTZ COLLIERY			13 FEB 1916		BOIS GRENIER MIL CEM		BORN CORNSAY COLLIERY.
BRENNAN	M	SGT	27	/42	C									POSS FROM EASINGTON TWO SONS IN THE NAVAL BRIGADE
BRETT	Pat	PTE	27	/825	C	158 CITY RD	NEWCASTLE	5/1/15	31/3/19	KR para 392	DECEMBER 17.		TO ARMY RESERVE CLASS P.	CPL.
BRITT	P	PTE	27	/835	D	BELTS BLDGS	WINLATON			KR para 392	AUGUST 16		TO 11th, 1st BNS.	LSGT.
BRITTON	Dan	PTE	27	/86	D	SHERBURN STATION	SHERBURN COLLIE				JULY 16			AWOL CT S/LAND 14/6/15, 5/7/15, 14/8/15, 26/8/15.
BRITTON	James	PTE	27	/28	A	27	SHERBURN COLLIE	12/1/15			JULY 16, SEPTEMBER 16.		TO 11th, 1st BNS, ATTACHED AOC, CLASS Z RESERVE.	34CCS 2/7 EVAC 5/7 HOSP MANCHESTER,WND RFOOT,AGE 4
BROGAN	A	PTE	27	/1387	A			21/4/15	10/2/19	GUNSHOT WOUNDS			TO 24/27th, 9th BNS ATTACHED 103 TRENCH MORTAR BTY	AGE 33.
BROOKS	John	PTE	27	/819	C	MORTON VILLAGE	SHIREMOOR	12/1/15		3 SEPT 1916		THIEPVAL MEM		LCPL, BORN EARSDON.
BROOMEFIELD	David	PTE	27	/30	A	83 CHURCHWAY	NORTH SHIELDS	14/1/15						
BROWN	C	PTE	27	/1457	A		LEMINGTON ON TY				JULY 16.			
BROWN	E	PTE	27	/70	D									
BROWN	Geo W	PTE	27	/831	D		SOUTH SHIELDS			27 APRIL 1918	SEPTEMBER 16, FEBRUARY 18	KLIEN VIERSTRAAT BRIT CEM	TO 22nd, 20th, 18th BNS.	LCPL, AGE 23 BORN NORTH SHIELDS.
BROWN	H	PTE	27	/1485	B									
BROWN	Hnry	PTE	27	/844	B	70 SMOKEY ROW FRAM M	DURHAM CITY	7/1/15		30 MAY 1918	SEPTEMBER 16, JUNE 18.	SOISSONS MEM	TO 14th BN.	BN M/GUN SECTION, HOSP BRISTOL 7/16 WND ANKLE
BROWN	J	PTE	27	/51	C		HEXAM				AUGUST 16			
BROWN	J	PTE	27	/838	A	9 VICTORIA PLACE	BIDDICK				JUL,SEP16,SS FEB17,MAR17		TO 18th, 22nd BN, CLASS Z RESERVE.	
BROWN	J	PTE	27	/846	D 30									
BROWN	J T	SGT	27	/1406	A		WHITE LE HEAD				OCTOBER 16, FEBRUARY 18.		TO 1st, 27th, 24/27th, 1/7th BNS, CLASS Z RESERVE.	
BROWN	Jn Tm	PTE	27	/810	B		CHILTON MOOR			28 APRIL 1917		ARRAS MEM		
BROWN	John	PTE	27	/33	A	22 CLEPHAN ST	DUNSTON	14/1/15			SEPTEMBER 16			ALSO IN THE LIST OF THE FIRST 50 TO JOIN 24TH.
BROWN	John	PTE	27	/805	A					1 JULY 1916		THIEPVAL MEM		BORN HIGGLETON MAIN YORKS.
BROWN	Stan	PTE	27	/43	A		SUNDERLAND			1 JULY 1916		THIEPVAL MEM		

NAME	INITI	RANK	BN	NUMBE	COMP	ADDRESS	TOWN_VILL	ENLISTED	DISCHARG	CAUSE_DIS	WOUNDED	BURIED	TRANSFER	ADD
BROWN	Thos	PTE	27	/81	A		BRANDON COLLIER	7/1/15					TO LABOUR CORPS.	
BROWN	W	PTE	27	/56	C		EASINGTON LANE	26/12/14	2/11/18	KR para 392	AUGUST 16		TO DEPOT.	
BROWN	Wm	PTE	27	/26	B	7 ALMA PLACE	GRANGE VILLA			15 MARCH 1916		BREWERY ORCHARD CEM		BORN DURHAM.
BROXUP	G W	PTE	27	/64	D	22 SIMPSON ST	NORTH SHIELDS	29/12/14	19/12/17	GUNSHOT WOUNDS	AUGUST 16.		TO 3rd BN.	BELLHOUSTON HOSP GLASGOW 7/16, WND IN LEGS.
BRUCE	Wm	PTE	27	/845	A	15 SPELTER WORKS RD	SUNDERLAND	7/1/15					TO 23rd, 20th, 18th BNS, CLASS Z RESERVE.	
BRYAN	R E	PTE	27	/80	A		BISHOP AUKLAND	8/1/15	11/10/17	WOUNDS	JULY 16		TO 3rd BN.	
BUCKLE	Ralph	LCPL	27	/34		11 COUNCIL HOUSES	ANNFIELD PLAIN	14/1/15		22 OCT 1917	JULY 16, SEPTEMBER 16.	TYNE COT MEM	ATTACHED 103 LTMB, TO 24/27th BN.	8 PERCY AVE CATCHGATE, BORN CATCHGATE.
BUCKLEY	J M	PTE	27	/1508	B		NEWCASTLE							AWOL 27/7/15, 25/8/15 IN COURT 28/7/15, 7/9/15.
BULLER	G H	CPL	27	/47	C	6 MILLGARTH	PENSHAW						TO 14th BN.	
BULMER	Jas	PTE	27	/828	C	FRAMWELLGATE	DURHAM CITY	12/1/15		7 OCT 1916	APRIL 16, AUGUST 16.	CITE BON JEAN CEM		BORN GUISBOROUGH, IN SOLDIERS DIED AS BOWMAN JAS
BUNCE	David	PTE	27	/88	B	99 BROOMSIDE LANE	DURHAM CITY	8/1/15					TO MACHINE GUN CORPS.	MGC No 302298.
BURKE	James	SGT	27	/53	C	110 BURBANK ST	WEST HARTLEPOOL			18 MARCH 1916		BREWERY ORCHARD CEM		RESCUED BY Lt MARSHALL FROM THE ENEMY WIRE.
BURNICLE	JohnR	PTE	27	/803	A		SUNDERLAND			KR para 392	AUGUST 16.			AWOL 25/8/16 COURT SUNDERLAND
BURNS	J	PTE	27	/813	B			28/12/14	29/3/16	MYALGIA			TO 30th BN.	DID NOT SERVE OVERSEAS.
BURROWS	J	PTE	27	/66	A	37 KING ST	SHOTTON COLLIER	30/12/14	31/1/19	KR para 392	MAR 17, JUN 17, JULY 18.		TO 1st GARRISON BN, 26th, 25th BNS, ARMY RESERVE C	6 QUALITY ROW SHOTTON COLL 1918.
BURTON	J	PTE	27	/842	A		EASINGTON COLLI	4/1/15	9/2/18	GUNSHOT WOUNDS	JULY 16, SEPTEMBER 16.		TO DEPOT.	34CCS 2/7 EVAC 5/7,BRISTOL 11/7/16,AGE 33 WND LLEG
BUSHEL	J	PTE	27	/806	A									
BYGATE	Wm	PTE	27	/807	D	3 WELLFIELD TERR	WINDY KNOOK			29 MAY 1918		SOISSONS MEM	TO 24/27th BN, ATTACHED 8th ENTRENCHING BN, 12/13t	AGE 40, NOK 17 DODDINGTON VILLAS WINDY KNOOK
CAFFERY	Thos	PTE	27	/138	D	95 CARNABY TERR	GATESHEAD	28/12/14	26/10/18	GUNSHOT WOUNDS	DECEMBER 17		TO 10th, 9th, 14th BNS, DEPOT.	LCPL, DESERTED 20/2/18.
CAIRNS	John	PTE	27	/148	B	34 FRONT ST	NEWBOTTLE			1 JULY 1916		GORDON DUMP CEM		
CALLAGHAN	T	PTE	27	/865	C	14 VERIN ST	GATESHEAD							
CALLAN	Newry	CPL	27	/91	A	GREEN ST	EAST HETTON	18/1/15	31/1/19	KR para 392	JULY 16, OCTOBER 16.		TO ARMY RESERVE CLASS P.	BROTHER Chas IN 24NF.
CALVERT	T	PTE	27	/116	C	JOHN ST	WITTON PARK	4/1/15	23/5/18		JULY 16		TO ROYAL INNISKILLING FUSILIERS.	
CAMERON	T	PTE	27	/114	C			6/1/15	28/10/18				TO DEPOT.	DID NOT SERVE OVERSEAS.
CAMPBELL	David	PTE	27	/881		TOWER HOUSE	NEWCASTLE	7/1/15					TO 1st GARRISON BN.	DESERTED 16 NOVEMBER 1917.
CAMPBELL	J	PTE	27	/137	A			23/12/14	12/10/18				TO DEPOT.	DID NOT SERVE OVERSEAS.
CAMPBELL	T	CPL	27	/122	C	16 CROSS ROW	HEBBURN							
CANT	Jas	PTE	27	/121	B	45 GEORGE ST	NEWCASTLE							ALSO ON D COY 30th BN ROLL.
CARLOW	T	PTE	27	/130	C	2 FOURTH ST	WARDLEY				OCTOBER 16.		TO HIGHLAND LIGHT INFANTRY.	
CARMAN	Alf	PTE	27	/887	C	NORTH VIEW	SHERBURN HILL			1 JULY 1916		BLIGHTY VALLEY CEM ATHUILE		BORN KELLOE.
CARMAN	Jas	PTE	27	/891	D	EAST ST	BROOMPARK	5/1/15	26/3/18	SICK	AUGUST 16.		TO DEPOT.	34 CCS 1/7/16 EVAC 5/7/16 WND L FOOT, AGE 24.
CARMICHEAL	G	PTE	27	/140	D		WALKER				JANUARY 1917		TO 22nd BN, CLASS Z RESERVE.	ACPL.
CARNEY	J	PTE	27	/873	C	6 KETTLEDRUM ST	WEST STANLEY							
CAROLINE	Jas L	PTE	27	/112	B	25 CAMDEN LANE	NORTH SHIELDS							
CARR	Alf	PTE	27	/880	D	29 DRAGON VILLA	DURHAM CITY	7/1/15					TO 24/27th, 11th BNS, ROYAL FUSILIERS(24th BN).	FRANCE 27 11/1/16 TO 9/8/17,24/27 10/8/17 TO 3/7/1
CARR	G	PTE	27	/93	A		BISHOP AUKLAND	2/1/15	24/2/17	WOUNDS	JUNE 16, JULY 16.		TO DEPOT.	
CARR	John	PTE	27	/1526	D	33 THORPE AVE	CROOKHILL	24/7/15	1/4/19	KR para 392			TO ARMY RESERVE CLASS P.	CPL.
CARR	P	PTE	27	/867	C			1/1/15	7/8/16	MYALGIA			TO 30th BN.	DID NOT SERVE OVERSEAS. ON BN ROLL AS COOR P.
CARR	R M	PTE	27	/119	C	1 ROBINSON LANE HIGH	SUNDERLAND							
CARR	T S	PTE	27	/136	A			28/12/14	26/10/18				TO DEPOT.	DID NOT SERVE OVERSEAS.
CARR	W	PTE	27	/857	A									
CARR	Wm	PTE	27	/103	A	2 BOOTHS COTTAGES	SHERBURN	7/1/15	25/1/19				TO MACHINE GUN CORPS(34th BN), CLASS Z RESERVE.	MGC No 151954.
CARRUTHERS	Gordn	PTE	27	/1543	A 24	8 WATLING ST	LEADGATE			1 JULY 1916		THIEPVAL MEM	TO 24th BN.	MISSING AUGUST 16, BORN ANNFIELD PLAIN.
CARTER	E H	PTE	27	/129		19 SIXTH ST SOUTH	EASINGTON COLLI						TO 2nd GARRISON BN, CLASS Z RESERVE.	
CARTER	N	PTE	27	/886	D		NEWCASTLE	5/1/15	7/2/18	WOUNDS	OCTOBER 16.		TO DEPOT.	LCPL, 3 CCS 2/7/16 EVAC 2/7/16.
CARTY	C	PTE	27	/133	A		SUNDERLAND				AUGUST 16		TO SOUTH LANCASHIRE REGT.	
CASEY	B	PTE	27	/141	D			28/12/14	2/7/16	SICK			TO 30th BN.	DID NOT SERVE OVERSEAS, AGE 29.
CASTLING	F	PTE	27	/859	A								TO 25th, 1/4th, 9th BNS, CLASS Z RESERVE.	
CASTLING	Frank	PTE	27	/144	A	14 OFFICE SQUARE	LINTZ COLLIERY						TO 24/27th, 12/13th BNS, CLASS Z RESERVE.	SGT
CASTLING	P	PTE	27	/855	A		LEADGATE			1 JULY 1916		THIEPVAL MEM		
CAULFIELD	H	SGT	27	/160	A		STANLEY	30/1/15	18/10/16	GUNSHOT WOUNDS	JULY 16		TO DEPOT.	SEE ALSO 27/98.
CAULFIELD	J	CPL	27	/98	A		STANLEY	2/1/15	11/10/17	SICK			TO 3rd BN.	
CAVAN	Peter	CQMS	27	/1363	B	15 EGERMONT GARDENS	GATESHEAD						TO 3rd BN, COMMISSIONED.	
CAVANAGH	F Tom	PTE	27	/863			CLEATOR MOOR	31/12/14						ORE MINER DESERTED 31/12/14 AGE 24, 5'3''.
CHAPLIN	Wm	LSGT	27	/139	D	145 CHADWICK ST	CORNSAY COLLIER			1 JULY 1916	OCTOBER 16	THIEPVAL MEM		
CHARLTON	John	PTE	27	/153	A			21/12/14	22/8/17	SICK			TO DEPOT.	
CHARLTON	JohnJ	PTE	27	/142	D		SOUTH SHIELDS				SEPTEMBER 16		TO ROYAL DEFENCE CORPS.	LCPL,FRANCE 11/1/16 TO 6/7/16,AWOL 24/8/15 SSHIELD
CLARK	Jas S	PTE	27	/110	B		SEAHAM HARBOUR			1 JULY 1916		BAPAUME POST CEM		LCPL, BORN BOLDON COLLIERY.
CLARK	R	PTE	27	/146				22/12/14	7/6/15	INNEFFICIENT				
CLARKE	Bernd	PTE	27	/883	D	50 LAURENCE ST	HORDEN						TO LABOUR CORPS.	LAB CORPS No 400439.

NAME	INITI	RANK	BA	NUMBE	COMP	ADDRESS	TOWN_VILL	ENLISTED	DISCHARG	CAUSE_DIS	WOUNDED	BURIED	TRANSFER	ADD
CLARKE	C	PTE	27	/860	D									
CLARKE	JohnW	PTE	27	/131	D	24 THERESA ST	SOUTHMOOR						TO 8th, 12/13th BNS, CLASS Z RESERVE.	
CLARKSON	Wm	PTE	27	/1462	C	25		22/7/15	5/10/17	KR para 392			TO DEPOT.	
CLASPER	Henry	PTE	27	/113	A	92 BROCK ST	NEWCASTLE						TO 24/27th, 9th BNS, CLASS Z RESERVE.	
CLASPER	Thos	PTE	27	/850			BYKER	21/12/14						LABOURER DESERTED AGE 21, 5'8''.
CLEMENT	J	PTE	27	/877	D								TO 24/27th, 11th, 12/13th BNS, CLASS Z RESERVE.	ACPL.
CLEST	T	PTE	27	/101	A	11 CLOCKWELL ST STHW	SUNDERLAND	8/1/15		KR para 392				NAME POSSIBLY CLEET ALLOTTED NEW No 204180.
CLISH	J M	PTE	27	/135	D		EASINGTON				JULY 16			
CLOSE	J J	PTE	27	/156	C	FRONT ST	LOW PITTINGTON							
COATES	Thos	PTE	27	/102	A	20 HOPPER ST	SUNDERLAND				AUGUST 16			LSGT, AWOL CT S/DLAND 17/8/15.
COLEMAN	J	PTE	27	/854	A									DESERTED 22 MAY 1917.
COLEMAN	Jos	PTE	27	/884	D			5/1/15	17/7/17	SICK			TO 85th TRAINING RESERVE BN.	
COLEMAN	W H S	PTE	27	/109	B					KR para 392				
COLLIN	J	PTE	27	/124									TO 1st GARRISON BN, CLASS Z RESERVE.	
COLLING	J P	PTE	27	/159	A		NEW SHILDON	21/12/14	6/5/18	VDH	APRIL 16		ATTACHED 10th KOYLI, TO 3rd BN NF.	ACPL. HOSPITAL CHATHAM.
COLLINS	James	PTE	27	/879			CARDIFF	2/1/15						SEAMAN DESERTED 2/1/15 AGE 39, 5'8''.
COLLINS	P	PTE	27	/872	C		GRANGETOWN				SEPTEMBER 16.		TO 8th, 16th BNS, CLASS Z RESERVE.	34 CCS 2/7/16 EVAC 5/7/16 WND FOREHEAD
COMERFORD	M	PTE	27	/147	A	184 CLAVERING AVE	DUNSTON	22/12/14	8/3/17	SICK			TO DEPOT.	IN BAND
COMMON	Thos	PTE	27	/97	A	2 MILL HOUSE AYERS Q	SUNDERLAND	7/1/15						
CONLIN	J	PTE	27	/889	D	111 FRAMWELLGATE	DURHAM CITY							
CONN	Geo	PTE	27	/145	B	1 GREGSON TERR	SEAHAM COLLIERY			1 JULY 1916		BAPAUME POST		
CONNOLLY	Wm	PTE	27	/132	C	58 HERBERT ST SCOTSW	NEWCASTLE			7 OCT 1916		CITE BON JEAN CEM		
CONNOR	T	PTE	27	/126	C		GATESHEAD				SEPTEMBER 16		TO 23rd, 16th BNS, CLASS Z RESERVE.	
CONNOR	Thos	PTE	27	/853	B	24 WYNDHAM ST	CLEATOR MOOR			1 JULY 1916		PUNCHEVILLIERS MIL CEM		MISSING OCTOBER 1916.
CONROY	M	PTE	27	/862	B	247 CHESTNUT ST	HIRST	30/12/14	23/8/17	GUNSHOT WOUNDS	OCTOBER 16.		TO DEPOT.	
CONVERY	F	PTE	27	/858		14 WILLIAM STREET	LINTZ COLLIERY	23/12/14					TO ROYAL NAVAL DIVISION	MINER DESERTED AGE 19, 5'7'', RND No TZ/4385.
CONWAY	P	PTE	27	/120		42 JOHN ST	HEBBURN NEWTOWN						TO 1st GARRISON BN, 12/13th BN, CLASS Z RESERVE.	
COOK	G	PTE	27	/861	B									
COOK	J	PTE	27	/866	B									
COOK	J	PTE	27	/888	A									
COOKE	Jos M	PTE	27	/152	C			21/12/14	14/12/15					DID NOT SERVE OVERSEAS.
COOPER	B	PTE	27	/108	A									
COOPER	W	PTE	27	/1521	A	24 70 GREY ST	NORTH SHIELDS	19/7/15	15/11/17	GUNSHOT WOUNDS	OCTOBER 16.		TO 24th BN, DEPOT.	LCPL.
COOPER	Wm	PTE	27	/876	C	230 PILGRIM ST	NEWCASTLE			1 JULY 1916		THIEPVAL MEM		LCPL, MISSING OCTOBER 16.
CORY	John	LCPL	27	/134	D	2 WEST ST	SHERBURN HILL						ATTACHED 103 BDE HQ, 24/27th, 11th BNS, CLASS Z RE	CQMS ON A LIST, AWOII ON MR.
COSTELLOE	J	PTE	27	/158	C	10 BUSTY TER	SHILDON	21/12/14	1/4/18	SHELLSHOCK			TO 3rd BN.	
COULSEY	Rupt	PTE	27	/96	B	16 POTTER ST	SHOTTON COLLIER	7/1/15		2 JULY 1916		MEAULTE MIL CEM		BORN TOFTHILL CO DURHAM.
COULSON	J R	PTE	27	/890	B									
COULSON	W	PTE	27	/1388	D		BLYTH				DECEMBER 16.		TO 8th, 9th BNS, CLASS Z RESERVE.	
COURTNEY	J	PTE	27	/117	C			7/1/15	17/6/16				TO 30th BN.	DID NOT SERVE OVERSEAS.
COURTNEY	J	PTE	27	/851				21/12/14	1/11/16	SICK			TO DEPOT.	
COWAN	W	PTE	27	/1461	A			1/6/15	13/4/18	GUNSHOT WOUNDS			TO LABOUR CORPS, 16th BN NF, DEPOT.	
COWIE	A P	PTE	27	/1503	C		CAMPERDOWN				AUGUST 16, AUGUST 18.		TO 16th, 20th, 25th BNS, CLASS Z RESERVE.	34CCS 2/7 EVAC 5/7,21 AMBTR 6/7,18 GHOSP,SHIP 7/7
COWLEY	Dan	PTE	27	/874	C		DURHAM CITY	11/1/15		KR para 392				AWOL 8 JULY 1915, H/O TO ESCORT 10/7/15.
COX	W	PTE	27	/1486	C		WALLSEND	24/6/15	31/12/17	GUNSHOT WOUNDS	SEPTEMBER 16.		TO 3rd BN.	
COXON	Jas	PTE	27	/864	B		TANFIELD				OCTOBER 16.		TO 30th, 8th BNS, DURHAM LI(11th BN), CLASS Z RESE	DURHAM LI No 46195.CPL.
COYNE	JohnT	CPL	27	/115	C	QUEENS HEAD YARD	DURHAM CITY						TO 24/27th, 25th, 12/13th BNS, CLASS Z RESERVE.	
COYNE	P	LCPL	27	/1459	C								TO ROYAL DEFENCE CORPS.	IN FRANCE 11/1/16 TO 21/7/16.
CRAGGS	J	PTE	27	/157	D								TO LABOUR CORPS.	
CRAIG	A	PTE	27	/878	A	40 CHARLOTTE ST	NORTH SHIELDS							
CRAIGIE	Rob	PTE	27	/151	B		HEDLEY				APRIL 16		TO 23rd, 2nd BNS, CLASS Z RESERVE.	
CRANNER	Thos	PTE	27	/92	A	38 COVENT GARDEN ST	SUNDERLAND	7/1/15		15 MAY 1916		BECOURT MIL CEM		
CRANSTON	J	PTE	27	/868	C		LOW FELL				SEPTEMBER 16.			
CRAWFORD	E G	CSM	27	/1361	B	22 ST MARYS TERRACE	HARTON				AUGUST 16.		TO 3rd BN, CLASS Z RESERVE.	CONV HOSP KIDDERMINSTER 7/16.
CRAWFORD	Wm L	PTE	27	/106	B	2 SHAWS ROW	HETTON							
CROMBIE	D	PTE	27	/870	C	23 PARADE HENDON	SUNDERLAND				AUGUST 16.			HOSP LONDON 7/16 WND ABDOMEN
CROMBIE	Pat	PTE	27	/95		29 HARDWICK STREET	SUNDERLAND	2/1/15						LABOURER DESERTED AGE 38, 5'5'', AWOL 5/2/16 CT SU
CRONIN	Pat	PTE	27	/104	A	58 MILBURN ST	GATESHEAD	7/1/15		1 JULY 1916		THIEPVAL MEM		NOK 6 BACK BATEY TERR GATESHEAD. BORN LONDON.
CROSBY	Robt	PTE	27	/111			SOUTH SHIELDS	6/1/15						LABOURER DESERTED 2/4/15 AGE 25, 5'7''.
CROSSEY	Chas	PTE	27	/154	A	19 MITCHELL ST	SOUTHMOOR			24 JULY 1916		ETAPLES		BORN WILLINGTON, NOK 13 MURRAY ST WEST STANLEY.

NAME	INITI	RANK	BA	NUMBE	COMP	ADDRESS	TOWN_VILL	ENLISTED	DISCHARG	CAUSE_DIS	WOUNDED	BURIED	TRANSFER	ADD
CROW	Ralph	PTE	27	/107	B		FATFIELD			6 SEPT 1916		ABBEVILLE		
'CROWTHER	J	PTE	27	/1506	C	10 CHATHAM PLACE	NEWCASTLE							
CUMMINGS	J	PTE	27	/1472	A	18 THE SIDE	NEWCASTLE	9/6/15	11/6/16	SICK			TO DEPOT.	
CUNNINGHAM	Joe	SGT	27	/852	B	MULLARTOWN ANNALONG	GLISSDIMOND Co			12 DEC 1917	SEPTEMBER 16	NEUVILLE VITASSE MIL CEM	TO 8th, 27th, 24/27th BNS.	3 CCS 2/7 EVAC 2/7/16 GSW, CSM AGE 21.
CUNNINGHAM	John	PTE	27	/849	A		SUNDERLAND			14 MAY 1916		MERICOURT MIL CEM		
CURRAN	J	PTE	27	/882	A		HOUGHTON LE SPR	6/1/15	24/10/17	SICK	AUGUST 16.		TO DEPOT.	
CURRAN	John	PTE	27	/155	C	40 UPTON ST TEAMS	GATESHEAD	21/12/14	11/3/18	SICK	FEBRUARY 17		TO 24th BN, DEPOT.	
CURRAN	Wm	LSGT	27	/100	A	BOWDEN CLOSE	SUNDERLAND			28 APRIL 1917		ARRAS MEM		SGT.
CURRY	Thos	PTE	27	/143	D	21 CAROLINE ST	HETTON LE HOLE				AUGUST 16, FEBRUARY 17.			
CURRY	Wm	PTE	27	/125	C		SOUTH SHIELDS	14/1/15		KR para 392				ACPL.
DALE	Geo	PTE	27	/201	C	68 MISSION YD NEW EL	DURHAM CITY	7/1/15	16/10/18				TO DEPOT.	DID NOT SERVE OVERSEAS, AGE 46 AWOL 17 JULY 1915.
DALEY	John	LSGT	27	/161	A	37 BACK NORTH TERR	SEAHAM			1 JULY 1916		THIEPVAL MEM		SGT, BORN WHITEHAVEN, MISSING OCTOBER 16.
DANKS	Rich	PTE	27	/164	A	JOHNSON SQUARE	HASWELL				JULY 16		TO 3rd BN, CLASS Z RESERVE.	
DARWIN	Geo	PTE	27	/906	C 24	18 BELVEDERE ST	WORKINGTON			1 JULY 1916		THIEPVAL MEM	TO 24th BN.	MISSING SEPTEMBER 16.
DAVENPORT	James	PTE	27	/921			BISHOP AUKLAND	28/12/14						LABOURER DESERTED 28/12/14 AGE 35, 5'3''.
DAVIDSON	Ernst	PTE	27	/895	A	13 BURROWS ST	SOUTH SHIELDS	14/1/15		KR para 392	OCTOBER 16.			EMPLOYED REDHEADS SHIPYARD
DAVIDSON	Geo	PTE	27											AWOL 31/7/15 COURT GATESHEAD. AGE 30.
DAVIDSON	T	PTE	27	/907	C	40 PAGE STREET	SUNDERLAND						TO ROYAL ENGINEERS.	
DAVIES	John	PTE	27	/190		1 SHAFTO TERR	SHIELDROW			1 JULY 1916		THIEPVAL MEM		BORN HOUGHTON LE SPRING.
DAVISON	G H	PTE	27	/922	D	15 ROBINSON TERR	SUNDERLAND						TO 24/27th, 11th BNS, CLASS Z RESERVE.	
DAVISON	J	PTE	27	/194	D								TO LABOUR CORPS.	
DAVISON	J	PTE	27	/203				11/1/15	1/1/18	ARTHRITIS			TO 3rd BN.	
DAVISON	M	LCPL	27	/182	A	104 CHARLES ST	BOLDON COLLIERY	29/12/14	3/2/19	KR para 392	AUGUST 18		TO ARMY RESERVE CLASS P.	
DAWSON	Edwd	PTE	27	/167	A	47 LAMPTON ST	SHERBURN HILL			30 APRIL 1917	SEPTEMBER 16	WARLOY MIL CEM		LCPL, BORN LEAMSIDE.
DAWSON	H	PTE	27	/176					29/1/19				TO 1st BN, CLASS Z RESERVE.	3CCS 2/7 EVAC 3/7,GSW,3rd SCOT GHOSP GLASGOW 11/7
DAWSON	Jos	PTE	27	/188	A	2 MIDDLE RD	GATESHEAD						TO 3rd BN.	
DAY	DavdE	PTE	27	/909	C	5 UPTON ST	GATESHEAD				MARCH 16.		TO LABOUR CORPS(169 A E COY).	AWOL 13/12/15 IN COURT GATESHEAD AGE 17.
DEFTY	G	PTE	27	/199	C	27 BRAMWELL ST	SUNDERLAND	6/1/15	3/2/19	KR para 392	JANUARY 18		TO ARMY RESERVE CLASS P.	
DENT	W	RQMS		/1446	C 27									
DENVER	W	PTE	27	/905	B								TO 24/27th, 8th BNS, CLASS Z RESERVE.	
DERBYSHIRE	Walt	PTE	27	/1514	A 24	427 GRANT ST	BROOMPARK				JULY 16		TO 24th, 11th, 24/27th, 19th, 8th, 19th BNS, CLASS	24th BN TRENCH RAID 25/26th JUNE 16,MINER ESH COLL
DEVENISH	John	PTE	27	/183	D		NEWCASTLE			1 JULY 1916		THIEPVAL MEM		
DEVLIN	Frank	PTE	27	/893			GATESHEAD			1 JULY 1916		GORDON DUMP CEM		
DEWS	J	PTE	27	/172	B									
DINNING	Thos	PTE	27	/200	A	GALLONS YARD	FELLING SHORE	6/1/15	24/5/18	GUNSHOT WOUNDS	JUNE 17		TO 3rd BN, ARMY RESERVE CLASS P.	AR P, 3/2/19.
DITCHBURN	J	PTE	27	/192	D	45 HARTINGTON ST	SUNDERLAND				OCTOBER 16		TO 24/27th, 11th BNS, CLASS Z RESERVE.	
DIXON	Ern A	PTE	27	/1478	A	96 JOHN ST	BLAYDON						TO 24/27th, 14th, 3rd(D COY) BNS, CLASS Z RESERVE.	SERVICE WITH 3rd BN MAY HAVE BEEN PRIOR TO 14th BN
DIXON	J W	SGT	27	/1370	C					KR para 392			TO 24/27th BN.	
DIXON	J orW	PTE	27	/911	A		NEWCASTLE				MARCH 17.			
DOBBINSON	Geo	LCPL	27	/894	A	10 JUBILEE ST PITY M	DURHAM CITY			1 JULY 1916		THIEPVAL MEM		CPL, BORN FRAMWELLGATE DURHAM, MISSING OCTOBER 16.
DOBSON	John	PTE	27	/916	A	50 LAWRENCE ST HENDO	SUNDERLAND			22 OCT 1917	AUGUST 18(GAZ)	TYNE COT MEM	TO 25th BN.	
DOBSON	Pat	PTE	27	/181	C	30 LAWRENCE ST	SUNDERLAND			1 JULY 1916		THIEPVAL MEM		NOK 22 COUSIN ST HENDON, BORN SEAHAM HARBOUR.
DOBSON	Ralph	PTE	27	/205	D	8 WILLIAM ST	HETTON DOWNS	12/1/15	6/4/19		JULY 16		TO KO YORKSHIRE LI, WEST YORKS, DUKE OF WELLINGTON	34 CCS 2/7/16 EVAC 5/7/16 SHELLSHOCK.
DOBSON	Thos	PTE	27	/175	B	35 WALWORTH ST	SUNDERLAND			28 MARCH 1918	SEPTEMBER 16	POZIERES MEM	TO 14th, 12/13th, 14th BNS.	25 AMBTR 5/7, 18 GHOSP SHIP 9/7/16 WNDED L LEG.
DOCHERTY	J	PTE	27	/917	B			29/12/14	7/2/19	SICK			TO 24/27th, 9th BNS, DEPOT.	AGE 26.
DODDS	Edw	PTE	27	/195	D	50 FRAMWELLGATE	DURHAM CITY	6/1/15	1/4/19	KR para 392			TO 24/27th, 19th BNS, ARMY RESERVE CLASS P.	
DODDS	Jos W	PTE	27	/193	D	24 SCHOOL TERR	SOUTHMOOR	7/1/15		1 JULY 1916		THIEPVAL MEM		BORN TOW LAW, MISSING OCTOBER 16.
DODDS	L	PTE	27	/169	A		LEADGATE			KR para 392	OCTOBER 16		TO 25th, 1/5th, 1/6th, 1st, 19th BNS.	3 CCS 2/7/16 EVAC 2/7/16, NEW NUMBER 243147.
DODDS	T	CPL	27	/186	C									
DOLAN	J	PTE	27	/179	B	25 STAFFORD ST	SUNDERLAND				AUGUST 16		TO LABOUR CORPS.	HOSP SOUTHEND ON SEA 7/16, COY F/BALL TEAM.
DONNELLY	D	PTE	27	/180	C			29/12/14	12/10/17	SICK			TO DEPOT.	
DONNELLY	JnPat	PTE	27	/185	A	12 BK HIGH ST	WALLSEND	7/1/15			JULY 16			34 CCS 2/7 EVAC 5/7/16,WND R THIGH, AGE 36, LCPL.
DONNELLY	Jos	PTE	27	/178	B	37 HILL ST	NEW SILKSWORTH			3 JULY 1917	1 JULY 16	SUNKEN RD CEM BOISLEUX	TO 14th BN.	3 CCS 2/7/16 EVAC 2/7/16.
DONNELLY	T	PTE	27	/1426	B	WHITEHOUSE LANE	USHAW MOOR							
DONNELLY	Thos	PTE	27	/189	D	6 FORD COURT	BLACKHALL MILL						TO 24/27th, 8th BNS, CLASS Z RESERVE.	SERGEANT.
DONNISON	John	LCPL	27	/910	D	PLOUGH INN	HASWELL PLOUGH	7/1/15					TO 24/27th, 11th BNS, ROYAL FUSILIERS(24th BN).	FRANCE 27 11/1/16 TO 9/8/17,24/27 10/8/17 TO 3/7/1
DOOLEY	P	PTE	27	/898	A	MONKWEARMOUTH	SUNDERLAND				SEPTEMBER 16.		TO SCOTTISH RIFLES.	34 CCS 2/7/16 EVAC 5/7/16 GSW HAND.
DORRITT	JohnR	CPL	27	/173	B	33 WILSON ST TEAMS	GATESHEAD				SEPTEMBER 16		TO CLASS Z RESERVE.	15 NUNS LANE GATESHEAD 1918.
DORRITT	JohnW	LCPL	27	/915	D	96 PINE ST TEAMS	GATESHEAD				OCTOBER 16.		TO 10th BN, CLASS Z RESERVE.	SEE ALSO 27/173 CPL J R DORRITT.
DOSH	J	PTE	27	/177	B		SEAHAM HARBOUR				JULY 16		TO LABOUR CORPS.	

NAME	INITI	RANK	BA	NUMBE	COMP	ADDRESS	TOWN_VILL	ENLISTED	DISCHARG	CAUSE_DIS	WOUNDED	BURIED	TRANSFER	ADD
DOUGLAS	Geo E	PTE	27	/904	C	12 OUSTERLEY TERR	CRAGHEAD	7/1/15			JULY 16.		TO KINGS SHROPSHIRE LIGHT INFANTRY.	3CCS 2/7 EVAC 2/7/16,3rd NTHN GHOSP SHEFFIELD 7/16
DOWNEY	F	PTE	27	/908	C		SOUTH SHIELDS	4/1/15	31/3/19	KR para 392	AUGUST 16.		TO ARMY RESERVE CLASS P.	
DOYLE	Benj	PTE	27	/162	A	68 BACK STATION	HEBBURN			1 JULY 1916		BAPAUME POST CEM		BORN TYNE DOCK. NOK 6 BIDDICK INN TERR FATFIELD.
DOYLE	Lawrn	CPL	27	/1357	D		DARLINGTON			26 DEC 1917	SEPTEMBER 16	BISHOPWEARMOUTH	TO 3rd BN.	LCPL,34 CCS 2/7 EVAC 5/7/16 GSW+FRACTURES BORN GAT
DREW	Alf	PTE	27	/198	B	26 EIGTH ST	BLACKHALL				JULY 16, AUGUST 16.		TO LABOUR CORPS, ROYAL FUSILIERS.	
DRINKALD	John	PTE	27	/902	B	5 BREWERY BANK	SWALWELL	7/1/15		1 JULY 1916		THIEPVAL MEM		
DRUMMOND	J R	PTE	27	/920	A		SOUTH NEWSHAM				AUGUST 16.		TO MACHINE GUN CORPS.	
DRYSDALE	Rob	PTE	27	/918	D		WASHINGTON			9 APRIL 1917	SEPTEMBER 16.	BAILLEUL RD ST LAURENT BLAGNY		BORN NORTH SHIELDS.
DUFFY	B	PTE	27	/168	D									
DUFFY	J	PTE	27	/163				21/12/14	6/9/16				TO 30th BN.	DID NOT SERVE OVERSEAS.
DUFFY	James	PTE	27	/196						KR para 392				SHOWN ON MRC AS 26/196.
DUFFY	Jas W	PTE	27	/166	A		PELTON FELL			9 APRIL 1917		ARRAS MEM		
DUFFY	Jos	PTE	27	/1546	A	9 BROOK ST	SUNDERLAND	4/6/15	8/8/17	KR para 392	AUGUST 16			HOSP ABERDEEN 7/16 SHRAPNEL WNDS R ARM.
DUGGAN	Jas	PTE	27	/171	B	29 BURLEIGH ST	SOUTH SHIELDS			3 JULY 1916	1 JULY 1916	MERICOURT		SGT,BORN BOLDON,DIED 64 FLD AMB,MINER ST HILDA COL
DUNN	Geo W	PTE	27	/204	D	122 DERWENT WATER RD	GATESHEAD				SEPTEMBER 16		TO 27th, 16th, 1/7th BNS, CLASS Z RESERVE.	
DUNN	Rob H	PTE	27	/913	D	3 ALBERT ST CHESTER	SUNDERLAND			4 APRIL 1918	AUGUST 16.	BRAY MIL CEM BRAY SUR SOMME	TO 8th, 16th BNS.	AGE 26.
DURKIN	Wm	PTE	27	/1436	A		SWINFORD Co MAY			1 JULY 1916		THIEPVAL MEM		MISSING OCTOBER 16.
EARLY	F	PTE		/1497	B 27									No ALSO ALLOCATED TO KEOGH .
EARLY	J	PTE	27	/210	B		SEAHAM			KR para 392				
EARLY	T	PTE	27	/1496	B	TOWER HOUSE PILGRIM	NEWCASTLE							No IN IRISH HEROES 1497.
ECCLES	Rob	PTE	27	/208	A	5 VANE ST	CONSETT	8/1/15		1 JULY 1916		THIEPVAL MEM		MISSING OCTOBER 16.
ECCLES	Wm	LCPL	27	/212	C	58 MEDOMSLEY RD	CONSETT				SEPTEMBER 16		TO 1st, 23rd BNS, CLASS Z RESERVE.	34CCS 2/7 EVAC 5/7/16 WND LARM, AGE 26 REP POW 12/
EDGAR	T	PTE	27	/206	A									34CCS 8/7/16 EVAC 106 AMBTR R/MATIC FEVER,AGE 41.
EDINGTON	G	PTE	27	/219	D	47 BACK NORTH ST	NORTH SHIELDS							
EGAN	D	PTE	27	/1484	D	16 BEECH ST	THROCKLEY						TO LABOUR CORPS.	
EGAN	Pat	PTE	27	/217	D	146 NELSON ST	LEADGATE						TO LABOUR CORPS.	
EGERTON	Wm	PTE	27	/1527			WALLSEND			1 JULY 1916	JUNE 16	THIEPVAL MEM		IN BAND
ELCOATE	Robt	PTE	27	/218	D	23 QUARRY ST	TANTOBIE						TO LABOUR CORPS(GAR GD COY).	LABOUR CORPS No 407096.
ELDERBRANT	John	PTE	27	/213	C	78 SOMERSET ST	GATESHEAD			24 OCTOBER 1917	MARCH 17	BERERAIN MIL CEM	TO 24/27th, 9th BNS.	LCPL, SNIPER, BORN BIRMINGHAM.
ELGY	T H	PTE	27	/211	C		OLD PELTON	6/1/15	13/5/18	WOUNDS	SEPTEMBER 16		TO ARMY RESERVE CLASS P.	
ELLIOTT	J S	PTE	27	/216	D									
ELLIOTT	Jos	PTE	27	/926	B	50 SOUTH MARGARET ST	HETTON LE HOLE	7/1/15		1 JULY 1916		THIEPVAL MEM		MISSING FEBRUARY 17, AGE 27.
ELLIOTT	T	PTE	27	/927	A		BOLDON COLLIERY			KR para 392	OCTOBER 16.		TO 25th, 1/4th BNS.	ALLOTED NEW NUMBER 204562.
ELLIOTT	ThosW	PTE	27	/928	D		BEBSIDE			1 JULY 1916		BAPAUME POST CEM		
ELLIS	C	PTE	27	/1400	D		GATESHEAD				NOVEMBER 16, MARCH 17.		TO 16th, 1/7th BNS, CLASS Z RESERVE.	
ELSEY	Ben	PTE	27	/215	D	22 RYHOPE ST	RYHOPE	14/1/15			NOVEMBER 16		TO 24/27th, 11th BNS, CLASS Z RESERVE.	SHELLSHOCK.
ELSEY	RichH	PTE	27	/214	C	21 BACK IVY ST	SOUTH SHIELDS	8/1/15	11/1/17	SICK			TO DEPOT.	
ELVES	R	PTE	27	/220	A	38 STAVORDALE ST	DAWDON						TO LABOUR CORPS(837 LAB COY).	
EVANS	Jos	PTE	27	/209			CROOK	3/1/15						MINER DESERTED 6/5/15 AGE 30, 5'8''.
FAGAN	G	PTE	27	/934	B		WORKINGTON				OCTOBER 16.		TO LABOUR CORPS.	LAB CORPS No 11547.
FAHEY	James	PTE	27	/255	D	66 SALVIN STREET	SPENNYMOOR				SEPTEMBER 16		TO LABOUR CORPS, GLOUCESTERSHIRE REGT.	
FAIL	David	CPL	27	/936	A	9 GREENS TERR	SOUTH SHIELDS	14/1/15		1 JULY 1916		THIEPVAL MEM		SGT, AGE 20, MINER AT ST HILDA COLLIERY.
FAILL	David	SGT	27	/1413	A	127 SECOND ST	SHOTTON COLLIER						TO 25th BN, CLASS Z RESERVE.	CSGT ESCAPED FROM 25th BN HQ BUNHILL ROW 21/3/18
FAILL	W	PTE	27	/1416	A	127 SECOND ST	SHOTTON COLLIER						TO 12/13th BN, CLASS Z RESERVE.	
FAIRLESS	G	PTE	27	/233	C	24 NORTH ST	BRANDON	6/1/15	7/4/17	WOUNDS	AUGUST 16		TO DEPOT.	114 AMBTR 3/7,18 GHOSP,SHIP 5/7/16,WND R ARM.
FAIRLESS	John	SGT	27	/244	D	37 SPELTER WKS RD	SUNDERLAND	31/12/14	6/9/17	SICK			TO DEPOT.	CPL.
FAIRLESS	Wm	PTE	27	/227	A	16 CLIFFORD RD	SOUTHMOOR						TO 2nd BN, CLASS Z RESERVE.	DESERTED 10/12/17.AWOL 6/7 21/7 COURT 9/7 26/8/15.
FALLON	James	PTE	27	/252	A		SHERIFF HILL			10 APRIL 1917	AUGUST 16	ROCLINCOURT	TO 22nd BN.	CPL.
FARISH	Flem	PTE	27	/257	B		BRANDON	21/12/14	29/3/16				TO 30th BN, REENLISTED R ENGINEERS TRF TO TANK COR	SERVED WITH 179 TUNNELLING COY R.E.
FARLEY	G	PTE	27	/256	B									
FARLEY	J	SGT	27	/242	D									ALSO ON D COY 30th BN ROLL.
FARRINGTON	J	PTE	27	/947	C									
FATHERLEY	F T G	PTE	27	/1511				12/7/15	30/4/16	UNFIT			TO 1st GARRISON BN.	AGE 41
FAWCETT	J	PTE	27	/1458	A		NEWCASTLE	25/5/15	19/10/17	SHELL WOUNDS	AUGUST 16.		TO 8th, 16th BNS, DEPOT.	
FAWELL	Leo W	PTE	27	/930		3 STATION LANE GILES	DURHAM CITY	5/1/15	29/1/16				TO 30th BN.	DID NOT SERVE OVERSEAS.
FAY	Tim	SGT	27	/231		8 BACK STEPNEY ST	NEWCASTLE	7/1/15		14 APRIL 1917		ETAPLES		
FEE	A E	PTE	27	/226	A		HEDDON ON THE W	4/1/15	21/7/17	GSW R THIGH.	SEPTEMBER 16		TO DEPOT.	
FEE	R	PTE	27	/251	A								TO CLASS Z RESERVE.	
FELTON	R	PTE	27	/230	C	HIGH ST	BRANDON	**/1/15		KR para 392	JULY 16, AUGUST 16.			HOSP MANCHESTER WND L SHOULDER.
FENWICK	E	PTE	27	/258	A		ASHINGTON				SEPTEMBER 16		TO GREEN HOWARDS.	

NAME	INITI	RANK	BA	NUMBE	COMP	ADDRESS	TOWN_VILL	ENLISTED	DISCHARG	CAUSE_DIS	WOUNDED	BURIED	TRANSFER	ADD
FENWICK	J B	PTE	27	/1398	D		BEBSIDE	24/4/15	1/4/19	KR para 392	JUNE 16, SEPTEMBER 16.		TO ARMY RESERVE CLASS P.	CPL.
FENWICK	J W	SGT	27	/241	D			10/1/15	27/7/18	SHELLSHOCK			TO 3rd BN.	
FENWICK	John	LCPL	27	/238	C	17 BURN ST	GATESHEAD			10 APRIL 1917	OCTOBER 16	ROCLINCOURT VALLEY MIL CEM	TO 21st BN.	
FENWICK	Rich	PTE	27	/1531	C	39 CHANDLESS ST	GATESHEAD			21 AUGUST 1918	SEPTEMBER 16.	RAILWAY CUTTING CEM	TO 8th, 1st BNS.	
FERGUSON	Archi	PTE	27	/938	D	14 NEWBRIDGE ST	NEWCASTLE	8/1/15			SEPTEMBER 16.			
FERGUSON	J	PTE	27	/239	C	28 BEECH ST	SOUTH SHIELDS	9/1/15	3/7/16	WOUNDS	APRIL 16		TO DEPOT.	CPL.
FERGUSON	J J	PTE	27	/945										STILL SERVING 1920 WITH REGULAR BN IN IRAQ.
FERGUSON	W	PTE	27	/950	B		SOUTH SHIELDS				DECEMBER 16.		TO LABOUR CORPS.	
FERRISS	J	PTE	27	/228	B		FENCEHOUSES	5/1/15	6/3/18	GUNSHOT WOUNDS	NOVEMBER 16		TO ARMY RESERVE CLASS P.	
FERRY	Wilsn	PTE	27	/234	C	45 ROSE AVE	SOUTHMOOR			1 JULY 1916		THIEPVAL MEM		BORN SUNDERLAND, NOK 86 MAPLE ST SOUTHMOOR.
FIDLER	Isaac	PTE	27	/931	B		WHITEHAVEN			14 JULY 1917	OCTOBER 16.	THIEPVAL MEM	TO 23rd BN.	MISSING DECEMBER 17, SHOWN AS LIV STOCKPORT IN GAZ
FINN	Edw	SGT	27	/942	C	3 GRACE TERR	SUNDERLAND	7/1/15			FEBRUARY 16, NOVEMBER 16.		TO CLASS Z RESERVE.	WOUNDED R ARM.
FISHER	JohnG	PTE	27	/1376	D		HOUGHTON LE SPR				OCTOBER 16.		TO 24th, 14th, 12/13th BNS, CLASS Z RESERVE.	LCPL, HOSP FISHPONDS BRISTOL 7/16.
FITZPATRICK	Jas	PTE	27	/232	C	DIXON ST	BLACKHILL							
FITZPATRICK	Noel	PTE	27	/1449	A 24	8 HIGH ST	JARROW						TO 24th, 22nd, 26th, 1st BNS, CLASS Z RESERVE.	SCOUT TOOK PART IN TRENCH RAID 25/26th JUNE 16.
FLAHERTY	E	PTE	27	/243	D	24 WHITFIELDS BLDGS	NEWCASTLE	24/7/15	27/7/19		SSHOCK JUNE 17		TO LABOUR CORPS.	IN BN BAND.
FLECK	R	PTE	27	/933	A	17 RAY STREET	SOUTH SHIELDS							
FLEMING	Doug	PTE	27	/246	D		WHITEHAVEN			1 JULY 1916		THIEPVAL MEM		
FLETCHER	Jas W	PTE	27	/250	D	1 KENSINGTON TERR	DUNSTON			16 JUNE 1917	SEPTEMBER 16	BOULOGNE EAST CEM	TO 16th BN.	BORN SACRISTON, AGE 28, NOK 6 CHAPEL ST DUNSTON.
FLETCHER	Wm	PTE	27	/225	A	7 FELL ST ST PETERS	NEWCASTLE	7/1/15		22 JUNE 1916		FEILLY STATION CEM		BORN WREKETON
FLYNN	R	LCPL	27	/240	D		SUNDERLAND				AUGUST 16		TO LABOUR CORPS.	3 CCS 2/7/16 EVAC 2/7/16.
FOLEY	Barth	PTE	27	/1537	C 24	21 SHOTTON STREET	HARTFORD COLLIE			1 JULY 1916		THIEPVAL MEM	TO 24th BN.	MISSING SEPTEMBER 16, BORN SUNDERLAND.
FOLEY	Jas	PTE	27	/941	C	119 VINE ST	GATESHEAD	29/10/14						
FOLEY	P	SGT	27	/223	A					KR para 392				AWOII, SGT DRUMMER IN BAND.
FOLEY	Peter	PTE	27	/948		16 RHODES ST	WALKER	7/1/15					TO 19th, 14th, 12/13th, 14th BNS, CLASS Z RESERVE.	NOT OVERSEAS WITH TYNESIDE IRISH.
FOLEY	T	PTE	27	/237	C	64 RAILWAY ST	RYHOPE	9/1/15	7/11/17	WOUNDS	APRIL 17		TO DEPOT.	
FORBES	T	PTE	27	/951	C	6 CLARA ST	WINLATON							
FORD	J	PTE	27	/224	A		NEWCASTLE	4/1/15	28/9/17	GUNSHOT WOUNDS	JULY 16		TO 3rd BN.	
FORSTER	J	SGT	27	/236	C			8/1/15	22/8/16	WOUNDS	MARCH 16		TO DEPOT.	
FORSTER	J	PTE	27	/247				20/12/14	20/10/15				TO 30th BN.	DID NOT SERVE OVERSEAS.
FOSTER	D	CPL	27	/1477	D									
FOSTER	Frncs	LCPL	27	/937	B		HEXAM			1 JULY 1916		THIEPVAL MEM		CPL.
FOSTER	JohnT	LCPL	27	/254	A 30	1 DUKE ST	GATESHEAD						TO 3rd BN, CLASS Z RESERVE.	
FOSTER	Ralph	PTE	27	/221	B	12 BROOMSIDE LANE	DURHAM CITY	7/1/15						
FOSTER	T	PTE	27	/943	D		NEWCASTLE				SEPTEMBER 16, NOVEMBER 18		TO 23rd, 12/13th, 11th BNS, CLASS Z RESERVE.	
FOSTER	Tom W	PTE	27	/934	D		HEWORTH			9 SEPT 1916		THIEPVAL MEM		CPL.
FOSTER	W	PTE	27	/944	D		NEWCASTLE				JULY 16.			
FOTHERGILL	Thos	PTE	27	/932	A	53 CLEVELAND ST	SOUTH SHIELDS	14/1/15		12 JULY 1917	SEPTEMBER 16.	YPRES MENIN GATE MEM	TO 11th, 10th BNS.	LCPL, BORN SOUTH SHIELDS.
FOWLER	W	PTE	27	/222	A									
FRAIN	Anthy	PTE	27	/939	C	27 THRIFT ST	SOUTH SHIELDS	8/1/15					TO 24/27th, 11th, 1st BNS, CLASS Z RESERVE.	ACPL.
FRANCIS	M	SGT	27	/235	C	195 FRONT ST	EASINGTON LANE							ALSO ON D COY 30th BN ROLL.
FRAZER		CPL	27	/253	C 30									
FULLALOVE	J	PTE	27	/949	A		THORNLEY	21/12/14	5/9/17	SICK	JULY 16.		TO 3rd BN.	
FULLARD	Archi	PTE	27	/249		23 SOMERSET ST	GATESHEAD			26 OCT 1917	JULY 16	TYNE COT MEM	TO 25th, 1/5th BNS.	DESERTED 26 JANUARY 1916. CT G/HEAD AGE 27.
FULTON	James	PTE	27	/248	B		HIGH FELLING	23/12/14		KR para 392	JULY 16		TO 8th, 16th, 1/5th BNS.	LABOURER DESERTED 29/5/15,34 CCS 2/7 EVAC 5/7/16
FURNESS	J	PTE	27	/229									TO 1st GARRISON BN, CLASS Z RESERVE.	
GALLAGHER	J	PTE	27	/277		78 RAILWAY ST	RYHOPE						TO 1st GARRISON BN.	STILL SERVING 1920.
GALLAGHER	J J	PTE	27	/969	D								TO 24/27th, 19th(W COY) BNS, CLASS Z RESERVE.	LCPL.
GARDNER	Alf	PTE	27	/299	D	51 CARLTON ST	NEWCASTLE	7/1/15						
GARDNER	F	PTE	27	/1364	B									
GARDNER	Jas	PTE	27	/297	B	43 SPEN RD	HIGH SPEN	4/1/15	3/3/19	KR para 392			TO ARMY RESERVE CLASS P.	
GARDNER	Mich	PTE	27	/260	C	5 NORTHUMBERLAND SQU	WINLATON	7/1/15		3 SEPT 1916		THIEPVAL MEM		
GARDNER	Rob	PTE	27	/273	C	41 WEST ST	HIGH SPEN	5/1/15	8/11/18	SICK	NOVEMBER 16.		TO 24th BN, DEPOT.	
GARLAND	T	PTE	27	/269	B	6 STOBBART ST MNKWRM	SUNDERLAND	8/1/15						
GARNHAM	Err T	PTE	27	/1487	C	37 STAVORDALE ST	DAWDON			1 JULY 1916		THIEPVAL MEM		BORN TWIXELL NTHBLD, MISSING OCTOBER 16.
GARTHWAITE	Fredk	PTE	27	/275	B	30 DOCK ST	TYNE DOCK	14/1/15						
GATTISS	Wm	PTE	27	/293	D	16 BENSHAM CRESENT	GATESHEAD			15 JUNE 1918	OCTOBER 16.	MAGNABOSCHI ITALY	TO 11th, 1st, 11th BNS.	BORN HEWORTH, AGE 40 WHEN KILLED.
GEARY	W	PTE	27	/1451	D								TO LABOUR CORPS.	LABOUR CORPS No 398693.
GETTINGS	Archi	PTE	27	/958	B	54 BACK WAYMAN ST	SUNDERLAND			28 DEC 1917	NOVEMBER 16.	ST MARTIN CAVALAIRE	TO 1st, 21st BNS.	BORN SOUTH SHIELDS, SHOT IN LEG 7/16.
GIBBON	Jos	PTE	27	/267	A	10 PEARSON ST	STANLEY			1 JULY 1916		THIEPVAL MEM		

NAME	INITI	RANK	BA	NUMBE	COMP	ADDRESS	TOWN_VILL	ENLISTED	DISCHARG	CAUSE_DIS	WOUNDED	BURIED	TRANSFER	ADD
GIBSON	Andw	PTE	27	/965	C	83 SOUTH ELDON ST	SOUTH SHIELDS	14/1/15						
GIBSON	C	PTE	27	/268	B	30								
GIBSON	J	PTE	27	/285	D	2 KENDAL ST	SUNDERLAND						TO 85th TRAINING RESERVE BN.	
GIBSON	J	PTE	27	/957	B	DEPTFORD	SUNDERLAND	5/1/15	31/3/19	KR para 392	OCTOBER 16.		TO 11th, 26th, 22nd BNS, ARMY RESERVE CLASS P.	
GIBSON	JohnE	PTE	27	/276	B	28 EMMA ST	CONSETT	9/1/15	5/8/18	GUNSHOT WOUNDS	NOVEMBER 16		TO COMMAND DEPOT ALNWICK.	15 ROSEMOUNT CONSETT 1918.
GIBSON	T	SGT	27	/286	D	30								
GILL	Mich	PTE	27	/953	A	2 QUEEN ST EAST	SUNDERLAND	7/1/15		1 JULY 1916		THIEPVAL MEM		BORN FENAGH Co CARLOW.
GILL	Thos	PTE	27	/296	A	43 RUSSELL ST	BRANDON COLLIER	6/1/15	17/11/16	WOUNDS	OCTOBER 16.		TO DEPOT.	
GILLAND	J	PTE	27	/274	B									
GILLESPIE	Peter	PTE	27	/961	B	3 RAILWAY ST	LANGLEY PARK	5/1/15	28/8/18	GUNSHOT WOUNDS	AUGUST 16.		TO DEPOT.	
GILROY	Bernd	PTE	27	/966	C		NEW BRANCEPETH	14/1/15			MARCH 16.			
GIRLING	Edwin	PTE	27	/959	B		SOUTH SHIELDS			1 JULY 1916		THIEPVAL MEM		
GOODWIN	R	PTE	27	/291	D	12 STRANGEWAYS ST	DAWDON				OCTOBER 16.			
GOONAN	J	PTE	27	/261									TO 1st GARRISON BN, CLASS Z RESERVE.	
GORDON	J	PTE	27	/975	B		WIGAN	28/12/14	31/3/19	KR para 392	AUGUST 16.		TO DEPOT, ARMY RESERVE CLASS P.	CPL.
GORMAN	John	PTE	27	/967	C	16 TRINITY ST	NORTH SHIELDS	14/1/15			SEPTEMBER 16.			CPL. ALLOTED NEW NUMBER 88641.
GRADY	J	PTE	27	/960	B			5/1/15	26/2/18	DAH			TO ARMY RESERVE CLASS W.	
GRAHAM	Frncs	PTE	27	/287	A	VICTORIA BDS NEWCAST	SUNDERLAND			1 JULY 1916		OVILLIERS MIL CEM		BORN THROCKLEY.
GRAHAM	G	PTE	27	/1371	C		TYNEMOUTH	31/3/15	18/7/16	28 NOV 1916		TYNEMOUTH	TO DEPOT.	LCPL.
GRAHAM	John	PTE	27	/964	C	21 ESHWOOD ST	NEW BRANCEPETH	12/1/15			OCTOBER 16.			34 CCS 2/7/16 EVAC 5/7/16 WND L FOOT
GRAHAM	Jos	PTE	27	/265	B	11 HILLS YARD	WALKER	4/12/14	4/4/16	27 DEC 1920		ALL SAINTS NEWCASTLE	TO 30th BN.	DID NOT SERVE OVERSEAS, AGE 56.
GRANT	Jas W	PTE	27	/974			SOUTH SHIELDS			19 FEB 1915		SOUTH SHIELDS		
GRAY	E A	PTE	27	/282	C									
GRAY	G	PTE	27	/289	D	QUEENS HEAD YARD	DURHAM CITY				MAY 16, AUGUST 16.			
GRAY	Tom J	SGT	27	/298		19 SHAKESPEAR ST STH	SUNDERLAND	14/1/15		28 MAY 1915		SOUTHWICK		
GRAY	Wm	PTE	27	/963	C	10 CAMDEN STREET	SUNDERLAND			16 APRIL 1918		TYNE COT MEM	TO 19th, 9th, 20th, 9th BNS.	AGE 23, BORN NEWCASTLE.
GRAYSON	W	PTE	27	/283	B								TO MACHINE GUN CORPS.	MGC No 71032.
GREATHEAD	Geo	PTE	27	/271	B	27 ROTHSAY ST	SUNDERLAND							
GREAVES	Ralph	PTE	27											AWOL 15/8/15 COURT NEWCASTLE 7/9/15
GREAVES	Rich	PTE	27	/956	A	375 EAST ST	BROOMPARK	7/1/15					TO 24/27th, 11th BNS, CLASS Z RESERVE.	6 THIRD ST WHEATLEY HILL.
GREEN	Forst	PTE	27	/954	A	9 JAMES ST	SOUTH HETTON	2/1/15	24/8/17	SICK			TO DEPOT.	
GREEN	G	PTE	27	/1495	C		HAMSTERLEY COLL	30/6/15	10/12/17	GUNSHOT WOUNDS			TO 3rd BN.	NAME GIVEN AS BREEN.
GREEN	John	PTE	27	/290	D		SOUTH SHIELDS			26 OCT 1917	OCTOBER 16.	TYNE COT MEM	TO 1/5th BN.	BORN EAST RAINTON.
GREEN	John	SGT	27	/952	A	9 JAMES ST	SOUTH HETTON	7/1/15		1 JULY 1916		THIEPVAL MEM		BORN EASINGTON.
GREEN	Mich	PTE	27	/1544	A	24 CO-OP BLDGS	ANNFIELD PLAIN			19 MAY 1916		BECOURT MIL CEM.	TO 24th BN.	BORN WITTON GILBERT, AGE 21.
GREEN	T	PTE	27	/1515	C		WEST STANLEY				SEPTEMBER 16		TO 16th, 1st BNS, CLASS Z RESERVE.	
GREEN	Thos	PTE	27	/968			SUNDERLAND	21/12/14						LABOURER DESERTED 21/12/14 AGE 21, 5'9''.
GREEN	Wm	PTE	27	/278	C	20 PARMETER ST	SOUTHMOOR	14/1/15		1 JULY 1916		THIEPVAL MEM		MISSING OCTOBER 16, BORN CRAMLINGTON.
GREENER	R	PTE	27	/294						KR para 392			TO 2nd GARRISON BN.	
GREENSIDE	J W	PTE	27	/295	A	21 MARY ST	WEST STANLEY	21/12/14	21/7.17	GUNSHOT WOUNDS	AUGUST 16.		TO DEPOT.	
GREENWELL	S	PTE	27	/292	D		FENCEHOUSES				SEPTEMBER 16.		TO 24/27th, 8th BNS, CLASS Z RESERVE.	
GREEVES	J	LCPL	27	/281	C		SOUTH SHIELDS				SEPTEMBER 16			SGT.
GREGORY	T	PTE	27	/279	C	15 WEST ST	SHOTTON COLLIER	21/12/14	1/11/17	WOUNDS			TO DEPOT.	30 FIRST ST HORDEN.
GREY	Wm	PTE	27	/970			DURHAM CITY	22/12/14						LABOURER DESERTED 22/12/14 AGE 21, 5'3''.
GRIMES	Peter	PTE	27	/1529	C 24	18 FRONT ST	LINTZ COLLIERY			1 JULY 1916	FEBRUARY 16.	THIEPVAL MEM	TO 24th, 27th BNS.	BORN BIRTLEY.
GROVES	Andrw	CPL	27	/263	A	68 SMOKEY ROW FRAM M	DURHAM CITY	7/1/15					TO 30th BN(D COY), LABOUR CORPS.	SGT LAB CORPS No 30004.
GUNN	Jos	PTE	27	/971			THORNABY			22 AUGUST 1915		NORTH ORMSEBY		
GUY	Rob	PTE	27	/962	B	16 RAILWAY ST	LANGLEY PARK	8/1/15			AUGUST 16.		TO 23rd, 22nd, 8th BNS.	SHOWN ON MR AS KIA.
GUY	Thos	PTE	27	/270	B	THE FORD	WITTON GILBERT	7/1/15		1 JULY 1916		THIEPVAL MEM		BORN USHAW MOOR.
HACKETT	J	PTE	27	/1012	C									
HACKETT	R	PTE	27	/1480	B									
HAINING	W	PTE	27	/1549	D									
HAINSWORTH	JohnW	PTE	27	/309	A	22 FRANKLIN ST	SHIELDFIELD			1 JULY 1916		THIEPVAL MEM		MISSING OCTOBER 16, BORN MIDDLESBOROUGH.
HALDER	John	PTE	27	/344	D	35 MAXWELL ST	SOUTH SHIELDS			1 JULY 1916		THIEPVAL MEM		MISSING OCTOBER 16.
HALES	Jas	PTE	27	/1025	C	2 HUDSON ST	NORTH SHIELDS				AUGUST 16.			
HALL	G	PTE	27	/1024	B		SOUTH SHIELDS				NOVEMBER 18.			
HALL	J	PTE	27	/319	B									
HALL	Jos L	PTE	27	/324	B	57 MILTON ST	SOUTH SHIELDS			1 JULY 1916		THIEPVAL MEM		BORN WEST STANLEY.
HALL	P Y	PTE	27	/1011	C		SOUTH SHIELDS	17/1/15	10/10/17	UNFIT	SEPTEMBER 16		TO 10th, 9th BNS.	
HALL	R	PTE	27	/1021	D		USWORTH	30/12/14	10/4/17	WOUNDS	OCTOBER 16		TO DEPOT.	

NAME	INITI	RANK	BA	NUMBE	COMP	ADDRESS	TOWN_VILL	ENLISTED	DISCHARG	CAUSE_DIS	WOUNDED	BURIED	TRANSFER	ADD
HALL	T	PTE	27	/352	C	2 HOBSON TERR	BIDDICK							
HALL	T	PTE	27	/1003	B	3 McGOWANS COURT	WHITEHAVEN			3 NOV 1918	SEPTEMBER 16.	WHITEHAVEN	TO LABOUR CORPS(367 LAB COY).	
HALL	Thos	PTE	27	/357	C	DOCK HOTEL	TYNE DOCK	14/1/15					TO ROYAL DEFENCE CORPS.	IN FRANCE 18/5/16 TO 9/9/16.
HALL	Thos	PTE	27	/1014	C		SOUTH SHIELDS			1 JULY 1916	APRIL 16.	BECOURT MIL CEM		AWOL 11/9/15 CT SOUTH SHIELDS 13/9/15.AGE 18.
HALL	Thos	PTE	27	/1027	B	32 EDITH AVENUE	USWORTH COLLIER			1 JULY 1916		THJIEPVAL MEM		MISSING NOVEMBER 16, BORN EASINGTON LANE.
HALL	W	SGT	27	/355			NEWCASTLE				AUGUST 16		TO 11th, 27th, 24/27th BNS.	ALLOCATED NEW NUMBER 93358.
HALL	Wm	PTE	27	/327	C	1 CAROLINE ST	HETTON LE HOLE			1 JULY 1916	SEPTEMBER 16.	GORDON DUMP CEM		LSGT.
HANDS	Thos	PTE	27	/1006	C	22 GEORGE ST	BLAYDON			1 JULY 1916		THIEPVAL MEM		MISSING OCTOBER 16.
HANRATTY	W	PTE	27	/328	C	26 FRONT ST	LINTZ COLLIERY			KR para 392	SEPTEMBER 16		TO 11th BN.	34 CCS 2/7, 21 AMBTR 5/7, 18 GHOSP, SHIP 9/7/16
HANSON	T W	PTE	27	/1405	B		NORTH SHIELDS				SEPTEMBER 16.		TO 11th BN.	SGT.
HANSON	Thos	PTE	27	/350	D	2 GEORGES TERR	BEARPARK	5/1/15	15/10/17	GUNSHOT WOUNDS	OCTOBER 16		TO 3rd BN.	LCPL.
HARBOTTLE	ChasJ	PTE	27	/346	D	38 SOUTH PELAW SQ	CHESTER LE ST	4/1/15	19/3/18	GUNSHOT WOUNDS	JULY 16		TO ARMY RESERVE CLASS W.	BANKFOOT COLLIERY ROLL OF HONOUR.
HARDY	Thos	PTE	27	/1026	B	20 BRICKGARTH	HETTON LYONS						TO 24/27th, 19th(Y COY) BNS, CLASS Z RESERVE.	AWOL 15/12/15 CT HOUGHTON LE SPRING, SGT.
HARGRAVE	Fred	PTE	27	/345	D		LOW PITTINGTON			1 JULY 1916		THIEPVAL MEM		BORN CHOPPINGTON
HARKER	Rich	PTE	27	/1460	A		WARDLEY			9 APRIL 1917	JUNE 16.	ARRAS MEM	TO 25th, 20th BNS.	
HARLAND	Thos	PTE	27	/312	B	40 DOCTOR ST	SEAHAM			1 JULY 1916		THIEPVAL MEM		MISSING OCTOBER 16, BORN EASINGTON LANE.
HARPER	H	CPL	27	/1552	C	30				KR para 392			TO 30th, 27th, 25th(A COY)BNS.	SGT REPORTED MISSING 21/3/18.
HARRINGTON	E	PTE	27	/331	C									
HARRISON	J	PTE	27	/1501	C	17 RIVER ST	NEWCASTLE	6/7/15	17/5/16	SICK			TO 30th BN.	DID NOT SERVE OVERSEAS, AGE 39.
HARRISON	Jos	LCPL	27	/308	A		SUNDERLAND			20 JUNE 1916		ALBERT MIL CEM		
HARRISON	S	PTE	27	/300	A		NORTH SHIELDS				SEPTEMBER 16			21 AMBTR 6/7,18 GHOSP,6 C DEPOT 7/7,SSHOCK AGE 38,
HARTFIELD	J	PTE	27	/1013	C								TO 24/27th, 8th BNS, CLASS Z RESERVE.	
HARTLEY	J	PTE	27	/304	B		SHOTTON COLLIER							
HARVEY	J	PTE	27	/311	A		DURHAM CITY				AUGUST 16.			
HARVEY	J W	LCPL	27	/987	A		NEWCASTLE				JULY 17.			
HARVEY	Jas B	CPL	27	/986	A	16 STANLEY TERR STAN	CROOK			1 JULY 1916		THIEPVAL MEM		LSGT, BATTALION PHYSICAL TRAINING INSTRUCTOR.
HARVEY	Mich	CPL	27	/1020	A	16 STANLEY TERR STAN	CROOK			24 JAN 1919	OCT 16	CROOK RC CEM	TO 3rd BN, ATT LINE OF COMS SIGNALS APO1, LABOUR C	HOSP HARROGATE 7/16,GASSED,LAB CORPS No 517640.
HARVEY	Wm Hy	PTE	27	/340	D	79 SOMERSET ST	SILKSWORTH	7/1/15					TO 18th, 23rd BNS, CLASS Z RESERVE.	7 MILLER TERR 1918.
HAUGHEY	Mich	PTE	27	/1338	C	45 PLANTATION ST	LEADGATE			1 JULY 1916		THIEPVAL MEM		BORN MIDDLESBOROUGH, MISSING OCTOBER 16.
HAZEL	Thos	PTE	27	/1016	D	86 ESHWOOD ST	NEW BRANCEPETH	12/1/15					TO 13th BN, CLASS Z RESERVE.	PRISONER OF WAR MAY 17.
HAZZARD	Thom	PTE	27	/990	B	18 CHURCH ST	CLEATOR MOOR	14/1/15		1 JULY 1916		THIEPVAL MEM		IN DYCH AS HAGGARD.
HEATHERTON	Jos	PTE	27	/977	B		NEWCASTLE			1 JULY 1916		THIEPVAL MEM		PARENTS LIVING 16 PITT ST MANCHESTER.
HEDLEY	J	PTE	27	/1008	C		FENCEHOUSES				SEPTEMBER 16.		TO 20th, 22nd BNS, ROYAL DEFENCE CORPS.	FRANCE 27 11/1/16 TO 5/7/16,20 18/3/17 TO 25/9/17,
HEDLEY	J	PTE	27	/1010	C		FENCEHOUSES				AUGUST 16			3 CCS 2/7/16 EVAC 5/7/16 WND R THIGH AGE 27.
HEDLEY	J T	PTE	27	/321	B	71 PINE ST TEAMS	GATESHEAD	22/12/14	14/11/17	WOUNDS	AUGUST 16		TO DEPOT.	
HENAGHAN	J	PTE	27	/984				8/12/14	21/8/17	STAMMERING			TO 30th BN.	
HENDERSON	Frank	LCPL	27	/1017		22 HEDLEY ST	SOUTH SHIELDS	14/1/15		20 JUNE 1916		ALBERT COM CEM EXT		AGE 21.
HENDERSON	J	PTE	27	/314	B	44 POPLAR ST	SOUTHMOOR	21/12/14	27/8/17	GUNSHOT WOUNDS			TO 85th TRAINING RESERVE BN.	
HENDERSON	T	PTE	27	/336	C		NEWCASTLE				FEBRUARY 18			
HENDERSON	T	PTE	27	/1417	A									
HENNESSY	John	PTE	27	/1030	A	1 UNION ST	LEMINGTON ON TY						TO 24/27th, 11th, 19th BNS, CLASS Z RESERVE.	
HEPPLE	J W	PTE	27	/983		2 MODEL ST	SEAHAM						TO 1st GARRISON BN, CLASS Z RESERVE.	
HERON	Hugh	PTE	27	/313	B	42 BIRKS RD	CLEATOR MOOR			1 JULY 1916		BECOURT MIL CEM		AGE 39.
HERON	J	PTE	27	/978	A		GATESHEAD				JANUARY 17, MARCH 17.			
HERON	Jos	PTE	27	/317	B	1 LANGLEY TERR	NEW KYO			29 MARCH 1918	SEPTEMBER 16	ARRAS MEM	TO 1st BN.	3 CCS 2/7/16 EVAC 2/7/16. BORN HOLYHILL.
HERON	P	PTE	27	/1507	C	JANET ST	BYKER	12/7/15			JULY 1916		TO 25th, 26th, 25th BNS, KINGS OWN YORKS LI(2/4th	TRANSFERED BACK TO NF ALLOTTED NEW No 89307.
HERRON	W	PTE	27	/305	C			8/1/15	6/6/18				TO DEPOT.	DID NOT SERVE OVERSEAS.
HESLOP	H	PTE	27	/1002	B	19 TAYLOR ST	SOUTHMOOR		12/2/19				TO 10th BN, KINGS OWN YORKSHIRE LI(2/4th BN), CLAS	AVL 25 TOWNLEY ST STANLEY 1918, KOYLI No 63413
HEWITSON	J G	PTE	27	/1435	B		BIRTLEY STATION						TO 9th, 27th, 24/27th, 19th, 2nd BNS, CLASS Z RESE	
HICKMAN	Jos	SGT	27	/323	B		LINTZ COLLIERY			29 MARCH 1917		POZIERES MEM	TO 24/27th, 19th BNS.	POS 4 SCHOOL ST LINTZ?
HIGGINS	A	PTE	27	/1029	C	49 BRICKGARTH	HETTON LYONS			KR para 392				BROTHERS DANIEL IN RE, THOMAS IN RGA.
HIGGINS	G	PTE	27	/1031	B	49 BRICKGARTH	HETTON LYONS				SEPTEMBER 16			BROTHERS DANIEL IN RE, THOMAS IN RGA.
HIGGINSON	Chas	PTE	27	/1420	B	31 JANE ST	EPPLETON						TO LABOUR CORPS.	LAB CORPS No 396983.
HILL	Reubn	PTE	27	/1022	D	37 QUARRY ST	NEW SILKSWORTH	31/12/14	1/8/17	GUNSHOT WOUNDS	SEPTEMBER 16 SS/CK NOV 16		TO 3rd BN.	18 GHOSP 6/7/16 CONV DEPOT 12/7/16 AGE 22.
HILLARY	J	PTE	27	/301	A									
HIND	Wm	PTE	27	/1028	A		GATESHEAD			1 JULY 1916		THIEPVAL MEM		
HINDS	John	PTE	27	/998	B		SHERBURN HILL			23 APRIL 1917	JANUARY 17.	ARRAS MEM		LCPL MENTIONED IN BN WAR DIARY 22/12/16.
HODGE	John	PTE	27	/318	D	23 JOICEY TERR	OXHILL	22/12/14	9/8/18	GUNSHOT WOUNDS	AUGUST 16.		TO 20th BN, DEPOT.	HOSP DULWICH WND FOOT MINER TANFIELD LEA COLLIERY.
HODGKINSON	T	PTE	27	/334	C									
HODGSON	G	PTE	27	/1555	D		NEWCASTLE				SEPTEMBER 16.		TO 1st, 27th, 24/27th, 19th BNS, CLASS Z RESERVE.	

NAME	INITI	RANK	BA	NUMBE	COMP	ADDRESS	TOWN_VILL	ENLISTED	DISCHARG	CAUSE_DIS	WOUNDED	BURIED	TRANSFER	ADD
HODGSON	Geo W	PTE	27	/995	B	8 NORTHUMBERLAND ST	SUNDERLAND				AUGUST 16.		TO 23rd BN, CLASS Z RESERVE.	IN COY FOOTBALL TEAM.
HOGG	Ralph	PTE	27	/354	B		NEWBOTTLE			1 JULY 1916		THIEPVAL MEM		
HOLDER	J	PTE	27	/342										
HOLLAND	J	PTE	27	/342	D									
HOLLANDS	Wm	PTE	27	/1001	B	1 JOHNSONS HILL	SOUTH SHIELDS			1 JULY 1916		THIEPVAL MEM		IN BN BAND ALSO IN COY FOOTBALL TEAM.
HOLLYMAN	T	PTE	27	/999	C			31/12/14	8/6/16	KR para 392				
HOLMES	Alex	PTE	27	/335	D		SUNDERLAND			1 JULY 1916		THIEPVAL MEM		
HOLMES	Jhn W	PTE	27	/310	A	2 JOICEY TERR	BILLQUAY	11/1/15	4/12/18	GUNSHOT WOUNDS	SEPTEMBER 16		TO 12/13th BN, DEPOT.	AGE 35.
HOLMES	W	PTE	27	/337	D		WITTON PARK	29/12/14	18/9/16	WOUNDS	JULY 16		TO DEPOT.	
HOOD	Fred	PTE	27	/330	C	13 GREEN ST	SEAHAM	26/12/14	17/1/19		6/6/17(GAVRELLE)		TO 10th BN, CLASS Z RESERVE..	22 CANADIAN HOSP, CANTERBURY HOSP 10/6/17. SHUN
HOPE	G	PTE	27	/989	B			2/1/15	25/4/19	KR para 392			TO 24/27th, 8th BNS, DEPOT.	
HOPE	Rich	PTE	27	/315	B	5 MITCHELL ST	SOUTHMOOR			25 MARCH 1917	SHELLSHOCK MAY 17.	HABARACQ MIL CEM.		CPL, BORN BOLDON.
HOPPER	Alb E	PTE	27	/320	B	11 VICEROY ST	SEAHAM HARBOUR			11 MARCH 1917		FABOURG DE AMIENS ARRAS	TO 1st, 27th BNS.	LSGT, BORN DOVER.
HOPPS	Edgar	PTE	27	/1489	C		COXHOE			30 MARCH 1917	SEPTEMBER 16.	BROWNS COPSE CEM		BORN THORNLEY
HOPWOOD	Geo T	PTE	27	/325	C	6 LUMSDEN ST TEAMS	GATESHEAD						TO 24/27th, 9th BNS, CLASS Z RESERVE.	81 CARNABY TERR 1918, No GIVEN AS 355.
HORNE	Harry	PTE	27	/341	D		LONDON			19 DEC 1917		TYNE COT MEM	TO 1/4th BN.	
HORNER	Wm	PTE	27	/1015	D	13 DURHAM ST	SHERBURN HILL			25 NOV 1916		FABOURG DE AMIENS CEM ARRAS	TO 19th BN.	AGE 20.
HORSMAN	Rob	PTE	27	/360	A	71 PINE ST	GRANGE VILLA						TO 24/27th, 8th BNS, CLASS Z RESERVE.	
HOURIGAN	Rob	PTE	27	/356	B		HETTON LE HOLE			1 JULY 1916		THIEPVAL MEM		BORN EPPLETON, MISSING OCTOBER 16.
HOUSE	J	PTE	27	/991	B		SOUTH SHIELDS	4/1/15	6/10/16	GUNSHOT WOUNDS	SEPTEMBER 16.		TO DEPOT.	LCPL, 34 CCS 1/7/16 EVAC 1/7/16 AGE 19.
HOWARD	Geo	PTE	27											AWOL 9/8/15 COURT GATESHEAD AGE 25.
HOWARD	R	SGT	27	/1362	B								COMMISSION IN LOYAL NORTH LANCASHIRE REGT(5th BN).	AWO2.
HOWARTH	CuthL	PTE	27	/349	D	30 CHILTON ST	SUNDERLAND	12/1/15						
HOWE	E	PTE	27	/985	B			12/1/15	12/4/18	GUNSHOT WOUNDS			TO 3rd BN.	
HOWE	John	LCPL	27	/307	A		SUNDERLAND			1 JULY 1916		THIEPVAL MEM		
HOWE	Jos	PTE	27	/332	A	8 BROUGHAM ST STHWCK	SUNDERLAND			1 JULY 1916		THIEPVAL MEM		
HOY	T	PTE	27	/981	C	4 LOW CHARE	CHESTER LE ST				OCTOBER 16.		TO 22nd BN, CLASS Z RESERVE.	2 G HOSP 4/7/16 H SHIP 5/7/16 AGE 19 WND BREAST.
HUGGINS	Alb E	PTE	27	/303	A	27 STONE ROW	GRANGE VILLA			KR para 392			TO 19th BN, ATTACHED 257 TUN COY RE, 1/5th BN.	LIVING 4 WHITLEY GREENS BLACKHOUSE EDMONDSLEY 1914
HUGHES	J T	SGT	27	/1336	A								TO 24/27th, 25th, 9th BNS, CLASS Z RESERVE.	
HUGHES	James	PTE	27	/359	C	KENMIRE HSE KENMIRE	FELLING			12 OCT 1916		PLOEGSTEERT MEM		AGE 25.
HUGHES	R	PTE	27	/348	D	41 GLADSTONE ST	SUNDERLAND							
HUGHES	T	PTE	27	/980	A								TO 24/27th, 11th BNS, CLASS Z RESERVE.	
HUGHES	Thos	PTE	27											AWOL 14/9/15 COURT S SHIELDS
HUGHES	Tom	PTE	27	/351			SOUTH HETTON			1 JULY 1916		THIEPVAL MEM		MISSING OCTOBER 16.
HUGHES	Wm Hy	PTE	27	/996	B	BUSHBLADES FARM	TANTOBIE	7/1/15		28 APRIL 1917		ROCLINCOURT VALLEY CEM	TO 20th BN.	BORN CATSHILL WORCESTERSHIRE.
HUGO	J	PTE	27	/316	B		WHITEHAVEN				SEPTEMBER 16		TO 1st, 27th, 24/27th, 19th(Z COY), CLASS Z RESERV	SGT.
HUMBLE	James	PTE	27	/326	C	3 FRONT ST	LINTZ COLLIERY				NOVEMBER 16, MARCH 17.		TO 23rd BN, CLASS Z RESERVE.	
HUMBLE	Wm	PTE	27	/1009	C		FRIARSIDE			1 JULY 1916		THIEPVAL MEM		
HUNT	John	PTE	27	/302	A	4 RAILWAY ST	LANGLEY PARK	14/1/15		1 JULY 1916		THIEPVAL MEM		BORN CORNSAY. SEE 27/1000.
HUNT	Sam	PTE	27	/1000	B	11 RAILWAY ST	LANGLEY PARK	14/1/15		2 JULY 1916		WARLOY MIL CEM		BORN CORNSAY COLLIERY. SEE ALSO 27/302.
HUNTER	R H	PTE	27	/333	B			28/12/14	6/9/16	SICK			TO 30th BN.	
HUNTER	T	PTE	27	/1492	A									
HUNTER	Thos	LCPL	27	/1019	D		MURTON			1 JULY 1916		THIEPVAL MEM		
HUTLER	L	PTE	27	/1004	C								TO 24/27th, 11th BNS, CLASS Z RESERVE.	
HYLTON	Jonas	PTE	27	/339	D	FRONT ST	SHERBURN HILL	7/1/15		24 FEB 1916		BAILLEUL COM CEM EXT		BORN WASHINGTON, FIRST SHERBURN HILL FATALITY.
INGRAM	T A	CPL	27	/362	B									ALSO ON D COY 30th BN ROLL.
IRVING	Wm	PTE	27	/1033			SEAHAM HARBOUR	21/12/14						MINER DESERTED 10/5/15 AGE 21, 5'6''.
IRWIN	J	PTYE	27	/1034	C	2 LORN BLDGS	EAST BOLDON						TO 24/27th, 8th, 12/13th BNS, CLASS Z RESERVE.	
IRWIN	Thos	PTE	27	/1037	D	20 MURRAY ST	WEST STANLEY	14/1/15		27 MAY 1918		SOISSONS MEM	TO 24/27th, 8th, 1/4th BNS.	LCPL, BORN PELTON.
IRWIN	Wm	PTE	27	/1384	D	BANKHEAD HOUSE 25 GI	HEXAM				OCTOBER 16.		TO 9th, 18th, LAB CORPS(848 LAB COY) DWR(13 GAR BN	27 11/1/16 TO 5/7/16, 9 12/7/17 TO 28/7/17, 18 29/
IVERS	John	PTE	27	/1339	B	SPRINGWELL	GATESHEAD	14/1/15		1 JULY 1916		THIEPVAL MEM		MISSING OCTOBER 16.
IVESON	G	PTE	27	/1036	D	28 FRAMWELLGATE	DURHAM CITY				OCTOBER 16.		TO SCOTTISH RIFLES.	BATH WAR HOSP 11/7/16
IVESON	John	PTE	27	/1032	B	7 ROSA ST WESTOE	SOUTH SHIELDS			5 JULY 1916		DAOURS COM CEM EXT	TO 24th BN.	BORN GILESGATE DURHAM, 34CCS 2/7/16 DIED IN CCS
IVESON	Robt	PTE	27	/361	A	4 BELLES VILLAS GILE	DURHAM CITY						TO ROYAL DEFENCE CORPS.	R DEFENCE CORPS No 50033.
IVEY	John	LCPL	27	/1035	D	4 JOHN ST SQUARE	CONSETT			1 JULY 1916		THIEPVAL MEM		BORN WASHINGTON.
JACKSON	E	PTE	27	/377	C								TO LABOUR CORPS, ROYAL SUSSEX REGT.	
JACKSON	W	PTE	27	/1041	C									
JAGGERS	Alex	PTE	27	/383	D	64 COMMERCIAL RD	SOUTH SHIELDS			1 JULY 1916		THIEPVAL MEM		LCPL, MISSING OCTOBER 16,AWOL 25/8/15 CT S SHIELDS
JAMES	J	PTE	27	/372	B									
JAMIESON	R	PTE	27	/381	A	44 SCHOOL TERR	SOUTHMOOR							77 BACK GEORGE ST NEWCASTLE 1919.

NAME	INITI	RANK	BA	NUMBE	COMP	ADDRESS	TOWN_VILL	ENLISTED	DISCHARG	CAUSE_DIS	WOUNDED	BURIED	TRANSFER	ADD
JARVIS	E	PTE	27	/382	D			6/1/15	24/9/18	TRENCH FEET			TO 27th, 26th BNS.	
JEFFERSON	Henry	PTE	27	/379	D	NELSON ST	HIGH PITTINGTON						TO LABOUR CORPS(165 LAB COY).	
JENKINS	W	PTE	27	/370	B			30/12/14	22/5/18	SHELLSHOCK			TO 24/27th BN, DEPOT.	
JEWITT	J W	PTE	27	/384	D		GATESHEAD				JANUARY 17.		TO ROYAL INISKILLING FUSILIERS(6th BN).	
JOBLING	J F	PTE	27	/369				29/12/14	3/4/16	SICK			TO 30th BN.	DID NOT SERVE OVERSEAS.
JOBLING	L	PTE	27	/363	A		NEWCASTLE				JUNE 16, AUGUST 16.			
JOBSON	J J	PTE	27	/374	C	12 EAST ADA ST	MURTON COLLIERY						TO 24/27th, 11th BNS, CLASS Z RESERVE.	
JOHNSON	F	PTE	27	/367	B	3 OFFICE SQUARE	LINTZ COLLIERY	26/12/14	13/12/17	PARALASIS	SEPTEMBER 16		TO DEPOT.	
JOHNSON	J	PTE	27	/365	A									
JOHNSON	J	PTE	27	/376		3 TURNERS BLDGS	SACRISTON						TO 2nd GARRISON BN, CLASS Z RESERVE.	
JOHNSON	J J	PTE	27	/1045	A								TO 24/27th, 11th, 8th BNS, CLASS Z RESERVE.	
JOHNSON	R	PTE	27	/1414										
JOHNSON	R W	PTE	27	/368	B								TO 24/27th, 11th BNS, ROYAL FUSILIERS(24th BN).	FRANCE 27 11/1/16 TO 3/7/18, 11 4/7/18 TO 28/8/18,
JOHNSON	Rob	PTE	27	/1415	C	1 VEGHILL SOUTHWAITE	CARLISLE			3 SEPT 1916	SEPTEMBER 16.	THIEPVAL MEM		BORN LONGBENTON.
JOHNSON	T	PTE	27	/1044									TO 2nd GARRISON BN, CLASS Z RESERVE.	
JOHNSTONE	Henry	PTE	27	/378			NEWCASTLE	4/1/15						LABOURER DESERTED 4/1/15 AGE 41, 5'4''.
JONES	J	PTE	27	/1038	A		DUBLIN				AUGUST 16			
JONES	Jos E	PTE	27	/385	A			9/1/15	27/8/17	SICK			TO DEPOT.	AGE 36.
JORDAN	J	PTE	27	/380	B			6/1/15	19/10/16	SICK			TO DEPOT.	
JORDAN	J R	PTE	27	/387	A									
JORDAN	John	PTE	27	/375	C	76 BYKER BANK	NEWCASTLE			1 JULY 1916		THIEPVAL MEM		
JORDAN	Jos	PTYE	27	/1418	C	21 PEMBERTON ST	HETTON LE HOLE	9/1/15	15/7/18	SICK			TO DEPOT.	
JOYCE	J	PTE	27	/364	A		NORTH SHIELDS				SEPTEMBER 16			21 AMB TR 6/7, 18 GHOSP,6CONV DEPOT,SSHOCK,AGE 29,
JOYCE	W	PTE	27	/371		1 SCHOOL ROW	SHOTTON COLLIER	30/12/14	31/3/19				TO 1st GARRISON BN, 26th BN.	
KAIL	John	PTE	27	/1054									TO LABOUR CORPS.	LAB CORPS No 677077.
KEATING	W	PTE	27	/1057	D						FEBRUARY 16.		TO ROYAL ARMY MEDICAL CORPS.	
KEEGAN	C	PTE	27	/1052	C	22 CAROLINE ST	HETTON LE HOLE	24/12/14	25/12/17	SICK			TO 3rd BN.	IN COURT FOR ASSAULT MARCH 1915.
KEEGAN	J	PTE	27	/1490						KR para 392			TO 1st GARRISON BN, 2nd BN.	ENTERED SALONICA 20/12/15
KEELING	J	PTE	27	/1055	C	12 HIND ST	SUNDERLAND				OCTOBER 16.			34CCS 2/7 EVAC 5/7,HOSP ABERDEEN 7/16 WND RHIP,LLE
KELL	W	PTE	27	/405	C	33 JOICEY ST	SHERBURN HILL				OCTOBER 16.		TO LABOUR CORPS, ROYAL FUSILIERS.	HOSP WARRINGTON 7/16 WND ARM,LAB CORPS No 578131.
KELLY	B	PTE	27	/395	B	4 RUSSELL SQUARE	SHIELDFIELD	9/1/15	11/1/18	GUNSHOT WOUNDS	AUGUST 16.		TO 3rd BN.	
KELLY	E	LCPL	27	/400	C		NEWCASTLE	29/12/14	18/3/18	GUNSHOT WOUNDS	MARCH 16, SEPTEMBER 16.		TO 14th, 24th, 20th, 3rd BNS.	AWOL 17/12/15 IN COURT 31/12/15.
KELLY	Edwd	PTE	27	/1051			NEWSHAM	24/12/14						MINER DESERTED AGE 19, 5'4''.
KELLY	Jos	PTE	27	/1061	C	10 MAYNARDS ROW GILE	DURHAM CITY				AUGUST 16.		TO CLASS Z RESERVE.	34 CCS 2/7/16 EVAC 5/7/16 WND R LEG, AGE 19.
KELLY	P	PTE	27	/1431	B		FENCEHOUSES				JULY 17.		TO ARMY SERVICE CORPS.	
KELLY	W	PTE	27	/391	B						MARCH 16			
KEMP	A	PTE	27	/401	D	92 PARK ST	DARLINGTON				APRIL 16		TO 24th, 27th, 24/27th, 14th BNS, CLASS Z RESERVE.	BROTHER J W KEMP KIA 2nd NF 24/4/15.
KEMP	Wm	PTE	27	/388	A	13 VINE ST	SUNDERLAND	7/1/15						AWOL 9/8/15 IN COURT GATESHEAD, AGE 25.
KENDALL	W	PTE	27	/1056	C			30/12/14	16/3/18.	GUNSHOT WOUNDS	APRIL 16.		TO ARMY RESERVE CLASS P.	
KENNEDY	J	PTE	27	/1050	A	50 GRASHORN RD	FRISINGTON				JUNE 16.			
KENNEDY	John	PTE	27	/1049	B		WARDLEY	21/12/14		4 SEPT 1916		ADANAC MIL CEM		MINER DESERTED 4/15 AGE 20, 5'4'' PROMOTED LCPL.
KENNEDY	JohnT	PTE	27	/1547	C	21 CLARENCE TERR	WILLINGTON	9/2/15	1/4/19				TO ARMY RESERVE CLASS P.	
KENNEDY	Peter	PTE	27	/1047	B	JACKTREES RD	CLEATOR MOOR			29 AUGUST 1917		HAGRICOURT MIL CEM		
KENNEDY	R	PTE	27	/397	C									
KENNEDY	R	LCPL	27	/398	C		GATESHEAD	31/12/14	28/2/17	WOUNDS	AUGUST 16.		TO DEPOT.	CPL.
KENNY	Thos	PTE	27	/1053	A	55 EDITH AVENUE	USWORTH			4 OCT 1918	JULY 1916	GREVILLIERS BRIT CEM	TO YORK AND LANCASTER REGT(2/4th BN).	AGE 26,Y&L No 57664, 16 SINGLE ROW USWORTH COLLIER
KEOGH	Rich	PTE	27	/1048	B	108 BOWTHORN RD	CLEATOR MOOR			9 APRIL 1917	JANUARY 17.	ROCLINCOURT VALLEY CEM	TO 25th BN.	BORN MARYBOROUGH QUEENS Co.
KEOGH	Thos	PTE	27	/1497			MARYBOROUGH QUE			4 SEPT 1916		ADANAC MIL CEM	FROM SOUTH IRISH HORSE.	ENTERED FRANCE 20/1/15,SOUTH IRISH HORSE No 1005.
KERVIN	W	PTE	27	/1046	B	11 PETER ST HARRIS V	FRIZINGTON	21/12/14	4/2/18	WOUNDS			TO DEPOT.	
KILBRIDE	J	PTE	27	/1424	D		COUNDON				NOVEMBER 16.			
KING	Art J	PTE	27	/1060	D		ANNITSFORD			11 SEPT 1916		CONTAY MIL CEM		ACPL.
KING	F C	PTE	27	/399	C	3 CLIFFE TERR HENDON	SUNDERLAND				JULY 16			34 CCS 1/7/16 EVAC 5/7/16 WND CHEST & BACK AGE 26.
KIRBY	John	PTE	27	/1059	D	6 RUSSELL ST TEAMS	GATESHEAD	8/1/15			AUG 16, FEB 18, JUNE18.		TO 20th BN, CLASS Z RESERVE.	HOSP BLACKPOOL 1918, SEE 26/1018 KIRBY D.
KIRKBRIDE	W	PTE	27	/407	A	54 FRANCIS ST	SOUTH SHIELDS	10/1/15	31/1/16	SICK			TO 30th BN.	DID NOT SERVE OVERSEAS.
KIRKUP	J C	PTE	27	/396	B	53 JACKSON SQURE	ANNITSFORD						TO 24/27th, 11th, 1st BNS, CLASS Z RESERVE.	SGT.COULD POS LIVE 13 LYTONN ST SOUTH SHIELDS
KNAPP	J W	PTE	27	/392	A	53 FRANCIS ST	SEAHAM HARBOUR	22/12/14	10/6/18	GUNSHOT WOUNDS			TO DEPOT, ARMY RESERVE CLASS P.	SGT, TO P RES 5/3/19.
KNAPPER	Jos W	PTE	27	/404	D	56 FRANCIS ST	SEAHAM HARBOUR			10 APRIL 1918	AUGUST 16.	TROIS ARBRES MIL CEM	TO 16th, 1/5th BNS.	BORN HANLEY STAFFORDSHIRE.
KNIGHTS	Chas	PTE	27	/390	A		LOWESTOFT			6 OCT 1916		TROIS ARBRES MIL CEM.		ACPL.
KOSSICK	R	PTE	27	/1058	A									
LAIDLAW	T	PTE	27	/1086	A	35 BUSTY TERR ELDON	BISHOP AUKLAND						TO 26th, 9th BNS, CLASS Z RESERVE.	LCPL

NAME	INITI	RANK	BA	NUMBE	COMP	ADDRESS	TOWN_VILL	ENLISTED	DISCHARG	CAUSE_DIS	WOUNDED	BURIED	TRANSFER	ADD
LANCASTER	R	PTE	27	/1443	A									
LANG	J	PTE	27	/427	D		SUNDERLAND				SEPTEMBER 16.		TO MACHINE GUN CORPS.	3 CCS 2/7/16 EVAC 3/7/16 GSW, MGC No 71036.
LANGAN	John	PTE	27	/415	B	11 THIRD STREET	HORDEN COLLIERY				SEPTEMBER 16		TO LABOUR CORPS.	LAB CORPS No 407705.
LANGLANDS	Rich	PTE	27											AWOL 25/5 COURT NEWCASTLE 26/5/15
LAVERTY	Pat	PTE	27	/1076	B	10 CROSSFIELD ROAD	CLEATOR MOOR	14/1/15		KR para 392	AUGUST 16.		TO 14th BN.	
LAWLER	Jas J	PTE	27	/1085		1 VALE ST SCOTSWOOD	NEWCASTLE	21/12/14						LABOURER DESERTED 21/12/14 AGE 28, 5'3''.BORN MIDD
LAWRENCE	J W	CPL	27	/424	D		HETTON LE HOLE	7/1/15	16/8/17	GUNSHOT WOUNDS	OCTOBER 16		TO 24th, 27th, 3rd BNS.	
LAWSON	H	PTE	27	/1079	C		NEWCASTLE				SEPTEMBER 16.		TO DURHAM LI, NORTH STAFFORDSHIRE REGT.	BATH WAR HOSP 11/7/16
LAWSON	T	PTE	27	/423	A 24								TO 24th, 30th BNS.	ALSO ON D COY 30th BN ROLL.
LAWSON	Wilf	PTE	27	/1392	D		BLYTH			2 JULY 1916		MEAULTE MIL CEM		
LAYBOURN	John	PTE	27	/1407			CRAWCROOK			12 SEPT 1916		INDIA	TO 2nd GARRISON BN.	
LEARMOUTH	Jos	PTE	27	/426	D	1 PRUDHOE COURT	NEWCASTLE			1 JULY 1916		THIEPVAL MEM		NOK 138 NEWGATE ST NEWCASTLE.
LEASLEY	Chas	PTE	27	/428	A		GATESHEAD	12/1/15					TO 24/27th, 9th BNS, CLASS Z RESERVE.	
LEE	Rich	PTE	27	/1070	B	50 SOUTH MARGARET ST	SOUTH HETTON	7/1/15						
LEITHER	Thos	PTE	27											AWOL 11/7 16/7 2/9 2/10/15 COURT GATESHEAD AGE 18.
LENAGHAN	Mich	PTE	27	/1081	D	29 ENGOS ST	LEMINGTON ON TY	14/1/15			SEPTEMBER 16.			
LENG	Harry	PTE	27	/1071		8 AVON STREET	SUNDERLAND	2/1/15						ROPEMAKER DESERTED 2/1/15 AGE 19, 5'7''.
LEONARD	John	PTE	27	/1445		111 STATION RD	EASINGTON			1 JULY 1916		THIEPVAL MEM		NAME APPEARS ON AVL WITH TI No AND ALSO 71379 RFA
LEWIS	J	PTE	27	/411	A	16 VICTORIA COTTAGES	FELLING			21 AUGUST 1917		FELLING		LCPL.
LEWIS	Wm Ja	SGT	27	/408	A		NEWRY Co ARMARG			21 JUNE 1916		HEILLY STATION CEM		
LIDDLE	Alf	PTE	27	/425	C 25	27 CUTHBERT ST	BLAYDON				SEPTEMBER 16		TO 30th(B COY), 25th, 12/13th, 1/7th BNS, CLASS Z	34 CCS 2/7 EVAC 5/7,21 AMBTR 6/7,18 GHOSP,14/7 6 C
LIDDLE	D	PTE	27	/1072	B		SOUTH SHIELDS			KR para 392	NOVEMBER 16.			
LILLEY	A	PTE	27	/413		76 STATION RD	EASINGTON						TO 1st GARRISON BN, CLASS Z RESERVE.	
LINDLEY	R	PTE	27	/1077	C		EASINGTON LANE	6/1/15	6/9/16	VDH	SEPTEMBER 16.		TO DEPOT.	34 CCS 2/7/16 EVAC 5/7/16 HIP WND AGE 26.
LINDSEY	HerbN	PTE	27	/418	B	14 OXCLOSE ST	WASHINGTON STAT			4 JULY 1916		MERICOURT MIL CEM		BORN SPENNYMOOR.
LISHMAN	W	PTE	27	/420	C								TO 24/27th, 21st, 25th BNS, CLASS Z RESERVE.	
LITHGOW	A	PTE	27	/416	B		BISHOP AUKLAND				AUGUST 16.			SEE ALSO 27/1074 LITHGOW L BISHOP AUKLAND.
LITHGOW	Tom W	PTE	27	/1074	B	4 THOMPSONS YARD	BISHOP AUKLAND			1 JULY 1916		THIEPVAL MEM		MISSING OCTOBER 16.
LITTLE	R	CQMS	27	/412	A									
LLOYD	J	PTE	27	/1396	D								TO 24/27th BN, ROYAL DEFENCE CORPS.	FRANCE 11/1/16 to 9/8/17, 24/27 10/8/17 TO 7/1/18.
LLOYD	Walla	SGT	27	/409	A		NEWCASTLE			1 JULY 1916		THIEPVAL MEM		
LOATES	W	PTE	27	/1446		2 LUCY ST TOWNLEY	STANLEY	14/6/15	19/12/18	GUNSHOT WOUNDS			TO DEPOT.	AGE 32.
LOATES	W	PTE		/1531	D 27					KR para 392			TO 24/27th, 25th, 12/13th BNS.	ON MR AS 27/ No ALSO ALLOCATED TO FENWICK R.
LOCKWOOD	Henry	PTE	27	/1082		TOWER HSE PILGRIM ST	NEWCASTLE	11/1/15						MINER DESERTED 11/1/15 AGE 24, BORN MORLEY YORKS.
LOGAN	Ralph	PTE	27	/1381	D	VULCANS PLACE	BEDLINGTON			8 SEPT 1916	SEPTEMBER 16	FLAT IRON COPSE MIL CEM		AGE 18.
LONG	Wm	PTE	27	/1441	B		BENTON			1 JULY 1916		SERRE RD No 2 CEM+THIEPVAL MEM		BODY RECOVERED AFTER THIEPVAL MEM COMPLETED
LONSDALE	Wm	PTE	27	/414	B	WHITFIELD STREET	CROOK			1 JULY 1916		THIEPVAL MEM		AGE 29.
LOUGHEAD	Sam F	PTE	27	/1385	D	12 HAUGH LANE	HEXAM						TO 22nd BN, CLASS Z RESERVE.	
LOUGHRAN	J	PTE	27	/1471	D	68 MORPETH ST	SPITTAL TONGUES			KR para 392				
LOVE	Stan	PTE	27	/1068	A	7 NEWCASTLE ST	NORTH SHIELDS			13 MAY 1916		BECOURT MIL CEM		BORN TYNEMOUTH, AGE 33.
LOWDEN	L	PTE	27	/422	C			5/1/15	15/3/18	GUNSHOT WOUNDS			TO 3rd BN.	34 CCS 2/7/16 EVAC 5/7/16, WND L LEG, AGE 36.
LOWE	W	PTE	27	/1069	C		SOUTH SHIELDS	1/1/15	31/3/19	KR para 392	AUGUST 16.		TO 10th, 8th BNS,ARMY RESERVE CLASS P.	
LOWERY	Geo	PTE	27	/1084	D		CROOK			KR PARA 392	AUGUST 16.			34 CCS 2/7/16 EVAC 5/7/16 WND NECK.
LOWERY	JohnB	PTE	27	/1062	A	59 DIXON ST BENSHAM	GATESHEAD	22/12/14	20/11/18	KR para 392	SEPTEMBER 16, DECEMBER 17		TO 8th, 16th BNS, DEPOT.	
LUGTON	J	SGT	27	/1064	A		SOUTH SHIELDS	22/12/14	13/12/16	KR para 392	OCTOBER 16.		TO DEPOT.	3 CCS 2/7/16 EVAC 3/7/16 GSW.
LUMSDEN	G	PTE	27	/1380	D		CHOPPINGTON				1 JULY 16			21 AMBTR 6/7,18 GHOSP,SHIP 7/7,SSHOCK+GAS AGE 18.
LYDON	M C	PTE	27	/417		5 SOUTH PLANTATION R	TRIMDON						TO 1st GARRISON BN, CLASS Z RESERVE.	
LYNCH	C	PTE	27	/1455	C									
LYNN	W	PTE	27	/1075	B	32 DOCK STREET	TYNE DOCK	14/1/15		KR para 392	NOVEMBER 16.		TO 1st BN.	3 CCS 2/7/16 EVAC 3/7/16 SHELL WND
LYONS	P	PTE	27	/1083			JARROW	11/12/14						LABOURER DESERTED 7/5/15 AGE 20, 5'10''.
MACKAY	R D	PTE	27	/1131	B								TO 24/27th, 11th BNS, CLASS Z RESERVE.	
MADDEN	Rich	CPL	27	/492	D	30 GREEN ST	WASHINGTON				JULY 16.		ATTACHED 103 LTMB, TO 23rd, 27th, 24/27th, 9th BNS	CSM 103LTMB.
MAGERATICH	J	PTE	27	/482	B			6/1/15	9/9/16	WOUNDS	MARCH 16		TO 34th BN.	
MAHONE	T	PTE	27	/1139	B			5/1/15	19/10/17	SICK			TO DEPOT.	
MAIN	Jas	PTE	27	/1126	A	CHIRTON	NORTH SHIELDS			11 APRIL 1918	AUGUST 16.	PLOEGSTEERT MEM	TO 11th, 1/5th BNS.	HOSP TORQUAY 7/16,LCPL NEW NUMBER 243137.
MAIN	W	PTE	27	/518				28/12/14	22/9/15	KR para 392			TO 30th BN.	DID NOT SERVE OVERSEAS.
MALLABURN	Thos	PTE	27	/490	B	4 WEAR TERR	WASHINGTON STAT			1 JULY 1916		THIEPVAL MEM		NOK 19 DERWENT TERR WASHINGTON STN.
MALLOY	John	PTE	27	/1129	B	28 DUKE ST	CLEATOR MOOR	14/1/15		15 JULY 1916		BOULOGNE EAST MIL CEM		
MANNING	Thos	PTE	27	/1134	C	2 WOOD ST	USWORTH			17 OCT 1918	AUGUST 16.	HIGHLAND CEM LE CATEAU	TO ROYAL INNISKILLING FUSILIERS(6th BN C Coy).	BORN MONKWEARMOUTH, AGE 29, RINNISF No 21565..
MARGA	W P	PTE	27	/521			ATHERTON LANCS	29/12/14					TO 2nd GARRISON BN.	DESERTED 5/11/15 AGE 25, 5'5''.

NAME	INITI	RANK	BA	NUMBE	COMP	ADDRESS	TOWN_VILL	ENLISTED	DISCHARG	CAUSE_DIS	WOUNDED	BURIED	TRANSFER	ADD
MARRATY	J	PTE	27	/497	C			29/6/15	5/3/19	KR para 392			TO ARMY RESERVE CLASS P.	ASGT.
MARRS	Jos W	PTE	27	/491	B	19 BARCLAY ST	SUNDERLAND	12/1/15			AUGUST 16, AUGUST 18.			LCPL.
MARSHALL	A	LCPL	27	/475	A	50 HENRY ST	EAST BOLDON						TO LABOUR CORPS.	LAB CORPS No 397013.
MARSHALL	J	PTE	27	/1135	C	22 FORE ST	JESMOND	8/1/15	25/7/17	GUNSHOT WOUNDS	AUGUST 16.		TO 3rd BN.	34 CCS 2/7/16 EVAC 5/7/16 WND L LEG
MARSHALL	W L	PTE	27	/1512	D									DESERTED 15/9/15 IN COURT 21/9/15. DESERTED 24/5/1
MARTIN	J E	PTE	27	/1124	A		FELLING	29/12/14	30/11/17	WOUNDS	AUGUST 16.		TO DEPOT.	
MASON	Math	PTE	27	/515	D		FERRYHILL			1 JULY 1916		THIEPVAL MEM		
MASON	Thos	PTE	27	/1140	D	75 QUEEN ST	NORTH SHIELDS	8/1/15			SEPTEMBER 16.		TO 23rd, 9th BNS, CLASS Z RESERVE.	34CCS 2/7 EVAC 5/7/16,EMPLOYED AT BACKWORTH COLLIE
MASON	Wm	PTE	27	/478	A	7 PERCY ST	NORTH SHIELDS	26/12/14	11/3/19	KR para 392			TO 1st, 14th BNS, ARMY RESERVE CLASS P.	
MASON	WmJks	PTE	27	/1137	C		SOUTH SHIELDS	14/1/15			AUGUST 16.			3rd NTHN GHOSP SHEFFIELD 10/7/16.
MATHEWSON	Rob	PTE	27	/489	A	8 BYKER BLDGS BYKER	NEWCASTLE			1 JULY 1916		BAPAUME POST CEM		MISSING OCTOBER 16.
MAYNE	F	PTE	27	/1442	A									
MAYNE	R B	SGT	27	/1123	A	13 MORPETH ST	NEWCASTLE				SEPTEMBER 16.		TO 85th TRAINING RESERVE BN, CLASS Z RESERVE.	2 GHOSP 5/7/16 HOSP SHIP EGYPT AGE 20, ACSGT.
MECHEN	J	LCPL	27	/493	C								TO ROYAL DEFENCE CORPS.	FRANCE 11/1/16 TO 7/5/17.
MEEK	C H J	PTE	27	/513	D	ESTHER PIT COTTAGES	BURNHOPEFIELD			12 APRIL 1918	AUGUST 16.	PLOEGSTEERT MEM	TO 25th, 1/4th BNS(ATTACHED 149 TRENCH MORTAR BTY)	NEW NUMBER 204612, BORN DRYBROOK GLOUCS, AGE 36.
MELIA	M	CQMS	27	/1386	C		JARROW				MAY 17, 19 OCT 17.		COMMISSION NORTHUMBERLAND FUSILIERS, TO 26th BN.	CSM
MELLON	J	PTE	27	/1133	C		WHITLEY BAY				SEPTEMBER 16.			2 GHOSP 4/7 EVAC 5/7,BATH HOSP 11/7/16,WND RTHIGH.
MENHAM	J	CSM	27	/1467	D								FROM 9th BN(C COY).	ENL 1886,SERVED,NWFRONTIER,SOUDAN,SAFRICA.NF No 17
MERRINGTON	D	PTE	27	/488	B		HETTON LE HOLE				AUGUST 16, DECEMBER 17.			
METCALFE	M	PTE		/572	D 27		HOUGHTON LE SPR				MARCH 16, JULY 16			
METCALFE	R	PTE	27	/487	B		FENCEHOUSES				NOVEMBER 16			
MIDDLETON	Thos	PTE	27	/483	B		HETTON			9 APRIL 1917	OCTOBER 16	ROCLINCOURT VALLEY CEM	TO 24th BN.	BORN WAKEFIELD.
MILBURN	John	CPL	27	/1356			GATESHEAD				AUGUST 16.		TO 23rd BN, DURHAM LI(15th BN), CLASS Z RESERVE.	DLI No 46559.
MILES	J W	PTE	27	/1127	A		NEWCASTLE	5/12/14	18/8/17	GUNSHOT WOUNDS	OCTOBER 16.		TO 3rd BN.	
MILLER		CPL	27	/503	B 30									
MILLER	Adolp	PTE	27	/500	C		SUNDERLAND			1 JULY 1916		THIEPVAL MEM		MISSING OCTOBER 16.
MILLER	R	PTE	27	/1125	A		SEAHAM				SEPTEMBER 16.			
MILLER	Sam	PTE	27	/502	A	21 PARMETER ST	SOUTHMOOR	11/1/15	21/2/19	KR para 392	SEPTEMBER 16.		TO 3rd BN, ARMY RESERVE CLASS P.	34 CCS 2/7/16 EVAC 5/7/16.
MILLS	JohnE	PTE	27	/1138	D	23 ROBINSON TERR HEN	SUNDERLAND			29 MAY 1917	SEPTEMBER SSHOCK DEC 16.	ETAPLES.	TO 1st BN.	34CCS 2/7/16 EVAC 5/7/16 WND KNEE+WRIST
MILLS	Jos	PTE	27	/1141	D	23 ROBINSON TERR HEN	SUNDERLAND				JULY 16.			
MILLS	Thos	PTE	27	/1120			NEWCASTLE	8/1/15						DRILLER DESERTED 8/1/15 AGE 19, 5'4''.
MILNE	Geo N	PTE	27	/1136	C	4 WALLIS ST	SOUTH SHIELDS	14/1/15						
MITCHINSON	J	CPL	27	/479	B		NEWCASTLE				MARCH 17.		TO LABOUR CORPS.	SGT. LAB CORPS No 401692.
MONKHOUSE	Naylr	PTE	27	/506	D		GATESHEAD	22/12/14						LABOURER, DEST 24/5/15 AGE 27, 5'7'',AWOL 15/9 CRT
MONOGHAN	Jas	PTE	27	/525	D	81 SOUTHEY ST	GATESHEAD	14/12/14	28/8/18	GUNSHOT WOUNDS	OCTOBER 16		TO DEPOT.	
MONTGOMERY	Sam	PTE	27	/1144	A	22 BK WESLEY TERR	HIGH FELLING	4/1/15	19/2/19	KR para 392	SEPTEMBER 16.		TO 8th, 12/13th BNS, DEPOT.	21 AMBTR 6/7 18 GHOSP,6 CONV DEPOT 7/7/16 SSHOCK,
MOONEY	M	PTE	27	/496	C		SUNDERLAND				MARCH 17.			
MOORE	Fred	PTE	27	/484	A	34 CLYDE ST	SUNDERLAND	12/1/15						
MORGAN	Frank	PTE	27	/1421	C	DIXONS BLDGS	CATCHGATE			25 APRIL 1917		ARRAS MEM		
MORLEY	Pat	PTE	27	/1130			CHARLESTOWN Co	23/12/14						MINER DESERTED 23/12/14 AGE 26, 5'9''.
MORRIS	John	PTE	27	/1128	A	27 WEST ST	ESH COLLIERY				SEPTEMBER 16.		TO 10th BN, CLASS Z RESERVE.	34CCS 2/7 EVAC 5/7/16 WND L LEG AGE 24.
MOSELEY	J	PTE	27	/514	D		NEWCASTLE				OCTOBER 16.		TO 21st, 14th BNS, CLASS Z RESERVE.	34 CCS 2/7/16 EVAC 5/7/16 WND FACE & WRIST AGE 42.
MULKERN	Mich	PTE	27	/476	C	38 ALEXANDER ST	NEWCASTLE	7/1/15						
MULLEN	Felix	PTE	27	/1122	A	264 RAILWAY ST	LEADGATE	14/1/15			SEPTEMBER 16.		TO ROYAL DEFENCE CORPS.	3CCS 2/7 EVAC 2/7/16 GSW, FRANCE 11/1/16 TO 5/7/16
MULLIGAN	JohnJ	PTE	27											AWOL 25/8/15 COURT GATESHEAD AGE 26.
MUNRO	M	PTE	27	/499	C		JARROW			KR para 392	SEPTEMBER 16			34 CCS 1/7/16 EVAC 5/7/16 WND R FOOT, AGE 34.
MURPHY	Hugh	PTE	27	/474		27 EMBLETON ST	DAWDON COLLIERY	2/1/15	18/2/18	MALARIA			TO 2nd GARRISON BN, 3rd BN.	
MURPHY	J	PTE	27	/495	C						MARCH 16.			
MURPHY	Jn Jo	PTE	27	/508	A 24		MIDDLESBOROUGH			29 SEPT 1916	SEPTEMBER 16	NORTH ORMSBY	TO 24th BN.	
MURPHY	John	PTE	27	/480		1 STAITHES LANE	MORPETH			15 JUNE 1917		ARRAS MEM	TO 14th BN.	AGE 38, BORN LIMERICK.
MURPHY	John	PTE	27	/510	D		MORPETH				SEPTEMBER 16.		TO LABOUR CORPS.	LAB CORPS No 219621.
MURPHY	P	LCPL	27	/1121	A		WORKINGTON				OCTOBER 16.			
MURPHY	Pat	PTE	27	/509	D	12 MORTIMOR ST	BLACKHILL						TO EAST YORKS(3rd BN).	E YORKS No 39227.
MURRAY	A C	PTE	27	/504	D									
MURRAY	J	PTE	27	/522	A									
MURRAY	J J	PTE	27	/517	C									
MURRAY	Jn Wm	PTE	27	/1145	B	38 PRINCESS ST	CONSETT	7/1/15		4 DEC 1917	OCTOBER 16. DECEMBER 17.	MENDINGHEM CEM	TO 8th, 16th BNS.	
MURRAY	JohnT	PTE	27	/477				4/1/15	8/9/17	ACCIDENT			TO 3rd BN.	AGE 44.
MURRAY	M	PTE	27	/511	B									
MURRAY	Pat	PTE	27	/485	B		WORKINGTON			22 JUNE 1917		STANLEY NEW CEM Co DURHAM	TO 85th TRAINING RESERVE BN.	DIED HOME.

NAME	INITI	RANK	BA	NUMBE	COMP	ADDRESS	TOWN_VILL	ENLISTED	DISCHARG	CAUSE_DIS	WOUNDED	BURIED	TRANSFER	ADD
MURRAY	Peter	PTE	27	/1146	D	12 FRONT ST	USWORTH						TO 24/27th, 8th BNS, CLASS Z RESERVE.	
MURRAY	Robt	PTE	27	/520	A		NEWCASTLE		24/4/19		AUGUST 16.		TO KINGS OWN YORKSHIRE LI, CLASS Z RESERVE.	FRANCE 26/8/15, 3CCS 2/7/16 EVAC 3/7/16.KOYLI No 3
MURRAY	T	PTE	27	/516				26/12/14	29/1/16	KR para 392			TO 1st GARRISON BN, DEPOT.	
MURRAY	Thos	PTE	27	/1494	D	GLENREE	BALLINA Co MAYO			1 JULY 1916		THIEPVAL MEM		LCPL.
McADAM	Geo	PTE	27	/1093		311 SUNDERLAND RD	GATESHEAD	29/12/14	20/12/17	GUNSHOT WOUNDS	SEPTEMBER 16.		TO DEPOT.	
McADAM	Geo	PTE	27	/1099			GATESHEAD	4/1/15						LABOURER DESERTED 29/5/15 AGE 19, 5'8''.
McAVOY	S	PTE	27	/454	B	42 WYNDHAM ST	CLEATOR MOOR	21/12/14	1/8/17	GUNSHOT WOUNDS	OCTOBER 16		TO 3rd BN.	
McBEATH	AlbtH	PTE	27											AWOL 26/5/15 COURT SUNDERLAND.
McCABE	J	PTE	27	/435	D									
McCABE	John	PTE	27	/465	A	48 DERWENT ST	BLACKHILL	26/12/14	11/3/19	KR para 392	SEPTEMBER 16		TO 1st BN, ARMY RESERVE CLASS P.	
McCANN	Bennt	SGT	27	/1104	C	18 MORTIMER ST	BLACKHILL				OCTOBER 16.		TO CLASS Z RESERVE.	34CCS 2/7 EVAC 5/7 HOSP BIRMINGHAM, AGE 20.
McCARTHY	M	PTE	27	/467	D		NEWCASTLE	28/12/14	29/6/17	SICK	MAY 17.		TO 3rd BN.	
McCARTNEY	Edw	SGT	27	/1096	A	30 DOCTOR ST	SEAHAM	7/1/15			OCTOBER 16			SEE ALSO 25/494.
McCLUSKEY	R	PTE	27	/464	D									
McCLUSKEY	T	PTE	27	/471	A									
McCOMBE	Thos	PTE	27	/439	B	6 LADYSMITH TERR	WHITEHAVEN			1 JULY 1916		BAPAUME POST		
McCONNELL	Jas	PTE	27	/459		57 WALTER ST	JARROW					JARROW		DID NOT SERVE OVERSEAS, AGE 27.
McCOURT	B	PTE	27	/457									TO 1st GARRISON BN, CLASS Z RESERVE.	
McCOURT	Mich	PTE	27	/437	A	31 VICTORIA COURT	CONSETT	7/1/15		1 JULY 1916		THIEPVAL MEM		MISSING OCTOBER 16.
McCRANN	E	PTE	27	/1113	B					KR para 392			TO 14th BN.	
McCRUM	Geo	PTE	27	/449	C	35 JOHN ST	SOUTHMOOR	14/1/15			SEPTEMBER 16		TO 1st BN, CLASS Z RESERVE.	
McDERMOTT	Pat	PTE	27	/443	B		FENCEHOUSES			1 JULY 1916		THIEPVAL MEM		MISSING OCTOBER 16.
McDERMOTT	W	PTE	27	/448				9/1/15	4/4/16	SICK			TO 30th BN.	DID NOT SERVE OVERSEAS.
McDONALD	J S	PTE	27	/1098	B	23 WESLEY LANE	FELLING	7/1/15	1/4/19	KR para 392	AUGUST 16, AUGUST 18.		TO 23rd BN, ARMY RESERVE CLASS P.	
McDOWALL	Jas	PTE	27	/1117	B		ANNALONG Co DOW			28 APRIL 1917	OCTOBER 16	ARRAS MEM	TO 14th, 24th, 27th BNS.	34 CCS 2/7/16 EVAC 5/7/16 NECK WND.
McDOWELL	David	PTE	27	/461	B		WEST RAINTON					HEILLY STATION CEM		
McDOWELL	Jas	PTE	27	/1119	B	52 BOWTHORN RD	CLEATOR MOOR			1 JULY 1916		THIEPVAL MEM		BORN GARGENCY Co DOWN, MISSING OCTOBER 16.
McELEAVEY	Wm	PTE	27	/473	D	48 LOW ALBION STREET	WITTON PARK	7/1/15		12 FEB 1916		Y FARM CEM BOIS GRENIER		AGE 42, BORN BISHOP AUKLAND.
McGARRY	Jas	PTE	27											AWOL 24/5/15 COURT NEWCASTLE 31/5/15
McGARRY	P	PTE	27	/436									TO 2nd GARRISON BN, CLASS Z RESERVE.	
McGEE	J P	LSGT	27	/468	A	7 GLADSTONE ST	USWORTH COLLIER						TO 2nd, 12/13th BN, CLASS Z RESERVE.	ALSO ON A COY 30th BN ROLL.
McGEE	Mich	PTE	27	/1091	A	31 EDITH AVENUE	USWORTH							
McGEE	P	PTE	27	/1519		38 STAPLE ROAD	JARROW	13/7/15	15/11/15	INNEFFICIENT			TO 30th BN.	DID NOT SERVE OVERSEAS, AGE 24.
McGEE	Peter	PTE	27	/1092		31 EDITH AVENUE	USWORTH	28/12/14	20/10/15	SICK			TO 29th BN.	DID NOT SERVE OVERSEAS.
McGINN	Owen	PTE	27	/1432	A	7 ARGYLE PLACE	NEWCASTLE				AUGUST 16.			AWOL 14/8/15 IN COURT 23/8/15.
McGOUGH	Arth	PTE	27	/1109	D	5 CONSETT TERR	CONSETT			1 JULY 1916		THIEPVAL MEM		BORN BLACKHILL, MISSING OCTOBER 16.
McGOUGH	Wm	PTE	27	/1111	C	64 CALIFORNIA ST	SEAHAM	10/1/15	31/3/19	KR para 392	SEPTEMBER 16, JUNE 18.		TO 12th, 19th, 25th BNS, ARMY RESERVE CLASS P.	
McGREGOR	Ed S	PTE	27	/450	C		NEWCASTLE					VENDEGNES MIL CEM	TO 2nd, 12/13th BNS.	
McGURK	A	PTE	27	/446	B		HAZELRIGG	9/1/15	1/4/19	KR para 392	AUGUST 16		TO 8th, 16th, 1/5th BNS, ARMY RESERVE CLASS P.	
McHENRY	Wm	LCPL	27	/1094	B		WORKINGTON			1 JULY 1916		BAPAUME POST CEM		LSGT.
McHUGH	Thos	LCPL	27	/442	B		TYNE DOCK			1 JULY 1916		THIEPVAL MEM		BORN SOUTH SHIELDS, MISSING OCTOBER 16.
McKEATING	W	PTE	27	/1112	B			11/1/15	5/10/17	KR para 392	1 JULY 16.		TO 80th TRAINING RESERVE BN.	34CCS 2/7/16 EVAC 5/7/16 WND R ELBOW, AGE 21.
McKENNA	Geo	LCPL	27	/1101	B		MIDDLESBOROUGH			4 SEPT 1916	SEPTEMBER 16.	THIEPVAL MEM		ACPL REPORTED NOT WOUNDED DECEMBER 16 GAZETTE.
McKENNA	T	CQMS		/1445	D 27									No ALLOTTED TO LEONARD.
McKEOWN	John	PTE	27	/444	B	89 CROMWELL RD	BILLQUAY							
McKEOWN	Wm	PTE	27	/458	B		BYKER			1 JULY 1916		THIEPVAL MEM		DESERTED 21/6 CT 13/8/15, AWOL 9/10 CT 11/11/15
McKINLEY	H	PTE	27	/472	D	5 ROSE ST	PENSHAW							
McLAIN	N	PTE	27	/1090	B		BURNHOPEFIELD	28/12/14	15/9/17	GUNSHOT WOUNDS	OCTOBER 16.		TO 3rd BN.	
McMANN	Ross	PTE	27	/1105	C	19 BARCLAY ST MONKWR	SUNDERLAND	14/1/15						
McMENZIE	JohnF	PTE	27	/1439	D	16 CHARLES ST	DINNINGTON				AUGUST 16.		TO 20th, 25th, 9th, 1st BNS, CLASS Z RESERVE.	
McMULLEN	A	PTE	27	/1116	B	101 BOWTHORN RD	CLEATOR MOOR				JULY 16.			
McNAIN	E	PTE	27	/445				9/1/15	15/11/15				TO 30th BN.	DID NOT SERVE OVERSEAS.
McNALLY	J	PTE	27	/462	BV									
McNALLY	John	LCPL	27	/469	B	33 BUTTES RD	CLEATOR MOOR	14/1/15		9 SEPT 1916		THIEPVAL MEM		SGT BORN KILLINGWORTH NTHBLD.
McNALLY	P	PTE	27	/1469	B			6/6/15	17/5/16					
McNALLY	Wm	SGT	27	/438	D	6 DIXON ST	BLACKHILL	4/1/15	12/4/18	SYNOVITIS			TO ARMY RESERVE CLASS P.	
McNANEY	W	PTE	27	/1095	A					22 DEC 1916		HARTON ST PETERS	TO 30th BN.	
McNEICE	F J	RSM	27	/1367	B								COMMISSION IN NORTHBLD FUS(Lt+QM 19th BN 2nd TYNES WITH 19th BN FROM 24/8/17.	
McNIEL	Sim G	PTE	27	/451	C	11 COUNCIL HOUSES CA	ANNFIELD PLAIN	14/1/15			AUGUST 16.		TO 14th, 10th BNS, CLASS Z RESERVE.	LCPL.
McNINLEY	J	PTE	27	/1110	D			9/1/15	12/8/16	FLATFEET			TO DEPOT.	

NAME	INITI	RANK	BA	NUMBE	COMP	ADDRESS	TOWN_VILL	ENLISTED	DISCHARG	CAUSE_DIS	WOUNDED	BURIED	TRANSFER	ADD
McNULTY	Chas	PTE	27	/1097	B		GATESHEAD			4 SEPT 1916	SEPTEMBER 16.	ADANAC MIL CEM		BORN NEWCASTLE.
McPARLIN	J	PTE	27	/1115	C		GATESHEAD	29/12/14	13/10/18	KR para 392	JANUARY 17.			
McQUEEN	G	LCPL	27	/431	A									
McQUILLAN	Rich	LCPL	27	/1107	D	23 HARDWICK ST	SUNDERLAND			1 JULY 1916		THIEPVAL MEM		MISSING OCTOBER 16.
McQUILLAN	S	PTE	27	/456	C									
McSTRAW	Geo H	CPL	27	/1118	B	180 BOWTHORN RD	CLEATOR MOOR			15 FEB 1916		BAILLEUL MIL CEM		LSGT, BORN CLEATOR MOOR.
McSWEENEY	P	SGT	27	/1103	C									
McWILLIAMS	P	PTE	27	/1108	D	31 LAVERY ST	BILLQUAY	9/1/15	12/4/18	WOUNDS	AUGUST 16.		TO 21st, 10th, 3rd BNS.	
NAISBETT	John	PTE	27	/1148	A	17 BOWLBY ST	HOUGHTON			1 JULY 1916		THIEPVAL MEM		SEE ALSO 27/535 PTE Joseph.
NAISBETT	Jos	PTE	27	/535	C	17 BOWLBY ST	HOUGHTON LE SPR			1 JULY 1916		THIEPVAL MEM		SEE ALSO 27/1148.
NAREY	James	PTE	27	/542		20 FAIRLESS ST	NEWCASTLE						TO 1st GARRISON BN, CLASS Z RESERVE.	
NATHAN	Dan	PTE	27	/1153			BURNLEY	2/1/15						RIVETTER DESERTED 2/1/15 AGE 19, 5'4''.
NAVIN	John	PTE	27	/1476	B	MINERS HOMES	HALTWHISTLE			4 JULY 1916		ETAPLES		34 CCS 2/7/16 EVAC 4/7/16 WND L LEG.
NEAL	Corn	PTE	27	/529	A	39 DOUGLAS TERR	USWORTH	7/1/15						NAME COULD BE SPELT 'NEIL'
NELSON	Benj	LCPL	27	/1151	C	310 SOUTH ELDON ST	SOUTH SHIELDS			11 MAY 1916		BECOURT MIL CEM		ACPL, AGE 20.
NEWCOMBE	E	PTE	27	/534	C 30		NEWCASTLE				NOVEMBER 16		ATTACHED 7th MANCHESTERS, TO 25th, 1/5th BNS, CLAS	ALLOTED NEW NUMBER 243175.
NEWCOMBE	H	PTE	27	/544	B	6 SIMPSONS BLDGS	OLD SHILDON	23/12/14	11/1/17	SICK	AUGUST 16.		TO 85th TRAINING RESERVE BN.	
NEWTON	J	SGT	27	/541	D 30									
NEWTON	J	PTE	27	/1389	D						APRIL 16.			
NEWTON	J T	PTE	27	/531	B		ASHINGTON				MARCH 17		TO 24/27th, 19th(W COY) BNS, CLASS Z RESERVE.	
NICHOLSON	J E	PTE	27	/526	C		GATESHEAD	2/1/15	4/10/16	WOUNDS	OCTOBER 16.		TO DEPOT.	
NICHOLSON	John	PTE	27	/546	D		SCOTLANDGATE			12 MAY 1917	AUGUST 16.	ARRAS MEM	TO 9th BN.	
NICHOLSON	JohnJ	PTE	27	/533	B	52 BRUSSELS ST	GATESHEAD				JANUARY 17.		TO 1/4th BN.	NICHOLSON E W 43664 4th BEDFORDS AVL 1918.
NICHOLSON	Wm	PTE	27	/1154	D	1 KEMPS BLDGS FRONT	HASWELL	7/1/15					TO 1st GARRISON BN, 21st, 1st BNS, CLASS Z RESERVE	
NOLAN	J C	PTE	27	/545	B					KR para 392				
NOLAN	J E	PTE	27	/527	A									
NOLAN	J E	PTE	27	/528	A		BIRTLEY			KR para 392	JULY 16.			
NOLAN	John	PTE	27	/538		5 BEACON RD	NEWTON ON THE M			3 MAY 1917		ARRAS MEM	TO 16th, 1st BNS.	BORN QUBEC Co DURHAM, AGE 30.
NOLAN	Mart	PTE	27	/1147	A		BIRTLEY	30/12/14	28/2/18	GUNSHOT WOUNDS	SEPTEMBER 16.		TO ARMY RESERVE CLASS P.	3 CCS 2/7/16 EVAC 2/7/16 GSW
NORMAN	Augst	PTE	27	/1152	C	STANLEY HOUSE	HORDEN COLLIERY			27 FEB 1916		RATION FARM CEM		BORN WEST STANLEY.
NORMAN	Horce	PTE	27	/530	A	11 WOODFIELD ROW	CROOK						TO 10th BN, CLASS Z RESERVE.	
NORWOOD	Mel O	PTE	27	/536	C	78 GILESGATE	DURHAM CITY			28 APRIL 1917	JANUARY 17.	BROWNS COPSE CEM	TO 11th, 27th BNS.	LCPL.
NORWOOD	T	PTE	27	/537	C	78 GILESGATE	DURHAM CITY				AUGUST 16			3rd NORTHERN GEN HOSP SHEFFIELD 10/7/16.
NURSE	JohnJ	PTE	27	/540	D		HEBBURN			10 SEPT 1917	JUNE 16.	HARGICOURT MIL CEM.	TO 27th, 21st, 24th, 21st BNS.	BORN JARROW, AGE 43 16 GLEN ST HEBBURN NEWTOWN.
O'BRIEN	P	PTE	27	/554	C	SEWAGE WORKS STH CHU	BISHOP AUKLAND			KR para 392	OCTOBER 16.		TO 85th TRAINING RESERVE BN.	ASGT.
O'BRIEN	R	PTE	27	/561				22/12/14	15/11/15	RHEUMATISM			TO 30th BN.	DID NOT SERVE OVERSEAS.
O'CONNELL	D	SGT	27	/551	B		CONSETT	12/1/15	10/4/17	WOUNDS	OCTOBER 16.		TO DEPOT.	
O'CONNER	F	PTE	27	/556	C			28/12/14	27/7/18	SICK			TO 30th BN.	DID NOT SERVE OVERSEAS, ALSO ON D COY 30th BN ROLL
O'CONNER	P	PTE	27	/557	D	87 DYSON TERR	NEW SEAHAM							
O'CONNOR	Thos	PTE	27	/1156	A	6 HESLOP ST SOUTH CH	BISHOP AUKLAND			13 MAY 1916		BECOURT MIL CEM		CPL, AGE 35.
O'HAGAN	P	PTE	27	/550	A			9/1/15	5/3/19	KR para 392			TO 18th, 24/27th BNS, ARMY RESERVE CLASS P.	SGT.
O'HARA	John	CPL	27	/1162	D	68 ELSWICK ST	GATESHEAD				SEPTEMBER 16.		TO LABOUR CORPS.	BORN ACLARE.
O'NEAL	Roger	PTE	27	/1161	D		FENCEHOUSES			15 APRIL 1918	MISS OCT 16, JUNE 18.	MENDINGHEM CEM	TO 26th, 18th BNS.	BORN DUBMIRE HETTON LE HOLE,WND NOT MISS DEC 16
O'NIELL	Mich	PTE	27	/1160	A	59 BERKS RD	CLEATOR MOOR	14/1/15		KR para 392	SEPTEMBER 16.			LCPL.
O'NIELL	Rich	PTE	27											AWOL 20/98/15 COURT GATESHEAD AGE 44.
O'NIELL	Rodck	PTE	27	/1155	A		FENCEHOUSES				OCTOBER 16.		TO LABOUR CORPS.	
O'NIELL	Thos	PTE	27	/1158	A		GATESHEAD				JANUARY 1917		TO 24/27th BN,ATT 8th ENTRENCHING BN, 25th, 9th, 8	CPL CLASS Z RESERVE.
O'RIELLY	Hugh	PTE	27	/555	C	BREWERY LANE	FELLING			1 JULY 1916		BECOURT MIL CEM		BORN BYKER, AGE 38.
OLIVER	Thos	PTE	27	/552	A	9 SLATERS HOUSES	WHITE LE HEAD	8/1/15			AUGUST 18.		TO 25th BN.	LCPL.
ORMSTON	Thos	CPL	27	/553	B	5 GRENVILLE TERR	NEWCASTLE	7/1/15			OCTOBER 16		TO CLASS Z RESERVE.	SGT, IN COY FOOTBALL TEAM.
ORR	J C	PTE	27	/560	C	21 RIVER ST	SOUTH SHIELDS				SEPTEMBER 16.		TO MACHINE GUN CORPS.	3rd SCOTTISH G HOSP GLASGOW 11/7/16
OSWALD	J	PTE	27	/1528	C 24	3 NORTH VIEW	LINTZ COLLIERY	26/7/15	13/11/18	GUNSHOT WOUNDS	JULY 16.		TO 24th, 22nd BNS, DEPOT.	
OSWALD	R	SGT	27	/558	D	6 RAILWAY VIEW	WASHINGTON STAT	2/1/15	1/3/17	WOUNDS	JULY 16.		TO DEPOT.	34 CCS 2/7/16 EVAC 5/7/16 GSW BACK.
OWENS	Frncs	PTE	27	/548	A	21 DALE ST	BLACKHILL	12/1/15		KR para 392				
OWENS	Peter	PTE	27	/549	A	82 ALICE ST	SOUTH SHIELDS	14/1/15		KR para 392	OCTOBER 16		TO 20th BN.	
OXLEY	Jas	PTE	27	/559	A	61 CHURCH ST	BOLDON COLLIERY			1 JULY 1916		THIEPVAL MEM		BORN PITTINGTON.
PALMER	E	PTE	27	/575	B			9/1/15	18/9/16	FRACTURES				
PALMER	J	PTE	27	/574				9/1/15	15/11/17				TO DEPOT.	
PARKER	Jos	PTE	27	/587	D	47 BEAUFORT ST	GATESHEAD	14/12/14	5/3/19	KR para 392			TO 24/27th, 23rd BNS, ARMY RESERVE CLASS P.	
PARKIN	F	PTE	27	/582	D	7 BELLA ST TEAMS	GATESHEAD				SEPTEMBER 16.		TO 25th, 1/4th BNS, CLASS Z RESERVE.	ALLOTED NEW NUMBER 204604.

NAME	INITI	RANK	BA	NUMBE	COMP	ADDRESS	TOWN_VILL	ENLISTED	DISCHARG	CAUSE_DIS	WOUNDED	BURIED	TRANSFER	ADD
PARKIN	Robt	LCPL	27	/572	B	27 SWAN ST	BEARPARK COLLIE	8/1/15	10/5/18	MYALGIA	OCTOBER 16		TO ARMY RESERVE CLASS W.	
PARKS	J	PTE	27	/583	D	32 2nd ROW SWINBURNE	SEAHAM						TO ROYAL DEFENCE CORPS.	IN FRANCE 11/1/16 TO 30/12/17.
PARR	H	PTE	27	/1173	C	12 DOUGLAS TERR	USWORTH						TO CLASS Z RESERVE.	PRISONER OF WAR MARCH 1917.
PATRICKSON	R	PTE	27	/1166	A		HETTON LE HOLE				JUNE 16, SEPT 16, MAR 17.		TO CLASS Z RESERVE.	34 CCS 2/7/16 EVAC 5/7/16 WND ARM+LEG AGE 19.
PATTERSON	F	PTE	27	/571	B									
PATTERSON	Jn Ts	PTE	27	/576	C	51 CONSTANCE ST	CONSETT	12/1/15		3 SEPT 1916		THIEPVAL MEM		WIFE LIVING 7 CHURCH ST LEADGATE.
PATTERSON	Wm Hy	PTE	27	/580	C	3 PROVIDENCE PLACE G	DURHAM CITY			24 MAY 1917		ARRAS MEM		BORN SHERBURN HOUSE DURHAM.SEE 25/1217 SAME ADDRES
PATTON	T	LCPL	27	/584	D	1 HALL ST	SOUTH HETTON				JANUARY 17, AUGUST 18.		TO 12th, 24/27th BNS, CLASS Z RESERVE.	SGT.
PEACOCK	J	PTE	27	/577	C	12 MARSHALL WALLIS R	SOUTH SHIELDS	9/1/15	30/10/17	WOUNDS			TO 3rd BN.	
PEARSON	Jn F	PTE	27	/565	A	6 FINCHALE TERR HEND	SUNDERLAND			1 JULY 1916	SEPTEMBER 16	THIEPVAL MEM		MISSING DECEMBER 16.
PEARSON	John	PTE	27	/1176	C	9 BLUE QUARRIES RD	GATESHEAD						TO 12/13th BN, CLASS Z RESERVE.	ALSO ON C COY 30th BN ROLL AS /1170.
PEARSON	N	PTE	27	/578	C		SUNDERLAND	10/1/15	22/5/18	GUNSHOT WOUNDS	FEBRUARY 18.		TO 24/27th BN, DEPOT.	
PEARSON	T	PTE	27	/1164	A	5 GILES PLACE	HEXAM						TO 8th BN, CLASS Z RESERVE.	
PEARSON	Wm	PTE	27	/573				9/1/15	29/1/16	SICK			TO 30th BN.	DID NOT SERVE OVERSEAS.
PEASE	C	PTE	27	/1175	D								TO 24/27th BN, CLASS Z RESERVE.	ON B COY 30th BN ROLL AS PEARSON.
PENMAN	Thos	PTE	27	/1171	C	21 CLEVELAND ST	SOUTH SHIELDS			13 SEPT 1917		HARGICOURT BRIT CEM	TO MACHINE GUN CORPS(103 MG COY).	MGC No 71034, AGE 22.
PENTLAND	Jos	PTE	27	/1167	B	9 EDWARD ST	BLAYDON			1 JULY 1916		GORDON DUMP CEM		BORN SWALWELL.
PESCODD	N S	PTE	27	/581	D	4 VANE TERR	SUNDERLAND	27/12/14	9/5/17	WOUNDS	OCT 16		TO DEPOT.	SHOWN LIVING BLAYDON IN GAZ.
PHILIPS	Thos	PTE	27	/585	D	17 WILLIAM ST	CONSETT				AUGUST 16.		TO LABOUR CORPS.	FRACTURE L KNEE, AGE 36, LABOUR CORPS No 436993.
PICKEN	Fred	PTE	27	/1178	A	35 HAMILTON ROW	WATERHOUSES	7/1/15		7 OCT 1918	SEPTEMBER 16.	ST MARIE CEM LE HAVRE	TO ROYAL INNISKILLING FUSILIERS(6th BN).RIF No 215	34 CCS 2/7 EVAC 5/7, 2nd BRISTOL 11/7/16, AGE 22
PIGGFORD	Edw	PTE	27	/568		1 SUNDERLAND ST	BRANDON COLLIER						TO 1st GARRISON BN, CLASS Z RESERVE.	
PINCHEN	Jas	PTE	27	/569	B	6 CAMDEN ST	NEWCASTLE			KR para 392			TO 21st, 10th, 1/5th BNS.	
PLUSE	Thos	PTE	27	/1165	A	STAITHES HOUSES WATE	WASHINGTON			1 JULY 1916		THIEPVAL MEM		MISSING OCTOBER 16.
POLLARD	E	PTE	27	/566	A									POSIBLY BENJAMIN, 46 SPEN RD HIGH SPEN ???
POTTER	S	PTE	27	/1177	D		NEWCASTLE				JULY 16.			
POTTS	A A	PTE	27	/570	B	19 JOHN ST	SILKSWORTH				JULY 16		TO EAST YORKSHIRE REGT (10th & 8th BNS), 1/6th NF.	ALLOTTED NEW NUMBER 64957.
POWTON	Jos A	PTE	27	/1174		10 FRANCIS ST	CROOK						TO 2nd GARRISON BN, CLASS Z RESERVE.	
PRINCE	Jas	LCPL	27	/1179	A					3 AUGUST 1916	AUGUST 16.	READING BERKS		34 CCS 2/7/16 EVAC 5/7/16, HOSP READING 11/7/16.
PRINGLE	Geo W	PTE	27	/1169	B	13 SOUTH VIEW AUTON	DURHAM CITY			1 JULY 1916		THIEPVAL MEM		BORN ALDIN GRANGE DURHAM.
PRINGLE	H	PTE	27	/1180	C 24								TO 24th, 30th BNS.	ALSO ON D COY 30th BN ROLL.
PRINGLE	John	PTE	27	/579	A	27 ANN ST	EAST STANLEY	11/1/15	31/3/19		JULY 16.		TO ARMY RESERVE CLASS P.	34 JOICEY SQUARE STANLEY 1918.
PRINGLE	John	PTE	27	/588	C	7 SUSSEX ST	SUNDERLAND			11 MAY 1917	SEPTEMBER 16.	FABOURG DE AMIENS CEM ARRAS	TO 8th, 9th BNS.	3rd SCOTTISH GEN HOSP GLASGOW 11/7/16,AGE 34.
PRIOR	R	PTE	27	/1168	B		SOUTH SHIELDS	7/1/15	14/3/17	WOUNDS	SEPTEMBER 16.		TO DEPOT.	IN COY FOOTBALL TEAM.
PRITCHARD	Edw	LCPL	27	/563	A	61 MARSDEN ST	SOUTH SHIELDS	14/1/15					TO 24/27th BN, CLASS Z RESERVE.	
PULLEN	Wm	LCPL	27	/589	B		SOUTH SHIELDS			1 JULY 1916		THIEPVAL MEM		MISSING OCTOBER 16.
QUINN	C	PTE	27	/593				29/12/14	30/10/17	SICK			TO 1st GARRISON BN, DEPOT.	
QUINN	H	CPL	27	/591	B			4/1/15	4/4/16				TO 30th BN.	DID NOT SERVE OVERSEAS.
QUINN	H P	CPL	27	/594	D	4 UPPER MILL ST	GATESHEAD		31/3/19	KR para 392			TO MACHINE GUN CORPS(34th BN).	MGC No 151953. ACSGT.
QUINN	J	PTE	27	/592				28/12/14	15/9/16				TO 30th BN.	DID NOT SERVE OVERSEAS.
QUINN	Jas	PTE	27											AWOL 21/7/15 COURT NEWCASTLE 9/8/15
QUINN	M	PTE	27	/1183	B		WHITEHAVEN	11/1/15	16/2/18	GUNSHOT WOUNDS	SEPTEMBER 16.		TO DEPOT.	IN COY FOOTBALL TEAM.
QUINN	Turn	PTE	27	/1182	C	1 BUSH INN YARD	GATESHEAD	6/1/15	13/12/18	GUNSHOT WOUNDS	JUN,SEP,DEC16,DEC17,JAN18		TO 16th, DEPOT.	21 AMBTR 6/7 18 GHOSP C DEPOT 9/7/16 LCPL, AGE 23,
RAFFERTY	D	PTE	27	/626	D		BEDLINGTON			KR para 392	OCTOBER 16.		TO 1st BN.	34 CCS 8/7 EVAC 22 AMB TR 9/7/16 WND RTHIGH,AGE 39
RAFFERTY	John	PTE	27	/1212	B	TOWER HOUSE PILGRIM	NEWCASTLE	7/1/15			SEPTEMBER 16.		TO ROYAL DEFENCE CORPS.	FRANCE 11/1/16 TO 21/12/16, 2/3/17 TO 6/5/17.
RAINEY	John	LCPL	27	/617	C	49 NEW BRIDGE ST	NEWCASTLE	14/1/15						
RAMSHAW	James	PTE	27	/627	D	11 STANLEY TERR	SHINEY ROW			18 MARCH 1916		BREWERY ORCHARD CEM.		BORN SCOTSWOOD.
RAMSHAW	Jas	PTE	27	/1198	C		HOWDEN ON TYNE			1 JULY 1916		THIEPVAL MEM 1996		LCPL, BORN WILLINGTON QUAY, KIA AUGUST GAZ.
RATHBONE	Chas	PTE	27	/613	C	19 WILFRED ST PALLIO	SUNDERLAND			1 JULY 1916		THIEPVAL MEM		
RAYNE	John	SGT	27	/628	D		HOLYWOOD Co WIC			15 OCT 1917		BRANDHOEK MIL CEM	TO LABOUR CORPS(164 LAB COY).	LABOUR CORPS No 386442.
READY	J	PTE	27	/611				9/1/15	29/3/16				TO 30th BN.	DID NOT SERVE OVERSEAS.
REAH	T	PTE	27	/609	C								TO 2nd BN, ATTACHED 5th ENTRENCHING BN, CLASS Z RE	
REAVELY	Math	PTE	27	/1210	A	70 OFFICE ST	LITTLEBURN	7/1/15		4 OCT 1917	OCTOBER 16.	BARD COTTAGE CEM YPRES	TO 8th BN.	MACHINE GUN SECTION., HOSP EDMONTON 7/16.
REAY	J	PTE	27	/1206	D	JOICEY ST	SHERBURN HILL			KR para 392	JULY 16.			
REDMAN	W A	PTE	27	/603		24 NORTH PLANTATION	TRIMDON						TO 2nd GARRISON BN.	
REDPATH	E	PTE	27	/1185	C 24	69 TAYLOR ST	SOUTH SHIELDS	31/12/14	22/9/16	SICK 29/11/18		HARTON ST PETERS	TO 24th, 27th BNS, DEPOT.	AGE 23.
REGAN	J	PTE	27	/634	B		SOUTHWICK	29/12/14	12/12/17	WOUNDS	NOVEMBER 16, JANUARY 17.		TO DEPOT.	
REGAN	P	PTE	27	/629		1 WALKERS BLDGS	WASHINGTON						TO 1st GARRISON BN, CLASS Z RESERVE.	
REID	J J	PTE	27	/614	C									
RENFORTH	J	PTE	27	/623	D	89 WESLEY ST	SHIELDFIELD							
RENNIE	R W	PTE	27	/1397	B		NORTH SHIELDS				SEPTEMBER 16.		TO 23rd, 22nd BNS, CLASS Z RESERVE.	BATH WAR HOSP 11/7/16

NAME	INITI	RANK	BA	NUMBE	COMP	ADDRESS	TOWN_VILL	ENLISTED	DISCHARG	CAUSE_DIS	WOUNDED	BURIED	TRANSFER	ADD
RENTON	D	PTE	27	/1452	B		NEWCASTLE				SEPTEMBER 16.		TO 20th, 27th, 24/27th, 18th BNS, CLASS Z RESERVE.	IN COY FOOTBALL TEAM.
RENWICK	W	PTE	27	/621	B	20 BROUGH BLDGS	BYKER BANK							
REYNOLDS	A	PTE	27	/1204	D	33 PERCY ST	JARROW						TO 24/27th, 8th, 1/7th BNS, CLASS Z RESERVE.	
REYNOLDS	J	PTE	27	/624	D	TOWER HOUSE	NEWCASTLE	12/1/15			AUGUST 16.		TO ROYAL ENGINEERS.	34 CCS 2/7/16 EVAC 5/7/16, WND L FOOT, AGE 27.
REYNOLDS	J	PTE	27	/1213	D		NEWCASTLE				JULY 16.		TO LABOUR CORPS.	3 CCS 2/7/16 EVAC 2/7/16 GSW
RICHARDS	S	PPTE	27	/1203	D	73 JAMES ARMITAGE ST	SUNDERLAND				1 JULY 1916		TO 14th, 12/13th, 14th BNS, CLASS Z RESERVE.	345 CCS 1/7 EVAC 5/7/16 WND L ANKLE AGE 24
RICHARDS	Wm	PTE	27	/1208	A	32 FOURTH ST	SOUTHMOOR	8/1/15			JULY 16.		TO 24th, 9th BNS.	
RICHARDSON	F	PTE	27	/1191	B	278 SOUTH ELDON ST	SOUTH SHIELDS				JULY 16			
RICHARDSON	Geo W	PTE	27	/1192	B	21 JOHN ST	SOUTH SHIELDS		16/2/19		DECEMBER 16.		TO 1st, 16th, 1/6th BNS, K O YORKSHIRE LI(15th BN)	
RICHARDSON	J	PTE	27	/1200	C	5 ORMOND ST	SOUTH SHIELDS				SEPTEMBER 16.		TO 23rd, 19th(Z COY), CLASS Z RESERVE.	
RICHARDSON	John	PTE	27	/598	A		WILLINGTON QUAY			1 JULY 1916		THIEPVAL MEM		
RICHARDSON	M	PTE	27	/630	D	24 NORTH ST	SACRISTON				SEPTEMBER 16.		TO 24/27th, 11th BNS, ATTACHED 17 CORPS HQ, CLASS	
RICHARDSON	T	PTE	27	/622	D	20 CORNER HOUSE	WINLATON	22/12/14	28/7/17	GUNSHOT WOUNDS	MAY 16, JUNE 16.		TO 3rd BN.	
RICHARDSON	Thos	PTE	27	/1184	A	37 SECOND ST	HORDEN	7/1/15		1 JULY 1916		THIEPVAL MEM		LCPL
RIDDLE	D W	PTE	27	/633									TO 1st GARRISON BN, CLASS Z RESERVE.	
RIDDLE	W	PTE	27	/1190	B									
RIDLEY	T	LCPL	27	/610	D 30	1 DUNDAS ST	SUNDERLAND				JULY 16, SSHOCK DEC 16.			
RILEY	Arth	PTE	27	/1211	D		HEXAM			1 JULY 1916		THIEPVAL MEM		BORN RIPPONDEN YORKS. KIA AUGUST GAZ.
RILEY	H E	PTE	27	/619	B	BOWTHORN RD	CLEATOR MOOR	21/12/14	4/2/17	KR para 392	JANUARY 17.		TO DEPOT.	CPL.
ROACHE	J	ACPL	27	/636									TO 2nd GARRISON BN, CLASS Z RESERVE.	
ROBERTS	T	PTE	27	/620	C	47 ALDERSON ST	SOUTH SHIELDS			KR para 392	AUGUST 16.		TO 25th, 1/4th BNS.	ALLOTED NEW NUMBER 204599.
ROBERTSHAW	Robt	PTE	27	/625	B	62 RAVENSWORTH RD	DUNSTON						TO CLASS Z RESERVE.	CPL IN M/G SECTION.
ROBINSON	A	PTE	27	/1205	D	100 CORBRIDGE ST	BYKER	20/1/15						
ROBINSON	Edw	PTE	27	/1209	D	49 NEW BRIDGE ST	NEWCASTLE	7/1/15						AWOL 22/8/15 IN COURT 2/9/15.
ROBINSON	J	PTE	27	/612	C		NORTH SHIELDS	18/1/15	13/3/18	GUNSHOT WOUNDS	OCTOBER 16		TO ARMY RESERVE CLASS P.	
ROBINSON	J	LCPL	27	/1199				11/1/15	22/11/15	EPILEPSY			TO 30th BN.	DID NOT SERVE OVERSEAS.
ROBINSON	Jonas	PTE	27	/615	C	13 LUCY ST TOWNLEY	STANLEY	14/1/15		4 NOV 1918		LANDRECIES BRIT CEM	TO GLOUCESTERSHIRE REGT(1/5th BN).	MISSING OCTOBER 16,48 MARY ST WEST STANLEY 1914.
ROBINSON	M	PTE	27	/1197	C			11/1/15	28/8/17	SICK			TO 25th, 27th BNS, DEPOT.	
ROBINSON	R	PTE	27	/599	A			4/1/15	5/3/19	KR para 392			TO 24/27th, 9th BNS, ARMY RESERVE CLASS P.	
ROBINSON	W	PTE	27	/1196	B		SOUTH SHIELDS				OCTOBER 16.		TO ROYAL DEFENCE CORPS.	FRANCE 11/1/16 TO 9/7/16.
ROBINSON	W	PTE	27	/1454	D									
ROBINSON	Wm	PTE	27	/1410			FELLING			1 JULY 1916		THIEPVAL MEM		
ROBSON	A	SGT	27	/607	B									
ROBSON	G	SGT	27	/1193	C 30									
ROBSON	J W	PTE	27	/608	B									
ROBSON	James	LCPL	27	/601	A			6/1/15	27/8/16	SICK			TO 30th BN(A COY).	DID NOT SERVE OVERSEAS, AGE 32.
ROBSON	Jas H	LSGT	27	/631	C 30		TYNEMOUTH			24 AUGUST 1917		TYNE COT MEM	TO KINGS OWN YORKSHIRE LI(6th BN).	ON C COY 30th BN ROLL, KOYLI No 42977.
ROBSON	John	PTE	27	/597	A	49 PREST ST	GATESHEAD	7/1/15			SEPTEMBER 16		TO LABOUR CORPS.	LAB CORPS No 403518.
ROBSON	John	PTE	27	/605	B	51 PREST ST TEAMS	GATESHEAD				OCTOBER 16		TO 20th 18th, 14th BNS, CLASS Z RESERVE.	
RODGERS	John	PTE	27	/596	A	2 HILL TERR	MIDDLETON IN TE			1 JULY 1916		THIEPVAL MEM		BORN STARTFORTH YORKS.
RODGERS	P	PTE	27	/1195	C	6 BRAITHWAITES COURT	CLEATOR MOOR							
RODGERS	T	PTE	27	/602									TO 2nd GARRISON BN, CLASS Z RESERVE.	
ROONEY	J	PTE	27	/1188	D		SPENNYMOOR	29/12/14	7/11/18	SICK	SEPTEMBER 16.		TO 24th, 11th BNS, DEPOT.	
ROUELL	Tom W	CPL	27	/1186	A		BISHOP AUKLAND			1 JULY 1916		THIEPVAL MEM 1996		KIA AUGUST GAZ.
ROWELL	Frank	PTE	27	/1207	B	27 PARK TERR	SWALWELL	7/1/15		1 JULY 1916		THIEPVAL MEM		
ROWELL	Robt	PTE	27	/1202	B		KIBBLESWORTH				APRIL 18.			AWOL 31/7, 2/9/15 IN COURT GATESHEAD, AGE 35.
ROWNTREE	James	PTE	27	/618	C		NEWCASTLE			1 JULY 1916		THIEPVAL MEM		MISSING OCTOBER 16.
RUSSELL	Rob	PTE	27	/604	B	49 GROSVENOR ST	GATESHEAD							
RUTHEN	R	PTE	27	/600	C		WALKER				MARCH 16		TO 24/27th, 25th, 9th BNS, CLASS Z RESERVE.	
RUTTER	M	PTE	27	/1194	C								TO MACHINE GUN CORPS RE ENLISTED 1920.	
SAINT	Cuthb	PTE	27	/678	C	40 CHURCH WAY	NORTH SHIELDS			7 JAN 1918		BUCQUOY ROAD CEM	TO 24/27th BN.	AGE 42.
SAMS	Berti	PTE	27	/1234	C	2 GEORGE ST	BISHOP AUKLAND			23 SEPT 1917	AUGUST 16.	BAGRICOURT MIL CEM	TO 22nd BN.	
SANDERSON	W H	PTE	27	/697	B	WATERLOO	BLYTH				JULY 16			REPORTED IN HOME HOSP 7/16.
SAWYERS	J	PTE	27	/1242	D	2 CHURCH ST	BOLDON COLLIERY				AUGUST 16.			
SAYERS	Thos	LSGT	27	/660	B	115 JANET ST	NEWCASTLE	6/1/15	17/11/16	VDH			TO DEPOT.	
SCOLLEN	John	PTE	27	/663	B		SEAHAM			1 JULY 1916	APRIL 16	THIEPVAL MEM		BORN DENTON BURN, IN BATTALION BAND.
SCOTT	GeoWK	PTE	27	/1513	C 24		TYNEMOUTH			24 APRIL 1917		BROWNS COPSE CEM	TO 24th BN.	AGE 20.
SCOTT	J	LCPL	27	/662	B								TO 24/27th, 11th BNS, CLASS Z RESERVE.	
SCOTT	J B K	PTE	27	/655	B	11 YEOMAN ST	NORTH SHIELDS	8/1/15			SEPTEMBER 16.			
SCOTT	J G	CPL	27	/673	C									IN BATTALION BAND.

NAME	INITI	RANK	BA	NUMBE	COMP	ADDRESS	TOWN_VILL	ENLISTED	DISCHARG	CAUSE_DIS	WOUNDED	BURIED	TRANSFER	ADD
SCOTT	JohnW	PTE	27	/693	B	58 WOULDHAVE ST	SOUTH SHIELDS			7 JULY 1916		BOULOGNE.		BORN NORTH SHIELDS, MINER ST HILDA COLLIERY.
SCOTT	T	PTE	27	/1536	C 24			12/8/15	15/2/18	VDH			TO 24th BN, ARMY RESERVE CLASS W.	
SCOTT	T R	PTE	27	/1255				30/12/14	17/5/16	SICK			TO 30th BN.	DID NOT SERVE OVERSEAS.
SCOTT	W	PTE	27	/1560	B 24					KR para 392				
SELBY	Wm	PTE	27	/1342	A	OLD WHEATBOTTOM	CROOK				MARCH 17.		TO 1st, 27th BNS, CLASS Z RESERVE.	
SELLARS	J	PTE	27	/677	C		GATESHEAD	30/12/14	24/8/17	GUNSHOT WOUNDS	APRIL 16, OCTOBER 16.		TO 85th TRAINING RESERVE BN.	3 CCS 2/7/16 EVAC 2/7/16.
SEWELL	A	PTE	27	/698	B								TO 24/27th, 19th(Z COY) BNS, CLASS Z RESERVE.	
SEYMOUR	T W	SGT	27	/639	A	35 DALE ST	BLACKHILL	26/10/14	16/10/17	WOUNDS	JULY 16		TO DEPOT.	HOSP WARRINGTON 7/16 WND LEG,ARM,THIGH.
SHANE	L	PTE	27	/1220	B	100 CORBRIDGE ST	BYKER	20/7/15		1 JULY 1916		THIEPVAL MEM		MISSING OCTOBER 16.
SHARKEY	Denni	PTE	27	/646	A	43 BRADLEY SQUARE	LEADGATE	2/1/15	18/3/18				TO 30th BN(D COY), DEPOT.	DID NOT SERVE OVERSEAS.
SHAUGHNESSY	Eddy	PTE	27		D	HENRY STREET	SEAHAM							
SHAUGHNESSY	Lew	PTE	27		D	HENRY STREET	SEAHAM							
SHAUGHNESSY	Sam	LCPL	27		Sigs	HENRY STREET	SEAHAM							TRANSCIPT OF INTERVIEW STATES D COY 27th BN.
SHAW	A	PTE	27	/659	B	11 ABBEY ST SOUTHWIC	SUNDERLAND	6/1/15	3/4/18	SICK			TO ARMY RESERVE CLASS P.	
SHEPHERD	Wm Hy	PTE	27	/691	D							FAMPOUX MIL CEM		BORN BURNMUSTON YORKS,MINER ST HELENS COLLIERY B/A
SHUTTLEWORTH	Jas A	PTE	27	/1247	D	11 REED ST	NORTH SHIELDS			1 JULY 1916		THIEPVAL MEM		BORN TYNEMOUTH, MISSING OCTOBER 16.
SIDDLE	Rob	PTE	27	/638	A	8 ANNES TERR EASINGT	DUNSTON	8/1/15		27 APRIL 1918		TYNE COT MEM	TO 24/27th BN, ATTACHED 8th ENTRENCHING BN, 12/13t	BRICKLAYER DESERTED 21/5/15 AGE 29, 5'4''.
SIMOND	Alb	PTE	27	/1219	A		SOUTHWICK	8/1/15			SEPTEMBER 16.			
SIMONETTE	J C	PTE	27	/1533	C									
SIMONETTE	Jas E	PTE	27	/671		3 SCARBOROUGH RD BYK	NEWCASTLE	14/1/15					TO 2nd GARRISON BN, CLASS Z RESERVE.	
SIMONETTE	Jos	PTE	27	/670	C	295 WELBECK RD BYKE	NEWCASTLE	11/1/15	31/3/19	KR para 392	JANUARY 17.		TO 9th, 23rd, 1st BNS, ARMY RESERVE CLASS P.	
SIMONETTE	Thos	PTE	27	/669	C	48 BENSON RD BYKER	NEWCASTLE	14/1/15					TO ROYAL DEFENCE CORPS.	FRANCE 11/1/16 TO 26/5/17, AWOL 29/11 CT 4/12/15.
SIMPSON	Chas	CSM	27	/1360	A	17 MATAFAN ST	NEWCASTLE			1 JULY 1916		THIEPVAL MEM	FROM 1st BN.(MENTIONED IN DESPATCHES BOER WAR)	ENL 1886 SERVED CRETE,SOUDAN,NWFRONTIER,SAFRICA.
SIMPSON	Geo	PTE	27	/1236	C		WILLINGTON			1 JULY 1916		THIEPVAL MEM		LCPL BORN BISHOP AUKLAND, MISSING OCTOBER 16.
SIMPSON	J	PTE	27	/656	B									
SIMPSON	J	PTE	27	/1224	D		DURHAM CITY	5/1/15	13/3/18	GUNSHOT WOUNDS	JULY 16.		TO DEPOT.	
SIMPSON	Jas	PTE	27	/667	B	119 COMMERCIAL RD	SOUTH SHIELDS	11/1/15	10/2/19	GUNSHOT WOUNDS			TO 24/27th, 19th BNS, DEPOT.	AGE 26.
SIMPSON	R	PTE	27	/1227	C		SOUTH SHIELDS	6/1/15	16/5/18	SHELL WND 28/6/	MAY 18.	HARTON ST PETERS		
SIMPSON	T	PTE	27	/650	A			4/1/15	23/10/17	SICK			TO DEPOT.	
SIMPSON	W	PTE	27	/1215		10 WALKER ST TEAMS	GATESHEAD	4/1/15						MINER DESERTED AGE 22, 5'8'', BORN WINLATON.
SLATER	A	PTE	27	/1340	D									
SLATER	ThosS	PTE	27	/674	C	24 ERNEST PLACE GILE	DURHAM CITY	30/12/14	30/10/17	WOUNDS	JULY 16.		TO 3rd BN.	
SLOANE	W	PTE	27	/645	B		NEWCASTLE				JANUARY 17.			
SMAILES	Thos	PTE	27	/675	C		SOUTHMOOR				AUGUST 16			3rd NORTHERN GEN HOSP SHEFFIELD 8/7/16.
SMITH	Alf	PTE	27	/685	D	47 RAWLING RD	GATESHEAD			1 JULY 1916		THIEPVAL MEM		LCPL, MISSING OCTOBER 16, BORN BENSHAM.
SMITH	H	PTE	27	/686	A									
SMITH	H R	PTE	27	/1235	C	8 LOGAN ST	LANGLEY PARK	28/12/14	25/6/18	GUNSHOT WOUNDS				
SMITH	J	PTE	27	/695	A	69 CHURCH ST	SEAHAM				JULY 16.		TO 16th, 8th BNS, CLASS Z RESERVE.	REPORTED LIVING GATESHEAD WHEN WOUNDED 7/16.
SMITH	J	PTE	27	/1226									TO 24/27th, 19th(Z COY) BNS, CLASS Z RESERVE.	
SMITH	J	PTE	27	/1231	C								TO LABOUR CORPS.	
SMITH	J K	PTE	27	/644	D 30			2/1/15	18/2/18				TO 30th BN(D COY), DEPOT.	CPL, DID NOT SERVE OVERSEAS.
SMITH	Jos	PTE	27											AWOL 22/12/15 COURT SOUTH SHIELDS.
SMITH	M	PTE	27	/684	D			18/12/14	1/4/16	VDH			TO 30th BN.	
SMITH	P	LCPL	27	/690	D	25 STAFFORD ST	SUNDERLAND	26/12/14	13/10/17	KR para 392	OCTOBER 16		TO DEPOT.	LSGT.
SMITH	P	PTE	27	/694	D	HEDLEYS BLDGS	SHIREMOOR				SEPTEMBER 16.			
SMITH	Robt	PTE	27	/1244	D	8 CROQUET ST	CHOPWELL	21/12/14	14/3/18	GUNSHOT WOUNDS	JULY 16.		TO 3rd BN.	
SMITH	Thos	PTE	27	/1248	A	30 AUSTRALIA ST	SEAHAM	21/12/14	31/3/19	KR para 392			TO 24/27th BN, ARMY RESERVE CLASS P.	LCPL.
SMITH	W	PTE	27	/688	A	16 DURHAM ST	SHERBURN HILL							
SMITH	W	PTE	27	/1228	C	97 NORTH VIEW	CHILTON MOOR						TO 24/27th, 14th, 12/13th BNS, CLASS Z RESERVE.	
SMITH	W W	PTE	27	/683	D	38 QUEBEC ST	ESH COLLIERY						TO 3rd BN.	
SMITH	Wm	PTE	27	/1249		24 MAUD ST	LEMINGTON ON TY						TO 2nd GARRISON BN, ATTACHED NF CATTERICK(1918), Z	
SMITHERS	Math	CPL	27	/640	A		SOUTH SHIELDS			1 JULY 1916		THIEPVAL MEM		
SNAITH	W	PTE	27	/680	D	55 VICTORIA RD	GATESHEAD						TO 24/27th, 22nd BNS, CLASS Z RESERVE.	
SNOWBALL	J	LSGT	27	/1230	C	35 BUTTES BLDGS	SWALWELL				JULY 16.		TO CLASS Z RESERVE.	34 CCS 1/7 EVAC 5/7/16 WND L LEG CQMS AGE 26.
SNOWBALL	John	PTE	27	/1239	A	69 PRINCESS ST	SOUTH SHIELDS	14/1/15						
SOUTHERN	John	PTE	27	/1250		12 BRUSSELS ST	GATESHEAD			15 JULY 1916		GATESHEAD		BORN ST HELENS LANCS, AGE 18.
SPEDDING	Geo	PTE	27	/1222	D	10 NORTH VIEW	SHERBURN HILL	8/1/15		2 MARCH 1919		PITTINGTON	TO 9th, 16th, 1/7th BNS, LABOUR CORPS(534 AGR COY)	BORN RYHOPE, LAB CORPS No 491543.
SPEDDING	J	PTE	27	/666	B	22 PARMETER ST	SOUTHMOOR	11/1/15					TO 9th, 16th, 1/7th BNS, CLASS Z RESERVE.	MINER DESERTED AGE 22, 5'10'', BORN USHAW MOOR.
SPENCE	G S	PTE	27	/1251	C									
SPENCE	Tom J	PTE	27	/682	D	25 BROOK ST	SEAHAM			1 JULY 1916		THIEPVAL MEM		MISSING OCTOBER 16.

NAME	INITI	RANK	BA	NUMBE	COMP	ADDRESS	TOWN_VILL	ENLISTED	DISCHARG	CAUSE_DIS	WOUNDED	BURIED	TRANSFER	ADD
SPITTY	J	PTE	27	/1253			CRAGHEAD				AUGUST 16.		TO ROYAL DEFENCE CORPS.	IN FRANCE 11/1/16 TO 3/7/16.
SPOORS	Thos	PTE	27	/654	A	48 BRUSSELS ST TEAMS	GATESHEAD	8/1/15					TO LABOUR CORPS(783 LAB COY).	LAB CORPS No 397103.
SPOTTISWOOD	T	PTE		/669	C	27	SOUTH SHIELDS				OCT 16			
STEAD	Pat	PTE	27	/1233	C	66 SOUTH DEMPSTER PL	FELLING			3 DEC 1917	JULY 16.	NOEX LE MINES MIL CEM	TO 16th, 24th, 8th BNS.	
STENISON	J	PTE	27	/1237	D		NEWCASTLE				OCTOBER 16.			
STEPHENSON	Chris	PTE	27	/1241	D		SHILDON			1 JULY 1916		THIEPVAL MEM		BORN MIDDRIDGE YORKS.
STEPHENSON	D	SGT	27	/651	A									
STEPHENSON	E	CPL	27	/676	D		STAITHES				JULY 16.		TO 2nd BN, ATTACHED 6th ENTRENCHING BN.	
STEPHENSON	T	PTE	27	/1232	C		SOUTH SHIELDS				JANUARY 18.		TO 24/27th BN, CLASS Z RESERVE.	
STEPHENSON	T	PTE	27	/1238	C		SOUTH SHIELDS			4 JULY 1920	OCTOBER 16.	HARTON ST PETERS	TO LABOUR CORPS(848 LAB COY).	BATH WAR HOSP 11/7/16, LAB CORPS No 471237.
STEPHENSON	Thos	PTE	27	/1229	C	2 HOYSTON VILLAS	BILLQUAY			27 MAY 1918		SOISSONS MEM	TO 24/27th, 12/13th BNS.	SGT.
STEPHENSON	W H	PTE	27	/1399	D									3 CCS 2/7/16 EVAC 2/7/16 GSW.
STEWART	R	PTE	27	/641	A	6 CROSS ROW FARRINGD	SUNDERLAND							
STEWART	Thos	PTE	27	/1243	D	97 FRAMWELLGATE	DURHAM CITY	7/1/15			JULY 16.		TO 23rd, 12/13th BNS, CLASS Z RESERVE.	BORN WESTMORLAND.
STEWART	W	CSM	27	/1524	C			27/7/15	11/9/17	WOUNDS	FEBRUARY 16		TO 3rd BN.	
STOBART	K T	PTE	27	/1225	B						SEPTEMBER 16.			
STOBART	W	PTE	27	/1217	A									
STONEHOUSE	ThosD	PTE	27	/696	C	4 GARBUTTS BLDGS	BISHOP AUKLAND			7 OCT 1916		CITE BON JEAN CEM		BROTHER IN A COY 26BN, BORN HOUGHTON LE SPRING.
STOREY	Ben	PTE	27	/1221	A	30 JOHN ST	CONSETT	5/1/15	23/10/17	GUNSHOT WOUNDS			TO DEPOT.	
STOTHART	J	PTE	27	/665	B									
STOTHART	T W	LCPL	27	/648	A									
STRAKER	G	PTE	27	/657	B		PENSHAW				SEPTEMBER 16.			
STRANGHAN	G	PTE	27	/1341	C						1 JULY 1916			2 GHOSP 4/7, SHIP 5/7/16 AGE 37, WND BUTTOCKS.
STRATHERN	J E	PTE	27	/1218	A	19 GRASMERE ST	BLACKHILL				JULY 16.		ATT DIV SALVAGE COY, TO 26th, 1/7th BNS, CLASS Z R	
SUDDICK	R	PTE	27	/1456	D			20/1/15	27/3/17	SICK			TO DEPOT.	
SUDDICK	R E	PTE	27	/1257	D		FENCEHOUSES	22/12/14	23/11/18	SICK	NOVEMBER 16.		TO 22nd, 16th BNS, DEPOT.	
SUDDICK	W	PTE	27	/1256	D		FENCEHOUSES				JULY 16.		ATTACHED 103 MACHINE GUN COY.	34 CCS 2/7/16 EVAC 5/7/16 WND L LEG AGE 24.
SWINBANK	Geo	PTE	27	/1223	A	29 STEVENSON STREET	BOWBURN	8/1/15			JULY 16.			NORTH EVINGTON HOSP LEICESTER 8/7/16
SWINDELLS	F	PTE	27	/1433									TO 2nd GARRISON BN, CLASS Z RESERVE.	
TANSEY	P	PTE	27	/1260	A			9/1/15	4/2/18	KR para 392			TO 24/27th, 14th BNS, DEPOT.	
TATE	RichW	PTE	27	/1267	C		COPELEY			14 MARCH 1916		BREWERY ORCHARD CEM		MINER AT ST HELENS COLLIERY,
TAYLOR	J	PTE	27	/713				6/1/15	28/8/17	SICK			TO 1st GARRISON BN, DEPOT.	
TAYLOR	Jos T	PTE	27	/1274	D	34 HAUGH LANE	HEXAM				SEPTEMBER 16.		TO 1/6th BN.	21 AMBTR,18 GHOSP 6/7,SHIP 9/7,AGE 18, WND SSHOCK.
TAYLOR	Thos	PTE	27	/718	D	18 WILSON TERR	SILKSWORTH	7/1/15		3 JULY 1916	1 JULY 16	PUNCHEVILLIERS		3 CCS 2/7/16 DIED IN CCS 3/7/16,BORN STOCKTON.
TAYLOR	Thos	PTE	27	/1258	D	30 MOOR PIT CATCHGAT	ANNFIELD PLAIN	14/1/15		1 JULY 1916		GORDON DUMP CEM		BORN PELTON.
TAYLOR	W	PTE	27	/716	C									
TEMPERLEY	W	PTE	27	/1482	C					20 APRIL 1919		BRANDON		
TENNANT	P	PTE	27	/701	A			30/12/14	4/4/16				TO 30th BN.	DID NOT SERVE OVERSEAS.
TENNETT	Norm	PTE	27	/1263	A	115 FORT ST	SOUTH SHIELDS			1 JULY 1916		THIEPVAL MEM		
TERRELL	Alf	PTE	27	/1266	C	61 JOHN WILLIAM ST	SOUTH SHIELDS			1 JULY 1916		GORDON DUMP CEM		LCPL, EMPLOYED BOLDON COLLIERY.
THOMAS	James	PTE	27	/1275			CARDIFF	4/1/15						FITTER DESERTED 4/1/15 AGE 31, 5'9''.
THOMPSON	A	PTE	27	/721	D									ALSO ON D COY 30th BN ROLL.
THOMPSON	A	PTE	27	/725	A	30								
THOMPSON	Alex	PTE	27											AWOL 9/6/15 COURT NEWCASTLE 17/6/15 POS 27/721
THOMPSON	C	PTE	27	/715	C									
THOMPSON	Fred	PTE	27	/1409			FRIZINGTON			5 JULY 1916		ST SEVER CEM ROUEN	TO 24th BN.	
THOMPSON	H	PTE	27	/722	D		NEWCASTLE				DECEMBER 16.			
THOMPSON	J	PTE	27	/702	A									
THOMPSON	J	PTE	27	/719	D			31/12/14	7/8/17	SICK			TO 3rd BN.	
THOMPSON	J	SGT	27	/720	D	76 VILLAGE LANE	WASHINGTON		25/1/19				TO MACHINE GUN CORPS(34th BN), CLASS Z RESERVE.	RSM 34th BN MGC, MGC No 152013.
THOMPSON	J	PTE	27	/1277		BOYAL ST	MONKHESLEDON						TO 1st GARRISON BN, CLASS Z RESERVE.	
THOMPSON	J R H	PTE	27	/723		126 CUTHBERT ROAD	GATESHEAD			2 SEPT 1917		TYNE COT MEM	TO DURHAM LI(12th BN).	DLI No 44110, AGE 35 BORN SOUTH SHIELDS.
THOMPSON	J W	SGT	27	/707	B								TO 23rd, 27th, 24/27th,WEST INDIES REGT(8&11th BNS	AWOII TO CLASS Z RESERVE.
THOMPSON	Sam	LCPL	27	/1273	A	26	WORKINGTON			28 APRIL 1917		ARRAS MEM	TO 26th BN, KINGS OWN YORKSHIRE LI(9th BN).	KOYLI No 43088.
THOMPSON	T	PTE	27	/1408	C									
THOMPSON	W	PTE	27	/1468	B									
THOMPSON	Wm	PTE	27	/1268	B	8 WEST VIEW BRANSTY	WHITEHAVEN			3 DEC 1917		MENDINGHEM CEM	TO 16th BN.	
THORNTON	J	CPL	27	/712									TO 1st GARRISON BN, CLASS Z RESERVE.	
THREFALL	Edw	PTE	27	/709	B	1 ATKINSONS BLDGS	BIRTLEY				SEPTEMBER 16.		TO 24/27th, 19th(Z COY) BNS, CLASS Z RESERVE.	
TIERNEY	J	PTE	27	/728	A		BEDLINGTON	15/12/14	3/5/18	GUNSHOT WOUNDS	JULY 16.		TO 3rd BN.	

NAME	INITI	RANK	BA	NUMBE	COMP	ADDRESS	TOWN_VILL	ENLISTED	DISCHARG	CAUSE_DIS	WOUNDED	BURIED	TRANSFER	ADD
TIGHE	J	SGT	27	/717	D	51 ELDON ST	SOUTH SHIELDS			KR para 392	SEPTEMBER 16.			CSM, WOUNDED BOTH FEET.
TIGHE	J	PTE	27	/1271	A		WHITEHAVEN				APR 16, SEP 16, DEC 18.			34 CCS 2/7/16 EVAC 5/7/16 WND L FOOT.
TISSEMAN	R E	PTE	27	/714	D		SOUTH SHIELDS				OCTOBER 16.			
TODD	Alb E	PTE	27	/711	C	8 ESHWOOD ST	NEW BRANCEPETH	14/1/15			JUNE 16.			CPL.
TODD	John	PTE	27	/1428	B	38 LUCKER ST	LEMINGTON ON TY						TO 3rd BN, LANCASHIRE FUSILIERS(1/8th BN).	
TONER	John		27	/1383	C 30	12 ROSEBERRY TERR	CONSETT	14/1/15					TO 30th BN(C COY).	
TONER	P F	CPL	27	/1270	B			19/12/14	15/3/18	GUNSHOT WOUNDS			TO 3rd BN.	IN BAND.
TONER	Peter	PTE	27	/1269	B	2 WEST STRAND	WHITEHAVEN			1 JULY 1916		THIEPVAL MEM		BORN CASTLE WELLAN Co DOWN, IN BN BAND.
TONER	Wm	LCPL	27	/703	A	52 DERWENT ST	BLACKHILL	12/1/15		11 SEPT 1917	AUGUST 16	ZUYDCOOTE MIL CEM	TO 1st, 16th(A COY) BNS.	HOSP HALIFAX 7/16, AGE 30.
TOOLE	N	PTE	27	/1481	D									
TRAINER	P	PTE	27	/1262	B		WORKINGTON			KR para 392	JULY 16.		TO 10th, 24/27th BNS.	
TRAYNOR	Jas	PTE	27	/1556	B 30		CLEATOR MOOR			24 OCT 1918		BERMERAIN MIL CEM	TO 30th(B COY), 26th, 9th BNS.	LCPL.
TREMBLE	J	PTE	27	/708	B	59 NORTH ST	WINLATON	11/1/15	21/12/17	SICK			TO DEPOT.	
TULIP	J	LCPL	27	/726	D									18 G HOSP 6/7/16 TO BASE 17/7/16 AGE 39.
TURNBULL	A	PTE	27	/727	A		BEBSIDE				OCTOBER 16.			3 CCS 2/7/16 EVAC 2/7/16
TURNER	A	CPL	27	/710	C									
TURNER	FranJ	PTE	27	/1276	A	175 BOTTLE BANK	LEADGATE			1 JULY 1916		THIEPVAL MEM		AGE 23.
TURNER	Rob D	PTE	27	/1344	D		MURTON			1 JULY 1916	SEPTEMBER 16.	THIEPVAL MEM		CPL.
TURNER	Wm P	PTE	27	/1343	D	19 HENRY ST	NEW SILKSWORTH			11 FEB 1916		Y FARM CEM BOIS GRENIER		BORN HAMSTERLEY, LCPL.
TWEEDY	John	PTE	27	/1259	A	43 SPENCER ST	GATESHEAD	14/1/15		15 MAY 1917	OCTOBER 16.	FELLING	TO 20th BN, DEPOT.	
TYRIE	W	SGT	27	/1450	B								TO 27th, 24/27th, 11th BNS, CLASS Z RESERVE.	
UDALE	JohnR	PTE	27	/731	D	9 CLIFF TERR	SUNDERLAND			KR para 392				
URWIN	Mich	PTE	27	/730	C	10 MASON ST	BYKER	7/1/15			SEPTEMBER 16.		TO HIGHLAND LIGHT INFANTRY.	HOSP MANCHESTER 7/16
USHER	Alf	PTE	27	/1279	A	20 STAVORDALE ST	DAWDON			6 JULY 1916		HEILLY STATION CEM		BORN SILKSWORTH, AGE 20.
VASEY	W	PTE	27	/1280			DURHAM CITY				JULY 16.		TO ROYAL ARMY MEDICAL CORPS.	
VENUS	Jas W	PTE	27	/1281	C		NEWCASTLE			KR para 392	AUGUST 16.		TO 25th, 1/5th BNS	ALLOTED NEW NUMBER 243194.
WADE	ThosA	PTE	27	/1308	A 30		BEAMISH			3 MARCH 1917		SAILLY-AU-BOIS MIL CEM	TO DURHAM LI(18th BN).	DURHAM LI No 49701.
WAGGOTT	J	PTE	27	/753	A 30	62 CUTHBERT ST	BLAYDON				DECEMBER 17.		TO 30th BN(A COY),16th,1/4th,1/5th BNS,Z RESERVE.	NOT OVERSEAS WITH TYNESIDE IRISH.
WAKE	J	PTE	27	/1328	B			10/1/15	14/2/19	KR para 392			TO DEPOT.	
WAKE	J T	PTE	27	/1284	A		SUNDERLAND				MARCH 18.		TO 24/27th, 25th, 12/13th BNS, CLASS Z RESERVE.	
WAKELEY	John	LCPL	27	/763	B 30	508 JOHN WILLIAMSON	SOUTH SHIELDS	14/1/15					TO 30th BN(B COY),1/4th,11th BNS,Z RESERVE.	NOT OVERSEAS WITH TYNESIDE IRISH.
WAKENSHAW	C	PTE	27	/746	C									
WALKER	John	PTE	27	/1347	C	15 PERKINS ST STH CH	BISHOP AUKLAND			1 JULY 1916		THIEPVAL MEM		MISSING OCTOBER 16.
WALKER	W	PTE	27	/774	D					KR para 392			TO 25th, 1/4th BNS.	ALLOTED NEW NUMBER 243199.
WALKER	Wm	PTE	27	/750	A	24 TOWNLEY TERR	HIGH SPEN			1 JULY 1916		THIEPVAL MEM		MISSING OCTOBER 16.
WALL	Ben W	PTE	27	/762	D	3 CLARKES BLDGS	NORTH SHIELDS	14/1/15	30/1/19				TO MACHINE GUN CORPS(34th BN), CLASS Z RESERVE.	MGC No 152010.
WALLACE	James	PTE	27	/772	D		HEXAM			1 JULY 1916		THIEPVAL MEM		
WALLEY	J	PTE	27	/1391									TO 1st GARRISON BN, CLASS Z RESERVE.	
WALMSLEY	W	PTE	27	/756	D	13 WALKERS BLDGS	WASHINGTON STAI							
WALTERS	Isaac	PTE	27	/1548	C		SOUTH SHIELDS			11 MAY 1916		BECOURT MIL CEM		
WALTERS	J G	PTE	27	/1301	C		SOUTH SHIELDS				OCTOBER 16.		TO 16th, 11th BNS, CLASS Z RESERVE.	34 CCS 1/7/16 EVAC 5/7/16 WND TOES, AGE 21.
WALTON	Cuthb	PTE	27	/1322	D	1 SIXTH ST	BASINGTON	5/1/15	1/8/19	KR para 392			TO 1/5th BN., DEPOT.	KING GEORGES HOSP LONDON 1918.
WALTON	D	PTE	27	/784	A 24	2 RICHMOND ST	NEWCASTLE				JULY 16.		TO LABOUR CORPS.	
WALTON	E	PTE	27	/1375	B 24								TO 24th, 24/27th, 9th BNS, CLASS Z RESERVE.	
WALTON	Henry	PTE	27	/1331	C	35 JOHN WILLIAMSON S	SOUTH SHIELDS	14/1/15						
WALTON	J T	PTE	27	/1314	D		NEWCASTLE	22/12/14	25/7/17	WOUNDS	AUGUST 16.		TO 3rd BN.	
WANLESS	R	PTE	27	/1542	B 24								TO 24th, 24th/27th BNS, CLASS Z RESERVE.	
WARD	ChasE	PTE	27	/783	B		NEWBURN			1 JULY 1916		THIEPVAL MEM		MISSING OCTOBER 16. BORN ROUGHTON NORFOLK.
WARD	Geo F	PTE	27	/1345	A		ANNFIELD PLAIN	14/1/15			SEPTEMBER 16.		TO LABOUR CORPS.	
WARD	Mich	PTE	27	/751	D	7 REDHAUGH BRIDGE RO	GATESHEAD	8/1/15	10/7/17	KR para 392	OCTOBER 16.			LABOURER DESERTED 29/5/15 AGE 28,5'5''AWOL 9/7/15.
WARD	T	PTE	27	/755	D	1 RITCHIE TERR	WASHINGTON STAT	9/1/15	31/3/19	KR para 392	SEPTEMBER 16, JANUARY 18.		TO 24/27th BN, ARMY RESERVE CLASS P.	ASGT.
WARD	T J	PTE	27	/768	D									
WARDLAW	J	PTE	27	/1382	D								TO 25th, 22nd, 12/13th, 1st BNS, CLASS Z RESERVE.	
WARDLE	Arth	PTE	27	/739	C	21 PARK TERR	WEST MOOR	7/1/15			SEPTEMBER 16.		TO DURHAM LI, LONDON REGT, MIDDLESEX REGT.	34 CCS 2/7/16 EVAC 5/7/16
WATERS	John	PTE	27	/747	D	2 WESTBURN TERR	CRAWCROOK	8/1/15					TO 24/27th, 14th BNS, CLASS Z RESERVE.	ASGT.
WATERS	W	PTE	27	/1438	A		NEWCASTLE	21/5/15	27/10/16	WOUNDS	AUGUST 16.		TO 85th TRAINING RESERVE BN.	
WATSON	A	PTE	27	/1300	C			23/12/14	6/6/17	SICK			TO 18th, 22nd BNS, 80th TRAINING RESERVE BN.	
WATSON	G J	PTE	27	/1302	C	HAZELRIGG	DUDLEY	14/1/15			OCTOBER 16.			34 CCS 2/7/16 EVAC 5/7/16 SSHOCK AGE 18.
WATSON	Geo	PTE	27	/737	C	16 CARLTON ST	SHIELDFIELD	7/1/15		1 JULY 1916		THIEPVAL MEM		POS LIVING 76 STEPNEY LANE NEWCASTLE 1915.
WATSON	H	PTE	27	/1329				8/1/15	26/11/15	SICK			TO 30th BN.	DID NOT SERVE OVERSEAS.

NAME	INITI	RANK	BA	NUMBE	COMP	ADDRESS	TOWN_VILL	ENLISTED	DISCHARG	CAUSE_DIS	WOUNDED	BURIED	TRANSFER	ADD
WATSON	JohnW	PTE	27	/1330	A	16 HYDE ST	SOUTH SHIELDS	14/1/15						AWOL IN COURT SOUTH SHIELDS 4/12/15.
WATSON	Jos	PTE	27	/1172		WATERSIDE	SWALWELL			1 JULY 1916		THIEPVAL MEM	TO 20th BN.	
WATSON	M	PTE	27	/740				5/1/15	18/10/17	SICK			TO 1st GARRISON BN.	
WATSON	Wm	PTE	27	/749	D	84 CLIVE ST	NORTH SHIELDS				SEPTEMBER 16.			
WATTS	J	PTE	27	/1294			OLDHAM	28/12/14					TO 2nd GARRISON BN.	LABOURER DESERTED 5/11/15 AGE 42, 5'7''.
WAUGH	A	PTE	27	/1313	D	1 BRAMWELL LANE	HEWORTH	22/12/14	31/3/19	KR para 392			TO 26th, 9th BNS, ARMY RESERVE CLASS P.	
WAUGH	T	PTE	27	/1283	A	37 MIDDLE ST	NETTLESWORTH	22/12/14	1/4/19	KR para 392	AUGUST 16.		TO 1st, 24/27th BNS, ARMY RESERVE CLASS P.	
WEATHERALL	Wm	PTE	27	/764	C	49 BUCKINGHAM ST	NEWCASTLE			27 AUGUST 1917		BELLICOURT MIL CEM.	TO 24/27th BN.	BORN PITTINGTON, LCPL.
WELDON	W	PTE	27	/1325		38 BONDGATE	BISHOP AUKLAND						TO 1st GARRISON BN, CLASS Z RESERVE.	
WESTHEAD	E	PTE	27	/779	D									
WHALLEY	Arth	PTE	27	/766	C	10 ROBERTS ST WESTOE	SOUTH SHIELDS			1 JULY 1916		THIEPVAL MEM		BORN SILVERDALE STAFFORDSHIRE.
WHALLEY	Math	PTE	27	/1311	C	58 WALKER ST	GATESHEAD			27 MAY 1918	FEBRUARY 18.	SOISSONS MEM	TO 24/27th, 14th BNS.	CPL, AGE 26.
WHARTON	David	PTE	27	/1315	D	83 FLEMING ST TEAMS	GATESHEAD						TO 24/27th, 11th BNS, CLASS Z RESERVE.	
WHEATLEY	John	PTE	27	/1321	D		BISHOP AUKLAND	5/1/15	31/3/19	KR para 392	OCTOBER 16.		TO 1st, 12/13th BNS, ARMY RESERVE CLASS P.	BEAUFORT WAR HOSP FISHPONDS BRISTOL 8/7/16.
WHELAN	P	PTE	27	/1317			CLEATOR MOOR	28/12/14						MINER DESERTED 1/5/15, AGE 37, 5'6''.
WHINTHORPE	John	PTE	27	/1427			HEBBURN	12/5/15						LABOURER DESERTED 12/5/15 AGE 30, 5'5''.
WHITE	Chas	PTE	27	/769	B	30 BACK SHUTTLES, TEAMS	GATESHEAD				DECEMBER 18.		TO 19th, 14th BNS, CLASS Z RESERVE.	
WHITE	Rob E	PTE	27	/733	C	21 STEPHENSON ST	MURTON	2/1/15	8/9/17	GUNSHOT WOUNDS	AUGUST 16.		TO DEPOT.	HOSP SOUTHAMPTON 7/16
WHITLOCK	John	PTE	27	/1290	A	47 CORNISH ST	SEAHAM	7/1/15						
WHITLOCK	Wm	PTE	27	/1319	D	47 CORNISH ST	SEAHAM	4/1/15	9/9/16	VDH			TO 34th BN.	
WHITTAKER	J	SGT	27	/1282	B									ALSO ON D COY and B COY ROLLS 30th BN.
WHITTIT	ThosS	PTE	27	/1291	A	CLAVERING HOUSE	NEWCASTLE	7/1/15			OCTOBER 16.		TO 1st, 1/7th BNS, CLASS Z RESERVE.	3 CCS 2/7/16 EVAC 2/7/16 GSW.
WHITTON	Geo W	PTE	27	/776	D		SHOTTON COLLIER			7 AUGUST 1917	OCTOBER 16	NIEUPORT MEM	TO 16th BN.	34 CCS 2/7 EVAC 5/7/16 WND R THIGH AGE 31.
WHITTON	J T	PTE	27	/775	D		SHOTTON COLLIER	28/12/14	14/3/19	KR para 392			TO 24/27th, 19th BNS, ARMY RESERVE CLASS P.	
WIGLEY	Geo T	LSGT	27	/1318	D	FRONT ST MOUNT PLEAS	CROOK				AUGUST 1918.		TO 24/27th, 14th BNS, CLASS Z RESERVE.	AWOII.
WILCE	R	PTE	27	/1316	B		CARLISLE	21/12/14	8/9/17	WOUNDS	OCT 16		TO 3rd BN.	
WILD	Hen S	PTE	27	/1287	A	20 LONG ROW	LITTLETOWN	8/1/15			JULY 16.			34 CCS 2/7/16 EVAC 5/7/16 WND L LEG, LCPL.
WILKINSON	Henry	PTE	27	/765	A	10 BICKNALL ST	TRIMDON							
WILKINSON	Jos	PTE	27	/738	C		NEWCASTLE			25 APRIL 1917		BROWNS COPSE CEM		SGT.
WILKINSON	R	PTE	27	/1350	A	HEXAM TERR	KELLOE							
WILKINSON	S	PTE	27	/771	C	CHAPEL ROW	SHERBURN COLLIE	29/12/14	6/8/17	KR para 392	AUGUST 16.		TO 80th TRAINING RESERVE BN.	LCPL, HOSP COLCHESTER 7/16 WND SHOULDER.
WILKINSON	T	PTE	27	/752									TO 1st GARRISON BN, CLASS Z RESERVE.	
WILKINSON	Wm A	PTE	27	/748		2 GREENFIELD ST	GATESHEAD	6/1/15	27/4/17	WOUNDS			TO DEPOT.	AWOL 17/6/15 IN COURT 3/7/15.
WILLIAMS	I	PTE	27	/786	B		CHESTER LE ST				OCTOBER 16.			
WILLIAMS	J	PTE	27	/1297	C								TO 24/27th, 14th BNS, CLASS Z RESERVE.	
WILLIAMS	J	PTE	27	/1309	C								TO 25th, 1/4th BNS, CLASS Z RESERVE.	ALLOTED NEW NUMBER 204582.
WILLIAMS	S	PTE	27	/1352	A		MIDDLESBOROUGH				SEPTEMBER 16.			
WILLIAMS	T	PTE	27	/1354	D		HETTON DOWNS				SEPTEMBER 16, APRIL 18.			LCPL, BATH WAR HOSP 11/7/16.
WILLIAMSON	E	PTE	27	/767	D		BLACKHILL				JULY 16.			
WILLIAMSON	Henry	PTE	27	/1288	A	2 HILL ST	SILKSWORTH	7/1/15			AUGUST 16, MAY 18.		TO 8th BN, CLASS Z RESERVE.	
WILLIAMSON	J	PTE	27	/1402	D		TANTOBIE				JANUARY 17, MARCH 17.		TO ROYAL DEFENCE CORPS.	FRANCE 27 11/1/16 to 8/1/17, BASE NF 9/1/17 to 29/
WILLIAMSON	Jas	PTE	27	/742	C	25 SIXTH ST	EASINGTON COLLI	5/1/15	18/7/16	WOUNDS	APRIL 16.		TO DEPOT.	
WILLIS	T	PTE	27	/1348	B									
WILSON	G	LCPL	27	/1285	A		RHODE ISLAND US				DECEMBER 16.		TO 24/27th, 14th BNS, CLASS Z RESERVE.	SGT.
WILSON	Geo W	PTE	27	/781	D		FERRYHILL			1 JULY 1916		THIEPVAL MEM		
WILSON	Geo W	PTE	27	/1379	D	178 PARKER ST BYKER	NEWCASTLE	14/1/15			DECEMBER 16.		TO ROYAL DEFENCE CORPS.	IN FRANCE 11/1/16 TO 6/7/16.
WILSON	J	CPL	27	/773	D		MARLEY HILL				OCTOBER 16.		TO WEST YORKSHIRE REGT, CLASS Z RESERVE.	34CCS 2/7 EVAC 25 AMBTR 5/7,18 GHOSP,SHIP 9/7/16.
WILSON	J	PTE	27	/1307	C								TO ROYAL ENGINEERS.	
WILSON	Jack	PTE	27	/735	C	36 EDITH AVENUE	USWORTH COLLIER				MARCH 17.		TO LABOUR CORPS.	
WILSON	Jas	PTE	27	/1304	C	98 LAUREL ST	WALLSEND			7 JULY 1916		ST SEVER CEM ROUEN.		** TRUE NAME RUFUS BROOKSBANK BORN BRIDLINGTON. **
WILSON	JnBkw	PTE	27	/1320	D	59 WAYMAN ST	SUNDERLAND	5/1/15	31/12/17	GUNSHOT WOUNDS			TO 3rd BN.	
WILSON	JohnG	PTE	27	/758	C	25 NEWTON CAP BANK	BISHOP AUKLAND	9/1/15	31/3/19	KR para 392	OCTOBER 16, DECEMBER 17.		TO 8th, 16th BNS, ARMY RESERVE CLASS P.	HOSP FISHPONDS BRISTOL 8/7/16
WILSON	M G	PTE	27	/757	A			9/1/15	23/2/18	SCIATICA			TO DEPOT.	
WILSON	Math	LCPL	27	/743	C	1 WEST VIEW TEMPLETO	CONSETT	5/1/15	18/8/17	SICK			TO DEPOT.	
WILSON	R	PTE	27	/1312	D	THE COLLIERY ST HELE	BISHOP AUKLAND							
WILSON	Rob B	PTE	27	/759		46 WESTMINSTER ST	GATESHEAD	11/1/15	17/8/16	29 AUGUST 1916	JULY 16	SALTWELL CEM	TO 30th BN(B COY).	HOSP MANCHESTER,AGE 28,DIED OF PERITONITIS.
WILSON	Thos	PTE	27	/761	C		NEWCASTLE			13 APRIL 1917	SEPTEMBER 16.	ARRAS MEM	TO 1st BN.	
WILSON	ThosW	PTE	27	/1346	A	26 THE SQUARE	WARDLEY COLLIER	14/1/15		4 SEPT 1917	AUGUST 16.	DOZINGHEM MIL CEM	TO 24th, 22nd BNS.	BORN FELLING.
WILSON	W	PTE	27	/741	C		WASHINGTON	5/1/15	29/3/17	SICK	SEPTEMBER 16, MARCH 17.		TO DEPOT.	
WILSON	W	PTE	27	/1349									TO 19th, 14th, 9th, 14th, 24/27th, 19th, 9th BNS.	DESERTED 1 JULY 1919.

NAME	INITI	RANK	BA	NUMBE	COMP	ADDRESS	TOWN_VILL	ENLISTED	DISCHARG	CAUSE_DIS	WOUNDED	BURIED	TRANSFER	ADD
WILSON	W	LSGT	27	/1401	D	6 CHAPEL LANE SANDGA	NEWCASTLE	26/4/15	2/10/16	SICK 17/8/17		ALL SAINTS NEWCASTLE	TO DEPOT.	AGE 31.
WINTER	Chris	PTE	27	/1303	C		BEAMISH	7/1/15			MARCH 17.			
WINTER	Henry	PTE	27	/736	C	146 CHURCH ST	NORTH SHIELDS	7/1/15			OCTOBER 16.			
WINTER	J G	PTE	27	/732	C	COMMERCIAL ST	CROOK						TO 24/27th, 14th BNS, CLASS Z RESERVE.	
WINTER	Jas	PTE	27	/785	B		NEWBURN			1 JULY 1916		THIEPVAL MEM		
WISHART	A	PTE	27	/1466		35 FELL ST St PETERS	NEWCASTLE				OCTOBER 18			
WOLFENDALE	Wm	PTE	27	/777	d	11 MARIA ST	SILKSWORTH			1 SEPT 1918	AUGUST 16.	HAC CEM ECOUST ST MEIN.	TO 25th, 1st BNS.	
WOMBWELL	T	PTE	27	/1353	D		NEWCASTLE	12/1/15	5/9/17	WOUNDS	APRIL 16, JULY 16.		TO 3rd BN.	AWOL 12/12/15 IN COURT 24/12/15.
WOOD	D	PTE	27	/778	B		SEAHAM COLLIERY	28/12/14	20/12/17	KR para 392	OCTOBER 16.		TO DEPOT.	
WOOD	J	SGT	27	/734	C		WEST STANLEY			KR para 392	JULY 16.			
WOOD	J	PTE	27	/780	B		WASHINGTON STAT				JULY 16.		TO ROYAL INNISKILLING FUSILIERS(6th BN).	
WOOD	T	PTE	27	/1292	C	70 NEWCASTLE ST	BRANDON COLLIER						TO 9th BN, CLASS Z RESERVE.	
WOOD	T B	LSGT	27	/1299	B	30 TRUMPET TERR	CLEATOR MOOR			KR para 392	SEPTEMBER 16.			
WOOF	John	PTE	27	/754	D	21a BURN ST	GATESHEAD			2 JULY 1916		MEAULTE MIL CEM		
WOOLAGHAN	J	PTE	27	/1298	B	26 WYNDHAM ST	CLEATOR MOOR			5 OCT 1917		BROWNS COPSE CEM ROUEX	TO ROYAL WARWICKSHIRE REGT(1/8th BN).	R WARWICKS No 29677.
WOOLAGHAN	Thos	PTE	27	/1306	B		WHITEHAVEN		6/2/19				TO MACHINE GUN CORPS, CLASS Z RESERVE.	MISS OCT 16,NOT MISS DEC 16, MGC No 139837.
WOOLAGHAN	W	PTE	27	/782	B									
WRAITH	Rob R	PTE	27	/760	A	9 ST LAWRENCE RD	NEWCASTLE	14/1/15			SEPTEMBER 16.		TO 24/27th, 11th, 1st BNS, CLASS Z RESERVE.	
WRIGHT	Rob W	PTE	27	/1286	A	24 NEWGATE ST	NEWCASTLE	7/1/15		KR para 392				
YELLOW	Wm	PTE	27	/790	B	60 SOUTH TERR	ESH WINNING	7/1/15	3/1/17	WOUNDS			TO DEPOT.	
YOUNG	J	PTE	27	/1334	B		WHITEHAVEN						TO 18th, 1st BNS, CLASS Z RESERVE.	REPORTED MISSING SEPTEMBER 16.
YOUNG	Syd	PTE	27	/1335	A	44 ALBION ST BENSHAM	GATESHEAD	7/1/15		1 JULY 1916	OCTOBER 16.	THIEPVAL MEM		AGE 20, NOK 29 DIXON STREET GATESHEAD.
YOUNG	Wm	PTE	27	/789	B	7 MAUD ST	LEMINGTON ON TY						TO 22nd, 3rd BNS, CLASS Z RESERVE.	1st SOUTH AFRICAN GEN HOSP ABBEVILLE 1918.
YOUNG	Wm W	PTE	27	/1355	A	29 VICTORIA ST	SHOTTON COLLIER			12 MARCH 1916		SEAHAM	TO 30th BN.	10 CHURCH ST HASWELL 1916.

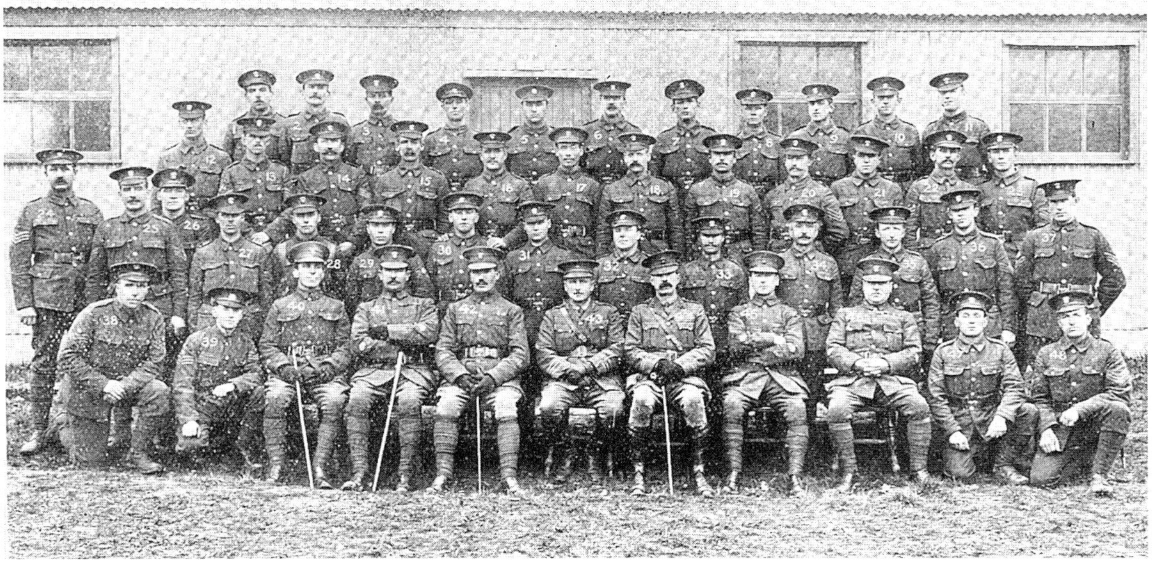

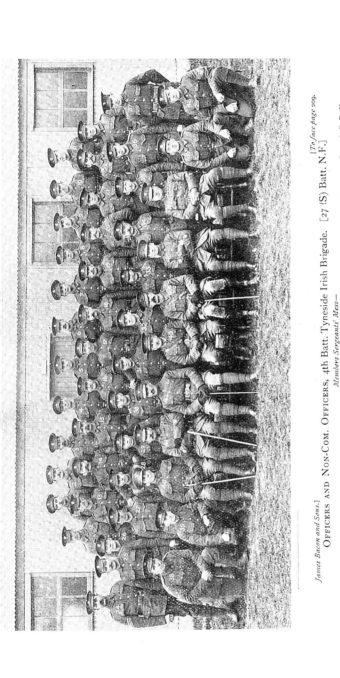

James Bacon and Sons.] [To face page 209.

OFFICERS AND NON-COM. OFFICERS, 4th Batt. Tyneside Irish Brigade. [27 (S) Batt. N.F.]

Members Sergeants' Mess—

1. C.Q.M.S. Little.
2. Sgt. McSweeney.
3. ,, Scott.
4. ,, O'Connell.
5. ,, McCann.
6. ,, Dixon.
,, Snowball.
8. Sgt. Burke.
9. ,, F. ster.
10. ,, Hickman.
11. ,, Wood.
12. ,, Wilson.
13. ,, Howard.
14. ,, Stephenson.
15. Sgt. Groves
16. ,, Francis.
17. ,, Fairless.
18. ,, Allen.
19. ,, Foster.
20. ,, Hopper.
21. ,, Finn.
22. Sgt. Caulfield.
23. ,, Thompson.
24. ,, Oswald.
25. ,, Raine.
26. ,, McNally.
27. ,, Thompson.
28. ,, Main.
29. Sgt. Tyrie.
30. ,, Cunningham.
31. ,, Wigley.
32. ,, Wood, J.
33. ,, Sayers.
34. ,, Daly.
35. C.Q.M.S. McKenna.
36. Sgt. Hughes
37. C.Q.M.S. Melia.
38. ,, Cavan.
39. S.-Sgt. Hammond.
40. C.S.M. Crawford.
41. ,, Stewart.
42. R.S.M. McNeice.
43. Lt.-Col. G. R. V. Steward.
44. Capt. F. W. S. Buckman.
45. R.Q.M.S. Dent.
46. C.S.M. Menham.
47. Sgt. Fenwick.
48. ,, Armstrong.

Appendix VII

ALHABETICAL NOMINAL ROLL
OTHER RANKS
30th NORTHUMBERLAND FUSILIERS
TYNESIDE IRISH RESERVE BATTALION

DUE TO POSTINGS AND RENUMBERING
FIGURES FOR THE RESERVE BATTALION
ARE INCONCLUSIVE

NAME	INITI	RANK	BA	NUMBE	COMP	ADDRESS	TOWN_VILL	ENLISTED	DISCHARG	CAUSE_DIS	WOUNDED	BURIED	TRANSFER	ADD
ADDY	Willi	PTE	30	/ 346			HOLMFIRTH			28 MARCH 1918		POZIERES MEM	TO 13th, 12/13th BNS.	
ALLEN	A	RSM		/1506	B									ORIGINAL BN UNCONFIRMED.
ALSOP	H	PTE	30	/ 302			HOLMFIRTH				NOT WND MAY 17		TO 13th, 12/13th, 23rd, 9th BNS, CLASS Z RESERVE.	
ANDERSON	J	PTE	30	/ 170	B									
ANDERSON	J	CPL		/1230	A									ORIGINAL BN UNCONFIRMED.
ANDERSON	J	PTE		/1290	A									
ARMITAGE	H	PTE	30	/ 382									TO 13th, 12/13th, 23rd BNS, CLASS Z RESERVE.	
ARMSTRONG		PTE	30	/ 143	B									
ARMSTRONG	H	PTE	30	/ 266	A		OAKENSHAW				AUGUST 16			
ASPLAND	C	PTE	30	/ 29	C									
ATKINSON	H	PTE		/ 872	C									
ATKINSON	R	PTE	30	/ 118	C		NEWCASTLE				JANUARY 17			
AUSTIN	T W	LCPL		/1332	D	24 FOURTH ST SOUTH	EASINGTON COLLI							
AUTY	J H K	PTE	30	/ 359				20/1/16	31/8/16	SYNOVITIS				DID NOT SERVE OVERSEAS.
AVERY	H	PTE	30	/ 227	C									
BAILES	H	PTE		/ 98	A									ORIGINAL BN UNCONFIRMED.
BAILEY	J W	PTE	30	/ 340		31 PROVIDENCE ROW	BRADFORD			16 JUNE 1917		ARRAS MEM	TO 13th BN.	BORN BAILDON YORKS.
BAINBRIDGE	A	PTE		/1370	A									ORIGINAL BN UNCONFIRMED.
BARAS		PTE		/ 777	D									
BARETT	J	CSM		/ 98	B									ORIGINAL BN UNCONFIRMED POS 24/ OR 25/.
BARLOW		CPL	30	/ 362									TO 9th BN, ROYAL FUSILIERS(17th BN).	FRANCE 9 15/8/18 TO 28/8/18, 17 RF 29/8/18 TO 7/9/
BARLOW	J F	PTE	30	/ 262	C								TO ROYAL FUSILIERS.	STUDENT USHAW COLLEGE, R FUS No GS/93455.
BARRON	Wm	PTE	30	/ 18	B		BOWSDEN	25/10/15	28/2/19	KR para 392	OCTOBER 16		TO 24th BN, DEPOT.	ACPL, VOLUNTARY AID HOSP CHELTENHAM 8/7/16.
BARTLE	S	LCPL	30	/ 334			NEWCASTLE	11/12/15	26/6/17	GUNSHOT WOUNDS	MARCH 17		TO 19th BN, DEPOT.	
BATCH	Chas	PTE	30	/ 349		9 SIGOTT ST	HUDDERSFIELD			16 JUNE 1917		ARRAS MEM	TO 13th BN.	BORN RAMSEY HUNTINGDON.
BATEY	J W	PTE		/ 308	D									POS 24/.
BATEY	W H	PTE		/ 668	B									
BATTYE	W	PTE	30	/ 307						KR para 392			TO 13th BN.	
BAYNE	F	PTE		/ 694	D									
BEAUTIMAN	T	PTE	30	/ 202				6/12/15	22/12/17	SICK			TO DEPOT.	
BECKWITH	Willi	PTE	30	/ 393		9 NORTHFIELD TERR	SLAITHWAITE			11 JUNE 1918		TROIES TOWN CEM	TO 13th, 12/13th BN.	
BELL	G	PTE	30	/ 37	A									
BELL	J R	PTE	30	/ 309	A								TO LABOUR CORPS.	
BELL	R	PTE		/ 772	C									
BENNETT	E	PTE	30	/ 336						KR para 392			TO 27th, 13th, 24/27th, 19th BN.	
BINNS	A	PTE	30	/ 331			QUEENSBURY				JAN 18		TO 9th, 1st BNS, CLASS Z RESERVE.	
BIRKENSHAW	W	PTE		/ 877	C									
BIRNEY	Thoma	SGT	30	/ 292		23 ROWLANDSON TERR	FELLING			27 MAY 1918		LA VILLE AUX BOIS	TO 1/5th BN.	AGE 27.
BLACK	A J	PTE	30	/ 209	C									
BLACK	G W	PTE	30	/008	A									
BLACK	G W	PTE	30	/ 8	A									
BLACK	J	PTE		/ 873	C									
BLAKE	S R	PTE	30	/ 177	C	CONYERS RD	BYKER	5/10/15					TO LABOUR CORPS.	LAB CORPS No 216627.
BOLTON	R	PTE	30	/ 39	A									
BOYD	J	PTE	30	/ 85	D									SHOWN AS /86 ON BN ROLL.
BRABAN	J	PTE		/ 49	D									POS 26/ OR 27/.
BRANNEN	James	PTE	30	/ 155	A	5 JAMES ST	WHICKHAM			28 APRIL 1917	MISS OCT 16	ARRAS MEM	TO 25th BN.	SHELLSHOCK DEC 16.
BRANNIGAN	J	PTE	30	/ 165	B		ANNITSFORD			6 AUGUST 1916		CABERET ROUGE CEM	TO 24th BN.	
BRENNAN		PTE		/ 42	D									POS 26/ OR SGT M 27/.
BRINDLEY	T D	CPL	30	/ 150	A			29/11/15	31/3/19	KR para 392			TO ARMY RESERVE CLASS P.	DID NOT SERVE OVERSEAS?? CHECK
BROWN		PTE	30	/ 124	D									
BROWN	David	PTE	30	/ 73	C	6 PRINCE CONSORTS RD	JARROW			1 JULY 1916		THIEPVAL MEM	TO 24th BN(B COY).	MISSING AUGUST 16.
BROWN	J	PTE	30	/ 36	A									
BROWN	M	PTE	30	/ 56	C									
BRUCE	T	PTE	30	/ 216	C									STUDENT AT USHAW COLLEGE
BUCKLEY		LCPL		/ 91	D									25/ OR 26/.
BURGOYNE	Rob M	PTE	30	/ 105	B		WALKER			14 MARCH 1917		FABOURG DE AMIENS	TO 25th BN.	
BURKE	S	PTE	30	/ 54	B	12 GEORGE ST	BLAYDON							
BURNEY	Franc	CPL	30	/ 235	C			28/1/16	20/12/18	GASSED 6/4/18			TO 5th TR BN, 8th, 25th, 3rd BNS, COMMISSIONED.	AGE 21,TO FRANCE 6/17,TO UK 9/17,HOSP LONDON.
BURR	H	PTE		/ 71	C									

NAME	INITI	RANK	BA	NUMBE	COMP	ADDRESS	TOWN_VILL	ENLISTED	DISCHARG	CAUSE_DIS	WOUNDED	BURIED	TRANSFER	ADD
BURTON	A F	CPL		1045	A									POS CQMS WND IN HOSP ROUEN 7/16, NOT TI.
BYRNE	J	LCPL	30	144	C	BACK ST	CHESTER LE STRE						TO ROYAL ENGINEERS.	RE No 248786, WR267156.
CAFFERY		PTE	30	121	D									
CAIRNS	W	PTE		654	B									ORIGINAL BN UNCONFIRMED.
CAMPBELL	J	PTE	30	213	C			3/12/15	2/11/18	GUNSHOT WOUNDS			TO 19th, 14th BNS, DEPOT.	
CAPSTICK	J	PTE		1553	B									ORIGINAL BN UNCONFIRMED.
CARNEDY	J	PTE	30	16	D	52 NEWTON ST	FERRYHILL							
CARNEY	T	PTE		826	C									POS 26/
CARR		PTE		430	A									ORIGINAL BN UNCONFIRMED.
CARR	M	CPL		1207	A									NOT T.I.
CARRUTHERS	R	PTE		838	D									
CARSON	J J	LSGT	30	2	C									PALLBEARER TO SGT FINAN.
CARTWRIGHT	J	LCPL	30	383			HUDDERSFIELD	1/5/16	16/9/18	GSW	APRIL 18		TO DEPOT	
CASSIDY	John	PTE	30	66	C	LUCKER COTTAGE	BELFORD			26 OCT 1917	DECEMBER 16	POELCAPPELLE BRIT	TO 24th, 25th, 1/7th BNS.	AGE 25.
CAVANAGH	John	PTE	30	1462	B	4 NORTH STREET	BRANDON COLLIER						TO 3rd BN.	ORIGINAL BN UNCONFIRMED. 25/ OR 27/?
CHARLTON	Edwar	PTE	30	123			ST ANTHONYS NEW			17 AUGUST 1918		TANNAY BRIT CEM	TO 25th, 9th BNS.	CORRECT NAME EDWD CHARLTON WINTER, AGE 40.
CHARLTON	T	PTE	30	267	A									
CHEETHAM	W	PTE	30	211	B									
CHILD	W	SGT		854	B	12 STRATFORD ROAD	HEATON							PROB 24/.
CHRISTOPHER	Richa	PTE	30	251	C	HENDERSYDE MARINE AV	MONKSEATON			29 SEPT 1918		UNICORN CEM VENDHUIL	TO 27th BN, HEAVY BRANCH MGC, TANK CORPS.	SGT COMMISIONED NOV 16, Lt 16th BN TANK CORPS.
CLANCY	Mathe	SGT	30	225	C	19 SANDRINGHAM TERR	BENTON			10 APRIL 1917		WARLINCOURT HALT CEM	TO KINGS OWN YORKSHIRE LI(9th BN).	KOYLI No 42976,BORN GATESHEAD,STDT AT USHAW COLLEG
CLARKE	T H	PTE	30	100	B									
CLAZIE	Rober	PTE	30	38	A		COLDSTREAM			7 DEC 1918	SEPTEMBER 16	NEUF BRISACH CEM	TO MACHINE GUN CORPS(206 MG COY).	POW MARCH 1918,DIED OF EXSPOSURE,MGC No 71037.
CLIFFORD	J W	PTE	24	379										
CLIFFORD	T C	PTE	30	233	C									STUDENT AT USHAW COLLEGE.
COCKBURN	R	PTE	30	89	A									
COE	S B	PTE	30	187	C									
COLEMAN	J W	PTE	30	244	B			25/1/16	22/8/16	SICK			TO DEPOT.	DID NOT SERVE OVERSEAS.
COLEMAN	Peter	PTE	30	153	C	3 GLOUCESTER ST	MIDDLESBOROUGH			1 JULY 1916		THIEPVAL MEM	TO 24th BN.	MISSING SEPTEMBER 16.
COLLINS	Harry	PTE	30	369			CLAYTON YORKS			31 MARCH 1918		POZIERES MEM	TO 13th, 9th, 23rd, 1/5th BNS.	
COLLINS	J R T	PTE	30	146	A									
CONNOR	J	PTE	30	135	A									COULD BE 25/.
COOPER	F	CSGT	30	689									TO 9th BN, ROYAL FUSILIERS(17th BN).	FRANCE 9 15/8/18 TO 28/8/18, 17 RF 29/8/18 TO 7/9/
COOPER	J	PTE		885	A	402 LEWIS STREET	GATESHEAD							ORIGINAL BN UNCONFIRMED.EMPLOYED GATESHEAD STATION
CORCORAN	J	PTE	30	421	A									POS 24/421. UNCONFIRMED.
COTTON	J	PTE		736	B									
COULSON	J	PTE	30	255	A									
COULTER	R	PTE		917	C									
COUPLAND	F	LCPL	30	439				25/5/16	31/7/17	WOUNDS			TO DEPOT.	
COXON	R	PTE		1503	A									ORIGINAL BN UNCONFIRMED.
CRAM		CQMS		1479	C									
CRANGLE	G	PTE	30	314	B									STUDENT AT USHAW COLLEGE
CRANGLE	J H	PTE	30	214	B									
CRAWFORD	Richa	PTE	30	232	C			../1/16	6/3/18		4/10/17		TO KINGS OWN YORKSHIRE LI 6th, 9th BNS.	STDNT AT USHAW COLLEGE,ENTERED FRANCE DEC 16.
CRIBBENS	Thos	PTE	30	122	A			22/11/15	27/12/16	SICK			TO 24th, 30th BNS.	
CROWBIE	R S	PTE		91	B									ORIGINAL BN UNCONFIRMED MAY NOT BE TI.
CUNNINGHAM	D	PTE	30	219	C									STUDENT AT USHAW COLLEGE.
CUNNINGHAM	H P	SGT	30	182	B								TO 24th, 1/5th, 17th BNS.	STILL SERVING APRIL 1920
CUNNINGHAM	T	PTE	30	734	B									
CUNNINGHAM	T	PTE		150	B									COULD BE 24/ OR 27/.
CUNNINGHAM	W	PTE	30	420	A									NOT TYNESIDE IRISH BUT SERVING WITH 30th BN.
CURRY	R H	PTE		117	B		USWORTH				AUGUST 16			
CUSWICK	D	PTE	30	711	A									
DAGG	W	PTE	30	13	A									
DALEY	W	CPL		177	D									POS 26/.
DANSKIN	W	PTE	30	125	C									
DAVIDSON	T	PTE	30	234	B									
DAVIS	F	PTE		302	A									NOT TYNESIDE IRISH BUT SERVING WITH 30th BN.
DAWSON	J	PTE	30	82	C									
DELANEY	P	CPL	30	768	B								COMMISSIONED.	STUDENT AT USHAW COLLEGE.

NAME	INITI	RANK	BA	NUMBE	COMP	ADDRESS	TOWN_VILL	ENLISTED	DISCHARG	CAUSE_DIS	WOUNDED	BURIED	TRANSFER	ADD
DENT	Geo W	PTE	30 /	79	B		NEWCASTLE			30 SEPT 1916	FEBRUARY 17	THIEPVAL MEM	TO 24th BN.	
DENT	Wm	PTE	30 /	265	B				29/9/19				TO MACHINE GUN CORPS(34th BN), CLASS Z RESERVE.	MGC No 152011. MUST HAVE BEEN 24/27th BN ALSO.
DICKIE	G	LCPL	30 /	149	C									
DICKINSON		LCPL	/	1489	C									
DILLON	P	PTE	30 /	229	C									STUDENT AT USHAW COLLEGE.
DINSDALE	T	PTE			C									
DIXON	C	CPL	30 /	94	A									
DIXON	F	PTE	30 /	114	D									
DOCK	Wm	CPL	30 /	131	C	30 RICHARDSON ST	CARLISLE			26 APRIL 1918		TYNE COT MEM	TO 8th, 25th BNS.	
DODD	J	PTE	30 /	280	A									
DODDS	T W	PTE	30 /	274									TO 25th, 1/7th BNS. REMAINED IN THE ARMY	ALLOTED NEW Nos 292088 AND 80036, GSM 'IRAQ'
DONNOLLY		PTE	30 /	260	A									
DOW	M	PTE	/	9	B									NOT TYNESIDE IRISH BUT SERVING WITH 30th BN.
DOYLE	J	PTE	30 /	109	D									
DOYLE	J W	PTE	30 /	269	A									
DUNNE	P	PTE	30 /	203	C									
DYSON	Harol	PTE	30 /	358			RIPPONDEN			4 OCT 1917		TYNE COT MEM	TO KINGS OWN YORKSHIRE LI(6th, 9th BNS).	KOYLI No 43017, AGE 38.
EBDON	G	PTE	/	899	C									
EDMINSON	G	PTE	30 /	268	A									
EDMONDSON	Berti	PTE	30 /	385			BARNOLDSWICK			21 APRIL 1917		ARRAS MEM	TO 13th, 10th, 9th BNS.	
EGAN	L	SGT	/	132	D									
ELLEN	G W	PTE	30 /	103	C		LONDON				OCT 16, JAN 18.			
ELLIOTT		PTE	/	887	C									
ELLIOTT	T W	SGT	30 /	485									TO 9th BN, ROYAL FUSILIERS(17th BN).	FRANCE 9 15/8/18 TO 28/8/18, 17 RF 29/8/18 TO 7/9/
ELLIS	W	PTE	30 /	299				1/12/15	4/4/17	NEPHRITIS			TO 10th BN, DEPOT.	
EMMOTT	E	PTE	30 /	342				2/12/15	4/12/17	WOUNDS			TO 13th BN, DEPOT.	
ENGLISH	R	PTE	30 /	75	B									
FANNING		CSM	/	1369	C									
FARNAN	J	PTE	30 /	286									TO 9th BN, CLASS Z RESERVE.	
FEATHERSTONE	Alber	PTE	30 /	343		12 LEAMINGTON TERR	ILKLEY			23 DEC 1916		VERMELLES MIL CEM	TO 13th BN.	
FEE	Austi	PTE	30 /	230	C	16 ALBERT TERR	BLAYDON						COMMISSIONED TO ROYAL AIR FORCE.	STUDENT AT USHAW COLLEGE,18 MONTHS IN T IRISH.
FELL	A A	PTE	30 /	368				28/3/16	18/8/16	SICK			TO 34th BN.	DID NOT SERVE OVERSEAS.
FISH	J	PTE	/	295	A									NOT TYNESIDE IRISH BUT SERVING WITH 30th BN.
FISHER	G	PTE	30 /	305	A									
FISHER	T	SGT	/	1621	A									ORIGINAL BN UNCONFIRMED.
FLATLEY	Thos	CPL	30 /	242	B		CHARLESTOWN Co			28 APRIL 1917		ARRAS MEM	TO 24th BN.	ALSO SGT D COY 30th BN.
FLYNN	Charl	PTE	30 /	222	C			../1/16	9/11/17		9/4/17		TO KINGS OWN YORKSHIRE LI 6th, 9th BNS.	STUDENT AT USHAW COLLEGE,ENTERED FRANCE DEC 16.
FORTUNE	J	PTE	30 /	90	A		FELTON			KR para 392	OCTOBER 16		TO 24th, 25th, 1/5th BNS.	ALLOCATED NEW NUMBER 204631.
FOSTER	J T	PTE	/	245	A									
FOWLER	J R	PTE	30 /	92	A									
FOX	J	PTE	30 /	9	B		BEDLINGTON	18/10/15	30/1/19	KR para 392	OCTOBER 16		TO 25th, 8th, 16th, 1/6th BNS, ARMY RESERVE CLASS	BATH WAR HOSP 11/7/16
FRANCIS		SGT	30 /	23	D									
FRAZER		CPL	30 /	253	C									POS 27/.
GARDNER	T	PTE	30 /	246	B									
GENT	W	PTE	/	980	A									
GIBBON	R	PTE	30 /	307	A									ON MRC AS 24/.
GIBBONS		LCPL			C									
GIBBONS	John	CPL	30 /	117	C			16/11/15	19/2/18		EASTER MONDAY 1917		TO 3rd BN.	STUDENT AT USHAW COLLEGE, HOSP BRIGHTON.
GILL	Benja	PTE	30 /	332				21/11/15	4/1/18	GASSED			TO 3rd BN.	
GILLESPIE	G	PTE	/	1394	A									ORIGINAL BN UNCONFIRMED.
GILROY	R	PTE	/	1322	A									
GOLIGHTLY	R	PTE	30 /	169	B									
GRACE	J	PTE	30 /	198	C									
GRAGAN		PTE	30 /	220	C									
GRAHAM	H	PTE	30 /	301	A									
GRAHAM	J	PTE	30 /	195	C									
GRAHAM	J N	PTE	30 /	44	A								TO 19th BN, ATTACHED 10th ENTRENCHING BN, 14th BN,	
GRANT	A	PTE	30 /	738	C									
GREEN	J	LSGT	/	1483	C									
GREEN	R	PTE	30 /	81	B									

NAME	INITI	RANK	BA	NUMBE	COMP	ADDRESS	TOWN_VILL	ENLISTED	DISCHARG	CAUSE_DIS	WOUNDED	BURIED	TRANSFER	ADD
GREENAN	C	PTE		/ 186	C									
GUTHERIE	A	PTE	30	/ 113	B									
GUTHRIE	A	PTE	30	/ 137									TO 25th BN.	DESERTED 7/9/18.
GUY	W	PTE	30	/ 3	A	3 NAPIER ST	NEWCASTLE	5/10/15						
HAGGERTY	T	PTE	30	/ 135	C									
HAILS	M	PTE		/ 259	C									
HALL	Georg	PTE	30	/ 58		JOY GARDENS	KELSO			1 JULY 1916		THIEPVAL MEM	TO 25th BN.	MISSING OCTOBER 16
HALL	J	PTE	30	/ 11	D									
HALPIN	W	PTE		/ 279	C									POS RICHARD, CORNSAY COLLIERY, PROB 26/.
HAMILTON	J J	PTE	30	/ 193	A			20/10/15	17/10/17	SICK			TO 25th BN, DEPOT.	
HANCOCK	A D	PTE	30	/ 652	B									
HANLON	T	PTE		/ 312	C									PROB 26/
HARVEY	J H	SGT		/ 263	B									COULD BE 24/ 25/ OR 30/?
HAY	W	PTE	30	/ 72	C								TO 24th, 25th, 20th, 12/13th, 1/4th, 12/13th BNS,	3 CCS 4/7/16 EVAC 11/7/16 APPENDICITIS.
HEENEY	J E	PTE	30	/ 666	B									
HELLIWELL	A	LCPL	30	/ 365									TO 13th, 22nd, 10th BNS, CLASS Z RESERVE..	
HELLIWELL	H	PTE	30	/ 391				11/5/16	17/10/19	KR para 392			TO DEPOT.	
HENDERSON	W	PTE	30	/ 134	A									
HENDRY	R	PTE		/ 968	C									
HERBERT	Louie	PTE	30	/ 78	B	5 MARINO CRS CLONTAF	DUBLIN			10 APRIL 1918	SEPTEMBER 16.	PLOEGSTEERT MEM	TO 25th, 26th, 1/5th BNS.	AGE 21.
HERDMAN	J	PTE		/1369	D									POS 25/1367 HERDMAN A.
HERRON	J P	CPL		/ 955	B									
HODGKINSON	C	PTE	30	/ 196	A									
HOGG	E	PTE	30	/ 133	A									
HOGGINS	P	PTE	30	/ 97	A	9 COPELAND TERR	SHIELDFIELD						TO 24th, 25th, 1/4th BNS, ROYAL DEFENCE CORPS.	34CCS 2/7 EVAC 5/7,5th GHOSP LEICESTER 11/7/16, AG
HOLLAND	T	PTE		/1332	D	17 MARGARET ST	WASHINGTON STAT							
HOLT	R	PTE	30	/006	A									
HOOD	J	LCPL	30	/2877	B									
HOPE	J L	LCPL	30	/ 191	C								TO 24th, 12th, 12/13th BNS, CLASS Z RESERVE.	
HOPKINS	J	PTE	30	/ 34	A									
HORNSBY	Thoma	LCPL		/1196	D	BOTTLE BANK	BLACKHILL	12/11/14						ALSO ON D COY 24th BN ROLL. BUT NOT 24/1196.
HORTON	F	PTE	30	/ 371						KR para 392			TO 13th, 12/13th BNS.	
HOWARD	Chas	PTE	30	/ 323			MOSSBY			23 DEC 1916			TO 13th BN.	
HOWEY	W	PTE		/1331	A									
HOYLE	Willi	PTE	30	/ 330			HALIFAX			4 OCT 1917		TYNE COT MEM	TO 13th, 12/13th BN.	
HUDSON	C	PTE		/ 994	A									ORIGINAL BN UNCONFIRMED.
INGLIS	J	PTE		/ 355	C									
IRSKINE	J	CPL		/ 174	D									
IRWIN		PTE	30	/ 126	D									
JACKSON	Alb D	LCPL	30	/ 115	B		JARROW			1 JULY 1916		THIEPVAL MEM	TO 25th BN.	MISSING OCTOBER 16.
JACKSON	Clar	PTE	30	/ 163	B		WAKEFIELD			14 OCT 1918		BLARGIES MIL CEM	TO 25th BN.	
JAMESON	W	PTE	30	/ 660	B									
JOBSON	John	PTE	30	/ 46	A	HECKLEY FENCE	ALNWICK			1 JULY 1916		THIEPVAL MEM	TO 24th BN.	MISSING AUGUST 16, AGE 19 BORN BELFORD.
JOHNSON		PTE		/ 861	C									
JOHNSON	E	PTE	30	/ 17	B									
JOHNSON	Edwd	LCPL	30	/ 116	B		BURNHOPEFIELD			1 JULY 1916		THIEPVAL MEM	TO 24th BN.	MISSING AUGUST 16.
JOHNSTON	Albt	CPL	30	/ 60	C		MINDRUM MILL						TO 24th, 24/27th, 20th, 22nd, 9th BNS, CLASS Z RES	
JONES	Chas	CPL	30	/ 464	C	THE CROWN HOTEL	HAWSE			1 JUNE 1917		HENIN COM CEM EXT	TO KINGS OWN YORKSHIRE LI(9th BN).	KOYLI No 42986, AGE 19.
JOYCE	M	PTE	30	/ 276	A	30 DOUBLE ROW	HEDLEY HILL							
JOYCE	T	PTE	30	/ 86	C		NEW BRANCEPETH				OCTOBER 16			
KEENAN	H	LCPL		/ 327	D									PROB 25/.
KEIGHLEY	J	PTE	30	/ 252	C									
KERSHAW	Harry	LCPL	30	/ 315		39 HARKER ST LOWMOOR	BRADFORD			4 OCT 1917		TYNE COT MEM	TO KINGS OWN YORKSHIRE LI(9th BN).	KOYLI No 42953, AGE 21
KIDD	J R	PTE	30	/ 291	A									
LACEY	G	PTE		/ 843	A									ORIGINAL BN UNCONFIRMED POS 24/.
LACY	L	PTE	30	/ 248	C									
LAHIFF	R	SGT		/1026	D									
LAPPER	H	SGT	30	/ 449									TO 8th, 25th, 12/13th BNS, CLASS Z RESERVE.	
LAW	R	PTE	30	/ 374				11/12/15	10/1/19	SHRAPNEL WOUND			TO 13th BN.	AGE 23.
LAZZARI	J	SGT	30	/ 87	A	5 KINGSLEY TERR	RYTON				AUGUST 16.		TO 25th BN, CLASS Z RESERVE.	3 CCS 2/7/16 EVAC 3/7/16 GSW.

NAME	INITI	RANK	BA	NUMBE	COMP	ADDRESS	TOWN_VILL	ENLISTED	DISCHARG	CAUSE_DIS	WOUNDED	BURIED	TRANSFER	ADD
LEADBITTER		PTE		/ 396	D									POS 26/.
LINCOLN		SGT		/ 543	D									
LINDSAY	P	PTE	30	/ 655	B									
LIVELY	M	PTE	30	/ 112	B			15/11/15	26/7/17	SHELLSHOCK			TO 3rd BN.	
LOCKHART	G	PTE	30	/ 50	A									
LONGSTAFF	H	PTE		/ 23	B									NOT TYNESIDE IRISH BUT SERVING WITH 30th BN.
LONSDALE	H	PTE	30	/ 335				12/2/16	6/2/17	KR para 392			TO 13th BN.	
LOYDEN	John	PTE	30	/ 273						19 APRIL 1918		ETAPLES MIL CEM	TO LANCASHIRE FUSILIERS(2/5th BN).	LF No 31476.
MACKIN	Peter	PTE	30	/ 236	B		BLYTH							LETTER IN SOUTH SHIELDS GAZ 29/7/16.
MAFFIN	Georg	PTE	30	/ 160	B								TO GORDON HIGHLANDERS.	GORDONS No 31712.
MAITLAND	Willi	PTE		/ 523	A	163 LWR CUTHBERT ST	GATESHEAD		14/12/18				TO KINGS OWN YORKSHIRE LI 6th, 9th BNS.	KOYLI No 42950, SGT.
MALLINSON	G F	PTE	30	/ 325						KR para 392			TO 13th, 24/27th, 8th BNS.	
MARTIN	J	PTE	30	/ 120	C									
MASON	J	PTE	30	/ 657	B									
MATHEWS	J	PTE	30	/ 247	B									
MATHEWSON	R	PTE	30	/ 279	A									
MATHIE	J	CQMS		/1373	D									
MEAD	W	PTE		/ 434	C									
MEARNS	W	PTE		/ 452	C									
MIDDLEMASS	J	CPL		/ 409	C									POS 24/ OR 26/.
MILNER	O	PTE	30	/ 261	A									
MINGAY	J H	PTE		/ 129	C									
MINGAY	T H	PTE		/ 237	C									
MITCHELL	H A	PTE	30	/015	A									
MONAGHAN	Lesli	PTE	30	/ 127	C	65 GORDON ST	GATESHEAD			1 JULY 1916		THIEPVAL MEM	TO 25th BN.	
MORELAND	Willi	PTE	30	/ 189	A		CLEATON			26 OCT 1917		TYNE COT MEM	TO 19th, 14th, 1/7th BNS.	
MORGAN	C J	LCPL	30	/ 152	A									
MULLANEY	M	PTE		/ 442	C									
MULLANEY	W J	PTE		/ 437	D									
MULLEN	C H	CPL	30	/ 205	C								TO 25th BN, ROYAL FUSILIERS(24th BN).	FRANCE 25 19/2/18 TO 30/8/18, 24RF 31/8/18 TO 6/1/
MULLER	F	LCPL		/ 524	D									
MULLIGAN	M	PTE	30	/ 241	B								TO 25th BN, CLASS Z RESERVE.	
MURDIE	E	PTE	30	/ 637	A									
MURPHY	J	PTE	30	/ 206	B									
MURPHY	John	PTE	30	/ 83	C			8/11/15	29/11/17	SICK			TO DEPOT.	
MURRAY	J	PTE	30	/ 243	B									
McARDLE	J	CPL		/1157	C									prob 25/.
McCLUSKEY	G	PTE	30	/ 271	D									
McCORMACK	Arthu	CPL	30	/ 231	C	47 PARK RD	CONSETT	29/1/16	27/9/18	GUNSHOT WOUNDS	APRIL 1918		TO 1/4th BN.	STUDENT AT USHAW COLLEGE, ENTERED FRANCE EASTER 19
McCOY	Edwd	PTE	30	/ 6	C	24 24 MELBOURNE ST	NEWCASTLE			1 JULY 1916		THIEPVAL MEM	TO 24th BN.	
McDERMOTT	Berna	LCPL	30	/ 190	C				14/2/19				TO KINGS OWN YORKSHIRE LI 6th, 2nd BNS, CLASS Z RE	STUDENT AT USHAW COLLEGE. KOYLI No 42964.
McDERRMOTT	T	PTE	30	/ 338				17/8/14	12/3/18	SICK			TO ARMY RESERVE CLASS W.	
McDOUGALL		PTE	30	/ 65	C									
McELDUFF	J	SGT	30	/ 402		PACK HORSE INN	CROOKGATE						TO 18th, 14th(A COY) BNS, CLASS Z RESERVE.	
McGEE	J	CPL		/1114	C									ORIGINAL BN UNCONFIRMED.
McGLORY		PTE	30	/ 180	D									
McGOUGH	E	PTE	30	/ 240	C									STUDENT AT USHAW COLLEGE.
McGUINESS	R	PTE		/ 463	A									ORIGINAL BN UNCONFIRMED POS 27/463?
McGUIRE	G	PTE		/ 354	A									ORIGINAL BN UNCONFIRMED POS 24/?
McHUGH	T	PTE	30	/ 254	A									
McINTYRE	F	LCPL	30	/ 207	B									
McKEE	H	PTE	30	/ 142	C									
McKEOWN	John	LCPL	30	/ 21	B		HEBBURN			27 OCT 1918	OCTOBER 16	BERLIN STAHNSDORF	TO 25th, 27th, 16th, 14th BNS.	BORN JARROW DIED WHILST A PRISONER OF WAR.
McKEVER	James	LCPL	30	/ 110	B		NEWCASTLE			1 JULY 1916		THIEPVAL MEM	TO 25th BN.	
McKIRGAN	John	PTE	30	/ 119		46 UPPER BRANCH ST	SOUTHBANK			19 NOV 1916		BAILLEUL	TO 24th BN.	BORN BALLYMENA.
McLAREN	W	PTE	30	/ 68	C									
McMAHON	Georg	PTE	30	/ 166	D				28/1/19				TO KINGS OWN YORKSHIRE LI 6th, 2nd BNS, CLASS Z RE	
McMAHON	Phili	PTE	30	/ 215	C					9 APRIL 1917			TO KINGS OWN YORKSHIRE LI 6th, 9th BNS.	
McMASTERS	M	SGT		/1653	D									
McNALLY	J	PTE		/1171	A									ORIGINAL BN UNCONFIRMED POS 24/ OR 25/

NAME	INITI	RANK	BA	NUMBE	COMP	ADDRESS	TOWN_VILL	ENLISTED	DISCHARG	CAUSE_DIS	WOUNDED	BURIED	TRANSFER	ADD
McNAMEE	Josep	LCPL	30	245	B		CLEATOR MOOR			13 AUGUST 1916		THIEPVAL MEM	TO 9th BN.	
McNEIL	J	SGT		1206	D									
McNIFF	Franc	PTE	30	228	C			../1/16				CERISY GAILLY CEM	COMMISSIONED ATTACHED ROYAL FLYING CORPS.	STUDENT AT USHAW COLLEGE,SGT POSTED CADET SCHOOL. PROB 25/?
McPEAK	J	PTE		485	D									
McWILLIAMS		PTE		212	C									
NAYLOR	Arthu	PTE	30	351		2 COMMERCIAL CRES	HUDDERSFIELD			14 APRIL 1917		ARRAS MEM	TO 13th BN.	
NAYLOR	Arthu	PTE	30	304			HUDDERSFIELD			16 JUNE 1917		ARRAS MEM	TO 13th BN.	
NELLES	J	PTE	30	99	A	252 HIGH ST	GATESHEAD							
NESBIT	Wm	PTE	30	33	B		SHEDLAW			17 DEC 1918		BELGRADE CEM NAMUR	TO 25th, 14th BNS, ROYAL FUSILIERS(24th BN).	FRANCE 25 16/3/16 TO 11/4/18, 14 18/7/18 TO 28/8/1
NICHOLS	J	LCPL	30	164	A									
NICHOLSON	Frank	PTE	30	322										
NICHOLSON	R	PTE		858	C									
NOBLE	Geo D	PTE	30	392			HUDDERSFIELD			29 AUGUST 1918		VIS-EN-ARTOIS MEM	TO 13th BN, RIF BDE(DEPOT), ATT 1/5th LONDON REGT	RIF BDE No 45178.
NORMAN	D	PTE	30	185	A									
NORTH	E	PTE	30	308						KR para 392			TO 13th BN.	
NUGENT	J	PTE		183	C									
O'CONNER	D	PTE	30	223	C									STUDENT AT USHAW COLLEGE, WOUNDED.
O'HAGAN	B	LCPL		556	C									
O'REILLY	H	PTE	30	200	C								TO 25th BN.	DESERTED 7 NOVEMBER 1917.
OATES	P	PTE	30	386									TO 13th, 12/13th, 25th BNS, CLASS Z RESERVE.	
OCONNOR	Franc	PTE	30	272		33 EDITH ST	CONSETT			23 MARCH 1917		ARRAS MEM	TO MANCHESTER REGT(17th BN).	MAN REGT No 43198, BORN LONGBENTON.
OHARE	James	LCPL	30	257	A	68 ELSWICK ST	NEWCASTLE			30 JULY 1916		ARRAS MEM 1996	TO 25th BN.	ON 30th BN ROLL AS OHARE 30/259, BORN GATESHEAD.
ONIELL		PTE		176	C									
ONIELL	Jos	PTE	30	148	A		HEBBURN			1 JULY 1916		THIEPVAL MEM	TO 25th BN.	
ORANGE	Jas	PTE	30	161	B	21 REDHEUGH BRIDGE R	GATESHEAD						TO 25th BN, LABOUR CORPS(281 A E COY), NF.	STILL SERVING JAN 1921, LABV CORPS No 368901
ORD	Rober	LSGT		570	D									
ORIVRDEN	T	PTE	30	157	A									
OUSTON	C	PTE		1361	C									
OVINGTON	T	PTE	30	837	A									
OWENS	J	LCPL	30	151	A									
PAGAN	W	PTE	30	52	A			27/10/15	12/12/17	SICK			TO 25th BN, DEPOT.	
PARKER	J	PTE	30	172	B									
PARKER	J	SGT		543	D									
PARNABY	A S	PTE	30	475				15/5/16	31/8/16	SICK				DID NOT SERVE OVERSEAS.
PARVIN		PTE		1160	C									
PEARSON	F	CQMS	30	401				6/1/15	9/10/19	KR para 392			TO DEPOT.	DID NOT SERVE OVERSEAS.
PEARSON	J	PTE		1170	C									
PECKSTON	Cuthb	PTE	30	217	C					22 MARCH 1918		ARRAS MEM	COMMISSIONED, TO 25th BN.	STUDENT AT USHAW COLLEGE.
PETERS	A W	SGT	30	253									TO 1/4th BN.	
PETERSON	C A	PTE		106	B									
PHELAN	D	PTE	30	14	A									
PHILIPS	G A	PTE	30	249	C									STUDENT AT USHAW COLLEGE.
PHILIPS	J	PTE	30	221	C									STUDENT AT USHAW COLLEGE, PRISONER OF WAR.
PHILIPS	T	PTE		886	C									
PHILLIPS	R	PTE		1513	B									ORIGINAL BN UNCONFIRMED.
PIGG	J W	LSGT			B									
PLATT	Harry	PTE	30	356		32 CLOSE HILL LANE	NEWSOME			22 SEPT 1916		THIEPVAL MEM	TO 13th BN.	BORN HUDDERSFIELD.
POLLARD	R	PTE	30	130	B			16/11/15	17/6/16	KR para 392				DID NOT SERVE OVERSEAS.
PORTER		PTE		530	D									
PRINGLE	A	PTE	30	26									TO MACHINE GUN CORPS.	
PRINGLE	Wm Dr	PTE	30	28	B		BERWICK			1 JULY 1916		THIEPVAL MEM	TO 25th BN.	
PRIOR	Felix	PTE	30	264	B	NESTFIELD ST	DARLINGTON		21/2/18				TO KINGS OWN YORKSHIRE LI 6th, 9th BNS, COMMISSION	STUDENT AT USHAW COLLEGE. KOYLI No 42963.
PROCTOR		PTE		571	D									
PRUDHOE	A H	PTE	30	630	A									CORRECT No PROBABLY 27630 PRUDHOE A L.
QUINN	C	PTE		1002	A								TO LABOUR CORPS.	
QUINN	J	PTE		173	C									
QUINN	P	PTE	30	002	A									
RAMSHAW	John	PTE	30	5	C	24 69 DUNSTON ST	HEBBURN			28 SEPT 1918	JULY 16	BUCQUOY RD MIL CEM	TO 24th, 12/13th, 8th BNS.	RAMSHAW S PTE NF AT ABOVE ADDRESS NO REGT No.
REAY	W B	PTE	30	300	A									
REILLY	P	PTE	30	12	A		SOUTH SHIELDS	20/10/15	12/4/18	GUNSHOT WOUNDS	JUNE 18.		TO 3rd BN.	

NAME	INITI	RANK	BA	NUMBE	COMP	ADDRESS	TOWN_VILL	ENLISTED	DISCHARG	CAUSE_DIS	WOUNDED	BURIED	TRANSFER	ADD
REYNOLDS	J	PTE	30	/ 154	A		ALFRETON	1/12/15	22/12/17	GSW	JANUARY 17		TO 24th, 1st, 3rd BNS.	
RICE	W	PTE	30	/ 208	A		LIVERPOOL	17/11/14	19/4/17	GUNSHOT WOUNDS	JULY 16		TO 25th, 3rd BNS.	
RICH	L	PTE		/ 884	C									
RICHARDS	G S	PTE		/ 961	C									
RICHARDSON	J	LCPL		/ 637	C									ORIGINAL BN UNCONFIRMED 24/ OR 26/.
RICHMAN	J	PTE		/ 967	C									
RIDDELL	W	PTE		/ 272	A									NOT TYNESIDE IRISH BUT SERVING WITH 30th BN.
RILEY	M	PTE		/ 807	C									
RILEY	N	PTE	30	/ 104	B									
ROBSON		LCPL			C									
ROBSON	E	PTE	30	/ 428	A									
ROBSON	F	PTE		/ 304	A									NOT TYNESIDE IRISH BUT SERVING WITH 30th BN.
RODGERS	W	PTE		/ 210	C									
ROGAN	J	PTE		/1265	A									
ROGERSON	J W	LCPL	30	/ 31	B									
ROONEY	Josep	PTE	30	/ 76	B		HEWORTH			1 JULY 1916		BAPAUME POST MIL CEM	TO 25th BN.	MISSING OCTOBER 16.
ROONEY	T	PTE	30	/ 77	B								TO 25th BN, ROYAL FUSILIERS(24th BN).	FRANCE 25 10/3/16 TO 30/8/18, 24RF 31/8/18 TO 18/9
ROSS	J	PTE		/ 567	D									
RUSSELL	A	PTE	30	/001	A	44 Jas ARMITIDGE ST	SOUTHWICK							
SAVAGE	J	PTE	30	/ 145	B								TO 1st GARRISON BN, CLASS Z RESERVE.	
SCOTT	Edmun	PTE	30	/ 295		19 LUSTRE STREET	KIEGHLEY			22 SEPT 1916		THIEPVAL MEM	TO 13th BN.	AGE 19. SHOWN ON TM AS 32/295.
SCOTT	J	PTE		/ 239	C									
SCOTT	J W	PTE	30	/ 188	A									
SCOTT	R	PTE	30	/ 45			MELDON				OCTOBER 16		TO 24th BN.	ALLOTTED NEW No 85781.
SCOTT	R J	PTE		/ 623	D									PROB 26/?
SHEEHAN	John	CPL	30	/ 168	B		CAHERCIVEEN			1 JULY 1916		THIEPVAL MEM	TO 25th BN.	MISSING OCTOBER 16.
SIM	W G	PTE	30	/ 735	B									
SIMONS	James	PTE	30	/ 178	C	259 KIRK ST	BYKER			1 JULY 1916		THIEPVAL MEM	TO 24th BN.	MISSING AUGUST 16.
SIMPSON	J T	PTE		/1447	C									ORIGINAL BN UNCONFIRMED.
SIMPSON	R	PTE		/ 869	C									
SIMS	R	PTE		/1447	A									ORIGINAL BN UNCONFIRMED.
SINCLAIR	J S	PTE		/1372	A									ORIGINAL BN UNCONFIRMED.
SKIPPER	Wm	PTE	30	/ 107	B		TYNEMOUTH			26 MARCH 1918	OCTOBER 16	POZIERES MEM	TO 25th, 16th, 1/6th BNS.	
SKIPPERS	J T	LCPL	30	/ 147	A									
SMART	E M	LCPL	30	/ 175	C		GATESHEAD				FEB 17,		TO 24th BN, CLASS Z RESERVE.	MISSING AUGUST 16, WND+PRISONER OF WAR FEB 17.
SMITH	Ernes	PTE	30	/ 329			HALIFAX			24 AUGUST 1917		TYNE COT MEM	TO KINGS OWN YORKSHIRE LI(6th BN).	KOYLI No 42980, AGE 35.
SMITH	F W	ACQM	30	/ 421									TO 9th BN, ROYAL FUSILIERS(17th BN).	FRANCE 9 15/8/18 TO 28/8/18, 17 RF 29/8/18 TO 7/9/
SMITH	H	SGT		/ 37	D									
SMITH	J	PTE	30	/ 312									TO 13th, 1/5th BNS, CLASS Z RESERVE.	
SMITH	J W	PTE	30	/ 636	A									
SMITH	L	PTE		/ 240	B									NOT TYNESIDE IRISH BUT SERVING WITH 30th BN.
SMITH	T P	PTE	30	/ 562				8/12/15	31/8/16	KR para 392(iii				
SPENCE	J	PTE		/1284	D									PROB 25/1285 SPENCE J.
STEBBINGS	H	PTE	30	/ 337									TO 13th BN, CLASS Z RESERVE.	
STOTHERT	J	PTE	30	/ 74				26/10/15	2/7/16	KR para 392				DID NOT SERVE OVERSEAS.
STRICK		CPL		/ 653	B									
SWAN	R	PTE	30	/ 64	C									
SWAN	T	PTE	30	/ 69	C		WOOLER				OCT 16			
SWEENEY	M	PTE	30	/ 128	C		SHIELDFIELD				OCTOBER 16		TO 25th BN, ROYAL INNISKILLING FUSILIERS(6th BN).	
TAGGART	J	PTE	30	/ 20	B		NEWCASTLE	27/10/15	20/4/17	WOUNDS	OCTOBER 16		TO 25th BN, DEPOT.	
TATE	J B	PTE		/ 768	B									NOT TYNESIDE IRISH BUT SERVING WITH 30th BN.
TAYLOR	Jos C	PTE	30	/ 201		23 DEPTFORD ROAD	SUNDERLAND			9 APRIL 1917		COJEUL BRITISH CEM	TO KINGS OWN YORKSHIRE LI(9th BN).	KOYLI No 42995, BORN DURHAM AGE 21..
TAYLORSON	S W	PTE	30	/ 258	A									
TEAHEN	Denni	PTE	30	/ 136	B	4 SECOND STREET	BLACKHALL COLLI				OCTOBER 16		TO DURHAM LIGHT INFANTRY.	DLI No 373404.
TERRY	S	PTE	30	/ 315						KR para 392			TO 12th, 12/13th, 9th, 23rd BNS.	
THOMPSON	Fred	PTE	30	/ 420									TO MACHINE GUN CORPS(34th BN), CLASS Z RESERVE.	MGC No 151960.
THOMPSON	G T	LCPL	30	/ 91	A									
THOMPSON	J	PTE	30	/ 24	D									
THOMPSON	J H	PTE	30	/ 19	B									
THOMPSON	R	PTE	30	/ 1	B		SOUTH SHIELDS	31/8/15	30/1/19	KR para 392	AUGUST 16		TO 25th BN, ARMY RESERVE CLASS P.	

NAME	INITI	RANK	BA	NUMBE	COPP	ADDRESS	TOWN_VILL	ENLISTED	DISCHARG	CAUSE_DIS	WOUNDED	BURIED	TRANSFER	ADD
THORBURN	W	PTE		/ 906	C									
TIERNEY	J	PTE	30	/ 111	D	48 PRINCE CONSORT RD	JARROW				JUL OCT 16		TO 24th, 14th, 24th, 14th BNS	DESERTED 10/6/18, SEE ALSO 24/1626.
TIERNEY	T	PTE		/1264	C									
TIGHE		PTE		/ 162	D									POS 24/.
TIGHE	Adolp	LCPL	30	/ 204	C	125 DURHAM RD	TUDHOE		28 SEPT 1918			DUISANS BRIT CEM	TO 24th, 8th BNS.	AGE 23, NOK KILLARNEY HOUSE TUDHOE GRANGE.
TINLIN		PTE	30	/ 51	A									
TODD	J	PTE	30	/ 658	B									
TONOR	J	PTE		/1383	C	12 ROSEBERRY TERR	CONSETT	14/1/15						
TOUGH	J	CPL		/1499	D									
TUMELTY	Austi	CPL	30	/ 224	C		DURHAM CITY	../3/16	10 NOV 1917			ARRAS MEM	COMMISIONED ROYAL DUBLIN FUSILIERS(11th BN) OCT 16	STUDENT AT USHAW COLLEGE, KILLED ON A NIGHT PATROL
TURNER		LCPL			C									
TURNER		LSGT		/ 17	D									
TURNER	D	PTE	30	/ 140	C									
TWEDDLE	R S	LSGT			B									
TWEEDY	A	PTE	30	/ 96	A									
URWIN	J	PTE	30	/003	A								TO DURHAM LI.	CORRECT No 28003.
USHER	F	PTE	30	/ 95	A									
USHER	W	PTE	30	/ 93	A									
WAITE	J M	SGT	30	/ 194	D			30/12/15	15/9/16	KR para 392			TO DEPOT.	DID NOT SERVE OVERSEAS.
WALKER	F	LSGT		/1296	A									ORIGINAL BN UNCONFIRMED.
WALKER	J E	PTE	30	/ 294		38 KING ST YEADON	LEEDS		6 JUNE 1917			ARRAS MEM	TO 13th BN.	
WALSH	J T	CPL		/ 728	D									
WANGLE	W	PTE	30	/ 179				9/12/15	23/9/17	SICK			TO 24th, 27th, 3rd BNS.	
WATERS		LCPL			C									
WATERS	J	PTE	30	/ 67	C								TO 24th, 20th, 22nd BNS, CLASS Z RESERVE.	
WAUGH	J	PTE	30	/ 55	A								TO 24th, 22nd, 26th BNS.	
WELLANDS	T F	PTE		/1295	C	75 NEW ELVET	DURHAM CITY						TO ROYAL ENGINEERS(3 Mech Sect).	RE No 324213. 42 HALLGARTH ST 1918.
WELSH	J	PTE	30	/ 138	B									
WESTGARTH	F	PTE	30	/ 654	B									
WHEATLEY	J H	PTE		/1301	C									
WHEEL	W	PTE	30	/ 22	D			2/11/15	8/3/16	INNEFFICIENT				DID NOT SERVE OVERSEAS, AGE 41.
WHITE		PTE		/ 871	C									
WHITE	R	CPL	30	/ 49	A								TO 24th BN(C COY), CLASS Z RESERVE.	34 CCS 2/7 EVAC 5/7/16 WND SHLDR+BACK,AGE 19.
WHITNAM	F	PTE	30	/ 339									TO 13th, 12/13th BNS, CLASS Z RESERVE.	
WILD	E	PTE	30	/ 197	B									
WILKINS	T	PTE	30	/054	A									
WILLIAMS	J T	PTE	30	/ 184	C					KR para 392			TO 24th BN.	
WILLIAMS	S	CPL		/1496	A									ORIGINAL BN UNCONFIRMED.
WILLIAMSON	F	PTE	30	/ 318				3/12/15	13/7/18	WOUNDS			TO 13th, 26th, 16th BNS, DEPOT.	
WILLS	J	PTE		/ 965	C									
WILSON	C	PTE	30	/ 70	C		COLDSTREAM				OCT 16		TO 24th BN.	TOOK PART IN TRENCH RAID 5/6th JUNE 1916.
WILSON	G	PTE		/ 891	C									
WILSON	T	PTE		/1289	C									
WOOD	J A	PTE	30	/ 141	A			24/11/15	31/3/16	INNEFFICIENT				AGE 19, DID NOT SERVE OVERSEAS.
WOODWARD		PTE		/ 749	D									POS 26/, 3 OSWALD COURT DURHAM.
WOODWARD	G W	PTE		/ 749										
WRIGHT	John	LCPL	30	/ 162	B	38 SEAVIEW ST	SHANKHILL		10 APRIL 1918			PLOEGSTEERT MEM	TO 1/4th BN.	SGT, AGE 22.
YULE	A A A	PTE		/ 59	D									

NAME	INITI	RANK	BA	NUMBE	TOWN_VILL	ENLISTED	DISCHARG	TRANSFER
ARMDTRONG	Edwd	PTE	24	/1640	WHITE LE HEAD	19/7/15	7/2/16	TO 30th BN.
ARMSTRONG	Edwd	PTE	24	/1301	GATESHEAD	19/12/14	30/12/14	HAD SERVED 4th VOLUNTEER BN DURHAM LI.
ARMSTRONG	J H	LSGT	24	/957				
ARMSTRONG	Jn Js	PTE	24	/515	BLAYDON	7/11/14	8/3/15	HAD SERVED 3YRS IN THE VOLUNTEERS.
ARMSTRONG	Rich	PTE	24	/906	WEST HARTLEPOOL	9/11/14	1/12/14	HAD SERVED IN DURHAM LI VOLUNTEERS.
BOWES	Art W	CPL	24	/564				TO LABOUR CORPS.
BROWN	A	PTE	24	/1383				
CARR	W	CPL	24	/430				TO 30th BN.
CUNNINGHAM	H	PTE	24	/429				TO 30th BN.
FLINTOFF	T	CPL	24	/1210				TO ROYAL ENGINEERS.
GILLESPY	J	PTE	24	/1394				TO 30th BN.
GILROY	R	PTE	24	/1322				TO 30th BN.
GRIEVES	C	PTE	24	/1509	LEAMSIDE			TO KING'S OWN YORKSHIRE LI, ROYAL ENGINEERS.
MULLARKEY	T	CPL	24	/642	BEDLINGTON			
MURPHY	Mich	PTE	24	/88	BLACKHILL	3/11/14	9/12/14	
McDONNELL	F	PTE	24	/1624	LIVERPOOL			COMMISIONED 27th BATTALION 2/7/15.
SCOTT	W		24	/1560				
ROBSON	Jothn	PTE	24	/115	GOSFORTH	3/11/14	8/1/15	
ROBSON	Thos	PTE	24	/370	THORNLEY COLLIE	6/11/14	30/1/15	HAD SERVED IN RGA VOLUNTEERS.
ROBSON	Wm	PTE	24	/1268	BEDLINGTON	21/12/14	7/1/15	
TAIT	JohnC	PTE	24	/1052				TO LABOUR CORPS.
VAUGHTON	A	PTE	24					TRIED BY FGCM AT ERGUINGHEM 8/3/16, NOT FOUND ON MR.
WALTON	E	PTE	24	/1375				

NAME	INITI	RANK	BA	NUMBE	TOWN_VILL	ENLISTED	DISCHARG	TRANSFER
ARMSTRONG	Thos	PTE	25	/757	NEWCASTLE	14/11/14	27/4/15	
LYNES	James	PTE	25	/1057	GATESHEAD	19/11/14	10/6/19	TO 30th BN(23/7/15), 1st GARRISON BN(7/8/15), 200 LAB COY.

NAME	INITI	RANK	BATTA	NUMBE	TOWN_VILL	ENLISTED	DISCHARG	TRANSFER
BRENNAN	John	PTE	26	/42	SOUTH SHIELDS	26/11/14	15/3/15	JOINED BN 25/1/15.
ARMSTROMG	Geo	PTE	26	/763	NEWCASTLE	14/12/14	23/4/15	

NAME	INITI	RANK	BA	NUMBE	TOWN_VILL	ENLISTED	DISCHARG	TRANSFER
ROBSON	Wm	PTE	27	/1393	NEWCASTLE	23/4/15	31/7/15	
PATTERSON	Geo	PTE	27	/1498	HEDLEY HOPE			